Wicked Words

Also by Hugh Rawson

A Dictionary of Euphemisms & Other Doubletalk

A Dictionary of Quotations from the Bible
(with Margaret Miner)

The New International Dictionary of Quotations
(with Margaret Miner)

An Investment in Knowledge
(with Hillier Krieghbaum)

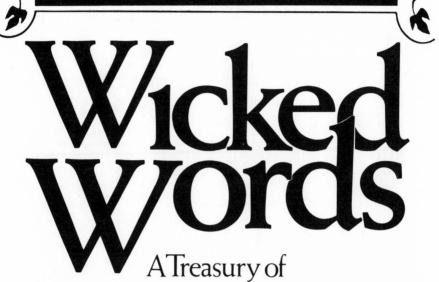

Wicked Words

A Treasury of
Curses, Insults, Put-Downs,
and Other Formerly Unprintable
Terms from Anglo-Saxon Times
to the Present

HUGH RAWSON

Crown Trade Paperback/New York

Published by Crown Publishers, Inc., 201 East 50th Street, New York, New York 10022. Member of the Crown Publishing Group.

CROWN TRADE PAPERBACKS and colophon are trademarks of Crown Publishers, Inc.

Printed in the U.S.A.

Library of Congress Cataloging-in-Publication Data

Rawson, Hugh.
  Wicked words / by Hugh Rawson.
    p. cm.
  1. English language—Slang—Dictionaries. 2. English language—Etymology—Dictionaries. 3. English language—Obscene words—Dictionaries. 4. Blessing and cursing—Dictionaries.
5. Invective—Dictionaries. 6. Swearing—Dictionaries. I. Title.
PE3721.R38 1989
427—dc19   89-672
                                                         CIP

ISBN 0-517-59089-1

10 9 8 7 6 5 4 3 2 1

First Paperback Edition

To Kate and
The Great Merlini

SOURCES AND METHODS

Most sources are identified in passing in the text, but some have been used so regularly as to deserve special acknowledgment. First is the *The Oxford English Dictionary*, edited by Sir James Murray, which I have used in the compact edition published by Oxford University Press in 1971, and the four supplements to it, edited by R. W. Burchfield, published between 1972 and 1986. Other especially helpful general works have included: *The American Thesaurus of Slang* by Lester V. Berrey and Melvin Van den Bark (Thomas Y. Crowell, 1953); *New Dictionary of American Slang*, Robert L. Chapman, ed. (Harper & Row, 1986); *A Dictionary of American English* by Sir William Cragie and James R. Hulbert (University of Chicago Press, 1938–44); *Slang and Its Analogues* by J. S. Farmer and W. E. Henley (1890–1904, Arno Press, 1970); *A Classical Dictionary of the Vulgar Tongue* by Captain Francis Grose (1796, edited and annotated by Eric Partridge, Barnes & Noble, 1963); *The American Language* by H. L. Mencken (Alfred A. Knopf, 1936, and its supplements of 1945 and 1948, as well as the one-volume abridged edition, edited and updated by Raven I. McDavid, Jr., with David W. Maurer, 1963); *A Dictionary of Slang and Unconventional English* by Eric Partridge (Macmillan, 1970); and the *Dictionary of American Slang* by Harold Wentworth and Stuart Berg Flexner (Thomas Y. Crowell, 1975), which remains very useful, since it includes dated citations, which were dropped from its successor, *New Dictionary of American Slang*.

Somewhat more specialized but of great value within their particular areas were: the *Dictionary of American Regional English*, Frederick G. Cassidy, ed. (Belknap Press of Harvard University Press, Vol. 1, 1985); *A Dictionary of Soldier Talk* by Colonel John R. Elting, Sergeant Major Dan Cragg, and Sergeant First Class Ernest Deal, all U.S. Army, Ret. (Charles Scribner's Sons, 1984); *I Hear America Talking* by Stuart Berg Flexner (Van Nostrand Reinhold, 1976); *Listening to America* by Stuart Berg Flexner (Simon & Schuster, 1982); *Americanisms* by Mitford M. Mathews (University of Chicago Press, 1966); *Language of the Underworld* by David W. Maurer, ed. by Allan W. Futrell and Charles B. Wordell (University Press of Kentucky, 1981); *The Lore and Language of Schoolchildren* by Iona and Peter Opie (Oxford University Press, 1959); *Shakespeare's Bawdy* by Eric Partridge (E.P. Dutton, 1960); *Dr. Bowdler's Legacy* by Noel Perrin (Atheneum, 1969); Vance Randolph and George P. Wilson, *Down in the Holler: A Gallery of Ozark Folk Speech* (University of Oklahoma Press, 1953); *A Dictionary of International Slurs* by A. A. Roback (1944, Maledicta Press, 1979); *The Joys of Yiddish* by Leo Rosten (McGraw-Hill, 1968); *Safire's Political Dictionary* by William Safire (Random House, 1978); and *Slang and Euphemism* by Richard A. Spears (Jonathan David, 1981). My own *A Dictionary of Euphemisms & Other Doubletalk* (Crown, 1981) also was helpful, of course, as the counterpart of the present work.

Two periodicals of particular value were *American Speech* (University of Alabama Press, from 1925) and *Maledicta* (Maledicta Press, from 1977). For etymologies, I have relied principally on *The Random House Dictionary of the English Language* (second edition, Stuart Berg Flexner, ed., 1987), *The American Heritage Dictionary of the English Language* (1st edition, William Morris, ed., 1969), and *An Etymological Dictionary of Modern English* (Ernest Weekley, 1921, Dover Publications, 1967).

Unless otherwise specified, all quotations from the Bible are from the King James or Authorized Version of 1611. Release dates for most of the films that are cited come from *Leonard Maltin's TV Movies & Video Guide* (Signet, revised annually).

The dates that I have given for the introductions of new words and meanings often come from the *OED*. The dating is not precise, of course. Many words, especially taboo terms and slang expressions, may be used for many years before appearing in the written record—or that portion of it scanned by the readers who have supplied citations for the *OED* and other dictionaries. Searches in magazines, newspapers, underground literature, and other specialized works often produce earlier dates for particular usages than are given in standard reference works. Still, the evolution of the language is well handled in the *OED*, with its immense number of dated citations. This great dictionary is necessarily the starting point for anyone who seeks to track the way words have been used over periods of many years. Even its omissions, which are few, are significant.

Many individuals have gone out of their way to furnish me with examples of usage and to help me verify or clarify examples already in hand. Only some contributors are named in the text. All are greatly thanked, however. I am especially indebted to Susan Arensberg, David F. Costello, Robert W. Creamer, Ira Konigsberg, David E. Koskoff, E. C. Krupp, Barbara Livesey, Herbert B. Livesey III, Jim Meir, Robert Nadder, Catherine S. Rawson, Kenneth Silverman, and Claire Sotnick. My children, Nathaniel and Catherine Rawson, and my sister-in-law, Mary E. Miner, a teacher who really listens to her students, were of great help in supplying information about school yard sayings. Joanne Caldara and Susan Rogers provided editorial assistance as well as typing.

I am particularly grateful to Paul Heacock, who suggested the idea for this book, and to Brandt Aymar, Lisa Pliscou, and Mark Hurst for their patience and skill in shepherding the project along the way to publication.

Finally, I am extremely fortunate to be married to a fine writer and editor, Margaret Miner. This book has benefited in a great many ways from her advice and criticisms. All things considered, she has been quite patient, too.

Hugh Rawson,
April 1989

Which hurts a child more, a "dirty" word he hears or sees, or the picture of handsome young adults smoking cigarettes with rapt enjoyment? Which does more damage to an impressionable young mind, a view of uncovered skin or evidence of mendacity in the politician and huckster?

Theodor Rosebury,
Life on Man, 1969

Wicked Words

INTRODUCTION

The Anatomy of Wicked Words

Sticks and stones may break my bones,
But names will never hurt me.

Of all the bits of folk "wisdom" that are handed down from generation to generation, this has to be one of the most misleading. Names do hurt. Words are
weapons. Bones heal faster than psyches. And verbal attacks frequently serve not
just in lieu of physical violence but as a prelude to it.

Consider the role that words played in the rioting that surrounded the
Democratic National Convention in Chicago at the end of August 1968. The
antiwar demonstrators who converged on the convention generally were unarmed.
Language was their principal weapon against the police who sought to control
them. Naturally, the demonstrators used the most powerful words they knew.

Stressing the way language led to violence, *Rights in Conflict*, the report on the
riot by the President's Commission on the Causes and Prevention of Violence,
included such statements from witnesses as:

> There were stones thrown, of course, but for the most part it was
> verbal. But there were stones being thrown. But the police were respond-
> ing with tear gas and clubs and every time they could get near enough to
> a demonstrator they hit him.

And from another observer:

> It seemed to me that only a saint could have swallowed the rude
> remarks to the officers. However, they went to extremes in clubbing the
> yippies. I saw them move into the park, swatting away with clubs at girls
> and boys in the grass.

Unusually for a government document, this report, better known as "The
Walker Report," after commission chairman Daniel Walker, included the actual
words that were employed by participants in the riot, which resulted in hospitaliza-
tion of at least 101 demonstrators and 49 police, with perhaps another 1,000
demonstrators being treated elsewhere. "Extremely obscene language was a contributing factor to the violence described in this report," wrote Mr. Walker in a
prefatory note, "and its frequency and intensity were such that to omit it would
inevitably understate the effect it had."

Because of the chairman's insistence on faithfully transcribing the terminology,
the Government Printing Office refused to print the commission report, and *The
New York Times*, the nation's newspaper of record, toned down the historical record
in this manner (12/2/68):

> . . . Chants of "＿＿ the pigs" and "dirty pigs" drowned out exhortations
> from the speaker's stand to "sit down." One demonstrator waved a placard

1

at the police. It pictured a young man burning his draft card and was captioned, "_____ the draft."

The *Times'* account also serves as a litmus test of sort, showing the differences in the strengths of the taboos on two terms, one a participle and the other a noun:

An officer shouted, "Let's get the _____ bastards!"

In this same period, words also were singled out as the chief provocation of the tragedy at Kent State University on May 4, 1970, when members of the Ohio National Guard fired upon antiwar demonstrators. The students did hurl some missiles at the guardsmen, but not many reached their targets; the distances were too great. As James A. Michener reported in *Kent State: What Happened and Why* (1971):

> Worse, in a way, than the missiles were the epithets, especially when launched by coeds. A steady barrage of curses, obscenities and fatal challenges came down upon the Guard, whose gas masks did not prevent them from hearing what they were being called. Girls were particularly abusive, using the foulest language and taunting the Guardsmen with being "shit-heels, motherfuckers, and half-ass pigs." Others called them less explosive but equally hurtful names: "toy soldiers, murderers, weekend warriors, fascists." . . .
> Guardsmen knew the words, but many of them had been reared in homes where it would have been unthinkable for even the toughest man to use them; to hear them in common usage by girls who could have been their sisters produced a psychic shock which ran deep. . . . the girls had removed themselves from any special category of "women and children." They were tough, foul-mouthed enemies. . . .

The guardsmen took this abuse for less than half an hour before turning on their tormentors and discharging sixty-one shots in three ragged volleys. They hit thirteen students, killing four—two young men and two young women. None of the soldiers sustained a serious injury.

Of course, scenarios of similar sort frequently are played out on a personal level. For example, there was the episode on Geraldo Rivera's television show, taped November 3, 1988, when a guest, Mr. John Metzger, a member of the White Aryan Resistance Youth, said of another guest, Mr. Roy Innis, chairman of the Congress of Racial Equality, that he was "sick and tired of Uncle Tom here, sucking up and trying to be a white man." Result: Mr. Innis jumped out of his chair and began to choke Mr. Metzger. Members of the audience joined in the fracas. So did other guests on the program, including Mr. Bob Heick, director of the American Front, and Mr. Michael Palash, director of Skinheads of National Resistance. The chief casualty was the host, Mr. Rivera, a onetime amateur boxer, who suffered a broken nose.

The words that led to violence in the foregoing instances were of various sorts—conventional obscenities; the standard *pig* metaphor for police; a political epithet (*fascist*); some specialized slurs (*toy soldier*, etc.); and an ethnic insult with a literary origin (*Uncle Tom*).

But what makes these words so "bad"? Why should they provoke such violent responses? There is nothing inherently pejorative about most of them and even the worst ones can be used in a nonthreatening way. We can refer to a *pig* in a barnyard without agitating anyone. *Uncle Tom* and *toy soldier* are innocuous in and of themselves. *Bastard*, once heavily tabooed, was such a tame term in the 1960s that even a very proper paper like *The New York Times* would print it.

The answer, of course, lies in the context. The meanings of words change considerably, according to who says them, to whom, and in what circumstances. Hillfolk may call each other *hicks* and *hillbillies* in a friendly sort of way, but if a city slicker addresses them by those terms, the rural residents are likely to take umbrage. A Jew can get away with referring to another Jew as a *kike*, but it is very hard for a *goy* (not a very complimentary term itself, by the way) to use *kike* without appearing anti-Semitic. *Virgin* doesn't raise eyebrows in church, but it was banned from Hollywood soundtracks for many years. *Brother-in-law* can lead to blows when used as a form of address in some parts of the world, since the speaker's implication is that he has had sexual intercourse with the other person's sister. A young man in York, England, was fined the equivalent of $126 in 1984 for uttering the otherwise innocuous *meow* to a German shepherd, who happened to have a police sergeant in tow.

The meanings of words also change over time. A *knave* was once a boy-child, not necessarily a roguish one; a *girl* was a child of either sex; a *hussy* was a housewife; a *boor* was a farmer; a *villain* was a serf. *Crap* used to be the chaff or dregs of something, such as the residue that settles at the bottom of a keg of beer. Mark Twain, whose vocabulary most definitely included the slang of his period, rendered *crop* as *crap* in *The Gilded Age* (with Paul Dudley Warner, 1873), thus indicating the relative newness of the presently dominant meaning of this word. Jane Austen referred in *Emma* (1816) to boarding schools where "young ladies for enormous pay might be screwed out of health and into vanity"—not a sentence that any writer today would commit to paper. Because of the changes in the meanings assigned to words, the choice of a particular one—*girl*, say, when an adult female is meant—sometimes conveys more information about the social class, education, and attitudes of the individual who employs it than about the person supposedly described.

The way a word is spoken or said also is important in determining its meaning. For example, *bastard* and *bugger* (a sodomite, technically) as well as the obsolete *whoreson*, have their familiar, non-abusive uses. ("He's a cute little bugger, isn't he?") The great Oedipal insult that so shocked soldiers at Kent State can be employed in much the same way, as in "We will joyfully say, 'Man, he's a motherfucker'" (Bobby Seale, in Robert L. Chapman, *New Dictionary of American Slang*, 1986). *Bitch* can be applied to a woman with no insult intended. The final words of Jonathan Swift's last letter to his lifelong friend, Esther Johnson (Stella), were "Agreeable Bitch" (6/6/1713), and the term continues to be used affectionately and admiringly, as noted by Claude Brown: "Cats would say, 'I saw your sister today, and she is a fine bitch.' Nobody was offended by it" (*Manchild in the Promised Land*, 1965). Among loggers in the Pacific Northwest, *son of a bitch* long ago became a harmless term, so that one woodsman might greet another with, "Hi, you red-eyed son-of-a-bitch!" (*American Speech*, 12/25).

Spoken a different way in other circumstances, any of these terms may become offensive. For instance, the unnamed hero of Owen Wister's *The Virginian* does not mind it when his friend Steve affectionately calls him a "son-of-a-____"

(the dash is in the original, 1902), but when the bad man, Trampas, addresses him this way, he draws his pistol and produces the immortal reply: "When you call me that, *smile!*" And the novel's narrator, pondering the different responses to the same epithet, concludes: "So I perceived a new example of the old truth, that the letter means nothing until the spirit gives it life."

The power of a word as well as its meaning depends greatly on the setting in which it is used. Double standards abound. Traditionally, "gentlemen" were allowed to use taboo words among themselves which, if uttered when "ladies" were present, would be considered unforgivable breaches of decorum. Carried to ridiculous lengths in the past (*breast, leg,* and *pregnant* are among the words that have been avoided in mixed company), this dichotomy has almost evaporated, thanks largely to women's liberation, and it is now common to hear females using the same four-letter words as males, especially in moments of stress or anger—when they are *pissed off,* for example. Other double standards remain. Words that are acceptable enough in informal situations are supposed to be avoided on formal occasions; the language of the streets is taboo in the living room. For many Americans, the most shocking thing about the White House transcripts, released by President Richard M. Nixon in 1974, was the revelation that locker-room language was used frequently in the Oval Office. The transcripts were peppered with "expletive deleteds" and "characterization omitteds" which took attention away from the substance of the conversations.

The ultimate absurdity is reached when fearful people search for "bad" meanings where none exist. Both the Federal Bureau of Investigation and the Federal Communications Commission are said to have investigated Richard Berry's rock 'n' roll song "Louie Louie," playing the version recorded by the Kingsmen in 1963 at different speeds in order to determine if the lyrics are dirty. (As originally written by Mr. Berry, they're not, but the singers slurred them so much that it was hard to tell.) The theory here apparently was that there must be something wrong about anything young people liked so much.

And in *anno Domini* 1988, William Cole's anthology *I'm Mad at You* was placed on the restricted shelves of elementary school libraries in North Kansas City, Missouri, because it contained Eve Merriam's "Mean Song," which is comprised largely of bad-sounding but meaningless words, as in

> Snickles and podes,
> Ribble and grodes:
> That's what I wish you.
> A nox in the groot,
> A root in the stoot
> And a gock in the forebeshaw, too.

Sound does contribute to meaning, of course. It obviously is only one factor, and not the dominant one, since words with the same sounds have widely different meanings—and *duck* and *luck* are not 75 percent obscene. Still, there appears to be something inherently "bad" about some letters and combinations thereof. Thus, the letter *l* leads into an unseemly number of sexy words: *lascivious, lecherous, lesbian, lewd, libertine, licentious, low-minded, lubricious, lurid, lustful,* and [*sinful*] *luxuriousness.* Among others. The letters *sn,* meanwhile, produce more than their share of words with noxious meanings, including *snake, sneak, snitch, sniveling, snob, snoop, snooty,* and *snotty.*

The derogatory impact of many words also seems to be enhanced by a hard *k* or *g* sound, as in *cock, coon, kike, jerk, nigger, pig, spic,* etc., and by the use of alliteration and rhyme, as in *boob tube, claptrap, crumb bum, flim-flam, gobbledygook, goo-goo, rinky-dink, ticky-tacky,* and *wishy-washy*.

Many innocent words also are avoided simply because they sound like other terms having low meanings. It was because of the resemblance in sound that farmers and other, more refined people began shying away from *ass* and *cock* in the mid-eighteenth century, saying *donkey* and *rooster* instead. The active imagination can make extremely farfetched associations. *Aspic, buttress, curtail, rapier, sects,* and *titter* were among the words that students at Emory University in Atlanta, Georgia, avoided in the 1930s, according to a study by Professor J. M. Steadman, Jr. (*American Speech,* 4/35). More than half a century later, it is almost a sure bet that one can bring conversation to a halt at even the most sophisticated cocktail party by saying "Jane is crapulent," meaning only that she is eating or drinking too much, or that "Frank is a cunctator," referring to his tendency to delay before acting on anything.

The meanings of words are so dependent on context, on the spirit with which they are employed, and on what is in the mind of the person who sees or hears them that it is tempting to argue that they are intrinsically meaningless. Somehow, however, communication does take place, albeit with much misunderstanding. Perhaps it is better to think of words as bottles of wine. The wine may change as it ages, and people may argue about whether it is really good or bad. No one doubts, however, that the bottle does contain something besides air, and it is even possible for most people to agree most of the time on the nature of what is inside. Messages do get through, both good and bad.

The messages conveyed by "bad" words are of three types: the profane, the obscene, and the insulting. Each represents a different form of abuse. Profanity abuses sacred belief: It is irreligious, by definition and by origin, coming from the Latin *pro* (before, outside) + *fanum* (temple). Obscenity abuses the body, the temple of the self: It derives from the Latin *obscēnus,* probably from *caenum* (filth). Obscenity includes pornography, from the Greek *pornē* (prostitute) + *graphein* (to write [about]) and scatology, from the Greek *skatos* (dung, shit) + *logy* (the science or study of). Insult abuses other individuals, typically in terms of their ethnicity, nationality, religion, political persuasion, sex, mental disabilities, or physical peculiarities: It comes from the Latin *insultāre* (to leap upon).

Religious people have made many efforts over the years to reinforce the Third Commandment with laws and other regulations to abolish profanity. For example, an Act of Parliament of 1606 made it a crime, punishable by a fine of ten pounds, for anyone in any theatrical production to "jestingly or profanely speak or use the Holy Name of God, or of Christ Jesus, or of the Holy Ghost, or of the Trinity, which are not to be spoken but with fear and reverence." More than three hundred years later, the Hollywood production code of 1930 included a clause to the same effect: "Pointed profanity (this includes the words *God, Lord, Jesus Christ*—unless used reverently—*hell, s.o.b., damn, Gawd*), or every other profane or vulgar expression, however used, is forbidden."

Another notable landmark in the war against profanity is George Washington's General Order to the Continental Army of July 1776: "The general is sorry to be informed that the foolish and wicked practice of profane cursing and swearing, a vice hitherto little known in an American army, is growing into fashion. He hopes

5

the officers will, by example as well as influence, endeavor to check it, and that both they and the men will reflect that we can have little hope of the blessing of Heaven on our arms if we insult it by our impiety and folly."

The shock power of profanity has declined greatly over the years, however. From past proscriptions of profanity, we know that swearing must have been common, as well as disturbing, at least to true believers; otherwise it would not have been necessary to erect formal bans in the first place. Today, the official and semiofficial proscriptions have been discarded, and profanity itself raises few eyebrows. Exclamations such as *damn, goddamn, hell, Jesus, Jesus H. Christ,* and *Jesus Christ on a bicycle* (or *crutch*) are seen and heard frequently, but they are not nearly as troubling to most people as other words available for expressing surprise, anger, disgust, or whatever.

The deterioration of profanity has been noted by a number of observers, the only real disagreement being on when it began. Americans, with a relatively short national history, tend to date the decline to the Civil War. The British take a longer view. In what still stands as the most perceptive analysis of the subject, Robert Graves argued in *Lars Porsena, or The Future of Swearing and Improper Language* (1936) that standards of profanity had been slipping in England since about 1600, except for periods of wartime amelioration.

Graves linked the deterioration of profanity principally to religion, taking his title from the opening lines of one of Macaulay's *Lays of Ancient Rome:*

> Lars Porsena of Clusium
> By the Nine Gods he swore
> That the great house of Tarquin
> Should suffer wrong no more.

Graves' point, of course, was that Lars Porsena was in an enviable position with so many gods to swear by, compared to Christians who have only one God. And even that One sometimes is said to be dead. Graves also cited a number of other causes for the decline of profanity, including "the effect on swearing of spiristic belief, of golf, of new popular diseases such as botulism and sleepy sickness, of new forms of scientific warfare, of the sanction which the Anglican Church is openly giving to contraception, thereby legitimatizing the dissociation of the erotic and progenitive impulses [and of] gallantly foul-mouthed feministic encroachments on what has been hitherto regarded as a wholly male province. . . ." Within its terms, his treatment is, as noted, definitive.

More specifically, Protestantism seems to be largely responsible for the present sad state of profanity. Where the most taboo words in Roman Catholic countries tend to be the blasphemous ones—oaths in the name of the Father, Son, or Virgin Mary—the truly offensive terms for Protestants are those that refer to intimate parts of the body and its functions. That this is basically a religious rather than national or cultural distinction is suggested by the earthy vocabulary of Chaucer in pre-Reformation England. For Chaucer and his courtly audiences, *ers* (arse), *fart,* and *queynt* (cunt) simply did not have the same strength as to later Protestant generations. His standards were the same as those of Dante and Boccaccio in Roman Catholic Italy—and Dante put blasphemers, not users of obscenity, in the seventh circle of the Inferno (along with murderers, suicides, perverts, and other violent offenders against God and Nature).

Another indication of the different weighting given to profanity in Protestant and Catholic cultures is the difference in the penalties assigned for the offense. Where Parliament prescribed a fine of ten pounds in 1606, the summary of Spanish laws issued in Roman Catholic New Orleans by Alexander O'Reilly on November 25, 1769, provided that "he who shall revile our Savior, or His mother the Holy Virgin Mary, shall have his tongue cut out, and his property shall be confiscated, applicable one-half to the public treasury and the other half to the informer." Judging from language taboos, Protestants generally are more terrified of their bodies than their Lord.

Obscenity, meanwhile, has been of public concern only for the past couple hundred years. In fact, neither England nor the United States had any antiobscenity statutes until the nineteenth century, when improvements in public education combined with developments in printing technology to create a popular demand for the kind of literary works that previously had circulated without restriction among society's elite. At the same time, better methods of reproducing drawings, along with the invention of photography, made it possible to produce what were politely called *French prints* and *French postcards* (or *American cards* in France). The pictorial works attracted an even larger audience, of course, since one did not even have to be literate in order to appreciate them.

In prior centuries, when printed materials were not disseminated widely, books were expensive, and reading was limited mainly to aristocrats. Censorship then tended to be concerned with political and religious matters rather than decency. People who could read were allowed to decide for themselves what made good reading. Thus, the Council of Trent in 1573 decided that there was no harm in publishing a version of Boccaccio's *Decameron* in which sinful nuns and priests had been changed into sinful lay people. And in 1708, when a printer, James Read, was hauled into court for having published *The Fifteen Plagues of a Maidenhead,* Lord Justice Powell dismissed the indictment, saying:

> This is for printing bawdy stuff but reflects on no person, and a libel must be against some particular person or persons, or against the Government. It is not stuff to be mentioned publicly; if there should be no remedy in the Spiritual Court, it does not follow there must be a remedy here. There is no law to punish it, I wish there was, but we cannot make law; it indeed tends to the corruption of good manners, but that is not sufficient for us to punish.

Subsequently, judges did begin to make law, but even so prosecutions for obscenity tended to cover other concerns. Thus, Edmund Curll was convicted in 1727 of corrupting public morals by publishing *Venus in the Cloister, or the Nun in Her Smock,* though this title had been in print in English since at least 1683; Curll, however, was a political gadfly, whose other offenses included printing privileged proceedings of the House of Lords as well as a "seditious and scandalous" political memoir (for the latter, he stood an hour in the pillory). Another great corrupter of public morals, John Wilkes, eventually did jail time for publishing a bawdy poem with many four-letter words, *An Essay on Woman* (1763), but the radical Mr. Wilkes (much honored in America for his sympathies with the colonists) was prosecuted principally for political reasons.

Which is not to say that everything was permissible at all times in public prior to the nineteenth century. Many of our euphemistic expressions for sexual and related matters are considerably older, indicating the earlier reluctance to speak openly on these topics. Shakespeare, for example, is full of references to sexual intercourse, typically in such allusive phrases as "the act of darkness" (*King Lear*), "act of shame" (*Othello*), "making the beast with two backs" (*Othello*), and the more complicated "groping for trouts in a peculiar river" (*Measure for Measure*, the phrase referring to fishing in a private stream).

Shakespeare also contains a great many sexual puns—e.g., "Pistol's cock is up" (*Henry V*)—but he never used explicitly the most tabooed of the many words for the analagous female part, though it obviously was part of his vocabulary. Thus, he also punned in *Henry V* on the French *con*, but the closest he came to employing the English equivalent was in *Twelfth Night* (1600–02), when he had Malvolio spell out the dread word: "By my life, this is my lady's hand. These be her C's, her U's, and ['n] her T's; and thus makes she her great P's."

Many similar pre-Victorian examples could be cited. Suffice it to say that the Hebrew totally lacks words for the male and female sexual parts, the male member being referred to as "that organ" and the female counterpart as "that place." The Bible also is replete with such delicate allusions to the act of evacuating the bowels as "Saul went in [to the cave] to cover his feet" (*I Samuel*, 24:3) and "when thou wilt ease thyself abroad, thou shalt . . . turn back, and cover that which cometh from thee" (*Deuteronomy*, 23:13).

Obscenity in our culture is essentially a function of social class. It always involves words that are, by definition, vulgar—from the Latin *vulagāris*, equivalent to *vulg(us)*, the common people. (Pornographic works that do not rely heavily on obscenity are comparatively few and far between, the leading exception being John Cleland's *The Memoirs of a Woman of Pleasure*, a.k.a. *Fanny Hill*.) The vulgar terms are old ones, of course, often described delicately as Anglo-Saxon words, though not all of them are. By contrast, the most acceptable, upper-class words tend to be imports, typically of Latin or French derivation, e.g., *copulation, enceinte, defecation, derriere, micturition, penis, pudendum*, and so forth.

Note, too, that definitions of vulgarity vary considerably. Commenting on two words that are now considered quite beyond reproach, Isaac D'Israeli (father of Benjamin) had this to say in *Curiosities of Literature* (1791–1823):

> A lady eminent for the elegance of her taste, and of whom one of the best judges, the celebrated Miss Edgeworth, observed to me that she spoke the purest and most idiomatic English she had ever heard, threw out an observation which might be extended to a great deal of our present fashionable vocabulary. She is now old enough, she said, to have lived to hear the vulgarisms of her youth adopted in drawing-room circles. To *lunch*, now so familiar from the fairest of lips, in her youth was known only in the servants' hall. An expression very rife of late among our young ladies, *a nice man*, whatever it may mean, whether that man resemble a pudding or something more nice, conveys the offensive notion that they are ready to eat him up!

To some extent, fastidiousness about not using vulgar, lower-class words dates to the Norman Conquest, when the new aristocracy spoke French, but the lines of demarcation, as we now know them, were not really drawn until about the middle of the eighteenth century, when the middle classes began to make their weight felt socially. Until the early 1700s, even refined people casually used what later came to be regarded as low words. The King James Bible of 1611, for instance, includes *dung, piss,* and *whore.* At the court of Queen Anne (1702–14), *arse* was heard frequently, even from the lips of maids of honor. Country people at the opening of the eighteenth century habitually spoke of *cocks* and *haycocks,* not *roosters* and *haystacks.* The *breast* of the plow had not yet become the *bosom* of the plow. When Lady Mary Wortley Montagu wished to describe the uninhibited behavior of the wife of the French ambassador upon receiving visitors in 1724, the word she used was *pissing.*

The new middle-class morality was inspired in part by religious revival in both the colonies and Great Britain. (*Methodism,* meaning the practice of following a method, was coined as a derisive term in 1729 by students at Oxford where John and Charles Wesley held their first meetings, but nonetheless accepted quickly by them.) It also was a reaction to the profound changes that were taking place in society, especially in England, as the factory system was being established, the land enclosed by absentee owners, and the countryside depopulated (Oliver Goldsmith, *The Deserted Village,* 1770). London, as a result, became swollen with people who were cut off from their traditional roots and inhibitions. The metropolitan scene, as described by Tobias Smollett in *The Expedition of Humphry Clinker* (1771), may seem familiar to those who walk the streets of some twentieth-century cities:

> The plough-boys, cow-herds, and lower hinds, are debauched and seduced by the appearance and discourse of those coxcombs in livery, when they make their summer excursions [to the city]. They desert their dirt and drudgery, and swarm up to London, in hopes of getting into service, where they can wear fine clothes, without being obliged to work; for idleness is natural to man. Great numbers of these, being disappointed in their expectation, become thieves and sharpers; and London being an immense wilderness, in which there is neither watch nor ward of any signification, nor any order or police, affords them lurking-places as well as prey.

By the end of the 1700s, proto-Victorianism was in full bloom. The change in sensibilities is evident from a letter by Sir Walter Scott, relating how his grand-aunt, Mrs. Keith Ravelstone, had asked him when he was a young man in the 1790s to procure her some books by Aphra Behn, which she fondly remembered from her own youth. A playwright as well as a novelist, Behn, 1640–89, was the first Englishwoman to write professionally. Her best known novelette was *Oroonoko, or the History of a Royal Slave;* her plays included such thrillers as *The Forced Marriage, or the Jealous Bridegroom* and *The Amorous Prince.* Scott had reservations about the request, telling his elderly relative that "I did not think she would like either the manners, or the language, which approached too near that of Charles II's time to be quite proper reading." Nevertheless, since "to hear was to obey," Scott sent his "gay old grand-aunt" some of Behn's works in a well-sealed package, marked "private and confidential." Scott continues:

> The next time I saw her afterwards, she gave me back Aphra, properly wrapped up, with nearly these words: "Take back your bonny Mrs. Behn; and, if you will take my advance, put her in the fire, for I have found it

impossible to get through the very first novel. But is it not," she added, "a very odd thing that I, an old woman of eighty and upwards, sitting alone, feel ashamed to read a book which, sixty years ago, I have heard read aloud for the amusement of large circles, consisting of the finest and most credible society in London."

Efforts to root out vulgarisms picked up steam in the early nineteenth century with the work of the great expurgators, who wished to render the literature of the past suitable for women and children of their own, more fastidious time. The leaders in this field were Henrietta Maria (known usually as Harriet) Bowdler and her brother, Thomas, whose *Family Shakespeare* appeared in 1807 (an enlarged edition was published in 1818) and Noah Webster, whose edition of the Bible "with Amendments of the language" (i.e., no *piss, whore,* etc.) came out in 1833.

High-minded people also began banding together during this period to campaign publicly against obscenity in word and picture. These self-appointed arbiters of public morality formed such pressure groups as the Boston Watch and Ward Society, the New York Society for the Suppression of Vice, and, on the British side of the Atlantic, the Organization for the Reformation of Manners, later called the Society for the Suppression of Vice. (The witty Reverend Sydney Smith, 1771–1845, maintained that the Society should be called a society for suppressing the vices of persons whose incomes did not exceed five hundred pounds a year.) The societies initiated private prosecutions for obscenity and indecency under the common law and pressed for the enactment of formal statutes to require the government to enforce the new morality. Their efforts to criminalize materials that they regarded as indecent (including, most particularly, not just salacious matter but publications for educating the public in the techniques of birth control) culminated in the Obscene Publications Act of 1857 in Great Britain and the Comstock Act of 1873 in the United States. These laws were enforced so rigorously that for many years even scholarly works were reduced to ∫---, etc., while ordinary dictionaries ordinarily omitted this and similar words altogether.

Today, censorship of language is but a shadow of its former self, thanks to a series of court decisions, particularly those that overturned the legal bans against James Joyce's *Ulysses* (admitted to the United States in 1933) and D. H. Lawrence's *Lady Chatterley's Lover* (decriminalized in 1959 in the United States and 1960 in the United Kingdom). Of course, the court decisions reflected changes in society at large, with the trend toward permissiveness having been accelerated by two world wars, during which linguistic and other taboos (such as those against killing people) were flouted so often as to numb everyone's senses.

The desire to shelter women, children, and the masses from words that might give them bad ideas continues to be manifested, however, by the different degrees of freedom of expression allowed in different media. Books, which are read by relatively few people, enjoy the most leeway, at least at the adult level. Magazines and newspapers, which have larger audiences, tend to censor themselves. Meanwhile, the media that cast the widest nets—the movies, TV, and radio—also have the severest restrictions placed upon them, both internally in the form of self-censorship and externally through industry codes and government regulation.

In particular, efforts continue to restrict access of minors to "adult" periodicals as well as books (up to and including such rousers as *The Adventures of Huckleberry Finn, The Catcher in the Rye,* and *The American Heritage Dictionary*). The film rating system is well established, with the result that no self-respecting child wants to see anything that is labeled G (for "general") and some people wish to have song lyrics subjected to a similar system. Censorship of high school newspapers has been sanctioned by the Supreme Court of the United States, as has the right of school authorities to restrict the freedom of student speech even when it is not notably coarse, e.g., *Bethel School District No. 403 v. Fraser*, a 1986 decision in which the Court upheld, seven to two, the three-day suspension of a senior who urged the election of a friend for student office on the grounds that "he is a man who is firm—firm in his pants . . . a man who will go to the very end—even the climax for each and every one of you." (The friend won the election.)

Protection of the young also seemed to weigh heavily in the 1978 decision in which the Supreme Court upheld by a five to four vote the Federal Communications Commission's authority to ban certain words from the airwaves. The case was precipitated by a single complaint from a man who happened to tune in on a car radio, while traveling with his young son, to a broadcast in 1973 by New York's WBAI-FM of comedian George Carlin's "Seven Dirty Words" routine. All this, even though most American children know—albeit not always with a complete understanding—most of Mr. Carlin's words, along with many others of the same ilk. Parents who think differently are advised to query their dears on this point; the ensuing dialogue is likely to be enlightening to both generations.

In fact, the relaxation of the taboo against obscenity has led to a noticeable decline in wit. Elegant retorts of the sort attributed to Oscar Wilde, Winston Churchill, George Bernard Shaw, and Dorothy Parker continue to be treasured in large part because no one has since come close to matching them. Thus, when a woman (variously reported as Nancy Astor and a "female heckler") told Churchill, "If you were my husband, I would put strychnine in your coffee," he replied, "Madam, if I were your husband, I should drink it." And when a passerby commented, "There goes that bloody fool, Oscar Wilde," the great Oscar improved the occasion by remarking to a companion, "It's extraordinary how soon one gets to be known in London!" Today, by contrast, when a male heckler called Edward I. Koch a "war criminal," the future mayor of New York City was quoted as replying "**** off!" (*New Yorker*, 9/10/79). Meanwhile, personal observations by passersby in the city streets of today are likely to elicit only the crudest of replies: *Up yours* is about as nice as they get. In an age when anything goes, there is no longer a necessity for cleverness, and the level of public discourse sinks to the lowest common denominator, often of four letters.

While the barriers against profanity and obscenity have eroded, new ones have been erected to protect against personal insult. Captain Frederick Marryat, a distinguished naval officer before he turned to writing, noted the distinction in *Mr. Midshipman Easy*, published in 1836, the year before Victoria became Queen: "We are not strait-laced, — we care little about an oath as a mere *expletive*; we refer now to swearing at *others*, to insulting their feelings grossly by coarse and intemperate language. We would never interfere with a man for d___g his *own* eyes, but we deny the right of his d___g those of *another*." (A sensitive observer of fashions in language, Marryat has a female character in his 1834 novel, *Peter Simple*, insist on being served "lily turkey *bosom*, if you please." He also recorded in his *Diary in America*, published in 1839, the local aversion to *leg*, which extended, so he was told by one woman, to the point that some people "always say limb of a table, or limb of a piano-forte.")

For most people today, the most offensive words are those that disparage individuals according to race, religion, sex, and ethnic extraction, or focus on their physical and mental handicaps and peculiarities. We know from examining our stock of words, however, that people have always reviled one another and that bluntness has not always been considered poor form or, as it frequently is today, a matter of libel. The present meanings of words—their denotations and connotations—preserve the attitudes of previous generations just as surely as the strata of rocks record the history of the earth.

For example, it is clear that foreigners have almost always been targets of disparagement. The ancient Greeks looked down upon rude, crude *barbarians*, and the pejorative sense of that word persists. Similarly, negative connotations have become attached to *Goth, Hun, Philistine, Vandal,* and the names of other peoples. Jews have long objected to the use of *Jew* (*down*) as a verb; Gypsies and the inhabitants of Wales, though their complaints have not been registered as clearly, also are sensitive to the verbs *to gyp* and *to welsh* (as on a bet).

National rivalries can be traced by the appearance in English of many negative phrases involving *Dutch* and *French*, e.g., *Dutch comfort*, false comfort; *Dutch courage*, false bravery fueled by alcohol; *Dutch uncle*, not a real uncle; *French leave*, departure without notice; and *French pox*, syphilis. By the same token, the waves of immigrants to the United States were greeted with insults from those who had arrived shortly before. Thus, the Polish jokes of today merely continue the time-honored tradition of disparaging other nationalities, including the Chinese (a.k.a. *chinks* and *slopes*), the Germans (a.k.a. *krauts* and *jerries*, among other derogations), the Italians (*Eyetalians, macaronis, meatballs*), and, most notably, the Irish (both the *lace curtain* and *shanty* divisions). Typical Irish jokes included: Q. What are Irish apricots? A. Potatoes. Q. What is an Irish banjo? A. A shovel. Q. What is an Irish buggy? A. A wheelbarrow, said to be the world's greatest invention since the Irish learned from it how to walk on their hind legs. Even within the same ethnic group disparaging distinctions have been drawn. Thus, *kike* was popularized in the United States by assimilated German Jews, referring to Jews in later waves of immigration from Eastern Europe.

No group has escaped, not even the English (*French leave* in French is *filer à l'anglaise*), the *gringos*, and the *wasps*. As A. A. Roback, who was a great collector of ethnic insults (he called them ethnophaulisms), noted in the preface to his *A Dictionary of International Slurs:* "Undoubtedly some lay person will interpose the question: Why confine oneself to slurs and not include also the complimentary allusions? The answer is simple. There are practically none of the latter."

The same rule applies to words for other social groups. Cityfolk have always disparaged countryfolk (*bumpkins, hicks, hillbillies, rubes,* etc.) and the places they live in (*the boondocks, hicksville, podunk,* and *the sticks*). *Heathen* originally translated as "dweller on the heath"; *peasant* did not become a term of abuse until the sixteenth century; *zany*, from the diminutive of *Giovanni*, got its buffoonish sense through association with the hillfolk of the province of Bergamo, Italy. "Normal" people have always picked on people who seem different, whether because they are *airheads, blockheads, dolts, dunces, fools, imbeciles, lamebrains,* or *morons* ("special" is a preferred term today); because they are *cracked, loony, nuts,* or *off their rockers* ("suffering from mental or emotional dysfunction"); or because they are *fatties, lefties* (the words for "left" in Latin and French, respectively, are *sinister* and *gauche*), *shorties,* or have other unusual physical characteristics. (Long-armed Abraham

Lincoln often was referred to as a *baboon* or *gorilla*—and not just in Southern newspapers.)

Of all the outgroups, the largest and longest suffering is the tribe of women. This is apparent from the decline in the social status of such feminine titles as *dame, madam,* and *mistress* (along with the previously mentioned *hussy,* from *housewife*) and *yenta,* Yiddish for a coarse woman, but from the Italian *gentile,* kind, gentle, and ultimately noble, highborn.

The traditionally low status of women also is indicated by the way in which masculine terms with negative connotations tend to become feminized. Thus, *wench* comes from the Old English *wenchel,* meaning a child of either sex; *harlot* referred to a male servant, rascal, or buffoon before obtaining its present whorish sense; a *hoyden* was a country bumpkin; and a *shrew* was a wicked or mischievous man. (This pattern continues, with feminine words, in turn, being foisted off on homosexuals; e.g., *fairy; punk,* now a catamite but originally a female prostitute; *nancy,* from the female personal name; and *sissy.*)

There are patterns, too, in the way disparaging terms are formed. Among the most common categories of insult are:

Animal. Very few animal names have not been used as epithets at one time or another. From general terms such as *beast, brute,* and *animal* itself, to such specifics as *coon, crab, hog, jackass, jellyfish, rattlesnake, skunk, wolf,* and *worm,* the effect is to deny the target his or her humanity. Birds are particularly popular in the lexicon of animal derogation, especially as insults for the human female, a.k.a. *chicken, goose, hen, quail,* and, of course, *bird,* as well as for anyone who is lacking in brains, i.e., *as dumb as a dodo, as crazy as a coot, cuckoo,* or a *dupe* (from *de huppe,* the hoopoe, an Old World bird). Other prominent representatives of the animal kingdom in this category of insult include: the *horse* (the female *harridan, jade,* and *nag* all have equine origins); various types of *dog,* e.g., *bitch, cur, mongrel, mutt* (which actually comes from *mutton*), and *puppy;* such *insects* and *vermin* as the *drone, flea, fly, louse, maggot,* and *termite* (the last being an especially popular American metaphor for their Vietnamese opponents during the long war in that country); and other primates, including *ape, baboon, gorilla,* and *monkey.* Only rarely does the traffic go the other way, with derogatory human terms being applied to animals. *Parasite* is one such. To the ancient Greeks, the term denoted a professional diner-out—one who paid for his meals by flattering his host; biologists didn't begin using *parasite* until the eighteenth century.

Anatomy. People frequently are demeaned by referring to them in terms of their apparatus for excretion and procreation as though the part is equal to the whole. This figure of speech, wherein a less inclusive term stands for a more inclusive one, or vice versa, even has its own technical name: synecdoche. Women, especially, are degraded by being described purely as sexual objects. *Beaver, cunt, piece (of ass), pussy, quim, snatch, tail,* and *twat* are among the words that are used to denote both a woman and her genitals. Which is not to imply that men are exempt from this form of synecdoche, e.g., *cock, dick,* and *prick,* all of which have less inclusive as well as more inclusive uses.

Foods. Your enemy is what he eats. The French have long been reviled as *frogs,* the Germans as *the Boche* (cabbageheads) and as *krauts* (from *sauerkraut*), the British as *limeys,* the Mexicans as *chili eaters,* the Italians as *spaghetti benders,* and so on. Many foods also serve as metaphors for nonsense, e.g., *applesauce, baloney, banana oil, beans, mush, pap,* and *tripe.* And women, again, often are characterized as edible objects. *Cookie, cupcake, lamb chop, sugar, sweetie pie, (hot) tamale, tart,* and *tomato* are only some of the toothsome terms for woman. (To engage in oral-genital sex is *to eat,* of course, a metaphor that has been extended into such expressions as *box lunch* and *hair pie.*) Bad cars are *lemons,* black people who act as if they were white inside are *Oreos,* weaklings are *milksops* and *milquetoasts,* especially if they *can't cut the mustard anymore.* And so it goes, through the entire range of comestibles.

Names and nicknames. Personal names, both masculine and feminine, often are used as generics for entire groups of people as well as ways of addressing individuals whose real names are not known, or not worth knowing. Many of these derogations are true eponyms, deriving from the names of real people or from famous fictitious ones, e.g., *Benedict Arnold, chauvinist, Judas, martinet,* and *quisling,* in the first case, and *Alibi Ike, babbit, goody two-shoes, pander,* and *Peeping Tom* in the second. The insulting connotations usually come through most clearly when the familiar form of a name is used, as in *Chico, Charlie, Heinie, Hymie, Jack, Mick, Paddy, Uncle Tom,* and, in the case of women, *biddy* (from *Bridget*), *doll* (from *Dorothy,* but with the strong implication that the woman is a plaything), *jill* (closely related to *jilt*), *moll* (from *Mary,* the type specimen being Daniel Defoe's Moll Flanders), and *suzie* (commonly a prostitute, and for emphasis, *sidewalk suzie*). The demeaning effect of diminutives also is apparent in such terms as *Commie, homo,* and *pinko.* Mispronunciations, short forms, and nonstandard variants of ethnic names have a similar impact, e.g., *Canuck, Eyetalian, Hebe* (popularized without derogatory intent in the show-business newspaper *Variety*), *Injun, Jap, nigger, Polack* (which appears in *Hamlet*), and *prushun.*

Occupations. Clusters of words with pejorative meanings around certain vocations reveal society's traditional estimates of them and their practitioners. Agricultural laborers and small farmers—i.e., *apple-knockers, clodhoppers, goober grabbers, nesters, peasants, rednecks,* etc.—have always been looked down upon, not surprisingly considering the general bias against rural residents. It also seems that hardly anyone has a good word to say for servants, judging from the present meanings of *flunky, henchman, hireling, lackey, minion,* and *slave* (the last of which is ultimately an ethnic slur, deriving from *Slav*). *Peddlers* tend to have a negative image, as do *cadgers* (street sellers originally), *hucksters,* and *mongers* of various sorts (e.g., *costermonger, rumormonger, scandalmonger,* and *whoremonger*); so do *beggars, freeloaders, leeches* (an animal epithet), *moochers, panhandlers,* and *sponges* (yet another member of the much maligned animal kingdom). Among white-collar professionals, the members of the bar seem to be in especially bad odor, as indicated by the existence of *mouthpiece, pettifogger,* and *shyster* (the latter's etymology has been much debated, but it now seems clear that it comes from the German word for excrement). *Lawyer* itself has picked up so many bad connotations that most learned counsel prefer to be referred to as *attorneys* instead; in time, *attorney* is likely to become burdened with negative associations, too.

The general trend in the meanings of words, it is clear, is down. A great many of our terms of disparagment began as good or neutral characterizations of peoples, places, farmers, servants, and so on. Bad meanings tend to drive out good ones. This is the semantic equivalent of Gresham's Law in economics, i.e., bad money—

coins that were underweight or debased—will drive good full-weight money out of circulation, since people will tend to keep the better coins for themselves, stashed away in mattresses or whatever.

Exceptions to this rule exist in language if not finance. Some terms have escaped their original moorings almost completely, notably a number of jazz words (e.g., *boogie-woogie*, referring to secondary syphilis, and *jelly roll*, referring to the vulva), whose low meanings were lost as the music and the language of the subculture were adopted by the culture at large. *Jazz* itself originally was a verb meaning "to copulate."

Other words undergo cycles, changing back and forth from "good" to "bad." For example, *Negro* (from the Spanish or Portuguese *negro*, meaning "black") has swung in and out of favor a couple of times over the past two hundred and fifty years, as successive generations try to escape the labels of the past. When *Negro* is accepted, *black* is a term of opprobrium—and vice versa. In the political arena, *liberal* started out in politics in the early 1800s as an attack word, was transmuted into a positive term, and has recently been cast back into outer darkness, becoming mentionable only as *the L-word*.

Efforts also have been made, sometimes successfully, to rehabilitate "bad" words. Social and political activists work the hardest at this, flaunting pejorative terms as a consciousness raising technique. For example, *Chicano* (from the Spanish *chico*, boy) began as a derogatory term. This was true, too, of *Yankee* (of disputed origin, but most likely from the Dutch *Janke*, Little John), popularized prior to the American Revolution by British soldiers, who did not intend it as a compliment, but proudly adopted by the colonials after the Battles of Lexington and Concord. Overweight people, meanwhile, have begun trying to take the sting out of *fat*, banding together in the National Association to Aid Fat Americans; homosexuals have defiantly adopted *faggot* and *dyke*; some prostitutes have opted for *whore* (long considered a very bad word, but perhaps not one originally, being cognate to the Latin *cara*, dear); and, going about as far as one can go, "A few women artists," as Gloria Steinem has noted, "dubbed their new imagery *cunt art* in celebration of the discovery that not all sexual symbols were phallic" ("Words and Change," 1979).

The activists are swimming against the linguistic tide, however. "Bad" words far outnumber "good" ones. For example, *Roget's International Thesaurus* (fourth edition, revised by Robert L. Chapman, 1977) contains 89 synonyms for *drunk*, compared to 16 for *sober*, and 206 for *bad person* compared to 82 for *good person*. The synonyms for *unchastity* in the *Thesaurus* fill 140 lines, occupying exactly four times as much space as those for *chastity*. For *unchaste woman*, 34 synonyms are listed; for *unchaste man*, 24. No synonyms at all are given for *chaste woman* and *chaste man*.

Thanks to Gresham's Law, the imbalance between positive and negative words is likely to become even greater as time goes on. Surveying the condition of the language, the Reverend Richard Chenevix Trench, D.D. (1807–86), a leading philologist of his period as well as a divine, commented in a lecture: "[I]t is a melancholy thing to observe how much richer is every vocabulary in words that set forth sins, than in those that set forth graces. . . . How much wit, yea, how much imagination must have stood in the service of sin, before it could possess a nomenclature so rich, so varied, and often so heaven-defying as it has."

Indeed, the richness of the vocabulary of sin is a source of continual, not-so-melancholy fascination and edification for the unrepentant, all the world over. Thus, Amanda Bennett reported in *The Wall Street Journal* (7/23/84), on a visit to the village of Gaojia in China (she was the first outsider to visit the village since the Cultural Revolution of the 1960s and apparently the first foreigner ever to stay there overnight): "Eventually, the Liu family relaxes enough to tease me a bit. . . . Mr. Liu masters the English words 'Hi,' 'bye' and 'okay' on an evening stroll through the fields. Then, he grows thoughtful. 'Can you teach me any bad words?' he asks."

A

abortion. A failure. As dyspeptic Thomas Carlyle (1795–1881) said of Charles Lamb (1775–1834): "Poor Lamb! Poor England! when such a despicable abortion is named genius!" *Abortion* has only recently begun to escape the taboo that became attached to it as a result of its association with a formerly illegal operation. For years, newspapers refused to print the word and Hollywood censors kept it out of film soundtracks. The customary evasions were *criminal operation* in the United States and *illegal operation* in the United Kingdom. *Miscarriage* also was used frequently in lieu of the other term, as in the film version of John O'Hara's *Ten North Frederick* (1958). The taboo was strong enough that it even affected *miscarriage*. Thus, in Margaret Mitchell's *Gone with the Wind* (1936), Rhett Butler tells Scarlett, "Cheer up, maybe you'll have a miscarriage," just before she tumbles down the stairs and has one, but in the film that was made from the book (1939), Clark Gable mentions only the possibility of her having an "accident." Today, despite the decriminalization of the procedure (*Roe v. Wade*, 1973), advocates of women's reproductive rights still honor the old taboo when they say they are *pro-choice*, not *pro-abortion*, or that they favor *therapeutic interruption of pregnancy*. See also SQUEAL.

adder, deaf as an. A serpentine simile for the hard of hearing. ". . . Ralph was deaf as an adder" (Charles Dickens, *Nicholas Nickleby*, 1838–39). The idea that adders are deaf goes back at least to biblical times: "Their [referring to wicked judges] poison *is* like the poison of a serpent; *they are* like the deaf adder *that* stoppeth her ear" (*Psalms*, 54:4). Variations include *deaf as a white cat* (white cats are reputed to be stupid as well as deaf), *deaf as a post* (or *doorpost*), and *deaf as a doornail*. The adder is especially notable because it is said to go deaf on purpose, stopping up its ears to avoid hearing the snake charmer who has been summoned to drive it away. The adder does this by putting one ear to the ground and sticking its tail into the other. The first adder to perform this feat actually was *a neddre* or *a nadder*, not *an adder*. The present spelling dates from 1300–1500, when the article and the noun were divided incorrectly. The same thing also happened about the same time to the housewife's *napron*, the carpenter's *nauger*, and in reverse, to the type of salamander formerly known as *an ewt*. See also VIPER.

agitator. Activist. *Agitator* is an attack word, often elaborated as *outside agitator*, an almost all-encompassing term. For instance, noting the Southern penchant for blaming racial troubles on *outside agitators*, Justice Hugo Black pointed out that this term could even "be made to fit papers like the *Times*, which is published in New York" (*New York Times Co. v. Sullivan*, 1964). And as recently as 1976, the pastor of the Baptist Church in Plains, Georgia (home of President Jimmy Carter), made headlines when he told reporters that the congregation had adopted a resolution barring "niggers and civil rights agitators" from membership (*New York Times*, 11/2/76).

Agitators started out as *agents*. They first appeared on the political scene in 1647 when the common soldiers of Cromwell's army elected representatives to lay their grievances (lack of pay, especially) before their officers and Parliament. In its earliest uses the word often appeared as *adjutator*, possibly due to confusion with the military *adjutant*, but the context was in keeping with an older sense of *agitate*, i.e., to act as an agent. By the early nineteenth century, stirrers up of the body politic frequently were described as *agitators*. The Irish patriot Daniel O'Connell (1775–1847) was known to his admirers as "the great agitator" as well as "the Liberator." Not everyone admired O'Connell, of course, and his agitations may have contributed to the term's disparaging connotations, which have been evident since at least the middle of the last century. See also COMMIE, GOON, and MILITANT.

albatross. An impediment or JINX. "Tradition is the albatross around the neck of progress" (Bill Veeck, *New York Times*, 1/3/86). Originally a sign of good luck—because of its habit of following ships for days on end, providing sailors with their only companionship in otherwise desolate southern seas—the albatross has acquired a sinister significance because of the bad luck that supposedly comes from killing one. "Instead of a cross, the Albatross / About my neck was hung" (Samuel Taylor Coleridge, "The Rime of the Ancient Mariner," 1798). The Ancient Mariner shot his albatross with a crossbow and his fellow sailors hung the dead bird around his neck in order to make it clear to the fates that he alone was to blame. The incident is based remotely on fact. Coleridge and William Wordsworth had planned to collaborate on a poem about the origin of evil. The poem never got written because the styles of the two poets didn't mesh. While discussing it, however, Wordsworth told Coleridge the story of George Shelvocke, a buccaneer who was pursued by bad weather after one of his officers shot a black albatross while rounding Cape Horn in 1720. In actuality, having a dead albatross around one's neck would be very bad luck indeed, as a typical bird weighs fifteen to twenty-five pounds and has a wingspread of nine to twelve feet. A wonderful glider but an otherwise clumsy creature, the albatross also is known as the gooney bird. See also BIRD, GOON, and JONAH.

Alibi Ike. A person who is always making excuses, from the baseball playing protagonist of "Alibi Ike," a short story by Ring W. Lardner: "His right name was Frank X. Farrell, and I guess the X stood for 'Excuse me.' Because he never pulled a play, good or bad, on or off the field, without apologizin' for it. 'Alibi Ike' was the name Carey wished on him the first day he reported South" (*How to Write Short Stories*, 1924). The basic *alibi* is Latin for "elsewhere," and this was the strict meaning of the word when alleged perpetrators first began using it, e.g., "The prisoner had little to say in his defence; he endeavored to prove himself Alibi" (John Arbuthnot, *Law Is a Bottomless Pit*, 1712).

Ananias. A liar. "An Ananias historian has tried to write a history that would make John Brown a demon, a thief, and a murderer . . ." (Kansas State Historical Society, *Collections*, 1888). The reference is biblical—to Ananias, who sold a piece of land, but held back part of the price instead of donating the whole of it to the Apostles. "But Peter said, Ananias . . . why hast thou conceived this thing in thine heart? thou has not lied unto men, but unto God. And Ananias hearing these words fell down, and gave up the ghost . . ." (*Acts*, 5:3–5). Sapphira, wife to Ananias, was privy to his secret, and she also "yielded up the ghost" when confronted with the lie. See also LIAR.

animal. A human being without human qualities. "I say, let's get these animals off the streets. Forty-eight hours after conviction, into the gas chamber" (Wally George, "Hot Seat" KDOC-TV, Anaheim, California, in *Columbia Journalism Review*, 5-6/84). "They were attacked because they were defenseless, because they were easy targets for the animals that did it" (Israeli Defense Miniser Yitzhak Rabin, referring to Arabs who had killed twenty-one Jews in a synagogue in Istanbul, in *New York Times*, 9/10/86).

Animal, from the Latin *anima*, air, breath of life, is a comparatively new word, not often used in English prior to 1600. (It does not appear in the King James version of the Bible, of 1611.) Previously, the designation for what we call an *animal* was *beast*, or, a still older term, *deer*, as in "But mice, rats and such small deer Have Tom's food for seven long year" (William Shakespeare, *King Lear*, 1607). Shakespeare knew the modern word, however—and also how to use it contemptuously: "His intellect is not replenished, he is only an animal, only sensible in the duller parts" (*Love's Labor's Lost*, 1588–94).

On the lighter side, two-footed *animals* also are encountered today on college campuses, living together in *animal houses* (fraternities or sororities), as in the film *National Lampoon's Animal House* (1978). See also BEAST, BRUTE, MONSTER, YAHOO, and ZOO.

Ann. A white woman to a black person—or a black woman who acts too much like a white one. "While *Miss Ann*, also just plain *Ann*, is a derisive reference to the white woman, by extension it is applied to any black woman who puts on airs and tries to act like Miss Ann" (Geneva Smitherman, *Talkin and Testifyin*, 1977). See also CHARLIE, PADDY, and UNCLE TOM.

ape. A person who looks or acts like a big monkey. *To ape* is to mimic one and *to go ape* is to go wild or crazy—in effect, to be *out of [one's] tree*. The devil used to be considered *God's ape* and the same phrase was applied to natural-born fools. However the term is used, the connotations are pejorative. Thus, as mimic: "Report of fashions in proud Italy, Whose manners still our tardy apish nation Limps after in base imitation" (William Shakespeare, *Richard II*, 1595–96). Then there was John Porter, jailed in Boston in 1664 for calling his father a "Liar, and simple Ape, shittabed." (Porter didn't get along very well with his mother either. According to Kenneth Silverman's *The Life and Times of Cotton Mather*, 1984, Porter called his mommy a "Rambeggur, Gamar Shithouse, Gamar Pisshouse" and "the rankest sow in town.") Some two centuries later, *ape* also was the operative word when Algernon Charles Swinburne savaged Ralph Waldo Emerson as "a gap-toothed and hoary-headed ape . . . who now in his dotage spits and chatters from a dirtier perch of his own finding and fouling . . ." (letter, 1/30/1874). See also BABOON, GORILLA, JACKANAPES, and MONKEY.

apologist. Originally a person who defends or vindicates with arguments, as might a lawyer, philosopher, or champion of Christian doctrine, the term has fallen on hard times. "In the vocabulary of verbal representation, an *advocate* is a persuasive spokesman and has a positive connotation, as in the title assumed by Ralph Nader, 'consumer advocate'; an *apologist* is a propagandist, once meaning an explicator of God's word but now only used to mean a slavish mouthpiece . . ." (William Safire, *Safire's Political Dictionary*, 1978). See also LAWYER.

apparatchik. A second-order dysphemism, bearing the same relation to BUREAU-CRAT as bureaucrat does to civil servant or administrator. "And they said, 'Why would you resign?' and I replied, 'Because I don't want to be regarded as an apparatchik, an organization man who does whatever the organization wants" (Robert H. Bork, testimony, Senate Judiciary Committee, 9/16/87). The *apparatchik* is a product of the Russian revolution, the *apparat* being the party machine, and the *chik* being a zealous member of it. Even in its original setting, the term has disparaging connotations. Thus, speaking of Konstantin U. Chernenkov, upon his elevation as General Secretary of the Communist Party: "I don't think you can reduce him to the simplistic image of an incompetent, colorless Soviet apparatchik" (Dmitri K. Simes, *New York Times*, 2/14/84).

appeaser. One who placates, settles, or soothes; from the Latin *ad* (to) + *pais* (peace). Up until the Prime Ministership of Neville Chamberlain (1937–40), *appease, appeasement,* and *appeaser* were neutral words. It was the failure of his policy of concessions to Hitler, often described by himself as "methods of appeasement," that gave these terms their present negative connotations. Now they are fine words for blackjacking anyone who seems ready to discuss differences with foreign powers before going to war with them. Thus Senator William E. Jenner (Republican, Indiana), whose fulminations had the genuine rhythm of nineteenth-century frontier "bad" talk, drew on *appeaser* when attacking General George C. Marshall as "an errand boy, a front man, a stooge, or a conspirator for this administration's crazy assortment of collectivist cutthroat crackpots and communist fellow-travelling appeasers" (Forrest C. Pogue, *George C. Marshall: Statesman, 1945–1959,* 1987). See also DOVE.

apple, bad (or **rotten**). A no-good person, especially one who is likely to lead others astray, contaminating them as does the proverbial rotten apple in a barrel. "Of this group of 12 maybe there were 2 bad apples, but not John—John is definitely good" (*New York Times,* 2/12/87, quoting the neighbor of a young white man who had been accused of participating in an attack on three black men who had the misfortune of wandering into their neighborhood in Queens). The essential image is of some antiquity: "An evil soul producing holy witness Is like a villain with a smiling cheek, A goodly apple rotten at the heart" (William Shakespeare, *The Merchant of Venice,* 1596–98).

The apple's connotations are not all bad; for example, everything may be said to be in *apple-pie order* or it may be that Agatha is the *apple of my eye,* but in most folk sayings, the fruit's symbolic meaning tends to be negative. Thus, an *applehead* is a slow-witted person, as in " 'You sir,' thundered the Old Arbitrator [umpire Bill Klem], 'are an apple-head' " (*New York Times,* 9/24/51), and an *apple-knocker* is a farmer, or HICK, to a city slicker, who thinks that apples are harvested by knocking them off trees. To tell someone *to go climb a sour apple tree* is the functional equivalent of telling them *to go jump in the lake,* or more rudely, to go to hell, and for a woman *to fall off the apple tree* is to lose her virginity. *To upset the applecart* is to ruin a plan (from 1796), and occasionally elaborated in the mixed metaphorical threat, "I'll upset your applecart and spill your peaches". Meanwhile, an *apple-polisher* is a flatterer or, more rudely, a BROWN-NOSE(R) (apparently from the custom of schoolchildren of getting in good with their teachers by presenting them with shiny apples), while *applesauce* is just one of many food terms for nonsense (see BALONEY). Much more could (but will not here) be written about the significance of the apple in Western culture. Possible starting points for such an essay include the facts that the apple's genus name, *malus*, means "evil" in Latin; that the fruit of the tree of knowledge in the Garden of Eden probably was not an apple but an apricot; and that the romantic-sounding Avalon, of Arthurian legend, means "Apple Island" in Celtic. See also COSTERMONGER.

apron strings, tied to [someone's]. To be unduly subject to one's wife or mother; in other words, to be a WIMP, or a SISSY, depending on whether the strings are tied to a man or a boy. "He could not submit to be tied to the apron strings even of the best of wives" (Thomas Babington Macaulay, *The History of England from the Accession of James II*, 1849). The phrase dates to at least the sixteenth century, when it had a specific legal meaning, *apron-string hold* or *tenure* referring to tenure of an estate by virtue of one's wife or during her lifetime only.

arch-. A prefix for heaping additional odium upon one's chosen enemy, converting him into an *archenemy*. This reverses the prefix's usual meaning of chief, highest, or leading, as in *archangel*, *archbishop*, *archdeacon*, or *archduke*. On the downside, other *arch*'s include *archcriminal*, *archknave*, *archrogue*, *archseducer*, *archtraitor*, *archvillain*, and *archwag*. The frequent use of the prefix in the negative sense is what led to the development of the secondary meaning of *arch*, to describe clever, cunning, mischievous, or roguish behavior. All forms of *arch* come from the architectural *arch*, which, in turn, probably derives ultimately from the Latin *arcus*, a bow, whence also comes the *arc* of a circle and the *arcade* of an amusement park. See also ULTRA-.

armchair. The comfortable, often overstuffed symbol of domesticity makes a convenient prefix for denigrating thinkers as opposed to doers. The general implication is that the stay-at-home who offers advice or theories after the fact is less expert—and not nearly as brave—as the active participant in affairs. The flavor of the term is conveyed well by the following 1885 citation from the *OED*: "Mr. Chamberlain . . . met the expostulations . . . of his moderate allies with sneers at . . . 'the arm-chair politicians.'" Other examples of the *armchair* construction include *armchair athlete*, *armchair critic*, *armchair general*, *armchair historian*, *armchair professor*, *armchair* (a.k.a. *grandstand* or *Monday morning*) *quarterback*, *armchair strategist*, and *armchair traveler*. See also ULTRA-.

Asiatic. Crazy, abnormal; from the Spanish-American War, for someone who had spent too much time in the Far East, and later extended, often in the phrase, *gone Asiatic*, to anyone who seemed deranged. "Only solitary sailors who had gone Asiatic went to cathouses without first getting bombed" (James Earl Thompson, *Tattoo*, 1974). Indicative of the taint that became attached to *Asiatic* in politer civilian circles: "*Asian Review*. Volume XLIX, Number 177. January 1953 . . . After 68 years of existence the widely circulated quarterly hitherto known as the *Asiatic Review* makes a slight but important change of designation. . . . The term 'Asiatic' has come to be regarded with disfavour by those to whom it applied, and they feel entitled to be brought into line with usage in regard to Europeans, Americans, and Australians" (*Times Literary Supplement*, 2/6/53). See also GOOK and RAGHEAD.

ass. All asses are divided into two distinct species—those with four legs and those with two—but even so it is not always possible to tell them apart at first glance. For example:

There was a young lady from Madras
Who had a magnificent ass;
  Not rounded and pink,
  As you probably think—
It was grey, had long ears and ate grass.

The ambiguity caused by using the same word for the animal and the anatomical part is not always resolved as neatly as in the above limerick (from 1940, number 1,581 in G. Legman's remarkable collection, *The Limerick*, 1969). Careful analysis of context often is required to determine what is meant. Thus, the ASPCA might have brought charges against Vice President George Bush after he remarked that "we tried to kick a little ass last night" (*New York Times*, 10/14/84), except for the context . . . the reference being to his campaign debate with Geraldine A. Ferraro. On the other hand, when former U.N. ambassador Andrew Young admitted, regarding some fellow Democrats, "A lot of folks I thought were smart asses are a lot smarter than I thought they were" (*New York Times*, 8/30/84), the allusion most likely was to the four-legged JACKASS. (This wasn't a very edifying campaign. For Barbara Bush's contribution to it, see BITCH.)

But what is the deep linguistic structure—animalistic or anatomical—that supports such a phrase as *ass in a sling*, as in, "Got my head in the clouds, ass in a sling, feet planted firmly on the ground, and both guns blazing from the hip" (Los Angeles [where else?] *Reader*, 4/1/83)? It has been seriously suggested that this metaphor for partial incapacitation originated because donkeys are so awkward that they can't stand on just three feet and so have to be supported in slings when being shoed. This explanation is exceedingly picturesque but, alas, no trace of an ass sling has ever been found amidst the ruins of any smithy—and none was ever needed, since donkeys are capable of raising one foot at a time without toppling over. A much likelier explanation is that the sling in this instance is similar to the sling for a broken arm, but larger, and that this fanciful description for one who is so thoroughly defeated, whether by life or by drink, that he can hardly move, is an anatomical allusion, fundamentally.

In general, it seems the four-legged species of ass is meant whenever the allusion is to slowness, foolishness, stupidity, or clumsiness—qualities that have been attributed to the animal from time immemorial, e.g., "People captured the Donkey by the following stratagem. Being forsooth a tardy beast and having no sense at all, it surrendered as soon as men surrounded it!" (T. H. White, *The Bestiary*, twelfth century, tr. 1954). Commonly encountered subspecies, in addition to the previously mentioned *smart ass*, include *complete ass, dumb ass, half ass, horse's ass* (see HORSE), *stupid ass*, and *wise ass*. As an insult, the term is as old as the hills. Thus, a fragment of ancient Greek repartee involves a fresh young man who met an old woman driving a herd of animals and said, "Good morning, mother of asses," only to be topped with the reply, "Good morning, my son!" Over the years, the term has been so generalized that the quadrupedal meaning is but a faint etymological memory. Consider, for example, the unseemly spectacle of one animal abusing another animal with this term: " 'Stop it, you *silly* ass,' cried Rat from the bottom of the boat" (Kenneth Grahame, *The Wind in the Willows*, 1908).

Meanwhile, the anatomical ass figures prominently in a variety of expressions, particularly when threats of a personal nature are being made, e.g., *your soul is God's, but your ass is mine, I'll whip your ass,* and *your ass is grass and I'm the lawn mower* (? *ex*

Isaiah 40:6, "All flesh *is* grass"). This piece of anatomy also is the subject of such classic children's rhymes as:

> Oh they don't wear pants
> In the southern part of France,
> But they do wear grass
> To cover up their ass.
> (personal communication,
> Mamaroneck, New York, ca. 1941)
>   and
> I'm Popeye the sailor man,
> I live in a frying pan.
> I turn on the gas
> And burn off my ass,
> I'm Popeye the sailor man.
> (personal communication,
> Brooklyn, New York, 1982)

Asses in both senses first appeared in English around 1000 A.D. One sense comes from the animal's Latin name, *asinus*. The other comes from—and for many years appeared only as—the British *arse*, which, in turn, comes from an Indo-European root, *ers*, to be wet. In different forms, this root meant "dew" and "that sprinkles or ejects semen." In the first case, it led to such modern words as *rosemary* and RHUBARB, and in the second case to *arse*.

The evolution of the modern American (anatomical) *ass* from the traditional British *arse* is part of a general dropping of *r* before *s*, a pronunciation change that began in about the fifteenth century. The shift also is seen in such pairs as *burst/bust*, *curse/cuss*, *first/fust*, and *horse/hoss*, as well as in the name of the fish, the *barse*, now known as the *bass*. Just when this happened in the case of *arse/ass* is difficult to tell, the written record being woefully incomplete on account of the taboos attached to both words for many years. Still, there are clues, direct and indirect.

The earliest example of *ass* in its so-called vulgar and dialectical sense in the *Oxford English Dictionary* is from 1860. The reference there is to the *ass of the block*, a term that sailors used to describe the deep-scored line for carrying a rope through a pulley or block; earlier, in the eighteenth century, this same item had been called the *arse of the block*. But the word was certainly current prior to 1860. For example, Abraham Lincoln, some years before becoming president (1861), wrote a humorous piece involving such spoonerisms as *bass-ackwards* and *jass-ack*, as well as *tow-curd* (Mark E. Neely, Jr., *The Abraham Lincoln Encyclopedia*, 1982). Lincoln's earlier knowledge of the term in its modern sense also can be inferred from a poem sent to him in 1860 by his friend Ward Hill Lamon. This poem depends for its humor on unusual word breaks (*I like ass-bestus* is one such) and is a fine example of nineteenth-century American "bad" talk. It refers to the Democratic presidential nominating convention of 1860, which met first at Charleston, South Carolina, broke up over the question of including a pro-slavery plank in the platform, and then resumed in Baltimore, minus representatives from the eight cotton states, who had bolted from the party, foreshadowing their secession from the Union. For present purposes, the second verse is the key one:

And when they got to Charleston, they had to,
    as is wont
Look around to find a chairman, and so they took
    a Cu-
shing, who is known throughout the land
As most prodigious "pumpkins" when the niggers
    is on hand

Then, an ultra southern platform, they made and
    tried to pass
When up jumped all the Douglas men and quickly
    showed their as-
tonishment, at proceedings such as these,
For a platform made to suit the South, the
    North would never please

And they made another, that on it, all might sit
When the South got mad as fury and swore they'd
    on it sh-
-ow that down among the chivalry in their
    peaceful
    sunny land
There was not a single Cotton State on its planks
    would land

When Douglas found his chances were scarcely
    worth a shuck
He bade his delegates go home, to take a
    little fu-
-rther time, in order as you see
To meet again in Baltimore on some one to agree

Other evidence for the use of *ass* in lieu of *arse* is indirect, depending upon the avoidance principle. For instance, toward the end of the eighteenth century even earthy farmers began calling their asses *donkeys*—the latter being described in the *OED* (1893–97) as "a recent word." The point, of course, is that proto-Victorians were using *donkey* (perhaps from the pet name *Duncan*) because of the double meaning that *ass* already had acquired. As Captain Francis Grose explained, when defining Johnny Bum: "A he or jack ass; so called by a lady that affected to be extremely polite and modest, who would not say . . . ass because it was indecent" (*A Classical Dictionary of the Vulgar Tongue*, 1785).

The search for the primordial *ass* can be carried back even further, though the evidence becomes more tenuous with the passage of time. The dropping of the *r*'s in allied words provides some help. Thus, dictionaries record the first *boss* in 1815, the first *bust* in 1764, and the first *cuss* in 1775. *Bass* doesn't appear until 1802, but the pronunciation shift is evident from *base* (1586) and *bace* (ca. 1440). With *ass* the trail leads—as it so often does when questions arise about creative use of language—to William Shakespeare. He obviously knew the word in its quadrupedal sense. In *Hamlet* (1601–02), for example, the princely

Dane exclaims in one of his moments of despondence, "Why, what an ass am I!" But in the same play, the hero announces, "Then came each actor on his ass." The suspicion of a pun here—on *arse* pronounced *ahs*—is reinforced by Hamlet's scornful comment in the same exchange about the actors' "Buzz, buzz." As Eric Partridge points out (*Shakespeare's Bawdy*, 1948), this was the Bard's way of rendering in print the vulgar fart-like noise known to bad actors in modern times as the RASPBERRY. Clinching the argument for the Elizabethan understanding of the word in both senses is the weaver in *A Midsummer Night's Dream* (1594), who is transformed into an ass/donkey and who Shakespeare named Nick Bottom.

The taboo on *arse* and *ass* dates to the fastidiousness of the eighteenth century, preceding the full-blown Victorianism of the nineteenth. For example, in 1787 (*OED*), the innocent water pepper, *Polygonum hydropiper*, once commonly known as *arsesmart*, or *ass-smart*, first appears as "smart weed." And the otherwise uninhibited Captain Grose often resorted to dashes in his dictionary, as in "ASK MY A—E. A common reply to any question; still deemed wit at sea," and "BLACK A—SE. A copper or kettle. The pot calls the kettle black a-se." Interior evidence shows, however, that only a couple of generations before Grose, the term was bandied about in the very best of circles. For instance, the maids of honor at the court of Queen Anne seem to have gotten much amusement out of tricking dullards into asking a question to which they could reply, "Mine arse." This was known as "selling a bargain." Grose explains one way the feat was accomplished: "A lady would come into a room full of company apparently in great fright, crying out, 'It is white and follows me!' On any of the company asking, 'What?', she sold them the bargain by saying, 'Mine a--e.'" Be it also noted that the reign of Queen Anne (1702–14) is acknowledged on the high authority of the *Encyclopaedia Britannica* (1926) to have been "one of the most brilliant in the annals of England." Whatever the fact of that matter, *arse* was not often printed in full in Great Britain until well into the twentieth century. Frederic Manning was considered "extremely daring," according to Eric Partridge, to include all four letters in *Her Privates We* (1930). In the interim, the staid British chuckled over obituaries on such personages as R. Supwards and, in the case of a youth named Longbottom, the headline: ARS LONGA, VITA BREVIS. This was about as far as family publications could go.

Naturally, the blackout print did not prevent *arse* and *ass* from being used conversationally, the former appearing primarily in British English and the latter in American English. Herewith, a sampling of the more common variations on the *asinine* theme:

ass (*about* or *around*), to. To fool around; schoolboy talk.

ass-deep. Very deep. "The snow is ass-deep to a man in a jeep" (Robert Leckie, *March to Glory*, 1960).

assed up. Confused, muddled; a euphemism for "fucked up."

asshole. A stupid person. "Well, who was the asshole that did? It is Liddy?" (President Richard M. Nixon, White House tape, 6/23/72). This particular vulgarism is of historic significance, occurring in a recording that helped prove that Nixon had started to participate in the cover-up of the Watergate break-in just six days after it occurred and that he had lied to the nation many times when denying this. Release of the transcript on August 5, 1974, left him no choice but to resign, which he did four days later.

This vulgarism also appears in a great many phrases, especially in military talk, e.g., *asshole buddy*, a close friend or pal; *to keep a tight asshole*, an allusion to the tendency of frightened people to lose control of their bowels; R.A., said to stand for *regular asshole* as well as Regular Army; *asshole to belly button*, which is to be in very close formation; and the standard instruction of sergeants to soldiers as they police an area, "All I want to see is assholes and elbows" (personal communication, Fort Dix, New Jersey, 11/56).

ass-kisser. A sycophant, a brown-noser; often abbreviated *A.K.* In British English, the *arse* form is more common, e.g., "[British Foreign Minister] Ernest Bevin . . . declared on one occasion in 1948 that the President [Truman] would 'lick any Jewish arse that promised him a hundred votes' " (Leonard Mosley, *Marshall: Hero for Our Times,* 1982). See also *kiss ass* below.

ass man. One who is successful (sexually) with women; a Don Juan. *Ass* here is an anatomical displacement. See *piece of ass* below.

ass over teakettle. Upside down, head over heels; *arse over turkey* in British English, or *arsy varsy.* The last dates to at least the sixteenth century; the *varsy* was formed by changing the pronunciation of *versus,* Latin for "turned," to duplicate the sound of the *arsy.*

ass peddler. A prostitute, either male or female.

asswipe(r). Toilet paper or a substitute; an incompetent or foolish person. The term is old; Chaucer knew it as *erswisp.* One of history's greatest authorities on bad talk, François Rabelais, addressed this subject in memorable detail in *Gargantua* (1534, tr. 1694), with the protagonist describing the various materials he had used for the purpose, including—among others—calfskin, a hare, a pigeon, a lawyer's bag, and a penitent's hood. Gargantua's conclusion: "there is no ass-wiper like a well-downed goose, if you hold her neck between your legs. . . . You get a marvelous sensation." Then there is the classic reply by a disgruntled composer to one of his critics: "I am sitting in the smallest room of my house with your review before me. Soon it will be behind me" (Max Reger, 1873–1916). The same thought has been attributed to Voltaire and others. Thus, from the conclusion of a lament, *The Poet's Condition,* by an impoverished Grub Street writer, Thomas Brown (1663–1704):

> And tell how doleful the case is;
> If I don't move your pity,
> To make short of my ditty,
> 'Twill serve you to wipe your arses.

badass. A tough person, especially a mean or malicious one. "A marine who postures toughness is sarcastically labeled a *bad ass* or *hairy-assed marine*" (*American Speech,* 10/56). The acronym *BAM,* however, does not stand for Bad Ass Marine, but for Broad-Assed Marine, i.e., a female marine (from World War II). See also BAD.

bare-ass. Naked, sometimes abbreviated *B.A.* by kids when they go skinny-dipping.

barrel ass, to. To move fast, especially when driving.

bug up [one's] ass, to have a. To be very touchy or irascible, especially about wanting to do things one's own way; more politely, *to have a bug up [one's] nose.*

burn [one's] ass, to. To anger, often used reflexively. "But what really burned my ass was a meeting [Red Sox manager Eddie] Kasko held in spring training in '72" (Sparky Lyle and Peter Golembock, *The Bronx Zoo,* 1979).

busy as a one-legged man in a ass-kicking contest. Very busy indeed.

candy-ass. A weakling or sissy. "Here was a man [Richard M. Nixon] who . . . labeled 'candy-ass' a Secretary of the Treasury [and future Secretary of State,

George P. Shultz] who balked at using the tax system to punish citizens he considered 'enemies' " (Anthony Lewis, *New York Times*, 8/2/84). Sensitive souls have euphemized this one as *candy-ankle*.

chew ass, to. To berate, to bawl out, especially in the military. *To chew* (or *kick*) *ass* (and *take names*) means that the verbal abuse will be followed by other punishment.

cover [one's] ass, to. To protect oneself; especially in a bureaucratic setting, often abbreviated *C.Y.A.*, for *Cover Your Ass*. Another variant: "The story seemed an assiduous exercise in ass-covering . . ." (*Columbia Journalism Review*, 11-12/83).

fat (or *lard*) *ass*. Having large buttocks. See also FAT.

get your ass in gear, to. To get moving, usually an imperative.

haul ass (or *tail*), *to*. To move (out) quickly, to hurry up. The expression dates to World War I. Lenny Bruce's use of it helped lead to his prosecution for obscenity in New York City in 1964. He had asserted that women generally—and, by strong implication, Jacqueline Kennedy, in particular—"haul ass to save their asses," and of all the scatalogical things Bruce ever said, this was the remark that seemed to offend the most sensibilities. Certainly, the prosecution made the most of it, and he was convicted. For more on this case, see TIT.

have [one's] head up [one's] ass, to. To be stupid or to act that way. By implication: *Pull your head out* to someone who is acting in a *stupid-ass* manner or, rhetorically, *Isn't it dark in there?* This last may be followed with the offer: *I'd give you a match to see with, except you might explode*.

kick ass, to. To abuse or beat up, either physically or verbally (see George Bush's remark at the beginning of this entry). "For the fourth game in a row, we came out and started kicking ass and scored runs and hit the ball like I couldn't believe" (Lyle and Golembock, *op. cit.*). See also *to chew* (*kick*) *ass* (*and take names*) variant above.

kick in the ass. A personal setback, disappointment, or defeat; euphemistically, a *kick in the pants* (or *tail*). In either case, the kick is metaphoric and the pain is to the psyche, not the seat. *To kick [someone] in the pants* is to propel that someone into action.

kiss [one's] ass, to. To boot-lick, so to speak; sometimes abbreviated *K.A.* "Asked about his being criticized by American Jews for having played host to a visiting Libyan goodwill mission, Mr. [Billy] Carter replied, 'They can kiss my____ as far as I'm concerned now' " (*New York Times*, 2/16/79). The expression has been around for some time. For example, Captain Francis Grose included an entry on the subject: "KISS MINE A-SE. An offer, as Fielding observes, very frequently made, but never, as he could learn, literally accepted. A kiss mine a-se fellow; a sycophant." See also the citation from Fielding's *Shamela* in DAMN.

Not to know [one's] ass from [one's] elbow (or *from a hole in the ground*, or *from third base*, or *from a double-barreled shotgun*, or from whatever other item comes quickly to the speaker's mind). Not to know very much at all.

pain in the ass. A nuisance; an obnoxious person or thing, euphemized as *pain in the neck*. "You should have been a hemorrhoid because you're such a pain in the ass" (novelty card, New York, 1981, *Maledicta*, 1981).

piece of ass (or *tail*). A woman regarded as a sex object; an act of sexual intercourse. "He . . . thought she was a flaming, fabulous piece of ass" (Judith Krantz, *Scruples*, 1978). Here, *ass* and *tail* are bywords, of course, for nearby anatomy. In the first case, *ass* echoes the anterior meaning of its Indo-European root, *ers*. As for *tail*, it has long had double meanings in both masculine and feminine senses, standing for the penis (in Latin, *penis* = tail) as well as for what Chaucer's Wife of Bath called her "likerous [lecherous] tayl," not meaning her rump. None of this should be taken to imply that men do not appreciate well-shaped feminine backsides. There is even a technical term to describe beautiful buttocks—*callipygian*, after the name of a famous statue of Venus. Sir Thomas Browne referred to "callipygae" as "women largely composed behinde" (*Pseudodoxia Epidemica*, 1646). He may have had tongue in cheek. Today a callipygian woman might be described admiringly as *having an ass you could plant a flag on*. Strangely, *piece of ass* has been dated in writing only to 1942 and *The Thesaurus of American Slang* (Lester V. Berrey and Melvin Van den Bark), where it is lumped in with the synonymous *piece* (or *hunk*) *of tail*, or *skirt*, or *butt*. The expression is almost certainly much older than this, however. See also PIECE, TAIL, and TIGHTASS.

play grab-ass, to. To fondle, not necessarily the buttocks; in extended use, to fool around.

raggedy ass. Raw, as a recruit; green; sloppy and poorly disciplined, or *ragbags*; from World War I, if not before, unto modern times: "Respect what man, you raggedy-assed little fuck?" (Robert Flannagan, *Maggot*, 1971).

stick it (or *stuff it*) *up your ass.* A most contemputous suggestion, usually expressed as an emphatic rejection of another person, plan, or idea; for emphasis, *stick it up your ass and holler fire*. The expression also may be euphemized as *stick it in your ear*. In whatever form, this is the moral equivalent of *go fuck yourself* and it may, in fact, be combined with that expression, e.g., *go fuck yourself in the ass and give yourself some brains*. See also STICK IT TO [SOMEONE] and UP YOURS. The grossness of the vulgarity is mitigated slightly by knowing that the notion is not unique to our time and culture. Thus, a common Hungarian curse, whose popularity may reflect the importance of the horse to Attila and the Huns, has been translated somewhat discreetly as "horse's member up your anus" (John Simon, *Paradigms Lost*, 1980). And Reinhold Aman, founder of *Maledicta: The International Journal of Verbal Aggression*, reports that the oldest curse he has ever found—from ancient Egypt—starts out "May a donkey copulate with you!" (*Maledicta*, Summer 1977). This curse appears frequently in documents of the Twenty-third Dynasty (749–21 B.C.), the idea being that those who do not abide by legal agreements deserve this particular fate. In full, the curse goes: "If you do not obey this decree, may a donkey copulate with you! May a donkey copulate with your wife! May your child copulate with your wife!" All of which goes to show that the art of cursing has not advanced a great deal in the past couple thousand years. You can, as the saying goes, bet your you-know-what on that.

B

babbitt. A narrow-minded, self-satisfied, middle-class materialist. "Bohemia is a state of mind inhabited by those who, whether or not they are creative or particularly intellectual, like to stand on the margins and scoff at the babbitts" (Vance Packard, *The Status Seekers*, 1959). The progenitor: "His name was George F. Babbitt. He was forty-six years old now, in April 1920, and he made nothing in particular, neither butter nor shoes nor poetry, but he was nimble in the selling of houses for more money than people could afford to pay" (Sinclair Lewis, *Babbitt*, 1922). See also BOURGEOIS and PHILISTINE.

babe in the woods. An inexperienced or naïve person; an easy mark; one who is wet behind the ears. The allusion is to an old story, and a sad one, *The Children in the Wood*, which is preserved as a ballad as well as a play (both from 1601). It seems that a rich man in Norfolk died, leaving his young son and daughter in the care of an uncle, with the proviso that the uncle would inherit if the children should happen to die. Thus tempted, the uncle hired two men to kill the children. One of the men relented and killed his partner instead of the children, but left them in the forest. All sorts of bad things then happened to the uncle—his cattle died, his sons died, he himself died in jail—and the hireling, caught in connection with another crime, later confessed all. But none of this helped the innocent babes in the wood, who died after having been abandoned there.

baboon. A subhuman. "When Maud Malone Devlin, nine months pregnant, discovers her husband Jack has just had a fling with her gorgeous Scandinavian birth instructress, she confirms what she has always suspected: that all men are baboons" (Maureen Baron, in-house editorial bulletin, New American Library, 9/17/86). The term is venerable. For example, the prototypical Frenchman in John Arbuthnot's *The History of John Bull* (1712) was Lewis Baboon—a pun upon *Bourbon*. (The French had yet to metamorphose into FROGs.) Later, in the eighteenth century, a standard insult was "You are a thief and a murderer, you have killed a baboon and stole his face" (Captain Francis Grose, *A Classical Dictionary of the Vulgar Tongue*, 1796). Not even the greatest of men have been exempt from such abuse, e.g., "[*The Appeal*] was noticeably free from vituperation, calling the President 'Mr. Lincoln,' instead of the 'Illinois Baboon' " (A.D. Richardson, *The Secret Service*, 1865). The long-armed Lincoln often was portrayed in simian terms. See also GORILLA.

The etymology of *baboon* is uncertain. It may have been applied to people—simpletons or ninnies—before becoming attached to a particular breed of monkey. The earliest-known example of the word occurs in a thirteenth-century manuscript in which the Old French *babouin*, a gaping figure, refers to a person who gawks at the statues in front of Notre Dame while his purse is cut from behind. The idea that the *baboon* is a simpleton fits in well with the word's Indo-European root, *baba,* which imitates the unintelligible babbling of a baby, and which also gives us BARBARIAN. People who act like baboons are said to engage in *baboonery* (from ca. 1840). One of the preferred replies to "See you later, alligator" is "See you soon, baboon." See also APE.

baby. An infantile person, frequently a SISSY or CRYBABY. "That great baby you see there is not yet out of his swaddling clouts" (William Shakespeare, *Hamlet,* 1601–02). Today, the insult probably is employed most often by those who are barely out of babyhood themselves, e.g., a schoolyard taunt heard in Brooklyn, New York, in 1983:

> Baby, baby—
> Stick your head in gravy.
> Wash it out with bubble gum,
> And send it to the Navy.

backbiter. One who secretly slanders another, biting him while his back is turned. The term already was at least a couple hundred years old when Chaucer used it: "The backbiter wole torne al thilke goodnes up-so-doun" (*Canterbury Tales,* 1387–1400).

back-stabber. Like a BACKBITER, but worse—actions speaking louder than words. The expression reeks of Renaissance intrigue, but has been dated only to 1906 in the *OED,* with the earliest example illustrating a figurative *back-stabber,* not an actual one: "I will tell you my idea of a false friend and back-stabber—to sweat the workman for a personal profit and fawn on him for political profit; to promise old-age pensions for votes and having got the votes, to refuse them" (*Westminster Gazette,* 1/6/06). One presumes that former White House chief of staff Donald T. Regan also had figurative knives in mind when he told the congressional committees investigating the Iran-Contra connection that he wasn't worried about taking "spears in the breast" so much as "knives in the back"—alluding to the intrigues within the Reagan White House (7/30/87). See also DOUBLE-CROSSER.

bad. Evil, false, unsound, degenerate; not good, not right, not true—the list could easily be extended, for the word has a raft of noxious meanings, alone and in such combinations as *bad actor, badass, bad blood, bad debts, bad dude, bad egg, bad girl, bad man, bad-mouth, bad news, bad off, bad-tempered,* and so on. The quintessential "bad" word is, however, also a very good example of how language reflects and reinforces the values of male-dominated heterosexual society. *Bad* derives from the Anglo-Saxon *baeddel,* a hermaphrodite; the related *baedling* is even worse, meaning an effeminate fellow or sodomite. Thus, the equation of the word with "evil," starting in the thirteenth century, is in perfect keeping with traditional attitudes of straight-thinkers toward that which is different (i.e., unnatural, perverted, depraved, immoral, or evil—pick one). In black English, however, the word's meaning reverses itself, e.g., "The slang had changed. . . . when somebody would say something about a bad cat, they meant that he was good. Somebody would say, 'That was some bad pot,' meaning it was good. You really got high" (Claude Brown, *Manchild in the Promised Land,* 1965). This, of course, is the voice of the counterculture, a looking-glass world wherein bad traits may have survival value—in the short run at least. See also the reversibility of STINK.

bag. A woman, usually an ugly one or a prostitute. For emphasis, an *old bag*. "I don't chase around with filthy bags" (Percy Marks, *The Plastic Age*, 1924). The woman who is a *bag* is not necessarily a *bag woman* (or *lady*), meaning a woman, sometimes a homeless one, who carts many possessions around town in shopping bags; nor is she a *bag woman* in the sense used by Representative Adam Clayton Powell, Jr. (Democrat, New York) on March 6, 1960, when he brought a million-dollar libel suit upon himself by identifying Esther James as a *bag woman* for the police, meaning she collected bribes for them from gamblers. (The case helped end a memorable political career. When Powell failed to appear for trial, Ms. James was awarded damages, and when he failed to pay up, he was cited for contempt of court, with the result that he could no longer come to New York to appear before his constituents, since he would be arrested if he did.)

In its primary feminine sense, *bag* parallels the older *baggage* and may well be an abbreviation of it. Originally just a collection of portable packages, *baggage* has referred to women since the sixteenth century, probably because the *baggage trains* of armies traditionally included loose-living camp followers, e.g., "Every common soldier carrying with him his she-baggage" (Robert Johnson, *The Worlde*, 1601). The term might sometimes be used playfully of a young and *pert baggage* or a *saucy baggage*, but the intimations of immorality were always close to the surface. Thus, speaking of Hester Prynne and her scarlet "A": "But she,—the haughty baggage, —little will care what they put on the bodice of her gown!" (Nathaniel Hawthorne, *The Scarlet Letter*, 1850). In an entirely different context, a *bag* is part of the male anatomy—and this leads to complications for those who are especially sensitive to double meanings. In the Ozarks, for example, "A paper bag is always called a *sack* or a *poke*, since bag means scrotum . . . and is too vulgar for refined ears" (Vance Randolph and George P. Wilson, *Down in the Holler*, 1953). See also DOUCHE BAG and WHORE.

bah. An exclamation of impatience or contempt, first recorded in 1600 (*OED*), and used most memorably by Charles Dickens ("Bah," said Scrooge. "Humbug!", *A Christmas Carol*, 1843). The expression is by no means obsolete: " 'Bah, humbug,' Senator Alan K. Simpson, a Wyoming Republican, said when Senator [Patrick] Leahy [Democrat, Vermont] was finished and had left the hearing room" (*New York Times*, 12/17/87). See also HUMBUG, POOH-BAH, and UGH.

balls. The testicles; a relatively modern (perhaps as recent as the nineteenth century) shortening of the much older *ballocks*. The latter is not slang but Standard English, traceable to ca. 1000; thus, from an Anglo-Saxon manuscript of the period, "*Testiculi*, beallucas" (Thomas Wright, *A Volume of Vocabularies*, 1857). Today, the base word is heard most often in such figurative expressions as *to bollix up*, which is the same as the newer *ball up* (foul up, or *balls-up* in British English) and *ballocks*, which is British for nonsense or rubbish, synonymous with *balls* or *all balls*, used on both sides of the Atlantic. An early American example: " 'If I were to stop thinking about you, you'd evaporate.' 'Which is balls,' observed the second boy judicially, again in the slang of his period . . ." (Owen Wister, *Philosophy 4: A Story of Harvard University*, 1903). The anatomical sense of *ballocks/bollix* is not entirely obsolete, however. The *OED* includes an example of this form of *ballocks* from as recently as 1966, and it seems quite likely that somewhere some children still sing the ditty, heard in Johnson County, Iowa, around 1900 and reported in *American Speech* (4/49):

Yankee Doodle had a cat,
And he was full of frolics,
And all the mice and rats
That came around,
They grabbed him by the bollix.

The anatomical *ball*, like the original *ballocks*, has had a number of figurative spin-offs, including *ballbuster*, which is either a hard task or taskmaster; *to have [someone] by the balls*, which is to have [someone] in a defenseless position; and *ballsy*, which is to be strong and nervy—a term that has slipped so far from its original mooring that it can be applied to females: "I want to show ballsy women who get laid—or who can say, 'No, I don't want to' " (TV producer Liz Bolen, *New York* magazine, 5/29/78).

The copulative verb, *to ball [someone]*, seems to be an Americanism of relatively recent (1960s) vintage; it probably derives from the *ball* that is a lot of fun, as in *to have a ball* at a dance or other social gathering. In British slang, however, the social and anatomical senses were associated in such now obsolete phrases as *buff ball* and *ballum rancum*, e.g., Captain Francis Grose's definition of the latter: "A hop or dance, where the women are all prostitutes. N.B. The company dance in their birth-day suits" (*A Classical Dictionary of the Vulgar Tongue*, 1796). A synonym in Grose's day was *buttock ball*, referring originally to the swinging dance but extended to include the act of copulation.

See also BUNK and CULL(Y).

baloney. Nonsense, rubbish—the most common of the many foods that are used as terms of disparagement. "You have to admire President Reagan's bravery at his last news conference, but you don't have to swallow his baloney" (James Reston, *New York Times*, 3/22/87). While frequently serving as a euphemism for the stronger BALLS or BULLSHIT, *baloney* has been improved in various ways, e.g., *bull-oney*, *phony baloney*, *balloey* (a portmanteau word, from *baloney* + *hooey*), *verbaloney* (another portmanteau), and *globaloney* (*global* + *baloney*, introduced by Representative Clare Boothe Luce (Republican, Connecticut), in her maiden speech to the House in February 1943. The *baloney* that is nonsense dates to the 1920s. The expression was popularized by New York Governor Alfred E. Smith in the 1930s, one of the refrains of his campaign speeches in 1936 being "No matter how thin you slice it, it's still baloney." Smith obviously associated the word with the *bologna* sausage (in turn, from Bologna, Italy), but the linguistic connection has not been proved beyond doubt. Another possibility is that the exclamation derives from *polony*, which is the sausage that British eat instead of *bologna*, and which derives in its turn from the Gypsy *pelone* (testicles). Whatever, it seems that a food is at the root of the expression. Other foods—many of them, like bologna, mixtures of different items—that have acquired derisive meanings include:

applesauce. "I tell you folks, all politics is applesauce" (Will Rogers, *The Illiterate Digest*, 1924). Utter nonsense may be characterized as *concentrated applesauce*. A related meaning of *applesauce* is "insincere flattery," whose origin was explained in *Century Magazine* this way: " 'Applesauce' means a camouflage of flattery, and is derived from the boarding-house trick of serving plenty of this cheap comestible when richer fare is scanty" (Autumn 1929). See also APPLE, BAD.

asparagus. Because many people don't like it? See also *spinach* below.

banana oil. Nonsense, especially of the insincere or unctuous sort; also as an interjection, *bananas!* See also BANANA.

balderdash. The word is recorded first (*OED*, 1596) as referring to froth or frothy liquid, though some etymologists suspect the sense of frothy, jumbled, meaningless words may be older. It also has denoted a mixture of liquids, such as milk and beer or adulterated wine, as well as—getting back to language—filthy or obscene writing or talk. "I am almost ashamed to quote such nauseous balderdash" (Lord Macaulay, *The History of England from the Accession of James II*, 1849). A variant is *bladderdash*, where the *bladder* is a puffed-up bag that contains nothing but wind or hot air. See also BARMY and BLATHERSKITE.

beans. An interjection of disbelief, as in *aw, beans;* also *full of beans*, which is to be full of nonsense (or energy). The latter phrase may have something to do with the gaseous condition that arises from consuming too many beans. It parallels *full of hops* and *full of prunes*, both of which imply foolishness as well as high spirits—and both of which also have cathartic effects.

farrago. A confused mixture, as of ideas; from the Latin word for mixed fodder for cattle and, thus, a relative of *farina*, *barley*, and *bran*.

flummery. Similar to *applesauce* in that it has the added connotation of insincere flattery. Now a light, bland food, such as custard, *flummery* originally was a coagulated concoction of slightly fermented flour or oatmeal. A variant, with both culinary and nonsense meanings, is *flummadiddle*.

fudge. Nowadays, the interjection usually brings the stickly candy to mind, but it may actually be related to the verb *to fudge*, meaning to fake or to fit together in a makeshift way. Another, more remote possibility is that it honors a seventeenth-century English seaman, Captain Fudge, who, upon returning home from a voyage, however bad the condition of his ship, "always brought home his owners a good cargo of lies; so much that now, aboard ship, the sailors, when they hear a great lie told, cry out, 'You *fudge* it' " (Isaac D'Israeli, *Curiosities of Literature*, 1791–1823). Etymologists doubt this theory, although the existence of Captain Fudge is confirmed by another source, a letter written in 1664, which adds that he was known as "Lying Fudge." The U.S. State Department sometimes is called *the fudge factory*.

gallimaufry. A jumble, a ridiculous medley; originally a stew of leftovers, from the French *galimafrée*, perhaps from *galer*, to live a gay life, and *mafrer*, to eat voraciously.

goulash. Another stew; specifically, among criminals, false information.

hash. See HASH.

hodgepodge. Also a jumble of different elements and originally a stew of various vegetables and meat; the word is a variant of *hotchpotch*, wherein the cooking *pot* is evident. "Mr. [Paul] Screvane found the report 'a hodgepodge of what everybody knows, of what others have said, and what some people have been whispering back of the hand' " (*New York Times*, 12/31/64).

horseradish. Another everyday relish, similar (semantically) to *applesauce*.

mishmash. A meaningless jumble of unrelated items; a reduplication of *mash*, itself a soft and pulpy mixture of grain or some other substance, from ca. 1450, and sometimes pronounced *mishmosh* under the mistaken apprehension that it is a Yiddish word.

mush. Another somewhat unappetizing mixture of foods. See MUSH.

nuts. See NUT.

oil. Probably short for *banana oil*: "Aah, stop the oil, will you?" (Jerome Weidman, *I Can Get It For You Wholesale!*, 1937). See also BANANA.

pap. Semi-liquid food for babies; see PAP.

pastiche. Not, strictly speaking, a bad thing in and of itself, but in an artistic context, frequently, a working together of diverse fragments from other sources with satirical intent; from the Italian *pasticcio*, a pasty or meat pie, in turn from the Latin *pasta*, dough, paste.

potpourri. A miscellany, especially a literary production of disparate and incongruous elements. *Potpourri* is French for *olla podrida*, a highly seasoned stew; literally, a putrid pot, from *olla*, pot + *podrida*, rotten.

spinach. Popularized by E. B. White's caption to a *New Yorker* cartoon by Carl Rose (Mother: "It's broccoli." Child: "I say it's spinach and I say the hell with it," 12/8/28), and probably an independent invention of Mr. White's. The vegetable appeared earlier, however, in *gammon and spinach* (or *spinnage*), which was nineteenth-century thieves' slang for "nonsense" or "humbug." Opinion is divided as to whether the *gammon* referred to the spiel of the person who sold *gammon*, meaning bacon, or to the trick, or "game," that a sharper or con man played on his victim. "What a world of gammon and spinnage it is, though, ain't it!" (Charles Dickens, *David Copperfield*, 1850). See also VEGETABLE.

vanilla. Besides its use as an exclamation of disbelief, this is a code word for "pretty girl" in soda fountains, where a cry of "Vanilla!" alerts the kitchen help to "Come take a look at what just walked in." Stuart Berg Flexner suggests in *I Hear America Talking* (1976) that the sense of nonsense may have resulted from *vanilla* being uttered too often by undiscriminating soda jerks (the-little-wolf-who-cried-girl-effect). Whatever is *plain vanilla*, finally, is simple, unadorned, and unimaginative, as in "What the White House needed after Mr. Bork's defeat, [Kevin Phillips] continued, was 'a plain vanilla Republican, not more conservative intellectuals with esoteric ideological fish to fry' " (*New York Times*, 11/11/87).

The preceding list is merely a sampling of the food words that also mean nonsense. Others, cited in *The American Thesaurus of Slang*, include *apple butter, apple strudel, beef, bunch of ant paste, bunch of tripe* (see TRIPE), *duck soup, flap sauce, hamburger, leaping oysters, lentil soup, load of clams, noodle soup,* and *stewed rhubarb* (see RHUBARB). See also BUNK, KRAUT, and the many food terms for low intelligence in BLOCKHEAD.

bamboozle. To cheat, to deceive. ". . . fellow writers, felt obliged to go on record that they, and the literary world at large, had not been bamboozled somehow: Hemingway was not nearly as good as had originally been thought" (*New York Times*, 11/17/85). A word of unknown origin, *bamboozle* surfaced around 1700. Jonathan Swift did not like it when he heard it, and he included *bamboozle* among a list of new "Words invented by some Pretty Fellows" that he thought should be expunged from the language (*Tatler*, 9/26/1710). Others on Swift's list that have also withstood the test of time despite his opinion of them include *banter, bully, mob,* and *sham*. A secondary meaning of *bamboozle*, now apparently obsolete, is "to render pregnant," as in the following social note from Brooklyn, New York, on January 30, 1807: "Heard that D. Stoothoff's wench got bamboozled by his Negro Sam, an old Married Etheopian" ("Gleanings from John Baxter's Journals, 1790–1826," *American Speech*, 10/65). See also HUMBUG.

banana. A crazy person. Thus, one vice presidential candidate on another: "Mondale has called Bob [Dole] a bananna [*sic*]" *Birmingham* (Alabama) *Post-Herald*, 10/27/76). In the plural, the word means "nonsense," often as an interjection, *bananas!*, or raving insanity, usually in the phrase, *to go bananas.* ". . . it's no wonder you find women once proud of their mid-thirtyish poise and hard-won professional competence going bananas" (*Mother Jones,* 5/83). Variations include *banana-cake,* a crazy person (similar to *fruitcake*); *bananahead,* a stupid person; *banana oil,* nonsense; *Bananasville,* whose residents have all *gone bananas;* and *whamfartbananas,* which is to go bananas and then some, as in "I'm going whamfartbananas already. I'll be a basketcase by the time I'm confirmed, you realize that" (*Analog,* 2/77).

Nor does this exhaust the metaphor. The *banana* suggests the penis, therefore sex, as in a popular English music hall song of the WWI period, "I had a banana / with Lady Diana." From this idea, it follows naturally that *to have one's banana peeled* is a figure of speech for copulation. Almost inevitably, PBS used a banana for demonstrating proper condom use in a TV show about AIDS (11/6/87), leading to a protest from the International Banana Association. "The choice of a banana rather than some other, inanimate prop constitutes arbitrary and reckless disregard for the unsavory association that will be drawn by the public and the damage to our industry that will result therefrom," wrote Robert Moore, IBA president. "The banana is an important product and deserves to be treated with respect."

As picturesque as all these are, however, none quite matches Reginald Paget's description of Prime Minster Anthony Eden at the time of the Suez crisis in 1956: "He is an overripe banana, yellow outside, squishy in." See also BALONEY and NUT.

banana republic. Any small country in Central America whose economy depends upon fruit exports and, in extended use, a denigration of any country at all that is considered weak and, as nations go, laughable. Thus, speaking of the Federal Republic of [West] Germany, Horst Ehmke, a Social Democrat legislator, said, "Abroad we were being ridiculed as an operetta nation, a banana republic" (*New York Times,* 2/2/84).

bandit. A partisan. "According to a new Führer order bandits captured in battle are to be shot" (Lieutenant Kurt Waldheim, General Staff daybook entry, 8/8/43, referring to opposition to the Italian 11th Army by irregular troops in northwestern Greece, *New York Times,* 5/2/86).

Authoritarian governments commonly use *bandit* to criminalize political or military resistance to them, e.g., ". . . every armed nationalist who doesn't agree with the central government [of the USSR] is a 'bandit' . . . Similarly, any participant in a camp rebellion and any participant in an urban rebellion is also a 'bandit' " (Aleksandr I. Solzhenitsyn, *The Gulag Archipelago, 1918–1956,* 1974). Another country with this tradition is China: "Chiang [Kai-shek] had spent much time in Nanchang during the four years of his First, Second, Third, Fourth and now [1934] his Fifth 'annihilation' campaign against the 'Red bandits' " (Harrison E. Salisbury, *The Long March,* 1985). See also GANG and TERRORIST.

barbarian. An uncouth, uncultured, uncivilized person, especially one who is fierce and brutal. Thus, speaking of the Libyan leader Colonel Muammar el-Qaddafi: "I find he's not only a barbarian but he's flaky" (President Ronald Reagan, press conference, 1/7/86). See also FLAKY.

The *barbarian* is the quintessential outsider. The word comes from *bárbaros,* the ancient Greek term for anyone who couldn't be understood because he didn't speak Greek. It derives ultimately from *baba,* an Indo-European root that imitates the incoherent speech of a baby (*babble*, BABY, BABOON, and BLAH are others that share this root). Originally a relatively neutral term for a foreigner, the Greek word began to acquire pejorative connotations following the Persian invasions of Greece under Darius and Xerxes in the fifth century B.C. Plato said: "I thank God that I have been born a Greek and not a barbarian, a freeman and not a slave, a man and not a woman; but above all that I have been born in the age of Socrates." The original application of the word to language remains when we say that a *barbarous* writer has committed a *barbarism*. See also GOOK, GOTH, GOY, GRINGO, HUN, TARTAR, VANDAL, and, for what the barbarians think of the people who gave them their name, GREEK.

barf. To vomit or as a noun, that which is cast up; in extended use, an expression of strong disgust, as in "I am totally barfed out" (San Fernando Valley Girl Talk, ca. 1983). Though relatively new, having been dated so far only to the mid-1950s, *barf* is of unknown origin. Best guess is that it imitates the sound of retching. The term has been elaborated into *barf bag*, a paper convenience for airline passengers who have been overcome by what the airlines choose to call "motion discomfort." The negative associations of the word are strong enough that it also has been euphemized as *frab*, which is an example of Reverse English (along with *enob* and *mosob*). See also PUKE.

barmy. Foolish, flighty, empty-headed. Thus, speaking of Tony Benn, a fellow Labour Party member said: "Tony may be a bit barmy but tell me what national political leader isn't" (*New York Times*, 3/1/84). *Barm* is a yeasty froth or head that forms on beer when it is poured out. Technically, then, to be *barmy* is to be light-headed. *Barmy froth*, meaning a flighty, empty-headed fellow, dates to the sixteenth century. *Balmy*, in this same sense, is a nineteenth-century variant of *barmy*. See also *balderdash* in BALONEY.

basket case. Helpless; flat on [one's] back. "Spain is not yet an economic basket case" (*Newsweek*, 11/1/82). The expression arose in the miltary, originally referring to quadruple amputees. People who are sound physically but suffering from shell shock or other mental impairment also may be referred to as *basket cases*.

bastard. An illegitimate child; a despicable person; a SON OF A BITCH. The term has been so overused that it has lost much of its force, with the result that speakers frequently feel the need to embellish it in various ways, e.g., "Where have you been you stupid prick bastard?" (Ring Lardner, Jr., *The Ecstasy of Owen Muir*, 1954). In extended, attenuated, and even friendly contexts, a *bastard* can be any person, chap, fellow, guy—even a thing, as in, "Well, George, we knocked the bastard off" (Sir Edmund Hillary to George Lowe, first words upon descending from the summit of Mount Everest, 5/28/53, Walt Unsworth, *Everest: A Mountaineering History*, 1981).

Though heavily tabooed for most of the past couple of centuries because of its association with unbridaled sexuality, *bastard* has not always been an insult. It derives from *fils de bast*, son of a packsaddle, the notion being that the child was conceived in irregular circumstances. In olden times, when this happened a lot, the term did not carry a great deal of emotional freight and was used in place of the surname that the child otherwise would have had, e.g., William the Bastard, commonly referred to this way in his lifetime (1027–87), though school texts today usually call him William the Conqueror. The word does not seem to have gained much force as an epithet until the eighteenth century, when it began superseding WHORESON and acquired that word's pejorative connotations. Thus, François Rabelais, a brave author indeed, lambasted critics: "As for you, little envious prigs, snarling bastards . . . you will soon have railed your last: go hang yourselves" (*Pantagruel*, tr., Peter A. Motteux, 1737). With examples like this before him, Captain Francis Grose mistakenly interpreted *bastard* as a slang word, including it along with the piquant *bastardly gullion* (a bastard's bastard) in *A Classical Dictionary of the Vulgar Tongue* (1796).

The taboo was never so strong that the word disappeared, of course. Rather, it tended to be restricted to use by males and it rarely appeared in print in its principal, illegitimate sense. Normally, it was replaced by such euphemisms as *love child, natural child, outside child, wood's colt,* and the still wilder, "Darling, I'm the son of a seacook," (*Arsenic and Old Lace,* film, 1944). The taboo was reflected by the gradual disappearance of *bastard* as an adjective to denote that which is inferior, impure, or of a hybrid nature, as *bastard cannon, bastard wine, bastard goose,* etc. For example, polite bird-watchers now refer to the *bastard wing* (the small group of feathers attached to the first joint of a bird's wing and corresponding to the human thumb) as the *alula,* which is a coinage of the eighteenth century (from the Latin *ala,* wing), when English was being prettied up for Victorian times.

Class differences in the use of *bastard* also have been noted. For instance, Robert Graves pointed out that among the lower classes the term was regarded as an unforgivable insult while upper classes tolerated it, perhaps because so many of the latter have "noble or even royal blood in their veins . . . under the courtesy title, 'natural sons and daughters' " (*The Future of Swearing and Improper Language,* 1936).

The rough talk of soldiers in World Wars I and II did much to break down the taboos against "bad" words, more so in the case of *bastard* in Great Britain and the Commonwealth countries than in the United States. In Australia, for instance, the term is bandied about quite freely in public, e.g., Prime Minister Gough Whitlam's comment in 1974 to his supporters: "I do not mind the Liberals . . . calling me a bastard. In some cases, I am only doing my job if they do. But I hope you will not publicly call me a bastard, as some bastards in the Caucus have" (*Wall Street Journal,* 6/27/83). In the United States, by contrast, the government mounted an investigation to identify the leaker after *The Washington Post* reported (2/18/82) that Secretary of State Alexander Haig had referred during a departmental meeting to British Foreign Secretary Lord Carrington as a "duplicitous bastard." See also BUGGER, GIT, MONGREL, and WHORESON.

bat. A prostitute, i.e., a nocturnal creature, also called *fly-by-night.* Similar terms for women who ply their trade after the sun goes down include *nightbird, nighthawk,* and *owl.* The French, meanwhile, have the even quainter *hirondelle de nuit,* or night swallow. See also QUAIL.

battle-ax. A belligerent and formidable woman, usually an older one and frequently one's wife. "Say, there was a battle-ax if you ever see one. She had a face on her that'd fade flowers" (George Ade, *Artie,* 1896). Legend has it that the term honors the women who produced Battle-Ax Cut Plug chewing tobacco at a processing plant in Lexington, Kentucky, around the turn of this century. Little red axes adorned the tin tags attached to the plugs and the women workers, being of a rather rough-and-ready nature, came to be known to the local gentry as *battle-axes*. The term is said to have spread from this. The story is supported only with anecdotal evidence, however, and—alas—is probably too good to be true. See also HARRIDAN.

bawd. A madam or prostitute; she who runs a *bawdy house*—the latter term still considered strong enough that family newspapers have been known to isolate it within quotation marks, presumably to keep the contamination from spreading, e.g., "The Government agency responsible for insuring 14,000 of the nation's banks has acquired a financial interest in some unusual assets lately: fleets of tuna boats and taxis, an X-rated movie, a 'bawdy house' and a high-priced copy of the Koran" (UPI, 12/9/76). *Bawd* is a venerable word, dating to the fourteenth century, probably a shortening of *bawdstrot* (for the *strot* part, read: *strut*), and in turn from the Old French *baude*, lively, bold; the Old High German *bald*, bold; and, ultimately, the Indo-European root *bhel*, which refers to a bold swelling and whose derivatives (up to and including the personal names *Archibald* and *Leopold*) tie in with the idea of tumescent masculinity. In keeping with all this, it should come as no surprise that *bawd* originally was applied to men more often than to women—to procurerers rather than procuresses. As often happens (see BITCH for other examples), the meaning of the tainted term gradually was limited to women exclusively, a process that was completed about 1700. By the end of that century, Captain Francis Grose was distinguishing between a *bawd* and a *cock bawd*, the latter being "the male keeper of a bawdy house" (*A Classical Dictionary of the Vulgar Tongue*, 1796). See also PANDER and WHORE.

bazoo. A person's mouth, especially when loud or boastful words emanate from it; perhaps from the Dutch *bazuin*, trumpet. "Shut yer big bazoo!" (*Saturday Evening Post*, 4/24/48). The *bazoo* should not be confused with another instrument, the KAZOO.

beast. One who is deficient in human qualities. Thus, sermonizing on "The Old-Time Gospel Hour," broadcast by two Sacramento, California, radio stations in March 1984, the Reverend Jerry Falwell described the parishioners of the Metropolitan Community Church as "brute beasts, part of a vile and satanic system" (UPI, 9/25/85). The members of this congregation rated as *beasts* in the reverend's eyes because they were homosexuals, and his choice of words made news because he denied having uttered them, offered to pay $5,000 if it could be proved that he had said them, and then was ordered by a court to ante up when a tape recording was produced. In the back of Mr. Falwell's mind, perhaps, was the Biblical *beast*, which is the antichrist, and whose minions are known by the sign, *the mark of the beast*, which is 666: "and there fell a noisome and grievous sore upon the men which had the mark of the beast, and *upon* them which worshipped his image" (*Revelations*, 16:2). See also ANIMAL, BRUTE, and PIG.

beaver. The female genitals or an entire woman; usually but not necessarily pejorative in the extended sense, with female CB'ers sometimes applying the term to themselves, as in "This is Little Beaver from Tallahassee." The genital *beaver*, as opposed to the strictly nonsexual *eager beaver* (so far dated only to 1943), the apparently older *work like a beaver* (*OED*, 1741), and the basic dam-building animal (whose name comes from the Old English *beofor*, to skin), was popularized by *Ball Four*, a best-seller of 1970, in which Yankee pitcher Jim Bouton outraged his teammates by telling how some of these professional practitioners of the national pastime passed their own free time. In Bouton's words: "A beaver shooter is, at bottom, a Peeping Tom. . . . I've seen guys chin themselves on transoms, drill holes in doors, even shove a mirror under a door." Related expressions include *beaver chaser, beaver fever* (i.e., HORNY), *beaver flick, beaver pose,* and *shooting beaver* (female exhibitionism, similar to *mooning* or *shooting moon*, which is—or was, in the 1960s—the public display of naked buttocks, also known as, when placed firmly against car windows, *pressed ham*). Another variant is *Bucky,* as in "He's a real Bucky," i.e., HORNY, the reference being to Bucky Beaver, who starred in Ipana toothpaste commercials in the 1960s (personal communication, Mark Hurst, 2/1/89).

Beaver seems to have acquired its sexual meaning comparatively recently. This sense is included in the 1975 supplement to the *Dictionary of American Slang* (Harold Wentworth and Stuart Berg Flexner) but not the 1967 edition of that work. *Beaver shooting*, however, was defined in a report on student slang at the Columbus campus of Ohio State University as "A mild form of voyeurism consisting of scanning the girls' dormitory windows for whatever visual pleasures they might offer" (*American Speech*, 2/67). An early example of *beaver* appears in a limerick that was first published in 1927 and later incorporated by G. Legman into his massive collection *The Limerick*, 1969. The item in question is number 1,160:

> There was a young lady named Eva
> Who went to the ball as Godiva,
> But a change in the lights
> Showed a tear in her tights,
> And a low fellow present yelled, "Beaver!"

As the limerick suggests, *beaver* probably originated as a street cry—a code word that men could call out to other men, advising them that if they looked sharp, a woman without underpants might be seen; *cooze* and *zitz* have been used the same way. This sense of the word most likely derived from *beard*, since *beaver* (meaning the pelt of the dam-building animal) is slang for *beard* and *beard* has referred to the female pubic hair as well as male facial hair since at least the seventeenth century. (Captain Francis Grose defined *beard splitter* as "A man much given to wenching" in *A Classical Dictionary of the Vulgar Tongue*, 1796.) The linguistic association is reinforced a number of levels. Thus, *beaver* also is shorthand for *beaver hat*, and *hat* is another old byword for the female genitals ("hat," according to Grose, "because frequently felt"). Again, a nickname for the *beaver* (animal) is *flat tail*, and TAIL is a very old word for the female genitals (Chaucer used it in this sense in the fourteenth century). Moreover, small furry animals often serve as metaphors for the female genitals: *Squirrel shooting* (see SQUIRREL) is the same as *beaver shooting*, and a *mink* is an especially attractive or high-class *beaver*. (Similar synonyms include CAT, MON-KEY, and PUSSY.) Finally, "Let's go beaver shooting," has some of the same nonsensical appeal as "Let's go watch the submarine races," an invitation to park and neck that was popularized ca. 1955 by the disc jockey Murray the K. Given all this, it is not hard to see why the sexual *beaver* has caught on—and why the term probably will be with us awhile. See also PIECE.

beetlebrain. A person of low intelligence, i.e., one who has all the smarts of an insect; hence, the comic strip character Beetle Bailey. Beetles have been regarded as dumb since at least the sixteenth century: "Beetle-braines cannot conceive things right" (*OED*, pre-1604). See also INSECT.

beggar. A mean or low fellow (poverty breeds contempt), from ca. 1300 and still extant: "Shanna's eyes narrowed as she gritted, 'You vulgar beggar, they should hang you for a molester of women!' " (Kathleen E. Woodiwiss, *Shanna*, 1977). See also BUM, MOOCHER, and PANHANDLER.

belch. A burp or to burp, and an example of changing fashions in "bad" talk, *burp* being a euphemism from ca. 1930 for the much older *belch* from ca. 1000. Our Victorian ancestors objected to *belch*, as they did to most other Standard English words for the body's parts and functions, with the *Oxford English Dictionary* specifying of *belch* that it is "now *vulgar*" (Volume B, 1882–88). Americans were nearly as prudish. *Belch* was cited as "coarse" or "obscene" by 25 out of 361 respondents in a study by J. M. Steadman, Jr., of verbal taboos among students at Emory University in Atlanta, Georgia (*American Speech*, 4/35). On the vulgarity scale, this put *belch* ahead of WHORE (24 mentions), BASTARD (22) and NASTY (18), though leaving it far behind such other zingers as BELLY (the top-rated term, with 87 mentions), STINK (69), *guts* (59, see GUTLESS), and PUKE (51). The sheer blandness of these terms makes one suspect that Steadman's students did not report all the dirty words they knew. The study cannot be totally dismissed, however, since it fits in with other evidence. In the case of *belch*, as late as 1942 the censors in the Hays office were still trying to discourage Hollywood producers from using the term in movies.

Over the years, *belch* has had other low meanings in extended use by criminals, hobos, and circus-types. Thus, *to belch* can be to complain, to protest, or to rat or inform upon, as in "I feel good that I didn't belch on a pal, because that's the code I was raised on" (Morris Lipsius, *New Yorker*, 12/1/51). *Belch* also is an old word for a poor kind of beer, one that caused imbibers to burp, whence the name of the Shakespearean character Sir Toby Belch (*Twelfth Night*, 1600–02).

belly. A very old word, dating to the tenth century (from the Old English *belig*, bag), usually avoided by fastidious types, who would rather discuss frontal anatomy in terms of the Latin *abdomen* (from *abdere*, to hide away) or the French *stomach* (from *estomach*, and ultimately the Greek *stomachos*, gullet). *Belly* was not regarded as an especially bad word until the eighteenth century, when incipient Victorians started to get *stomachaches* instead of *bellyaches*. Previously, people had spoken freely of consuming *belly-cheer* and *belly-timber* (food); of giving other people a *bellyful* (a thrashing or drubbing); and of taking a *belly-plea* (a plea of pregnancy by a woman convicted or a capital offense, for which purpose every well regulated jail had a resident male "child-getter"). By the early nineteenth century, however, *belly* had come to be considered so vulgar that editors on both sides of the Atlantic took it out of the Bible. Dr. Benajmin Boothroyd systematically dropped the term from his *New Family Bible and Improved Version* of 1824 and Noah Webster did the same when he revised the Bible for Americans in 1833. (Boothroyd also converted a girl's navel, or *belly button*, into her *waist*, while Webster did a thorough cleansing job, deleting such other lewd words as DUNG, STINK, SUCK, and WHORE.) Children, of course, relish words that adults will pick up only with tongs. Thus, Robert Graves reported in *The Future of Swearing and Improper Language* (1936) that little East Enders in London loved to embarrass passing clergymen and respectable old ladies by reciting:

Pa's out and Ma's out, let's talk dirt!
Pee-poh-belly-bottom drawers.

See also BREAST.

Benedict Arnold. A traitor. Arguably General George Washington's best field commander during the American Revolution, his name became synonymous with treachery after his plot to hand over West Point to the British was discovered in 1780. "The *Press Register*, a Mobile newspaper that had reported Mr. [Jefferson B.] Session's nomination for the Federal district judgeship, said yesterday that Senator [Howell T.] Heflin [Democrat, Alabama] had become a Benedict Arnold by his vote and 'forever sullied what heretofore was an admirable record of public service' " (*New York Times*, 6/7/86). See also JUDAS, QUISLING, and TRAITOR.

berk. A fool—or worse. "The Tories were burglars, berks and bloodlusters" (John Osborne, *Paul Slickey*, 1959). The term is Cockney rhyming slang of the lowest sort. *Berk* is an abbreviation of *Berkshire Hunt*, where *Hunt* rhymes with an ancient word for the female pudendum. Sometimes the intermediate term is construed as *Berkeley Hunt*, with the result that *Berkeley* also has the same double meaning as *berk*. Rhymes on unstated themes are fairly common in Cockney talk. For example: *Bristols* are breasts or titties (from Bristol cities); *china* is a pal or mate (from china plate); *cobblers* are testicles or balls (from cobblers' stalls or, perhaps, awls); and *elephants* is to be drunk (from elephant's trunk). In other instances, the speaker may go so far as to articulate the rhyme word, e.g., *ham and eggs*, legs; *hit-or-miss*, kiss; *plates and dishes*, kisses; *plates of meat*, feet; and *twists and twirls*, girls (the last may be of American origin). The visitor to Great Britain should take care not to confuse *berk* or *Berkeley* with *Berkeleys*, which are breasts, and which perhaps come from the Gypsy word for this part of the anatomy, *berk* or *burk*—*berkia* when both are meant—rather than from the infamous *Hunt*.

bilk. A cheat or to cheat; not often encountered as a noun nowadays but a fighting word in some circles a century or so ago. From a report on a visit to the Western Territories after the Civil War: ". . . the most degrading epithet that one can apply to another is to pronounce him 'a bilk.' No Western man of pluck will fail to resent such concentrated vituperation. The term was entirely novel to me, and I first asked its meaning of a landlord, who explained by saying that 'a "bilk" is a man who never misses a meal and never pays a cent' " (A. K. McClure, *Three Thousand Miles Through the Rocky Mountains*, 1869). The term is an old one, included in the cheating sense in the first edition (1785) of *A Classical Dictionary of the Vulgar Tongue* by Captain Francis Grose, who noted that "Bilking a coachman, a box-keeper, and a poor whore, were formerly, among men of the town, thought gallant actions." The word's origin is uncertain, but the best guess is that it is an alteration of *balk*. It appears first (*OED*, 1651), as a term in cribbage, *to bilk*, meaning to balk or spoil an opponent's score by consigning relatively unusable cards to the crib. See also CHEAT.

bimbo. A dumb woman, especially a young and promiscuous one; a girlfriend, tramp, or prostitute. "In New York, a puckish bond trader says he wants to set up an independent company to cater to traders' whims. He would call it 'Limos, Bimbos & Lines,' providing, as he claims securities firms do informally, a limousine, a woman in a hotel room, and cocaine for customers" (*Wall Street Journal*, 9/12/83). Jack Conway (d. 1928), a *Variety* staffer, popularized *bimbo* in the sense of a dumb woman. The word also has served as a masculine epithet, referring to tough guys, dummies, and men in general—usually contemptuously. Both female and male meanings surfaced in the opening decades of this century. The male sense may actually be the older of the two, but it has become subordinate to the other. (See BITCH and HARLOT for other examples of pejorative terms that have become feminized.) The word is sometimes abbreviated *bim* in both the female and male senses, while the former also appears as *bimbette*. Both forms of *bimbo* probably derive from the Italian *bambino*, baby. See also BROAD and GROUPIE.

bird. A disrespectful sound, and insulting gesture, and a generally disparaging characterization of any man or woman, but especially of a convict, homosexual, or slow-witted person.

In the aural sense, the *bird* is the same as a boo, Bronx cheer, or RASPBERRY. This is British theatrical slang, first recorded in the early nineteenth century. Originally, the *bird* or *the big bird* was goose, the term referring to hissing not booing. When the critics in the stalls got going, it was said *the goose is loose*. And the audiences of the day showed little civility. Thus, Charles Lamb reported on the opening-night reception of his play *Mr. H.*: "Damn 'em how they hissed! It was not a hiss neither, but a sort of frantic yell, like a congregation of wild geese, with roaring something like bears, mows and mops like apes, sometimes snakes, that hiss'd me into madness (letter to Thomas Manning, 10/11/1805). Poor Lamb. He even admitted to joining in the hissing so that no one would realize he was the author.

By extension, *to give [someone] the bird* or *the big bird* is to dismiss that person, figuratively or perhaps actually, as from a job. The symbolic meaning of the term flows naturally from this, *bird* also being the technical name of the well-known hand gesture that is made with middle finger upraised. Casey Stengel got the message across, but much more cleverly, one Sunday in May 1919. When the crowd in Brooklyn's Ebbets Field, which had been riding him all afternoon, booed and applauded mockingly as he stepped up to the plate in the seventh inning, the mighty Casey turned around toward the stands, bowed, and doffed his cap, revealing a small bird—a sparrow—that fluttered away, causing the boos to dissolve into laughter (Robert W. Creamer, *Stengel: His Life and Times*, 1984).

But *giving* or *throwing the bird* is not always a laughing matter. For example, photographs of antiwar protestors at Kent State University show many young men and women making this gesture at members of the Ohio National Guard prior to the soldiers' opening fire on the students, killing four of them, on May 4, 1970. The special grand jury convened that October to investigate the shootings "appears to have been especially incensed at this, and indicted one young man, who had already been struck by a bullet, for a felony which carried a punishment as high as three years in jail and $10,000 fine. One national magazine justified the fatal shooting of Jeffrey Miller on the grounds that he had made an indecent gesture against the Guard" (James A. Michener, *Kent State: What Happened and Why*, 1971).

This grand jury could not bring itself to indict any of the guardsmen who fired their weapons, however.

As a metaphor for a person, *bird* is of considerable antiquity. Back in the thirteenth century, a *bird* was a young man or woman, a maiden, and, alas, sometimes a WHORE or *bird of the game* (see QUAIL). In the old-time, feminine sense, there seems to have been some confusion with an even more ancient word, *burde*, and perhaps with *bryde*, bride. The modern female *bird*, meanwhile, is a Britticism, exported to the United States in the early 1960s, e.g., "This bird is almost human" (*Alfie*, film, 1966). See also CHICKEN.

Bird has always had masculine meanings, too, however. For instance, in the argot of Elizabethan con men, *the bird* was glossed as "The fool that is caught" (Robert Greene, *The Black Book's Messenger*, 1592). Among the same set of people, a *queer bird* was "one that came lately out of prison . . . He is commonly a stealer of horses" (?John Awdeley, *The Fraternity of Vagabonds*, 1561). From the seventeenth through the nineteenth centuries, a *whore's bird* was the moral equivalent of a WHORESON or, as we now say, a BASTARD. Today, the term frequently connotes duffer-like eccentricity, typically in such combinations as *odd bird, old bird,* and *queer bird* (the latter's meaning has shifted for the better). Because convicts are kept in cages, they are *jailbirds* (from the seventeenth century) as well as *yardbirds* (much newer, probably from the twentieth century). Male homosexuals also qualify as *birds* or *birdies*, and to go on the *bird circuit* is to make a tour of gay bars across the country. "If only that St. Paul's crowd . . . would not mistake *him* for a bird" (F. Scott Fitzgerald, *This Side of Paradise*, 1920).

Bird also appears in various proverbial expressions and sayings, such as TV comedian George Gobel's refrain "Well, I'll be a dirty bird." (The original dirty bird is the shitpoke, so-called on account of its habit of defecating when taking to wing.) Finally, anything that is entirely irrelevant, worthless, trivial, and more than faintly ridiculous can be dismissed as being *(strictly) for the birds*. Popularized during World War II, this seems to be a sanitized version of a longer expression, *shit for the birds*, the allusion being to the practice of birds eating the droppings of horses, cattle, and other animals (*American Speech*, 10/57).

See also ALBATROSS, BUZZARD, CANARD, CANARY, CHICKEN, COCK, CROW, DODO, DOVE, DUCK, FINK, GOOSE, JAY, JINX, KIBITZ, PEACOCK, PELICAN, QUAIL, and VULTURE.

bitch. The correct term for a female dog and usually an insult when applied to a female human; of obscure origin, possibly related to the Latin *bestia* (beast). The "usually an insult" covers up a number of exceptions. For example, *bitch* can be used in an affectionate and admiring way, as demonstrated by the last words of Jonathan Swift's last letter to Stella (Esther Johnson, 6/6/1713): "as I was coming into town, and just received your letter, I said aloud—Agreeable Bitch." This fond meaning has withstood the test of time, e.g., ". . . me making sure that my ole lady doesn't see me with this foxy bitch on the back of my bike" (letter to *Playboy*, 7/78). The term also is common among blacks: "To Johnny, every chick was a bitch. Even mothers were bitches. Of course, there were some nice bitches, but they were still bitches. . . . Cats would say, 'I saw your sister today, and she is a fine bitch.' Nobody was offended by it. That's just the way things were. It was easy to see all women as bitches" (Claude Brown, *Manchild in the Promised Land*, 1965). All is relative, of course, as Ernest Borneman noted in an interview with Reinhold Aman (*Maledicta*, Summer 1979):

If a black man hears a white man use the word "black," he at once thinks it is a racial insult. If a Jew hears a non-Jew use the word "Jew," he immediately thinks it's an anti-Semitic remark. A black man can say lovingly to his woman, "You sweet black bitch," but let a white man say that to his black girl friend and hell will burst open.

Bitch and the adjectival *bitchin'* may also have positive meanings in nonhuman contexts. Thus, when speaking of something as fine as, say, a new red convertible, "That's a bitch," translates as "That's great," and young Billy intends it as a compliment when he tells Norman in *On Golden Pond* that "That canoe is really bitchin' " (Ernest Thompson, 1979).

Finally, still in the category of exceptions, *bitch* once referred to males as well as females, e.g., "I can tell you landlord is a vast comical bitch . . ." (Henry Fielding, *Tom Jones*, 1749). The masculine sense is dated by the *Oxford English Dictionary* to before 1500 and it was still current in the early nineteenth century, as evidenced by the journal of Marjory Fleming, who died in 1811 (of measles, aged eight): "Today I pronounced a word which should never come out of a lady's lips it was that I called John an Impudent Bitch."

Marjory's comments show how strong the taboo against *bitch* had grown by the beginning of the nineteenth century. This is an example of proto-Victorianism at work. The *Oxford English Dictionary* (the letter B was prepared in the 1882–88 period) specified that the word as applied to a woman was "Not now in decent use; but formerly common in literature," and it provided no examples of the word in any sense at all from after 1833, four years before Victoria became queen.

The taboo against the term stemmed from its associations with a dog in heat. To call a woman a *bitch* was to imply that she was not only a prostitute but worse—that she was lewder and more lascivious even than a professional retailer of sex. Captain Francis Grose characterized this as "the most offensive appelation that can be given to an English woman, even more provoking than that of whore, as may be gathered from the regular Billingsgate or St. Giles answer—'I may be a whore, but can't be a bitch' " (*A Classical Dictionary of the Vulgar Tongue*, 1796).

The offensiveness of the word became so great that people began avoiding it even in its proper canine context. Instead they resorted to such euphemisms as *doggess, dog's lady, lady dog, lust dog, puppy's mama* (or *mother*), *she dog*, and *slut pup*. For example, the great lexicographer, Dr. Samuel Johnson (1696–1772), told the following story on himself: "I did not respect my mother, though I loved her; and one day, when in anger she called me a puppy, I asked her if she knew what they called a puppy's mother" (H. L. S. Thrale Piozzi, *Anecdotes of the Late Samuel Johnson, LL. D.*, 1786).

The sheer opprobrium of the word as applied to females apparently led people to stop using it as an epithet for males. This kind of thing happens fairly often to words with bad meanings. They may start off applying to men only, or to both men and women, but the women frequently are left holding the bag, so to speak. For example, a HARLOT originally was a male buffoon or rascal; a BAWD was a pander, a go-between, usually a man rather than a woman; a *tomboy* actually was a boy, not a girl; and even GIRL started out as a neutral term, referring to a child of either sex up into the fifteenth century. (See also BOY, BUFFOON, and PANDER.) The apotheosis of *bitch* in its feminine sense comes from a letter by William James to H. G. Wells (9/11/1906): "A symptom of the moral flabbiness born of the exclusive worship of the bitch-goddess *success*."

Inhibitions against *bitch* have relaxed in the twentieth century, thanks in large part to the frequency with which this and other taboo words were used in World Wars I and II. At the same time, the meaning of *bitch* has become adulterated, so that it no longer stands for WHORE. Common current forms include *a bitch* (anything bad or difficult, as in "Frank got drunk as a bitch today," or "My calculus course is a bitch"), *to bitch* (to gripe or grumble), *bitch box* (a loudspeaker), *bitch off* (to annoy, as in "That bitches me off"), *bitch session* (a group of complainers in the act thereof), *bitch up* (to confuse or botch up), *bull bitch* (a woman with masculine traits), and the omnipresent SON OF A BITCH. (Another term, worth resurrecting out of the mists of the nineteenth century, is *bitchrell*, or poor poetry, coined by John Keats on the model of "doggerel.") By 1962, *bitch* was admitted to Hollywood soundtracks (*Advise and Consent*). Still, the term has to be handled with care. Vice President George Bush's wife, Barbara, honored the old taboo when referring to Geraldine A. Ferraro, then campaigning for her husband's office, as "that four-million-dollar—I can't say it, but it rhymes with 'rich' " (10/8/84). Next day, she took it all back, telling reporters: "Of course I would never call Congresswoman Ferraro a witch." Her husband's press secretary, Peter Teeley, compounded the offense by referring to Mrs. Ferraro as "too bitchy" (10/11/84). He later tried to take this back by saying that he meant *bitchy* in the sense of *crabby*, but he did not bother to explain what dictionary he was using. The 1972 supplement to the *Oxford English Dictionary* defines "bitchy as "*a*. Sensual, sexually provocative. *b*. Malicious, catty." Pick one.

See also DAME, DOG, SLUT, and, for more Bush-league talk, refer to ASS.

blabbermouth. One who talks too much, who runs off at the mouth; especially a tattletale or revealer of secrets. The basic *blab*, meaning a person who does not control his tongue, is very old (Chaucer used it) and of uncertain origin (it may imitate, as does *babble*, the chatter of a baby). See also BLUBBERMOUTH.

blackguard. A scoundrel, an unprincipled person. "[George IV's] tutor, Bishop Richard Hurd, said of him when he was fifteen years old that he would be 'either the most polished gentleman or the most accomplished blackguard in Europe—possibly both'; and the latter prediction was only too fully justified" (*Encyclopaedia Britannica*, 13th ed., 1926). *Blackguard* has been dated to 1535, appearing first as "Black Guard." It is not certain whether the original reference was to a group of attendants dressed in black or to the scullions and other menials who traveled with a noble family from one residence to another and with an army from camp to camp. Both senses were current later in the century and it is possible that either was a play upon the other. The term also has evolved into an adjective and a verb to cover those who act like *blackguards* or talk as though they were raised in the gutter. "One of my foul-mouthed visitors was described as 'the blackguardin'est feller that ever set foot in this town' " (Vance Randolph and George P. Wilson, *Down in the Holler*, 1953). See also ROGUE and SCOUNDREL.

blah. Banal nonsense, often repeated for emphasis: *blah, blah, blah*. In the plural, *the blahs* is a physical condition popularized in the 1960s by Madison Avenue as a means for marketing a tablet that goes "plop, plop, fizz, fizz," etc. Based on the earlier *blah feeling*, this term quickly found its way into nonmedical contexts, e.g., "The radicals are suffering from a case of the blahs" (*Life*, 12/12/69). See also BUNK and UGH.

blatherskite. Nonsense, or the noisy, talkative person who spews it forth; from *blather* or *blether*, to talk nonsense or to babble, and *skite*, a contemptible person, a voider of excrement (see also CHEAPSKATE). Variants include *bladderskate* (where the *bladder* is a bag full of air or wind), *blathergab*, and *bletherskate*. *Blither*, as in *blithering idiot*, also is another form of *blather*. The epithet was popularized in America about the time of the Revolution by the old Scotch song "Maggie Lauder," which includes the lyric "Jog on your gait, ye bletherskate" (F. Sempill, ca. 1650). See also BUNK, IDIOT, and MOTORMOUTH.

bleeding heart. A liberal. "I'm not a lover of Communists . . . or bleeding hearts" (*Seven Days in May*, film, 1964). Popularized in the 1930s by newspaper columnist Westbrook Pegler (1894–1969), the label implies that anyone who supports government programs for poor people must have an unduly soft heart and, very likely, a soft head, too, perhaps even an EGGHEAD. Thus, quoting one of Seattle's finest, patrolman Ed Burkhart, on the question of caring for that city's homeless people: "The bleeding hearts talk about helping them. I think we ought to keep the pressure on to encourage them to go somewhere else. If we provide 400 new beds, we get 400 new tramps" (*New York Times*, 12/2/86). The antithesis of the *bleeding heart* is the *tough-minded realist*, whose characteristics have been defined by Russell Baker this way: "As a general rule of thumb, any person described in political journalese as 'tough-minded,' 'level-headed' and 'realistic'—all in one paragraph—can safely be regarded as a man who would make Attila the Hun, by comparison, seem like a 'bleeding heart' " (*New York Times*, 1/16/72). See also GOO-GOO and LIBERAL.

blighter. A contemptible fellow; British, apparently from *blight*, the idea being that the *blighter* is like a disease or parasite. *Blighter* and *blight* are of surprisingly recent vintage. The former has been dated to the nineteenth century and the latter to the seventeenth. *Blight*'s origin is unknown. See also PARASITE.

blockhead. A stupid person; in effect, someone with a block of wood for brains. "No man but a blockhead ever wrote, except for money" (Dr. Samuel Johnson, 4/5/1776, in Boswell's *Life* of the great lexicographer, 1791). Incidentally, after the doctor told a stupid maid that she was one, Boswell commented: "I never heard the word blockhead applied to a woman before, though I do not see why it should not, when there is evident occasion for it" (3/22/1776, *op. cit.*).

Dating to 1549 (*OED*), *blockhead* is one of the oldest of a large family of *-head* insults. They are closely related to the *-brain* family (see LAMEBRAIN). Most of the *-head* words describe the cranium in terms of its presumed density, or lack thereof (*airhead*, *bubblehead*, and so on); its shape (*jarhead*, *jughead*, *pinhead*); and its composition (*blockhead*, for example). The last category includes a large subset of food terms, which is not too surprising, considering that stupid people utter a lot of nonsense, and nonsense itself often is conceived as an unpalatable food. (see BALONEY). Herewith, a lightly annotated list of the more common *-head*s:

addlehead (also *addlebrain*, *addlecap*, *addlepate*, or simply *addled*). Stupid people have been said to be *addled* upstairs since around 1600. The term suggests that the *addlehead* is a muddler, and that the muddle itself is putrid. *Addle* originally denoted stinking urine or other liquid filth.

airhead. The term's popularity dates from the 1980s. "A little early, aren't you, airheads?" ("Miami Vice," WNBC-TV, New York City, 9/16/84). The expression condenses the older "[someone who] doesn't have anything between the ears but air." See also *empty-headed* below.

applehead. The metaphor may also imply that the stupid one is an apple-knocker or HICK. See also APPLE, BAD, and COSTERMONGER.

beanhead. Beans are small, of course.

blunderhead. One who makes many mistakes or blunders, from the seventeenth century; perhaps an alteration of *dunderhead*, below.

bonehead. One with a thick head, especially a stubborn person or one who acts without thinking, as does the baseball player who pulls a *boner* or *bonehead* play by, say, throwing to the wrong base; from 1908 (OED) but recorded half a century earlier as an adjective, *boneheaded* (1864, *Dictionary of American English*). *Bonehead* students may also *bone up* on subjects, but the verb comes from the name of the editor of a set of translations, Bohn's *Classical Library*, widely used by American college students in the early nineteenth century as *ponies*, i.e., trots. An exceedingly dumb person may be said *to be bone from the knees up*.

bubblehead. An airhead, in effect. "Bubble-head Henry Wallace . . ." (Westbrook Pegler, syndicated column, 3/11/52).

bullhead. From the seventeenth century; an obstinate person as well as a stupid one.

cabbagehead. The earliest example of a brainless *cabbagehead* in the OED comes from a work by the first Englishwoman to make a go of it as a professional writer; "Thou foul filthy *cabbage-head*" (Aphra Behn, *False Count*, 1682). See also KRAUT.

cerealhead. A child's insult; see DUMB/DUMMY.

cheesehead. "You let this cheesehead . . . insult me . . . ?" (Raymond Chandler, *The Big Sleep*, 1939). See also CHEESY.

chowderhead. The expression dates to the early nineteenth century and apparently continues the sequence of *cholter-, jolter-,* and *jolthead*, all with the same meaning. The last of these is the oldest (OED, 1533); it suggests that the stupid person got that way by being knocked on the head too often. Today, we would say that a *jolthead* is *punch-drunk* (making use of a term coined by Dr. Harrison S. Martland, *Journal of the American Medical Association*, 10/13/28).

chucklehead. From the eighteenth century, and probably from the *chuck* or *chock* of wood, making this an exact equivalent to *blockhead*, but with overtones today of one who laughs foolishly when there is nothing to laugh at.

clodhead. A lump of earth for brains; from the seventeenth century. See CLOD and CLODHOPPER.

clunkhead. Popularized by Arthur Godfrey on radio and television in the early 1950s (*Dictionary of American Slang*, 1975); possibly from *clunker*, for anything that is old, beat-up, and doesn't work well, as a rattletrap automobile.

cod's head. See COD.

cork-headed. Light-headed; not much there.

deadhead. Not only a stupid, boring person but from the 1840s one who doesn't pay his way, a FREELOADER, and in our own time a fan of the rock group, The Grateful Dead. A variation on the brainless theme: "Most of the inhabitants were dead from the neck up" (John Dos Passos, *The 42nd Parallel*, 1930).

dumbhead. From the nineteenth century; a translation of the German *dummkopf*, where *kopf* = head and *dumm* = stupid. See also DUMB/DUMMY.

dunderhead. From the seventeenth century; perhaps from the Dutch *donder*, thunder, implying that the stupid one has been scared witless by a thunderclap, with help from the association with *blunder*. "Shall I be called as many blockheads, numsculls, doddypooles, dunderheads . . . and other unsavoury appelations" (Laurence Sterne, *Tristram Shandy*, 1767).

empty-headed. "He would not allow me to praise a lady then at Bath; observing, 'She does not gain upon me, Sir; I think her empty-headed'" (James Boswell, reporting on a conversation with Dr. Johnson, 4/26–28/1776, *Life of Samuel Johnson*, 1791). The expression was more than a century old when Johnson used it (*OED*, 1650).

fathead. From 1842. See FAT.

featherhead (or *-brain*). Again, the noun, from 1845, seems to have developed from the adjective: "Many Gentlemenes . . . estates are deplumed by their featherheaded wives" (Nathaniel Ward, *The Simple Cobler of Aggawam in America*, 1647). See also FEATHERWEIGHT.

fiddlehead (or *-brain*). As empty as a fiddle. *Fiddle-brained* dates to 1650. See also FIDDLE-FADDLE.

flathead. "Greenhorns, flatheads!" (Mark Twain, *Huckleberry Finn*, 1884).

fluffhead. A person, usually a woman, not noted for vigorous intellect. See also FLUFF.

fuckhead. An extremely dumb person, or one who is mixed-up emotionally, or one "who keeps talking while the author is trying to concentrate" (Eugene Landy, *The Underground Dictionary*, 1971). The underlying idea is that sexual excess addles one's brains. See also JERK.

giddyhead (or *-brain* or *-pate*). A form of dizzy, lightheaded stupidity; from the Middle English *gidy*, mad, foolish, and the Old English *gydid*, insane, as through possession by a god.

hardhead. From the sixteenth century, frequently a person who is noted for obstinacy as well as stupidity; not to be confused with the modern *hardhat*, a construction worker, frequently a flag-waving conservative.

jarhead. The head often is regarded as a pot of some sort; see CRACKPOT, for instance. *Jarhead* has enjoyed other deprecatory meanings, especially in the American South, where it has been used to denote both a black male and a mule.

jughead. The type specimen is the dimwitted Jughead Jones, sidekick of the hero of the *Archie* comics. Though usually regarded as a male epithet, *jug* actually began as a female name, a sixteenth-century pet form of *Joan* or *Judith*. See MOLL for more about this and other female names. Parallelling *jarhead* in modern use, a *jughead* also is a horse or mule that is hard to train.

knothead. From 1940, at least. See *knucklehead*.

knucklehead. Popularized in the U.S. Marines in World War II. "Knothead: an unintelligent Marine; knucklehead: a knuckle lower than a knothead" (*American Speech*, 10/48).

lardhead. A variation on the *fathead* theme; twentieth century. See also LARD.

loggerhead. A log is a block of wood, of course, and *loggerhead* has been used to mean *blockhead* since Shakespeare's time: "Ah you whoreson loggerhead!" (*Love's Labor's Lost*, 1588–94).

lunkhead. A nineteenth-century Americanism, probably from *lump*, meaning a heavy, dull person, and perhaps the earlier (ca. 1400) *lump of clay*, meaning a soulless person. "So the duke said these Arkansas lunkheads couldn't come up to Shakespeare" (Mark Twain, *Huckleberry Finn*, 1884). See also LUNK.

meathead. From the 1940s, an updating of *fathead* (see above), perhaps influenced by MEATBALL; popularized by the TV show "All in the Family" (1971–83), whose lead character, Archie Bunker, continuously referred to his son-in-law as "Meathead," except when he was really mad, in which case the mildly liberal son-in-law became a "Polack pinko meathead." Indicative of the show's national impact in its second season: "An angry new bride writes to an advice columnist saying she'd stopped speaking to her father after he kept introducing her new husband at the wedding reception as 'my new Meathead.' The columnist advises forgiveness" (*TV Guide*, 9/3/83).

melonhead. Apparently a twentieth-century elaboration of the nineteenth-century *melon,* with the same meaning, alluding to the seeming greenness of a stupid fellow (Eric Partridge, *A Dictionary of Slang and Unconventional English,* 1970). *Watermelonhead* also has been reported (*American Speech,* Fall–Winter 1974).

moonhead. American, from the early twentieth century, rare; probably a derivative of *moonstruck.* See LUNATIC.

mudhead. Also a native of Tennessee (*Dictionary of American English,* 1838).

muddlehead (or *-pate*). The adjective, *muddle-headed,* dates to the eighteenth century, and the noun, *muddlehead,* to the nineteenth. A *muddlehead* is the same as a *mudhead.* The confused *muddle* apparently arises from the Middle Dutch *moddelen,* to make muddy.

mule-headed. See MULE.

mullethead. A nineteenth-century Americanism, probably referring originally to the fish (compare *cod's head*); possibly influenced by the earlier British use of *mull* and *mullhead* to refer to a simpleton.

mushhead. See MUSH.

muttonhead. Literally, a sheephead; from 1768 as *mutton-headed* (OED) and from 1804 as *muttonhead* (*Dictionary of American English*). See also MUTT.

noodlehead. A *noodle* has been a simpleton or stupid person since the mid-eighteenth century and *noodle* by itself is slang for the head, making *noodlehead* something of a redundancy. "The words ninnyhammer, noodle, and numscull are frequently bandied to and fro betwixt them" (John Hawkesworth, *The Adventurer,* 1753). The OED says this sense of *noodle* is of "obscure origin," but its coming into vogue at about the same time as MACARONI seems more than coincidental. See also *Yankee Doodle* in YANKEE. *Noodle,* in the sense of to act the fool, also appears to be the chief component of *canoodle,* to fondle, pet, or neck—an Americanism that dates to the middle of the last century and which is still encountered occasionally in dark places. "*Canoodlin'*—A Maine nicety for pleasurable dalliance between the sexes, meaning mostly the casual kind—the kind in the *bushes* or behind the *chip pile*" (1975, in Frederic G. Cassidy, *ed., Dictionary of American Regional English,* 1985).

peahead. The reference is not so much to the vegetable as to the alleged size of the brain. Or, a variation on the theme: "The Hon. Member disagrees. I can hear him shaking his head" (Canadian Prime Minster Pierre Trudeau, quoted in Nancy McPhee, *The Book of Insults,* 1978).

peanuthead. Another small vegetable. See also PEANUT.

pighead. Stubborn as well as stupid; from 1620 (Ben Jonson) as *pigheaded* and from 1889 in the short form (OED). See also PIG.

pinhead. "There's just as many pinheads on State Street as you'll find out in the woods" (George Ade, *Artie,* 1896). "How many pinheads can dance on an angel?" (*Los Angeles Reader,* 4/1/83).

pointed (or *pointy*) *head*. "Bless your pointed little head" (college slang, in *American Speech*, 10/48). *Pointy head* frequently is reserved for attacks on intellectuals, the implication being that their tapering heads would fit neatly into DUNCE caps. "As an aide to Gov. George Wallace of Alabama and his national campaign director in 1970–71, I helped the Gov'nuh blame it all on those 'integrating, scallywagging, race-mixing, pointy headed liberals who can't even park their bicycles straight' " (Tom Turnipseed, *New York Times*, 8/30/84). Despite the difference in shape, a *pointy head* is essentially the same as an EGGHEAD.

potatohead. Not necessarily an Irishman; a redundancy, similar to *noodlehead*, since *potato* alone is slang for the head. *Potato-headed* is dated to 1832 in the OED. In modern, 1980s parlance, a person who spends too much time watching a TV, a. k. a. the *boob tube*, is a *couch potato*.

pothead. Originally a smoker of marijuana, especially a heavy smoker, a *weed head*, but in extended use anyone who acts as if his or her brains are addled. "Erica Buehrens said a problem youngster at Hunter [High School in New York City] is known as a 'J.D.' (as in juvenile delinquent), a 'druggie' or a 'pothead' " (*New York Times*, 2/2/89). The *pot* that fills the *head* probably comes from the Mexican Spanish *potiguaya*, marijuana leaves. Other druggies include *hophead* (from 1911, where *hop* is opium) and the newer *acidhead*, *basehead*, and *crackhead*. See also junkie in JUNK.

puddinghead. As *pudding-headed* from 1726 (OED) but best memorialized as the eccentric hero of Mark Twain's *Pudd'nhead Wilson* (1894). A *puddinghead* is a soft head and *pudding-hearted* is an old term for one who is softhearted or squishy in a cowardly way. The idea probably comes from the oldest sense of *pudding* as a kind of sausage or a haggis in which entrails and other unmentionables are cooked inside an animal's stomach. There is also a strong suggestion here, however, that the *puddinghead* has become stupid through excess masturbation, also known as *pulling [one's] pudding*, where *pudding* is old slang for the penis (from the eighteenth century and probably from *pudendum*. See also JERK). The *pudding* in the child's rhyme, "What's your name, / Pudding-and-tame, / Ask me again, / And I'll tell you the same," seems to have an entirely different origin, referring to a fiend or devil, Pudding-of-Tame, who is mentioned in Samuel Harsnet's *Popish Impostures* of 1603 (Iona and Peter Opie, *The Lore and Language of Schoolchildren*, 1959).

pumpkinhead (or *-pate*). A big vegetable without very much inside and another redundancy, a *pumpkin* also being a swelled-up, self-important, stupid person. The metaphor appears as early as 1607 in the form *pumpion-headed*. In Colonial America, *pumpkinheads* also had much in common theologically and politically as well as physically with the close-cropped Roundheads of the old country: "Newhaven is celebrated for having given the name *pumkin-heads* to all New-Englanders. It originated from the Blue Laws, which enjoin every male to have his hair cut round by a cap. When caps were not to be had, they substituted the hard shell of a pumkin" (Samuel Peters, *A General History of Connecticut*, 1781).

rockhead. A hardhead; also in the phrase *to have rocks in [one's] head*. Dated to the 1950s in the *Dictionary of American Slang*, but probably substantially older. In baseball, *to pull a rock* is to make an error. Note the parallel to *bonehead*, listed earlier.

saphead. The adjective, *sap-headed*, dates to the 1600s. See also SAP.

shithead. Of uncertain antiquity; not recorded until the twentieth century. Also known as *shit-for-brains*.

softhead. From 1650 (OED). See also *soft-brained* in LAMEBRAIN.

spaghettihead. Like a *noodlehead.* "You wonder why kids are spacey? Watch enough of this and you turn into a spaghetti-head" (Thomas Yacavone, of East Hartford, Connecticut, commenting on the wonders of MTV, *New York Times*, 8/25/87).

squarehead. A German or Scandinavian; Australian slang, from 1903 (Farmer and Henley, *Slang and Its Analogues*); applied especially to German soldiers in World War I and later to anyone on the dull or stupid side. See also SQUARE.

tackhead. A pinhead, in effect.

thick-headed (or *-skulled* or just *thick*). *Thick* is used here in the sense of dense, another word for describing mental as well as material states. Shakespeare recognized both meanings of *thick:* "He's a good wit? Hang him, baboon! His wit's as thick as Tewksbury mustard" (*Henry IV, Part II*, 1596–97). *Thick-skulled*, from the middle of the seventeenth century, predates *thick-headed* (1801) and *thickhead* (1871).

weak-headed. See WEAK-.

woodenhead. Another kind of *blockhead:* "I . . . saw the coronation procession, which seventy or eighty thousand woodenheads besides were looking at" (Thomas Carlyle, letter to his wife, 9/8/1831).

wooly-headed (or *-brained* or *-witted*). Absentminded people have been said *to be gathering wool* since the sixteenth century and simpleminded people to be *woolly-headed* since the seventeenth. In nineteenth-century America, black people also were derided as *woolly-heads*, without reference to their intelligence, as were the abolitionists who sympathized with them. See also UNCLE TOM. The original wool-gathering metaphor seems to go back to the act of collecting tufts of wool from hedges and bushes in sheep pastures—a task that apparently was assigned to children and the simpleminded.

bloodsucker. A person who consumes the lifeblood of another (i.e., the other person's money); an extorter. The representatives of the IRS or its equivalent often have been regarded as *bloodsuckers*, e.g., "I . . . cast my Eye . . . upon a certain Tax-gatherer . . . ask'd the Devil, whether they had not of that sort of Blood-suckers, among the rest, in their Dominions" (Sir Roger L'Estrange, tr., *The Visions of Don Francisco de Quevedo Villegas*, 1668). See also LEECH and VAMPIRE.

bloody. Very. This seemingly innocuous term was heavily tabooed in Great Britain from ca. 1750 to ca. 1920. Previously, the intensive had been used casually in the best of circles. Thus, Dean Swift reported in a letter to Stella (1711) that "It was bloody hot walking to-day," and Samuel Richardson, a notably refined writer, observed without undue shuddering: "He is bloody passionate. I saw that at the Hall" (*Pamela*, 1742). But times were changing quickly. Samuel Johnson included the word in *A Dictionary of the English Language* (1755), but in this form: "Very: as *bloody* sick, *bloody* drunk. (*This is very vulgar*)." On the other side of the Atlantic and fifteen years later, the good citizens of Boston probably were aware of the vulgar connotation when they baited British redcoats: "Come you Rascals, you bloody-Backs, you Lobster Scoundrels; fire if you dare, G-d damn you" (*Massachusetts Gazette Extraordinary*, 6/21/1770). This was rather brave of them, if not foolhardy, considering that just three months before the *bloody-Backs* had fired into a crowd, killing three outright and wounding eight others, two of whom subsequently died (the Boston Massacre).

The onset of the taboo against *bloody* coincides with the increase in linguistic prudery that presaged the Victorian Era but it is hard to say what the precise cause was in the case of this specific word. Attempts have been made to explain the term's extraordinary shock power by invoking etymology. Theories that it derives from such oaths as "By our Lady" or "God's blood" seem farfetched, however. More likely, the taboo stemmed from the fear that many people have of blood, and, in the minds of some, from an association with menstrual bleeding. Whatever, the term was debarred from polite society during the whole of the nineteenth century. Even approximations were suspect. Thus, in 1887 the title of Gilbert and Sullivan's *Ruddygore* was changed to the present *Ruddigore* because the original was deemed too close to *bloodygore*.

The taboo against *bloody* began to ease in the early years of the twentieth century. George Bernard Shaw used it in *Pygmalion* (1914), causing a great sensation (Eliza: "Walk! Not bloody likely. I am going to take a taxi."), and people flocked to the play, partly to have their ears assaulted by the dread word. Still, newspapers—always among the strongest bastions of public morality—would not print the term, resorting instead to *b____y* and to such euphemisms as *blinking, blooming,* and *pygmalionly*. The constant repetition of the word by soldiers during World War I contributed further to the demise of the taboo. They not only used it as an adjective of all work but elaborated it into such combinations as *abso-bloody-lutely, hoo-bloody-rah,* and *of-bloody-course*. The more literate ones also enjoyed reciting a turn-of-the-century poem, variously entitled "The Australian Poem" and "The Great Australian Adjective." It begins:

> A sunburnt bloody stockman stood,
> And in a dismal bloody mood
> Apostrophized his bloody cuddy [donkey]:
> "This bloody moke's no bloody good,
> He doesn't earn his bloody food.
> Bloody! Bloody! Bloody!"

Still, old taboos die hard. As late as 1936, the residual power of this one was great enough to cause Robert Graves to genuflect before it. Reprinting a version of the Australian epic in *The Future of Swearing and Improper Language,* he evaded the word in this manner:

> The sunburnt ____ stockman stood,
> And, in a dismal ____ mood,
> Apostrophized his ____ duddy

And so on, for four more verses—quite a tribute to the enduring shock power of what also has been called, most discreetly, "The Shavian Adjective."

blow. A word of many meanings, not all of them low. For example, *to blow* is to leave, as in "Let's blow this joint." It also is to squander, as in "He blew his inheritance at the racetrack"; to botch something, especially through one's own error, as in "It was an easy grounder but the shortstop blew it"; and to treat someone to something, as in "I'll blow you to a meal tonight." On the rude side, to tell someone *to go blow* is to tell that person to scram; to make tracks.

In the military, meanwhile, *blow it out your barracks bag* (or *your B-bag* or *your footlocker*) is a common way of cutting off anyone who is spouting a lot of malarkey. (In its original form, from World War II, this expression appears as *blow it out your ass.*)

Also: *to blow off [one's] mouth* is to talk too much; *to blow hot and cold* is to be inconsistent; *to blow the gaff* is to betray a secret (the *gaff* being a concealed device for rigging a roulette wheel or other gambling game in the operator's favor); *to blow smoke* or *one's own horn* is to boast; a *blowhard* is a boaster or windbag; *to blow the lid off [something]* is to expose a scandal; *to blow the whistle on [someone]* is to do the same; *to blow [someone away]* is to kill someone, literally or figuratively; *to blow off steam* is to vent emotion, whether by swearing or by talking too much; *to blow up* is to lose one's temper, as is *to blow a fuse* or *a gasket* and *to blow [one's] top* or *cork* or *stack* or *wig* or almost any other imaginable covering. Many of these expressions are of considerable antiquity. For instance, Aesop told a fable about *blowing hot and cold; to blow the gaff* was preceded by *to blow the gab,* in the sense of "To confess, or impeach a confederate" (Captain Francis Grose, *A Classical Dictionary of the Vulgar Tongue,* 1785); and people have been *blown away* for at least a couple hundred years: "I ordered . . . the artillery officers to prepare to blow them away" (*Monthly Review,* 1776). As originally used, however, the latter phrase did not connote *blowing away* with a pistol or rifle. Rather, this was the technical term for dispensing military justice to a traitor, mutineer, or other bad person by binding him to the muzzle of a cannon, and firing.

Among the many meanings of *blow,* of which the foregoing are just a sampling, the most common in the modern era involve oral-genital sex, whether as a verb, *to blow [someone],* or an adjective, typically in the form of *blow job* (the title of a 1964 film by Andy Warhol on the subject). The really surprising thing about the sexual senses is how new they seem to be. Neither verb nor adjective appear in the *Oxford English Dictionary*'s 1972 supplement—and the editors of that volume did not have blinkers over their eyes, as a casual perusal of its contents will demonstrate. Both forms are included in the 1975 *Dictionary of American Slang,* but without citations— indirect evidence of their newness. Meanwhile, *The Thesaurus of American Slang,* of 1953, has *blow job* but only in the then-current, now-archaic sense of "jet plane," as in "A P-59 jet propelled Airacomet, affectionately called the 'blow job' by flyers, will make several flights . . . in 1946" (San Francisco *Examiner,* 7/26/45). The term is superficially a euphemism for SUCK (the witticism "Suck—don't blow" apparently dates at least to the 1960s). The sexual sense may derive from *blowoff,* meaning the ending, finish, or climax of something (from *to blow off steam*). The connection here is made in a 1939 glossary of "Prostitutes and Criminal Argots" by David W. Maurer: "To BLOW (YOU) OFF. To hold intercourse through the mouth" (*Language of the Underworld,* 1981). In addition, Maurer recorded *blower* as "A French girl. Also indicated by the phrase *she stoops to conquer.*" (Prostitutes and thieves' mistresses also were called *blowers* from the seventeenth through the nineteenth centuries, but this *blower* seems to be a variant of the Gypsy *blowen,* with the same meaning. It may be significant, too, that in the eighteenth and nineteenth centuries, the penis was sometimes referred to as a *whorepipe*—adding a new dimension to the phrase "to pay the piper.") Whatever the source, the word seems to have filled a need and since gaining currency has been extended to include the act and activity as performed by either sex. It has also occasioned more than its share of puns. Thus, from Ray Allen Billington's *Limericks Historical and Hysterical* (1981):

A bitter new widow, quite tough,
To her mate's ashes said in a huff,
  "You've diddled young girls,
  Never brought me no pearls,
And wanted me to blow you—so puff."

blubbermouth. A weepy person; a CRYBABY. "Men Are Bigger Blubbermouths Than Women" (headline, *National Enquirer*, 9/13/83). *Blubber* is ultimately of ono-matopoeic origin, imitating the bubbling sounds of a baby. It has been used this way, usually contemptuously, since ca. 1400. The sense of bubbling inherent in the word also gave rise to the swollen *blubber* that is fat. This, in turn, is responsible for *blubberhead*, meaning a fathead or stupid person, as well as the obese *blubber-belly*, *blubber-cheeks*, *blubber-guts*, and the picturesque *to sport blubber*, an eighteenth-century put-down for "a large coarse woman, who exposes her bosom" (Captain Francis Grose, *A Classical Dictionary of the Vulgar Tongue*, 1796). See also BLABBERMOUTH and FAT.

bobo. A stupid person; probably from the Spanish *bobo*, fool. "The difference between telling someone he is a nutsy-bobo to his face or in, say, an anonymous note is not insignificant. If you're going to insult someone to his face (which is the only decent thing to do and God bless you), remember that you can still get away with almost anything if you say it with a smile, and you might as well use your front teeth while you still have them" (Richard Coniff, *New York Times Magazine*, 9/18/83). "Bobo, made famous [in baseball] by Bobo Newsom, is now used less as a nickname than as a derogatory label for any player who is thought of as the manager's pet ('He's the old man's bobo')" (Zander Hollander, ed., *The Encyclopedia of Sports Talk*, 1976). See also BOOB and NUT.

Boche. A German. *Boche* is French slang from the nineteenth century, perhaps a relic of the Franco-Prussian war (1870–71). It is short for *alleboche*, of uncertain origin, but probably a blend of *Allemand*, German, and *caboche*, skull, hardhead, from the Old French *caboce*. The last term, as it happens, also is the source of the English *cabbage*, so a *Boche* is, in effect, a *cabbagehead*. See also BLOCKHEAD and KRAUT.

bohunk. Originally an immigrant from Hungary to the United States, *bohunk* later was applied indiscriminately to Czecks, Letts, Poles, and Slavs generally. The implication usually is that the *bohunk* is a clumsy, stupid, boorish, lower-class lout who works with his back, not his brains. Middle-class Americans whose ancestors had gotten off the boat a generation or so earlier used to bandy the term about rather freely. "I told her not to fall in love with a Bohunk but if she ran across a Standard Oil Magnate to nab him" (Harry S. Truman, letter to his future wife, Elizabeth Virginia Wallace, 5/3/11, in the *New York Times*, 3/14/83). The word dates to the turn of this century (*OED*, 1903). Although preceded slightly in print by *hunk* (1896), it probably was formed by collapsing together and slightly altering *Bohemian* and *Hungarian*. See also HUNK.

bonkers. Eccentric, crazy; if totally out of it, then *stark staring bonkers* or *stone fucking bonkers*. The term is British and of obscure origin. It appeared first in the 1920s in the sense of "tipsy" or "light-headed" and has since crossed the Atlantic. "The

Secretary [of the Interior, James G. Watt] has gone bonkers. It's time the white-coat people took him away" (Gaylord Nelson, former Democratic senator from Wisconsin and chairman of the Wilderness Society, *New York Times*, 1/2/83). It has been suggested that *bonkers* comes from the *bomb*, which rattles one's brains, or from the *bonk* on the head, which does the same. See also MAD.

boob. A stupid person, a dolt; from *booby*, also a dolt as well as the gannet, thought to be a dumb bird. ". . . he found himself surrounded by boobs: Everybody was, in one way or another, incompetent, ignorant or venal" (William F. Buckley, discussing David Stockman's account of life in the Reagan Administration, syndicated column, 4/30/86).

Usually in language, an animal name is established first, then applied disparagingly to people, but here the opposite may have occurred. The word probably derives from the Spanish *bobo*, fool, in turn from the Latin *balbus*, stammering. The oldest example of human *booby* in English comes from ca. 1600; the first citation for a *winged booby* from 1634 (*OED*). Superior people often characterize their fellow citizens—the public generally—as *boobies*. Thus, Herbert Asquith, Prime Minister of Great Britain (1908–16), asserted that Liberal newspapers were "written by boobies for boobies."

The clipped *boob* dates to the early twentieth century, as in—from one of baseball's greatest pitchers—"There's a poor 'boob' in the hospital now that stopped one with his head" (Christy Mathewson, *Pitching in a Pinch*, 1912). This was a favorite epithet of H. L. Mencken, who combined it with *bourgeoisie* to form *booboisie*, one of several HLM-isms to make it into standard dictionaries (with *bootician*, a bootlegger, and the better known *ecdysiast*, a stripteaser). Just why *booboisie* stuck in the public consciousness is not clear. It was merely one of a number of *boob* terms proposed by Mencken in a column on February 15, 1922; those that didn't stick included *boobariat*, *booberati*, *boobarian*, and *boobomaniac*. One of Mencken's friends, Siegfried Weisberger, attracted national attention when closing his Baltimore bookstore by proclaiming that "the age of the boob is upon us." This was in 1954, two years into the Eisenhower Administration. Mr. Weisberger may also have been concerned with the baleful influence of the *boob tube*, or TV, a.k.a. the *idiot box*. See also IDIOT.

In the plural, women have *boobs* or *boobies*, which are breasts, and which have nothing to do with either dolts or gannets, this form of the word deriving from *bubbies*, an Elizabethan term that formerly was Standard English for this part of the female anatomy. See also BREAST, DODO, and DUMB/DUMMY.

boogie. A black person. "I have seen that big boogie there mopping it up" (Ernest Hemingway, *To Have and Have Not*, 1937). *Boogie's* origin is uncertain, but it may come from the name of the hobgoblin that scares children in the dark, the *bogey* or *bogeyman*. If so, this makes *boogie* the natural counterpart of SPOOK. For *boogie-woogie*, see JAZZ.

boondocks. The backwoods, the outback, any rural area, also called the *boonies* and inhabited by *boonierats*. "Those who have been feeling the public pulse out in the boondocks report a good deal of unrest" (*Spectator*, 3/12/65). The term apparently dates from the Philippine Insurrection (1899–1902), deriving from the Tagalog *bundok*, mountain, referring originally to remote, wild, rough country. The earliest examples of its use in writing, however, come only from the 1940s, e.g., *Out in the Boondocks* (James D. Horan and Gerold Frank, 1943). Among the younger set, *boondocking* also has become something of a euphemism for the petting that often takes place when couples retire to isolated places.

Similar geographic approximations for rural areas include *the brush; the bushes,* inhabited by *bushwhackers* (see also BUSH); *the clods; the flat,* usually referring to the prairie, though a *flatlander,* to a Vermonter, is anyone not native to the Green Mountain State (and not to be confused with a *flatbacker,* a prostitute, or a female from *Flatsville,* whose bust is small); *the Great American Jungle; hayseed country; hickdom; hoosierdom; jakedom; jay country; the rhubarbs* (apparently a blend of RUBE and *suburb*); *rubedom; the sticks* (also *stick country, stickdom,* and, in the case of a particular town, *Stickville*); and *(the) toolies* (from *Thule* in Greenland and, ultimately, *Ultima Thule,* an island, probably in the Shetlands, considered by the ancient Greeks to be the most northerly point in the world). See also HICK and PODUNK.

boondoggle. Make-work, especially when done at public expense; also a gadget, especially a lanyard of the sort made by Boy or Girl Scouts. ". . . we can carve out the boondoggles and pork" (President Ronald Reagan, State of the Union Address, 1/27/87).

Boondoggle appeared on the national scene in 1935 during an investigation of public relief expenditures in New York City. Mr. Robert Marshall, of 291 Garfield Place, Brooklyn, testified that he taught "boon doogles," which he described as "a term applied back in pioneer days to what we call gadgets today. . . . They may be making belts in leather, or maybe belts by weaving ropes, or it might be belts by working with canvas, maybe a tent or sleeping bag. In other words, it is a chamber of horrors where boys perform crafts that are not designed for finesse and fine work, but simply for a utility purpose" (*New York Times,* 4/4/35). The term's origin is unknown, though many guesses have been made, among them that it comes from Daniel *Boone's dog;* from the Scottish use of *boondoggle* to mean a marble that one receives without having worked for it; and—a wild stab indeed—that it has something to do with the activities of *boonierats* in the BOONDOCKS. The most popular theory—adopted by a number of dictionaries—is that the word was coined about 1925 by Robert H. Link, a Scoutmaster in Rochester, New York, originally as a nickname for his son and later extended to plaited thongs. It seems possible that the word is older, however, both in the sense of a handcrafted gadget and of time spent inconsequentially, e.g., "To the cowboy it meant the making of saddle trappings out of the odds and ends of leather, and they boondoggled when there was nothing else to do on the ranch" (*Chicago Tribune,* 10/4/35).

boor. A stupid, clumsy, ill-mannered fellow. "We went into a little drinking house where there were a great many Dutch boors eating of fish in a boorish manner, but very merry in their way" (*The Diary of Samuel Pepys,* 5/19/1660, Henry B. Wheatley, ed., 1892). Originally, from before 1500, a *boor* simply was a farmer. Like many other words for country dwellers (see HICK), this one quickly acquired pejorative connotations. The English, having picked it up from the Dutch (*boer,* farmer), began by associating the term with agricultural workers in foreign countries. Thus, the Dutch and Germans were said to have *boors,* whereas the English countryside was populated by upstanding *yeomen.* The word's pejorative meanings then were broadened to include rude, ill-bred rustics generally. For example, Florio's Italian-

English dictionary of 1598 lumped together "a lubber, a clowne, a boore, a rude fellow" in the definition for *grossolano*. (PEASANT evolved in the same way during this period.) Today, only in South Africa, where the Dutch farmers who colonized that country are known as Boers, is the term used without opprobrious connotations (and then only by a minority of the nation's population). See also BUMPKIN and DUTCH.

boot-licker. A toady; a sycophant; one who curries favor with a superior. The short form, *boot-lick*, may be used either as a noun, referring to the person, or as a verb, meaning the unsavory act. "He boot-licked around until he became a ward committeeman" (James T. Farrell, *Young Lonigan*, 1932). The expression is an Americanism and has been dated to before 1850. It may have originated as a euphemism, the boot standing in, so to speak, for a portion of the lickee's anatomy. See also ASS, BROWN-NOSE(R), SYCOPHANT, and YES-MAN.

bore. A tiresome person or activity. "Society is now one polished horde, / Formed of two mighty tribes, the *Bores* and the *Bored*" (George Gordon, Lord Byron, *Don Juan*, 1819–24). *Bore* came into English fairly late, around 1750, initially in the sense of *ennui*. Its etymology is unknown, though it may have something to do with the sense of drilling that is inherent in the kind of bore that is an auger. Within several decades, the word came into vogue in its modern sense: "BORE. A tedious, troublesome man or woman, one who bores the ears of his hearers with an uninteresting tale; a term much in fashion about the years 1780 and 1781" (Captain Francis Grose, *A Classical Dictionary of the Vulgar Tongue*, 1796). See also TWADDLE and WET BLANKET.

boss. Leader, employer. As an attack word, it crops up most often in politics. Thus, Theodore C. Sorensen amplified a reference in *Kennedy* (1965) to "Chicago's resolute Mayor and political leader, Dick Daley" in this manner: "It should be noted that powerful Kennedy supporters are referred to in this book as 'political leaders,' those in the opposition camp are called 'bosses.' By convention time, recognizing their inability to defeat him, most of the 'bosses' had become 'political leaders.' " The basic distinction between the *boss* and the *political leader* carries over to related sets of terms. "Politicians are grouped as 'reform' or 'regular'; thus reformers 'plan' while regulars 'plot.' Reformers are 'friends' while regulars are 'cronies.' And, of course, the classic distinction, reform personalities are 'leaders' while regulars are 'bosses' " (Brooklyn [New York] *Phoenix*, 10/9/75).

The word comes from the Dutch *bass*, meaning master or foreman, and was popularized after the Revolution in the United States by servants so imbued with the spirit of egalitarianism that they didn't want to address anybody as "Master." (For that matter, they didn't like "servant" either and thus were called, and called themselves, "the help.") The usage quickly spread and was extended to include associations of all sorts. Thus, Jean Lafitte was known to the pirates, smugglers, and murderers who inhabited his colony at Barataria (from ca. 1810) as *the Bos*. And it was the word's gangland use that eventually resulted in its development as a political term. The elements are coupled in the earliest example of a political *boss* in *A Dictionary of American English*: "The custom which makes . . . 'bosses' of the men who control election gangs [sic]" (J. G. Holland, *Sevenoaks, A Story of To-day*, 1875).

The adjective is *bossy*, and no one much likes to be characterized this way either. It dates from the same period as the political *boss* and typically is applied to minor functionaries and individuals who act like big *bosses* even though they are not, e.g., "There was a lady manager who was dreadfully bossy" (*Harper's Magazine*, 12/18/1882). See also CRONY, GANG, MACHINE, and REGIME.

bounder. One whose behavior leaps over the normal limits; in popular use in Great Britain by the 1880s; ordinarily restricted to males. "To speak of a man as a bounder is to allude to him as an outsider or cad" (London *Times*, 5/2/1890). See also CAD and HEEL.

bourgeois. Middle-class, materialistic, small-minded, extremely conventional. "How beastly the bourgeois is / especially the male of the species" (D. H. Lawrence, "How Beastly the Bourgeois Is," 1929). *Bourgeois* entered English in the sixteenth century, but did not become overwhelmed with disparaging connotations until the nineteenth, when Marx and Engels used it as a synonym for "capitalist," e.g., "The Bourgeois, not content with having the women and daughters of their wage-slaves at command . . . find it capital [pun intended?] amusement to seduce each other's wives" (*The Communist Manifesto*, 1848, tr. 1886).

The exact meaning of *bourgeois* has varied not only over time but according to the class of the person employing the term. " '*Bourgeois*,' I observed, 'is an epithet which the riff-raff apply to what is respectable and the aristocracy to what is decent" (Anthony Hope [Sir Anthony Hope Hawkins], *The Dolly Dialogues*, 1894). C. S. Lewis also observed this phenomenon during his lifetime (1898–1963) and commented perceptively upon it: "All my life the epithet *bourgeois* has been, in many contexts, a term of contempt, but not for the same reason. When I was a boy—a *bourgeois* boy—it was applied to my social class by the class above it; *bourgeois* meant 'not aristocratic, therefore vulgar.' When I was in my twenties this changed. My class was now vilified by the class below it; *bourgeois* began to mean 'not proletarian, therefore parasitic, reactionary.' Thus it has always been a reproach to assign a man to that class which has provided the world with nearly all its divines, poets, philosophers, scientists, musicians, painters, doctors, architects, and administrators" (*Studies in Words*, 1960).

Bourgeois is something more than a term of reproach in the Communist lexicon, however. Rather, it is the preface to a formal criminal charge. Thus, when announcing the downfall of the Gang of Four (see GANG), Hsinhua, the official news agency of the People's Republic of China, reported accusations that they were "typical representatives of the bourgeoisie inside the party and the unrepentant capitalist roaders who were still on the capitalist road" (*New York Times*, 10/22/76). Then there was the case of the young couple who were caught fornicating in what they thought was a secluded part of a Western Electric factory in the province of Sian. For this breach of Revolutionary decorum, factory leaders subjected them to public criticism for their "bourgeois life style" (*New York Times*, 10/12/77). See also BABBITT, LACE-CURTAIN, LUMPENPROLETARIAT, PHILISTINE, and PLEBEIAN.

boy. Man; almost always an insult today when referring to any male past the age of puberty. "A Federal judge [in Newark, New Jersey] held a lawyer in contempt today and fined him $1,000 for referring to a black man who brought a police brutality suit as a 'boy' and for disregarding rulings by the judge" (AP, 6/20/84).

The pejorative meanings of *boy* have come to the fore as a reaction against its use until recent times as a way of addressing servants in general and black males in particular. Typically, and especially in the American South, the black man remained a *boy* until he was forty or so, at which point he metamorphosed into an *uncle*. (A black woman was either a GIRL or an *aunt*.) This usage was sanctioned by the highest and most enlightened authorities, e.g., "You mentioned one letter which you wrote last Friday, and sent by the Secretary's boy" (Thomas Jefferson, *Writings*, 1764). See also UNCLE TOM.

Boy's menial associations are in keeping with its etymology, as it happens. The word appears to have referred to a slave before acquiring its meaning of a male child. The key links in the chain, as traced by the *American Heritage Dictionary* (1969), are the Middle English *boye*, originally a male servant or knave, which possibly came from the Norman French *abuie*, fettered, in turn from the Old French *embuier*, to fetter, the Vulgar Latin *imboiare*, to have a collar or fetters around the neck, and the Greek *boeiai*, oxhides or things. The pejorative sense also has spilled over into other contexts. Thus, *cowboys* survive and so do *playboys*, if only because of the magazine, but one hardly ever sees a *bellboy*, *houseboy*, or *tomboy* nowadays. Only in special situations can the word be used safely. For example, an ad for bourbon whiskey pictured some distillery employees, all of them white and well above voting age, with copy explaining, "Each of these boys can talk forever about Jack Daniel's" (*Smithsonian*, 8/80). It apparently was okay to call these men *boys* because it was understood that they were really *good old boys*.

bozo. A fellow, a guy, especially a big, stupid one. The modern perception of *bozo* has been influenced by Bozo the Clown who stars on "The Bozo Show," a children's television show that has been syndicated around the country since the 1950s. Prior to that, the clown was on records: "Bozo was created by Capitol Records in 1940 as a voice in a series of story-telling albums for children" (*Wall Street Journal*, 10/31/83). The word came before the clown, however. "He picks out the most glarin' weaknesses . . . of the other bozo" (*Collier's*, 12/11/1920). *Bozo* seems to be Spanish, but the exact origin is unclear, with different etymologists suggesting that the English term derives from *bozo* in the sense of "down growing on the cheeks of youths," *bozal* meaning "stupid, inexperienced," and the dialectical *boso* or "you people," which resembles a direct form of address (from the second-person plural, *vosotros*). See also CLOWN.

brain-damaged. No good. Thus, describing the administrative technique of Steven P. Jobs, cofounder of the Apple computer company: "If he hears something he doesn't like, he berates the offending employee, calling the idea or product 'brain-damaged' " (*New York Times*, 11/8/87). Even worse is to be *brain-dead*, a term that was popularized by the case of Karen Anne Quinlan, a young New Jersey woman who went into a deep coma in 1975 after having made the mistake of mixing alcohol with barbiturates. Although her brain had ceased functioning, and although she was removed from an artificial respirator in 1976, she remained alive, fed intravenously, until June 25, 1987. *Brain-dead* was modeled on the earlier *brain death* (1968), as distinguished from the cessation of other vital functions such as the heart and lungs, whose operations can be sustained mechanically by life-support equipment. *Brainsick*, referring to mental disease, madness, or foolishness, is still older, having been dated to the fifteenth century.

brat. A nasty child. Thus, John Adams on the subject of Alexander Hamilton: "I lose all patience when I think of [that] bastard brat of a Scotch peddler . . ." (letter to Benjamin Rush, 1/25/1806). *Brat* dates to the early sixteenth century and is of obscure origin. It may derive from a rough cloth called "brat" that was used as a makeshift covering, especially for infants. If so, the epithet originally was tantamount to calling someone a "rag" or, more specifically, a "diaper." People still resent the label. For example, when asked what disturbed him about crowds at tennis matches, John McEnroe complained: "People yelling 'Brat' or 'Superbrat.' I'll never understand why people do that" (*New York Times*, 1/16/84). See also SOREHEAD.

breast. A mammary gland; a taboo word, rarely seen in print or uttered in mixed company during most of the nineteenth century and much of the twentieth. The revulsion that proper people felt toward this word at the beginning of this period is apparent from the following exchange from Captain Frederick Marryat's *Peter Simple* (1834): "Fate had placed me opposite a fine turkey. I asked my partner if I should have the pleasure of helping her to a piece of the breast. She looked at me indignantly and said, 'Curse your impudence, sar; I wonder where you larn your manners. Sar, I take a lily turkey *bosom*, if you please.' " And well over a century later, people still were reluctant to use this anatomical term. "If people insist on talking about her breasts, she would rather they called them boobs, which is a way-out word . . . rather than breasts" (*Daily Mirror*, 8/27/68). See also BELLY, BOOB, and TIT.

broad. A woman, impolitely considered. "A member of the Dubuque [Iowa] Human Rights Commission has resigned in a dispute over his reference to female postal workers as 'stupid broads' " (UPI, 4/30/84). The term is an Americanism, dating to the early twentieth century. Opinions are divided as to whether it derives from one of *broad*'s standard subsidiary meanings (outspoken, coarse, loose, vulgar) or from one of the phrases in which the word commonly appears, such as *broad-minded* (perhaps reinforced by BAWD) or *broad-beamed* (a nautical metaphor originally, perhaps reinforced by *broad-gauge lady*, a British railroading metaphor for a woman with a large seat). It could also be that the modern feminine sense draws on all the foregoing associations, since the term originally denoted a coarse or loose woman, with low or broad morals, who spent a lot of time on her beam-ends—that is, a prostitute. In time, the slang meaning was broadened, so to speak, to include any girl or woman, not necessarily a bad one. This made it possible to use the word more or less affectionately, especially when one referred to herself. Thus, no one is reported to have walked out of the theater when Nellie Forbush sang Oscar Hammerstein's lyric about "Honey Bun [who] was broad where a broad should be broad" (*South Pacific*, 1949), nor did the title of Bette Midler's *A View from a Broad* (1980) prevent it from making some best-seller lists.

Nevertheless, polite people continue to shy away from *broad*. For example, consider what has happened in the world of track and field, where the *broad jump* has been relabeled the *long jump*. This change occurred about 1966, as evidenced by *The Encyclopaedia Britannica Book of the Year*: The 1966 volume lists the record for the "broad (long) jump," while the 1967 edition refers only to the "long jump," without parenthetical explanation. A member of the U.S. Olympic Committee told Robert W. Creamer, author of *Stengel: His Life and Times* (1984) and other books, that "We changed it [the name of the event] because of the connotation" (Creamer, personal communication, 6/9/82). Creamer continues: "He went on to point out that in French and Italian and so on it was called the 'long jump.' However, he also noted that 'pole vault' in those languages is 'pole jump' and the shot put is a 'throw,' so the shifting of just the one uniquely English term implies an overprotective concern for the niceties." The name change probably was motivated partly by the increasing participation of women in athletics and partly by the fear of television broadcasters that the event's traditional name might offend someone somewhere. It is possible, too, that the Olympians simply had grown tired of hearing jokes, such as the classic (ca. 1940) Moe Raft–Eddie Kaplan vaudeville routine:

Q. Can you do the broad jump?
A. You show me the broad, and I'll make her jump.

See also BIMBO and CHIPPIE.

brother-in-law. An unforgivable insult in many parts of the world when addressed to someone who is not really a brother-in-law. The impolite implication in Arabic, Swahili, and Urdu is that the speaker has been intimate with the other person's sister. A comparable American witticism for topping whatever another male has said, no matter how foul, is the retort: "That's what your sister said when I let her up." See also COUSIN.

brown-nose(r). A sycophant of the lowest sort, an *apple-polisher;* as a verb, the act of currying favor. The term has been dated to before World War II (*OED*, 1939) and was popularized during that conflict. "The Bronze Star Medal, supposedly in recognition of meritorious achievement, which blossomed profusely on the chests of staff officers not having sufficient rank to receive the Legion of Merit, was often known as the *Officers' Good Conduct Medal*, sometimes, more bitterly, as the *Brown Nose Medal* or *Brown Star*" ("American Army Speech in the European Theater," *American Speech*, 12/46). The sycophant may also be said *to brown [someone], to get nose with [someone]*, to be a *brownie* (also with allusion to a junior Girl Scout), or to receive *brownie points* (merit badges, in effect). This last reverses an older meaning of *Brownie*, a demerit, from a system for penalizing railroad workers that was devised in 1885 by George R. Brown, superintendent of the Fall Brook Railway. None of these *browns* should be confused with the British *browned off*, to be depressed, disgusted, or irritated—the equivalent of the American *pissed off*. Perhaps partly inspired by the older, puritanical *blue-nose*, the *brown-nose* image derives, of course, from the synonymous *ass-kisser* (or *-licker*). The color's connotations have given rise to many "brown" jokes, such as the following, which were collected at one of Manhattan's more exclusive private schools in 1984:

Q. What's brown and sits on the piano?
A. Beethoven's Last Movement.
Q. What's brown and joined the Army?
A. Gomer's Pyle.
Q. What's brown in the candy store?
A. Peter Paul's Mound.
Q. What's brown and sounds like a bell?
A. Dunnnng.

See also BOOT-LICKER.

brute. A human with unhuman qualities, especially one who is rude, crude, stupid, exceptionally strong, or prone to violence; as a term of disparagement, similar to but stronger than ANIMAL or BEAST. Real brutes don't commit *brutal* crimes, *brutalize* others, or set up *brutalitarian* regimes.

Soame Jenyns, whose book *A Free Enquiry into the Nature and Origin of Evil* (1757) was savaged by Dr. Samuel Johnson in a famous three-part review, leaned on *brute* in a sarcastic epitaph for Johnson, written after the doctor was safely dead (1784):

> Here lies Sam Johnson: —Reader, have a care,
> Tread lightly, lest you wake a sleeping bear;
> Religious, moral, generous and humane
> He was; but self-sufficient, proud and vain.
> Fond of, and overbearing in, dispute,
> A Christian and a scholar—but a brute.

buck. A man, especially an American Indian, black male, or, in Commonwealth countries, such as Australia and New Zealand, an Aboriginal. "*Buck* . . . now applied almost exclusively to male negroes as the opposite of *wench*" (*Dialect Notes III*, 1909).

The world combines the Old English *buc*, male deer, and *bucca*, he-goat, which fused prior to 1100. It was applied to men, as opposed to animals, as early as the fourteenth century. The connotations were not all bad, especially in the eighteenth century, when *bucks* were dashing, high-spirited young fellows (later, *bucks* degenerated into dandies or fops). As applied to nonwhites, however (from 1800), the term has always been disparaging, since it categorizes them as though they were animals. "I told the boys that we wanted 20,000 'bucks,' buck niggers, in Indiana this year" (*Congressional Record*, 6/1880). See also WENCH.

buckra. A white man, to a black person, principally in the southeastern part of the United States, almost always in a disparaging manner, the *buckra* being regarded as POOR WHITE TRASH. "Like the servants of most of the lordly planters of that day, Benny Bowlegs had but small esteem for the class whom he described as 'poor buckrah'" (W. G. Simms, *The Forayers; or, The Raid of the Dog-Days*, 1855). *Buckra* has been dated to the eighteenth century and remains current. It appears to be an Africanism, coming from the word for *master* in Efik, a language spoken by the Ibibio of southern Nigeria. See also WHITEY.

buffoon. A clown, a witless fellow, especially one given to coarse humor. Thus, referring to George Villiers, second Duke of Buckingham:

> Stiff in his opinions, always in the wrong;
> Was everything by starts, and nothing long;
> But in the course of one revolving moon,
> Was chymist, fiddler, statesman, and buffoon
> (John Dryden, *Absalom and Achitophel*, 1681)

The word derives from the Italian *buffare*, to puff. The allusion may be either to a light puff of air or to the comic gesture made with cheeks puffed out. The former seems more likely since clowns often are regarded as windy people. See also FOOL and WINDBAG.

bugger. One who practices sodomy (i.e., buggery) or, as a verb, the act thereof, but with many subsidiary meanings. As a noun: "Elliott . . . referred to Japanese-Americans as 'those slant-eyed buggers' " (*Columbia Journalism Review*, 1–2/85). And as a verb, from the wit and wisdom of Casey Stengel: "If I'm gonna be buggered I don't want an amateur handling the Vaseline pot" (Robert W. Creamer, *Stengel: His Life and Times*, 1984).

This term probably does *not* honor the memory of an Inquisitor, Robert le Bougre, who is said to have displayed indecent interest in this offense when questioning accused heretics. More likely, it comes from the general French *Bougre* (and Latin *Bulgarus*), meaning Bulgarian, the name commonly applied to Albigensian heretics in southern France in the twelfth and thirteenth centuries. Their doctrines were thought to have come from eastern Europe and they themselves were widely believed to practice what we now call *buggery* as a method of birth control. They had their reasons: They believed that matter in general was evil and that the human race in particular should not be perpetuated. At the same time, since the body was intrinsically so abhorrent, it didn't much matter what sexual (or other) activities it engaged in, so long as final absolution was given to the spirit—and so long as no babies were procreated along the way. (And whoever said that philosophy was dull sport?)

Bugger used to be one of the vilest epithets that any Englishman could hurl at another. Remarkably, the strength of the insult seemed to increase as one ascended the social ladder. Seeking to explain this peculiar social phenomenon, Robert Graves theorized in *The Future of Swearing and Improper Language* (1936) that the upper classes were touchier about the use of the term than the lower ones because homosexuality was more prevalent among the former than the latter. The taboo was sufficiently strong that the reduction of *bugger* to writing could be an actionable offense until the 1930s and even Graves carefully abbreviated it to *b*. Among the hoi polloi, and Americans, the word's meaning was broadened considerably to include any *chap* or *fellow*, and it was used endearingly as well as insultingly. Thus, *bugger* evolved into the moral equivalent of the generic SON OF A BITCH in such expressions as "Hello, you old bugger" or "He's a cute little bugger, isn't he?" The word also can be used in nonsexual ways as a noun, referring to any more or less undesirable thing, and as a verb, in the sense of "to ruin," "to spoil," or "to screw up," e.g., "we ran across information . . . that could actually bugger the investigation" (*Columbia Journalism Review*, 9–10/81).

Finally, *bugger* also has become an expletive-of-all-work, as in "I'll be buggered," "Bugger off," "Bugger you," or "Bugger all." The last of these translates as "damn all" or "nothing" (e.g., "Here we are in the middle of bugger all") and it gave Dylan Thomas, who died in 1953, one last guffaw from the grave when the fastidious BBC broadcast *Under Milk Wood* in 1954, without realizing that Llareggub, the fictional Welsh village that provided the play's setting, was a perverse as well as reverse name. See also BASTARD and BLIGHTER.

bull. The sexual potency of the animal made its name taboo in many parts of the land for a great many years. To get around this, a variety of euphemisms were used, especially when ladies were present. These included *cow brute, cow creature, cow's husband, gentleman cow, male cow, seed ox, top cow,* and so on. As late as 1917, *male cow* graced the pages of the *Journal of the American Medical Association* (November 17, page 24) and Vance Randolph reported in *American Speech* in 1929 that when he

63

asked "an unusually intelligent schoolmarm" in the Ozarks what she meant by "surly," she replied: "That's our name for male animal. We're kind of old-fashioned down here, you know. We couldn't come right out and say *top cow* like you-all do up North." So strong was the taboo that Ozarkians had to be careful with such words as *bullfrog, bull fiddle,* and *bullsnake* as well as geographical place names, such as *Bull Creek, Bull Mountain,* and *Bull Shoals.* In 1941, which is usually regarded as modern times, some of Randolph's neighbors were so offended by the appearance of the story of "Ferdinand the Bull" in a Sunday-school paper that they forbade their children ever to read this publication again (Vance Randolph and George P. Wilson, *Down in the Holler,* 1953). See also HORNY and NED IN THE FIRST READER.

bullshit. Nonsense and, as a verb, the act of spewing it forth, frequently with the implication that the nonsense is tantamount to a wilful lie. "Alfred JaCoby . . . calls Haiman's argument 'pure, unmitigated bullshit' " (*Columbia Journalism Review,* 5–6/84). "Go on, Dad. He's bullshitting you" (Ernest Thompson, *On Golden Pond,* 1979). The term has been euphemized as *B.S., booshwah, bushwa, bushwash, bull, pedigreed bull, prize bull, bovine excrement, heifer dust,* and so on. The basic material, also referred to as *basic sediment,* typically is slung in *bull sessions.* A person who is especially adept at *throwing the bull,* perhaps even using the nonsense as a cover for achieving a nefarious end, may be known as a *Spanish athlete* or *bullshit artist.* The person who recognizes the *BS* for what it is may declare, "I feel like a wagon wheel. Been through this bullshit before" (Herbert B. Livesey III, personal communication, 1984). See also BUNK.

The barnyard term appears rather late in dictionaries (ca. 1915 in the 1972 supplement to the *Oxford English Dictionary*), but is almost certainly much older. *Bull* in the sense of lies or exaggerated talk has been dated to the 1850s and *shit* with the same meaning was popularized by soldiers during the American Civil War. Still earlier, Americans often spoke of *flinging, slinging,* or *throwing the bull,* as in "he belonged to that numerous class, that it is perfectly safe to trust (as far as a tailor can sling a bull by the tail)" (Colonel Davy Crockett, *Col. Crockett's Exploits and Adventures in Texas,* 1836). It is even possible that the conjunction of the animal's name, its excrescence, and the sense of nonsense is purely fortuitous. One of the standard meanings of *bull* (from the sixteenth century, though now obsolete) is to fool, mock, or cheat (out of), and this kind of *bull* probably derived from the Middle English *bul,* falsehood, rather than from the animal. Other similar senses include the *bull* that is a blunder (used this way by Milton in 1642), a ludicrous jest, or a contradiction in terms (usually described as an *Irish bull*). These *bulls,* too, seem to have come from *bul,* falsehood, perhaps influenced by the Old French *boule,* bubble. While the Irish are justly famous for the self-contradictory *bulls*—e.g., "Gentlemen, it appears to be unanimous that we cannot agree" (attributed to Charles Stewart Parnell, 1846–91) and "In our family it is hereditary to have no children" (anonymous)—they seem not to have invented the art form. The earliest example of this kind of *bull* in the *OED* is from 1640 ("Dumbe Speaker! that's a Bull"), about a century before this sense of the word attached to the Irish. No *bull!*

bum. An idler, loafer, or ne'er-do-well; a beggar or, as a verb, to beg. "In a brief test for audio technicians, President Reagan referred to the Polish military Government as 'a bunch of lousy bums' " (*New York Times,* 10/11/82). The footloose *bum* is an Americanism, apparently deriving from the German *bummler,* an idler, and *bummeln,* a leisurely stroll, to waste time. In dates to the 1830s, thus coinciding with the appearance of many German immigrants in the United States. In keeping with the usual opinion of solid citizens toward those who drift from place to place, with no fixed occupation, the term was used in a disparaging manner from an early date, e.g., "Such ratty bums I never did see before in my life" (New Orleans *Lantern*, 4/9/1887). The pejorative connotations carried over into the word's secondary meanings; among them: a prostitute or other easily available woman, an inferior racehorse or other animal, a poor prizefighter, or almost anything else that is worthless, bad, or just not working, as in "The pimp's Cadillac had turned it into one flat hat, all right. . . . 'That is a bummed-out bonnet, Buckmore,' Gibson Hand clucked sadly" (Joseph Wambaugh, *The Glitter Dome*, 1981).

The disparaging senses of *bum* also are evident in such standard phrases as *bum rap, bum's rush, bum steer, crumb-bum* (see CRUMB), *ski bum, stew bum, stumblebum, tennis bum, bummer* (a bad experience), and so on. To take just one example: "In 1970, New London [Connecticut] changed the name of its Main Street to Eugene O'Neill Drive over the objections of Thomas J. Griffin, a former mayor, who called the playwright a 'stew bum' and asked, 'What did he do besides write plays?' " (*New York Times*, 10/9/88). Even among gentlemen of the road, the *bum* was viewed with disdain, as he frequently was a hopeless derelict or drunkard. "A hobo will work, a tramp won't, a bum can't" (CBS Radio Network, 8/25/52).

There are exceptions to all this, but not many. The old Brooklyn Dodgers were regarded affectionately by their fans as *dem bums* (but Brooklynites have always marched to the beat of a different drummer). The migrants who joined the IWW (Industrial Workers of the World, or Wobblies) around 1908 also sang a song with the refrain "Hallelujah, I'm a bum" (it provided the title of an Al Jolson film in 1933). Another Wobbly verse provides a darker, more traditional view of *bum*, however: It contrasts unemployed *bums* with established citizenry, rather to the disadvantage of the latter:

> The bum on the rods is a social flea
> Who gets an occasional bite,
> The bum on the plush is a social leech,
> Bloodsucking day and night.
> (Roger A. Bruns, *Knights of the*
> *Road: A Hobo History*, 1980)

The British also have used *bum* disparagingly to mean an idler or other worthless person, e.g., a limping couplet from Tom ("I do not love thee, Dr. Fell") Brown's *The Poet's Condition*: "My levee's all duns / Attended by bums" (pre-1704). This *bum*, however, comes from *bumble*, meaning a bumbler, bungler, or blunderer. More commonly, in British English, *bum* refers to what Samuel Johnson described in his *Dictionary of the English Language* (1755) as "the part on which we sit." ("Do you mean a chair, Doctor?" asked one of his few critics.)

This last, or posterior, *bum* is the oldest of the word's various forms (*OED*, 1387). It probably is of onomatopoetic origin, along with *bump*, another term for a roundish protuberance. Shakespeare knew the word in this sense. Thus, Puck tells of his pranks: "Sometimes for a three-foot stool [she] mistaketh me; Then slip I from her bum, down topples she" (*A Midsummer Night's Dream*, 1594–95). Because of this low meaning, *bum* was considered distinctly improper by the British for about a century and a half, starting around 1790. It was not forgotten during this period, of course, but merely relegated to underground literature and spoken ditties, such as:

Oh my finger, oh my thumb,
Oh my belly, oh my bum.

and

When to age of forty they come,
Men run to belly and women to bum.

Thus in *anno Domini* 1938, when the aforementioned Jolson film played in England, it was deemed necessary to change the title to *Hallelujah, I'm a Tramp*. (And proceeding in the other direction, from West to East, for the same anatomical-linguistic reasons and at about the same time, the title of the 1944 British film *Fanny by Gaslight* was changed for American consumption to *Man of Evil*.)

See also BEGGAR, LOAFER, and TRAMP.

bumpkin. A dull, awkward, country fellow; from the sixteenth century and probably derived from the Dutch *boomken*, a little tree, and apparently applied to a Dutchman—a short, squat person—before acquiring its rustic sense. The Dutch connection makes *bumpkin* a close cousin to BOOR; see also DUTCH.

bunk. Nonsense, as in "History is more or less bunk" (Henry Ford, *Chicago Tribune*, 5/22/16).

Bunk is short for *bunkum*, in turn from *Buncombe*, a county in North Carolina. The story is that in 1820, toward the end of the long and emotional debate on the Missouri Compromise, which settled the slavery question well enough to delay the Civil War for two generations, Representative Felix Walker, whose district included Buncombe, managed to get the floor and launch into a tedious, irrelevant speech. Anxious to start voting, other members complained, but Representative Walker said his constituents expected him to speak and so he was going to do so "for Buncombe." He kept on talking, and the term entered the language. The ultimate source of the word—the man for whom the North Carolina county was named—is Colonel Edward Buncombe. He was killed during the American Revolution, at the Battle of Germantown in 1777, and seems to have deserved better of his country.

Other forms of pretentious, insincere, essentially nonsensical talk or writing include:

bombast. Inflated, grandiloquent language. "I never knew Colonel North to be an absolute liar, but I never took anything he said at face value because I knew that he was bombastic and embellished the record, and threw curves, speed balls, and spitballs to get what he wanted, and I knew it and I knew it well" (Alan D. Fiers, chief, CIA Central American Task Force, testimony to congressional committees investigating the Iran-Contra connection, *New York Times*, 8/31/87). *Bombast*, sometimes supposed to be an eponym, from Theophrastus Bombastus von Hohenheim, a.k.a. Paracelsus (1490–1541), actually comes from *bombace*, cotton padding, in turn a corruption of the Latin *bombyx*, silk. The basic thought is the same, though the language is plainer, when a writer is criticized for *padding* a work with unnecessary words.

bosh. From the Turkish *boş*, worthless, empty; popularized by James J. Morier's novel, *Ayesha, The Maid of Kars* (1834).

claptrap. Originally, from the early nineteenth century, showy language intended to attract applause—that is, to *trap* the *clap*—but now more often empty, hollow, or misleading words. "Once again we hear the tiresome and silly complaint . . . that feminist organizations . . . are too white and too middle-class. Feminist leaders must disregard such claptrap" (letter, *New York Times*, 12/14/83).

cock and bull. See *cock-and-bull story* in COCK.

folderol (or *falderal* or *falderol*). From the first part of the nineteenth century, and apparently from the use of these syllables as a meaningless refrain in some songs, comparable to *tra-la-la.*

fustian. Similar in origin as well as meaning to *bombast*; in its oldest sense, from ca. 1200, the word denoted a coarse cloth of flax and cotton, from the Latin *fustaneus*, cloth, in turn probably from the suburb of Cairo where the cloth was manufactured, *Fostat.* "Yossarian was unmoved by the fustian charade of the burial ceremony" (Joseph Heller, *Catch-22*, 1961).

gasconade. To boast extravagantly; braggadocio. This is basically an ethnic slur, referring to the reputation of the inhabitants of the French province of Gascony. See also GASCON and *gasconade* in PEORIA.

rodomontade. Boastful blustering, from Rodomonte (rolling mountain), the brave but braggart Moorish king who appears in Matteo Maria Boiardo's *Orlando Innamorato* (1487) and its continuation by Lodovico Ariosto, *Orlando Furioso* (1516–33).

See also BALLS, BALONEY, BLAH, BLATHERSKITE, BULLSHIT, CODSWALLOP, CRAP, DRIVEL, EYEWASH, FIDDLE-FADDLE, FLAPDOODLE, FLIMFLAM, GARBAGE, GAS, GOBBLEDY-GOOK, HOCKEY, HOGWASH, HOKUM, HOOEY, HUMBUG, HYPE, JAZZ, JUNK, KIBOSH, MALARKEY, MOONSHINE, MUMBO JUMBO, MUSH, *nuts* in NUT, PHOOEY, PIFFLE, POPPY-COCK, ROT, RUBBISH, SHIT, TRASH, and TWADDLE.

bureaucrat. Public servant, a.k.a. *paper shuffler* and *pencil pusher*, unless the servant happens to be in the U.S. State Department, in which case he or she is a *cookie pusher* or member of *the striped pants set.* The disparaging sense of *bureaucrat* is apparent in its earliest known use in a letter of 1842 wherein Count Karl von Nesselrode, better known today for the pie that bears his name, is described as "the great bureaucrat of the great autocrat," meaning Nicholas I, Emperor of Russia. *Bureaucrat* comes from *bureaucracy*, invented earlier in the nineteenth century and also a word that always seems to raise the hackles of the user, e.g., "That vast net-work of administrative tyranny . . . that system of *bureaucracy*, which leaves no free agent in all France, except for the man at Paris who pulls the wires" (John Stuart Mill, *Westminster Review XXVIII*, 1837). Continuing the sequence: *Bureaucracy* comes from *bureau*, a writing desk with drawers used by public servants; *bureau* from the kind of coarse woolen cloth, *baize* or, in French, *bureau*, that was used to cover the piece of furniture; and the cloth *bureau* from the Late Latin word for a shaggy garment, *burra*, which also, considering the ridiculous appearance of the garment, seems to have given us *burlesque.* Which makes public servants and ecdysiasts distant cousins! See also APPARATCHIK, DUD, and GOBBLEDYGOOK.

burke. To suppress or hush up; to murder by suffocation. "Is Central America Ready for Self-Government?: 'Disappear,' to Burke" (headline for letter to *The New York Times*, 2/19/88). The term is an eponym, after William Burke (1792–1829), who, together with William Hare, enticed men to Hare's lodging house in Edinburgh, got them drunk, then suffocated them in order to obtain bodies for sale to Dr. Robert Knox, a leading teacher of anatomy. This was at a time when it was illegal to dissect bodies, except those of convicted murderers, and the demands of medical students for bodies to learn upon far outstripped the available supply. As a result, grave robbers, or resurrectionists, did a thriving business. Others, such as Burke and Hare, did not bother to wait for natural death and proper burial. The two Irishmen killed at least fifteen men, selling their bodies at from £8 to £14 per. After being arrested, Hare turned king's evidence and Burke was hanged. The notorious case helped persuade Parliament to pass the Anatomy Act of 1832, thereby legalizing and regulating the supply of bodies for dissection. And it also led with remarkable swiftness to the use of Burke's name as a verb, the crowd shouting "Burke him, Burke him." and "Burke Hare, too" as he was led to the gallows on January 28, 1829.

bush. Small-time, rinky-dink, second-rate, and most of all, when characterizing a person's behavior, unprofessional; from *bush league*, a baseball minor league. ". . . he rejected such epithets as 'selfish,' 'callous,' and 'ungrateful.' He chose 'inept,' an Ivy League euphemism for 'bush' " (Red Smith, *New York Times*, 12/20/77). The derogation sometimes appears in full and has proven useful enough to be adopted in nonathletic contexts, e.g., "He was . . . a bush-league Chicago gambler" (A. Hynd, *Public Enemies*, 1949). See also BOONDOCKS.

buttinski. One who pokes into other people's business; a meddler. "The friend belonged to the Buttinsky Family and refused to stay on the Far Side of the Room" (George Ade, *Girl Proposition 70*, 1902). The word is composed of *butt* (the kind a billygoat does) + *in* + *ski* or *sky* (a common ending of Eastern European sur-names). The ending of the surname was attached derisively to English words about the turn of this century, reflecting the prejudices of one generation of immigrants (principally German Jews in this case) toward a later generation of immigrants (principally Polish Jews in this case). Similar words of the period included *allrightsky* and *damfoolski*, but "only *buttinski* shows any sign of surviving" (H. L. Mencken, *The American Language, abr.* and *ed.* by Raven I. McDavid, Jr., 1979). See also KIKE, NOSEY PARKER, and WISENHEIMER.

buzzard. An untidy and contemptible person; one who takes unfair advantage by attacking others when they are in weakened condition. "With that technique, he [Roy Cohn] will ultimately defeat the buzzards of the Establishment bar, who reached new legal depths by waiting until a combative lawyer was on his deathbed and unable personally to contest 15-year-old charges of unethical conduct" (William Safire, *New York Times*, 8/4/86). *Buzzards* in human form have existed since at least the fourteenth century. Subspecies include the *blind buzzard*, meaning an ignorant or stupid person of either sex, and the *old buzzard*, almost always of masculine gender. *Between hawk and buzzard* is a British expression, dated to the seventeenth century and still current, for someone or something that is neither good (the *hawk* part) nor bad (the *buzzard*). Specifically, the phrase often was applied to tutors, governesses, and other adults who ranked above the servants in the great houses of England, but who were not the equals of the masters and mistresses of those establishments. Those who were *between hawk and buzzard* might be invited to the dinner table for dessert, but not to sit down with the family for dinner itself. In other, less formal contexts, *buzzard* may be a euphemism for *bastard;* *to be ragged as a buzzard's ass* is to be extremely unkempt; *to be poor as buzzard's dung* is to slide off the lower end of the poverty scale, and to act the part of a *jungle buzzard* is to beg from hoboes or to scavenge whatever food they have left in their jungles, or camps. See also BIRD, HAWK, and VULTURE.

byzantine. Complicated, devious; replete with intrigue. "Mix that metaphor! Sen. [John] Warner [Republican, Virginia] claims invocation of the War Powers Act would put U.S. forces in a 'byzantine thicket of quicksand' " (*Wall Street Journal*, 10/16/87). "Today, the word 'Byzantine' is often employed in a pejorative sense, which reminds us that the . . . failings in the later Roman world of the Theodosian Code, which gave birth to the Byzantine Empire, have not been forgotten: Bureaucracy is still recognized to be a danger" (Michael Grant, *The Fall of the Roman Empire—A Reappraisal*, 1976). See also BUREAUCRAT and PEORIA.

C

cad. A vulgar fellow, especially one whose actions have betrayed his lower-class origin; often, for emphasis, an *unspeakable cad*. "The Class system, and its conventions are no longer what they used to be, and *cad* is now an evasively defined word that has lost much of its sting. A cad used to be a jumped-up member of the lower classes who was guilty of behaving as if he didn't know that his lowly origin made him unfit for having sexual relationships with well-bred women" (Anthony West, *H. G. Wells: Aspects of a Life*, 1984). *Cad* is short for *caddie*, meaning an errand boy or gofer, which in turns comes from *cadet*, a noncommissioned officer or, originally, a younger son, from the diminutive of the Latin word for head, *capitellum*, little head. See also BOUNDER and HEEL.

cadger. A beggar. "A street-seller now-a-days is looked upon as a 'cadger,' and treated as one" (Henry Mayhew, *London Labour and the London Poor*, 1851). A *cadger* originally was a *carrier* (from ca. 1450), a middleman who collected produce from isolated farms, took the goods to market, and brought town wares back to the farmers on his return trips. Evidently, the itinerant cadgers did a lot of begging while trying to close sales. See also CODGER, MOOCHER, and PEDDLER.

caitiff. A villain, coward, or wretch; a despicable person. ". . . the wicked'st caitiff on the ground" (William Shakespeare, *Measure for Measure*, 1604). The base meaning of *caitiff* reflects the traditional view of victors toward the vanquished: It comes from *captivus*, the Latin word for a prisoner or captive. See also KNAVE.

canard. The French word for *duck* has become a byword for a hoax or absurdly false claim—making it a particularly good word to use when attempting to undercut charges brought against you. Thus, when Norwegians and Swedes started seeing what they thought were Russian submarines in their waters, Tass dismissed the reports as "propaganda canards emitting a foul stench" (AP, 5/4/83). The term usually is traced back to an old French expression, *vendre un canard à moitié*, to half-sell a duck—an impossible and, hence, fraudulent, sale. The figurative meaning, "to take in" or "to make a fool of," was well-established by 1611 when Randle Cotgrave defined a seller of such ducks as "a cousener, guller, cogger; foister, lyer" (*A Dictionary of the French and English Tongues*). This meaning of *canard* may also have been reinforced—or even inspired—by the readiness of ducks to swallow anything, as exemplified by the story, widely circulated, of a man who had twenty ducks, cut up one, and fed it to the other nineteen, who gobbled it down. Then he cut up another duck and fed it to the remaining eighteen, and so on, until the voracious ducks had consumed themselves and only one was left. See also GULL.

canary. A woman, sometimes a whore, and frequently but not necessarily a singer, a.k.a. *chirp* or *thrush*. "He acquired the art of making a canary understand that he wished to meet her on the corner at night by merely making a motion with his hands" (New Orleans *Lantern*, 10/6/1886). In the underworld, a *canary* is another kind of "singer," i.e., an informer, a.k.a. *nightingale,* PIGEON, or RAT. All prisoners, whether singers or not, once were regarded as *canaries.* Captain Francis Grose began his definition of *canary bird* with "jail bird, a person used to be kept in a cage" (*A Classical Dictionary of the Vulgar Tongue,* 1796). *Canary* comes from the Latin word for *dog,* the bird being native to the Canary Islands, named *Canariae Insulae* by the Romans on account of the large dogs, *canes,* that also inhabited them. See also BIRD and FINK.

cancer. Presently the most feared disease (though AIDS is coming on strong) and, hence, the most strongly tabooed, often euphemized in obituaries as *a long, prolonged,* or *incurable illness,* or simply not mentioned at all. "The fear surrounding cancer being even more acute [than in the case of TB], so is the concealment. In France and Italy it is still the *rule* for doctors to communicate a cancer diagnosis to the patient's family but not to the patient . . . In America, where—in part because of the doctors' fear of malpractice suits—there is now much more candor with patients, the country's largest cancer hospital mails routine communications and bills to outpatients in envelopes that do not reveal the sender, on the assumption that the illness may be a secret from their families" (Susan Sontag, *New York Review of Books,* 1/26/78).

Cancer (from the Greek word for *crab,* which is what Galen and other early physicians thought a swollen, cancerous tumor looked like) also has served since at least the seventeenth century as a metaphor for any evil that secretly eats away at something else. For example: "Sloth is a Cancer, eating up that Time / Princes should cultivate for Things sublime" (Thomas Ken, "Edmund, an Epic Poem," pre-1700). And, from one of the more memorable declarations of our own time: "We have a cancer within, close to the Presidency, that is growing. It is growing daily. It's compounded, growing geometrically now, because it compounds itself. That will be clear if I, you know, explain some details of why it is" (John W. Dean III to President Richard M. Nixon, 10:12–11:55 A.M., 3/21/73, *The White House Transcripts,* 1974).

candle to, can't hold a. A standard method of comparing one person to another—to the disadvantage of the person named, as in "Jerry can't hold a candle to John." The expression probably was devised soon after candles were invented. The root idea is that the person who holds a candle to provide light for a job is of less importance (being less skilled) than the person who actually does the work. Hence, not to be able to hold a candle for another person is to be truly inferior to them. "Though I be not worth to hold a candle to Aristotle" (Sir Edward Dering, *Fower Cardinal-Vertues of a Carmelite Fryar,* 1640). See also MUSTARD, CAN'T CUT THE and, for another example of a candle that can't be held, NINNY.

cannon fodder. Expendable people, i.e., food for cannon or fit only for consumption in other ways: "He'd bet those hostesses went mad about him; that's all they were, anyway, cannon fodder for the pilots" (John Le Carré, *The Looking Glass War,* 1965). The essential image is not new. Thus, from Shakespeare's *Henry IV, Part I* (1596):

PRINCE: I never did see such pitiful rascals.

FALSTAFF: Tut, tut, good enough to toss [on a pike], food for powder, food for powder. They'll fill a pit as well as better.

Canuck. A Canadian; specifically, a French Canadian. Despite the presence of the Vancouver Canucks team in the National Hockey League, the term usually is considered derogatory, especially when used by a non-Canadian. ". . . we don't have blacks but we have Cannocks [sic]" (letter to William Loeb, publisher, Manchester, New Hampshire, *Union Leader*, 2/24/72). This particular insult is of some historical importance, since it affected the course of American politics. The letter to Loeb attributed the comment to an aide to Senator Edmund Muskie (Democrat, Maine), then the front-runner in the contest for his party's presidential nomination. The aide supposedly made the remark at a meeting in Florida, and Muskie supposedly condoned it, telling the audience to "Come to New England and see." With two weeks to go before the New Hampshire primary, in which thousands of quondam French Canadians were eligible to vote, Loeb published the letter, together with a front-page editorial, headlined "Senator Muskie Insults Franco-Americans." Muskie lost his composure when responding to this assault and to a derogatory report about his wife that also appeared in the *Union Leader*, and his campaign proceeded to fall apart. The missive, which soon became known as "The Canuck letter," was arguably the most successful of the dirty tricks that were perpetrated on behalf of President Richard M. Nixon during the '72 campaign. Ken W. Clawson, White House deputy director of communications, later boasted privately—and denied publicly—that he had written the spurious letter. See also *ratfuck* in RAT.

The origin of *Canuck* is curiously uncertain. On the face of it, the word would appear to derive from the first syllable of Canada. Other guesses have been made, however, e.g., that it comes from *Johnny Canuck*, a cartoon character of the eighteenth and nineteenth century, similar to John Bull and Uncle Sam; that it comes from *Connaught*, originally used by French Canadians to refer to Irish immigrants; and that it is a variant of the Hawaiian *kanaka*, man, brought by whalers back to New England, whose residents then applied the term to their neighbors to the North. The last theory, as farfetched as it might seem, is reinforced by the earliest known spelling of the word: *Kanuk* (*OED*, 1835). Walt Whitman was edging closer to the modern spelling when he wrote—referring to all Canadians, not just those of French extraction—in *Leaves of Grass* (1855):

> Kanuck, Tuckahoe, Congressman, Cuff, I give them the same, I receive them the same.

carpetbagger. An outsider, usually a politician who runs for office in a district in which he or she has only recently become a resident. *Carpetbagger* was popularized during the years following the Civil War as a scornful epithet for Northerners who went South for political and financial gain. "I would sooner trust him [the black man] than the white scalawag or carpet-bagger" (*U.S. Public Documents, Number 1367*, 1868). The term had a prewar existence, however, the *carpet bag* having been a symbol since at least the 1840s for gentlemen who traveled light—particularly bankers, with few possessions, no permanent local residence, and a way of disappearing when most wanted. See also SCALAWAG and WILDCAT.

cat. (1) A man. The term has acquired flattering connotations in recent times. Thus, a *cat* can be a regular guy or one with advanced tastes in fashion or music (the *cool cat* or *hepcat*). Traditionally, however, the male human *cat* was a hobo or other itinerant with no fixed abode. This sense is in keeping with the classical image of the cat as the symbol of liberty, no animal being more opposed to restraint. Roman statues of the goddess of Liberty feature a cat at her feet. In a more general way, people have been characterized contemptuously as *cats* since at least the thirteenth century. For example: "I could endure anything before but a cat, and now he's a cat to me" (William Shakespeare, *All's Well That Ends Well,* 1602–03?).

(2) A spiteful person, usually a woman, frequently a whore, whence *cathouse* and, on the wide-open prairies of the Old West, *cat wagon*. The whorish sense is very old, e.g., from a poem of 1401: "Be ware of Christis curse, and of cattis tailis" (where *tailis* is being used in the third sense of *cat* below). The negative female associations of *cat* also appear in *catty* (see BITCH for an example) and *hellcat*.

(3) A woman's external genitals; the vulva. "The rest of them were putting cigarettes in their cats and puffing on them" (Paul Theroux, *The Great Railway Bazaar: By Train Through Asia,* 1975). This feat, by the way, always a popular one at men's—er—smokers, predates the invention of the cigarette. Thus, Captain Francis Grose defined *burning shame* in 1796 as "A lighted candle stuck into the parts of a woman, certainly not intended by nature for a candlestick" (*A Classical Dictionary of the Vulgar Tongue*). The genital sense of *cat* appears first in nineteenth-century "literature." It may have been inspired by the French *le chat,* which has the same double meaning in that language as it does in English, or by PUSSY, whose meanings parallel *cat* in both respects.

Cat appears in a great many combinations, phrases, and proverbs. To name a few of the more common: *catcall,* a derisive call or whistle, dating to before 1700 (*OED*); *cat fight,* a spiteful spate, as in "Colonel [George] Hamscher said . . . the conflict between the C.I.A. and the military was part of an 'interagency cat fight' " (*New York Times,* 1/10/85); *cat's paw,* a person who is used as the tool of another, from a fable about a smart monkey who used a cat's paw to rake chestnuts out of a fire; *cat on a hot tin roof,* a restless state made famous by Tennessee Williams's play of that name (1955), and which comes from an older phrase, *like a cat on hot bricks; raining cats and dogs,* a heavy downpour and an old one, as evidenced by Jonathan Swift's line, "I know Sir John will go, though he was sure it would rain cats and dogs" (*Genteel and Ingenious Conversation,* 1738); and *to let the cat out of the bag,* meaning to give away a secret, dated to 1760 in the *OED* and apparently stemming from the practice of rural sharpies of putting a cat in a bag, taking it to market, and trying to foist the bundle off on a unwary buyer as a tasty suckling pig (*to buy a pig in a poke* is a related phrase).

In addition, there are a number of particular breeds of *cat,* including:

the alley cat. A person with relaxed sexual standards; one who has the *morals of an alley cat;* specifically, a prostitute.

the catamaran. Not only a kind of boat but thanks to the feminine meaning of *cat,* a quarrelsome woman. "The cursed, drunken old catamaran" (Captain Frederick Marryat, *Peter Simple,* 1834).

the copycat. One who imitates the actions of another, as in the old riddle: Q. There were nine copycats in a boat and one jumped out. How many were left? A. Eight? Q. Wrong! There were none. The other eight jumped out, too, because they were copycats. . . . The *copycat* image is associated most strongly with the goings-on in grade-school classrooms, but the distribution of the species actually is widespread, as noted in a *New York Times* story datelined Brighton, England: "In the United States, Neil Kinnock may be known as the man who turned Senator Joseph R. Biden into a copycat orator. Here at the Labor Party's annual conference, he is trying to combat the more serious allegation that he wants to turn Labor into a copycat party" (9/30/87).

the fat cat. A rich person, especially a big contributor to political campaigns. *Fat cat* was coined by Frank R. Kent, of the Baltimore *Sun*, according to his colleague, H. L. Mencken, and was popularized in Kent's book *Political Behavior* (1928). In extended use, a *fat cat* may be anyone who enjoys special privileges of one sort or another. In the military, the term often crops up in verbal form, as *fatcatting*, to describe the cushy treatment that some officer or clever enlisted man has managed to wangle for himself.

the pussycat. The term can be used endearingly (*What's New, Pussycat?*, film title, 1959), but it has connotations of submissiveness and ineffectuality. "The problem is, the reporters aren't very fearsome. They're four pussycats trying to score in the world of '60 Minutes.' Lotsa luck!" (New York *Daily News*, 4/30/86).

the scaredy-cat. Another breed of cat commonly encountered on playgrounds and other places where youngsters congregate and engage in feats of derring-do—or don't dare, as the case may be. "You're a scaredy cat. Why don't you cry to your mama, you big scaredy cat?" (*Tolliver's Secret*, adapted by Amy Herrick, Packer Collegiate Institute, third grade play, 5/23/84).

the tomcat. A male who is on the make; one who is all dressed up, out on the town, and looking for female companionship. The expression also appears as a verb: "Some obscene significance is attached to the word tomcat. . . . to say that a boy is *tomcattin' around* means that he is seeking illicit romance, and such activities must not be mentioned in genteel conversation" (Vance Randolph and George P. Wilson, *Down in the Holler*). *Tomcat* dates from 1760 and the appearance of an anonymous work, *The Life and Adventures of a Cat*, whose hero was named Tom, and which was so popular that "Tom" became a favorite name for any male cat.

catamount. A fierce, sharp-tongued woman; a SHREW. "She was a dreadful cross-grained woman, a real catamount, as savage as a she bear that has cubs" (Thomas C. Haliburton, *The Clockmaker, or, The Sayings and Doings of Samuel Slick of Slickville*, 1835–37). *Catamount*, a catchall term for the cougar, lynx, mountain lion, and other wild felines, is a shortening of *catamountain*, in turn a condensation of *cat of the mountain*. See also WILDCAT.

cattle. Human beings, contemptuously considered. Traditionally applied to women (especially prostitutes), slaves, and other easy targets, the term is encountered most often today when people are being transported inhumanely in crowded *cattle cars*, as in "We took the train for Chattanooga. Our cars were cattle cars" (letter, *OED*, 5/4/1864).

cesspool. A repository for every kind of filth imaginable. For example: "I called the U.N. a cesspool. Is that really so terrible in view of the actions that have gone on there?" (New York City Mayor Edward I. Koch, *New York Times*, 9/30/83). *Cesspools* also figure prominently in the classic children's compliment: "Your eyes are like pools—cesspools; your ears are like flowers—cauliflowers; your teeth are like stars—they come out at night." This one probably has been handed down from one generation of children to another from time immemorial. Certainly, the Roman poet Martial (ca. 40–ca. 104 A.D.) was working this same vein when he said of an old floozy: "At night you take off your teeth just like your silk robe."

P.S.: The old imprecation, *bad cess to you*, doesn't seem to have anything to do with the *cess* that is in *pools*. More likely, this is a shortening of *success*, the phrase expressing the speaker's fond hope the person addressed will have bad luck.

chameleon. A changeable person, one with no fixed principles; from the well-known ability of the animal to vary its colors. The *chameleon* metaphor, dating to the sixteenth century, has enduring appeal to American politicians. Thus, Thomas Jefferson called Governor Edmund Randolph of Virginia "the poorest chameleon I ever saw, having no color of his own and reflecting that [of the person] nearest him" (Richard B. Morris, *Witnesses at the Creation*, 1985). And President Herbert Hoover termed his successor, Franklin D. Roosevelt "a chameleon on plaid" (James MacGregor Burns, *Roosevelt, The Lion and the Fox*, 1956). Most recently, Attorney General Edwin Meese III deployed *chameleon* in one of his attacks on the U.S. Supreme Court: "An active jurisprudence . . . is a chameleon jurisprudence, changing color and form in each era" (speech, 11/15/85). See also SPINELESS and TURNCOAT.

chamer. A stupid fellow, especially a stubborn one. "Stanley Reed was 'the Chamer,' which means fool, or dolt, or mule in Hebrew" (Supreme Court Justice Felix Frankfurter's private code-term for fellow Justice Stanley Reed, as recalled by Philip Elman, Columbia Oral History Project, 1983). See also DOLT, FOOL, MULE, and SCHNOOK.

charlatan. An impostor; one who pretends to having special knowledge or skill that he does not actually possess. "The quack, the charlatan, the jingo, and the terrorist can flourish only where the audience is deprived of independent access to information" (Walter Lippman, *Columbia Journalism Review*, 1–2/84). Not surprisingly, the word itself has a checkered history. It comes from the Italian *ciarlatano*, a mountebank, prattler, or babbler, in turn an altered form of *ceretano*, a seller of papal indulgences, from *Cerreto*, a village near Spoleto, whose inhabitants seem to have specialized in this sort of thing. See also QUACK, SWINDLER, ZANY, and, for more about place names, PEORIA.

Charlie (Charley). Any unknown man, such as the fun-loving *good-time Charlie*, but most often today a white male to a black person. The personal name may be prefixed with the meaningless honorific *Mr.* or converted into the nickname *Chuck*. In any case, the intent almost always is ironic if not downright derogatory. "Couldn't copy Charlie's good points an' live like men. So we copies his bad points . . . All it did was make us hate him all the more an' ourselves too . . . Seems to me the worst sickness a man kin have is the Charlie fever" (Charles Gordone, *No Place to Be Somebody*, 1969). *Charlie* is merely the latest in a series of black words for white people; see ANN, OFAY, *the man* in BOY, and WHITEY. Other minorities also have picked up on it (as they did with UNCLE TOM). Reporting on life in San Francisco: "And if somebody calls you Charlie when you're in the local Mexican-American barrio, you are almost certainly not of Hispanic ancestry" (*New York Times*, 7/16/84).

Whites have used *Charlie* in a disparaging sense, too. For example, in World War II a *washing machine Charley* was a Japanese photo reconnaisance plane, and in the Vietnam conflict (not really a war because there was no Declaration of it), the North Vietnamese and Vietcong were known variously as *Charlie, Victor Charlie, Mr. Charlie,* and even *Sir Charles*. In general military use, *Charley* also denotes any stupid or bumbling soldier, and *S.F.C.* in the barracks may not mean "Sergeant First-Class" but "Shit-Faced Charley." See also PADDY.

chatterbox. A person who never seems to stop talking, or as Captain Francis Grose defined the term two centuries ago: "One whose tongue runs twelve score to the dozen, a chattering man or woman" (*A Classical Dictionary of the Vulgar Tongue*, 1796). A variant is *chatterbug*. See also MOTORMOUTH.

chauvinist. Patriot. "I am a patriot; you are a chauvinist" (Anatol Rapoport, *Semantics*, 1975). The term comes from the surname of Nicholas Chauvin, a soldier so excessively devoted to Napoleon that he became a laughingstock first to his comrades and then to the nation at large, his name being attached to a flag-waving character in French vaudeville performances (from 1831). In our own century, the connotations of *chauvinism* have been extended to include excessive devotion to one's race (*white chauvinism*, ca. 1930) and one's sex (*male chauvinism*, ca. 1950), especially in the phrase *male chauvinist pig* (ca. 1970). This last has been used so often that it is now no longer necessary to articulate the adjoining words; they are understood. "The study reported that the 229 men questioned felt a male advocate of the feminist cause had more character, competence and sociability than his chauvinist counterpart" (*On Campus with Women*, 10/77). See also PIG and SEXIST.

cheap. Originally a neutral term, simply meaning a bargain or a barter, or a place where buying and selling is done, as in the shops of London's *Cheapside*, but from ca. 1500 an increasingly negative word, with connotations of inexpensiveness (*cheap talk, cheap flattery, dirt cheap* or, earlier, *dog cheap*); of low esteem (a woman may gain a *cheap* reputation—somewhat paradoxically by being overly generous); of stinginess; and of meanness or unfairness, e.g., a *cheap trick, cheap shot* (originally a football term for an unfair tackle), and *cheap shot artist,* for one who specializes in hits of this sort. "You can be sure that those who don't like the 600-ship Navy will use the Poindexter-North affair to take cheap shots at the naval service and the way we do business" (anonymous admiral, *New York Times*, 3/10/87).

The negative sense of *cheap* stems from the word's use in the phrase *goodcheap*, referring to a good bargain or something bought at low cost or on advantageous terms. This construction has been retained with positive connotations in French. For example, the name of the Parisian department store *Bon Marché* translates as "cheapness" (*bon*, good + *marché*, bargain). In English, the negative meaning can be softened, but only slightly, by sticking a vowel onto the end of the word as in *cheapie, el cheapo*, or, the short form: "The diverse delegates zeroed in on . . . vile and frugal (i.e., cheapo) publishers" (*Columbia*, 11/81). See also PENNY-ANTE, TACKY, and TIGHTWAD.

cheapskate. An excessively thrifty person; a TIGHTWAD. *Cheapskate* has pretty much replaced the nineteenth-century *cheap Jack* or *cheap John*, referring originally to a peddler of inferior—hence cheap—goods, and later to anyone acting in a cheap or stingy manner. The *skate* part, meaning a chap or fellow, apparently is an alteration of the Scottish *skyte*, a contemptible person, from *skite*, a voider of excrement. Literally, then, a *cheapskate* is a *cheap shit*. See also BLATHERSKITE.

cheat. A dishonest person, a practitioner of fraud, or the act of deceiving or swindling; one of the strongest accusations that can be made against another person. Literary gentlemen, in particular, seem to favor it. Thus, Robert Southey alleged of a far greater poet, Percy Bysshe Shelley: "He was a liar and a cheat; he paid no regard to truth, nor to any kind of moral obligation" (letter to Henry Taylor, 2/28/1830). And when James Macpherson threatened Samuel Johnson with physical violence for exposing the Ossian poems as a fraud (they were written by Macpherson, not by an ancient Gaelic poet), the doctor purchased a stout, six-foot oaken cudgel and replied: "Any violence offered me I shall do my best to repel; and what I cannot do for myself, the law shall do for me. I hope I shall never be deterred from detecting what I think a cheat by the menaces of a ruffian. . . . You may print this if you will" (letter to Macpherson, 1/20/1775).

Cheat derives from *escheat*, a legal term for the reversion of property to the state in the absence of legal heirs or claimants, or of the state's right to such confiscation. In medieval times, the officer who looked after the king's escheats was known as the *cheater*. This officer was not an especially popular person, and sometimes for good reason: "As a Cheater may pick the purses of innocent people, by showing them something like the King's broad seal, which was his own forgery" (*OED*, 1656). Thanks to such abuses, the dishonest connotations of the world evolved among thieves during the sixteenth and seventeenth centuries, gradually becoming standard. Variants include *cheatee*, one who is cheated; *cheatery*, the practice of cheating ("she wouldn't get the cheatery out of them," Harriet Beecher Stowe, *Uncle Tom's Cabin*, 1852); *cheater*, a rearview mirror as well as one who is unfaithful sexually; and *cheaters*, which can refer to false teeth, spectacles, and falsies or other padding for deceptively enhancing one's physical attributes. See also ROOK and SWINDLER.

cheesy. Inferior, shoddy, cheap; from 1896 (*OED*) and possibly from the aroma of overripe cheese. *Cheese* also has derogatory connotations in such phrases as *cheese eater* (a Dutchman), *cheesehead* (a dullard, see the example in BLOCKHEAD), and *the big cheese* (an important or self-important person). This last form of *cheese* doesn't appear to come from the dairy product, however, but from the Urdu *chiz*, thing. This word was popularized by Anglo-Indians in nineteenth-century London in such phrases as "the real chiz," meaning something good, first-rate, or highly becoming. The spelling quickly was changed and introduced in the new form to Americans: "Whatever is the go in Europe will soon be the cheese here" (Thomas Chandler Haliburton, *The Clockmaker, or, The Sayings and Doings of Sam Slick of Slickville*, 1837). Another nondairy *cheese* appears in the street cry, "Cheese it, da cops," which has been dated to the early nineteenth century (*Lexicon Balatronicum*, 1811) and is thought to be a corruption of "cease it." See also CHEAP, CHINTZY, and CORNY.

cherry. An inexperienced person, from the same word's use as slang for the hymen and, hence, a symbol of virginity. Both sexually and non-, the term has been extended to include males as well as females, usually in disparaging manner. For example: " 'I'll bet *you're* a cherry!' She puckered her lips and gave him tiny, teasing kisses. 'Cherry. Cherry. Cherr—' " (Earl Thompson, *Tattoo*, 1974). And in a non-sexual context during the war in Vietnam: "Replacement troops came in one or two at a time. They were simply Cherries at first. Inexperienced, they were a danger to be around, foolish to get close to in any way. This generic labeling isolated them. When a Cherry died, we didn't blink" (Roger Hoffman, *New York Times Magazine*, 5/12/85).

As a term for a young woman, *cherry* dates to at the least the mid-nineteenth century (variations included *cherry pie* and *cherry pipe*, the last a rhyme on yet another term for an eligible woman, *cherry ripe*). Just how and when the cherry came to symbolize virginity is not clear. For whatever it is worth, the tree itself is associated with the Virgin Mary in an Apocryphal story of a miracle performed by Christ while still in the womb. According to the tale—first mentioned in a Coventry Mystery of the fifteenth century and as recounted in the ballad "The Cherry Tree Carol"—Mary asked Joseph to pick a cherry for her while they strolled through an orchard or garden. When he brusquely refused, the unborn child caused the tree to bend down to give the Virgin its fruit. At the same time, the cherry is an old symbol of the shortness of life and the fleeting nature of its pleasures. The pleasures were particularly evident in medieval times in cherry orchards in the spring, when the fruit was picked and sold at cherry fairs. The fairs occasioned so much boisterous and licentious activity that they came to symbolize such happy albeit evanescent goings-on. The cherry fair is the ultimate source of the modern pop song "Life Is Just a Bowl of Cherries," which echoes a thought expressed by John Gower, a poet and friend of Chaucer, who said of the world, "For all is but a chery feire" (*Confessio Amantis*, 1393). On the flip side of this same coin is the graffito: "Life is a bowl of pits—somebody else got all the cherries" (*American Speech*, Fall 1980) See also PITS, THE and VIRGIN.

chestnut. A stale joke or anything else that is trite. The expression apparently comes from a play by William Dimond, *The Broken Sword* (1816). Recounting a favorite story, one of the characters says, "When suddenly from the thick boughs of a cork tree," only to be interrupted: "A chestnut, Captain, a chestnut . . . this is the twenty-seventh time I have heard you relate this story, and you invariably said, a chestnut, till now."

Chicano. A Mexican-American; originally a pejorative (from the Spanish *chico*, boy, perhaps reinforced by the word's use as a nickname, *Chico*), but made respectable by social activists as part of the ethnic consciousness raising of the late 1960s. Still, the word must be handled gingerly, as evidenced by the following advice from the *Los Angeles Times Stylebook* (Frederick S. Holley, 1981):

> Use *Chicano* as an abbreviated synonym for Mexican-American unless it is established that the individual prefers the latter. A reporter should establish the preference rather than make an assumption. Spanish-surnamed families that have been in California since the days of the dons should in particular not be called *Chicanos* unless they prefer it.

Chicano is a relative newcomer on the linguistic scene. Yet to be included in the *Oxford English Dictionary*, the word's first known appearance in print was as recently as 1947, in the summer issue of *Arizona Quarterly*, wherein the residents of a Tucson barrio were described as *"chicanos* who raise hell on Saturday night, listen to Padre Estanislao on Sunday morning and then raise hell on Sunday night" (Mario Suarez, "El Hoyo," *American Speech,* Fall 1969). See also MEXICAN.

chicken. A fowl label for a variety of different people who have in common the fact they are members of outgroups that are weak and put-upon. Thus, depending on context, a *chicken* is (1) a child or other young and inexperienced person; (2) a girl or young woman, especially an attractive one; (3) a timorous person or coward; or (4) a young male homosexual.

Chicken and *chick* have been applied to human offspring since before 1400 and in the beginning were not necessarily demeaning. The terms could even be used more or less affectionately, with groovy males referring to their female friends as *chicks, chickens,* and, in recent times, as *hip chicks* and *slick chicks. (Biddy,* a dialect word for a chicken, especially a young one, perhaps from the sound biddies make as they go about their business in the barnyard, can be used synonymously with the human *chick* in both masculine and feminine senses, e.g., a *Biddy League,* a basketball league for boys; see also the *Biddy* in MOLL.) In mainstream society, however, *chicken* has long been regarded as a less than flattering term for a woman, and it is hardly ever applied to one except in the phrase *no spring chicken,* which is not very flattering either, as it means one is past one's prime. This also is true of *chick* and its diminutive, *chicklet* (reinforced by the trade name of the small, sugar-coated gum bits), as in, "all the chicklets in my business, with their blow-dried hairdos, came along" (TV reporter Judy Licht, assessing her competition, *New York Times,* 10/19/86; see also TWINK). The basic comparison of women to birds is common, of course. See, for example, CANARY, PIGEON, QUAIL, and BIRD itself.

As an epithet for a timorous person, *chicken* has a long and dishonorable history, dating to at least the start of the seventeenth century. Thus, as Sancho Panza berated himself: "Heaven defend me, what a heart of a chicken have I!" (Miguel de Cervantes, *Don Quixote,* 1605, 1615). Variations include *chicken-hearted, chicken-livered, chicken-spirited,* and *hen-hearted.* " 'Come back here, you couple of chicken-livered cowards, and I'll thrash the two of ye!' " (Mark Twain, in an episode that his publisher persuaded him to cut from *Huckleberry Finn,* but which was included in *Life on the Mississippi,* 1883). And today, the *chicken* continues to adorn the escutcheons of the weak-kneed. For example, teenagers *play chicken,* often in cars (the game takes different forms; in one popular version, two cars are driven straight at each other until one driver *chickens out* by turning aside). Then there is *Chicken Little,* who feared the sky was falling down, as in ". . . we just had too many Chicken Littles in Congress in the last week who seemed to become hysterical over covert aid" (unnamed Reagan Administration official, *New York Times,* 4/15/84). The irony here is that the chicken actually is a brave bird, as evidenced by the ferocity of fighting cocks and the readiness of hens with chicks to attack much larger animals if they approach too near. See also COWARD.

When referring to a young male homosexual, *chicken* reverberates with all its other negative senses of youth, girlishness, and sissydom. This kind of *chicken,* often preyed upon by older men known as *chicken hawks* or *chicken queens,* goes back to the nineteenth century, with the earliest written examples coming from the language of seafaring men, who went on long voyages without women, e.g. from the *Congressional Record* of April 21, 1890: "In the hospital I saw an admirable illustration of the

79

affection which a sailor will lavish on a ship's boy to whom he takes a fancy, and makes his 'chicken,' as the phrase is."

Chicken also appears in various combinations, and when it does, it usually translates as "small." Thus, *chicken-breasted* is old English slang for "a woman with scarce any breasts" (*A Classical Dictionary of the Vulgar Tongue*, 1796); a *chicken-brain* or *chickenhead* is a dumb CLUCK or LAMEBRAIN; *to run around like a chicken with its head cut off* is to go crazy and act as if you don't have any brains at all; *chicken feed* is small change, and has been for at least a century and a half, e.g., "I stood looking on, seeing him pick up the chicken feed from the green horns and thought . . . men are such darned fools as to be cheated out of their hard earnings" (Colonel Davy Crockett, *Col. Crockett's Exploits and Adventures in Texas*, 1836); and, finally, *chickenshit* is a general term of disparagement for almost anything that is petty, worthless, annoying, and small-minded, especially in the military, where a *chickenshit* outfit is a unit in which regulations are enforced in fussy detail. This last is sometimes euphemized as *C.S.*, *chicken stuffing*, or just plain *chicken*, as in George Gobel's plaint, "How do you get out of this chicken outfit?" (TV show, 2/28/60). Kids also cry *chickie* as warning, but this is when they *lay chickie* acting as lookouts. Here, *Chickie, the cops* has the same force as *Cheese it, the cops* and the basic *chickie* probably relates less to the chicken *per se* than to another kind of bird that informs, i.e., the *stool pigeon* in PIGEON. See also COCK and HEN.

chimpanzee. A manlike ape. Speaking of Marlon Brando: "He has the manners of a chimpanzee, the gall of a Kinsey researcher, and a swelled head the size of a Navy blimp, and just as pointed" (Louella Parsons, in Charles Higham, *Brando: The Unauthorized Biography*, 1987). See also MONKEY.

Chinaman. A male Chinese; anyone who is easily victimized; a DUPE. "The Chinese greatly dislike the term *Chinaman* and *Chinee*, just as the Japanese dislike *Jap*" (H. L. Mencken, *The American Language*, Supplement I, 1945). A *Chinaman*, originally from 1772 (*OED*), was a dealer in porcelain. The modern meaning seems to be an American innovation, dating from 1849 and the California Gold Rush, which brought Chinese laborers as well as Easterners to the West Coast. "If I chose, I could enumerate a dozen more instances to prove that, in his own vulgar phraseology, Jack Perry has successfully played you for a Chinaman" (Mark Twain, *Virginia City* [Nevada] *Territorial Enterprise*, 8/19/1863). *Not a Chinaman's chance*, meaning no chance at all, or a slim one at best, also comes from the nineteenth century. (Earlier, this was known as a *dog's chance*; see DOG.) The chances of a *Chinaman* in the Old West can be gauged from a famous story about Judge Roy Bean, which seems to have appeared first in print in the El Paso, Texas, *Daily Times*, of June 2, 1884, and which might even have a shred of truth to it:

> Here is the latest on Roy Bean:
> Somebody killed a Chinaman and was brought up standing before the irrepressible Roy, who looked through two or three dilapidated law books from stem to stern, and finally turned the culprit loose remarking that he'd be d____d if he could find any law against killing a Chinaman [in B. A. Botkin, *A Treasury of American Folklore*, 1944].

See also CHINK and SLOPE.

Chinese. Confused, disorganized, badly executed, inferior. *Chinese* appears as a negative qualifier in numerous expressions, many of them originally British and dating to World War I, and all of them in keeping with traditional Western prejudices against the Chinese (see CHINAMAN and CHINK) and with the stereotypical beliefs that the inscrutable Chinese speak, talk, and act in unintelligible ways. For example:

Chinese ace. An inept aviator; one noted for *flying Chinese,* i.e., with Wun Wing Lo, or for making *Chinese landings* (see below).

Chinese attack. Not a real attack; just a lot of noise and other activity to confuse the enemy and take his attention away from the sector where the real attack is to take place.

Chinese blow. In baseball, an accidental or lucky hit.

Chinese burn. The British term for what American kids call an *Indian burn.* For the benefit of those who have blocked out memories of their childhood, the burning sensation is produced by taking another person's wrist and, with fists held close together, twisting the skin in opposite directions. See INDIAN GIVER.

Chinese compliment. Not a real compliment, but pretended deference to another.

Chinese copy. A slavishly exact copy; if of typewritten material, a copy that faithfully preserves all the original errors.

Chinese deal. A pretended deal; one that never materializes.

Chinese dolly. A filmmaking term for a shot in which a camera pans a scene while moving backward on tracks that are—naturally—slanted.

Chinese fire drill. A condition of much confusion, with everyone running around like chickens with their heads cut off; sheer chaos; specifically, among teenagers, a practical joke in which youngsters get out of a car that is stopped at a red light, run around it, and hop in and out of it even after the light changes, making other drivers think they will miss the green and then, presuming they have timed their movements correctly, all getting back into the car and speeding away just as the light changes to red again, leaving the other cars behind.

Chinese hat trick. An election-day fraud, whereby ten Chinese men vote early and often, changing their hats each time they appear at the polls.

Chinese home run. A cheap home run, struck in a small ballpark or down a short foul line.

Chinese landing. A bad landing, typically with Wun Wing Lo.

Chinese national anthem. The sound of an explosion, as of a bomb or shell; especially one that has landed far enough away for the speaker to be able to laugh at it.

Chinese puzzle. One without a solution.

Chinese Rolls-Royce. A Ford.

Chinese three-point landing. A crash.

See also DUTCH.

Chink (also **Chinky** and **Chinky-Chinky**). A Chinese. "I thumbed the bell. The door opened. A chink houseboy gave me the slant-eyed focus. 'Missa Tlenwick, him sleep. You go way, come tomollow. Too late fo' vlisito'.'" (Robert Leslie Bellem, "Killer's Harvest," *Spicy Detective,* 7/38, in Bill Pronzini, *Gun in Cheek,* 1982). *Chink,* from 1901 (*OED*), probably is the most common derogatory term for a Chinese. Thus, the Chinese entry in the "Ethnic Prejudice in America" series (Meridian, 1972), was "*Chink!*", edited by Cheng-Tsu Wu. (Other titles in the series were "*Kike!*", "*Mick*", and "*Wop!*"). See also CHINAMAN, DINK, and SLOPE.

chintzy. Unfashionable, inferior, cheap, stingy; from the brightly colored but inexpensive cloth. "The effect is chintzy and would be unbecoming" (George Eliot, letter, 9/18/1851). Or as Abigail Van Buren put it, when asked for an opinion on the restaurant manners of a wealthy woman who took home every bit of uneaten food, including crackers, carrot sticks, rolls, and other scraps from her own plate and those of her dining partners: "There is nothing wrong with it. If she were poor, she'd be 'chintzy.' But since she's rich, she's eccentric" (*New York Post*, 4/3/74). See also CHEAP, CHEESY, and SLEAZE.

chippie (chippy). A young woman, usually a promiscuous one, sometimes a whore. "John Bloom . . . is the creator of Joe Bob Briggs and of Briggs's escapist obsession with cheap movies and his rambling, low-rent, chippie-in-the-back-seat, county jail narratives" (*Columbia Journalism Review*, 11–12/83). It follows from this that a *chippie house* or *joint* is a brothel; that a *chippie chaser* is a skirt chaser; and that the act of chasing is *to chippie*, as in "Never chippied on your wife one time in eighteen years?" (Lenny Bruce, *How to Talk Dirty and Influence People*, 1972). It also says something about society's view of easily won young women that gamblers refer to suckers as *chippies* and that the term also denotes anything that is small or amateurish, as in the *chippie habit* of someone who is taking drugs on an irregular basis and in small quantities (still).

The origin of *chippie* has not been established satisfactorily. One theory is that is comes from *cheap*, a sound supposedly uttered by streetwalkers to attract customers. Another is that the original *chippies* worked in brothels in Mexico or the Southwestern United States, where the policy was to pay the girls with chips (much as taxi dancers used to be paid with paper tickets), which they turned back to the management for cash. A third theory is that *chippie* is related to the French *chipie*, a shrewish woman. Either of the latter two would fit fairly well with the earliest known example of the word in print: "This class of females are known by the gang as 'Chippies,' and most of them come from the slums, and work in the cigar and cigarette factories" (New Orleans *Lantern*, 10/27/1886, in *American Speech*, 2/50). See also BROAD and WHORE.

chiseler. A cheat; a petty crook; one who begs or borrows something, usually of small value, with little likelihood that it will be returned; a MOOCHER. "There is no place for the phony economics of the chiseler" (Secretary of Defense Charles E. Wilson, radio address, 2/23/51). Recorded first as a verb in a Scottish etymological dictionary of 1808, the term came into vogue in England in the 1830s, variously spelled *chizzel*, *chizzle*, *chizzell*, *chuzzle*, and finally, in the 1840s, as *chisel*. Possibly, this is a case of sound influencing meaning, with the ideas of cutting, paring, and shaving having been attached to an essentially unrelated word. Whatever, the term quickly crossed the Atlantic and moved inland, with the earliest American *chizzle* dating from 1834. By 1848, John Russell Bartlett assumed *chisel* was "a Western word" when preparing his *Dictionary of Americanisms*, and gave as an example "have chiselled the people of California out of a million dollars." Which is some *chiseling* indeed. See also FREELOADER and GOUGER.

Christ-killer. A Jew; a classic attack not often heard nowadays. Thus, in what has to be one of the less witty remarks made in the heyday of the Round Table at the Algonquin Hotel: "You goddamn Christ killer" (Alexander Woollcott to Franklin

Pierce Adams, in Howard Teichmann, *George S. Kaufman, An Intimate Portrait*, 1972). The epithet seems to have been fairly common in the nineteenth century, both in Britain and the United States. Eric Partridge characterized it as "proletarian and military ca. 1850–1915" (*A Dictionary of Slang and Unconventional English*, 1970), while H. L. Mencken noted that it "was familiar in my boyhood [b. 1880, Baltimore, Maryland] but has passed out with the decay of Bible searching" (*The American Language, Supplement I*, 1945).

chump. A slow-witted person, an easy mark. "Maybe manager Bancroft isn't regarded as a chump by baseball people" (*Sporting Life*, 5/27/1883). Perhaps inspired by *chunk* or *lump*, *chump* referred originally (ca. 1700) to a short, thick piece of wood, especially an end piece. From this, it was but a small step to equate the chump of wood with a person's head. Thus, a *chump* is a BLOCKHEAD and *to go off [one's] chump* is to go crazy. See also DUMB/DUMMY and KLUTZ.

clam. A closemouthed person; also one who doesn't talk a lot because he is on the stupid side, and hence, a sucker. "That lets you out, you know, you chowder-headed old clam!" (Mark Twain, *Screamers*, "Travelling Show," 1866). The *clam* that is a bivalve is cognate both to *clamp* and *clammy* (that which is sticky as well as cold). As slang for the mouth, the term is an Americanism dating to around 1800. Variants include *clam trap* and *clam shell*. Typically, early Americans used the term when telling someone else to be quiet, e.g., "Shet your clam . . ." (John Neal, *Brother Jonathan*, 1825). It follows from all this that the person who keeps his mouth shut is said *to clam up*. On the good side, a person may also be *as happy as a clam at high tide* (or *in high water*). Clams are happy then because the deep water protects them from being dug up by clammers with clam rakes.

clap. Venereal disease, usually gonorrhea. The four-letter word was taboo from around 1830 until after World War II—"*Obs.* in polite use," as the OED put it at about the midpoint of this period (Volume C., prepared 1888–93). Even now, so-called family newspapers tend to shun the word. Thus, when a venereal epidemic—contagious equine metritis—broke out at breeding stables in Kentucky, the professional journal *Science* reported that "The disease, which causes sterility in broodmares, was early on known as the 'Silver Jubilee clap' when it was first identified last year in England" (4/14/78). In its account for the general audience, however, *The New York Times* not only managed to avoid mentioning *clap* but ran its story under the headline "A Social Disease Among Horses."

Clap entered English in the seventeenth century, probably via the French *clapoir*, a venereal sore or bubo, in turn from *clapier*, the name of the place where the sore most likely was acquired, i.e., a brothel. The term was used freely as a noun and as a verb (one might be *clap'd* or *clap't*) for a couple hundred years prior to the onset of Victorianism. Swift, Pope, Steele, and other establishment authors used it, as did Dr. Samuel Johnson, a notably fastidious writer, both in "London" (1738), the poem that first brought him wide attention ("They sing, they dance, clean shoes, or cure a clap"), and in his great dictionary (1755). Before the century was out, however, the word had picked up sufficient taint for Captain Francis Grose to treat it as slang and include it in his *Classical Dictionary of the Vulgar Tongue*, 1796. The rest was silence, or almost so. Thus, speaking of the United States between the world wars: "*Venereal disease* was taboo . . . both *syphilis* and *gonorrhea*, so epidemic with no antibiotics available that they constituted a national health hazard, were censored in print by the federal government, even in medical journals that went through the mails. . . . The popular euphemism for having either disease was *burnt* [an old term—Captain Grose and Shakespeare before him knew the word in this sense], which also rapidly became taboo. *The clap* (very taboo) was the recognized colloquialism used by males; among the lower classes, especially in the South . . . it was believed that every young man should have it once to establish his manhood" (David W. Maurer, *American Speech*, Spring–Summer 1976).

Times have changed—though they still have a way to go in this case before we regain the free expression of the mid-eighteenth century. Note the conspiracy of silence surrounding Yale University's very first president: ". . . he's been totally ignored by Yale. I don't believe a college has been named for him! 'Semantically impossible,' a Yale official once told me" (Louis L. Tucker, letter, *Yale Alumni Magazine*, 5/85). The president's name: Thomas Clap.

clean [one's] clock. To defeat thoroughly; often expressed as a threat: "If you don't keep the hell away from Colly I'll clean your clock" (Peter De Vries, *Consenting Adults*, 1980). The phrase apparently originated in railroading, where *clean the clock* means to stop suddenly, causing the needle on the air brake gauge to drop back to zero (*Dictionary of American Regional English*, Volume 1, 1985). The expression fits well with *clean [one's] plow*, an agricultural metaphor for defeating or beating up [someone]; *clean [up] on*, with the same meaning; *take [someone] to the cleaners*, also a total defeat, usually financial; and, finally, *clock*, which can refer to a human face as well as to a time-telling device.

clinchpoop. A boor. This sixteenth-century term of contempt is obsolete, according to the *OED*, but at least one great mind is wrestling with the problem of reviving it. "I have been looking for an occasion to write the word 'clinchpoop' ever since stumbling over it in Joseph T. Shipley's 'The Origins of English Words.' . . . 'Clinchpoop' is a word that challenges writers to find the perfect setting for it" (Russell Baker, *New York Times*, 1/3/87). In theory, *clinchpoop* probably should be reserved for drunken mariners and other seagoing boors. This assumes that the *OED*'s guess about the word's formation is correct, i.e., "One who clinches or clenches the poops of vessels." This guess reeks of Victorian propriety, however. See also BOOR and POOP.

clod. A stupid person (literally, a lump of earth); dated to 1579 (*OED*). From "A Valentine to all our Mad readers": "Roses are red, / Violets are blue, / We make our bread, / On clods like you!" (*Mad* Super Special Number Twelve, 1973). See also BLOCKHEAD, CLOT, and KLUTZ.

clodhopper. A farmer, especially a stupid fellow. "The Trumans . . . were country people—'clodhoppers,' Harry called them—upright and respected but often in debt" (*New York Times*, 8/7/83). A *clodhopper* (*OED*, from ca. 1690) originally was just a ploughman, i.e., one who hopped over clods (perhaps with an allusion to *grasshopper*). The sense of lumpish stupidity was built into the word, however, thanks to the earlier use of CLOD, *clod pate, clod pole,* and *clod poll,* all in the sense of BLOCKHEAD. Later variants, referring to rustics, include *cloddy hop, clod jumper, clod knocker,* and, to stupid people in particular, *clodhead, clod polish,* and *clod-skulled.* See also HICK.

closet-. A private place where skeletons and such may be hidden from the light of day. "I just think we are seeing closet racism coming out into the open" (Bishop Desmond M. Tutu, on the policies of the United States, Great Britain, and Germany toward South Africa *New York Times*, 10/29/85). The idea that a secluded closet is fine place for secret doings is some centuries old, e.g., "There are stage-sins and there are closet sins" (*OED*, 1612–15). The combining form does not seem to have become popular, however, until the 1960s, when homosexuals began *coming out of the closet*. Those who kept their sexual orientation a secret were known as *closet queens* or *closet queers*. Others who have been known to keep secrets from the world include *closet addicts, closet conservatives, closet doves, closet drinkers, closet liberals*, and *closet Republicans*. The term's effect is similar to that of CRYPTO-.

clot. A stupid person, a CLOD (both *clot* and *clod* derive from the Old English *clott*, lump). "His wife has marital thrombosis—she's married to a clot" (G. Legman, "A Word for It!," *Maledicta I*, 1977).

clown. A person who is not to be taken seriously: a BUFFOON. "What do the USA and McDonald's have in common? Both are run by a clown named Ronald" (Los Angeles *Reader*, 4/1/83). "Two-thirds of them are clowns" (J. Peter Grace, chairman of President Ronald's cost-cutting panel, on the members of the U.S. Senate and House of Representatives, WPIX-TV, New York City, 8/5/84). "[Ivan] Boesky and the other clowns who have been breaking laws . . . are no excuse for business training to lapse into wimpish, socialistic sloganeering" (letter, *Yale Alumni Magazine*, Summer 1987). The oldest *clown* in the *OED* is dated to 1500–20; the reference is to a FOOL or jester, but it seems likely the word's primary sense then was of a rustic or other rural resident. Identical or closely related words in other languages carry the meaning of a log, lump, clod, and, hence, a clumsy boor, bumpkin, or lout. This, of course, is in full accord with the tendency to assign pejorative meanings to words for country dwellers. See also BOZO and HICK.

cluck. (1) A dullard or *chicken brain*; (2) a woman. For clarity, the first *cluck* often is coupled with *big* or *dumb*, as in "A thing like that don't happen to a dumb cluck like him every day" (James M. Cain, *The Postman Always Rings Twice*, 1934). The second *cluck* can be employed the same way as *chicken*, e.g., "Louise-Marie, to do her credit, was a game little cluck-cluck when it came to a show-down . . ." (*American Magazine*, 11/1913). See also DUMB/DUMMY.

cock. Whether referring to the whole man (a hearty *cock*, say, or a *cocky* individual) or to his instrument of procreation, the bird is one of the principal symbols of masculinity, along with BULL. The sexual overtones are so strong, in fact, that the name of the barnyard fowl has almost been lost in the United States, with the blander *rooster* (one who roosts) being the preferred term in polite society for most of the past two hundred years. The reluctance to say *cock* for fear of what other people will think one is thinking extends to additional words that incorporate the same nasty sound. Thus, no one today has any hesitancy about mentioning *apricots, haystacks*, and *weather vanes*, which have replaced words that our nice-nelly ancestors felt nervous about, i.e., *apricox, haycocks*, and *weathercocks*. These are typical of the changes that took place in the late eighteenth and early nineteenth centuries as proto-Victorians on both sides of the Atlantic began sanitizing the English language. Not even personal names were exempt. For instance, Amos Bronson Alcott, father to the famous Louisa May, changed the family name from *Alcox* (itself something of a comedown from the probable original, *Allcock*). As the magisterial editor of the *OED*, Sir James Murray, said in 1893 when he came to his entry on *cock*: "The current name among the people, but, *pudoris causa*, not permissible in polite speech or literature; in scientific language the Latin is used." And the Latin, of course, is *penis*, which was incorporated into English in the late seventeenth century, and which originally (to the Romans) meant *tail*—a slight displacement anatomically, but a large one psychologically.

The precise connections between the name of the potent cock and the human male, who likes to be regarded that way, too, are so ancient that they have been lost to lexicographic history. It has even been suggested that the anatomical meaning was inspired by comparison to the short pipe or spout for emitting fluid that is called a *cock* or *stopcock*, and which is traditionally equipped with a handle in the shape of a rooster or roosterlike comb. This is just guesswork, however, and it is at least as likely that the spigot was named after the anatomical organ as the other way around. Whichever came first, the association exists, and Albrecht Dürer made use of it, ca. 1497, in *Männerbad*, a woodcut of a group of men in a public bath. One of the men, almost naked, is leaning on a post from which a spigot protrudes. The pipe part curves down immediately in front of the man's lower pelvic region and the handle is shaped like a small barnyard cock. As Lorrayn Y. Baird points out in *Maledicta*, 1981, this is a "triple visual pun"—the stopcock, the barnyard cock, and the other one.

The earliest written example of man as *cock* in the *Oxford English Dictionary* comes from Chaucer (ca. 1386), and there the allusion is to a person who arouses others at daybreak. Later, in the sixteenth and seventeenth centuries, the term was extended to include the chief person or leader of a group (e.g., the *cock of the walk*) and to an especially plucky fighter (one with the spirit of a *gamecock*). Anatomically, the term doesn't appear in the *OED* (1972 supplement) until 1618: "Oh man what art thou? When thy cock is up?" (Nathaniel Field, *Amends for Ladies*). A generation earlier, however, Shakespeare indulged in all sorts of wordplay on the subject. For example, from *The Taming of the Shrew* (1593):

KATHARINA: What is your crest? A coxcomb?
PETRUCHIO: A combless cock, so Kate will be my hen.
KATHARINA: No cock of mine. You crow too like a craven. [N.B. in Elizabethan times, one of the standard meanings of *craven* was "a cock that will not fight."]

Still earlier, there is more iconographic evidence. An illumination in a mid–fourteenth-century French manuscript, now reposing in the Bodleian Library and described by Ms. Baird in *Maledicta*, shows a fox in the midst of what appears at first glance to be an ordinary henhouse raid: The fox runs away in the foreground, chased by a chagrined friar; several barnyard cocks and a castle are in the background. Close inspection, however, reveals the true source of the friar's grief, for instead of the expected barnyard cock in his mouth, the fox is running off with another visual pun.

Although long barred in polite circles from use on its own, *cock* has managed to insinuate itself into a great many expressions, both high and low, both "permissible" (as Sir James put it) and im-. For example:

cock ale. A good, strong beer, "mixed with the jelly or minced meat of a boiled cock, besides other ingredients" (*OED*) and reputed to have aphrodisiac effects—"A provocative drink," as Captain Francis Grose defined it (*A Classical Dictionary of the Vulgar Tongue*, 1796).

cock alley (or *lane*). "The private parts of a woman" (Grose again). Synonyms include *cock-hall, cock-inn, cockpit,* and *cockshire.* Within living memory, the most common graffito in what the British call "W.C.s" was a message imploring the reader to get in touch with "Miss Lucy Keeps, The Cockwell Inn, Tillit, Herts" (reported by Tim Healey in *Maledicta,* Winter 1980).

cockalorum. A small man with a big opinion of himself, from the early eighteenth century; probably from the strutting *cock* plus a pseudo-Latin suffix, though suspiciously close to the Dutch *kockeloeren,* to crow.

cock-and-bull story. An incredible tale, especially a long, rambling one; probably alluding to fables of the sort produced by LaFontaine (1621–95), in which cocks, bulls, and other animals do a lot of talking. One of the earliest, and most convoluted of all novels, Laurence Sterne's *Tristram Shandy* (1759) ends with the lines:

> L ____ d! said my mother, what is all this story about?—
> A Cock and a Bull, said Yorick—And one of the best of its kind, I ever heard.

And the expression remains current. Thus, after reading Philippine president Ferdinand Marcos's description of his resistance activities during World War II, a former U. S. Army captain, Ray C. Hunt, Jr., who was there at the time, said: "This is not true, no. Holy cow. All of this is a complete fabrication. It's a cock-and-bull story" (*New York Times,* 1/23/86).

cock-and-hen. Both sexes, figuratively speaking, as in *cock-and-hen-club* or *cock-and-hen-affair.* The basic phrase has been dated to the eighteenth century and may well be older, since *hen* has been used as the (human) female counterpart of *cock* for several centuries. See also HEN.

cock bawd. "A male keeper of a bawdy-house" (Grose, *op. cit.*). See also BAWD.

cock a snook. A well-known gesture of derision, with thumb on nose and other fingers extended, also known as *Queen Anne's Fan, The Spanish Fan, taking a sight, making a [long] nose, pulling bacon,* and *coffee milling* (with the little finger twirling as though grinding an imaginary coffee mill). *Snooks* is an old word of uncertain origin, used as a disrespectful reply to a stupid question—"Snooks!" The *cock* in *cock a snook* probably refers to the aggressiveness of the gamecock. See also FIG, NOT TO GIVE (or CARE).

cocked hat, knock into a. A dire threat to alter someone beyond recognition, as a circular hat is when its brim is tilted up to make a three-corner hat. "I told Tom I'd knock him into a cocked hat if he said another word" (J. K. Paulding, *Banks of Ohio,* 1833).

cock-eyed. A versatile term, with different meanings depending on context, i.e., cross-eyed, dead drunk, crazy, ridiculous, wrong, askew. The allusion originally may have been either to the marksman's squint when taking aim and cocking a firearm or to *cock* in the sense of something tilted up (as the hammer of a gun that is ready to be fired). In whichever case, the barnyard bird seems to be the ultimate source since the *cock* of a gun goes back to the matchlock era, when the firing mechanism actually was shaped like a rooster.

cockish. Of a woman: randy, wanton. "A cockish wench; a forward coming girl" (Grose, *op. cit.*).

cockney. A Londoner, traditionally one born within sound of Bow Bells, from ca. 1600, and usually pejorative. (See COXCOMB for *cockney* as an insult—directed at an American, yet.) *Cockney* comes from the Middle English for *cock's egg*, meaning an unusually small or misshapen hen's egg. The exact sequence by which this term became attached to Londoners has not been established. The progression seems to have been something like this: from malformed egg, to spoiled or pampered child, to sissy or milksop, to townsman (as perceived by the theoretically more rugged country types). Indicative of the country dweller's view of city folks is Captain Francis Grose's stab at the etymology of *cockney*: "A citizen of London being in the country, and hearing a horse neigh, exclaimed, Lord! how that horse laughs! A by-stander telling him that the noise was called *neighing*, the next morning when the cock crowed, the citizen, to show he had not forgot what was told him, cried out, Do you hear how the *cock neighs?*" (*A Classical Dictionary of the Vulgar Tongue*, 1796). For what the city people think about their country brethren, see HICK.

cock of the walk. The dominant man in any group; often a bully. *Walk* in the sense of an enclosure for fowl dates to the sixteenth century and *cock of the walk*, as applied to a person rather than a gamecock, goes back at least to the early eighteenth century. By contrast, a timid or cowardly person used to be called a *shy cock* (ca. eighteenth century). See also CRAVEN.

cock pimp. "The supposed husband of a bawd" (Grose, *op. cit.*).

cockquean. A low variant of *cotquean*, meaning an effeminate man, especially one who does women's work, or, alternatively, a woman who is coarse, vulgar, or masculine. Speaking of male *cotqueans*, we have it on the authority of the great essayist Joseph Addison (pre-1719) that "A stateswoman is as ridiculous a creature as a cotquean; each of the sexes should keep within its bounds." See also QUEEN.

cockroach. A person who scurries about pursuing many small projects; in general, any contemptible person. See ROACH.

cocksman. A man who is known for continually pursuing women—and catching more than his fair share, presumably on account of his sexual proficiency; a pun, perhaps on *marskman* or *coxswain/cock swain*.

cock-stand. An erection. The expression appears first in esoteric Victorian "literature." It probably is older.

cocksucker. A fellatrix or fellator; specifically a male homosexual and, in extended use, one of the two strongest terms of abuse (with MOTHERFUCKER) for any detested person or thing. The first dictionary to include the term seems to be *Slang and Its Analogue* (J. S. Farmer and W. E. Henley, 1891), which gives a one-word definition, *feliatrix*, this being a relatively innocent age, and provides no examples of usage. Lenny Bruce used the term in its modern, specific meaning during a performance on October 4, 1961, at the Jazz Workshop in San Francisco: "It's not a show—it's a bunch of cocksuckers, that's all. Damn fag show." Bruce was arrested for his choice of words, eventually tried, and, for once, acquitted. The power of the word may be due in part to its harsh sound, which is a blend of several phonic elements. As noted by Roger W. Westcott in "Labio-velarity and Derogation in English: A Study in Phonosemic Correlation (*American Speech*, Spring–Summer 1971): ". . . intrasyllabic and extrasyllabic repetitions can themselves be combined in various ways. Examples are *boob-tube* (palindromy and rhyme), *poppy-cock* (double palindromy and assonance), and *cock-sucking* [and] *mother-fucking* (palindromy, assonance, and rhyme)."

cocksure. Very sure, self-confident—often too much so. What late Victorians thought about when they heard this word can be inferred from the note that Sir James Murray felt compelled to add to the entry on it in the *OED*: "The word was originally perfectly dignified, and habitually used in the most solemn connexions." The exact origin of the term is unclear. The original allusion may have been to the sureness of a stopcock in preventing the flow of liquid, to the certainty that a cock will crow at daybreak, or to the reliability of the cocking mechanism of a gun. Shakespeare used the word in the latter sense in *Henry IV, Part I* (1596): "We steal as in a castle, cocksure."

cocktail. An American word that has been incorporated into practically all modern languages, including the Japanese, as other nations have taken to the drink. Curiously, no one knows for sure how *cocktail* arose. Many theories have been proposed, among them that it comes from the British *cock ale*, mentioned previously; from *cock's ale*, an alcoholic beverage given to fighting cocks; and from *coquetel*, a mixed drink introduced to Americans by French officers during the Revolution. The leading contender for the honor of being the source, however, is another French word, *coquetier*, eggcup. The theory here is that the drink itself derives from a cognac-based tonic, dispensed in *coquetiers*, ca. 1800, by an apothecary in New Orleans, Antoine Amédée Peychaud. The earliest example of the word in print comes from a newspaper far to the North—the Hudson (New York) *Balance*, May 13, 1806. This is not as surprising as might seem at first glance, since Hudson (1980 pop. 7,986) then was a fairly cosmopolitan place, being a stop on a major trade route (via the Erie Canal) to the West. As with other *cock* terms, this one also bothered modest people in the nineteenth century, e.g., "The Baltimore Clipper suggests that cocktails should henceforth be called rooster's shirts!" (New Orleans *Daily Picayune*, 10/25/1840). Note that this is a double euphemism, the obnoxious *tail* also being blotted out.

cock-teaser. A girl or woman who grants virtually every favor but the last; sometimes abbreviated *C.T.* The expression goes back at least to the nineteenth century. Farmer and Henley included it in *Slang and Its Analogues*, noting that it was equivalent to *cockchafer*. A large beetle, the *cockchafer*, really exists, but *chafer* in the slang sense means "one who makes warm, as by rubbing." (*Tease*, by the way, in the sense of *irritating* or *vexing*, derives ultimately from the ancient operation of wool carding, wherein fibers were teased apart with a large thistle, the teasel; an additional layer of meaning perhaps comes from the French *attiser*, to stir up [the fire], from which we also get *entice*.) *Cockchafer* has falled into disuse, but the *-tease, -teaser*, and *-teasing* forms remain common, especially among young people—which just goes to show that the Aquarian Age is not as liberated sexually as parents fear. ". . . I didn't want it to get around school that I was a 'cock tease'—any more than I relished the prospect of the nickname 'Do-It' Babcock. [*sic*] What was I to do . . . ?" (Lisa Alther, *Kinflicks*, 1975).

cock-up. British: a blunder, a foul up, a mess, perhaps from *cock* in the sense of something that is tilted up, over, and, in this instance, totally upside-down. "The American National Organisation of Women calls divorcees 'displaced homemakers' and a cock-up by an American doctor which results in your having the wrong leg amputated is a 'therapeutic accident' " (*Oxford Mail*, 8/4/83, reviewing Hugh Rawson: *A Dictionary of Euphemisms & Other Doubletalk*, 1981).

cocky. Bold, arrogant, conceited, like a barnyard cock; formerly lecherous, e.g., "He was not cockie enough to satisfie hir appetite" (William Thomas, *The Historie of Italie*, 1549).

cold-cock. To knock [someone] senseless, often encountered in the recumbant past tense, *cold-cocked*, as "Tom was cold-cocked when that rock hit him" (*American Speech*, 4/27). The expression probably derives from *knock a-cock*, once used to describe gamecocks or boxers who were knocked in a heap or senseless, with reinforcement from *cocked*, meaning *drunk* (and hence senseless) and *to knock [someone] cold.* See also COLD.

flat-cock. "A female" (Grose, *op. cit.*). In the southern part of the United States, where many early English expressions survive, *cock* is still used informally to refer to female as well as male genitalia.

horsecock. A military term for cold cuts, especially salami and bologna (World War II and probably earlier); also called *donkey dick*, or, more politely, *horse parts.*

hot cock. News, as in "What's the hot cock?" Variations, all indicating that the news or other account is not to be believed, include *bunch of cock, lot of cock*, and *to talk cock.* These terms may be influenced by *poppycock*, another word for nonsense or rubbish (from the Dutch *pappekak*, soft dung), but the principal ancestor seems to be *cock* as a nineteenth-century abbreviation for *cock-and-bull story.*

lobcock. And, finally, coming full circle to yet another *cock* that encompasses both an entire man and a piece of his anatomy, here is Captain Francis Grose's definition of this term: "A large relaxed penis; also a dull inanimate fellow" (*A Classical Dictionary of the Vulgar Tongue*, 1796).

See also COQUETTE, COXCOMB, PECKERWOOD, and PRICK.

cockamamie. Worthless, crazy, absurd. "You're not going to call me for the 50 millionth time and ask me the same dumb, stupid, cockamamie question, are you?" (sports-talk "host" Pete Franklin, WWWE, Cleveland, Ohio, *New York Times*, 10/13/86). The word seems to be a cockish corruption of *decalomania*, a craze for transferring decals from surface to surface—and, in the case of kids, to their skins—which has reached epidemic proportions at various times since the first recorded outbreak in 1862.

cod. A stupid person, a drunk, a hoax, an old person (not necessarily a CODGER, since *cod* was used this way long before the other appeared on the linguistic scene). More fully, an oaf or dumbhead might be called *a cod's head* or *a cod's head and shoulders* from the sixteenth through the nineteenth centuries. A synonym was *stockfish*, a generic term for the cod and its close relatives such as hake and whiting. When dried, these fish are thin, leading that overblown knight, Sir John Falstaff, to compare the young and slender Prince Hal to a *stockfish*, among other things: " 'Sblood, you starveling, you elf skin [probably meaning a snake's skin, not an eelskin], you dried neat's tongue [ox tongue], you bull's pizzle [pizzles were used for making whips], you stockfish! Oh, for breath to utter what is like thee!" (William Shakespeare, *Henry IV, Part I*, 1596).

Cod's origin is uncertain. The name of the fish may be related to another old meaning of *cod*, i.e., small bag. Perhaps the cod was thought of as a "bag-fish." Whatever, the bag sense also has resulted in *cod* meaning the scrotum, *cods* for testicles, and *codpiece*, the baglike affair worn by men in the middle ages to cover the opening in front of their breeches or hose, and frequently padded for special effect. These older senses persist in some rural parts of the United States, where Elizabethan English has not died out: "Cod still means scrotum or testicles in the Ozarks, and children giggle over such words as codfish and cod-liver oil. I have seen little girls blush when called upon to point out Cape Cod on a schoolroom map" (Vance Randolph and George P. Wilson, *Down in the Holler*, 1953). See also FISH.

codger. A senior citizen, male; usually in the phrase *old codger*. The term can be used affectionately, but is more often derogatory, with overtones of strangeness and eccentricity. *Codger* appears to have originated as a variant pronunciation of CADGER. See also COOT and FOGY.

codswallop. Nonsense, British-style. Thus, when Sir Fred Hoyle, an astronomer, dared challenge the authenticity of a famous bird fossil, paleontologists rose up to defend their turf: " 'It's rubbish,' Dr. Cyril A. Walker, a paleontologist at the [British] museum, said of Sir Fred's contention. . . . 'Codswallop,' echoed Dr. Alan J. Charig, a curator at the museum" (*New York Times*, 5/7/85). The word sounds as though it should be an old one, but the *OED*'s earliest example comes only from 1963. The *OED* says "Origin unknown," but it seems significant that *cod* is an old word for the scrotum and that *codswallop* is used derisively in the same way as the exclamatory *Balls!*. See also BALLS and COD.

cold. What's *cool* is usually good, but what's *cold* is almost always bad (inert, frozen, unconscious). The underlying association is of the absence of heat with the absence of life—of cold with death. This is recorded from the fourteenth century, though it probably is much older: "now in his colde grave—Alone withouten any compaignye" (Geoffrey Chaucer, *The Knight's Tale*, 1387–1400). There are exceptions. For instance, *to know something cold* (or *cold turkey*) is to know it very well, to have it down pat (see TURKEY), and a *cold war*, as unpleasant as that may be, is decidedly better than a hot one. The analogy is to death, however, when we say that someone has been *cold-cocked*, i.e., *knocked out cold* (see also COCK), or has *passed out cold*, or is unresponsive sexually and therefore *cold* or even *frigid*. Among the expressions in which *cold* plays a part:

   cold-blooded. Devoid of feeling or emotion, as opposed to *hot-blooded*; a relic of the medieval belief that the temperature of the blood controlled a person's temper.

   cold comfort. No comfort at all; from ca. 1325 (*OED*).

   cold cook. An undertaker; British slang from the 1800s. His place of business is the *cold cookshop*.

   cold deck. In card playing, a stacked deck, i.e., a well-prepared one; a mid–nineteenth-century Americanism.

   cold feet. A common symptom of fear or nervousness, since the 1890s.

   cold fish. An unemotional, unresponsive, unfriendly person.

   cold meat. A cadaver, from the eighteenth through the twentieth centuries on both sides of the Atlantic. It follows that a *cold-meat box* is a coffin, a *cold-meat cart* a hearse, and a *cold-meat party* a wake. *To make cold meat [of someone]* is to kill a person.

   cold shoulder. Studied contempt or neglect, usually in the phrase *to give, show,* or *turn the cold shoulder [to someone]*. The phrase seems to be Scottish, perhaps introduced to English by Sir Walter Scott. In its original context, the phrase referred not to a person's shoulder but to a shoulder of meat. The shoulder is an inferior cut, and the guest who is served this cold, instead of a fresh, warm roast, should realize that he has overstayed his welcome.

cold storage. A grave or cemetery, also a repository for ideas or projects for which there is no immediate use.

cold water. An agent for dampening and chilling someone's enthusiasm, from the early nineteenth century.

out in the cold. Neglected, abandoned, left to shift for oneself; from the nineteenth century but most recently and most famously in the title of John Le Carre's novel *The Spy Who Came in from the Cold* (1963).

Of course, sometimes the term merely refers to the state of the weather which, for example, may be described as being *as cold as hell, as cold as a witch's tit,* or *cold enough to freeze the balls off a brass monkey.*

See also HOT.

Commie. Traitor, enemy, foreigner, outsider, liberal, and, as an adjective, some- one or something that seems to exhibit such nefarious characteristics. "A liberal is a man who is constantly and simultaneously being kicked in the teeth by the commies and in the pants by the National Association of Manufacturers" (*Word Study,* 5/49). "I screamed, 'You dirty, filthy, stinky, crappy, Commie, dopey toilet! Thank God I don't have to resort to you . . . It's a shame there aren't laws to keep you and your kind out of a decent community. . Why don't you go back to where you came from?' " (Lenny Bruce, nightclub routine, ca. 1951, giving thanks that he was not the kind of comedian who had to depend on making dirty toilet jokes for a living, in Bruce, *How to Talk Dirty and Influence People,* 1972). See also TOILET.

Commie and *Comsymp* (the latter, a portmanteau, from *Communist* + *sympathizer,* coined by Robert Welch, founder of the John Birch Society) are more pejorative than the full *Communist,* as is usually the case in linguistic attacks (see PADDY). The basic term is employed widely, however, without too fine a regard for the actual politics of its targets. For example: (1) In Mobile, Alabama, after a Ku Klux Klan member was sentenced to death for murdering a young black man, his father, who happened to be the leader of the United Klans of America, denounced the court proceedings as the work of "liars and Communists" (AP, 2/2/84). (2) In Grand Prairie, Texas, a decent town boasting sixteen Baptist churches, a citizen protested at a City Council meeting against a proposal by local Buddhists to build a temple and monastery, saying, "We don't want the church or the Communist-type govern- ment they come from in our city" (*New York Times,* 8/3/84). (3) In the Nutmeg State, the Republican senatorial candidate in 1986, a Roger W. Eddy, characterized the Democratic incumbent, Christopher J. Dodd, as the "Communist Senator from Connecticut" because he opposed the Reagan Administration's efforts to aid the Contras in Nicaragua (*New York Times,* 11/5/86). And so it goes, back to that memorable speech on February 9, 1950, to the Ohio County, West Virginia, Women's Republican Club:

> While I cannot take the time to name all of the men in the State Department who have been named as members of the Communist Party and members of a spy ring, I have here in my hand a list of two hundred and five that were known to the Secretary of State as being members of the Communist Party and who nevertheless are work- ing and shaping the policy of the State Department. (Sen. Joseph R. McCarthy [Republican, Wisconsin], Wheeling [West Virginia] *Intelligencer,* 2/10/50).

The paper in the senator's hand, by the way, seems to have been a copy of a letter written three and a half years before by the then Secretary of State, James F. Byrnes, to a member of the House, containing statistics on security risks of all types, not just Communists. McCarthy knew the "205" was no good. The next day he said in a speech in Salt Lake City that he had "the names of 57 card-carrying members of the Communist Party." Still later, as reported by Richard H. Rovere in *Senator Joe McCarthy* (*1959*), he put the number at 81, then 10, then 116, then 1 (one), then 121, then 106. It was this kind of wild charge, of course, that led to Lenny Bruce's *Commie* toilet. N.B.: Senator McCarthy's "card-carrying" also has retained attack value. Thus, George Bush, shortly before receiving the 1988 Republican presidential nomination, told his party's platform committee that the Democratic nominee, Michael Dukakis, was "a card-carrying member of the American Civil Liberties Union" (*New York Times*, 8/18/88). See also AGITATOR, FELLOW TRAVELER, LEFT, PINKO, and RED. Compare: FASCIST.

condom. A sheath for the penis, also called a *safe, rubber, French letter, circular protector, disposable sanitary device,* and so on. Like most sexually charged words, *condom* was heavily tabooed for a great many years—in this case, practically from the time of the word's first known appearance in print (1706) until the latter part of the twentieth century. "A Gentleman of this House [Wills Coffee-House] . . . observ'd by the Surgeons with much Envy; for he has invented an Engine for the Protection of Harms by Love-Adventures, and has, . . . by giving his Engine his own Name, made it obscene to speak of him more" (*Tatler*, Number 15, 5/14/1709). The "Gentleman," supposedly, was a Dr. or Colonel Condom (or Cundum or Conton). Some say he was personal physician to Charles II; if so, the patient did not follow doctor's orders, as he had numerous royal bastards (Charles acknowledged fourteen and there probably were others; it seems that only the queen did not produce). All this makes a nice story but intensive research of medical and military records of the period has disclosed no trace of the eponymous Condom, and it seems likely that he is just the figment of the imagination of one of the patrons of Wills Coffee-House. Other guesses have been made at the word's origin—among them, that it derives from the name of a town in southwestern France, *Condom* (the English always attribute expertise to the French in affairs of this sort; witness the slang *French letter*, with the same meaning); that it comes from the Latin *condus* ("that which preserves," apparently referring to the health of the male); that the source is the medieval Latin *conduma,* house; and that it stems from *conundrum* (a problem without a satisfactory solution—and also an old slang term for a woman's most private part).

Whatever the etymology of the name, the item itself was in common use from 1700 on, though not much talked about in polite circles. Indicating the strength of the taboo, *condom* is one of the very few words that Sir James A. H. Murray excluded from the *Oxford English Dictionary* when he put Volume C to bed (1888–93). The social taboo was reinforced by law, of course. In the United States, contraceptives of all sorts were illegal for much of the nineteenth and twentieth centuries in many states. Not until 1965 was the legal ban entirely dissolved, with the Supreme Court holding a Connecticut law against birth control to be unconstitutional.

In the newly liberated age, it became possible to make jokes about what previously had been verboten: "The Republicans are thinking of changing the Republican Party emblem from an elephant to a condom, because it stands for inflation, halts production, and gives a false sense of security while one is being screwed" (Joseph Rosenberger, *The Death Merchant* #9: *The Laser War*, 1974). Or as a modern graffito has it: "Beware of Greeks bearing Trojans" (*American Speech*, Fall 1980). It took the threat of AIDS, however, to bring *condom* all the way out of the linguistic closet. In November 1986, Surgeon General C. Everett Koop recommended the device, using its proper name, as the best protection short of abstinence from AIDS, and TV commercials for the products began to appear in January of the following year, the first ones airing on KRON-TV, San Francisco. *Newsweek*, *The New York Times*, and other general-interest publications then announced that they would begin to accept ads, too. Even people who opposed the use of the device started to use the word publicly. "Encouraging frightened citizens to buy condoms and 'be safe' can only result in devastating consequences" (Representative William E. Dannemeyer [Republican, California], House subcommittee hearing, 2/10/86). As the *Times* noted: "The increasing public discussion of the condom, a birth-control device that was once unmentionable in many homes, has stirred debate among educators, religious leaders and parents" (2/12/87).

cony (or **tom cony**). A fool, a dupe, especially one easily cheated at cards. *Cony* is an antique word for *rabbit*, which today is used in much the same way; see RABBIT. *Cony* and *cony-catcher*, for the person who does the cheating, were popularized in a series of pamphlets by Robert Greene that exposed the techniques of Elizabethan rogues, con men, and cardsharps. "The poor man . . . is drawn in by these devilish cony-catchers, that at one cut of the cards [he] loseth all his money, by which means, he, his wife and children, is brought to utter ruin and misery" (*A Notable Discovery of Cozenage*, 1591). *Cony* had other low associations in the sixteenth and seventeenth centuries, thanks to its pronunciation (it rhymed with *money* or *honey*) and its use both as slang for the female pudendum, or *cunny*, and as a pet term for a woman—a parallel to *bunny* and PUSSY on both levels. It is because of the tabooed sexual sense that proto-Victorians began changing the pronunciation of *cony*, starting about 1800, to the modern, long *o* form, as in Coney Island.

coolie. An Asian or Indian, especially one of the lower classes. "In South Africa the word 'coolie' is used by some whites to describe Asians, and is bitterly resented by them as the word 'Kaffir' is resented by Africans" (*Guardian*, 10/4/67). "For us, agriculture was linked with backwardness and degradation. It was an occupation best suited to the 'coolies' [i.e., Indians] of the countryside" (Shiva Naipaul, *New Yorker*, 9/17/84). *Coolie* in the sense of native, unskilled laborer dates to the seventeenth century. The word probably comes from the name of an aboriginal tribe of Gujarat, India, the *Kulī* or *Kolī*, perhaps with some reinforcement from a nearly identical Tamil word, *kūli*, meaning "hire." See also DRUDGE, KAFFIR, and SLAVE.

coon. Short for *raccoon* and a derogatory term for a black person. "Terrel H. Bell, who served in Mr. Reagan's cabinet from 1981 to 1984 said the slurs [by mid-level Administration officials] included references to the Rev. Martin Luther King, Jr., as 'Martin Lucifer Coon' " (*New York Times*, 10/21/87). Then there is the white sheriff in the film *Mississippi Burning* (1988) who declares in the vernacular of the rural South in the 1960s that NAACP stands for "Niggers, Apes, Alligators, Coons, and Possums." Use of *coon* is by no means limited to whites, however. Thus Alton H.

Maddox, Jr., a militant African-American lawyer in New York, has termed the NAACP "the National Association for Coon People" (*New York Times*, 6/9/88). See also NEGRO.

The racial sense of *coon* was popularized by a hit song of 1896, "All Coons Look Alike to Me," by Ernest Hogan, a black man who used the word without being aware of its pejorative connotations. In our own time, the epithet was revived for public consumption by Norman Lear's TV creation, Archie Bunker (1971–83), whose dialogue was peppered with this and other ethnic slurs (see POLACK). During the show's second season, when it seemed to some that Archie's language was being toned down, Carroll O'Connor, who played the lead, explained that "We're not going to have him yell 'coon' every week just so we can keep up the reputation of being a racially pungent show" (*TV Guide*, 9/3/83).

Coon once had wider, whiter meanings. In the early nineteenth century, a *coon* could be either a frontiersman or a Whig (the party's parades featured live raccoons as well as coonskins and *to skin the same old coon* became a catch phrase for "to defeat the Whigs again"). Frontiersmen were still using the term toward the end of the century. Thus, as deputy sheriff in Custer County, Montana, ca. 1880, the fearsome mountain man John Johnson (called "Jeremiah Johnson" when Robert Redford played him in the film of that name) settled disputes by saying, "Wa'al, boys, this hez gone far 'nuff. An' whichever coon don't like thet, kin meet me now, hyar on ther spot, wi' fist, knives, clubs, or guns" (Raymond W. Thorp and Robert Bunker, *Crow Killer*, 1958). The racial sense developed early, however, e.g., "You half-niggers! you 'coon whelps! you snakes!" (Robert Montgomery Bird, *Nick of the Woods*, 1837). It seems significant, too, that one of the lead characters in America's first comic opera, *The Disappointment* (attr. Andrew Barton, 1767), is a black man named *Raccoon*.

Because of *coon's* disparaging use, most people today steer clear of the many phrases in which the word has appeared, e.g., *coon's age* (a long time, a.k.a. *dog's age*), *to go the whole coon* (to go all the way, *to go the whole hog*), and *to be gone coon* (to be ruined or lost, and apparently the oldest of a menagerie of similar sayings, e.g., *gone beaver, gone chick, gone gander, gone goose,* and *gone horse,* all the functional equivalents of the currently more popular *dead duck*). Folk etymology has it that *gone coon* originated during the Revolution when a coonskin-clad American spy, caught in a tree by a British solder, pleaded, "Don't shoot—I'll come down! I know I'm a gone coon." A notable exception to the rule about avoiding *coon* phrases was President Lyndon B. Johnson's vivid exhortation to American troops at Camranh Bay in South Vietnam:

"I salute you. Come home with that coonskin on the wall" (10/26/66).

coot. A fool, an insane person. ". . . Wanderer was defended by foxy lawyers who were capable of maintaining . . . that Wanderer was crazy as a coot . . ." (Alexander Woollcott, *Long, Long Ago*, 1943). The coot, a water bird, has been a byword since at least the eighteenth century for doltishness and madness, especially in such phrases as *crazy as a coot, old coot, silly as a coot,* and *stupid as a coot.* See also CODGER and DODO.

cop. A police officer. "Get me some cops to protect our policemen!" (Buster Keaton, *Cops*, film, 1922). *Cop* began as a slang term, popularized by criminals, who used it disparagingly, which is probably why FBI director J. Edgar Hoover tried in the 1950s to get everyone to stop using it. The term is an American shortening of *copper*, also meaning a police officer. The reference here is not to the traditional uniform, whose buttons are brass (see NANNY GOAT), not copper. Rather, *copper* was an expansion of an older sense of *cop*, meaning to grab or catch, which is what cops do to robbers. The older sense of the word is preserved in such expressions as *to cop*, meaning to steal; *to cop a plea*, to agree to a (lesser) charge; *to cop out*, to give up or escape (i.e., to seize an alternative to struggle); *to cop a feel*, and so on. *Cop* and *copper* for police officer have been dated to the mid-nineteenth century. *Cop*, meaning to grab, probably is a variant of the still older, now obsolete, *cap*, to capture or arrest, but it might also represent a borrowing either from the Gypsy *cop*, to steal, or the Hebrew *cop*, a hand or palm, used by a thief for snatching, and so—by extension, so to speak—a way of describing the act itself. See also FLATFOOT.

copperhead. A traitor; a disloyal person. The subversive meaning was established during the Civil War, when the term was applied to Northerners who sympathized with the Southern cause. Before that, *copperhead* had been used as an ethnic derogation for American Indians, Presbyterians, the descendants of the Dutch settlers of New York, and hostile peoples generally. See also MOSSBACK, SCALAWAG, SNAKE, and TRAITOR.

coquette. A flirt; also called a *cocat* or *cokitten*. The term is a feminine diminutive of the French *coq*, cock, and reflects the strutting, armorous propensities of the barnyard bird. Literally, it translates as "little cock." *Coquette* entered English in the early seventeenth century. See also COCK.

corny. Trite, unfashionable, mawkish; also (*pure*) *corn* or *cornball*. "Grown insolent and fat / On cheesy literature / And corny dramas" (W. H. Auden, *Nones*, 1951). *Corny* often is traced to *corn-fed*, meaning backward, provincial, or HILLBILLY, an expression used by big-city jazz musicians from at least the 1920s to describe old-fashioned country music. It seems, however, that there were *corny* jokes even before this. Going back to the 1890s, the companies that marketed seed corn throughout the midwest included jokes, riddles, and even cartoons in their seed catalogs. Talking about the catalogs that reached western Nebraska in the 1890–1910 period, Mari Sandoz reported in *American Speech* (10/46): "The jokes were all time-worn and over-obvious and were called *corn* catalog jokes or even *corn* jokes, and any quip or joke of that nature was called *corny*. . . . Later, when these seed houses put in radio stations and enlarged their business under the tremendous demand for the profitable new corn hybrids, the stations were called *corn* stations, and the jokes reached a much wider audience, augmented by songs, skits, and so on, but still the jokes in the early corn catalogs—time-worn and obvious, *corny*." See also CHEESY.

corpulent. Obese. The Latinate term (from *corpus*, body) may not seem to be a fighting word, but rotund people have feelings, too, and may be deeply offended by the characterization. Thus, when Leigh Hunt, while editor of *The Examiner*, wrote on March 22, 1812, of the Prince Regent (the future George IV) that "This Adonis in loveliness was a corpulent man of fifty," he and his brother John, the newspaper's publisher, were prosecuted for libel, convicted, and sentenced to two years in gaol. See also FAT.

costermonger. A seller of apples, especially the large apples called *costards*, and an old term of abuse. Shakespeare used "costermonger times" to mean an age when everything was reckoned only by its cash value (*Henry IV, Part II,* 1596–97). Washington Irving developed the idea further: "Thou art some scurvy costard-monger knave" (*Knickerbocker's History of New York,* 1809). *Costermongers* seem to have gotten a bad name because of "their low habits, general improvidence, love of gambling, total want of education, disregard for lawful marriage ceremonies, and their use of a peculiar slang language" (John Camden Hotten, *The Slang Dictionary,* 1859). There also were an awful lot of them—more than thirty thousand in London, ca. 1860. Because of its size and shape, *costard* also is an old term for a person's head. To say that "I'll rap you on your costard" is not only a threat but an insult, since it implies that the intended recipient of the blow also is an *applehead* or BLOCKHEAD. See also APPLE, BAD.

cotton-picking. A lowly job and, hence, a general term of disparagement, more or less equivalent to *damned.* Thus, in an open letter to a man who said he had caught a near-record bass, but then proceeded to eat it before it could be officially weighed: "It's time to show and tell about that fish, Otis. Otherwise, let's just forget about the whole cotton-pickin' thing" (*Atlanta Journal,* 9/2/84).

cousin. A person who is vanquished so easily that he seems to cooperate in his own defeat, almost as though he were part of the family; especially in baseball. "Cousin—a pitcher who is easy to hit" (George Herman Ruth, *Babe Ruth's Own Book of Baseball,* 1928). The term can be applied also to batters and even to entire teams. It was first used in the 1920s by one of Ruth's teammates on the Yankees, pitcher Waite Hoyt (Tim Considine, *The Language of Sport,* 1982). The modern sense is in keeping with the phrase *to make a cousin of,* meaning to deceive, impose upon, or hoax, which dates to the sixteenth century but rates an *Obs.* label in the *OED.* In its turn this form of *cousin* may be connected to the Elizabethan underworld *cozen,* to cheat, to defraud by deceit. From the seventeenth through the nineteenth centuries, a *cousin* might also be bawd, whore, or half-wit, which doesn't say much for family life in bygone times. See also BROTHER-IN-LAW and UNCLE TOM.

cow. A woman, especially a prostitute; formerly, also a timorous, easily *cowed* person, in such combinations as *cow-baby* and *cow-hearted.* "Cow. the Emblem of a Lazy, Dronish, beastly Woman, who is likened to a Cow" (Edward Phillips, *The New World of English Words; or A General Dictionary,* 1696). The low esteem in which cows are held also shows up in various expressions. Thus, a clumsy person may be said *to be awkward as a cow* or, worse yet, *to be awkward as a cow on skates,* and someone who *does not have cow sense* is pretty dumb indeed. A *cow town* is a small, isolated one, and a *cow college* is a little-known institution in the sticks, often an agricultural school (a *Moo U.*). Airline pilots, meanwhile, have been known to dismiss female flight attendants as *cow-pilots* (an even worse insult than *stewardess,* which also types by sex). Nor is it very flattering to be called *bovine*—witness the furor at fair Harvard, following the publicizing of a letter on Pi Eta Club stationery in which women invited to a club party were described as "a bevy of slobbering bovines fresh for the slaughter" (*New York Times,* 11/24/84). See also BULL, HEIFER, MAVERICK, and OX.

coward. A serious insult since at least the thirteenth century, the term comes from the Latin *cauda*, tail. The only question here is whether the allusion is to the tendency of a frightened animal to hold its tail between its hind legs or to the turning of tail in flight. In either case, the posture is ignoble: "Cowards die many times before their deaths, The valiant never taste of death but once" (William Shakespeare, *Julius Caesar*, 1599). Among children, the classic formulation is:

> Cowardy, cowardy custard,
> Can't eat bread and mustard.

This one also has been around for a while. The Christmas 1836 production at London's Adelphie Theatre was *Cowardy, Cowardy, Custard, or Harlequin Jim Crow and the Magic Mustard Pot* (Iona and Peter Opie, *The Lore and Language of Schoolchildren*. 1959).

See also CHICKEN; GUTLESS: LA-DE-DAH; LILY-LIVERED; MILKSOP; MILQUETOAST; MOLLYCODDLE; NAMBY-PAMBY; PANTY-WAIST; PUSSY; SISSY; SPINELESS; WEAK SISTER; WHITE FEATHER, TO SHOW THE; WIMP; WISHY-WASHY; WUSS; and YELLOW.

cowboy. An undisciplined or reckless person. "Do we want cowboys making national policy?" (Jonathan Kwitney, referring to rogue CIA agents, "All Things Considered," PBS, 8/27/87). The original *cowboys* (*OED*, from 1725) actually were just boys who looked after cows. The term acquired disparaging connotations during the American Revolution when Tory marauders in New York's Westchester County—sharply divided between Loyalists and Rebels—were labeled *cowboys*. In the next century, the *cowboys* were urbanized: "At the same time the streets appeared thronged with another set, hooting and howling, savage like, and in imitation of the licentious cow-boys and sooty chimney-sweeps in the suburbs of an ill-regulated city" (Middlebury [Vermont] *National Standard*, 2/27/1881). And twenty years later, the term was applied most memorably to a man who had really spent some time in Western saddles: "Now look, that damned cowboy is President of the United States." (Senator Mark Hanna [Republican, Ohio], on the succession of Theodore Roosevelt to the presidency, following the death of William McKinley, 9/14/01). See also DUDE.

coxcomb. A vain fop, a conceited fool, from *cock's comb*, originally a red strip of cloth, serrated like the comb of a rooster, that professional fools of the Middle Ages wore on their caps. The term has been applied as an insult to nonprofessional fools for the past four hundred years or so. Thus, John Adams dismissed a fellow founding father, Alexander Hamilton, as "an insolent coxcomb who rarely dined in good company where there was good wine without getting silly and vaporing about his administration, like a young girl about her brilliants and trinkets" (letter to Benjamin Rush, 1/25/1806). Adams also thought Hamilton was a BRAT. Then there was John Ruskin's criticism of one of James Abbott McNeill Whistler's paintings: "I have seen, and heard, much of Cockney impudence before now; but never expected to hear a coxcomb ask two hundred guineas for flinging a pot of paint in the public's face" (*Fors Clavigera*, 1877). Whistler, whose signature was a butterfly, stung like a bee, and sued Ruskin for libel, winning a famous victory but hardly any spoils (the jury awarded one farthing in damages). See also COCK, CROSSPATCH, and, for background on Whistler's suit, RUBBISH.

coyote. A contemptible person. "You blankety-blank, flop-eared, sheepheaded coyote, what did you say you took it for?" (William Sydney Porter [O. Henry], *Roads of Destiny*, 1909). A *coyote* may also be a resident of South Dakota, a. k. a. the Coyote State, or a flirtatious young woman, a. k. a. *wolfette* or *wolverine*. Meanwhile, in the southwestern United States, the term has been used since the nineteenth century as a derogation for any native American item, whether a plant or a person (usually an Indian or half-breed). Thus, referring to a person who makes most of his living by carrying other people piggyback across the Rio Grande from Mexico to the United States: "When the weather is wet and the river is tricky, he and his fellow 'coyotes' can make about $47 in a three-hour workday—exceptional pay by Ciudad Juarez standards" (*New York Times*, 3/9/84). See also WETBACK and WOLF.

crab. An irritable, disagreeable person. The term originally (pre-1300) alluded to the crusty disposition of the crabs that are crustaceans, but it later became associated with the bitterness of crab apples. Shakespeare had the latter sense in mind when writing *The Taming of the Shrew* (ca. 1593):

> PETRUCHIO: Nay, come Kate, come. You must not look so sour.
> KATHARINA: It is my fashion when I see a crab.
> PETRUCHIO: Why, here's no crab, and therefore look not sour.
> KATHARINA: There is, there is.
> PETRUCHIO: Then show it me.
> KATHARINA: Had I glass, I would.

A *crab* also is a body LOUSE; *to crab* is *to nag* or *to complain*, as in "Crab, crab, crab, that was all she ever did" (Dorothy Parker, *Big Blonde*, 1929); and *crabby* has appeared on the American political scene as a euphemism for something rather worse. See also BITCH.

cracker. A low-down Southern white, not necessarily from Georgia, though it sometimes is called the *Cracker State*. "I've been portrayed as a multimillionaire, right-wing, pistol-packing, redneck cracker, none of which is really true—except maybe the pistol" (Robert White, founder of the archconservative Duck Club, *New York Times*, 6/2/86). See also HICK.

The etymology of *cracker* takes us back to one of the first criminal syndicates in America, in this case the loosely organized gangs of horse thieves, counterfeiters, and slave-nappers that operated in the 1760s in the Carolinas and along the frontiers of Virginia, Maryland, and Georgia. What they stole in the Southern provinces, they sold in the North, and vice versa. The earliest reference to them comes in a letter of June 27, 1766, from Gavin Cochrane to the Earl of Dartmouth, in which Cochrane explained that this "lawless set of rascalls" were called *crackers* on account of their "being great boasters" (*American Speech*, 5/59). This sense of *cracker* is an old one, used by, among others, William Shakespeare: "What cracker is this same that deafs our ears With this abundance of superfluous breath?" (*King John*, 1594–97?). Other theories are that *cracker* derives from *corn-cracker* (corn being the principal ingredient of the diet of backwoodsmen) or from the predilection of teamsters in this part of the world for cracking their whips. Coming from the first observer, however, Cochrane's explanation seems to be the best. See also DIRT-EATER and REDNECK.

crackpot. A crazy person, a CRANK. "I don't think you would be talking about Adolf Hitler 40 years after the fact if he was some miniscule crackpot that jumped up on the European continent. He was indeed a great man, but also wicked—wickedly great" (Louis Farrakhan, press conference, 4/11/84, *New York Times*, 4/13/84). The allusion is to an easily cracked clay pot, of course; hence, the modern synonym, *psychoceramic*. *Crackpot* is not particularly old, dated only to 1883 in the *OED*, while the related mental *crack-up* and the British *crackers* are even newer. *Crackbrain*, meaning a crazy person or one with impaired intellect, dates to the sixteenth century, however, and such people have long been said *to be cracked*. "I could never see why Sir Roger [de Coverly] is represented as a little cracked" (Samuel Johnson, 4/18/1775, in Boswell's *Life*, 1791). *Crackpots* may make *cracks*, which are loud remarks, often boastful ones, as well as *wisecracks*. Any sharp, sudden noise, as of something breaking, qualifies as a *crack*, of course: "Excommunications . . . are but what our Famous Queen Elizabeth when Excommunicated by Pope Sergius, called them, the Popes crackfarts" (1569, in Edmund Hickeringhill, *Priest-craft, Its Character and Consequence*, 1705–07). See also CRAZY.

crank. An eccentric or crazy person; one with bizarre ideas; a grouch. "Cranks vary widely in both knowledge and intelligence. Some are stupid, ignorant, almost illiterate men who confine their activities to sending 'crank letters' to prominent scientists . . . others are brilliant and well-educated, often with an excellent understanding of the branch of science in which they are speculating" (Martin Gardner, *Fads and Fallacies in the Name of Science*, 1957). The person who is a *crank* has a mental kink, like that of the mechanical device whose handle is attached at right angles to its shaft. The word dates to ca. 1000, but wasn't used much in writing until the seventeenth century. The transfer of the mechanical metaphor to eccentric individuals seems to have been effected first by ingenious Yankees in the early decades of the nineteenth century.

crap. Labeled "coarse slang" when it finally gained entrance to the *OED* (1972 supplement), the term is nevertheless euphemistic for the stronger SHIT both in the literal, physical sense, and in extended uses where it stands for rubbish, nonsense, and insincere or downright deceitful talk, e.g., "It's the same old crap. One agency blames another and all the years of study are down the tube" (*New York Post*, 6/14/78). Or a quaint comeback reported by a visitor to Florida: "I know crap when I see it. Don't have to eat it to be sure" (personal communication, 1984). See also BUNK.

Perhaps the most interesting thing about *crap* is how recently it has acquired its excremental meaning. In the general sense of chaff, residue, or dregs of something (such as husks of grain or settlings of beer), the word dates to the fifteenth century. As the residue of people, it appears first in the late seventeenth century in the form of *cropping ken*, or privy (where the *ken* is a house and the *crop* may allude to the leftover crop that is left on the ground after harvesting). In the eighteenth and nineteenth centuries, people began paying visits to *crapping casas, cases,* and even *castles* (the latter presumably were furnished with euphemistic *thrones*). Thus, the excremental sense was in place before that eminent sanitary engineer Thomas Crapper (1837–1910) devised his valveless water waste preventer for W.C.s (1882). The short form, *crap*, doesn't appear in print either as a noun or verb referring to defecation until the mid-nineteenth century, however, and it took some years for this sense to contaminate the term. For example, Mark Twain rendered *crop* as *crap* when imitating the dialect of East Tennessee in the opening of *The Gilded Age* (1873): " 'Ole Drake Higgins he's been down to Shelby las' week. Tuck his crap down; couldn't get shet o' the most uv it; hit warn't no time to sell, he says, so he fotched it back again . . .' " It is unlikely that either Twain or his collaborator on this novel, Charles Dudley Warner, would have committed this word to paper if the coarse meaning were widely known at the time. Nowadays, it is all much different, of course, and it is impossible to use such words as *crapulence*, *craupulent*, and *crapulous* without causing bad thoughts to come to people's minds even though the long words, all having to do with eating or drinking too much, are entirely unrelated to the short one.

craven. Cowardly, also a COWARD; sometimes for emphasis, a *craven coward*. Of obscure etymology, but clear meaning from pre-1400: "Haa! crauaunde knyghte!" (*Morte Arthure*, 1871). Gamecocks that weren't game enough to fight also used to be known as cravens; see COCK and DUNGHILL.

crawfish. To retreat (as by crawling), to back out of a deal; especially in the Southeastern states. "No sooner did they see the old British Lion rising up . . . than they crawfished back to 49' " (*Congressional Globe*, 2/1/1848).

crazy. Insane. *Crazy* is a sixteenth-century offshoot of *craze*, which meant to break or to shatter, as a pane of glass, before being extended in the fifteenth century to include people who were *crazed* or broken down in body or mind. (The original sense survives in the *craze*, or tiny cracks, of a pottery glaze.) The oldest example of a crazy person in the *OED* comes from a letter that was written in the time of James I: "He was noted to be crazy and distempered before" (J. Chamberlain, 1617). As with other words for insanity, the meaning of this one has been extended gradually over the years to denote immoderate infatuation ("I'm crazy about you, baby"), impracticality ("It's a crazy idea"), and other departures from humdrum regularity. At the same time, the pejorative sense remains strong enough that the word is hardly ever applied today to people who really are crazy (usually known as the *mentally ill* instead). Much the same thing has happened to LUNATIC, MAD, and even NUT.

cream puff. A weakling, an easy mark; from the delicacy. "I remember my first campaign. My opponent called me a cream puff. That's what he said. Well, I rushed out and got the baker's union to endorse me" (Senator Claiborne Pell [Democrat, Rhode Island], *New York Times*, 2/13/87).

creep. A loathsome person, especially a stupid, worthless one. "A square don't know from nothin' and a creep is worse'n a jerk" (nightclub owner Toots Shor, quoted by Earl Wilson, New York *Evening Post*, 9/28/45). "For Archie [Bunker] was a loudmouthed disagreeable creep, and isn't it odd that we should have taken such a creature into our hearts" (Brendan Gill, *TV Guide*, 9/3/83).

The loathsome *creep* has been dated to 1876 (*OED*) and is probably a shortening of *creeper*, previously used in much the same way: "A gilded rascal, a low-bred despicable creeper" (William Rowley, *The Birth of Merlin*, ca. 1605). *Creeper* also acquired pejorative connotations from its use as a term for a sneak thief, especially one who worked in brothels. Such a *creeper* often is a prostitute who supplements her income by creeping out from beneath a bed and stealing a customer's money while he is otherwise engaged. An establishment in which this sort of thing occurs frequently is a *creep joint*. Thus, the modern, negative meanings of *creep* are in accord with the word's most ancient (pre-900 A.D.) associations with a low-down, stealthy, reptilian manner of locomotion. Of course, conservative politicians also wish to convey these associations when they characterize governmental programs to help individual citizens as *creeping socialism*. See also JERK, SQUARE, and WEIRDO.

cretin. A stupid fellow. "The Salvadoran Army has increased in size over the last four years and the cretins in Congress have refused to increase the number of advisers" (Robert K. Brown, editor and publisher of *Soldier of Fortune* magazine, *New York Times*, 9/5/84). *Cretin* comes from the Swiss French *crestin*, Christian, but is not really an ethnic insult, religious subdivision. Initially, from the eighteenth century if not before, the term was applied in the sense of "human" to distinguish the physically and mentally stunted *crestins* from nonhuman brutes. The medical condition cretinism is now known to be due to thyroid deficiency. See also MORON.

cripple. One who is disabled, handicapped, or impaired—a term that is hardly ever used of a person except in a disparaging way. "By now [1935] Talmadge courteously referred to Roosevelt as 'that cripple in the White House'" (Arthur M. Schlesinger, Jr., *The Politics of Upheaval*, 1960). And the usage remains current: "Interior Secretary James G. Watt said today that he had a mixed advisory group, with 'a black, a woman, two Jews and a cripple,' but he later apologized" (UPI, 9/21/83).

crocodile. A repacious person; especially a hypocrite, who affects sorrow with evil intent. "Beware of whores . . . for they be crocodiles, that when they weep, destroy" (Robert Greene, *The Black Book's Messenger*, 1592). The idea of hypocrisy goes back to the legend, first recorded in *The Travels of Sir John Mandeville* (ca. 1371), that the crocodile not only makes heartrending moans to attract its victims but actually sheds tears while devouring them. The symbolic value of the beast already was well established by Mandeville's time, however. Expatiating upon the crocodile's character, the author of a twelfth-century Latin bestiary noted: "Hypocritical, dissolute and avaracious people have the same nature as this brute—also any people who are puffed up with pride, dirtied with the corruption of luxury, or haunted with the disease of avarice—even if they do make a show of falling in with the justifications of the Law, pretending in the sight of men to be upright and indeed very saintly" (T. H. White, tr., *The Bestiary*, 1954). The epithet has not gone out of style. Thus, discussing his five wives, the film director and writer John Huston told an interviewer: "They were a mixed bag—a schoolgirl, a gentlewoman, a motion picture actress, a ballerina and a crocodile" (*New York Times*, 8/29/87). See also REPTILE.

crock. A worthless person, a good-for-nothing; typically, an elderly person, an *old crock*. The expression has been dated to the nineteenth century, but its origin is in doubt. It might derive either from the earthen crock that is a chamberpot or the Scottish *crock*, an old ewe, and hence, a worthless animal or person. See also CRONE.

crone. A withered old woman, a hag or witch; also an old word for an old ewe, a worn-out sheep with broken teeth. In English, the human sense appears in Chaucer's *Canterbury Tales* (1387–1400), nearly two hundred years before the sheepish sense is recorded, but both meanings probably derive from the Middle Dutch *caroonje, croonje,* old ewe, dead body, and ultimately from the Latin stem *carn-,* flesh (whence also such diverse terms as *carnal* and *carrion.*) See also CROCK and SHEEP.

crony. A close friend, usually with the implication that the *cronies* are partners in crime. The word surfaced in the 1660s as university slang for a good friend or pal, perhaps from the Greek *khronios,* long-lasting. The criminal associations appeared in the next century. Thus, Captain Francis Grose defined *crony* as "An intimate companion, a comrade: also a confederate in a robbery" (*A Classical Dictionary of the Vulgar Tongue,* 1796). In our own century, the term frequently is applied to politicians in power, the unstated charge being that the *cronies* have gotten into office through friendship rather than talent and that they are probably conspiring to do something bad as well. ". . . the Truman administration appeared to be foundering in a mess of corruption, cronyism, extravagance, and so forth" (Walter Lippmann, *Birmingham* [Alabama] *News,* 9/5/52). "Reformers are 'friends' while regulars are 'cronies' " (Brooklyn, [New York] *Phoenix,* 10/9/75).

crook. A thief; one who makes his living through crime. "I made my mistakes, but in all my years of public life I have never profited, *never* profited from public service. . . . I welcome this kind of examination because people have got to know whether or not their president is a crook. Well, I'm not a crook" (Richard M. Nixon, press conference, Associated Press Managing Editors Convention, Disney World, Florida, 11/11/73). That which is crooked is, by definition, not straight, and the word has long been used (from ca. 1200) for a trick, deceit, or other piece of guile. As applied to a person, however, the term is barely more than a century old. It appears to be an Americanism, with the earliest known example of its use in print coming, almost inevitably, from Chicago: "The *Times* still continues its attacks upon the Government officials in the interest of the Pekin and Peoria crooks" (*Chicago Tribune,* 2/6/1879). Country expressions for a worthless or untrustworthy person, albeit not necessarily a professional thief, include *crooked as a barrel of snakes, crooked as a dog's hind leg, crooked stick, so crooked he couldn't hide behind a corkscrew,* and *so crooked he can't lie straight in bed.* See also THUG.

crosspatch. A cranky, bad-tempered person, usually a female. Thus, from a nursery rhyme that was probably old when included in *Mother Goose's Melody: or Sonnets for the Cradle* (?Oliver Goldsmith, *ed.,* ca. 1765):

> Cross Patch draw the Latch
> Sit by the Fire and spin;
> Take a cup and drink it up,
> Then call your Neighbors in.

Cross dates to the sixteenth century in the sense of ill-tempered or peevish, while a *patch* during this period was a professional jester: "man is but a patched fool" (Shakespeare, *A Midsummer Night's Dream,* 1594–95). A *crosspatch,* then, began as a bad-tempered fool. Cardinal Wolsey (ca. 1475–1530) actually had a jester called

Patch, but the word probably is not an eponym. Wolsey's fool was really named Sexton. He most likely acquired *Patch* through Anglicization of the Italian *pazzo*, fool, with reinforcement from the multicolored patches of the traditional fool's garb; *patch* is an old variant of *piece*, and both forms are easily applied to people as well as to bits of cloth and other items. In *A Midsummer Night's Dream*, Bottom and his friends also are described as "a crew of patches, rude mechanicals." See also FOOL, PIECE, and SHREW.

crow. A woman or girl, usually an ugly or unpopular one, and often an elderly one, i.e., an *old crow*. "She is by no means a crow. In fact, she is rather nice-looking" (Damon Runyon, *Take It Easy*, 1938). In the past, the plainness of the crow has been used for insulting men, too. Thus, from one of literary history's more notable assaults: ". . . there is an upstart Crow, beautified with our feathers, that, with his *Tyger's hart wrapt in a Player's hyde*, supposes he is as well able to bombast out a blanke verse as the best of you: and being an absolute *Iohannes Fac totum*, is, in his owne conceit, the only Shake-scene in a countrey" (Robert Greene, attacking guess who, in *A Groatsworth of Wit*, 1592). Greene's allusion was to Aesop's tale about a crow that struts around in borrowed feathers.

Other common *crow* terms: *to crow*, to boast, as a fighting cock (but not a crow) does over a fallen opponent; *crowbait*, an old and worthless horse; and *to eat crow*, which is to consume that most unpalatable of all dishes—one's own words. The last phrase was popularized in the bitter presidential election of 1872 when Horace Greeley split from the Republican Party, which he had helped found, and ran against Ulysses S. Grant. Steadfast Republicans, and some Democrats, too, regarded Greeley as an unappetizing *crow* or *boiled crow*, e.g., "The chief leader of the Democratic party of Rhode Island, Hon. Thomas Steever . . . cannot and will not 'Eat Crow.' He prefers Grant to Greeley, and made a speech at Providence recently to that effect" (San Diego *Daily Union*, 9/13/1872). The phrase itself originated in a mid–nineteenth-century joke about a man who made a bet that he could eat anything, and thereupon was presented with a dish of roast crow. After taking a bite and chewing away, he announced, "Yes, I can eat crow! . . . but I'll be darned if I hanker after it" (from William Safire, *Safire's Political Dictionary*, 1978).

Finally, there is the *crow* that is a black person, from the eighteenth century, and probably the origin of *Jim Crow*, the title of a popular minstrel song by Thomas D. Rice (copyright 1828, and see COWARD for an early British example). By the 1840s, *Jim Crow* stood for segregation, as in the *Jim Crow car* (for blacks only) on a train. The phrase also continued to be used as a form of address to individual blacks and as a general description of the race. Thus, speaking to a youngster named Harry, "Come here, Jim Crow," or, referring to Topsy, "I thought she was rather a funny specimen in the Jim Crow line" (Harriet Beecher Stowe, *Uncle Tom's Cabin*, 1852). Field-workers for the *Dictionary of American Regional English* in 1965–70 were still eliciting *crow* in response to the question on "Nicknames . . . for people of foreign background . . . Negro." Thus, in the early 1960s, prior to the demise of segregation, that part of the University of Georgia's football stadium, where black citizens of Athens were required to sit, was known as the *crow's nest*. See also BIRD.

crud. A contemptible person; rubbish; any filthy, disgusting, or worthless thing. "Theodore Sturgeon once said that 90 percent of everything is crud" (*Playboy*, 2/84). *Crud* and the adjectival *cruddy* often serve as euphemisms for excrement ("Get the cruddy end of the stick," D. Levin, *Mask of Glory*, 1949), but they also are strong terms in their own right. "I think we do our cruddiest, our shoddiest work in April, May, and June" (Justice Harry A. Blackmun, on the Supreme Court's annual rush to churn out opinions before adjourning for the summer, *New York Times*, 7/25/88).

Crud is a variant of the coagulated, milky *curd*. One hopes that Miss Muffet was not aware of *crud*'s meanings, however, as they are uniformly noxious, including dried semen; diarrhea; unpalatable food; fungus, skin, and intestinal infections; and various other loathsome complaints, both real (especially venereal) and imaginary, often referred to as the *creeping crud*. See also GRUBBY and RAUNCHY.

crumb. A worthless person, a no-good. "I never wanted to be a crumb. If I had to be a crumb, I'd rather be dead" (Salvatore "Lucky" Luciano, 1897–1962, in Richard Norton Smith, *Thomas E. Dewey and His Times*, 1984). The adjective is *crumby* or *crummy*, for anything that is dirty or lousy, as in "It's such a crummy system—it just seems like a bog" (Joseph P. Kennedy II, *New York Times*, 12/4/85). The various *crumbs*, including *crumb-bum* (usually a lousy boxer or *stumble-bum*), *crumb-joint* (a flop house), and *crumb roll* (a bed or blanket roll), all have less to do with the mess that comes from crumbling bread than from the nineteenth-century slang use of *crumb* to mean a body louse or bedbug, e.g., "Fortunately, I am not troubled with the 'crumbs' now" (O. W. Norton, *Army Letters*, 1863). See also LOUSE.

crybaby. A common children's jeer, also occasionally directed at adults by adults. For example, quoting former Los Angeles Dodger manager Walt Aston, who had had it up to here with the griping of his ballplayers: "I'm tired of listening to you spoiled crybabies" (*New York Times*, 10/7/84). Children often work the insult into murderous little ditties, such as the following, which is common in both the United States and the United Kingdom:

> Cry, Baby, cry,
> Put your finger in your eye,
> And tell your mother it wasn't I.

This verse appeared in print as far back as 1842 in James O. Halliwell's *The Nursery Rhymes of England* and there is no reason to suppose it was new at the time. See also BLUBBERMOUTH.

crypto-. A person who conceals his or her true beliefs. "Pacifists or 'cryptos,' or that breed of degenerate intellectuals" (Winston S. Churchill, *Hansard Commons*, 1947). Though it can stand alone, as here, the term is encountered more often as a combining form in such constructions as *crypto-Communist, crypto-Fascist, crypto-Semite*, or, as in the following *New York Times* headline, "Marxism and Crypto-Marxism" (10/26/77). *Crypto-Fascist*, from 1940, may be the oldest of these. Whether as a separate word or a prefix, the term is inherently negative, implying secrecy and duplicity. It comes from the Greek *krypte*, hidden place. See also CLOSET- and ULTRA-.

cub. A young person, unformed and uninformed; frequently an *impudent cub*. "O thou dissembling cub! What wilt thou be when time has sown a grizzle on the case"

(William Shakespeare, *Twelfth Night*, 1600–02). The comparison of a young person to a cub comes from the medieval belief that bear cubs were born formless and licked into shape by their mothers. See also RUNT and WHELP.

cuckoo. A fool; out of one's wits, crazy. Thus, Prime Minister Margaret Thatcher dismissed the Bishop of Durham's criticisms of Tory policies: "After all, it wouldn't be spring, would it, without the voice of the occasional cuckoo?" (*New York Times*, 5/9/85).

The "insane" meaning of *cuckoo* probably is a tribute to the bird's monotonous call, whose repetition with clock-like regularity is enough to drive anyone up the wall. The essential inanity of the bird has been assumed for many years, witness "Cloudcuckooland," the name of the Utopian city in the air built by the leading characters of Aristophanes' *The Birds* (414 B.C.). It used to be that *cuckoo* also signified *cuckold*, i.e., a husband whose wife has been unfaithful to him (tradition-ally with another male). *Cuckold*, as it happens, derives from *cuckoo*, the association between the two words apparently stemming from the cuckoo's habit of laying its eggs in other birds' nests. In bygone times, to cry *cuckoo* after a married man was to let him know that his wife's lover was in the vicinity. This is the kind of intelligence that most husbands can do without, as noted by William Shakespeare in *Love's Labor's Lost* (1588–94):

> The cuckoo then, on every tree,
> Mocks married men; for thus sings he—
>   Cuckoo,
> Cuckoo, cuckoo! Oh, word of fear,
> Unpleasing to the married ear!

See also DODO, HORNY, and KOOK.

cull(y). A man, especially a fool, a dupe. "Man was by nature woman's cully made: / We never are but by ourselves betrayed" (William Congreve, *The Old Batchelor*, 1693). This term of abuse is slightly archaic but well worth reviving in view of its piquant etymology, as it descends ultimately from the Latin *coleus*, testicle. The metaphor also appears in the French *coullion*, a low fellow, an idiot, and a testicle; the Italian *coglione*, with the same array of meanings; and the older English *cullion*, ditto. See also BALLS and GULL.

cult. An organized group of people, religious or not, with whom you disagree. "Secretary of Commerce [Frederick B.] Dent charged that a 'vindictive and irre-sponsible cult' is seeking to force the resignation of President Nixon" (*New York Post*, 11/9/73). Even within strictly religious terms, *cult* may be counted as an attack word by those who regard their cult as a religion. "D'Antonio, Zlatos, and Reiterman all urge reporters to omit the word 'cult' from their stories on religious sects, no matter how cult-like a group may appear . . . use of the word 'cult' may place a reporter in libelous territory" (*Columbia Journalism Review*, 11-12/85).

cunt. The most heavily tabooed of all English words—generally not used by either males or females until adulthood; unspeakable in mixed company except as an insult or among those who are close if not intimate friends; and from the early eighteenth century through the mid-twentieth, printable only in underground literature and at the risk of criminal prosecution. The word may be employed in a strictly anatomical sense or as a term of abuse for a person, usually a woman but on occasion a man. Thus, speaking anatomically—and also demonstrating the lateness with which even a liberated woman of the twentieth century might encounter this word—Sheilah Graham reported in her memoir *A State of Heat* (1972) that as a chorine at the London Pavilion, "I heard all the four-letter words from 'cock' to 'cunt' and learned what they meant. . . . Where I had come from [in the city's East End] a 'cunt' was called a 'pussy cat' and a 'cock' was a 'John Thomas,' although I had not yet read *Lady Chatterley's Lover*." And as a term of abuse: "To call a man a cunt is to call him a woman: castrated, therefore not a man. To call a woman a cunt is to dismiss her absolutely: she is a O, a nullity" (Signe Hammer, New York *Village Voice*, 7/25/77). See also PUSSY.

The strength of the taboo surrounding this word is indicated by the extraordinary number of euphemisms and verbal roundabouts that have been devised for it. Some 650 synonyms for the word were included by J. S. Farmer and W. E. Henley in *Slang and Its Analogues*, which avoided legal difficulties in 1896 with the notice on its title page that the work was *"PRINTED FOR SUBSCRIBERS ONLY."* Despite all this, the word is not slang, just extremely old, with a more complete literary history than the four-letter word for copulation, which is its only serious rival to the claim of "most heavily tabooed term." It has been dated to the eleventh century, which makes it substantially older than the Latinate words that are commonly used in its place: *vagina*, dated to 1682 in the *OED*, and (more accurately but used less frequently, probably because of its "vulgar" sound) *vulva*, from 1548. The English word has cognates in other languages, ancient and modern, including the German *kunte*, French *con*, Old Norse *kunta*, Latin *cunnus*, and apparently the Basque *kuna* and the ancient Egyptian *qefen-t*. Its distribution suggests a link to some primordial term, implying quintessential femininity, perhaps *kuni*, the word for *wife* or *woman* in Nostratic, the hypothetical proto-language spoken in the Middle East prior to 10,000 B.C., from which most modern languages seem to have evolved. If so, the word is akin to *gwen-*, an Indo-European root that is ancestress to the modern Greek *gune*, wife or woman, as well as the English *quean*, meaning a prostitute; the royal *queen*; the *misogynist* who hates women; and the *gynecologist* who specializes in female medicine. Another possibility, which detracts only slightly from the word's antiquity, is that it derived directly from *ku-*, the hypothetical Indo-European base of a variety of Germanic words meaning "a hollow space or place, an enclosing object, a round object, a lump" (*American Heritage Dictionary*, 1969). This would make the tabooed term first cousin to such rousers as COD, *cote, cottage, cove, cubby(hole), cudgel*, and *keel*, as well as—an interesting convergence—*cock* (but in the sense of a heap of straw, a *haycock*, not the bird, the spigot, the penis, or the man). See also CONY.

At the very outset, when the word first appeared in English, it did not have the same force as today. In the *OED*'s oldest example of the term's use, from ca. 1230, it appears unabashedly in the name of a London thoroughfare, Gropecuntelane. Back in this plain-speaking era, when people's names often were based on physical peculiarities, the word also appeared in such forms as Godwin Clawecuncte, recorded in 1066; Gunoka Cuntles, 1219; and Bele Wydecunthe, 1328 (James McDonald, *A Dictionary of Obscenity, Taboo & Euphemism*, 1988). Geoffrey Chaucer, too, employed the word as occasion demanded in *The Canterbury Tales* (ca. 1387–1400), though with a different spelling: "And prively he caught hire by the queynte . . . And heeld hire hard by the haunchebones" (*The Miller's Tale*). And see DOTARD for another Chaucerian example. At about this same time, the term also crops up in a medical text: "In wymmen [the] neck of [the] bladdre is schort, & is maad fast to the cunte" (*Lanfranc's Science of Circurgie*, tr. ca. 1400).

During succeeding centuries, the word faded from use—at least in printed books of the better sort and in polite conversation. Thus Shakespeare did not use the term as openly as Chaucer, merely alluding to it with the expectation that audiences would get his puns. For example, in *Henry V* (1599), the French princess, Katharine, is shocked to learn that the English words *foot* and *gown* (rendered *coun* by the playwright) sound like the indecent *foutre* (fuck) and *con* in her own language. Then there is Hamlet's bantering with Ophelia about "country matters" in the third act of his play (1601–02), where the "country/cunt-ree" is firmly located below Ophelia's waist:

> HAMLET: Lady, shall I lie in your lap?
> OPHELIA: No, my lord.
> HAMLET: I mean, my head upon your lap.
> OPHELIA: Aye, my lord.
> HAMLET: Do you think I mean country matters?
> OPHELIA: I think nothing, my lord.
> HAMLET: That's a fair thought to lie between maids' legs.

Bolder still, Shakespeare even spelled out the word in *Twelfth Night* (1600–02), with the steward, Malvolio, deciphering the handwriting on a letter this way: "By my life, this is my lady's hand. These be her C's, her U's, and ['n] her T's; and thus makes she her great P's."

After Shakespeare, the word retreated further into the shadows. John Fletcher noted in *The Spanish Curate* (1622) that "They write *sunt* with a C, which is abominable." An exception was John Wilmot, second Earl of Rochester, who felt no need after the Restoration to resort to euphemisms (thus, of one of Charles II's mistresses: "Her Hand, her Foot, her very look's a Cunt"), but even so, his poems were not published until after his death in 1680 and then, though printed in England, this edition falsely bore "Antwerp" on the title page, as if it were an import. Other writers were more guarded. Thus, Andrew Marvell (1621–78) added some reverse English to "To His Coy Mistress" by punning on the antique Chaucerian form:

> . . . then worms shall try
> That long-preserved virginity,
> And your quaint honor turn to dust,
> And into ashes all my lust:
> The grave's a fine and private place
> But none, I think, do there embrace.

This example is footnoted in a college text, *Seventeenth-Century Prose and Poetry* (1946) by two distinguished professors, Robert F. Tristam Coffin and Alexander M. Witherspoon, who explain that "quaint" here means "Fastidious," with also "a suggestion of 'old-fashioned' "—which is, of course, just the other part of the Marvellous pun.

Later writers produced still other evasions for the word that almost everybody knew but which no one (well, hardly anyone) wished to see in print, e.g., graffiti not having changed much over the years, Theophilis Lucas's reference in *The Memoirs of Gamesters and Sharpers* (1714) to "a baudy monosyllable, such as boys write upon walls." (In fact, the simple *monosyllable* became one of the standard euphemisms for the anatomical part for much of the eighteenth and nineteenth centuries.) Matthew Prior (1664–1721) sidestepped the issue even more completely when ending his poem about Hans Carvel, a jealous old doctor who dreamed, while abed with his wife, that the devil gave him a magic ring that would prevent his being cuckolded so long as he wore it, upon which Carvel was awakened by his wife's vehement complaint: "You've thrust your finger God knows where!" (And *Carvel's ring* also became a euphemism for you-know-what.) Generally interpreted as a similar allusion is the abrupt ending of Laurence Sterne's *Sentimental Journey* (1768): "So that, when I stretched out my hand, I caught hold of the fille-de-chambre's _____." And at the end of the eighteenth century, when many of the attitudes that we associate with Victorianism already were in flower, Captain Francis Grose, though his subject was slang, felt compelled to resort to asterisks when he decided to include this word in the second edition (1788) of *A Classical Dictionary of the Vulgar Tongue*: "C**T. . . . a nasty name for a nasty thing." Thus delicacy was preserved, the asterisks apparently being less offensive to the eye than the thought of the word was to the mind.

When it came to underground literature, matters were different, of course. For example, Pietro Aretino (1492–1556), one of the fathers of pornography as we now know it (called by some "the Divine Aretino"), wrote a series of dialogues, in one of which the following case is made for the use of earthy language rather than high-flown metaphor:

> Oh, I meant to tell you and then I forgot: Speak plainly and say "fuck," "prick," "cunt," and "ass" if you want anyone except the scholars at the university in Rome to understand you. You with your "rope in the ring," your "obelisk in the Colosseum," . . . your "sword in the scabbard," not to mention your "stake," your "crozier," your "parsnip," your "little monkey," your "this," your "that," your . . . "job," "affair," "big news," "handle," "arrow," "carrot," "root," and all shit there is—why don't you say yes when you mean yes and no when you mean no—or else keep it to yourself?

Aretino's dialogues are of additional literary interest for serving as the model for such works as *L'Escole des Filles* (1655), which appeared in English as *School of Venus* (1688). It was the French version of this "novel"—consisting mainly of a discussion of sexual matters by two girls, Fanchon and Susanne—that was purchased on February 8, 1668, by His Majesty's Secretary of Naval Affairs, one Samuel Pepys. He characterized it as "the most bawdy, lewd book that I ever saw," and for this reason procured it "in plain binding, avoiding the buying of it better bound because I resolve, as soon as I have read it, to burn it." The next night, after consuming "a mighty good store of wine," he retreated to the privacy of his chamber, where he read the book "for information sake," then proceeded with the burning, "that it might not be among my books to my shame."

The social taboo of the sixteenth and seventeenth centuries against the *C-word* and other four-letter monosyllables was reinforced by law in the eighteenth and nineteenth centuries. The jurists were slow to act because at first there were, in fact, no laws against obscenity on the books. In 1708, an indictment against a printer, James Read, for publishing *The Fifteen Plagues of a Maidenhead* was dismissed because, in the words of the court, "There is no law to punish it: I wish there were: but we cannot make law. It indeed tends to the corruption of good manners, but that is not sufficient for us to punish."

In 1727, however, the judges decided that they could make law after all, when presented with the case of Edmund Curll, a printer, bookseller, and generally scurrilous fellow, who put out an esoteric work, *Venus in the Cloister, or the Nun in Her Smock*. The book had been printed in English as far back as 1683, but no one liked Curll, who was a political gadfly, too, and this time the court accepted the attorney general's argument what while every immoral act may not be indictable, "if it is destructive of morality in general; if it does or may affect all the King's subjects, it then is an offence of a public nature." Thus, Curll became the first person to be convicted of obscenity in the English-speaking world and his case became the precedent for later prosecutions.

Not all offenders were convicted, "progress" being made by fits and starts in this area, as in most others. For example, when John Cleland was hauled before the Privy Council in 1749 for having written *The Memoirs of a Woman of Pleasure*, a.k.a. *Fanny Hill*, he pleaded poverty, was reprimanded, and then given a pension of £100 annually on condition that he not repeat the offense—a creative solution that failed to keep Cleland from producing a similar albeit tamer work, *The Memoirs of a Coxcomb*. But Cleland was much better connected than Curll (the president of the Privy Council was a relative) and he did not actually employ any objectionable words in his otherwise objectionable book, Ms. Hill contenting herself with references to her "cleft of flesh," "hidden mine," "tender part," "furnace mouth," and so forth. Nevertheless, the trend toward censorship was clear, and it resulted eventually in the replacement of judge-made laws by the Obscene Publications Act of 1857 in Great Britain and the Comstock Act of 1873 in the United States—both of which, not-so-incidentally, then became bulwarks for suppressing the dissemination of information about birth control.

Still, the "nasty" word would not die. Robert Burns used it, though it was rendered as "c__t" when his *Merry Muses of Caledonia* (ca. 1790?) was published in 1911. John Keats also knew it and discussed its origin after a Mr. Redhall, who said "he did not understand anything but plain english", was persuaded to break the ice and "say the word out" (letter, 1/5/1818). Even Abraham Lincoln knew the word, as is apparent from the poem he received from a friend ca. 1860 (see ASS for the text). Of course, the anonymous author of *My Secret Life* (ca. 1890) also employed the term, over and over again, but got away with it because the original edition of his memoir was extremely small (only six copies authorized), with none offered for sale in regular channels.

Reflecting perfectly the tenor of the Victorian Age, this was one of the very few words that Sir James Murray knowingly excluded from the great *Oxford English Dictionary* (Volume C, 1888–93). That Murray was merely upholding middle-class morality is evident from the inclusion later on in Volume Q (1902) of the old "quaint-queynt" form, presumably on the theory that it would not unduly arouse certified Chaucerian scholars and that the masses would not find it under this spelling. Even here, however, the *OED* does not venture a definition of its own, but discreetly refers the reader to a citation from 1598 in which passing mention is made of "a woman's quaint or priuties."

Murray was fighting a losing battle, of course. By the time the last volume of the OED went to press (1929), the terrible word was well on its way to becoming printable again. World War I had a great deal to do with this, not that it was the only or even the immediate cause. Society was changing anyway, but the war almost certainly accelerated the demise of this and other linguistic taboos. All-male groups always seem to speak without much restraint, and soldiers of the American and British armies used this particular word so often that it began to lose its power. (Familiarity breeds acceptance, if not contempt). On the American side, *cunt cap*, the term invariably used by soldiers to designate what is officially called the "garrison cap," apparently dates to this period. And speaking of the British army, Eric Partridge reported in his notes on Grose's *A Classical Dictionary of the Vulgar Tongue* that "Among the soldiers in 1914–1918 the word was perhaps heard most often in some such phrase as 'you silly *or* you great c____,' though its literal application was frequent. Many avoided it; the others, if displeased with a rifle, a knapsack or indeed almost any object, occasion or person, would describe it as 'a c____.' " (The French, by the way, use their word in much this way, *con* also translating as "fool" or "imbecile." The term is used regularly in public with this meaning, e.g., the 1984 film, *Petit Con*, while continuing to enjoy its other meaning in other contexts.)

Though Partridge, writing in 1931, still felt constrained by social conventions and the law to use dashes, the necessary precedents already had been set in English for printing the dread word in full. James Joyce had likened the Dead Sea to "the grey sunken cunt of the world" in *Ulysses* (1922), a book that was banned in the United States until 1933 but hardly unread, demand for it being so great in the intervening years that it was printed clandestinely in large quantities, thereby depriving a near-blind author of his rightful royalties. Then there was D. H. Lawrence's *Lady Chatterley's Lover* (1928), which finally became admissible legally to the United States in 1959 and to England in 1960. In the interim, this book also appeared in both countries, but in expurgated editions, thus demonstrating again that it wasn't so much the author's ideas that offended as his choice of particular words for expressing them. And what was all the fuss about? Merely that Lawrence was using in fiction the same language that real people used in real life. He even realized—as Sheilah Graham reported in her memoir—that this word was one that many women did not learn when they were young. Thus, from a postcoital conversation between Mellors and his Lady: " 'Th'art good cunt, though, are'nt ter? . . .' 'What is cunt?' she said." In the United States, Judge Frederick van Pelt Bryan held that "at this stage in the development of our society, this major English novel does not exceed the outer limits of the tolerance which the community as a whole gives to writing about sex and sex relations" (decision, 7/21/59). In England, the next year, a jury reached the same conclusion following a five-day trial during which they not only heard arguments pro and con but read the book. When the jury returned its verdict of "Not Guilty," after deliberating for three hours on November 2, 1960, the audience cheered.

The next logical step, of course, is for social activists to attempt to convert the "bad" word into a "good" one, waving it like a banner as they mount the barricades. As noted by Gloria Steinem: "The feminist spirit has reclaimed some words with defiance and humor. *Witch, bitch, dyke* and other formerly pejorative epithets turned up in the brave names of small feminist groups. A few women artists dubbed their new female imagery *cunt art* in celebration of the discovery that not all sexual symbols were phallic" ("Words and Change," 1979, in *Outrageous Acts and Everyday Rebellions*, 1983). The efforts of the more radical feminists have not yet met with general approbation in the case of the last word, but they do accord with a common pattern of linguistic change. See DYKE, FAG, and FAT, for example.

cur. A despicable person. "[William] Loeb's kind of reverse 'Dear Sir, you cur' journalism was a throwback to the days of intense competition among papers" (*Columbia Journalism Review*, 11-12/81). *Cur* once was a neutral term for any dog, especially a watchdog or shepherd's dog (the shepherd's "trusty cur," as Dryden put it in 1697), but today the implication is that the *cur* is a mongrel. And the word is never intended as a compliment when applied to a human being, e.g., "Out, dog! Out, cur! Thou drivest me past the bound of maiden's patience" (William Shakespeare, *A Midsummer Night's Dream*, 1594–95). See also DOG and MONGREL.

curmudgeon. A grouch with redeeming qualities, especially one with an admirable talent for invective. The type specimen is Harold L. Ickes (1874–1952), Secretary of the Interior during the whole of Roosevelt's presidency and the first year of Truman's, who was called "the old curmudgeon" so often that he adopted the sobriquet when he wrote his *Autobiography of a Curmudgeon* (1943). Among the objects of this curmudgeon's displeasure were Senator Huey Long of Louisiana ("The trouble with Senator Long is that he is suffering from halitosis of the intellect. That's presuming Emperor Long has an intellect") and Governor Eugene Talmadge, of Georgia ("his chain-gang Excellency").

Curmudgeon dates to the sixteenth century. Samuel Johnson, who had apparently mislaid a slip of paper with his source's name on it, passed along the suggestion in his dictionary (1755) that the word arose as a faulty way "of pronouncing *coeur mechant*, Fr. an unknown correspondent." The French translates as "evil heart," but John Ash stumbled badly when following in Johnson's footsteps, deriving the term in his dictionary (1775) from *coeur*, meaning "unknown," plus *mechant*, meaning "correspondent." With this horrible example before them, the modern dictionary makers pass the word silently by, labeling its origin "obscure" or "unknown."

D

daffy. Mildly crazy, foolish, stupid; DIPPY or DIZZY. "A person who is 'wanting in the upper storey' is: bats, batty, barmy, crackers or crackpot, daffy . . ." (Iona and Peter Opie, *The Lore and Language of Schoolchildren*, 1959). *Daffy* apparently derives from the fourteenth-century *daffe*, a fool, and is probably related to *daft*, which started out (ca. 1000) meaning "gentle" or "meek." Our true opinion of these supposedly admirable qualities is indicated by *daft*'s shift in meaning to "stupid" as applied to animals (ca. 1325), then to "stupid" as applied to people (ca. 1450), and finally (1536, *OED*) to the now dominant sense of CRAZY. For similar sense developments, see STUPID.

dago. An Italian, Portuguese, or Spaniard, usually the former, as in: Q. Why does time fly in Italy? A. Because every time you turn around you see a day go. Logic suggests that the term was applied first to Spaniards, since it comes from the Spanish personal name *Diego*, James. From an early date, however, it was used without too fine a regard for national origins, e.g., "The negro Dago hanged for fiering Mr Powell's house," which comes from 1723 and is the oldest citation for the word in the *OED*. As more Italians came to this country, the word became attached particularly to them. Thus, after the Mafia gunned down the New Orleans police chief, David C. Hennessy, on Girod Street on October 15, 1890, the dying man was asked who did it. " 'Dagos,' whispered Hennessy, and collapsed . . . Before the end came, Hennessy said that he had not recognized any of his assailants, but that they were all Italians" (Herbert Asbury, *The French Quarter*, 1938). As an adjective, the cheap wine, *dago red*, was known to Californians as early as 1906. See also ITALIAN, SPANISH, and WOP.

daisy chain. A form of group sex in which three or more people, arranged in roughly circular fashion, simultaneously attempt to gratify each other. The term is thought to have originated in the (male) homosexual community but has since gone straight, even acquiring a nonsexual meaning in the business world, where it refers to a method by which three or more companies gratify each other while ripping off the public. For example, in a column about a $10,000 reward given to Dale Kuehn, a low-ranking government auditor, Mary McGrory reported that "an anonymous donor . . . thought Kuehn deserved a bonus for spilling the beans about a 'daisy chain' which poured oil through six Texas companies, jacking up the price at each resale before selling it to Florida Power Co.—which passed the $8.5 million overcharge on to its customers." (*New York Post*, 2/11/78)

dame. Any girl or woman. "These dames that write these books—they don't want to hear anything good. If you kill sentiment, you're a dead pigeon. The world runs on sentiment" (the president of Frank E. Campbell, The Funeral Chapel, Inc., referring to Jessica Mitford and her exposé of his industry, *The American Way of Death*, 1963, *New York Times*, 6/8/88).

Dame has been working its way down the social scale since the thirteenth century, when it denoted the abbess of a nunnery or other woman of high rank (from Latin *domina*, lady or mistress, the feminine form of *dominus*, lord or master). Stops along the way included such senses as that of the wife of a knight or baronet, the lady of the house, and the mistress of an elementary school. Today, the implication generally is that the *dame* is a rough-and-ready sort of the lower classes, e.g., "Women aren't women [in the 1935 novel *Decoy* by Michael Morgan]; they're dames, babes, skirts, tamales, dolls, floozies, chippies, and trollops" (Bill Pronzini, *Gun in Cheek*, 1982). Of course, with the exception of the antique *trollop, dame* and the synonyms in the preceding list also serve as markers of the social class of the person employing them. See also MISTRESS and YENTA.

damn. A comparatively mild oath that nevertheless has been tabooed for the past two hundred years or so. "Pointed profanity (this includes the words *God, Lord, Jesus Christ*—unless used reverently—*Hell, S.O.B., damn, Gawd*), or every other profane or vulgar expression, however used, is forbidden" (Motion Picture Production Code, 3/31/30). A special exemption had to be granted by the Code administrator to enable Clark Gable to utter the immortal line, "Frankly, my dear, I don't give a damn," in *Gone With the Wind* (1939)—and this was only after months of arguing, payment of a $5,000 fine by the producer, and shooting of the scene with the alternate line, "Frankly, my dear, I don't care."

Damn, deriving from the Latin *damnare*, to inflict loss upon or to condemn, doesn't appear in print in English until the sixteenth century, but obviously was in the air much earlier, since Joan of Arc is on record (1431) as referring to the English soldiers as the *Goddem*, alluding to their favorite expression. Shakespeare and other writers employed the term openly (see LOON for an example from *Macbeth*) up to the eighteenth century, when people of refinement in England and abroad (meaning the United States, too) began avoiding it. They did this by devising euphemisms, such as *darn, dang*, and *ding*, and by using dashes creatively, as in *d- -n* and *d- - -*. In this mode, the past participle often comes out *d_____d*, e.g., from a high point in *Shamela* ("Mr. Conny Keyber," a.k.a. Henry Fielding, 1741): "Yes (says he) and you are a d_____d, impudent, stinking, cursed, confounded jade, and I have a great mind to kick your a——. You, kiss —— says I." (See also ASS.) Victorians in the next century were still more reticent. As the Captain of the *H.M.S. Pinafore* (W. S. Gilbert, 1878) oh-so-politely put it:

> Bad language or abuse,
> I never, never use,
> Whatever the emergency;
> Though "Bother it," I may
> Occasionally say,
> I never use a big, big D.

Of course, the word continued in use despite the literary convention, with soldiers and sailors, especially, remaining faithful to the standards of Joan of Arc's time. Frederick Marryat, who had a distinguished career in the British Navy before becoming a novelist, catches the flavor of life aboard ship—despite the dashes—in

Peter Simple (1834), when a boatswain berates a sailor for spilling tar on a newly cleaned deck:

> . . . you d——d hay-making son of a sea-cock. Do it again, d—n your eyes, and I'll cut your liver out.

Digressing on the subject of language, Marryat continues:

> . . . common parlancy won't do with a common seaman. It is not here as in the Scriptures, "Do this and he doeth it" . . . but it is, "do this, d____n your eyes," and then it is done directly. The order to *do* just carries the weight of a cannon shot, but it wants the propelling power—the d____n is the gunpowder which sets it flying in the execution of its duty.

It was during this period, too, that the word became attached as a prefix in the Southern United States to YANKEE, as in "Take the middle of the road or I'll hew you down, you d'____d Yankee rascal" (*OED*, 1812).

Today, when we are surrounded by so many worse words, one would think that *damn* might have lost its power to shock and, in fact, it often is used as an intensifier, more or less equivalent to "very." Still, nervous nellies shy away from the term. A 1983 report from the American Library Association's young-adult services division listed *damn* as one of the words commonly removed from hardcover books when they were reprinted in paperback for children's book clubs (other no-no's included HELL, *thigh*, and BREAST). Adults are similarly protected: In *The Right Stuff* (1979), Tom Wolfe told how John Glenn admonished his fellow astronauts about playing around with the hero-worshipping cookies that congregated in Cape Canaveral bars. "Keep your damn zippers up," Glenn told the extramarital flyers, but in the 1983 film, the word somehow came out *darn*. And this was a full two generations after Gable's memorable utterance. See also GODDAMN.

deadbeat. One who does not pay his bills; a worthless fellow; a LOAFER or BUM. "[Roy Cohn] called the five committee members 'a bunch of deadbeat guys who could never get a significant job by election of the public or appointment by any responsible authority'" (*New York Times*, 11/17/85). The term is an Americanism, dated to 1863, perhaps a spin-off from the earlier use of *deadbeat* to signify one who was completely exhausted or "beat." See also CHEAT.

demagogue. A term for tarring political opponents whose arguments are uncomfortably effective. "What was the cause of my defeat? A system of grossest lies, a complete and unlimited use of the boodle of this country, a subsidized press, a lot of conscienceless demagogues that never ought to have even a name, a host of montebanks and jugglers sent us down" (Representative James Beauchamp "Champ" Clark [Democrat, Missouri], speech, 12/10/1894, commenting on an election defeat that proved to be only a momentary reverse in a long congressional career, including eight years as speaker of the house, 1911–19).

In ancient times, a demagogue simply was a popular leader or orator. Once the term acquired pejorative connotations in the seventeenth century, they quickly became dominant. It continues to see service in various forms, e.g., "One staff member of the House Intelligence committee describes Ashbrook's speech as 'pure and simple ACLU-demagoguery,' but adds that it was effective in garnering votes" (*Columbia Journalism Review*, 7-8/82). And as a verb, quoting Labor Secretary Bill Brock: "The Democrats are making a mistake by demagoguing this issue. That's a cheap-shot bill. It's a lousy. It really is a dumb bill. It's a stinking exercise in raw politics" (*New York Times*, 5/28/86). See also, in the order mentioned by Mr. Brock, CHEAP, DUMB, *lousy* in LOUSE, and STINK.

dense. Dumb; to be *dense* is to be *thick-headed.* "He will . . . put notions into her dense head" (*Poor Nellie*, 1887). For more on the composition of the human skull, see BLOCKHEAD.

devil. A wicked person, since the tenth century. Thus, from the diary of Samuel Pepys (1633–1703): "My wife did say something that caused me to oppose her . . . she used the word 'devil' which vexed me, and among other things I said I would not have her use that word . . ." Particular kinds of *devils* include unfortunate people, who are *poor devils*; assistants in print shops, who are *printer's devils* (from the *devil's tail*, the long, snaky wooden bar that the assistant used to activate an old-time press); and Caucasians, who are *white devils* in the lexicon of black Muslims.

Meanwhile, the hoary imprecations, *go to the devil* and *the devil take you*, dating from the fourteenth century, retain much of their old force among religious fundamentalists. Indicative of the devil's continuing power: Before the Pope appeared in Arizona State University's football stadium in Tempe in 1987, the institution's authorities tactfully covered up the huge sign bearing the team's nickname—the Sun Devils. Then there was the foofaraw in East Jordan, Michigan, that same year when a group of true believers petitioned the local school board to drop "Red Devils" as the nickname of the school's athletic teams. The board agreed to have the devil's face in the school's logo redrawn in less satanic style—"more positive and impish," as the board president put it—but the members declined to change the name. A difficulty here was that the most logical alternative, "The Crimson Tide," which was the school's former nickname, itself had been discarded in the 1940s because it seemed to local Cold War warriors to be too similar to "The Communist Red Menace" (*New York Times*, 2/19/87). See also HELL, HORNY, and SATAN.

dick. The penis; thus, a policewoman is a *Dickless Tracy*, a play on the underworld use of *dick* (as an abbreviated alteration of "detective") to refer to police officers in general and detectives in particular. Also encountered as a verb, and with a slightly different meaning: "Dick Nixon before he dicks you" (graffiti, from *American Speech*, Fall 1980). The precise origin of the term is obscure. The earliest record of the word in this sense comes from 1891 in *Slang and Its Analogues* by J. S. Farmer and W. E. Henley. The use of this particular male generic might come from *Donkey Dick*, a common name for a male jackass in the eighteenth century (see DONKEY). It also has been suggested by Eric Partridge that the name might derive from the large movable boom known as *derrick* (originally, not the name of a crane but of the gallows, with the name of this fearsome object coming from Derrick, a famous hangman at Tyburn at the start of the seventeenth century). Whatever the route, the anatomical dick almost certainly stems from a personal name, and it is just one of many such that have been bestowed upon this piece of male equipment. Among the standard ones: JACK, JOCK, *John, Johnny Come Lately, John Thomas, Mickey* (see

MICK), PETER, RANDY (lascivious, as well as *Randolph*), *Roger* (an old barnyard name for a bull), and *Thomas*. See also PRICK.

dingbat. A stupid or inept person, popularized by Archie Bunker on the TV show "All in the Family" (1971–83). *Dingbat* is an Americanism of uncertain origin, appearing first in print in 1838, apparently referring to some kind of alcoholic drink. Over the years it acquired other specialized meanings (e.g., money, a professional tramp or beggar, a muffin or bun, a typographical ornament) while also serving as a general word for any item whose true name is not known or which is not to be mentioned (such as the male genitalia, for instance). Other catchalls of this sort are *dingus, doodad, doohickey, gadget, gizmo, thingamabob*, and *whatchamacallit*. As for *dingbat*, it also was used in a derogatory manner pre-Bunker to denote a Chinese, an Italian, "a woman who is neither your sister nor your mother" (*American Speech*, 4/44), or "a pompous, bumbling, incompetent person serving in a position of authority" (*American Speech*, 12/68). See also DING-DONG and JERK.

ding-dong. A bumbler or silly person; also the penis. *Ding-dong* is one of several *d* words—including *ding-a-ling, doodle*, DINGBAT and DORK—that combine these two meanings. *Ding-dong's* ancestral form is not known; it might derive from the old (ca. fourteenth century) use of *ding* to mean a blow, since the penis often is regarded as a weapon, while stupid people—women as well as men—often are denigrated by referring to them in anatomical terms. As applied to a person, *ding-dong* also has the additional insult value of suggesting that the bumbling one makes mistakes with monotonous regularity. "Mr. O'Connor testified that he was surprised that 'someone of Jerry's knowledge, attitude, education—a cut above the average person on the street—why he would associate with such a ding-dong as Mr. Walker' " (*New York Times*, 3/28/86).

dinge. A black person. "The big dinge took him by surprise . . . the big black bastard" (Ernest Hemingway, *Winner Take Nothing*, 1933). The term also crops up in jazz, sometimes known as *dinge music*, wherein a *dinge* may be either a musician or a style of playing: "dinge, 'Negro vibrato' played with a very rapid, violent shake" (Lester V. Berrey and Melvin Van Den Bark, *The American Thesaurus of Slang*, 1953). *Dinge*, dated to 1848 as applied to black comes from *dingy*, itself a relatively new word, not known to Dr. Johnson when he compiled his *Dictionary of the English Language* (1755); it may be a variant of *dung*. The association of the term with people having dusky skins is nearly as old as our knowledge of the word itself: "DINGEY CHRISTIAN. A mulatto; or any one who has, as the West Indian term is, a lick of the tar-brush, that is, some negro blood in him" (Captain Francis Grose, *A Classical Dictionary of the Vulgar Tongue*, 1785).

dink. A Vietnamese; widespread American military use during the Vietnam conflict, 1961–75. "We called one of the Vietnamese employees at the advisory detachment where I was assigned in 1962 'dink,' because his favorite expression was 'You dinky dow, GI!' " (Dan Cragg, "Viet-Speak," *Maledicta*, 1982). *Dinky dow* is pidgin English for a Vietnamese expression meaning "crazy head," and it may be, as Cragg suggests, that this is the source of *dink*, the derogation. Among the other etymologies that have been suggested are that the term is a spin-off from *dink*, meaning something cheap and junky (*rinky-dink*); that it is an extension of the earlier (from 1920) Australian use of *dink* to mean a Chinese; and that it is a rhyme with CHINK. See also GOOK.

dippy. Crazy, foolish, stupid; probably from *dip*, and perhaps ultimately from *dipsomania* and the way *dipsomaniacs* act. "The old standby Newspaper, noted for its Powerful Editorials ever since the days of the Haves and the Wheelers, seemed to be going dippy with the rest of the outfit" (George Ade, *Hand-made Fables*, 1920). The basic *dip* also can be used as a prefix for constructing such synonyms as *diphead*, *dipshit*, and *dipstick*. *Dippy* also can be a suffix. Thus people whose brains have been addled by women are *doll-dippy*, and a person who has spent too much time in prison may become *stir-dippy*. See also MAD.

dirtbag (or **dirtball**). One who collects dirt; originally, from World War II, a garbage collector, but more frequently, in extended use, a filthy or despicable person. Thus, we have it on the authority of Senator Lowell P. Weicker, Jr. (Republican, Connecticut), that Rupert Murdoch, owner of the New York *Post* and many other media properties, is "the No. 1 dirt bag" in communications, having "caused hurt to many individuals" (*New York Times*, 1/28/88). As epithets go, *dirtbag* is equivalent to DOUCHE BAG and *scumbag* (see SCUM).

dirt-eater. A poor Southern white, a.k.a. *clay-eater*; also a pre–Civil War epithet among states-righters in the South for fellow Southerners who favored the Union. "Whether the North Carolina 'dirt-eater,' or the South Carolina 'sand-hiller,' or the Georgia 'cracker,' is lowest in the scale of human existence, would be difficult to say" (*Congressional Globe*, 1865). *To eat dirt* is quite another matter: This is comparable to eating one's own words, that is, to make a retraction or eat crow. See also CRACKER, CROW, and REDNECK.

ditz. A fool, a dope. "His parents, though, are ditzes—L.A. rich who are prisoners of their money, their shrinks, their own dim brains" (*Wall Street Journal*, 10/23/86). *Ditz* seems to be a relatively new word. It is included in the *New Dictionary of American Slang* (Robert L. Chapman, 1986), but not in the 1972 supplement to the *Oxford English Dictionary* or the other major slang dictionaries. It may be a back-formation from the adjective, *ditsy*, silly. Whatever, it is in complete accord with the sense of stupidity common to similar sounding words, e.g., DAFFY, DIPPY, DIZZY, DOTTY, and *dopey* (see DOPE).

dizzy. Scatterbrained, crazy, dumb. This is a very old word, which appears as a verb in the sense of "to act foolishly or stupidly" in the ninth century, long before acquiring the sense of "to make giddy," as from spinning around or looking down from a great height (ca. 1500). The term can be applied affectionately to men, e.g. that eminent member of the Gashouse Gang, St. Louis Cardinal pitcher Jay Hanna "Dizzy" Dean (whose brother Paul was called "Daffy"). Applied to women, however, the term frequently carries more than a hint of immorality. "Many of the local clergy last night warned the church members . . . against a 'Dizzy Blonde' company coming to one of the theaters soon" (*Kansas Times & Star*, 11/4/1889). See also DAFFY and FOOL.

dodo. This large but flightless bird, once native to Mauritius, has become a byword for stupidity (*dumb as a dodo*), for extinction (*dead as a dodo*), and for backwardness generally, e.g., "He belongs to the Dodo race of real unmitigated . . . Toryism" (Lisle Carr, *Judith Gwynne*, 1874). The qualities of the guileless dodo, which had no natural enemies on its island home, apparently were recognized immediately by the Portuguese who discovered Mauritius in 1507. The bird's name comes from the Portuguese *doudo*, simpleton, and its formal scientific name is no better, *Didus ineptus*. The ungainly dodo (swan-size or larger) succumbed to the depredations of man and other animals introduced by the sailors. The last record of a living dodo dates from 1681, when a visitor to the island noted in his journal that the bird's "fflesh is very hard." For more about brainless birds, see *booby* in BOOB, COOT, CUCKOO, DUPE, GOOSE, GULL, LOON, OSTRICH, PARROT, PIGEON, ROOK, TURKEY, and YOKEL, as well as the basic BIRD.

dog. The first of the animals to be domesticated and also a standard symbol of inferiority, abused linguistically in so many ways that one prefers to pass by in silence the question of what it says about man that he is so ready, in effect, to kick his oldest and best friend in the teeth. Stubb: "I will not tamely be called a dog, sir." Ahab: "Then be called ten times a donkey, and a mule, and an ass, and begone, or I'll clear the world of thee!" (Herman Melville, *Moby Dick*, 1851). Among the many extensions of the epithet's meaning:

A *dog* is a racehorse that doesn't run very fast, and a failure of any sort ("So many movies are *dogs*," *New Yorker*, 8/15/70); an ugly person, often a woman (see also MUTT); a worthless person, as in "Am I a dog that thou comest to me with staves?" (Goliath's complaint to the Hebrews when they sent a slip of a boy, David, to fight him (*I Samuel*, 17:43); or an untrustworthy person, as in Queen Margaret's warning of the treachery of the Duke of Gloucester, the future Richard III: "O Buckingham, take heed of younder dog! Look, when he fawns, he bites, and when he bites, His venom will rankle [cause festering] to the death" (William Shakespeare, *Richard III*, 1592–93). And at the end of the play, after Richard has been slain, his conqueror, the future Henry VII, announces: "The day is ours—the bloody dog is dead."

Today, the canine epithet often is applied to one's favorite enemies. Thus, Marxists speak of *capitalist running dogs*, *mad dogs*, or *stray dogs* (Libyan leader Muammar el-Qaddafi also used the latter on the British in 1984); Moslems refer to *Christian dogs*, as in Lebanon when gunmen came to a woman's house, "calling out, among other things, 'Open the door, Christian dogs' " (*New York Times*, 2/17/84); and Christians have used the term, too, as in—addressing a venerable Jew—"Dog of an unbeliever, whelp of a she-wolf; darest thou press upon a Christian, and a Norman gentleman . . ." (Sir Walter Scott, *Ivanhoe*, 1820).

But the denigration has never been limited to members of other groups, e.g., "COTTON MATHER, *You Dog, Dam you; I'l inoculate you with this, with a Pox to you*" (message attached to a grenade, tossed through the reverend's window, 11/14/1721, in retaliation for his advocacy of smallpox inoculations in Boston; from Kenneth Silverman, *The Life and Times of Cotton Mather*, 1984). The word doesn't even have to be articulated for the point to be made, as when a Florida prosecutor said of a murder defendant, "He shouldn't be out of his cell unless he has a leash on him and a prison guard at the other end of that leash" (the man was convicted but the prosecutor's choice of words led to a series of appeals that reached the Supreme Court, where it was finally decided, five to four, that the characterization was not quite poisonous enough to require a retrial; *New York Times*, 6/24/86).

Only rarely is *dog* used affectionately. *Dogged* persistence usually is construed as a commendable quality. As Samuel Johnson pointed out, "a man may write at any time, if he will set himself doggedly to it" (James Boswell, *The Life of Samuel Johnson, LL.D.*, 1791). Trouble is, not everyone may approve the result: "*Ulysses* is a dogged attempt to cover the universe with mud" (E. M. Forster, *Aspects of the Novel*, 1927). Others may sneer at those who *put on the dog* by getting all dressed up, though the display of finery is at worst a venial sin. The phrase may have a humble origin, however, deriving from the ordinary *dog collar*, the allusion being to the high, stiff collars that people wore when decking themselves out for special occasions in the 1890s. Also on the good side, young men about town used to be known as *gay dogs* (this was before *gay* acquired its present sexual orientation). Other members of this pack included *handsome dog*, *lucky dog*, and *old dog* (as well as *sad dog* and *sick dog*, especially on mornings after). Sometimes the simple *dog* suffices, as when two of Samuel Johnson's friends knocked on his door at three o'clock one morning, and asked him to come carousing with them. Johnson readily agreed, saying: "What, is it you, you dogs! I'll have a frisk with you." And the three stayed up drinking the whole night through, proving that not all dictionary makers are drudges all the time (Boswell, *op. cit.*). Such friendly *dogs* are in the minority, however. The connotations of mediocrity, worthlessness, and even cowardice are much more common, as exemplified by such constructions as:

black dog. In Queen Anne's reign (1702–14) a counterfeit coin, made of pewter instead of brass; later, a fit of melancholy, often in the phrase *the black dog is on his back.*

dirty dog. A contemptible person; among seafaring types: *you're a dirty dog and no sailor.*

dog, to. (1) To follow another person around, *to dog [one's] footsteps;* (2) To loaf or dodge work, *to dog [it].* "You're dogging it. I hate that" (karate instructor Paul Szantyr to lazy students, 1987). More strongly, also referring to loafing or shirking one's duty, *to whip [or fuck] the dog.*

dog-and-pony show. A carefully prepared performance or occasion, specifically, a press conference at which briefers trot out the facts (and sometimes put them through hoops). A variant, from a 1968 letter by an intelligence analyst in Vietnam: "We had a crash project to prepare a briefing on enemy strength as of 29 Feb. . . . I have never in my life assembled such a pack of truly gargantuan falsehoods. The reporters will think we are putting on a horse and dog show when we try to sell them this crap" (Commander James Meacham to his wife, *New York Times*, 1/4/85).

dogberry. The wild gooseberry and one of a number of plants in which the *dog*-prefix indicates an inferior item, unfit for human consumption, e.g., *dog cabbage, dog leek, dog parsley,* and *dog violets* (they don't have any smell). A bumbling public official may also be characterized as a *Dogberry,* but then the reference is to the foolish constable in Shakespeare's *Much Ado About Nothing* (1598).

dogbolt. An old (ca. fifteenth century) term for a contemptible person or other low wretch, especially one who is at the beck and call of another, perhaps originally referring to one person as the TOOL of another; also, a bolt or blunt-headed arrow, apparently of such little value that it was worth using only for shooting at dogs.

dogbreath. Bad breath, a.k.a. halitosis.

dogcatcher. Proverbially, the lowest and least important office in the land.

dog cheap. Very cheap indeed, since at least the early sixteenth century.

dog days. The worst part of summer, July and August, when the weather is so hot that even dogs are said to go mad. *Dog days* is a translation of the Latin *caniculares dies,* referring to the time of the year when the Dog Star, Sirius, rises and sets with the sun. Authorities, ancient and modern, disagree over the exact date and duration of the *dog days* because the helical rising of Sirius depends on latitude, epoch, and the brightness of the star (courtesy Dr. E. C. Krupp, Director, Griffith Observatory, Los Angeles, California). If a woman is said to be in her *dog days,* then she is menstruating. The idea is that she is especially bitchy at this time.

dog-eat-dog. Ruthlessly competitive, as applied to humans, despite the old saying, as applied to canines, that *dog will not eat dog.*

dogface. (1) An American soldier, especially an infantryman, or GRUNT, from at least 1935; possibly coined by sailors or marines, from the hang-dog expression of men returning from a long march. Soldiers have been wearing license-like *dog tags* around their necks since 1906, however, and living in *doghouses* (see below) for even longer. (2) Any despised person. "Mr. Spitz [Carl R., the conservative fund-raiser] was contemptuous of some of his contributors, she [Jane Esther McLaughlin, a onetime associate] said, and 'referred to two of his most ardent supporters as Dog Face and Ham Hocks' " (*New York Times,* 2/6/87).

dogfight. A melee, a free-for-all, whether among people, airplanes, or dogs.

dogfish. A sharklike person as well as a small shark.

doggone (it). A nineteenth-century American euphemism for "God damn," from the Scotch *dagone,* gone to the dogs, or perhaps a contraction of *dog on it,* a parallel to the antique *pox on it.*

dog-hearted. "Cruel, pitiless, malicious" (Samuel Johnson, *Dictionary of the English Language,* 1755).

doghouse, in the. In disfavor or disgrace. The *doghouse* that is a kennel or other small enclosure led American soldiers from the time of the Indian Wars to describe their tents as *doghouses, dog tents,* and, the prevailing term today, *pup tents.* And see *dogface* above.

dogie. A stray calf, frequently undernourished, as in the old cowboy song, "Git Along, Little Dogies"; from the 1880s and of obscure origin. A San Antonio stockman told John Lomax that *dogie* came from *doughguts,* used by cowboys to describe motherless calves who developed big stomachs because they were forced to eat grass before they were old enough to digest it (John A. and Alan Lomax, *Folk Song: U.S.A.,* 1975). But note how the connotations of neglect and inferiority in *dogie* tie in with the other linguistic associations with *dog.*

dog in the manger. A person who is so selfish that he will not let others use that which is useless to himself; from a fable by Aesop (ca. 620–560 B.C.) about a dog in a manger full of hay that snarled and bit, thus preventing the horse (or ox) from feeding.

dog Latin. "Barbarous Latin, such as was formerly used by lawyers in their pleadings" (Captain Francis Grose, *A Classical Dictionary of the Vulgar Tongue,* 1796). Variants include *dog English, dog Greek,* and, of course, that byword for inferior poetry, *doggerel,* formerly known as *dog rime.* A classic admonition to a bad poet: "Please curb your doggerel."

dogleg. Crooked, as a fence, a golf hole, or, of an untrustworthy person, "Frank is as straight as a dog's hind leg."

dog robber. An enlisted man who serves as an officer's orderly, valet, gofer, and general factotum; in extended use, a scrounger or sycophant. The term is an Americanism, dating from the Civil War, and seems to have been applied first to cooks, cooks' helpers, and others whose duties allowed them to hang around the mess, devouring all the leftovers and so leaving nothing for the dogs.

dog's age. A long time; synonymous with *hound's age* and *coon's age.* See COON.

dog's body. British: any junior person, especially one assigned to menial jobs; a midshipman in the Royal Navy.

dog's breakfast. A mess, something worthless. "The warders . . . have rejected the latest War Office offer as totally unacceptable. They feel the offer is a bit of a dog's breakfast" (London *Times,* 2/22/63).

dog's chance. The worst possible chance; from Roman times, the *canicula,* or losing throw at dice. See also *Chinaman's chance* in CHINAMAN.

dog's death. A mean and ignominious death, typically by hanging; in extended form, *to die a dog's death* or *die like a dog.*

dog's life. Not much of a life, as evidenced by the common observation when something bad befalls a person that such-and-such *shouldn't happen to a dog.*

dog's meat. "Anything worthless; as a bad book, a common tale, a villainous picture, etc." (J. S. Farmer and W. E. Henley, *Slang and Its Analogues,* 1891). *To eat dog* is to endure disgrace, comparable to eating dirt. See DIRT-EATER.

dog's portion. "A lick and a smell" (Captain Francis Grose, *A Classical Dictionary of the Vulgar Tongue* 1796). The phrase, "he comes in only for a dog's portion," had an additional piquant meaning in Grose's time, referring to "one who is a distant admirer or dangler after women."

dog's rig. "To copulate till you are tired, and then turn tail to it" (Grose, *op. cit.*). Grose did not say so, but in the interest of maintaining the semantic parallel, the copulation probably should be accomplished in the position variously known as *dog fashion, dog-style,* or *dog-ways.*

dog-tired. Very tired indeed.

dogs, to the. Ruination, a bad end; usually what the country, or the younger generation, is said to be going to, since at least the sixteenth century.

dog town. Originally, going back to the 1840s, a town that was overrun by dogs or, in the Western United States, a "town" of prairie dogs. Later, any small (or HICK) town, presumed to have more dogs than people and to be on the squalid side; also called *dogsburg* or—the fictional home of Al Capp's Li'l Abner—*Dogpatch.* See PODUNK.

hot dog. Show off, both as noun and verb. See HOT DOG.

lap dog. A pretty little person, small-minded, with a fierce bark and not much of a bite. "Had I not fed his lap-dog vanity . . . you would be Caroline Merton still" (Edward G. E. L. Bulwer-Lytton, *Alice, or the Mysteries,* 1838). Or, speaking of Vice President George Bush's efforts to ingratiate himself with conservative Republicans: "The unpleasant sound Bush is emitting, as he traipses from one conservative gathering to another is a thin, tinny 'arf'—the sound of a lapdog" (George F. Will, *New York Times,* 2/7/86). See also PUPPY.

mad dog. A crazy person or a malevolent one. ". . . treated for yellow fever or small-pox by this maddog doctor" (New Orleans *Lantern,* 5/7/1887). And speaking of Colonel Muammar el-Qaddafi, the Libyan leader: "Well, we know that this mad dog of the Middle East has a goal of world revolution" (President Ronald Reagan, press conference, 4/9/86). An offshoot of *mad dog* is *the hair of the dog that bit you,* meaning a drink taken to ward off the effects of having drunk too much the night before. This remedy for hangovers derives from the folk belief that hair from a rabid dog will cure a person who has been bitten by one.

red dog. Various negative meanings: a bank note of little or no value; a low grade of flour; and a relatively brainless brand of poker. Also a football maneuver. See RED DOG.

sick as a dog, as. Extremely sick. The phrase recalls the vivid image in *Proverbs*, 26:11: "As a dog returneth to his vomit, so a fool returneth to his folly."

top dog. A leading person, especially one who has gained his position through *dog-eat-dog* competition.

underdog. A person in an apparently losing position; frequently the object of sympathy. "L. Douglas Wilder, who defied predictions when he was elected Lieutenant Governor, has decided to raise money to help other underdogs seeking state or local office anywhere in the country" (AP, 12/3/85).

war dog. One who favors military solutions to political problems; a HAWK. "The gentleman regarded 54° 40′ men as 'war-hawks' and 'war-dogs!' " (*Congressional Globe*, 4/18/1846). The image is Shakespearean, from " 'Cry Havoc,' and let slip the dogs of war" (*Julius Caesar*, 1599).

yellow dog. Originally, a mongrel or cur, and popularized by Abraham Lincoln as a general symbol of inferiority. *Yellow-dog money* once had approximately the same value as *red-dog notes*, above, and *yellow-dog contracts*, since declared illegal, required workers to agree before being hired not to join a union during their term of employment.

See also BITCH, CUR, MONGREL, MUTT, PUPPY, SLUT, WHELP, and YAP.

do-gooder. A reformer, presumably soft-headed. The basic *do-good* has been dated to 1654 (*OED*) but the disparaging political sense appears to be a product of the 1920s. "The do-gooder . . . is all the hokum, all the blather and all the babble of the modern so-called 'social movement' " (*St. Louis Post-Dispatch*, 1/18/27). See also GOO-GOO.

doll. A double-edged endearment, since it relegates the woman to the position of pretty plaything. *Doll* is a pet form of *Dorothy* and has been used as a generic term (similar to MOLL from *Mary*) for any woman, especially a good-looking, empty-headed one, since the sixteenth century. The type specimen is Shakespeare's Doll Tearsheet, one of the denizens of the Boar's Head Tavern (*Henry IV, Part II*, 1596–97). Running a fairly close second is *Baby Doll*, as memorably portrayed by Carroll Baker in the 1956 film of the name, scripted by Tennessee Williams. Then there is the popular *Barbie Doll* (from the toy, of course; b. 1959), better developed physically than intellectually. Thus, speaking of the members of the Old Mission Beach Athletic Club in San Diego, California: "Their drink is the R.C. (rum and cola), their sport varies, and their feminine ideal is the overblown Barbie Doll with just enough sense to keep her pretty trap shut" (*Wall Street Journal*, 8/2/83).

P.S.: When accused of sexism, OMBAC members sigh heavily and say: "It's a nasty job, sexism, but *somebody's* got to do it."

See also BABY and DAME.

dolt. A stupid fellow. "The three greatest dolts in the world: Jesus Christ, Don Quixote, and I" (attributed to Simón Bolívar, 1783–1830). "I absolutely flailed away. I called [Raymond] Katz an amateur, a poseur, a dolt" (David Susskind, recalling an argument with a fellow producer, *New York Times,* 11/10/83). Dating to the seventeenth century, *dolt* appears to be a variant of *dull.* See also DULLARD and DUMB/DUMMY.

donkey. A symbol of stubbornness, stupidity, and the Democratic Party. *Donkey* surfaced as a slang word in the eighteenth century and was soon seized upon by fastidious people as a euphemistic substitute for ASS. Captain Francis Grose made the first known pass at the new word's etymology in *A Classical Dictionary of the Vulgar Tongue,* 1796): "DONKEY, DONKEY DICK. A he or jack ass; called a donkey perhaps from the Spanish or don-like gravity of that animal, intitled also the king of Spain's trumpeter." Other guesses of the word's origin include the possibilites that it derives from *dun* (brown) or from *Duncan,* a name often given by farmers to their asses. As applied to obtuse humans, *donkey* has been elaborated into such forms as *donkeydom, donkeyish, donkeyism,* and *donkeyship,* e.g., "His donkeyship determined / That he would yet have fun" (*St. Nicholas Magazine,* 2/1889). The phrase *donkey's years,* meaning a long time (similar to *coon's age* and *dog's age*) is a play on the length of "donkey's ears." See also ASS and MULE.

dope. A stupid person. "He called President Eisenhower a dope and Senator Eugene McCarthy a skunk" (obituary for publisher William Loeb in his own newspaper, the Manchester [New Hampshire] *Union Leader,* 9/14/81; see also SKUNK). It often is assumed that *dope's* stupid sense derives from the *dope* meaning narcotics, since people under the influence of opium, marijuana, cocaine, etc., tend to act *dopey.* This may simply be a case of linguistic convergence, however. The earliest example of a stupid *dope* comes from an 1851 glossary of words from Cumberland County, England, while the narcotic *dope* seems to be an American innovation, ca. 1870. The latter almost certainly derives from the Dutch *doop,* sauce, that is, a viscous substance, rather than, as has also been suggested, a rhyme with the first syllable of *opium.* The British *dope* seems to be a dialect word of uncertain ancestry. A likely progenitor, considering the derogatory way in which female words often are used, is *dopey,* meaning "A beggar's trull" (Captain Francis Grose, *A Classical Dictionary of the Vulgar Tongue,* 1785). See also DITZ, FOOL, SAD SACK, and YUCK.

dork. An eccentric person, an ODDBALL; also rendered as *doof, dirk,* and *dorf,* with all forms perhaps deriving from *dorbel,* a sixteenth-century term for a DUNCE or OAF. *Dork* also is a euphemism for the penis (analogous to DICK); thus, calling a man a *dork* is comparable to, but less offensive than, calling him a PRICK. See also DING-DONG and NERD.

dotard. An old, senile person, usually a man. "For certes, olde dotard, by your leave, / Ye shal have queynte right ynough at eve" (Geoffrey Chaucer, *Wife of Bath's Prologue,* 1387–1400).

   Dotard derives from *dote,* to act foolishly, to be weak-minded; whence also DOTTY. A *dotard* who rambles on and on may be said to be in his *anecdotage.* On the evidence of the Wife of Bath, the outlook for *dotards* in Chaucer's time was not completely bleak. Modern editions of *The Canterbury Tales* gloss her promised *queynte* variously as "pudendum" (Anchor Books Edition, 1961) and "sex (*lit.* female genitals)" (Signet edition, 1969). These are euphemistic evasions, of course, intended to shield twentieth-century college students from fourteenth-century forthrightness. For more about old people, see FOGY.

dothead. An Indian from India in the United States. The expression surfaced in Jersey City, New Jersey, in the fall of 1987, when local youths escalated their attacks on Indian immigrants from taunting to beating, and its use may be confined to that garden spot in the Garden State. "On the other side of town the other day . . . a group of teenagers giggled and joked about the beatings of 'dotheads' " (*New York Times*, 10/12/87). The same article noted that a letter to *The Jersey Journal*, which declared that "We will go to any extreme to get Indians to move out of Jersey City," was signed "The Dotbusters." The term apparently refers to the *bindi*, the cosmetic dot that Indian women put on their foreheads. See also GOOK.

dotty. Crazy, silly, feebleminded—especially as a result of being in one's *dotage* (a related word). *Dotty* dates to the fifteenth century and has the same root as *dote*, which meant to be crazy, to behave foolishly or stupidly, before being narrowed down to its modern sense of (foolishly?) lavishing extreme love or affection (upon someone). See also DOTARD, FOOL, and GAGA.

double-crosser. Technically, a cheater who cheats cheaters; generally, one who pretends to be a friend or ally while secretly acting otherwise. The term was popularized by gamblers in the early nineteenth century. The idea was to lure one or more people into an unlawful activity (the first *cross*) and then turn the tables on them (the second or *double cross*). For example: "Teemer declared, and Harlan did not deny, that a double cross was brought off. Teemer promised to sell the match, and finishing by selling those who calculated on his losing" (*Referee*, 8/21/1887). See also HEEL and TRAITOR.

double-dealer. A cheat; a sixteenth-century, card-playing metaphor that has gained general currency. "God . . . abhorreth . . . hypocrites and double dealers" (William Baldwin, *A Treatise of Morall Philosophie*, 1547). The word also can be employed to advantage as a verb or past participle. "I'd love to see Ike's face when he finds out that Tricky Dick, his partner in the fight against Democratic corruption, has been on the take for the last 2 years. . . . This should blow that moralizing, unscruplous, double-dealing son-of-a-bitch right out of the water" (*New York Post* editor James Wechsler, in Donald Hook and Lothar Kahn, *The Book of Insults & Irreverent Quotations*, 1980). See also FOUR-FLUSHER, PENNY-ANTE, and SWINDLER.

douche bag. A loathsome person, usually but not necessarily a woman. "Rufus is a douche bag" (*The Purple Rose of Cairo*, film, 1985). The point, of course, is that a male is doubly insulted when labeled with a female pejorative. Technically, the male should be called a *scumbag*. See also BAG and DIRTBAG.

dove. One who favors diplomacy in order to preserve or obtain peace, as distinguished from a HAWK. Doves and hawks use each other's names derisively, with doves generally coming off second-best in such exchanges, it being easier to talk tough than speak meek. The dove is an ancient symbol of peace, gentleness, and innocence. As Christ told his Disciples: "Behold I send you forth as sheep in the midst of wolves: be ye therefore as wise as serpents, and harmless as doves" (*Matthew*, 10:16). See also SERPENT.

In international politics, the dove has been associated with the Communists since Pablo Picasso presented his drawing of a dove of peace to the World Congress of Intellectuals in Wroclaw, Poland, in 1948. Domestically, the dove of peace was one of the symbols of antiwar demonstrators in the 1960s. Meanwhile, the dove-hawk division in American politics dates to the Cuban missile crisis of October 16–28, 1962. "The hawks favored an air strike to eliminate the Cuban missile bases. . . . The doves opposed the air strikes and favored a blockade" (Charles Bartlett and Stewart Alsop, *Saturday Evening Post*, 12/20/62). People who are caught in the middle—who are unsure what to do, or know what to do but fear to take a public stand—are known as *dawks*. See also PIGEON.

doxy. An old word for a loose woman, a beggar's wench, a prostitute, and sometimes, against all odds, a sweetheart. Not commonly encountered today, the word is preserved as if in amber by the remark that Bishop William Warburton (1698–1779) made to the Earl of Sandwich (of hero and grinder fame), when his lordship confessed to some puzzlement about the difference between *orthodoxy* and *heterodoxy*. Quoth the Bishop: "Orthodoxy is my doxy; heterodoxy is another man's doxy" (Joseph Priestly, *Memoirs*, 1831). Dating to the sixteenth century, *doxy* began as a cant word, used by thieves and other lowlifes. It is of uncertain origin, possibly deriving from the Germanic *dukk-*, a bundle, via either English *dock*, once used to mean a person's buttocks (hence *to dock* an animal's tail), or the Dutch *docke*, doll. The word is part of a famous Shakespearean entrance, when the rogue Autolycus opens Scene III, Act IV, of *The Winter's Tale* (1611) with a song:

> When daffodils begin to peer,
> With heigh! the doxy over the dale,
> Why, then comes in the sweet o' the year,
> For the red blood reigns in the winter's pale.

There is some debate of the *dale* part. Most scholars interpret the line to mean the *doxy* is coming over the valley, which may be so. On the other hand, as Gāmini Salgādo has pointed out in *Cony-Catchers and Bawdy Baskets* (1972), *dale* may also be a variant of (or pun upon) *dell*, which is not just a small valleylike depression in the earth, but also another cant word from the same period for a young girl; specifically, a virgin ("a young wench, able for generation, and not yet knowen or broken," Thomas Harman, *A Caueat or Warening for Common Cursetors, Vulgarely Called Vagabones*, 1567). If *dell*, the girl, is meant, then what Autolycus really is saying is that he prefers the experienced *doxy* to the untried *dell*—which seems as likely as the older woman coming across the valley. See also WHORE.

dreck. Junk, filth, or—the politest construction that can be put upon it—DUNG. From the Yiddish *drek*, with the same set of filthy, basically excremental meanings, the term has some of the qualities of a euphemism when introduced into an otherwise all-English conversation. In a Yiddish conversation, however, or among those who are familiar with that tongue, the effect of the word is different. "I would not recommend your using *drek* in front of my mother, much less yours, any more than I would approve of your using the sibilant four-letter English word for excrement" (Leo Rosten, *The Joys of Yiddish*, 1968). See also *TRAYF*.

drip. A dull, stupid person; a DROOP or WET BLANKET. The expression, dated to the 1930s, may derive from the earlier use of the word to mean nonsense, cheap flattery, or sentimental drivel. It appears on both sides of the Atlantic, with the stupid and sentimental senses tending to merge, e.g., "Someone considered over-affectionate is said to be soppy, sloppy, gormless, a drip, or a clot" (Iona and Peter Opie, *The Lore and Language of Schoolchildren*, 1959). See also SAP.

drivel. Stupid, childish language; nonsense. "The most abject drivel that has ever degraded paper" (Wilkie Collins, *The Moonstone*, 1860). Technically, *drivel* is spittle. The term has been applied to nonsense since the fourteenth century as a verb and since the nineteenth as a noun. Synonyms—encompassing words for nonsense as well as saliva—include *dribble*, DRIP, and *drool*. See also BUNK.

drone. An idler, a nonworker, with the strong implication that the *drone* is living off the labor of others; a mindless, boring person. For example, the Reverend Cotton Mather, who had no liking for the president of Harvard, John Leverett, while he was living, termed him after his death in 1724 an *"Infamous Drone"* (Kenneth Silverman, *The Life and Times of Cotton Mather*, 1984). See also INSECT.

droop. An especially languid DRIP, from the 1930s. "Don't be a droop" (Etta Kett cartoon, Topeka *Journal*, 4/23/40). Even worse is the *droopy drawers*—a mess of a person who is about as much fun as a WET BLANKET.

drop dead. An emphatic, scornful denial or rejection, sometimes abbreviated *D.D.* Often used by schoolchildren ("Do me a favor—drop dead!"), the remark is by no means limited to them, e.g., "Ford to City: Drop Dead," the pithy page-one headline with which the New York *Daily News* summed up President Gerald R. Ford's reaction to the city's request for federal aid when it was on the verge of bankruptcy (10/30/75). The headline is recognized as a classic and, as such, is subject to reuse: "New York to the Arts: Drop Dead" (New York *Village Voice*, 5/13/86).

Columnist Jimmy Breslin, who was present at the creation of the original headline, recalled its genesis this way: "Bill Brink wrote it with Mike O'Neill. It came out of the Garson Kanin line in *Born Yesterday*, 'Do me a favor, Harry. Drop dead.' They did it in fun first until they looked at it. Like, 'Here's one—"Ford to City: Drop Dead."' And then someone said, 'Holy Christ, yes! Put it in the paper'" (*New York* magazine, 4/11/88).

drudge. A menial person engaged in menial work, usually of a tedious sort; a HACK or SLAVE. No one ever put it better than the Great Cham of Literature, who defined *lexicographer* as "A writer of dictionaries; a harmless drudge" (Dr. Samuel Johnson, *Dictionary of the English Language*, 1755).

drunk. One who is intoxicated with alcohol—a boozehound, rummy, sot, souse, or wino if habitually so; a state of intoxication, a.k.a. blind, bombed, cockeyed, crocked, loaded, looped, pickled, plastered, polluted, potted, smashed, stewed, stiff, stinking, stoned, wiped out, zonked, and so on, these being only a few of the 350 + synonyms listed for *drunk* in the appendixes to the *Dictionary of American Slang* (Harold Wentworth and Stuart Berg Flexner, 1975). Frequently used in spoken English, e.g., Sam is "drunk," or "drunk as a skunk," or "so drunk he couldn't hit the ground with his hat in three tries," *drunk* does not often appear in print outside of fiction. This is because it is, so to speak, a loaded word—an open invitation to a libel suit. For this reason, newspapers may report that a senator, say, is a *bourbon-and-branchwater congressman*, or that he showed *lack of demeanor*, or that he seemed *tired*, but they almost never venture to refer explicitly to alcoholism unless or until the politician makes a public confession of addiction. Society's nervousness about using the word is also evidenced by the history of the word *drink*, whose past tense, *drank*, often was employed in place of the past participle, *drunk*, during the seventeenth to the nineteenth centuries, apparently because of the latter's alcoholic associations. Thus, even such a great stylist as Dr. Samuel Johnson could write, "He had . . . drank many a flaggon" (*Rambler*, Number 49, 1750).

duck. Any person, typically a low or rascally fellow. "Are you the duck that runs the gospel-mill next door?" (Mark Twain, *Roughing It*, 1872); as a verb, to dodge, avoid, or withdraw, as a duck does when it plunges underwater, and with the implication that he who *ducks* is getting away with something, whether it is a politician *ducking* a question or a bank teller *ducking out* to the race track.

    Duck appears in many combinations—e.g., *lucky duck*, *odd duck*, and *sitting duck*—and sometimes as an endearment, as *duck*, *ducks*, and *ducky*. As a rule, however, the label is to be avoided. Consider, for example:

    dead duck. A person with no chances of success; a goner.

    duck fucker. A possible progenitor of the alliterative exclamation, *fuck-a-duck* and a comparatively old job title, as evidenced by Captain Francis Grose's entry: "DUCK F-CK-R. The man who has the care of poultry on board a ship of war" (*A Classical Dictionary of the Vulgar Tongue*, 1796). The occupational description may be low sailor talk for *duck plucker*, but also has strong overtones of zoophilia.

    duck's disease. A person who has short legs. Grose recorded *duck legs*, with the same meaning, in 1796.

    duck soup. Anything that is easy to accomplish or, when referring to a person, easy to beat or cheat. "Them big yaps are duck soup for me" (Jim Tully, *The Bruiser*, 1936). The expression may derive from the *sitting duck* (see below), which is easy to shoot, or from the soup itself, proverbially easy to make.

    lame duck. An official whose power is limited by the common knowledge that he will leave office after completing his current term—usually. For an exception, consider the murky thought patterns of Alexander M. Haig, when considering the possibility of trying for the Republican presidential nomination: "I'm not throwing my hat into the ring. I don't want to be pushed prematurely into lame-duck status" (*New York Times*, 11/21/85). *Lame duck* started out in the eighteenth century as a British stock market term for jobbers who defaulted on their obligations, went bankrupt, and so limped out of Exchange Alley, with much mornful quacking.

    sitting duck. An easy mark, presumably from the fact that true sportsmen are supposed to shoot at ducks only when they are in flight. "Ever since Sinclair Lewis gave the first lessons in marksmanship, men of the Senator's type have been sitting ducks for the opposition" (*Harper's Magazine*, 4/1948). *Sitting ducks* frequently wind up as *dead ducks*.

See also QUACK.

dud. A worthless person; a LOSER or NEBBISH. "They don't have the guts to say, 'This guy is a dud because he doesn't agree with us,' so they put him through this ritual of being pecked to death by ducks" (Senator Alan K. Simpson [Republican, Wyoming], commenting on the Senate Judiciary Committee's rejection of the nomination of William Bradford Reynolds as associate attorney general, *New York Times*, 6/26/85). The contemptuous human sense has been dated to the early nineteenth century: "Applied to a thowless [spiritless] fellow . . . 'He's a soft dud'" (John Jamieson, *An Etymological Dictionary of the Scottish Language*, 1825). Other negative meanings—a *dud* (or bad) check, a *dud* (counterfeit) coin, a *dud* (unexploded) shell—came later, the *dud* shells being popularized in World War I. The worthless sense derives from *dud* or *dudde*, originally a rough cloak, but since the sixteenth century usually applied to clothes (*duds*), especially old ones or tattered ones. Thus the *dud* (person) is being dismissed, in effect, as an old rag. For similar formations, see BUREAUCRAT and WET BLANKET.

dude. Originally, from the 1880s, an overdressed dandy or fop; later, an Easterner or other citified type who traveled in the West or vacationed on a *dude ranch*, and still later, in our own time and especially among blacks, any young man, without pejorative meaning, unless otherwise specified. (Note that in Black English a *bad dude* may not be "bad" in the conventional sense; see BAD.) *Dude's* origin is not known, though the early emphasis on clothes suggests a connection with *duds*, and it is regarded generally as an Americanism, though the earliest example of its use in the 1972 supplement to the *OED* is from a Canadian newspaper: "The dude is one of those creatures which are perfectly harmless and a necessary evil to civilization" (*Prince Albert Times*, Saskatchewan, 7/4/1883). See also TENDERFOOT.

duffer. An incompetent person; a foolish or stupid one. The connections are not clear, but *duffer* may come from *duff*, thieves' slang from the eighteenth century for something that was worthless or fake—specifically, counterfeit money or goods that were passed off as smuggled or stolen in order to enhance their value. The incompetent *duffer* dates to 1842 (*OED*). Not until the 1890s did *duffers* begin *duffing* shots on golf courses, which they still do. See also FOGY.

dull. Not sharp mentally; stupid. *Dull* was used to describe people's wits several centuries before it was extended to the edges of swords, axes, and what-not ("dole hwette" crops up in a manuscript that was written prior to the year 1000). For emphasis, it has been elaborated into such picturesque expressions as *duller than a widder-woman's ax* and—here a cutting tool, a knife, really is meant—*so dull you could ride to mill on it* (Vance Randolph and George P. Wilson, *Down in the Holler*, 1953). A slow-witted person may also be called a *dullhead* or described as a citizen of *Dullsville* ("Frank is strictly from Dullsville"). A true master of words can make do with *dull* alone, however—as did Samuel Johnson, in characterizing poor Thomas Sheridan: "Why, Sir, Sherry is dull, naturally dull; but it must have taken him a great deal of pains to become what we now see him. Such an excess of stupidity, Sir, is not in Nature" (7/28/1762, from Boswell's *Life of Johnson*).

dullard. A stupid fellow; a fifteenth-century offshoot of DULL and still a useful word. As a former American ambassador to Russia, Malcolm Toon, said when appraising a new General Secretary of the Soviet Communist Party, Konstantin U. Chernenko: "The only impression I formed is that he was a dullard" (*New York Times*, 2/14/84). See also DOLT and DUMB/DUMMY.

dumb/dummy. Stupid; a brainless person. "Jerry Ford is so dumb that he can't fart and chew gum at the same time" (Lyndon B. Johnson, in Richard Reeves, *A Ford Not a Lincoln*, 1975). "I've learned some stunning slurs [while chauffering preschoolers] that would get special attention in an adult context. 'Diaper Dummy,' 'Cereal Head' and 'Stink Brain' are among my favorites" (Susan Baumann, *Litchfield County* [Connecticut] *Times*, 2/13/87).

Originally, going back to ca. 1000, a *dumb* person was one who lacked the power of speech. The extension of the word's meaning is in keeping with the popular assumption that people who can't express themselves must not understand anything either.

Dumb makes an excellent prefix or intensifier. For example: *dumb-ass, dumbbell, dumb blonde, dumb bunny, dumb cluck, dumb Dora, dumb-dumb* (a reduplication sometimes rendered as *dum-dum*, perhaps through confusion with the soft-headed bullet, which obtained its name, however, from Dum Dum, a town near Calcutta, where it was first manufactured at a British arsenal), *dumbhead* (a translation of *dummkopf*; see BLOCKHEAD), *dumb Isaac, dumb ox*, and *rumdum* (a stupid person as well as a drunkard). Variations include *dumbo* (also a person with big ears, thanks to the baby elephant whose ears were so large he used them as wings to fly in the 1941 Walt Disney cartoon film, *Dumbo*), and, of course, *dummy*, a sixteenth-century derivative of *dumb*, which also referred originally to muteness—*pace* Charlie McCarthy—rather than stupidity. See also DODO, LAMEBRAIN, and MORON.

dump. A run-down, shabby place, from *dump* in the sense of a heap of refuse, a.k.a. a sanitary landfill. "Do you think if I had any money I'd be living in a dump like the Chateau Blissac?" (P. G. Wodehouse, *Hot Water*, 1932). The word has acquired other unsavory meanings. For example *to take a dump* is to perform an act of defecation; *to dump* a fight or other contest is to lose it on purpose; *to dump* [*someone*] is to get rid of a person; and *to dump on* or *all over* [*someone*] is to criticize a person severely or to overwhelm the person with complaints or the like. Computer programmers have carried this last expression one step further, e.g., "Later she told a friend she had 'core dumped' on the boss. Translation: She had got everything off her chest, really unloaded" (*New York Times*, 2/19/84). All these meanings flow naturally from the word's earliest, thirteenth-century senses of a sudden fall or plunge, after which the thing dumped becomes refuse. To be melancholy or *down in the dumps* is another matter. Captain Francis Grose passed along the tongue-in-cheek explanation that this phrase derived "from Dumpos, a king of Egypt, who died of melancholy" (*A Classical Dictionary of the Vulgar Tongue*, 1796), but it seems more likely that this *dump* comes from the Dutch *domp*, a haze (the melancholy mind is gloomy), and a cognate to *damp*, whose oldest senses are of a vapor or mist—and a poisonous one at that.

dunce. A stupid fellow, a dimwit. "Blockhead! dunce! ass! coxcomb! were the best epithets he gave poor John" (John Arbuthnot, *The History of John Bull*, 1712). The term is an eponym, derived from the name of the great scholastic theologian, John

Duns Scotus (1265?–1308). Noted for his ingenious reasoning (his defense of the doctrine of Immaculate Conception earned him the title *Doctor Subtilis*), the influence of Scotus remained strong enough two centuries after his death for the rising humanists and reformers of the early sixteenth century to attack his followers as *Duns men* or *dunces*. The epithet initially referred to the hair-splitting arguments of the *Scotists*, as *they* called themselves, but the emphasis soon shifted, making the *dunce* a figure of ridicule in the modern sense before the century was out. See also *pointy head* in BLOCKHEAD.

dung. An execrable person. In the early years of the labor movement, in the eighteenth and nineteenth centuries, a *dung* was equivalent to the modern SCAB, that is, a person who continued to work while his fellows were on strike. Among tailors, in particular, a *dung* was one who agreed to be paid by piecework rather than by the day. The basic *dung* dates to before 1000 in the sense of decayed matter or manure for fertilizing the soil. By the thirteenth century, it was being applied to anything that was morally filthy, vile, loathsome, or contemptible. See also DINGE and SHIT.

dunghill. An expansion of DUNG from the sixteenth century. John Spencer caught the full flavor of the term in the second edition of his *Discourse Concerning Prodigies* (1665), terming "Paracelsus . . . a walking Dunghil (so offensive and corrupt his life)." From the sixteenth through the nineteenth centuries, a *dunghill* also was a coward and *to die dunghill* was to die a cowardly death, especially by repenting just before one was to be hanged. These expressions alluded to the *dunghill cock* or *dunghill craven*, which was the ordinary barnyard bird rather than a fighting game-cock. See also COCK, COWARD, and CRAVEN.

dupe. A person who is easy to fool or to trick into taking the part of another (a Communist *dupe*, for instance). The word surfaced in the early fifteenth century as underworld argot, a borrowing from the French *dupe*, in turn a contraction of *de huppe*, of a hoopoe—the hoopoe being an Old World bird, about the size of a thrush, that is supposed to be on the stupid side. The name of the hoopoe and, thus, the word *dupe* derives ultimately from the bird's cry—variously rendered as "Up-up" or "Hoop-hoop." See also DODO.

Dutch. A pejorative label pinned by English speakers on almost anything they regard as inferior, irregular, or contrary to "normal" (i.e., their own) practice.

The disparaging use of *Dutch* dates to the seventeenth century, when the English and the Dutch were building rival empires. (See also BOOR and BUMPKIN.) In the United States, the use of *Dutch* may have been facilitated through confusion with *Deutsch*, immigrant Germans making obvious targets for verbal abuse by red-white-and-blue-blooded Americans of one or two generations' standing. The Dutch themselves spoke English well enough to understand the unsavory connotations of the label and in 1934 Dutch officials were ordered by their government to stop using the term *Dutch*. Instead, they were to rewrite their sentences so as to employ the official *The Netherlands*. This edict made a few ripples on the linguistic pond but had no lasting effects, which is hardly surprising, given the profusion of *Dutch* phrases that have become part of the English language over the past three centuries. Among them:

Dutch act. Suicide. Thus, referring to a woman found hanging from a chande-
lier: "Some woman did a Dutch act at the Shepherd Arms" ("Kojak," WNEW-TV,
New York City, 2/19/82). *Dutch act* may derive from *do a Dutch*; see below.

Dutch(man's) anchor. Anthing left at home, especially when badly needed; from
the presumably apocryphal Dutch sea captain who explained, after his vessel went
onto the rocks, that he actually had a very good anchor but had left it at home.

Dutch angle. In filmmaking, a camera angle that deviates sharply from the
normal vertical or horizontal axis.

Dutch auction. A reverse auction in which goods are offered at progressively
lower prices until finally a bidder is found.

Dutch backgammon. A variation of the standard game in which it is advantageous
to roll low numbers with the dice instead of high ones.

Dutch bargain. A one-sided bargain, i.e., no bargain at all.

Dutch barn. One that has no sides, the roof being supported by pillars only.

Dutch bath. A sponge bath.

Dutch, beat the. An expression of astonishment or incredulity, as in "Doesn't that
beat the Dutch!"

Dutch book. A bookie, usually a small-time operator who is so dumb that he
consistently loses money; to *dutch a book* is the act of fouling up so badly that the
bookie will lose no matter which horse wins or, craftily, a scheme by others to
arrange their bets so that the bookie will lose and be driven out of business.

Dutch cap. A diaphragm, partly due to its resemblance to a small cap but also to
its popularization in Holland (though invented by a German, Dr. Wilhelm Mensinga)
through the work of the world's first birth-control clinic, opened there by Aletta
Jacobs in 1882. The *Dutch* epithet in this case is also in keeping with the common
tendency to give credit for sexually related breakthroughs to foreign nations, e.g.,
the CONDOM, known in England as the *French letter* and in France as *une capote anglaise*
(where capote = hooded cloak), and syphilis, known variously as the *French disease,
English disease, Spanish disease,* etc.

Dutch cape. A mirage; land that a sailor imagines seeing on the horizon.

Dutch cheer. Liquor.

Dutch clock. Depending on context, a bedpan or a wife.

Dutch comfort (or *consolation*). Cold comfort; in effect, "Thank God it's no worse."

Dutch concert. A hubbub, everyone playing or singing a different tune at once,
especially as a result of having had too much to drink

Dutch courage. False courage, inspired by liquor; also the liquor itself. "He
imbibes four doses of Dutch courage . . . Club members gather round and stand
him to further applications of 86-proof pluck" (*New York Times Magazine,* 3/18/84).
Also called *Geneva courage,* from the Dutch *jenever,* gin, and ultimately from the
Latin *juniperus,* juniper, the berry used to flavor it.

Dutch defense. A fake defense; retreat or surrender. In chess, the *Dutch defense* also
is a sham, but there the purpose is to attack, not retreat. This aggressive defense
was discussed in detail as early as 1779 in *Nouvel essai sur les echecs* by Elias Stein, a
resident of—where else?—Holland.

Dutch, do a. Run away, desert, in the sense of *French leave* (known to the French
as *filer à l'anglaise*); also a synonym for *Dutch act.*

Dutch, double (or *high*). Gibberish, or something that sounds like it, whether a
foreign language or English that is phrased so complicatedly as to seem nonsensical. In jump roping: the use of two ropes at once.

Dutch draught (or *drink*). A big swig; specifically, one that empties the cup or glass.

Dutch feast. A party at which the host gets drunk before the guests do.

Dutch flapdragon. "Dutch flapdragons, healths [drunk in] urine" (Thomas Middleton, *A Trick to Catch the Old One*, ca. 1606).

Dutch, get up one's. To become angry.

Dutch gold. An inferior alloy of copper and zinc, comparable to *German silver*, which is made of the same ingredients plus nickel.

Dutch grocery. An ill-kept grocery store.

Dutch have taken Holland, the. An old catchphrase for putting down the bearer of stale news, similar to, "Well, what do you know—Queen Anne [or Bess, or Mary, depending upon one's century] is dead."

Dutch headache. The aftermath of a *Dutch feast*; a hangover.

Dutch husband. A bed bolster.

Dutch, in. (1) In trouble or disfavor; (2) in prison; (3) pregnant.

Dutch leave. To desert; see *Dutch, do a* (above).

Dutchman if I do, I'll be a. A very strong refusal by an Englishman, meaning he would rather be a contemptible Dutchman than do whatever is asked.

Dutch medley. See *Dutch concert*.

Dutch, my old. A wife. Eric Partridge believed this to be a condensed form of "my old Dutch clock" (*A Dictionary of Slang and Unconventional English*, 1970). Another possibility is that it comes from *duchess*.

Dutch nightingale. A frog.

Dutch pennant. A frayed rope (nautical).

Dutch reckoning. An unitemized bill. "A verbal or lump account, without particulars, as brought at spunging or bawdy houses" (Captain Francis Grose, *A Classical Dictionary of the Vulgar Tongue*, 1796).

Dutch rose. The mark made when a sloppy carpenter misses a nail and dents the wood.

Dutch route. Suicide again.

Dutch sale. One that is made at low prices after the goods were offered for high ones; see *Dutch auction*.

Dutch steak. Hamburger.

Dutch straight. In poker, not a real straight, but one that is comprised of all even cards, as in 2, 4, 6, 8, 10, or all odd ones, as 3, 5, 7, 9, Jack; also called a *skip straight*.

Dutch, to talk. To speak gibberish.

Dutch treat. No treat at all, since each person is paying his or her own way. Variations include *Dutch date*, *Dutch lunch*, *Dutch supper*, and *Dutch party*.

Dutch turnpike. A roadway made by laying logs side by side, usually over marshy ground; a corduroy road.

Dutch uncle. Not a real uncle, but someone who has close enough standing to be able to speak plainly and severely, without too fine a regard for the listener's feelings.

Dutch widow. A whore.

Dutch wife. Originally a bed bolster, similar to a *Dutch husband*, but latterly a contrivance for masturbating with; occasionally, a full-scale replica, e.g., "He will liberate man from dependence on the opposite sex by constructing what seems to be known in Japan as a 'Dutch wife'; a kind of life-size mechanical doll with built-in electric heating and all the other refinements" (*Guardian*, 5/19/67).

So pity the Dutch, but before shedding all your tears for them, see also what English speakers have done to CHINESE, FRENCH, GERMAN, GREEK, IRISH, ITALIAN, MEXICAN, RUSSIAN, SCOTCH, SPANISH, SWEDE, WELSH, and even, for that matter, ENGLISH.

dweeb. A loathsome person; a CREEP or NERD. "Sandy is not some mere tedious South Street Seaport–frequenting, Ralph Lauren–encased, doorman-tipping dweeb who you would expect because, her life is so profoundly meaningless, to fall off the deep end of obsession" (New York *Village Voice,* 11/1/88). Popularized by teenagers, *dweeb* is of mysterious origin but appears, on the face of it, to be related to TWEEB.

dyke (or **dike**). A lesbian, especially a large, mannish, aggressive one, also called a *bulldyke* or *diesel dyke.* "Ann's 440, where Lenny opened in January of 1958 was a typical dyke toilet . . . a dark, clammy rendezvous for the femmes and butches" (Albert Goldman, *Ladies and Gentlemen, Lenny Bruce!!,* 1974). Originally a disparaging term, the word is gradually gaining respectability, at least among those who choose to flaunt their homosexuality, e.g., "Today the philanthropic North Star organization helps *Dykes Opposed to Nuclear Technology,* lesbians with small children are banded together in *Dykes and Tykes,* a lesbian newspaper is *Big Apple Dyke News*" (Leonard R. N. Ashley, "Dyke Diction," *Maledicta,* 1982).

The etymology of *dyke* is extremely obscure. It has been suggested that the word is a shortening of *hermaphrodite,* via *morphodite* and *morphodike,* all of which have long histories of use in a homosexual (but male) sense. Another possibility is that the term derives from *dike* meaning "to overdress," "to wear fancy clothes," *diked out* having been used in the same way as *decked out* in the United States since the 1840s. Arguing against both these theories is the fact that the word appears first in the long forms, *bulldiker* and *bulldyking,* both used in the 1920s by American blacks. No African antecedents have been found for the term, however, which leads to the possibility that this is basically just another backcountry, barnyard word, perhaps a combination of BULL and DICK.

E

eat. To partake of oral-genital sex. "But parents like the 36-year-old Mrs. Gore [wife of the Democratic senator from Tennessee]—many of whom grew up with rock 'n' roll—contend that a new degree of licentiousness has corrupted mainstream rock, [such as] 'Eat Me Alive,' a Judas Priest song that critics say described sex forced at gunpoint" (*Wall Street Journal*, 7/31/85). The sexual meaning of *eat*, an entirely innocent word in most contexts, is of uncertain antiquity but almost universally known. ("Almost" because this sense is missing from the *Oxford English Dictionary*'s 1972 supplement—the editors missed BLOW, too.) The oldest example of the sexual sense in the *Dictionary of American Slang* (1967) is from a novel published as recently as 1951, but a glossary of "Prostitutes and Criminal Argots," compiled by David W. Maurer in 1939 included "to EAT PUSSY. Cunnilingus" (*Language of the Underworld*, 1981).

Chances are the term had been around for a while when Maurer recorded it, since it fits closely with a host of other food metaphors for sex, particularly those in which the woman is regarded as a comestible or *dish* of some sort. Among them: *angel cake, baby cake, cherry pie* (*pie* alone is the vulva, also called *fur pie* or *hair pie*; see also CHERRY), *cookie, cupcake, cutie pie, dumpling, eatin' stuff* (also called *table grade*), *furburger* (commonly is known as a *box lunch*), *honey, honey bun, honey bunch, honey pie, hot* (or *sweet*) *patootie* (probably a play on *potato*, though *patootie* also is slang for the buttocks), *jelly roll* (see JAZZ), *lamb chop, lambie pie, muffin, peach, peaches, poundcake, sugar, sugar plum, sweetie pie, sweetums,* TAMALE, TART, *tomato,* and *white meat* (see WHITEY). Certainly, it did not take rock lyrics of the 1980s to introduce middle-class kids to the sexual meaning of *eat*. Witness the jokes that were making the rounds among high schoolers in the early 1950s in Westchester, New York:

> Q. What do you call a happy Roman?
> A. Gladiator.
>
> and
>
> Q. What is the square root of 69?
> A. Eight something.

More seriously, for what it says about our sexual hang-ups and the workings of the law, this is one of the words that got nightclub comedian Lenny Bruce in trouble—even though he translated it into another language! Thus, when Bruce opened at the Troubadour in West Hollywood on October 17, 1962 (the supposedly liberated 1960s), a detective in the crowd—especially chosen for the assignment because of his knowledge of Yiddish—took notes, which formed the basis of an official police report:

> During the course of the suspect's narration, he uttered obscene and offensive words including a reference to his ex-wife as being the type that

became upset when he entered the bathroom while she was "fressing" the maid. The term "fressing" is Yiddish and means "eating." . . . Throughout his narration suspect interjected the terms "schmuck" and "putz," which are Yiddish, and mean "penis." Suspect also used the word "shtup," a Yiddish word meaning sexual intercourse when used in the context the suspect used it. Also uttered during the narration by suspect were, etc., etc., etc.

Neither the Yiddish words nor the various Anglo-Saxon ones that the suspect used seemed to offend any of the people who had paid to hear his routine, but Bruce was subsequently arrested. (One wonders how many murders were committed in LA while the police busied themselves taking notes on Bruce.)

Perhaps the word eventually will rate an entry in the supplement to the supplement to the *OED*. *Fress* might deserve an entry, too. It has connotations of eating quickly and noisily; it's from the German *fress*, to devour.

For more about foods, see KRAUT.

egghead. An intellectual. "Adlai Stevenson once told what it was like to be the rare intellectual in politics. '*Via ovicapitum dura est*,' he said; the way of the egghead is hard" (*New York Times*, 10/28/82).

Egghead was popularized as a term for attacking intellectuals during the 1952 presidential campaign by the syndicated columnist Stewart Alsop, who had picked it up from his brother John. The remark was occasioned by a speech on atomic energy that Stevenson, the Democratic candidate, made in Hartford, Connecticut, on September 18. Impressed by the number of Republicans in the crowd who obviously approved of the speech, Stewart asked his brother, then working for the Republican candidate, Dwight D. Eisenhower, if this boded well for the GOP. But John wasn't worried. "Sure, Stew," he said, "all the eggheads are for Stevenson, but how many eggheads are there?" (*Saturday Evening Post*, 9/8/62). Stewart used the quote in his column, attributing it to a "rising Connecticut Republican," and it was quickly repeated elsewhere. John later told his brother that "the word sprang unbidden into his mind, with a mental image of a thin outer shell with mushy white stuff underneath." Stevenson tried to laugh off the epithet, saying, "Eggheads of the world unite; you have nothing to lose but your yolks," but this was wrong, as he also lost the election. This was not the first time the word was used, however, in a disparaging manner. For example, William Safire, with the help of one of his correspondents, tracked down a letter, written about 1918, in which Carl Sandburg reported that " 'Egg heads' is the slang here [Chicago] for editorial writers" (Safire, *I Stand Corrected*, 1984). At about this time, too, the novelist Warwick Deeping mentioned "A little eggheaded pedant" (*Second Youth*, 1919). One of the characters in the 1933 film *Hallelujah, I'm a Bum* also is called *egghead*—and it is of interest that Ben Hecht, coauthor of the screenplay, worked for the *Chicago Daily News* at the same time as Sandburg.

The idea of referring to a person as an egg is quite old, of course. "What, you egg! Young fry of treachery!" (William Shakespeare, *Macbeth*, 1606). People also have been characterized as being *bad eggs, good eggs, rotten eggs,* and *tough eggs;* as being *hard-boiled* and *soft-boiled;* and thanks to the nursery rhyme, as being *Humpty-Dumpties.*

Egg also is featured in proverbial expressions and comebacks, e.g., *to have egg on [one's] face,* to be embarrassed; *teach your grandmother to suck eggs,* said to one who presumes to give advice to a more experienced person; and *to lay an egg*, to fail, especially in the theater when a joke or an entire show, falls flat, and which perhaps derives from *duck's egg* or *goose egg* as a symbol for *zero*. Or, *to lay an egg* may derive from a nineteenth-century minstrel show joke. This possibility was suggested by Sherwood Cummings in *American Speech* (12/54), who cited Mark Twain's account in his autobiography of the routine:

> One of the things which always delighted the audience of those days [ca. 1850] until the minstrels wore it threadbare, was "Bones's" account of the perils which he had once endured during a storm at sea. The storm lasted so long that in the course of time all the provisions were consumed. Then the middleman would inquire anxiously how the people managed to survive.
>
> "Bones" would reply, "We lived on eggs."
>
> "You lived on eggs! Where did you get the eggs?"
>
> "Every day, when the storm was so bad, the Captain laid *to*."
>
> During the first five years that joke convulsed the house, but after that the population of the United States had heard it so many times that they respected it no longer and always received it in a deep and reproachful and indignant silence, along with the others of its caliber, which had achieved disfavor by long service.

See also INTELLECTUAL, LONGHAIR, and the *pointy head* in BLOCKHEAD.

eightball. A stupid person, a bumbler, especially one in trouble all the time (from *behind the eightball*, wherein the shooter in some forms of pool is in a bad position when the eight ball is between the cue ball and the ball he is supposed to pocket); also, a derogatory term for a black person. " 'Well, if you ask me, Barney is a combination of eight-ball, mick, and shonicker [Jew],' said McArdle . . ." (James T. Farrell, *Young Lonigan*, 1932.

elephant. A large person, with the implication that the person is clumsy, which is actually not true of real elephants, as they are quite graceful beasts. Two subspecies of the *elephant* family are the *rogue elephant* and the *white elephant*. The first beast is a loner, prone to violent rampages, e.g., "More than one Congressman has described the Central Intelligence Agency as a 'rogue elephant' " (*New York Times*, 6/13/85). The *white elephant*, in the sense of a costly or burdensome possession, goes back to the story that the kings of Siam would ruin a courtier they didn't like by presenting him with one of these animals, which had to be kept in sumptuous style because they were so greatly venerated. See also ROGUE.

elitist. Antidemocratic. To be among society's *elite*, or chosen, is one thing—usually a good thing—but to open oneself to a charge of being *elitist*, or of *elitism*, is to take a bath in very hot water. " 'Elitist' means a very inbred group of very rich people who go around telling everybody else what to do and how to suffer" (Edward I. Koch, *Mayor: An Autobiography*, 1984). Or as Sydney H. Schanberg said, commenting on the New York City mayor's *Mayor*: "He reserves his highest disdain and stereotyping for those he groups as 'liberals.' He calls them 'radicals' and 'elitists' and 'ideologues' and 'nuts and crazies' " (*New York Times*, 1/21/84). The application of the term is not limited to political controversies. For example, Jacques Barzun jumped on this word when he entered a dispute about the way history textbooks are written: "One is entitled to wonder how recently Joseph Gies has read the great historians he condemns as elitist and concerned only with battles and kings. . . . As to that purely pejorative word 'elitism,' it is clear that if the succession of events is the object of history, it must put forward the people who made things happen, the movers and shakers of the world" (letter, *New York Times*, 1/13/88). See also INTELLECTUAL and LIBERAL.

English. Not often used in a pejorative manner by speakers of English, the principal modern exception being the *English* (or *British*) *disease* (or *sickness*), which is a state of economic ill health, manifested by low productivity, e.g., "My honest opinion is that half this country [Australia] is coming down with the English disease: no one wants to work anymore" (Dr. Dennis Mackey, *Columbia Journalism Review*, 1-2/87). This fairly new *disease* should not be confused with the older (from the eighteenth century) *English malady* or *melancholy*, which is to suffer from the spleen, i.e., to be in low spirits, a complaint once regarded as being typically English.

The weakness of the English for flogging also is reflected in *English arts, culture,* or *guidance*, which are phrases that appear regularly, in ads of a very personal nature, as in "I am a dominant gal interested in submissive men. Let me turn you on to the delights of Eng arts. Must be sincere and generous. SASE 6791" (*Ace*, undated, ca. 1976). Other nationalities are rather harder on the English. The French, in particular, have devised opprobrious phrases for their traditional enemies, for example: *damné comme un Anglais*, damned as an Englishman; *méchant comme un Anglais*, ill-natured as an Englishman; *une capote anglaise*, literally, an English cloak, but actually what English-speakers call *a French letter; dents à l'anglaise*, buck teeth; *faire un lit à l'anglaise*, to make a bed the English way, i.e., not to bother to remove the covering; and *filer à l'anglaise*, to slip away or, as the English say, *to take French leave*. See also DUTCH and LIMEY.

eunuch. A man without balls, a weakling. "Screw the critics. They're like eunuchs. They can tell you how to do it, but they can't do it themselves" (Harry Cohn, 1891–1958, head of Columbia Pictures, in Norman Zierold, *The Moguls*, 1969). The man without testicles often is regarded as being so easily swayed as to lack principles as well; hence, the common phrases, *ideological eunuch, intellectual eunuch,* or *political eunuch*. For example: "The intellectual eunuch Castlereagh" (Byron, *Don Juan*, dedication, 1819), and, in our own time, Vice President Spiro Agnew's attack on Eastern Establishment types, whom he characterized as "ideological eunuchs, whose most comfortable position is straddling the fence" (speech, New Orleans, Louisiana, 10/19/69). Neither Byron nor Agnew, however, came close to matching Robert Burns, who used *eunuch* as the springboard for a remarkable assault (ca. 1791) on a critic, whose only good fortune is that he has remained unidentified: "Thou eunuch of language: thou butcher, imbruing [staining with blood] thy hands in the bowels of orthography: thou arch-heretic in pronunciation: thou pitch-pipe of affected emphasis: . . . thou pimp of gender: thou scape-gallows from the land of syntax: thou scavenger of mood and tense: . . . thou pickle-herring in the puppet-show of nonsense" (in Nat Shapiro, *ed., Whatever It Is I'm Against It*, 1984). See also INTELLECTUAL, SNOB, SPINELESS, and for Byron's epitaph for Castlereagh, PISS.

extremist. A nonmoderate, especially in politics; almost always disparaging whether referring to radicals of the left or the right. Only one major American politician has dared portray himself as an *extremist* in recent years, and that was Barry Goldwater, who proclaimed when accepting the Republican presidential nomination on July 16, 1964: "... *extremism in the defense of liberty is not vice! ... moderation in the pursuit of justice is not virtue!*" (italics in original). And Goldwater lost big. "Americans hate 'extremists' of all varieties. 'Left-wing extremists,' 'right-wing extremists,' 'moderate extremists' —Americans make no distinction. 'Extremists' are despicable" (Russell Baker, *New York Times Magazine,* 8/16/87). See also KOOK, LEFT, RADICAL, REACTIONARY, and RIGHT-WINGER.

Eyetalian (also **Eyetie, Eyeto, Eytie**). Italian, naturally; an Americanism, dated to 1840, which has since spread to other English-speaking peoples who have encountered Italians either in domestic life or on the battlefield. "The signor Brinio from Summerhill, the eyetallyano papal zouave to the Holy Father, has left the quay and gone to Moss Street" (James Joyce, *Ulysses,* 1922). See also ITALIAN. The *OED* labels *Eyetalian* a "jocular" formation, which is giving the term's users considerable benefit of doubt, as *Ayrabs, Scandihuvians,* and others usually fail to appreciate the playful humor of having their ethnic or national names mispronounced. See also HEBE, INJUN, and NIGGER.

eyewash. Nonsense, as in *that's so much eyewash.* Frequently the implication is that the nonsense is intended to flatter or fool the eye. *Eyewash* is weaker than *hogwash;* technically, it classes as *soft soap.* As nonsense, the term has been dated to the 1880s. It parallels, and perhaps derives from, an older expression of disbelief, *all my eye (and Betty Martin).* The origin of the last, which appears first in the short form, *all my eye,* in Oliver Goldsmith's *Good Natur'd Man* (1768), has been the subject of much speculation. It probably is *not* a vulgar post-Reformation rendering of a Roman Catholic prayer to St. Martin, patron saint of drunkards, beginning "O *mihi, beate Martine,*" a theory whose plausibility is dampened somewhat by the fact that no such prayer exists in the Breviary. Rather, *all my eye* and *eyewash* have more in common with the French *mon oeil,* which often is accompanied by a knowing wink or the pointing of a finger to the eye to emphasize that one doesn't believe a word of what has just been said—that it is just so much nonsense. See also BALONEY.

F

fag. A male homosexual. "Joyously they revel in the politics of hate, with plangent attacks on blacks and/or fags and/or liberals . . . (Gore Vidal, *Nation*, 3/22/86).

Fag generally is regarded as an Americanism, but its etymology is indecently obscure. One school of thought is that it is a clipping of *faggot*, with the same meaning. Another is that this kind of *faggot* might be an extension of *fag*. Arguing in favor of the first theory is that the homosexual *faggot* (1914) is slightly older than *fag* (1923), at least as far as the written record goes. Other possibilities abound, however. For example it has been suggested: (1) that the homosexual sense derives from the *fag* that is a cigarette, the point being that smoking cigarettes, as opposed to cigars, once was considered effeminate (note how the decadent Lord Henry Wotton is seen lying on a divan, smoking one cigarette after another, in the opening of Oscar Wilde's *The Picture of Dorian Gray*, 1891); (2) that it is a spin-off from, or perhaps reinforced by, the *fag* who performs menial tasks for older students in British public schools, where homosexuality is not unknown; (3) that it alludes to the faggots that fueled the fires in which sodomists and other heretics once were burned; and (4), a very long stretch indeed, that the modern meaning is due in part to *Fagin*, the corrupter of boys in Charles Dickens' *Oliver Twist* (1837–39). Then again, *faggot* also is an old term of abuse for a woman (*OED*, 1591); here, the woman is being dismissed as, in effect, a bundle of sticks. The metaphor has continued in service into the twentieth century, e.g., "That old faggot Mrs. Riordan" (James Joyce, *Ulysses*, 1922). Meanwhile, *to faggot* was nineteenth-century British slang for "To copulate; also to frequent the company of loose women" (J. S. Farmer and W. E. Henley, *Slang and Its Analogues*, 1893). The attractive thing about deriving the homosexual *fag* from the feminine-copulatory senses is that this makes a nice parallel with GAY, which also referred to the seamy side of heterosexual sex before it became a homosexual word.

Today, the principal difference between *fag* and *faggot* from a sexual standpoint is that the former is regarded as the more pejorative (as is true of diminutives and clippings generally; see JAP and PADDY, for instance). *Faggot* also has been used defiantly within the gay community, e.g., "Larry Kramer, author of *Faggots* (a semi-autobiographical novel about Fred Leamish, 'a 39-year-old faggot who must find true love by 40') . . . knows *faggot* is an insult, but he calls himself a *faggot* and shrugs, 'I'm pretty thick-skinned' " (Leonard R. N. Ashley, *Maledicta*, Winter 1979). The conversion of a derogatory term into a battle cry by radicals is not uncommon; for instance, see also DYKE and YANKEE. For emphasis, *fag* and *faggot* may also be elaborated into *faggotry, faggoty, fagocite, flaming faggot* (remembering those heretics), and *superfag*. A *fag hag* is a heterosexual woman who keeps company with homosexual men (see also HAG); a *fag bag* is a heterosexual woman who marries one. To call someone a *three-letter man* is another way of saying he is a *f-a-g*. And despite *faggot's* acceptance by some radicals, the short term remains very much a fighting word, e.g., "In 1978, Coonan and Featherstone were accused of killing Harold Whitehead—for calling a friend of theirs 'a fag'—in the middle of a crowded bar" (*New York Times Magazine*, 4/5/87). See also QUEER.

fairy. A gay man, especially one with feminine traits. ". . . [Cecil] Beaton was a true confessor, at least to his diary. Every time he was called a 'fairy,' a 'lulu,' a 'pansy,' a 'gladiola' or a 'queer,' he recorded the dreadful moment and squirmed a second time, on the diary page" (*New York Times Book Review*, 6/15/86). Or, an example of college humor in the early 1950s: "Q. Why do they have to nail all the windows at Harvard shut? A. To keep the fairies from flying out" (witticism, New Haven, Connecticut, ca. 1952). See also PANSY and QUEER.

Fairy's homosexual sense seems to be an American contribution to the language. The earliest known mention of the term occurs in the article "Sex and Art," by Colin A. Scott, in the January 1896 issue of *The American Journal of Psychology*: "Coffee-clatches, where the members dress themselves with aprons, etc., and knit, gossip and crochet; balls, where men adopt the ladies' evening dress are well known in Europe. 'The Fairies' of New York are said to be a similar secret organization. The avocations which inverts follow are frequently feminine in their nature." Independent confirmation of the existence of this "secret organization," also called the Circle Hermaphroditos, comes from *The Female Impersonators* (1922), an autobiographical work by Earl Lind (*pseud.*): "On one of my earliest visits to Paresis Hall [in New York City]—about January 1895—I seated myself at one of the tables. I had only recently learned that it was the androgyne headquarters—or 'fairie' as it was called at the time." Before being taken over by homosexuals, *fairy* had been a feminine word, referring in British slang to a debauched and/or ugly old woman, as in:

> Madame du Barry was a lively old fairy
> Who sold herself to the king;
> She got jewels and riches
> While other poor bitches
> Stayed pure and never got a thing.

In American slang, where the homosexual sense seems to have arisen, a *fairy* might also be debauched, but younger, as a girl who flits from man to man, e.g., "Poor Charles Earnest is so stuck on a fairy named Emma Brown that she can make him do anything she wishes" (New Orleans *Lantern*, 10/20/86). See also FLIT. Such gender changes, from feminine to homosexual, occur regularly (see GAY), mirroring the sex changes in other words, from male to female (see HARLOT).

fancy-pants. A sissy, a common insult from one child to another; also, an effete, overdressed man, as in *Fancy Pants* (film, 1950), a remake of *Ruggles of Red Gap* (1935), in which an English valet (Charles Laughton and then Bob Hope) winds up in the rugged American West. See also SISSY.

fancy-shmancy. Too fancy, pretentious. In the blending of Yiddish and English to form Yinglish, the sounds *sh-* (or *sch-*) and *shm* are used to deride and mock the words to which they are prefixed, as in *Santa-Shmanta* (attributed to Jack Paar, ca. 1962); the classic "Cancer-shmancer, as long as you're healthy," and Herblock's

141

takeoff on it, "Mutations, Smutations—Long As You're Healthy" (a cartoon on the Atomic Energy Commission, noted in *American Speech*, 12/61). Then there is the woman who told a friend that her son apparently had an Oedipus complex. "Oedipus-schmoedipus," said the friend, "so long as he loves his mother." See also SCHLEMIEL, SCHMUCK, and SCHNOOK.

fart. (1) to expel internal gas through the anus, or the discharge itself. "To break wind behind" (Samuel Johnson, *Dictionary of the English Language*, (1755). "A man who farts frequently is known as 'Whistle breeches.' The classification of farts is as follows: fiz, fuz, fizzy-fuz, poop, tally poop, tear your ass, the rattler, and the bath-tub bubble" (lumberjack talk from the Pacific Northwest, David F. Costello, 2/22/83).

2) A contemptible or just plain worthless person, often an *old fart, silly fart, stupid fart*, or *fartface*. "Lenny was outraged by Ruhe's performance. The little fart was stealing his act—that was how he saw it" (*Ladies and Gentlemen, Lenny Bruce!!*, Albert Goldman, from the journalism of Lawrence Schiller, 1974).

(3) Any activity or thing that is of no account, often as an expression of unconcern, as in *to not care a fart, to not give a fart, to not be worth a fart,* or *to not amount to a fart in a whirlwind.* " 'I don't give a fart for'n,' says the squire, suiting the action to the word" (Henry Fielding, *Tom Jones*, 1749).

(4) As a verb, to loaf or waste time, as in *to fart around* or *to fiddle-fart (around)*. "The dentist fiddle-farted for two hours while I suffered" (Robert L. Chapman, *ed., New Dictionary of American Slang*, 1986). See also FIDDLE-FADDLE.

Though regarded as a vulgarism by lexicographers and other representatives of middle-class society since the early nineteenth century, *fart* is not low slang but Standard English, and it was long accepted as such. An early form of the word appears in one of the very oldest English poems, "The Cuckoo Song" (ca. 1250) which begins "Summer is icumen in, Lhude sing cuccu!" The second verse of the song continues: "Bulluc sterteth, bucke verteth, Murie sing cuccu!" This terminology seems to have troubled our remote ancestors less than those that are nearer to us in time. For example, when Arthur Quiller-Couch annotated the lyric in *The Oxford Book of English Verse* (1916), he let readers know that *lhude* means "loud" and that *sterteth* means "leaps," but he passed by *verteth*, silently.

Of course, the word also was used by many writers of note in the intervening years, Geoffrey Chaucer, Ben Jonson, Sir John Suckling, and Jonathan Swift, among them. And Dr. Samuel Johnson, a relatively fastidious gentleman, illustrated its use in his *Dictionary of the English Language* with examples from Suckling:

> Love is the fart
> Of every heart;
> It pains a man when 'tis kept close;
> And others doth offend, when 'tis let loose

And from Swift:

> As when we a gun discharge,
> Although the bore be ne'er so large,
> Before the flame from muzzle burst,

> Just at the breech it flashes first;
> So from my lord his passion broke,
> He farted first, and then he spoke.

The word was not confined to strictly literary use by certifiably Great Authors, of course. For example, the first published version of the music and words of "Yankee Doodle," dating from the summer of 1775, differs somewhat from the rhyme that children learn at their mothers' knees today. Entitled "Yankee Doodle, or (as now Christened by the Saints of New England) The Lexington March," this was obviously a patriotic American composition, though published in London. (See also YANKEE.) As recorded by Kenneth Silverman in *A Cultural History of the American Revolution* (1976), the verse goes like this:

> Dolly Bushel let a Fart,
> Jenny Jones she found it,
> Ambrose carried it to the Mill
> Where Doctor Warren ground it.

Within a generation or so, however, incipient Victorians began to expunge this word from their vocabularies. The editors of *The Oxford English Dictionary* (Volume F, 1893–97) did not include any examples of the word from after 1825 and labeled it "Not now in decent use." Other dictionary makers followed suit. For example, it was excluded from the first edition of *Webster's New International Dictionary* (1909), as well as from the second edition (1934). Not until the appearance of the third edition (1961) was the word admitted.

Given this track record, it is amazing that people still talk openly of candles that *fizzle* and of fireworks that *fizzle out*, since the original meaning of *fizzle*, from the early sixteenth century, is "To break wind without noise" (*OED*). *Fizzle* comes from the older, now obsolete *fist*, meaning to break wind, whether quietly or not. In its turn, *fizzle* has engendered the short, bubbly *fizz*, which gives a new layer of meaning to the TV commercial, "Plop, plop, fizz, fizz, Oh what a relief it is."

fascist. Rigid, authoritarian, doctrinaire, but not necessarily related in any way to Benito Mussolini's Fascist government of Italy (1922–43). People whose politics are to the left frequently use *fascist* to smear those who are, or who seem to be, on the right. Thus, police officers at demonstrations in the 1960s often were referred to as *fascist pigs*. (See also PIG.) The term actually has a much wider application, however, and can be applied to almost anyone with whom one disagrees, e.g., "Jesus Christ assures us that the church will prevail against even the gates of hell. . . . It seems likely, therefore, that it will prevail against this society's fleeting passion for sex and fascist feminism" (Paul J. Masiclat, letter to *U.S. News & World Report*, 7/2/84). See also COMMIE.

fat. Obese, CORPULENT. "Nobody loves a fat man" (American proverb, in H. L. Mencken, *A New Dictionary of Quotations*, 1942). To live off *the fat of the land*, to reap *fat profits*, or to have a *fat part* in a play—all these are abundantly good things, even to lean people. As applied to individuals, however, *fat* usually is pejorative, if not downright derisive. An exception occurs in the case of those who have had their consciousness raised, such as the members of the National Association to Aid Fat

Americans who trundled off to a Fat Feminists conference in Norwalk, Connecticut, in the spring of 1987. To these women, *fat* is not a bad word. " 'We encourage the use of the word because it decriminalizes it,' said Victoria Reed, a 360-pound nurse at Norwalk Hospital" (*New York Times*, 4/1/87). Still, it seems the NAAFA has a way to go, considering that another of the conference-goers, 400-pound Karen Scott-Jones, was the president of a fat persons' support group, euphemistically named *Largesse*. And the nation's children, of course, still recite such lyrics as "Fatty, fatty, two-by-four, / Can't get through the bathroom door, / So he did it on the floor" (and, sometimes, "Licked it up and did some more"). Variations on the *fat* theme include:

fat ass. A broad-beamed person; also called a *buffalo butt.* See also ASS.

fat brain. An early form of fathead, below. "What a wretched and peevish fellow is this King of England, to mope with his fatbrained followers" (William Shakespeare, *Henry V*, 1599). This is one of many *-brain* suffixes; see LAMEBRAIN.

fathead. "[Talk show host Wally] George silences [guests] with shouts of 'Shut up, fathead,' 'Maniac,' 'Jerk,' or, as he loves to refer to Jimmy Carter, 'Moron' " (*Columbia Journalism Review*, 5-6/84). *Fathead* has been dated to the nineteenth century and the adjective, *fat-headed*, to the eighteenth. Shakespeare used *fat* alone to mean slow-witted and indolent, as a fat farmyard animal seems to be. This is one of many *-head* endings; see BLOCKHEAD.

fat-mouth. ". . . to talk too much, especially about somethin you don't know nothin bout, from Mandingo *da-ba*, literally 'big, fat mouth' " (Geneva Smitherman, *Talkin and Testifyin*, 1977).

fatso. A nickname for a fat person, usually bestowed with the worst of intentions; occasionally shortened, as in Fats [Thomas] Waller, the jazz pianist (1904–43).

fat-witted. Slow-witted, fat-headed; see also NITWIT. The insult need not be reserved for people who are heavyset, too, but it is perfect in such a case. As Prince Hal tells Falstaff; "Thou are so fat-witted . . . that thou hast forgotten to demand that truly which thou wouldst truly know" (Shakespeare, *Henry IV, Part I*, 1596).

See also LARD and the various *blubber* terms in BLUBBERMOUTH.

featherweight. Lighter than LIGHTWEIGHT. In boxing, a fighter has to be 126 pounds or less to be classified as a featherweight. Outside the ring, a *featherweight* is a weak person or one of little importance. "It would do your cousin a vast deal of good to run away from that feather-weight husband of hers" (Annie Edwardes, *A Girton Girl*, 1885). Somewhat similar is the *feather merchant*, a mental lightweight, often one who has floated into a job for which he is not equipped. A nice though seemingly nonce variant of this was the Republican salute to Franklin D. Roosevelt in 1936 as "The Feather-duster of Dutchess County" (*American Speech*, 2/37). Besides being light, feathers are soft and make comfortable beds; hence, also *feather merchant*, meaning a person who manages to make himself indispensable in a civilian job during wartime (also called a SLACKER) or, in the Navy, a sailor who manages to moor himself to a desk in an office. The softness of feathers is implicit, too, in *featherbedding*, used since at least the 1920s to characterize cushy jobs—superfluous ones on the railroads, especially—that involve little or no work (according to management). Earlier, the military had *feather-bed soldiers*, meaning those who had it soft, as in "Peter . . . determined to give his feather-bed soldiers some seasoning" (Washington Irving, *Diedrich Knickerbocker's History of New York*, 1848). See also *featherhead* in BLOCKHEAD and WHITE FEATHER, TO SHOW THE.

feh. Phooey. " 'Morals, ethics, feh,' he was quoted as saying. The Diamond Dealers Club said he had impugned the integrity of the 47th Street organization and its members and . . . suspended him for a year" (*New York Times*, 11/13/84). *Feh* is a Yiddish import, perhaps deriving from the German *pfui*. Leo Rosten maintains that it always should be pronounced forcefully, as though followed by an exclamation point, which is how he handled it in "Mr. K*A*P*L*A*N and the Unforgivable 'Feh!" (*The Return of H*Y*M*A*N K*A*P*L*A*N*, 1959). See also PHOOEY.

fellow traveler. A person who seems to tag along politically or intellectually with another; especially, one who sympathizes with Communism. "Fellow traveller . . . although an extremely useful term and deserving to survive . . . shows signs of being employed so widely and indiscriminately that it becomes mere vogue and probably discredited" (Eric Partridge, *Usage & Abusage*, 1957). Well, perhaps. Discredited it may be, but there are those who continue to employ it: "The Leesburg [Virginia] Garden Club, according to Lyndon H. LaRouche, Jr., is a 'nest of Soviet fellow travelers' " (*New York Times*, 4/11/86). Mr. LaRouche probably wasn't aware when he hurled this epithet at the Leesburg ladies that he was falling into the trap of adopting the language of the Enemy. The term is the English equivalent of the Russian *puputchik*, as used by Leon Trotsky in the early 1920s to describe writers who sympathized with the Bolshevik Revolution but were not taking active parts in remaking Soviet society. The term was employed in an extended sense in its first recorded appearance in English in an article, "Mr. Roosevelt and His Fellow-Travelers," by Max Lerner in *The Nation* (10/24/36): "The new phenomenon is the fellow-traveler. The term has a Russian background and means someone who does not accept all your aims but has enough in common with you to accompany you in comradely fashion part of the way. In this campaign both Mr. Landon and Mr. Roosevelt have acquired fellow-travelers." See also COMMIE and LACKEY.

fiddle-faddle. Nonsense. "When you add the words 'on Television' to the title it means you are adding guest stars and a certain amount of fiddle-faddle, too" (*New York Times*, 8/15/83). The expression has been used in this sense since 1671 (*OED*). It is a close cousin to *fiddle-de-dee* and *fiddlesticks*, both being used to describe "nothing" or "nonsense," and frequently employed as mild interjections to register impatience. "Fiddlesticks! it's nothing but the skin broken" (Thomas Hughes, *Tom Brown's School Days*, 1857). The *fiddlestick* is the bow for playing the fiddle. This expression sometimes appears as *fiddlestick's end*, which Captain Francis Grose thought due "to the ancient fiddlesticks ending in a point; hence metaphorically [*fiddlestick's end* is] used to express a thing terminating in nothing" (*A Classical Dictionary of the Vulgar Tongue*, 1796).

All the *fiddles* are in keeping with the disparaging use of *to fiddle* (since the sixteenth century) in the sense of to cheat, as in *to fiddle with the truth*, or to act idly or to fritter, as in *to fiddle away time* (a reflection of the attitudes of working stiffs toward grasshopper-like musicians). See also *fiddle-fart* in FART, *fiddlehead* in BLOCK-HEAD, and the basic BUNK.

fifth columnist. A subversive, a traitor; broadly, a person whose loyalty one wishes to impugn. ". . . like most of our Israeli fifth columnists, Midge [Decter] isn't much interested in what the *goyim* were up to before Ellis Island" (Gore Vidal, *Nation*, 3/22/86). *Fifth column* was coined during the Spanish Civil War. The circumstances that gave rise to the expression were described in a *New York Times* report of October 16, 1936: ". . . General Emilio Mola . . . stated he was counting on four columns of troops outside Madrid and another column of persons hiding within the city who would join the invaders as soon as he reached the capital." The phrase *fifth column* appeared in the *Times* the following day, and it quickly became a Loyalist (rightist) battle cry. General Mola died in a plane crash the following year, never having linked up with his *fifth column.* See also QUISLING.

fig, not to give (or **care**). To not care a bit. "And for his promises, and his offers to me, 'I don't value them of a fig— Not of a fig, Mrs. *Jewkes;* and then I snapt my fingers" (letter, Shamela Andrews to her mother, in Henry Fielding, *Shamela,* 1741). This expression of total unconcern may derive from the *fig* as a symbol of worthlessness (because figs are grown in such profusion) but, more likely, it is a spin-off from the contemputous Italian gesture, *la fica,* made by inserting the thumb between two fingers. In Italian, *fica* means both *fig* and *vulva* and the force of the gesture is comparable to the well-known visual insult with middle finger unpraised. The Italian term was known to Shakespeare and other sixteenth- and seventeenth-century English writers, who rendered it variously as *fico* and *figo* as well as *fig* and *fig of Spain,* e.g., "Die and be damned! And figo for thy friendship!" (*Henry V,* 1599).

The popularity in Italy of *fica* as a term of derision also is attributed in part to a memorable indignity visited upon the citizens of Milan in the twelfth century. In 1159, after a successful uprising against Frederick Barbarossa, the Holy Roman Emperor, the Milanese escorted the Empress Beatrix out of town, riding on a mule, facing backward. Unfortunately for them, Frederick retook Milan in 1162, and as punishment for their insult to Beatrix, he compelled his prisoners, upon pain of death, to extract with his or her teeth a fig from, as Farmer and Henley delicately put it, "the fundament of a mule" (*Slang and Its Analogues,* 1891). Each prisoner, upon performing this feat, had to announce *"Ecco la fica"* (Behold the fig), with the result that *far la fica* came into wide use as an expression of derision, e.g., *faire la figue* in French and *die Feigen weisen* in German. It helps not a bit to know that Barbarossa's "fig" probably was not the fruit but a "mule dropping" (comparable to a "horse apple"). Be all this as it may, the fruit itself—getting back to the hand gesture—has a long history as a sexual symbol, e.g., from, Aristophanes' *The Peace* (422 B.C.):

> Now live splendidly together,
> Free from adversity.
> Pick your figs.
> May his be large and hard.
> May hers be sweet.

See also *cock a snook* in COCK and SYCOPHANT.

fink. An odious person, especially an informer. "Justice [Antonin] Scalia referred to the person who disclosed the Government information in the hypothetical case as 'some fink in the Defense Department' " (*New York Times,* 2/17/87). The term appeared first during the labor strife of the late nineteenth century. It referred originally to a worker who spied on his fellows for management, or a similarly detested individual, such as a private detective, company guard, strike-breaker, or

SCAB. "*Fink* reputedly goes back to the Homestead strike of 1892" (H. L. Mencken, *The American Language, rev.* and *ed.* by Raven I. McDavid, Jr., 1979). The original connotations remain in place: "Except for being a rat, a fink, a scab, a thug, and a goon, he's one of the sweetest guys you'll ever meet" (Charles Williams, *Man in Motion*, 1959).

It has been suggested that *fink* arose as a rhyme on *Pink*, in turn an abbreviation of *Pinkerton*, the operatives of the Pinkerton detective agency once having been employed widely to put down strikes, including the exceedingly bitter one at the Carnegie Steel Company in Homestead, Pennsylvania. Another possibility is that the term comes from the German *fink*, "finch," which would fit with the use of the word to denote an informer, i.e., one who "sings," as does a CANARY.

A modern embellishment, from the 1960s, is *ratfink*, meaning an informer, traitor, or other person who is even more detestable than your average *fink.* See also RAT.

fish. As is only befitting, considering that fishing is one of humanity's oldest and most important occupations, the fish looms large in the language of contempt. In its most general sense, *fish* can be applied to any person, frequently in such derisive combinations as *cold fish, loose fish, odd fish, poor fish,* and *queer fish.* Beyond this, the term suggests an inexperienced person, one who can be easily outwitted, cheated, or—continuing the piscine metaphor—hooked. Daniel Defoe used the word in this sense in 1722 and it remains current. For instance, skilled poker players (SHARKs) are always on the lookout for novice *fish,* e.g., "For Dennis McLain . . . was also known to his teammates as The Dolphin because he was somewhat of a fish at the clubhouse card table and the track—a winner only on the mound" (*New York Times*, 3/20/85). In American prisons, newly admitted inmates also are known as *fish.* This usage dates to before 1915 and may have evolved from SUCKER, the term used by professional criminals to describe law-abiding citizen-victims as well as amateur criminals, who were easily caught, or hooked, by the police because they had no underworld ties and little or no experience in the proper conduct of crime. Here, the metaphor continues: *Fish* entering prison are admitted first to a holding cell known as the *tank,* where they either *sink* or *swim,* e.g., "The 'keeper' does not prepare the *fish* ahead of time for the ordeal that awaits them in the *tank* . . . new *fish* who do not learn immediately how to *swim* will undergo a devastating initiation rite [i.e., rape]" (Inez Cardozo-Freeman, with Eugene P. Delorme, *The Joint: Language and Culture in a Maximum Security Prison*, 1984).

Fish also has acquired various specialized meanings. The adjective *fishy* has been used to describe shady or dubious dealings since before 1850 (the allusion perhaps being to the slipperiness of fish). Sailors also have been known as *fish* (or *scaly fish*) for a couple of centuries. In addition, *fish* has a well-developed sexual history, being an old term for a woman, specifically a prostitute, and for a woman's most private part. Shakespeare made various plays on the word's sexual senses, e.g., from *Romeo and Juliet* (ca. 1595):

> SAMPSON: Therefore I will push Montague's men from the wall and thrust his maids to the wall. . . . Me they shall feel while I am able to stand. And 'tis known I am a pretty piece of flesh.
> GREGORY: 'Tis well thou art not fish. . . .

147

In Shakespeare's time, a *fish monger* was a BAWD or PIMP, and the *fishmonger's daughter* was a whore. This by no means exhausted the poetic imagination of the age—or of the bard. For instance, from *Measure for Measure* (1604):

MISTRESS OVERDONE: But what's his offense?
POMPEY: Groping for trouts in a peculiar river.
MISTRESS OVERDONE: What, is there a maid with child by him?

The allusion here is to poaching, since a "peculiar river" is not just a strange river but a privately owned one (the oldest senses of "peculiar" relate to private property), and those "trouts," of course, are not the kind of fish you fry.

The sexual senses of *fish* remained common in the nineteenth-century England, when *to have a bit of fish* was to engage in copulation and *to go to a fish market* was to visit a brothel. *Fish* (prostitute) and *fish business* (pandering) also have been reported in the United States (*American Speech*, 10/39) but neither is common today. More recently, *fish* has gained some popularity among male homosexuals as a strongly pejorative term for a female heterosexual (*American Speech*, Spring–Summer, 1970).

Fish and *fishing* also appear in a great many other sayings, such as *to fish in troubled waters, to have other fish to fry, to be a fish out of water, to be neither fish nor fowl,* and so on. Among those that have some value for putting down other people:

to drink like a fish. Said of a great imbiber of liquor; after consuming too much, the person becomes *fish-eyed*.

fish eater. A Roman Catholic, from the traditional R.C. abstention from meat on fast days; also called *guppy gobbler* and *mackerel snapper*. See also PAPIST.

fishface. A more common term of abuse in the seventeenth and eighteenth centuries than the twentieth, but well worth resurrecting.

fish story. A greatly exaggerated, often completely incredible tale. It seems likely that the propensities of fishermen in this regard have been recognized since the time of Jonah, but the earliest example of the phrase as such in the *OED* comes only from the nineteenth century: "A fish story! . . . In consequence of the shoals of white-fish which occupied and choked the channel between Bois Blanc Island and Amherstburgh, the steamboat could not pass" (*St. Louis Enquirer*, 12/8/1819).

fishwife. Originally, from the sixteenth century, merely a woman who sold fish, but within a hundred years, thanks to the foul and abusive language at the Billingsgate fish market in London, any shrewish, ill-tempered, loud-mouthed scold. See also *Billingsgate* in PEORIA.

a pretty kettle of fish. A mess, muddle, or quandary. " 'Here's a pretty kettle of fish,' cries Mrs. Tow-wouse" (Henry Fielding, *Joseph Andrews*, 1742). The expression is said to come from the Scottish custom of catching and cooking fish in large kettles during picnics or boating excursions along the Tweed and other rivers. The ironic twist to the phrase appears to reflect the traditional English disdain of all things Scottish (see SCOTCH), though for the English to criticize another nation's cooking seems also be a case of the pot calling the kettle black. See also CLAM, COD, CRAB, CRAWFISH, FRY, MACKEREL, OYSTER, SHARK, SHRIMP, and SPONGE.

flaky. In more or less ascending order of disparagement: unconventional, eccentric, bizarre, crazy. Thus, referring to threats by Libyan leader Colonel Muammar el-Qaddafi: ". . . how can you not take seriously a man that has proven he is as irrational as he is in things of this kind? I find he's not only a barbarian but he's flaky" (President Ronald Reagan, press conference, 1/9/86). See also BARBARIAN.

Flaky people are known, naturally, as *flakes*. The earliest examples of the term are from the sports world. "San Francisco Giants outfielder Jackie Brandt is thought to be the first ever to be described as flakey when he was given the nickname in the 1950s" (Tim Considine, *The Language of Sport*, 1982). The origin of the epithet is unclear. Some say that things Brandt was supposed to remember seemed to flake off from his mind and disappear. Or the term may derive from *flake out*, meaning to fall asleep, i.e., to be out of it. The latter explanation has the virtue of squaring with *flaky* in its postive senses of being totally relaxed, easygoing, or hanging loose, as in "I want a flaky chick" (Eugene E. Landy, *The Underground Dictionary*, 1971).

flannel-mouth. A smooth talker, a braggart, especially an Irishman, from at least 1870 unto modern times: "*Chaw-mouth* . . . refers to the Irishman's talkativeness and parallels the more common *flannel-mouth*" (American Dialect Society, *Publications*, XLII, 1964). See also IRISH.

flapdoodle. Nonsense. "Well, by and by, the king he gets up and comes forward a little, and works himself up and slobbers out a speech, all full of tears and flapdoodle . . ." (Mark Twain, *Huckleberry Finn*, 1884). "The allegation is flapdoodle" (Walter Goodman, *The New York Times*, 6/21/86).

Flapdoodle may have originated through sheer verbal exuberance. The OED terms it "an arbitrary formation," an explanation that also would apply to *fadoodle* and *flamdoodle*, both also meaning nonsense or foolish talk, and *dipsy-doodle*, which is especially deceptive nonsense or chicanery (in baseball, a *dipsy-doodle* or *dipsy-do* is a curve, i.e., a tricky pitch to hit). *Flapdoodle* is redolent with other possible etymologies, however, including the barnyard rooster who flaps his wings while crowing "Cock-a-doodle-doo!," and the *flap*, which is an old word for a breech-clout, and which in turn covers what is sometimes called a *doodle*. See also BUNK.

flatfoot. A policeman, especially a detective. "His name is P. C. Wallace but we [juveniles of Edinburgh, Scotland] call him old Walrus. When he has gone round the corner we call him names such as slop, natter knob, or flatfeet" (Iona and Peter Opie, *The Lore and Language of Schoolchildren*, 1959). The police sense is an American-ism, dating to around the turn of this century; *flatty* means the same and is equally old (*OED*, 1899). *Flatfoot* also has been used in an uncomplimentary way to characterize infantrymen (the Foot Guards in England, but also militiamen who can't march) and sailors (in the opinion of marines). See also COP, FLOOZIE (for another occupation that results in flat feet), and the *horse marines* in HORSE.

flea. An insignificant person, frequently one who jumps around a lot, actually or figuratively; anything else that is small, dirty, dilapidated, and of no account. "Nevertheless, Northcliffe was a volatile creature, so prone to hop from one political position to another that Lloyd George compared him to a flea" (*Columbia Journalism Review*, 3-4/83).

Flea appears in many combinations. A *flea-brain* is a person with a small one, a DUMMY; a *fleabag*, *-box*, *-house*, or *-trap* is a cheap lodging house or hotel, a flophouse; a *flea market* is a rag-tag collection of small booths or card tables (but a term that has risen to respectability as *junk* has become *collectibles*). Of these, *fleabag* seems to be the oldest, first recorded from 1839 (*OED*) in the sense of *bed*, a meaning that it retains. Depending on context, a *fleabag* also can be an inferior racehorse (paralleling one of the many meanings of DOG) or it can be a dilapidated, run-down, sleazy public place of almost any sort, e.g., a movie house or a cheap nightclub. *To have a flea in [one's] nose* is to be crazy or to be possessed by some wild idea or scheme (equivalent to having a bee in [one's] bonnet) and *to have a flea in [one's] ear* is an old (ca. 1430) expression for suffering a sharp reproof or rebuff, e.g., " 'Quarters!' he roared. And . . . we all slunk back to our places . . . every one with a red face, you may be certain, and a flea in his ear, as the saying is" (Robert Louis Stevenson, *Treasure Island*, 1883). See also LOUSE.

flibbertigibbit. A silly, talkative person; a woman, ordinarily. The word seems to be of onomatapoetic origin, from the older *flibergib*, imitating meaningless chatter. "Likewise we call a woman which delighteth much to hear tales and tell tales a flibergib, also trish-trash, tagnag or tagrag, hunch-lunch, riffraff, habnab, heave and hoe, clapperclaw, kickle-kackle" (Henry Peacham, *The Garden of Eloquence*, 1577, in Willard Espy's work of the same name, 1983).

flimflam. Nonsense, especially that which is intended to deceive or swindle, as in *Flim-Flam: The Truth About Unicorns, Parapsychology and Other Delusions* (book title, James Randi, 1980). *Flimflam*, dating from the first half of the sixteenth century, is one of many reduplications with pejorative meanings, e.g., *boo-hoo, claptrap, dilly-dally, dum-dum,* FIDDLE-FADDLE, FUDDY-DUDDY, GOO-GOO, HOITY-TOITY, *kickback,* POOH-POOH, RIFFRAFF, *rinky-dink, shilly-shally, ticky-tacky, tittle-tattle, twiddle-twaddle,* and WISHY-WASHY. This one probably is based on the Old Norse *film*, a mockery or lampoon, or some closely related but now lost word. It has given rise to *flam*, used by itself to describe nonsense in general and a lie or hoax in particular. See also BUNK and HUMBUG.

flit. An effeminate man; a male homosexual. "Sometimes it was hard to believe the people he said were flits and lesbians" (J. D. Salinger, *The Catcher in the Rye*, 1951). The allusion is to the flitty flight of a bird or other winged creature; specifically, in this instance, a FAIRY. See also QUEER.

floozie. A flashy, lower-class, not very bright young woman, especially a prostitute or one who, though strictly speaking an amateur, does not say no very often; also rendered *floosie, floozy, faloosie, flugie,* and *floogy,* as in Slim Gaillard's hit song of 1938 "Flat Foot Floogie with the Floy Floy." (Nonsense songs were in vogue back then, but the *flat foot* here seems to imply that the *floozie* had professional standing, while the *floy floy* may have referred to a veneral disease.) *Floozie* dates to the early twentieth century. Its origin is uncertain, but it may be a variation on *flossy*, meaning *saucy* or *showy*. See also DAME, FLATFOOT, and WHORE.

fluff. A young woman, lightly considered; often *a bit* (or *piece*) *of fluff* or, if frivolous or on the stupid side, a *fluffhead* (see BLOCKHEAD). The oldest feminine *fluff* in the *OED* is from 1903 and a work entitled *Fluff-hunters* by a "Majoribanks": "The guard was about to whistle, when a bit of fluff was blown up the platform, and before Webster had time to send up a petition for a safe journey, it (the fluff) had come to rest on the corner seat opposite him." See also PIECE.

The *fluff* that is a mistake or blunder seems to be a later development, stemming from nineteenth-century theatrical slang, wherein *fluff* referred to " 'Lines' half learned and imperfectly delivered. Hence, "TO DO A FLUFF = to forget one's part" (J. S. Farmer and W. E. Henley, *Slang and Its Analogues*, 1893).

flunky. A servant; specifically, in the Marxist lexicon, a hireling of a capitalist nation, usually the United States. "The jargon peculiar to Marxist writing (*hyena, hangman, cannibal, petty bourgeois, these gentry, lacquey, flunky, mad dog, White Guard,* etc.) consists largely of words and phrases translated from Russian, German or French . . ." (George Orwell, "Politics and the English Language," 1946). "Official booklets and newspapers [in North Korea] continue to attribute the division of the country to 'United States imperialism' and its 'pro-American flunkies' in the South Korean Government" (*New York Times*, 6/13/86).

Flunky almost always is contemputous even in nonpolitical contexts. The word is Scottish; it has been dated to the late eighteenth century and may be a diminutive of *flanker,* meaning a footman, or sideman, posted at the flank of a carriage or chair. See also LACKEY.

fly. Anything or anyone insignificant, except in the case of *a fly in the ointment,* when the small thing spoils all. Flies have been getting into ointment since biblical times. Thus, *Ecclesiastes,* 10:1 has: "Dead flies cause the ointment of the apothecary to send forth a stinking savour: so *doth* a little folly him that is in reputation for wisdom *and* honour." Other animals can have the same deleterious effect. In the Ozarks, an equivalent expression is *a mouse in the meal.* And Charles Lamb summoned up a veritable menagerie in *Elia,* 2nd Series (1840), when he declared that "A Poor Relation—is the most irrelevant thing in nature, — . . . a lion in your path, —a frog in your chamber, —a fly in your ointment."

On its own, however, a *fly,* or a person who is like one, is of not much account, e.g., "Aleyn answerde I count hym nat a flye" (Geoffrey Chaucer, *The Reeve's Tale,* ca. 1387–1400). More recently, *fly* also has gained disparaging connotations as a suffix in *barfly,* from 1910, a person who spends altogether too much time in taverns, and *shoofly* (sometimes *shoefly*), from 1877, a police officer, usually one in plain clothes, assigned to watch out for corruption or other misbehavior among fellow police officers—an internal spy, in other words.

From this swarm of bad associations, it follows naturally that *to have no flies on [one]* is a compliment, meaning that the recipient is alert, active, or without fault. The latter expression seems to have originated among cattlemen in the nineteenth century, either in the United States or Australia, the point being that flies do not settle on cattle that are continually moving around. This metaphor also continues: The flies that land on cattle and bite them are called *gadflies* (from *gad,* an old word for a sharp spike), and this term also is applied to bothersome people, typically those who irritate the body politic. See also INSECT.

fogy. An elderly person with outmoded ideas and outdated attitudes, or a younger person who exhibits such traits; usually preceded with *old,* regardless of age, to emphasize the backwardness of the *fogy.* "The New Right (or the Old Fogies) has put significant pressure on this Administration to halt the funding of Planned Parenthood clinics" (*Litchfield County* [Connecticut] *Times,* 4/11/86). Dating to the late eighteenth century, *fogy* is of mysterious origin. It may derive from either of two obsolescent senses of *foggy*, bloated (as flesh), or marshy (hence moss-covered). Other possibilities are that the word is related to *foggie*, a brownish (moss-colored) bumblebee, or *fogram*, also meaning an old-fashioned person and also often prefaced with *old*, as in Fanny Burney's 1775 diary note about "A parcel of old Fograms." The word also has acquired specialized senses in the military, where an *old fogy* in the late eighteenth and early nineteenth centuries was an elderly or invalid soldier, and *fogy pay*, continuing into the twentieth century, is longevity pay, which increases the longer one stays in the service. See also CODGER, DOTARD, DUFFER, FRUMP, FUDDY-DUDDY, GEEZER, MOSSBACK, and OLD MAID.

fool. A stupid person. "Probably the most serious insult current among [Japanese] drivers in traffic is *baka*—fool" (Charles Berlitz, *Passport to Japanese*, 1985). "[Michael N. Manley] opened what his party describes as 'a relentless campaign' to demand early elections, calling [Jamaican] Prime Minster Edward P. G. Seega 'an arrogant, stupid fool' " (*New York Times*, 2/10/85).

Deriving from the Latin *follis*, a bellows, i.e., a WINDBAG, the word has overtones of silliness as well as feeblemindedness that derive from the role of the traditional court jester who, depending upon the monarch's taste, might be either a professional wit and entertainer or a *natural fool*, who did not have to learn the trade but was born to it (see also DUMB/DUMMY). The term appears in a great many phrases, e.g., *silly fool, tomfool,* and *tomfoolery*. Then there are *to fool around, to make a fool of, to play the fool,* and such proverbial bits of wisdom as *a fool and his money are soon parted, a fool's bolt is soon shot,* and so on.

Though some court jesters were highly regarded in their own time, the pejorative senses have been uppermost for a great many years, e.g., "By my troth, I was seeking for a fool when I found you" (William Shakespeare, *As You Like It*, 1599–1600). Which is about on the same level as the following verse, variations of which are still to be found in school scrapbooks and other public places:

> Abraham Lincoln is my nam[e]
> And with my pen I wrote the same
> I wrote in both hast[e] and speed
> and left it here for fools to read

(Mark E. Neely, Jr., *The Abraham Lincoln Encyclopedia*, 1982, quoting an inscription in one of Lincoln's copybooks, written when he was in his mid-teens.)

Lincoln's *fool*, and Shakespeare's, are comparatively lighthearted specimens. In other contexts, and in the right hands, the word retains an awful power. Thus, from the conclusion of Jonathan Swift's *The Day of Judgment*, a poem so dark that he did not publish it while he lived:

> Jove, nodding, shook the heavens and said . . .
> "Offending race of human kind,
> By nature, reason, *learning* blind . . .
> You who in different sects were shamm'd,
> And come to see each other damm'd;
> (So some folk told you, but they knew
> No more of Jove's designs than you;)
> —The world's mad business now is o'er,

And I resent these pranks no more.
—I to such blockhead set my wit!
I damn such fools!—Go, go, you're *bit*."

Where *bit* is period slang for *deceived* or *tricked*. See also BUFFOON, CLOWN, COXCOMB, CROSSPATCH, FUNNY, JERK, JOKER, MOPE, SCURRILOUS, and ZANY.

foul ball. An undesirable person, an ODDBALL; in prizefighting, an inferior boxer. ". . . finally asked the uninvited guest, a real foul ball, to leave" (Tim Considine, *The Language of Sport*, 1982). The reference, of course is to the ball that is batted outside the fair territory of a baseball field.

four-eyes. A person who wears glasses, also called *glass-eyes* and *specs*. "Eyeglasses for those with poor vision are so accepted these days that even little children are no longer taunted by the nickname Four Eyes" (*New York Times*, 9/7/83). *Four-eyes* may have fallen into disuse among the younger set, as the *Times* suggests, but adults have employed variations on the theme within living memory: "[Baseball] players wearing glasses get it good. Lee Walls is Captain Midnight. Bill Virdon answers to Cyclops. Clint Courtney is the sealed beam catcher" (Joe Garagiola, *Baseball is a Funny Game*, 1980).

four-flusher. A faker, a bluffer. "He is a four-flusher, a ring-tailed, rip-snorting hell-raiser, and a grandstander" (*Emporia* [Kansas] *Gazette*, 1/13/1914). Dating from about 1900, the term refers to the stud poker practice of pretending that one has a five-card flush when four cards of the same suit are showing. It is one of many specialized poker terms to have entered the general vocabulary. See also PENNY-ANTE.

fox. A sly or crafty man; an attractive woman. The first sense is much the older, e.g., "And he [Jesus] said unto them, Go ye and tell that fox [Herod], Behold, I cast out devils, and I do cures to-day and to-morrow, and the third *day* I shall be perfected" (*Luke*, 13:32). The feminine sense, meanwhile, usually is regarded as black slang, popularized by the heavyweight boxer, Muhammad Ali, then called Cassius Marcellus Clay, who used it in the course of an interview with *Time* magazine in 1963. The analogy of women to foxes is of some antiquity, however (see VIXEN), and the term had some currency prior to Mr. Ali's employment of it, e.g., the 1956 film *The Foxiest Girl in Paris*. One also suspects a bad pun lurking in *foxhole inspection*, which has been the functional equivalent for Wacs since World War II of the GI's *short-arm inspection*, i.e., a medical check for VD.

  Fox also has other sneaky meanings. Thus, a *fox* may be a traitor and *to fox* or *fox up* can be to deceive, to balk or hinder, to ruin or foul up. *To be foxed* is to be drunk and, of course, a *foxy* person is to be guarded against (unless she is a she, and sometimes even then). "Wanderer was defended by foxy lawyers . . ." (Alexander Woollcott, *Long, Long Ago*, 1943).

Frankenstein. A monster that destroys its creator and, by extension, any destructive person, plan, institution, or group. " 'You may not believe me, Claude, but the white man was made by a colored scientist, in a test tube, man. He isn't even real. He's like a Frankenstein monster' " (Claude Brown, *Manchild in the Promised Land*, 1965). The confusion between the creator and the monster is common. The young medical student who creates the monster in Mary Wollstonecraft Shelley's novel *Frankenstein: or, The Modern Prometheus* (1818) is Victor Frankenstein. The monster itself is unnamed. See also ZOMBIE.

freak. An odd or unconventional person. "When long-haired, outlandishly dressed, drug-using hippies pilgrimaged to Haight-Ashbury in the early 1960s, they were quickly dubbed *freaks;* the pejorative appelation was both obvious and intended" (*American Speech*, Winter 1969). The allusion here is to the *freak* that appears in a *freak show.* Originally, going back to the sixteenth century, a *freak* was a sudden change of mind, a whim, capricious disposition, trick, or fancy. The sense of abnormality or monstrousness is fairly new; this kind of *freak* is short for *freak of nature* and is traced in the *OED* only to the 1880s. In the immediately preceding decades, by contrast, P. T. Barnum advertised General Tom Thumb and other attractions at the American Museum as "curiosities." Latterly, *freak* also has obtained other unfortunate meanings: a drug addict (a *coke freak, smack freak, speed freak,* etc.); a male homosexual (if he enjoys the passive role of voyeur, then he is a *peek freak*); or other sexual deviant (e.g., the *freak trick* who uses or abuses prostitutes in unusual and sometimes violent ways). Of course, tastes vary, as indicated by the graffito "The best things in life are freaky" (*American Speech*, Fall 1980).

As a suffix, *freak* denotes enthusiasm in such constructions as *ecofreak, food freak,* and *Jesus freak.* The oldest of these seems to be *camera freak,* dated to 1906 by a correspondent of William Safire's (*New York Times*, 2/15/81). *Freak* in this sense parallels the slightly older *fiend. Opium fiend* dates to at least the early 1880s (H. L. Mencken, *The American Language, Supplement I,* 1945). Some of the other fiends include the *camera fiend, dope fiend, kissing fiend,* and *sex fiend.* See also QUEER.

freeloader. One who lives off others; a MOOCHER or SPONGE. The most surprising thing about this word is its apparent newness. The oldest examples of its use date only to 1947, after which it became a vogue word, especially with reference to eating or drinking at another's expense. "Congressmen are great freeloaders" (L. Mortimer, *New York Times Book Review,* 4/15/51). The term may be an offshoot of *free-luncher,* meaning a person who goes to a bar that serves food, eats all he can, and doesn't buy any drinks. The noun has given birth to the verb *to freeload* and to the adjectival *freeloading,* e.g., "My lousy, free-loading bohemian family, all chiselers" (Saul Bellow, *Herzog,* 1964). See also CHISELER and LOUSE.

French. The English began speaking poorly of the French—as far as the written record goes, at least—in the sixteenth century, when gentlemen started to acquire the *French pox,* or syphilis (*OED,* 1503). In other countries, the same complaint was known as *the Neapolitan disease, the Polish disease, the Spanish disease,* and even *the English disease,* each nation blaming another. The English developed the idea better than most, however, producing a phalanx of synonyms, including *French ache, French compliment, French crown, French disease, French fever, French goods, French gout, French malady, French marbles, French measles, French mole,* and *French-sick.* Sometimes one might simply say that the *Frenchman* had come for a visit or that one had been *Frenchified.* (The latter also was used from an early date in a general, contemptuous sense, as in Ben Jonson's *Every Man Out of His Humour,* of 1597: "This is one Monsieur Fastidious Brisk, otherwise called the fresh Frenchified courtier.") In extenuation for the English, it should be noted that they were not the only ones to blame the French for the pox: "The French disease, for it was that, remained in me more than four months dormant before it showed itself, and then it . . . covered my flesh with certain blisters, of the size of six-pences, and rose-colored" *The Autobiography of Benvenuto Cellini*, 1588–71, tr. John Addington Symonds, 1927).

In keeping with the original venereal context, the use of *French* in English frequently refers to something sexual—a backhanded compliment to the presumed prowess of the Gauls in this department. Among the more common *French* phrases:

French (n). Bad language, as in "Please excuse my French"; from the nineteenth century.

French (v.). In the nineteenth century, to fail, as *French land* was said to do because of a crop disease called *frenching*, but in the twentieth century, usually a reference to oral-genital sex, as in "Hot raunchy schoolgirl, 22, with father fetish seeks corres. with older men. Love to have fun and frenching for hrs" (personal ad, *Ace*, undated, ca. 1976).

French arts (or *culture*, *tricks*, or *way*). Oral-genital activities, again, as in "Lonesome 50 Cauc male anxious to meet mature ladies for sensuous adult pleasures love fr arts" (*Ace, op. cit.*). These phrases were preceded by the marginally more explicit *French vice*, which seems to have first graced public print in accounts of a sensational divorce case in which a leading Liberal politician, Sir Charles Dilke, appeared as corespondent (*Crawford v. Crawford and Dilke*, 1885). See also GREEK.

French faith. "Unfaithfulness; duplicity. (A phrase occurring frequently in the sixteenth century)" (Abraham Roback, *A Dictionary of International Slurs*, 1979).

French fly. Spanish fly; seventeenth and eighteenth centuries.

French kiss. (1) Passionate kiss in which the tongue or tongues come into play. (2) Oral-genital activity. Both senses seem to be twentieth-century creations and both remain current—a particularly dramatic example of the way meaning changes according to context.

French leave. To depart without giving notice or, as the French say, *filer à l'anglaise*. "He stole away an Irishman's bride and took French leave of me and my master" (Tobias Smollett, *The Expedition of Humphry Clinker*, 1771).

French letter. What the French call *une capote anglaise*, English cloak; a CONDOM. From the mid-nineteenth century: "What Jenny's sister paid for French letters, I don't know, I used to pay nine pence each" (Anonymous, *My Secret Life*, ca. 1890; the reference here is undated but, interior evidence suggests, pre-1851).

French pig. A veneral bubo or swelling; the same as the *Winchester goose* in GOOSE.

French pigeon. A pheasant killed by mistake (presumably) in the partridge season; British, nineteenth century.

French postcard. A naughty one. "At one time the hobo enjoyed almost exclusively the 'French post cards' (called 'American cards' in France)" ("D. Stiff," *Milk & Honey Route*, 1931).

French print. Also a naughty one. "Young de Boots of the Blues recognized you as the man who came to the barracks, and did business one-third in money, one-third eau-de-Cologne, and one-third in French prints, you confounded, demure, old sinner" ((William Makepeace Thackeray, *Pendennis II*, 1850).

French tickler. A condom equipped with ridges or other protuberances.

French walk. "Ejecting one from a place forcibly; possibly from the method employed by French pirates to make prisoners walk the plank" (Sterling Eisiminger, "A Glossary of Ethnic Slurs in American English," *Maledicta*, Winter 1979).

See also DUTCH and FROG.

fringe. At the outer edge (of acceptable behavior); marginally loyal (politically). "The media became unwitting collaborators [with] fringe groups seeking a radical transformation of society" (Henry Kissinger, London *Sunday Times*, 4/14/85). ". . . much of the press seems to be drawn from a relatively narrow fringe element on the far left of society . . . and . . . is trying to tear down America" (presidential science adviser George A. Keyworth, *Columbia Journalism Review*, 11-12/85).

The most famous (or infamous) *fringe*, of course, is the *lunatic fringe*. This phrase was popularized—and perhaps coined—by Theodore Roosevelt: "There is apt to be a lunatic fringe among the votaries of any forward movement" (*History as Literature and Other Essays*, 1913). Note that *lunatic fringe* is equally applicable to leftists and rightists. For example, when Harry S Truman told Clark Clifford that most of the people around Franklin D. Roosevelt were "crackpots and the lunatic fringe," he was not talking about ultraconservatives (*The Journals of David E. Lilienthal*, 1964). On the other hand, T. H. Bell recalled his tenure as Education Secretary in the Reagan Administration this way: ". . . proponents of the doctrines of the extreme right . . . took [the President's] guiding principles and carried them to the lunatic fringes of ideological political thought" (*New York Times*, 3/13/86). See also LUNATIC.

frog. A Frenchman. ". . . wouldn't be surprised if he'd invite frogs, and even wogs." (Nancy Mitford, *Love in a Cold Climate*, TV version, WNET-NYC, 4/4/82). See also WOG.

Frog is an old insult, with the *Oxford English Dictionary*'s first example of a person who was said to be a "foule froge" coming from ca. 1330. Originally applied freely to all sorts of obnoxious individuals, the epithet's meaning gradually was narrowed to denote Jesuits and inhabitants of Holland, also called *froglanders*. For example, the Dutch character in John Arbuthnot's *The History of John Bull* (1712) is named Nicholas Frog; see also DUTCH and PADDY. The French meaning of *frog* became popular toward the end of the eighteenth century, when the English and French were waging war against each other all over the world. The disparagement may well reflect the abhorrence of the beef-loving English at the strange tastes of the French, also known commonly in this era as *frog-eaters* or *froggies*, who lived in a country known variously as *Frogland* and *Frogmore*. (It is standard procedure, of course, for one group or nation to ridicule another's diet: see KRAUT.) The froggie flavor of the Napoleonic era is conveyed in a broadside of 1803 (from Thomas Wright, *Caricature History of the Georges*, 1858, in *American Speech*, 12/48):

> But if they [the French] feel stout,
> Why, then let them turn out.
> With their maws stuff'd with frogs, soups and jellies;
> Brave Nelson's sea thunder
> Shall strike them with wonder,
> And make the frogs leap in their bellies.

The association between the French and amphibian critters is much older than this, however, going back to the ancient coat of arms of the City of Paris, which has three toads springing up ("salient," as heraldrists say, the rising stance signifying valor). It is because of this device that a Frenchman may also be dismissed as a *crapaud* (not quite as bad as it sounds, since *crapaud* is merely the French for "toad") or a *Johnny Crapaud*. Anglicized variants include *crapo* and *crappo*, e.g., "I well know that these crappoes of Frenchmen are but poor devils" (Herman Melville, *Moby Dick*, 1851). The French themselves referred to the natives of their capital city as *grenouilles* (frogs), apparently with the Parisian coat of arms in mind. At Versailles, in 1791, as the Old Regime was tottering toward the scaffold, worried courtiers often asked one another, *"Qu'en disent les grenouilles?"*, meaning "What do the frogs [i.e., people of Paris] say?" (*Brewer's Dictionary of Phrase & Fable, rev.*, Ivor H. Evans, 1970). And Paris once was home to a great many frogs and toads, real ones, with *Lutetia*, the name by which Caesar knew the place, translating as "Mud-land," thus explaining gastronomy, heraldry, and insult all at once.

Frog also can be applied to non-French persons, but then the insult is personal rather than ethnic. The usual form is *frog-face*, a term that has been used in medical journals to describe a particular deformity that results from a tumor in the nose. In a nonmedical context, Ernest Hemingway characterized Wyndham Lewis this way: "He had a face that reminded me of a frog, not a bullfrog but just any frog. . . . I do not think I had ever seen a nastier-looking man" (*A Moveable Feast*, 1964). See also FRENCH and TOAD.

fruit. A male homosexual, a loose woman, both senses from ca. 1930 and both perhaps deriving from *fruit*, meaning a young and inexperienced person, a dupe, i.e., one who is "easy pickings"; also an eccentric or crazy person, who is, as the saying goes, *as nutty as* (or *nuttier than*) *a fruitcake*. In the homosexual world, the term has been elaborated in various ways, e.g., *fruiter*, *fruit fly* (also a heterosexual woman who is attracted to *fruits*), *fruit merchant*, *fruit picker* (an ostensibly heterosexual man who occasionally seeks out homosexuals), *fruit stand* (a gay bar), and *overripe fruit* (a gay who is past his prime). A person—male or female—beneath the legal age of consent is *forbidden fruit*. See also NUT and QUEER.

frump. A dowdy, dull person, usually but not necessarily a woman. "When a proposed party was being plotted out, he would say, 'Oh, don't ask the So-and-So's, they are such frumps' " (W. Holt, *Beacon for the Blind*, 1915). *Frump* has been dated to the sixteenth century, referring originally to a sneer, a jeer, a derisive deception or hoax. It might be a shortening of *frumple*, a wrinkle. The modern meaning has been dated in the *OED* to 1817: "They voted me a prig, a frump, a fogram." See also FOGY.

fry. Insignificant people or things, considered collectively, usually as *small fry* or *young fry*, though they are not necessarily either small or young in fact, e.g., "Compared with [Sheridan], all other managers were small fry" (J. Payn, *Talk of the Town II*, 1885). *Fry* is unusual among animal terms in that its oldest senses have to do with human offspring rather than—now the dominant meaning—the spawn of salmon or other fishes. See also FISH.

fuck. To copulate, and the act of so doing, with many extended nonsexual meanings. The once awesome power of this term has declined in the past several decades, but it continues to find many uses, primarily as an adjective, epithet, exclamation, and intensifier. It is the prototypical example of the close, not to say intimate, connection between sex and violence in our culture, and it also provides a litmus test of society's controls over sexual expression.

For legal as well as social reasons, what often is referred to as the *F-word* was long excluded from conventional dictionaries. The first general dictionaries in modern times to include the word were *The Penguin Dictionary* (1965) and *The American Heritage Dictionary* (1969), though the publisher of the latter, Houghton Mifflin, subsequently tarnished its achievement by putting out a bowdlerized version, known variously as the "Clean Green" or "Texas" edition, in an effort to penetrate, so to speak, the high school market in the Southwest. In *The American Heritage Dictionary* and most other dictionaries, the steamy word is defined blandly in terms of copulation, coition, or sexual intercourse, with these words, in turn, being defined in terms of each other. In *The American Heritage Dictionary*, for example, the definition for *fuck* is "To have sexual intercourse with," while the definition for *sexual intercourse* is "Coitus, especially between humans," and that for *coitus* is "Sexual intercourse between two human beings."

The circularity in the dictionary definitions is due partly to fastidiousness and partly to a remarkable lacuna in our language. Even though (despite advances in artificial insemination) the activity remains essential to the propagation of the human and most other species, and even though (despite protestations to the contrary) it looms larger in the thoughts of most people than any other topic (except possibly food), the English language lacks another transitive verb that expresses the basic idea with any degree of vividness. Instead, we make do on formal occasions with scientific, Latinate, and euphemistic fig leaves, such as *to coit, to procreate, to generate,* and *to have intercourse* (or *relations*). Of course, normal people do not normally talk this way. But there are problems even with the less formal alternatives. *To have sex* is a barbarism of the first order, since sex is something that everybody has all the time anyway. *To make love, to sleep with,* and *to have a meaningful relationship* all involve interior contradictions, since love, sleep, and meaningfulness frequently are in short supply. The slangy *to make it* seems rather impersonal, as though the party of the second part were hardly involved; *to lay* may or may not be strictly accurate and most people are afraid to use it in writing because of the grammatical confusion with the past tense of *lie; jazz* has escaped its original mooring; and *ball, bang, hump, score, screw,* etc., all lack the versatility of the basic term. See also HUMP, JAZZ, LAY, and SCREW.

Of the alternatives, *screw* comes closest, with its many extended uses, such as *screw up, screw you, screw around,* but it is basically a euphemism, neither as forceful nor as versatile as *fuck,* which appears in many more combinations. Who ever heard of a *flying (Philadelphia) screw, mind-screw, rat screw, screwhead, screwface,* or *stupid screw,* for example? Or ever said *what the screw, fat screwing chance,* or *im-screwing-possible?* And the famous bon mot attributed to Dorothy Parker (1893–1967), upon being asked if she planned to come into the office someday soon, loses a lot when rendered, "Tell Mr. [Harold] Ross that I'm too screwing busy and vice versa." The same goes for the answer of W. C. Fields (1879–1946) to the question about why he didn't drink water, i.e., "Because fish screw in it." One might almost as well resort to *frig,* an old (sixteenth-century) term for "to masturbate," which has evolved into a euphemism for the tabooed term, or to the three-letter *fug,* featured prominently in Norman Mailer's *The Naked and the Dead,* which appeared in 1948, before it was safe legally to print the four-letter word. ("I know who you are," Tallulah Bankhead is said to have said upon meeting Mr. Mailer for the first time. "You're the man who doesn't know how to spell *fuck.*") Another variant of the same ilk and the same period was *flog,* as in "Well, when you get back there, tell them what . . . (he searched for the appropriate word, the *mot juste* as they say in the dugouts) . . . what *flogheads* they are. Tell them that for me" (Ed Linn, "The Kid's [Ted Williams'] Last Game," *Sport,* 2/61, ellipses in original).

The taboo on the sexually charged base term, combined with the lack of suitable synonyms, results in a fair amount of hypocrisy, as noted by the anonymous author of "An Ode to Those Four-Letter Words," which runs, in part:

Oh perish the use of those four-letter words
Whose meanings are never obscure;
The Angles and Saxons, those bawdy old birds,
Were vulgar, obscene, and impure.
But cherish the use of the weaseling phrase
That never says quite what you mean.
You had better be known for your hypocrite ways
Than vulgar, impure, and obscene.

Though a lady repels your advance, she'll be kind
Just as long as you intimate what's on your mind.
You may tell her you're *hungry*, you need to be *swung*,
You may ask her *to see how your etchings are hung.*
You may mention the *ashes that need to be hauled;*
Put the lid on her sauce-pan, but don't be too bold;
For the moment you're forthright, get ready to duck—
The woman's not born yet who welcomes "Let's fuck."

Oh banish the use of those four-letter words
Whose meanings are never obscure;
The Angles and Saxons, etc.

This little masterpiece is only mildly dated. As noted by Valerie Solanus in the *S.C.U.M. Manifesto* (1968, the same year she shot Andy Warhol):

The nicest women in our "society" are raving sex maniacs. But, being just awfully, awfully nice they don't, of course, descend to fucking—that's uncouth—rather they make love, commune by means of their bodies and establish sensual rapport; the literary ones are attuned to the throb of Eros and attain a clutch upon the Universe; the religious have spiritual communion with the Divine Sensualism; the mystics merge with the Erotic Principle and blend with the Cosmos, and the acid heads contact their erotic cells.

Even the fast-talking patrons of singles' bars in the 1980s tend to talk around the point (see MONKEY, for example). And when the word is heard, it is much more likely to be in an extended application than in its literal, sexual sense, e.g., Frank is a *fuckup*, or he is *fucking off*, or he *doesn't give a fuck*, or he is *fucking A-OK*, or *far fucking out*, among many, many possibilities. This tendency in the use of the word is epitomized by the story of the sailor, who tells his shipmates about his adventures on leave: "I had a fucking great time. First I went to a fucking bar where I had a few fucking drinks, but it was filled with de-fucking-generates. So I went down the fucking street to another fucking bar and there I met this incredibly fucking good-looking broad and after awhile we went to a fucking hotel where we rented a fucking room and had sex."

The poem about the Angles and Saxons also is correct in suggesting that the bawdy word is an antique one. In fact, it is not a slang term but Standard English, recorded first in Scottish poetry of the early sixteenth century. The oldest example in the *Oxford English Dictionary* is in the form *fukkit* (this is in the 1972 supplement, the word having been excluded when Volume F originally was compiled, 1893–97). The citation is from a poem, "Ane Brash of Wowing," by William Dunbar, composed sometime before 1503.

Thus, *fuck* has a considerably shorter literary history than most other highly tabooed four-letter words. Of course, the term probably was used for many years before Dunbar's employment of it. The shortage of old citations, however, makes the word's etymology impossible to trace. Its early appearance in the works of Dunbar and other Scottish writers suggests that it is a Northern word. By contrast, English writers of the sixteenth century employed such synonyms as *swive, jape,* and *sard*. Today, the first of these survives, but only marginally, in the minds of students of Chaucer ("Thus swyved was this carpenteris wyf!") and of fans of John Barth, who resurrected it in *The Sot-Weed Factor* (1960), a parody of historical novels. A *jape*, meanwhile, has become merely a joke and hardly anyone remembers that the proverb, "Go teach your grandmother to suck eggs" started off as "Go teach your Grandam to sard" (*OED*, 1659).

The modern word seems to be related to the Middle Dutch *fokken*, to strike, to copulate with, and perhaps to the Germanic *ficken*, also to strike and also to copulate with. In addition, it bears a suspicious resemblance to the now obsolete English *firk*, a word of all work, with such diverse meanings as to move sharply and suddenly, to cheat, to urge oneself forward, to move about briskly, to beat, to lash, and which—getting to the point under discussion—also was used by Shakespeare and other writers'in ways that suggest it either was a blood relative of *fuck* or a euphemism for it. For instance, in Thomas Dekker's *The Shoemaker's Holiday* (1599), the lead character, Simon Eyre, and his wife, Margery, discuss a worker named Firk in these terms:

SIMON: Quarrel not with me and my men, with me
　and my fine Firk; I'll firk you if you do.
MARGERY: Yea, yea, man, you may use me as you
　please, but let that pass.

Whatever their relationship to the modern word, the ideas of sex and violence seem to be conjoined in *fokken, ficken,* and *firk*, just as they are in such current slang expressions as *(gang) bang, jump, nail, knock (up), off* (meaning to kill as well as to copulate), and *sock it to [someone]*.

The aggressive component of *fuck*, in fact, is responsible for much of its power in nonsexual contexts, especially when used in defiant attacks upon the Establishment (as in the Free Speech Movement at the University of California at Berkeley in 1964) or, another example from the same period: "If we can't sit at the table, let's knock the fuckin' legs off—excuse me" (James Forman, executive secretary of SNCC, preparing people to march on Selma, Ala., 1965, film clip, WNET-NYC, 2/29/88).

The term's built-in aggression also is evident in such oft-heard expressions as *fuck it, fuck you (Jack* or *Charlie), fucked* (cheated or victimized, as by the famous *fickle finger of fate*), and *(go) fuck yourself*. Of these, the last probably is the most common, e.g., Secretary of State William P. Rogers' reply to General Alexander Haig, when Haig presented him in the spring of 1973 with President Nixon's request for his resignation: "Tell the President to fuck himself" (Bob Woodward and Carl Bernstein, *The Final Days*, 1976). Even on those occasions when the word is used sexually, the aggressive component tends to be large, as in such standard phrases as *to fuck [someone's] brains out* and the famous *four F's*—the motto by which every red-blooded teenage male wishes to live, but seldom does—*find 'em, feel 'em, fuck 'em, forget 'em.*

Just when *fuck* began to replace the older *swive* and *sard* cannot be determined with much precision. The word was included in John Florio's Italian-English dictionary, *World of Wordes* (1598), in the definition of *fottere*: "to jape, to sard, to fucke, to swive, to occupy." Writing at about this time, however, Shakespeare (1564–1616) did not use the term, though he seems to have alluded to it with *firk*, with the French *foutre*, and, in *The Merry Wives of Windsor* (1597), with his reference to the *focative case* as a springboard for puns on *carrot* and ROOT, both old bywords for the penis. Given Shakespeare's tremendous vocabulary, his silence on the point suggests that *fuck* already was known widely enough to be tabooed.

But the word continued to be used, of course. It appears in a dictionary as a main entry for the first time in Thomas Henshaw's *Etymologicon Linguae Anglicanae* (1671), according to Allen Walker Read's ground-breaking article on the history of this term ("An Obscenity Symbol," *American Speech*, 12/34). In practice, however, as far as the written record goes, it seems to have been employed principally in lewd works intended for specialized audiences. Thus, John Wilmot, second Earl of Rochester (1647–80), used it frequently in his occasional verse, as in the epitaph he is supposed to have written for Nell Gwyn:

> She was so exquisite a Whore,
> That in the Belly of her Mother
> Her Cunt was placed so right before,
> Her father fucked them both together.

A most amiable JADE, Nell probably took this in good grace, but if not, she at least had the last laugh by outliving the poet by seven years.

Even in the next century, the word remained printable. It was included in Nathaniel Bailey's *Universal Etymological English Dictionary* (1721) and John Ash's *New and Complete Dictionary of the English Language* (1775)—and Ash was a Baptist minister, yet. Samuel Johnson, however, omitted it from his *Dictionary of the English Language* (1755). When complimented by a literary lady for not having any improper words (BLOODY, BUM, and FART seem not to have ruffled her feathers) in his great work, Dr. Johnson is reported to have replied, "No, Madam, I hope I have not daubed my fingers. I find, however, that you have been looking for them."

Johnson was the arbiter of the age—the Great Cham of Literature, as Smollett put it—and his decision set the precedent for the next two-hundred-odd years for most lexicographers, including Noah Webster (Webster, in fact, thought Johnson had been lax, allowing too many vulgar words into his dictionary) and Sir James Murray, editor of the monumental OED. Even slang dictionaries were affected by prudishness of the period. Thus, Captain Francis Grose admitted the term to the various editions of his *Classical Dictionary of the Vulgar Tongue* (1785, 1788, and 1796), but only in the form of "F--k," and at the start of the next, Victorian century, the term was dropped altogether when his dictionary, slightly revised by "A Member of the Whip Club," was republished as the *Lexicon Balatronicum* (1811). Robert Burns—another Scotsman, note—used the word in his poems, e.g., "And yet misca's a poor thing / That fucks for its bread" (*Merry Muses of Caledonia*, ca. 1790?), and this citation was included in the entry on *fuck* in *Slang and Its Analogues* (J. S. Farmer and W. E. Henley, 1893). Burns was probably the last well-recognized author to employ the term in a literary way prior to the twentieth century (but when his works were republished in 1911, the operative word came out "f--k").

By this time, of course, the social taboo had been cast into law, with passage of the Obscene Publications Act of 1857 in England and the Comstock Act of 1873 in the United States. Farmer and Henley avoided legal difficulties with the notice on the title page of each volume of *Slang and Its Analogues* that it was "*PRINTED FOR SUBSCRIBERS ONLY,*" but the laws were applied more stringently to publications with wider circulations, even those of a scholarly nature. For example, Eric Partridge, annotating Grose's dictionary in 1931, was reduced to "*f--k*" (and "*c--t*"), while Allen Walker Read managed to write his aforementioned 1934 article without once using the term outright, referring instead to "this word," "our word," and so on. As late as 1959, Partridge had to explain to readers of *Origins*, his massive book on etymologies, that "F**k shares with c**t two distinctions: they are the only two Standard English words excluded from all general and etymological dictionaries since the 18th century and . . . outside of medical and other official or semi-official and learned papers, still cannot be printed in full anywhere within the British Commonwealth of Nations."

The threat of prosecution and loss of mailing privileges could keep the word out of print but not, of course, stop people from using it. And use it they did, especially during the First World War, when soldiers employed it so frequently that it began to lose its power. As John Brophy noted in *Songs and Slang of the British Soldier: 1914–1918* (with Eric Partridge, 1930):

> [This word] was so common indeed in its adjectival form that after a short time the ear refused to acknowledge it and took in only the noun to which it was attached. . . . From being an intensive to express a strong emotion it became a merely conventional excrescence. By adding -ing and -ingwell an adjective and adverb were formed and thrown into every sentence. It became so common that an effective way for the soldier to express this emotion was to omit this word. Thus if a sergeant said, "Get your ----ing rifles!" it was understood as a matter of routine. But if he said "Get your rifles!" there was an immediate implication of urgency and danger.

Thus, the war helped numb everyone's senses sufficiently to make it possible to return the word to print. For example, the *OED* included *windfucker*, a name for the kestrel and also a term of opprobrium for a person, from 1599, in the Wh-Wo section, published in 1926 (eleven years after the death of Dr. Murray, who had ignored the bird's alternate name, *fuckwind*). Not many people would think of looking for this word under W in a dictionary, however. Therefore, most of the credit (or discredit, depending on one's point of view) for breaking down the taboo on printing this term belongs to James Joyce (Private Carr: "I'll wring the neck of any bugger says a word against my fucking king," *Ulysses*, 1922) and D. H. Lawrence (Lady C., continuing a conversation included in the entry on the even more highly tabooed *C-word*: "Cunt! It's like fuck then." Mellors: "Nay nay! Fuck's only what you do. Animals fuck. . . . an' tha'rt a lot besides an animal, aren't ter?—even ter fuck," *Lady Chatterley's Lover*, 1928).

After many tribulations and a number of trials (the tribulations included the seizure and burning by the U.S. Post Department of copies of *The Little Review*, containing early installments of *Ulysses*, and the routine confiscation by the U.S. Customs Bureau of any of Lawrence's books), it was finally decided that the public would not be irreparably damaged by the circulation of these works in the United States and England. The key decisions came in 1933 in the case of *Ulysses* in the United States (upheld on appeal in 1934) and, in the case of *Lady Chatterley*, 1959 in the United States and 1960 in England.

Addressing the question of language in the *Ulysses* case, Judge John Woolsey wrote:

> The words which are criticized as dirty are old Saxon words known to almost all men and, I venture, to many women, and are such words as would be naturally and habitually used, I believe, by the types of folk whose life, physical and mental, Joyce is seeking to describe. . . . I am quite aware that owing to some of its scenes "Ulysses" is a rather strong draught to ask some sensitive, though normal, persons to take. But my considered opinion, after long reflection, is that whilst in many places the effect of "Ulysses" on the reader undoubtedly is emetic, nowhere does it tend to be aphrodisiac.
>
> "Ulysses" may therefore be admitted into the United States.

On appeal, the United States Attorney Martin Conboy, clutching at straws, tried to have the book banned for being irreligious instead of obscene, asserting that "whatever constituted a reflection on the Church was indecent." He lost, two to one, with the majority opinion by Judge Augustus N. Hand establishing the principle that "the proper test of whether a given book is obscene is its dominant effect," a guideline that was later elaborated into "whether to the average person, applying contemporary community standards, the dominant theme of the material taken as a whole appeals to the prurient interest" (Justice William Brennan, *Roth v. United States*, 6/24/57).

In passing, it is worth noting that the operative words are rarely articulated in trials of this sort. For example, at the outset of a suit in 1981 to require the school board in Baileyville, Maine, to return *365 Days*, a book about the experiences of American soldiers in Vietnam, to library shelves, Judge Conrad K. Cyr ruled "that no obscene words should be uttered in court, and that the principal word in question should be referred to simply as 'the word.' The proceedings thus often had a Biblical ring" (*New Yorker*, 1/16/84). Or earlier, in one of Lenny Bruce's many trials—this one in Chicago in 1963—the prosecutor conducted his case in the following vein: "I don't think I have to tell you the term, I think that you recall it . . . as a word that started with a 'F' and ended with a 'K' and sounded like 'truck' " (Bruce, *How to Talk Dirty and Influence People*, 1972). Following the Chicago principle, *duck*, as some unknown wit has pointed out, is seventy-five percent obscene. (Bruce was found guilty, but *365 Days* was restored to the shelves in Maine, thanks in part to the testimony of one of the school's teachers, Jean Spearin, who, when asked if students might not be corrupted by the words in the book, replied: "Well, if they are corrupted by words, they couldn't have had much moral fiber to begin with.")

The landmark *Ulysses* and *Chatterley* decisions did not erase the old taboos, of course, with the result that we are now in what can best be described as a state of flux. In the United States, standards of what is printable vary considerably according to region and to medium of communication. Book publishing is the freest, if only because books are relatively expensive compared to newspapers, say, so that fewer people read them and are affected by their contents. (Traditionally, the richer, better-educated, upper classes have been given more leeway to enjoy their vices; after all, they run society.) Even so, book publishers continued to censor themselves and their authors until after World War II; hence, Norman Mailer's *fug*. The major breakthrough came in 1951, three years after publication of Mailer's *The Naked and the Dead*, when James Jones was allowed to include *fuck* (though not *cunt* and *prick*) in *From Here to Eternity*. (Jones had fifty *fucks*, by one laborious count—down from 258 in the original manuscript.) J. D. Salinger's *The Catcher in the Rye*, published the same year, also included the word, e.g., "If you had a million years to do it in, you couldn't rub out even *half* of the 'Fuck you' signs in the world." Subsequently, John O'Hara in *Ten North Frederick* (1955), Allen Ginsberg in the poem *Howl* (1958), and a great many other writers took advantage of their new liberty to render in print the words that real people speak in real life. The freedom given to books as originally published in hardcover, however, is not always extended to low-cost softcover editions for mass audiences, especially if they include children or young adults. Thus, Barbara Beasley Murphy told a meeting of The Authors Guild on February 23, 1983, that the original edition of her *No Place to Run* contained the *F-word*, but that this was deleted from the paperback edition. (See GODDAMN and HELL for more about book publishing in recent American history.)

In the case of magazines, standards vary widely according to the images that editors have of their publications and their readerships. For example (and also illustrating the different standards that may be applied to spoken English and printed English even within the same, largely all-male group), *Business Week* managed to convey the message that Wall Street brokers have converted ticker symbols for some companies into coarse nicknames without actually printing what was being said in the exchanges:

> What floor traders call Shaer Shoe (SHS) and Technical Tape (TTI) cannot be printed in *Business Week*. Perhaps the heaviest cross any company has to bear was what the Street called the old Fairbanks Morse stock, whose symbol before the company vanished into Colt Industries was FKM. Recently, FKM reappeared on the Amex tape, and word spread like lightning around the Street that "FKM is back." The new butt of it all: Fluke Mfg. Co. (7/29/72).

In the 1980s, *New York* magazine, although its audience is concentrated in big, bad Gotham, still used dashes, as in f---in' (4/11/88), and *Publishers Weekly* rendered the term as "*f---ed*" (9/25/87). Meanwhile, the sophisticated *New Yorker*, which formerly resorted to **** (9/10/79), has since found the courage to print all four letters

(6/3/85), page 81). On the other hand, men's magazines (as opposed to men's business magazines) have never had qualms about using the word. Thus, Paul Newman, in a frank interview of the sort that Hollywood stars didn't use to give, told *Playboy* (7/68) how he and Martin Balsam once killed time while on location in Arizona by classifying the different kinds of fucking:

> We got all the psychological classifications. There was sport fucking. There was mercy fucking, which would be reserved for spinsters and librarians. There was the hate fuck, the prestige fuck—and the medicinal fuck, which is "Feel better now, sweetie?" It just goes to show you what happens when you're stuck on location on top of a mountain. Your mind wanders slightly.

As a rule, newspapers, with their broader circulations, will not print the word. Exceptions include alternative (formerly called "underground") papers and neighborhood publications. Thus, the Brooklyn, New York, *Phoenix*, has quoted a mugger, " 'Give me your fucking bike lady!' " (8/18/83). *The Wall Street Journal*, however, avoids the term, e.g., "The invitation: copies of the gloomy Newsweek cover emblazoned with a rude rejoinder: 'N.F.W.' Loosely translated: 'No Feasible Way' " (10/26/87). The nation's newspaper of record, *The New York Times*, also has yet to print the word—and, given its track record, seems unlikely to do so in the near future. The closest the *Times* came to *ratfuck* (see RAT) at the time of the Watergate scandal was "rat----" (10/16/72). Nor did the paper reprint Jimmy Carter's use of *screw* (though it has often admitted that word to its pages in the figurative sense, as in "They are saying their system is screwed up, corrupted," quoting an unnamed White House official on the subject of Soviet defectors, 11/6/85). Then there was the case of Boston *Globe* cartoonist Paul Szep, who used the Russian words *HA XY A* in a drawing on 5/27/83, and was suspended for a week without pay after several readers phoned in to complain that the phrase means "What the fuck."

In the newspaper field, controls also are especially tight on student publications. Thus, the editor of the *Pace Press* at New York's Pace University was required to resign in November 1985 after publishing an article about avoiding AIDS, which included such words as "ass fucking" and "cocksucking." Pace could get away with this since students don't enjoy very much in the way of free speech, as evidenced by the Supreme Court's decision in 1986 upholding the three-day suspension given to Matthew Fraser, of Bethel High School, Spanaway, Washington. Speaking on behalf of a friend who was running for vice president of the student organization, Fraser had described the nominee as "a man who is firm—he's firm in his pants, he's firm in his shirt . . . a man who takes his point and pounds it in . . . a man who will go to the very end—even the climax for each and every one of you." The Supreme Court decided, seven to two, that Mr. Fraser's language was "vulgar and offensive," though it is not clear that the other students were greatly offended, as they elected his candidate to office by a large margin. (See VULGAR for a note on the dissent.)

In the movie business, following the demise of the Motion Picture Production Code (see DAMN, for instance), almost anything goes, the only question being what rating it will get under the X-R-PG-G system that was established by the Motion Picture Association of America in 1968 to shield younger people from some things their parents might not want them to see or hear. Here, too, situational ethics apply. For instance (and providing, in passing, another example of how different media handle the same term): "One naughty word does not necessarily mean an 'R' rating anymore now that director Richard (*Superman*) Donner has won a potentially precedent-setting appeal over the rating of his latest film, *Inside Moves*. . . . [It] was automatically deemed an 'R' because one scene contained the word f---. After viewing the film, however, 13 members of the 15-man MPAA committee voted to change the rating to PG" (*New York Post*, 12/8/80).

In general, the most stringent controls over the use of language at present seem to be exercised by the Federal Communications Commission (though the liberalization of standards in movies has caused some ripples on TV as the products of the silver screen are transferred to the cathode ray tube). Considering the FCC's policy of deregulating practically every other aspect of the broadcasting business, its concern with language seems odd, not to say perverse—and in the psychological sense of that term. The key decision here came in a case involving a broadcast in 1973 by WBAI-FM in New York City of a comedy routine by George Carlin, called "The Seven Dirty Words." Upon receipt of a single complaint by an unnamed man who said he heard the broadcast in company with his young son on a car radio (did palsy prevent him from changing stations?), the FCC banned further use of the words, an edict that was upheld, five to four, by the Supreme Court of the United States in 1978. Newspapers all over the land reported this decision without saying what the seven dirty words were, though at least one, the Portland, Maine, *Press Herald*, came up with the creative idea of announcing that it would supply a copy of the original, uncut story, containing the words, to any reader who sent a stamped, self-addressed envelope to P.O. Box 1460 in the city. (A reminder to announcers later was taped on the wall of WBAI's master control room. Printed in Gothic script, it read: "And the Supreme Court affirmeth the F.C.C., thus saying unto the Broadcasters—Thou Shalt Not Saith these seven Sinful words: Shit, Fuck, Piss, Cocksucker, Motherfucker, Cunt or Tits. Repetitively, gratuitously, or when children are in the room.")

Not content with this success, the FCC has since (1987) restored a 1976 order that restricts so-called indecent programming (and also telephone transmissions) in much broader, much vaguer terms. This order defines indecency as "language or material that depicts or describes, in terms patently offensive as measured by contemporary community standards for the broadcast medium, sexual or excretory activities or organs." Violators may be fined or lose their operating licenses. One result of this change was that in 1988 the Pacifica Radio Network, including WBAI and four other stations, declined to broadcast a reading of Allen Ginsberg's *Howl*. The network had just spent about $100,000 in legal fees to defend itself against one obscenity complaint and could not afford another such victory.

Obviously, we still have a way to go before we attain the state of grace exemplified by the sweetly solemn thought, often attributed to John (see MISTRESS) Wilkes but probably written by his friend, Thomas Potter, son of an archbishop of Canterbury, in *An Essay on Woman*:

> . . . life can little more supply
> Than just a few good fucks and then we die

This poem, a parody of Pope's *Essay on Man*, was read to the House of Lords by the Earl of Sandwich on November 15, 1763. One noble member demanded that the reading cease, but others cried, "Go on! Go on!" Nevertheless, the House resolved that Wilkes be prosecuted for printing "a most scandalous, obscene and impious libel." (The libel part arose because notes on the poem were attributed to the learned Bishop of Gloucester, William Warburton, of DOXY fame, to whom Pope had bequeathed his copyrights.)

Wilkes's arrest was ordered and he departed the country instead of answering the charge, not to return for four years—and when he did, he was jailed for twenty-two months. This set the stage for an epic test of wills between the voters of Middlesex and the government. The voters elected the radical Wilkes to Parliament four times while he was in prison, and he was denied a seat four times on account of his conduct. As a result, "Wilkes and Liberty" became a rallying cry throughout the land and in the American colonies abroad. Not until 1774 did Wilkes return to Parliament, though he was elected alderman and sheriff of London in the interim.

The real question, however—not addressed in most history books—is whether Sandwich, in reading the poem to the House of Lords, was more anxious to embarrass Wilkes on account of their political differences or on account of a very personal grudge: Wilkes had smuggled a baboon in a trunk into a Black Mass being celebrated by the earl at a gathering of the Hell Fire Club (to which both men, former friends, belonged). Released at a critical moment, the baboon, attired in a devil's costume, had hopped onto the earl's back, bringing the ceremony to a crashing end—and scaring the bejesus out of his Lordship.

There is often more to censorship than meets the eye.

fuddy-duddy. A fussy, old-fashioned person; an old FOGY. "Mr. Mott wandered along the Promenade . . . looking at the damned old fuddy-duddies who cluttered it up" (D. Moffat, *Mott Family in France*, 1938). Of unknown origin, the term surfaced first in a dialect dictionary of 1899 as *duddy fuddiel*, a ragged fellow. This makes it substantially older than Elmer Fudd (b. 1938), the animated cartoon character who usually lives up to his name. Variants include *fuddie-duddie*, *fuddydud*, and *fudbucket*, as in "STUPID ME! I called a Hollywood palooka a 'fudbucket.' He grunted, 'Me kill you!'" (Los Angeles *Reader*, 4/1/83).

funky. Stinky, smelly, musty. "He kept cursing at her and telling her what a stinking, dirty, funky bitch she was" (Claude Brown, *Manchild in the Promised Land*, 1965). "I thought I heard Buddy Bolden say / 'Funky-butt, funky-butt, take it away!'" (Jelly Roll Morton, recording, "Buddy Bolden's Blues," 1939). "The adjective of Buddy Bolden's legendary coinage connoted the bodily aroma of women who frequented a dance floor back of town in humid New Orleans, where they slow-dragged to low-down blues or up-tempoed to the strains of ragtime, which reflected the speed-up of American life around the first decade of this century" (Peter Tamony, *American Speech*, Fall 1980).

The malodorous sense of *funk* is at least three centuries old (*OED*, 1623). Captain Francis Grose defined the term this way in 1785: "To smoke [tobacco]; figuratively, to smoke or stink through fear" (*A Classical Dictionary of the Vulgar Tongue*). Hence, to be in a *funk*, or *blue funk*, is to be in a state of great fright. Other variations, chiefly British, include a *funk*, which is a coward; *funkhole*, which is a place to hide, such as a foxhole; *funk it*, which is to panic and shrink away from something or to fail, or flunk, usually an exam in school. The term was applied to music around 1954 by black musicians for whom *funky jazz* represented a return to the low-down, earthy roots of New Orleans jazz, as opposed to the cool, progressive, West Coast style that had been developed by Stan Kenton, Dave Brubeck, and other well-schooled white musicians following World War II. "Critics are on the search for something a little more like the old, original, passion-laden blues; the trade name which has been suggested for it is 'funky' (literally 'smelly', i.e. symbolising the return from the upper atmosphere to the physical, down-to-earth reality)" ("F. Newton," *Jazz Scene*, 1959). The application of the word to music brought *funky* into fashion in a favorable sense, so that the flower children of the 1960s began *to funk*, that is, to swing, to *funky* music; to wear *funky* clothes; and to adopt a *funky* life-style. See also JAZZ and PUNK.

funny. Not so funny in such expressions as *funny business*, or underhanded business; *funny face*, a traditional children's taunt; *funny farm*, an institution for the insane; and *to make fun of*, to tease—sometimes unmercifully.

Fun has become *funny* in a comical sense only within the last couple hundred years. *Fun* originally referred to a trick, hoax, or practical joke. Samuel Johnson knew *fun* in the modern sense of "Sport; high merriment; frolicksome delight," but characterized it as "A low cant word" (*A Dictionary of the English Language*, 1755). It probably comes from the Middle English *fon*, fool, whence also *fond*, originally a foolish affection, and *fondle*. See also FOOL.

fussbudget (or **-box** or **-pot**). A person who fusses a lot, especially an old woman or someone who acts like one. "Her husband was old fuss-budget Frank" (Margaret Mitchell, *Gone with the Wind*, 1936). The *fuss-* prefix has been dated only to 1901 (*OED*) but is certainly much older. The expression may have been popularized in part by the career of General Winfield Scott (1786-1866), widely known as "Old Fuss and Feathers" on account of his obsession with procedures and fondness for elaborate uniforms.

fuzzy-wuzzy. Originally, from the 1880s, a Sudanese warrior, from his hairstyle; later, any dark-skinned native with kinked hair, especially a resident of Fiji or New Guinea.

In the beginning, it was possible to use the term with some respect. The *fuzzy-wuzzies*, after all, defeated General Charles "Chinese" Gordon rather decisively at Khartoum in 1885. Rudyard Kipling praised their valor: "So 'ere's to you, Fuzzy-Wuzzy, at your 'ome in the Soudan. . . . a pore benighted 'eathen but a first-class fighting man" (*Tommy Atkins*, 1890). Such epithets are always essentially negative, however, as evidenced by the term's use in the following context: "There are Chinks and Japs and Fuzzy Wuzzies and Ice Creamers and Dagos, and so forth" (Nancy Mitford, *Pigeon Pie*, 1940). See also GOOK and LONGHAIR.

G

gaffer. An old feller; originally a term of respect (a sixteenth-century contraction of *Godfather*), but not often used that way today, reflecting the general decline in status of aged people in modern society. ". . . words like . . . gaffer, geezer, codger, dotard, old-time, antediluvian, pre-adamite, don't help anyone to think kindly about the elderly" (Donna Woolfolk Cross, *Word Abuse*, 1979). See also FOGY.

gaga. Crazy, foolish. "Nola darling, you've just gone gaga, that's all. What do you mean by staying down there in that wretched malarial heat" (Edna Ferber, *Show Boat*, 1926). The term has been dated to 1905. It derives from the French *gaga*, a senile person, the French word in turn being the nonsense imitation of the sound of a DOTARD's stammering speech. See also DOTTY.

galoot. A clumsy, uneducated, ill-mannered person; especially a rustic or LOUT. "Hear ye! Hear ye! This honorable court's now in session; and if any galoot wants a snort afore we start, let him step up to the bar and name his pizen" (Judge Roy Bean, 1825?–1903; his standard way of opening court in Langtry, Texas, in the 1880s and '90s, from Ruel McDaniel, *Vinegarroon*, 1936). The word dates to the early nineteenth century, appearing first as nautical slang for a soldier—that is, an awkward fellow in the eyes of sailors. See also LUMMOX and the *horse marines* in HORSE.

gang. A group of hoodlums or thugs. The term is used frequently in politics to imply that one's opponents are criminals, e.g., China's *Gang of Four*, led by Mao Zedong's widow, charged in 1976 with attempting to "usurp party and state power." The United States also has political *gangs*. Thus, discussing politics in Honolulu: "The gang that got in there and did well by themselves will be replaced by another gang that will take care of themselves and their friends while the system suffers and the state suffers" (Thomas P. Gill, former lieutenant governor of Hawaii, *New York Times*, 12/30/85).

A *gang* originally (pre-1000) was a going, way, or passage, a sense that is preserved in *gangway*. The meaning was extended by the fourteenth century to sets of things that went together, such as horseshoes and cartwheels, and later widened further to include people, tools, animals, workmen (as in *railroad gang*), and slaves or prisoners (the members of a *chain gang* qualify doubly, since they are workmen as well as convicts). The oldest example of the depreciatory, criminal sense of the term in the OED comes from 1632: "Nutt the pirate . . . with all his gang of varlets" (Thomas Birch, *The Court and Times of Charles I*). Another early user of the word in this sense was the Reverend Cotton Mather, who told his congregation that "some of the *Witch Gang* have been fairly executed," referring to events in

Salem, Massachusetts (sermon, 8/4/1692). A person who belongs to a *gang* is a *gangster*. The last term is an Americanism and it seems to have been employed first in a political context: "The gangster may play all sorts of pranks with the ballot box, but in its own good time the latter will get even by kicking the gangster into the gutter" (*Columbus* [Ohio] *Evening Dispatch*, 4/10/1896). See also BANDIT, BOSS, GOON, MOB, and THUG.

garbage. Anything worthless. "He's a piece of garbage" (a defense lawyer's characterization of a prosecution witness in a criminal trial, "60 Minutes," CBS-TV, 2/9/86). *Garbage* also means nonsense, as in "That's a load of garbage"; profanity, as in "Joe has a garbage mouth"; and worthless literature, as in "She flew with voracious appetite to sate herself on the garbage of any circulating library" (Jane Porter, *Thaddeus of Warsaw*, 1803).

Garbage started off as a culinary term, referring to giblets or other animal entrails to be eaten: "Take fayre garbagyes of chykonys [chickens] . . ." (*Two Cookery Books*, ca. 1430). See also RUBBISH and TRASH.

gas. Empty talk, bragging, nonsense; hot air. ". . . our whole conception of what exists outside us, is based upon the sense of touch. We carry this even into our metaphors: a good speech is 'solid,' a bad speech is 'gas,' because we feel that gas is not quite real" (Bertrand Russell, *The ABC of Relativity*, 1969). The person who talks too much is, naturally, a *gasbag*. The metaphor dates in the 1840s and probably derives from the earlier comparison of puffed up people to gas-filled balloons. This comparison was being made as early as 1792, just nine years after the Montgolfiers put the first balloon into the sky. The word *gas* was coined by a Belgian chemist, J. B. van Helmont (1577–1644), to describe a "spirit" produced by burning charcoal. ". . . this spirit, hitherto unknown . . . I call by the new name *gas*" (*Ortus medicinae*, 1648). He based his new word on the Greek *khaos*, chaos. See also BUNK and WINDBAG.

gascon. A braggart; one who indulges in extravagant boasting. This is an ethnic slur, alluding to the inhabitants of Gascony in southwestern France. They were regarded as great boasters from at least the eighteenth century. Thus, from "Song," a poem by Tobias Smollett (1721–71): "A peacock in pride, in grimace a baboon, / In courage a hind, in conceit a Gascoon." Or as the young Gascon said, when asked what he thought of his first sight of the Louvre, "Very nice—it reminds me of the back part of my father's stable." D'Artagnan, the hero of *The Three Musketeers*, who managed to talk himself into duels with three renowned fighters as soon as he arrived in Paris, was a Gascon—as was his real-life model, Charles de Baatz D'Artagnan (1623–73). See also *gasconade* in PEORIA.

gay. A good old word, from the fourteenth century, that has become tarred in recent years as a result of its association with homosexuality. "There's no telling what bothers people. Take the residents of Gay Street in West Seneca, New York. More than half of the families living there petitioned for a street name change. From now on they want to be called Fawn Trail" (*New York Times*, 6/7/87).

The homosexual sense of *gay* derives from the word's use in the heterosexual underworld. Thus, back in the 1600s, a dissipated or immoral man might be described as a *gay fellow*, and in the 1800s, a *gay bit* (or *woman*) was a prostitute, who might be said to lead the *gay life*, to live and work in a *gay house*, and *to gay it* when copulating (men could *gay it,* too). What happened was that in London, New York, and other large cities in the nineteenth century, prostitutes and homosexuals, both outgroups, frequently lived in close association and used the same lingo. *Gay's* first appearance in a dictionary in its homosexual sense is in N. Ersine's *Underworld & Prison Slang,* of 1935: "*Geycat* . . . a homosexual boy." As far back as 1889, however, at the time of the Cleveland Street Scandal (involving post office boys in a male brothel in London's West End), a prostitute named John Saul used *gay* with reference to both male homosexuals and to female prostitutes when giving evidence to the police and in court. PUNK made a similar transition at about the same time, changing from an essentially feminine-heterosexual term to a masculine-homosexual one; FAG and QUEER may have done the same. For other words that seem to have arisen in the homosexual underworld of the late nineteenth century, see FAIRY and PANSY.

geek. One who has sunk to the lowest depths of degradation; in a carnival sideshow, the "wild man" who kills chickens by biting off their heads. "I have always found [Franklin Delano] Roosevelt an amusing fellow, but I would not employ him, except for reasons of personal friendship, as a geek in a common carnival" (Murray Kempton, in Nancy McPhee, *The Book of Insults,* 1978). *Geek* is a nineteenth-century variant of a much older word, *geck,* meaning a fool or one who is fooled. It dates from at least the sixteenth century, e.g., "Why have you suffered me to be imprisoned . . . And made the most notorious geck and gull that e'er invention played on?" (William Shakespeare, *Twelfth Night,* 1600–02). The word was popularized in its modern form by William Lindsay Gresham's novel, *Nightmare Alley* (1946), and the film starring Tyrone Power that was made from it (1947). Both *geck* and *geek* also can be used as verbs. " 'How do you ever get a guy to geek? Or is this the only one? I mean, is a guy born that way—liking to bite off the heads of chickens?' " (Gresham, op. cit.). Among schoolchildren in the late 1980s in New York City, and very likely elsewhere, a *geek* or *geekoid* was the same as a NERD. See also FOOL and GULL.

geezer. An old person, usually male. *Geezer* apparently is a Cockney pronunciation of *guiser,* one in disguise—specifically, a mummer wearing a mask. Dated only to 1885 (*OED*), the term originally was applied more often to women than to men, often in the form *old geezer.* See also GAFFER.

German. Curiously, considering all the trouble they inflicted upon other nations, the Germans have not inspired a great many ethnic slurs, at least not in their own name. As far back as the eighteenth century, a *German duck* was "Half a sheep's head boiled with onions" (Captain Francis Grose, *A Classical Dictionary of the Vulgar Tongue,* 1785), and later generations produced such unflattering references as *German comb,* the fingers; *German garden,* a beer garden; *German goiter,* a beer belly; *German gospel,* boasting; *German measles,* not real measles; and *German silver,* not real silver but a white alloy of copper, zinc, and nickel. In time of war, especially during World War I, *German* was shunned, with the result that dog owners began keeping *Alsatians* instead of *German shepherds,* while children stayed home from school with *liberty measles.* The true place of the Germans in the lexicon of derogation is revealed more clearly, however, by their various nicknames and the ways in which these terms are used; see also BOCHE, HEINIE, HESSIAN, HUN, JERRY, KRAUT, and PRUSHUN.

gigolo. A man who is kept by a woman; especially a young man who squires an older woman around town, dancing in attendance upon her. Since the man is cast in a female role, it is only appropriate the term describing him is feminine, from the French *gigolette*, a prostitute, a dance-hall girl. The term has only been dated to the post–World War I period: "A gigolo, generally speaking, is a man who lives off women's money. In the mad year of 1922 . . . a gigolo, definitely speaking, designated one of those incredible and pathetic male creatures . . . who, for ten francs, . . . would dance with any woman wishing to dance . . . in the cafes, hotels, and restaurants of France" (*Woman's Home Companion*, 11/22). The *gigolette*, in turn, comes from *giguer*, to dance, and *gigue*, a word that appears in English as well as French as the name of a particular kind of dance. See also JIG.

gink. A man, especially a poor, unfortunate one; a JERK. Thus, speaking of one, Jeff Davis, who set himself up in 1908 as the King of the Hoboes: "In the early years of his reign as monarch, King Jeff opened several establishments for his subjects, each euphemistically called 'Hotel de Gink' " (Roger A. Bruns, *Knights of the Road*, 1980). It has been speculated that *gink* might be related to the Scottish *ginkie*, a contemptuous term for a woman, or to a Turkish word for *catamite*. See also GOON and PUNK.

ginzo. A foreigner, especially an Italian or Italian-American, sometimes rendered as *guinzo* and probably a variant of GUINEA. "He is nothing but a ginzo out of Sacramento, and his right name is Carfarelli" (Damon Runyon, *Take It Easy*, 1939).

girl. A female child; a young, unmarried woman; a form of address once widely accepted by women of practically all ages but likely now to be taken as an insult in any kind of public setting unless the person is very young indeed. Thus, the New York State Commission on Judicial Conduct publicly reprimanded a justice of the State Supreme Court, Anthony T. Jordan, Jr., for saying to an attorney who appeared before him on December 7, 1981, "I will tell you what, little girl, you will lose." The "little girl," according to the commission's report, subscribed to by six of its nine members, "was clearly an epithet calculated to demean the lawyer" (*New York Times*, 3/1/83). It is even more insulting to call a young man a *girl*, of course, e.g., a famous end-of-the-halftime remark attributed to Texas A&M football coach Dana X. Bible on a Saturday when his team was being badly outplayed, "Well, girls, shall we go?"

The recent assignment of pejorative meanings to *girl* continues a well-established trend. Up to the middle of the fifteenth century, *girl* was a neutral term. This was because the word originally referred to a child of either sex. Back then, *girls* were divided into *knaves* or *knave girls*, which were boys, and *gay girls*, which were girl-girls. (See also KNAVE.) Once the term was restricted to females, however, negative meanings began to develop. By the seventeenth century, for example, a *girl* was a maidservant, a *girl-of-all-work*, as in "my wife, coming up suddenly, did find me embracing the girl . . . I was at a wonderful loss upon it, and the girle also" (*The Diary of Samuel Pepys*, 10/25/1668). (The quotation is from the standard edition of the diary, edited by Henry B. Wheatley, 1893–99. Wheatley used ellipses in place of those passages which, as he explained in his preface, "cannot possibly be printed." This particular ellipsis shielded Victorian readers from the fact that Pepys was embracing the maid "con my hand sub su coats" when Mrs. Pepys surprised them.) In the eighteenth century, a *girl* (or *woman*) *about town* was a whore, while a *kind girl* was one's mistress. And in the nineteenth century, the term was applied as easily to a horse as a human: " 'Cheer up, old girl,' said Tom, patting the bay mare on the neck . . ." (Charles Dickens, *Pickwick Papers*, 1836–37).

Today the *Gibson Girl* of the 1890s is only one of a host of *girls* that would have to be renamed if reincarnated. Other girlish types of the past include the *sewing machine girl*, the *typewriter girl*, the *telephone girl*, the *career girl*, the *sales girl*, and the *bachelor girl* (also called a *bachelorette;* her latchkey was said to be her symbol of independence).

So good-bye to all the once-acceptable *girls*. Good-bye to *the It Girl* (Clara Bow, who starred in the film, *It*, based on Elinor M. Glyn's 1927 bestseller with that title) and good-bye to her sisters, the *glamour, oomph, pin-up,* and *sweater girls.* Good-bye, too, to *girlie*, a nineteenth-century term of endearment for little girls that later was applied to *girlie shows* and *girlie mags*, featuring very big *girls* indeed. (This line also led to *girly burly* for a burlesque show.) And good-bye, perhaps, to the *college girl* and to the *Girl Scout*, who, it has been suggested, should be turned into a *Youth Scout*. (Don't laugh. Amid the linguistic ferment of the 1970s, *Campfire Girls* became *Campfire, Inc.*, and the *Boy Scouts of America* adopted *Scouting USA* as their "communicative" name.) Of them all, only the *Cosmo Girl* still unabashedly flaunts her wares, typically in full-page ads, down to the navel: "You *can* be loving and ambitious at the same time says my mentor magazine . . . I guess you could say that I'm That COSMOPOLITAN Girl" (*New York Times*, 1/22/87).

See also MOLL, TART, WENCH, and, for other formerly masculine words that have acquired pejorative feminine meanings, HARLOT and HOYDEN.

git. A worthless person, a fool or idiot; a British updating of *get*, in the sense of *beget*, meaning any offspring, but particularly a BASTARD. "That bald-faced, moon-faced, four-eyed git Garnett gristling on about Harold Wilson" (*The Listener*, 8/3/60). See also FOOL and IDIOT.

goat. A lecher, often an *old goat*, in tribute to the sustained interest of some gaffers in this sort of thing. "By temperament, which is the *real* law of God, many men are goats and can't help commiting adultery when they get a chance; whereas there are numbers of men who, by temperament, can keep their purity and let an opportunity go by if the woman lacks in attractiveness" (Mark Twain, Letter 8, in Bernard DeVoto, *Letters from the Earth*, 1962).

The goat has been a symbol of sin (the devil's cloven feet are those of a goat) and of lechery for hundreds of years. Thus, from a twelfth century Latin bestiary: ". . . the He-Goat is a lascivious and butting animal who is always burning for coition. His eyes are transverse slits because he is so randy" (T. H. White, tr., *The Bestiary*, 1954). And from Shakespeare, "It is impossible you should see this, Were they as prime [lustful] as goats, as hot as monkeys, As salt [eager] as wolves in pride [heat] . . ." (*Othello*, 1604). The proper Shakespearean adjective is *goatish*. See also HOT, MONKEY, and WOLF.

Goat does have other meanings. For instance, *goat* may also be a dupe or, especially in sports, a player who makes a game-losing play, e.g., quoting a Philadelphia 76er, after being stripped of the ball at the end of a basketball game with the Boston Celtics: "What happened out there won't haunt me. I don't feel like a goat" (*New York Times*, 5/23/85). This sense of *goat* probably derives from the concept of the *scapegoat*, who bears the sins of others. Then there is *to get [one's] goat*, which is to anger another person. This is an Americanism of mysterious origin though not very old (*OED*, 1910). The most common theory of the phrase's origin is that it comes from the practice of racehorse owners of keeping a goat in the stables as gentling influence upon high-strung thoroughbreds. The idea is that getting the goat away from the stables might assure gamblers of a disastrous finish for the favorite.

See also the *Judas goat* in JUDAS and NANNY GOAT.

gobbledygook. Meaningless words, blithering blather; governmental jargon, originally and especially. Invention of the word usually is credited to Representative Maury Maverick (Democrat, Texas), grandson of the MAVERICK, whose duties as chairman of the Smaller War Plants Corp. during the Second World War required him to attend committee meetings at which BUREAUCRATS ran on about "maladjustments co-extensive with problem areas," "alternative but nevertheless meaningful minimae," and so on. This inspired him to produce a formal order on March 30, 1944, banning "gobbledygook language": "Be short and say what you're talking about. . . . No more *patterns, effectuating, dynamics*. Anyone using the words *activation* or *implementation* will be shot." The word obviously filled a need, since it caught on immediately. "People ask me where I got gobbledygook," the congressman explained. "I do not know. It must have come in a vision. Perhaps I was thinking of the old bearded turkey gobbler back in Texas who was always gobbledy-gobbling and strutting with ludicrous pomposity. At the end of this gobble there was a sort of gook" (*New York Times Magazine*, 5/21/44). See also TURKEY.

Synonyms of *gobbledygook* include *bafflegab, federalese, officialese, Pentagonese*, and *Washington Choctaw. Officialese* (*OED*, 1884) is the oldest of these, but *bafflegab* probably has the widest currency. It is a product of the early 1950s: "Milton Smith, the assistant general counsel of the U.S. Chamber of Commerce, has coined a new word, 'bafflegab,' designed solely for Washington bureaucrats, or for UN bureaucrats, for that matter" (San Francisco *Call-Bulletin*, 3/4/52). See also BUNK and MALARKEY.

goddamn. Wretched, cursed, like DAMN, only more so; generally used as an exclamation or an intensifier (e.g., *inde-goddamn-pendent*, attributed to newspaper publisher Joseph Pulitzer, 1847–1911), without particular reference to Divine Damnation and, with this in mind, often rendered as *goddam*. The oath has been dated to the fifteenth century (though it is no doubt much older), when English soldiers used it with sufficient frequency to lead the French, including Joan of Arc, to refer to them collectively as the *goddems*. The spirit of the expression, and the traditional literary constraints upon it, are evident from Captain Frederick Marryat's *Mr. Midshipman Easy* (1836), wherein the chaplain of a naval vessel laments a verbal indiscretion:

> "I hope I have not sworn—I hope not."
> "Not a word," said Jack—"I was close to you all the time—you only said, 'God preserve us!' "
> "Only that? I was afraid that I said 'God d____n it!' "

By and large, the expression has not been tabooed as heavily in Protestant countries as the various sexual and excremental terms that also serve as exclamations and intensifiers. This situation is reversed in Roman Catholic countries, as evidenced by Dante, who indulges freely in obscenity, while consigning blasphemers to the seventh level of Hell, in the company of murderers, perverts, and the like. Which is not to say that the Protestants haven't tried to control profanity. Thus, the rising tide of Puritanism in England was marked in 1605 by Parliament's passage of "An Act to restrain the Abuses of Players," which provided for a fine of £10 for anyone who "in any stage play, interlude, show, may-game, or pageant [should] jestingly or profanely speak or use the holy Name of God, or of Christ Jesus, or of the Holy Ghost, or of the Trinity." The authors of this act would have happily seconded George Washington's general order in July 1776 to the Continental Army: "The General is sorry to be informed that the foolish and wicked practice of profane cursing and swearing, a vice hitherto little known in an American army, is growing into fashion. He hopes the officers will, by example as well as influence, endeavor to check it, and that both they and the men will reflect that we can have little hope of the blessing of Heaven on our arms if we insult it by our impiety and folly." In our own century, this attitude was encapsulated most succinctly in the Motion Picture Production Code of 1930, which ordained that "Pointed profanity (this includes the words *God, Lord, Jesus Christ*—unless used reverently—*Hell, S.O.B., damn, Gawd*), or every other profane or vulgar expression, however used, is forbidden."

While Hollywood soundtracks have since admitted far bolder terms, the old prohibitions remain, especially among religious fundamentalists, who, like Dante, tend to take a severer view of profanity than obscenity. Thus, Thomas Nelson, Inc., of Nashville, Tennessee, a major Bible publisher, will permit authors of its general books, which are marketed in Christian bookstores, only to go as far as *g-----n*. No one outside the religious trade paid much attention to this policy until 1983 when Nelson required Dodd, Mead & Co., then its subsidiary in big, bad New York, to cancel three titles because their authors refused to excise this and other dreadful words. In an article on the episode—and demonstrating that the term generally is considered printable in full, even by a fairly fastidious family newspaper—*The New York Times* reported: "Lewis W. Gillenson, president of Dodd, Mead, said that Nelson had insisted that certain 'four-letter words, excessive scatology and language that took God's name in vain' had to be eliminated . . . an executive of Nelson told him it was all right to print 'damn' but not 'goddamn.' The four-letter word for copulation was forbidden, but the four-letter word for defecation was permitted" (9/1/83). In drawing these fine distinctions, it seems that Nelson's executives were reflecting accurately the mores of the Bible Belt. As Barbara Beaseley Murphy, whose *No Place to Run* was put on the restricted shelves of two high-school libraries in Calhoun County, Alabama (along with *The Grapes of Wrath, The Catcher in the Rye,* and similarly dangerous titles), told a meeting of The Authors Guild: "Goddamn in Anniston is worse than shit and bastard and son of a bitch" (2/23/83). See also JESUS.

goldbrick. An idler; one who tries to get out of doing his share of the work, especially in the Army; as a verb, to loaf, etc. "The wise guy always complains when there is work to do. Sometimes [in the Army] he is called a Gold Brick" (*Reader's Digest*, 10/43). The expression has been dated to 1914, appearing first as a description of lieutenants appointed direct from civilian life. Such officers, it seems, had something in common with the older sense of the term, from the nineteenth century, referring to an ordinary brick, dolled up by a swindler to look like gold. Actually, the *gold brick* wasn't worth anything, of course. See also LOAFER.

goober-grabber. A native of Georgia, dating from before the Civil War and derived from the importance of the peanut among the state's agricultural product; in some parts of the South, also a wanton, lascivious woman, from *goobers* as a euphemism for the male genitals (i.e., *peanuts*, sight and sound reinforcing one another). A *goober* also is a stupid person. The word is an African import, from *nguba*. See also PEANUT.

goody-good(y). Someone or something so excessively good as to make one's stomach turn. "Baddybad Stephen led astray goodygood Malachi" (James Joyce, *Ulysses*, 1922). See also SISSY.

goody two-shoes. An obnoxiously good person, often a HYPOCRITE; a GOODY-GOOD(Y). Thus, from a letter to the editor of *The New York Times*: "How can you be so Goody Two-shoes Sunday morning [in an editorial] about a broadcast you don't think is fit to be shown and then go out Sunday night and show it on your three New York Times television stations?" (Don Hewitt, executive producer of "60 Minutes," 2/22/85). The original Goody Two-Shoes was the heroine of a nursery tale, "The History of Little Goody Two-Shoes," included in *Mother Goose's Melody: or Sonnets for the Cradle*, published by John Newbery around 1765. (He is best remembered today for the Newbery Award, given for the best children's book published each year.) The girl in the story was a very poor child who was so overjoyed at receiving a pair of new shoes that she pointed them out to everyone she met, saying, "Two shoes!"—whence the title. In time, she gained knowledge, and wealth, too. The author of this epic may well have been Oliver Goldsmith, who is known to have done a lot of work for Newbery in this period and who probably edited this edition of *Mother Goose* for him. See also CROSSPATCH.

goof. A stupid fellow, also called a *goofball*, or a silly mistake; a person who acts *goofy* or constantly *goofs up* (as opposed to *goofs around* or *goofs off*, which is something that even smart people do when they waste time). The stupid *goof* is the oldest of these, dating to around World War I. It may be an alteration of the obsolete *goff*, an awkward person, a fool, from the sixteenth century. "He calls the bishop Greybeard Goff, And makes his power a mere scoff" (*OED*, 1678). See also JERK.

goo-goo. A political reformer; specifically and historically (from the 1890s), an advocate of *Good Government* in Boston, New York, and other machine-ridden cities; in extended use, a naïve person, a BLEEDING HEART or DO-GOODER. "The entire story of 'Ethics in the Boesky Era . . .' is redolent of the sort of mawkish, goo-goo liberalism of which the Northeast, the Ivy League, and Yale have reeked for years" (letter to the *Yale Alumni Magazine*, Summer 1987). See also GOOK.

gook. A foreigner; usually an Oriental. "Rather than eat the gook maid's cooking, Capt. Holmes had dined, and dined well, in the Bachelor Officers' Mess . . ." (James Jones, *From Here to Eternity*, 1951). And in the extended Occidental sense: "We got that clock the summer we went to Europe, me an' Big Mama on that damn Cook's Tour, never had such an awful time in my life, I'm telling you, son, those gooks over there, they gouge your eyeballs out in their grand hotels" (Tennessee Williams, *Cat on a Hot Tin Roof*, 1955).

The origin of *gook* is uncertain but it may come from *gugu* or *goo-goo*, as used in the American military to refer to Filipinos from ca. 1899 when our "little brown brothers" (William Howard Taft's phrase) had the temerity to rise up in arms against the people who had taken them and their islands away from Spain. This *goo-goo* (as opposed to the domestic, political GOO-GOO) may imitate the babbling of a language the Americans didn't understand or—another school of thought— allude to the shape of native eyes, from the phrase *goo-goo eyes* (soft and seductive, from ca. 1900). Both theories fit with standard ethnic labeling practices: see BARBARIAN and SLANT. Whatever the source, *gook* was used widely in World War II and subsequent conflicts. Its harsh sound makes it ideal for dehumanizing the enemy. (See also TERMITE.) Thus, from a realistic novel of World War II: " 'Gooks don't have consciences like we do,' Jack's 'buddy' explained. 'Life don't mean nothing to them. They'll sell their wives, daughters, kids, like goddam livestock' " (Earl Thompson, *Tattoo*, 1974). And from real life in Vietnam: "And when you shot someone you didn't think you were shooting at a human. They were a gook or a Commie and it was okay . . ." (Michigan Winter Soldier Investigation, 1971, in Frances FitzGerald, *Fire in the Lake*, 1972). The expression has since been adopted by armies in other lands. As the commander of the white government's Selous Scouts in what was still Rhodesia told *The New York Times* (7/16/79): "My men have tracked down 68 percent of all the gooks killed in this war." (A dead *gook* in this war was called a *floppy*.) See also ASIATIC, CHINK, DINK, DOTHEAD, FUZZY-WUZZY, RAGHEAD, SLANT, SLOPE, WOG, and ZIP.

goon. A stupid person, an oaf; a ruffian or tough, especially one hired to intimidate workers.

The first kind of *goon* probably comes from *gony*, a sixteenth-century term for a booby or simpleton, which also forms the basis for the name of the awkward *gooney bird* (see ALBATROSS). *Goon* in this sense appeared first in print in 1921 and was popularized in the late 1930s by college students, whose collective fancy was taken by Alice the Goon, a large ugly creature in E. C. Segar's *Thimble Theater* (Popeye) comic strip. Soldiers also latched onto the word prior to World War II, with *goon* designating those who had the lowest scores on Army classification tests. (See also ZOMBIE.) The Popeye strip, by the way, also was partly responsible for the name of the ubiquitous General Purpose vehicle of WW II, thanks to the confluence of the name of one of its characters, Eugene the Jeep, and the military abbreviation *G.P.*

The second, strong-armed kind of *goon* surfaced during labor troubles of the Depression, as in the Woody Guthrie song from this era:

> There once was a union maid.
> She was never afraid
> Of goons and ginks and company finks
> And the deputy sheriff that made the raids.

This *goon*, however, may come from the Hindi *gunda*, also a hired tough. The Hindi term appeared in British newspapers as early as 1926: "A general round-up of goondahs, or roughs, took place this morning [in Calcutta]" (*Glasgow Herald*, 4/27/26). And it remains in use on the subcontinent: " 'Congress [Party] goondas are worse than MIC,' said one poster, using a Hindi term for 'hoodlum' to compare Mr. Brabha, a businessman, with methyl isocyanate, the toxic chemical that leaked from a Union Carbide Corporation plant here [Bhopal] Dec. 3, killing at least 2,000 people" (*New York Times*, 12/13/84). See also HOODLUM and, another Indian import, THUG.

goop. A stupid, ill-mannered fellow; a BOOR. "Americans are shocked when they go abroad and discover whole groups of people behaving like goops—eating with their fingers and, making noises and talking while eating" (*Scientific American*, 4/55). Credit for coining the word usually is given to Gelett Burgess, who used it in 1900 in a book title, *Goops, and How to Be Them* (he also launched *bromide*, in the sense of a conventional person or cliché, and *blurb*). Laurence Urdang, editor of *Verbatim: The Language Quarterly*, has pointed out, however, that Burgess might have gotten the word from the Polish *głupy* (stupid, fatuous), which tends to be pronounced by non-Slavic speakers of English as *gwoopy*, just a short phonetic step from *goop* (*American Speech*, Fall 1983). The *goop* that is an icky, viscous substance probably is a combination of *gooey* and *glop*.

goose. A foolish person, often a *silly goose*, and yet another example of the use of birds as symbols of stupidity; see DODO. The foolish *goose* is usually a woman or a feeble man, as in "You souls of geese, That bear the shapes of men, how have you run From slaves that apes would beat!" (William Shakespeare, *Coriolanus*, 1608).

In addition to the sense of foolishness, which has been around since at least the sixteenth century, the name of the bird has acquired a number of low sexual meanings. Thus a *goose* used to be a whore; the act of copulation; a bubo (a sign of venereal disease); or a person so infected. As prostitute and disease, the venereal *goose* was shorthand for *Winchester goose*, in honor of the bishops of Winchester, who, before the break with Rome (1534), licensed a number of brothels on property near their palace in London's Southwark borough (the flocks of prostitutes in the area also were called *Winchester pigeons*).

The sexual sense of *goose* may have led to the modern verb, *to goose [someone intimately]*, as applied first to people and later to engines and anything else that may be *goosed* into activity. The exact connection between verb and bird is a mystery, however. H. L. Mencken reported that "The preponderance of medical opinion . . . inclines to the theory that the verb was suggested by the fact that geese, which are pugnacious birds, sometimes attack human beings, and especially children, by biting at their fundaments" (*The American Language, Supplement I*, 1945). Another possibility noted by Mencken was that the verb "derived from the old custom of examining a goose before turning it out in the fields by feeling of its rear parts: if an egg could be felt it was kept in its pen for the day." So this remains one of the dark corners of lexicography.

See also GUNSEL.

gorilla. Nowadays a hoodlum or thug, a knuckle-dragger, or anyone with lots of brawn, not much brain, and a fondness for strong-arm tactics, but in a less inhibited era, one of the epithets pasted on Abraham Lincoln, known variously to his political opponents as *the Illinois gorilla* and *the original gorilla*. "The extreme virulence with which he abused the President, the administration, and the Republican party. . . . [Stanton] never spoke of the President in any other way than as 'the original gorilla' " (General George B. McClellan, *McClellan's Own Story*, 1871). See also BABOON.

The apish sense of *gorilla* was fairly new in long-armed Lincoln's time, though the word itself comes from antiquity. Used in the sense of "hairy savage" in the ancient Greek account of the circumnavigation of Africa by the Carthaginian, Hanno, ca. 425 B.C., the term was resurrected in A.D. 1847 by an American missionary aptly named Savage (Dr. Thomas S.).

Variations on the "gorilla" theme include *Chicogorilla*, a native of the "Second City" and a tribute to the reputation it gained when Al Capone's *gorillas* roamed its windy canyons, and *gayrilla*, which is a *gorilla* with a same-sex orientation, e.g., " 'Up against the wall, you gay-rilla!' Buckmore Phipps snarled" (Joseph Wambaugh, *The Glitter Dome*, 1981). Most guy *gorillas* are straight, however, assuming the following bit of juvenilia can be taken at face value:

> Knock, knock.
> Who's there?
> Gorilla.
> Gorilla who?
> Gorilla my dreams.

See also HOODLUM and THUG.

Goth. A rude, uncivilized person; especially one who goes out of his way to destroy artworks and other hallmarks of high culture. "A horrible Goth of a Scotchman" (*OED*, 1870). The Goths, a Germanic people who descended upon the Roman Empire in the early part of the Christian era, were divided into two main branches, the East Goths, or Ostrogoths, and the West Goths, or Visigoths. The latter also have received a bad press: "A recent story in a major international newspaper about the war in Afghanistan described this war as 'marked by cruelty of Visigothic proportions' " (History Book Club *Review*, 9/88). See also BARBARIAN and VANDAL.

gouger. A cheat, especially one who extracts exorbitant profit from any business transaction. This sense of the word appeared first in the United States in the early nineteenth century. "I have joined a society composed chiefly of young lawyers (here called 'Gougers')" (*A Dictionary of American English*, 1819). The sense of unfairness, in turn, derives from another practice of our founding fathers, i.e., the gouging out of a person's eyes in a free-for-all fight. This tactic was so common that some people became known as *Gougers*, e.g., "One of the officers being in a public house in Louisville was grossly insulted by one of those Virginia Gougers, a perfect bully" (*DAE*, 1787). Northerners fought this way, too, according to Captain Francis Grose, who explained that *to gouge* meant "To squeeze out a man's eye with the thumb: a cruel practice used by the Bostonians in America" (*A Classical Dictionary of the Vulgar Tongue*, 1796). See also CHEAT and CHISELER.

Governor of Massachusetts. A traditional playground epithet among boys for an unliked fellow, especially one acting too big for his britches. "Billy Martin kicks dirt at an umpire, who turns his back, and then Martin's lips can be seen clearly forming the words, 'Governor of Massachusetts,' whereupon the ump whirls around in a rage and gives the ejection sign" (Veronica Geng, *New York Times*, 9/23/88). Many adults who had forgotten the expression were reminded of it during the 1988 presidential campaign by Vice President George Bush's constant references to his opponent, Michael Dukakis, by his title, Governor of Massachusetts, rather than by his name—an artful, subliminal putdown.

goy. Gentile, heathen, non-Jewish. "The children of Roma and those of Israel . . . are . . . dispersed among the Gentiles, whom they hate and despise, under the names of Busnees and Goyim" (George Borrow, *Zincali; Or an Account of the Gipsies of Spain*, 1841).

The term comes from the Hebrew *goy*, a neutral word meaning "nation" or "people," which has acquired strong overtones of stupidity, illiteracy, and coarseness as a result of its association with non-Jews. Thus, it is not a compliment to be told that one talks like a *goy*, acts like a *goy*, is *goyish*, or has *goy* brains. (In Yiddish, a *goyisher kop*, meaning a Gentile head, is a slow-witted person.) "When endurance is exhausted, kindliness depleted, the effort to understand useless, the epithet, 'A goy!' is used—just as, I suppose, Armenians say 'Turk!' or Mexicans say 'Gringo!' or Frenchmen 'Boche!' . . ." (Leo Rosten, *The Joys of Yiddish*, 1968). See also SHIKSA.

Eminent authorities in semantics have made very fine distinctions between what is Jewish and what is *goyish*. For example: "To me, if you live in New York or any other big city, you are Jewish. . . . If you live in Butte, Montana, you're going to be goyish even if you're Jewish. Evaporated milk is goyish even if the Jews invented it. Chocolate is Jewish, and fudge is goyish. Spam is goyish and rye bread is Jewish. Negroes are all Jews. Italians are all Jews. Irishmen who have rejected their religion are Jews. Mouths are very Jewish. And bosoms. Baton-twirling is very goyish" (Lenny Bruce, *How to Talk Dirty and Influence People*, 1972). See also BARBARIAN and JEW (DOWN), TO.

greaseball. An Italian, Greek, Spaniard, Puerto Rican, or Latin-American; in general, any foreign-looking person with thick, black, possibly oily hair. (There may also be an allusion here to olive-oily cooking.) The epithet has been dated only to the 1930s. "I never speak of [Italians] as wops, guineas, dagoes, or grease balls" (Damon Runyon, *Take It Easy*, 1939). See also GREASER and WOP.

greaser. A Mexican, from as early as 1836 but popularized during the Mexican War (1846–48); in extended use, an Italian or other GREASEBALL. Thus, from a memoir of service against the Mexicans: "If twenty Dragoons can't whip a hundred greasers with the Sabre, I'll join the 'Doughboys' and carry a fence rail [i.e., a rifle?] all my life" (Samuel E. Chamberlain, *My Confession*, 1956, but written ca. 1859). "The Mexicans are called 'Spaniards' or 'Greasers' (from their greasy appearance) by the Western people" (George F. Ruxton, *Life in the Far West*, 1849). An apparently nonce form that appeared during the Gold Rush of 1849 is the girlish *greaserita*, as in "the fair greaserita" (*American Speech*, 5/68). Just about a century later, again in California and again referring to appearance, *greaser* metamorphosed into *young tough*, especially when astride a motorcycle in the Marlon Brando–James Dean manner. See also MEXICAN.

Greek. (1) Incomprehensible talk, gibberish; (2) anal intercourse, from the association of the ancient Greeks with pederasty, usually in such phrases as *Greek arts*, *Greek culture*, or *Greek way*. See also SODOMITE.

(1) ". . . those that understood him smiled at one another and shook their heads—but for my own part, it was Greek to me" (William Shakespeare, *Julius Caesar*, 1599). See also BARBARIAN and GRINGO.

(2) "Ca. female would like to combine photo sessions with pleasure. Love gr, fr [i.e., Greek, French] arts" (*Ace*, undated, ca. 1976). The Greek national anthem, it has been suggested, should be changed to "I'm Walking Behind You." See also FRENCH, ITALIAN, and TURK.

greenhorn. An inexperienced person, a novice or newcomer; hence, a simpleton or a sucker. "I suppose you are not hoaxing us? It is, I know, sometimes thought allowable to take a greenhorn in" (H. Rider Haggard, *King Solomon's Mines*, 1885).

Like the similar TENDERFOOT, the word applied originally (from the fifteenth century) to animals rather than people. The reference probably was to oxen with new, or green, horns. In the seventeenth century, the term was transferred to raw recruits in the Army and then to neophytes in general, especially easy marks. The simple *green* also has been used in much the same way over approximately the same span of time, e.g., "You're green; your credulous; easy to be blinded" (George Chapman, *Al Fooles, a Comedy*, 1605). Today, the callow one might also be called a *green-ass, greenie*, or described as being *as green as grass*. See also GULL.

gringo. A white U.S. citizen, a YANKEE, to Americans who live south of the Rio Grande; in extended use, any European, usually an English one. ". . . the charge will not seem so ridiculous in Grenada or elsewhere in the gulf or Central America. Gringo intervention is part of the region's history" (Tom Wicker, *New York Times*, 4/1/83). The contemptuous term first grated upon U.S. ears at the time of the Mexican War: "We were hooted and shouted at as we passed through, and called 'Gringoes' " (John Woodhouse Audubon, *Western Journal*, 6/13/1849).

Various etymologies for *gringo* have been proposed, the most picturesque being that the word arose from a mishearing by Mexicans of a verse by Robert Burns that was sung by homesick Yankee soldiers in 1846–48: "*Green grow the rashes, O.*" But the American Spanish *gringo* also means gibberish, from the Spanish *griego*, Greek, and it seems more likely, as Stuart Berg Flexner points out, that the literal meaning of the ethnic insult is "one whose language is 'all Greek to me' " (*I Hear America Talking*, 1976). See also GREEK and YANKEE.

gross out. Disgust. "Bored? Grossed out? Come to the Bistro" (sign, Vassar College, Fall 1968, in *American Speech*, Spring–Summer 1973). *Gross*, in the sense of that which is exceedingly coarse or wanting in decency, dates to the sixteenth century and continues to see service, as in *Gross Jokes* (Julius Alvin, 1983). *Gross out* seems to have been an improvement of college students in the 1960s. The term may also be used as a noun, e.g., "Fred is a *gross-out*"; and as an adjective, "That was a real *gross-out* [or *grossitating*] party last night." See GROTTY and SCUZ(Z).

grotty (groady, groddy, etc.). Disgusting, bizarre; teenage use from the 1960s, and still current in the 1980s at such centers of learning as Kent School in Connecticut (personal communication, Douglas Denham, 3/84). The term apparently is an abbreviation of *grotesque*.

groupie. An ardent fan; originally, from the 1960s, a young woman who followed rock groups around, expressing admiration for their music by orgiastic dancing in discotheques and orgies elsewhere. "His defense described the sisters as 'groupies', girls who deliberately provoke sexual relations with pop stars" (London *Times*, 9/17/70). See also BIMBO.

Groupie soon was extended to encompass aficionados, devotees, and enthusiasts in other walks of life, and without any sexual implications, but the disparaging overtones carried over into the new contexts, e.g., "Steve Doyle . . . is a groupie. No, not the kind of groupie that chases after rock singers. Steve's serious. He *works* for his idol, and his idol happens to be a presidential primary contender" (Lynn Sherr, "Here Come the Political Groupies," *Saturday Review*, 6/10/72). "Fill that room with 1500 assorted lawmen, law groupies (male) and their elegantly coiffured women and you have the Texas Ranger Sesquicentennial Anniversary Celebration" (Chet Flippo, "Law and Order Groupies of Texas," *Rolling Stone*, 9/27/73). See also the *junkie* in JUNK.

grubby. Dirty, grimy, slovenly, contemptible; more or less cruddy (see CRUD). "If you want to squander $40 million [on aid to the Contras] be my guest, but not a heritage of honor. Why sacrifice that for this grubby, sleazy little operation?" (Lowell P. Weicker, Jr. [Republican, Connecticut], Senate debate, 3/18/87). The oldest senses of *grub* involve digging, as in clearing ground of roots and stumps; hence, the idea of laborious toil to eke out an existence, as through hack work by impoverished writers in *Grubstreet*. Dr. Samuel Johnson managed to keep a completely straight face while defining the term: "*grubstreet*. Originally the name of a street in Moorfields in London, much inhabited by writers of small histories, dictionaries, and temporary poems; whence any mean production is called grubstreet" (*Dictionary of the English Language*, 1755). This thoroughfare now is only a historical memory. Its name was changed in 1830 to Milton Street (something of a euphemism, even though the Milton in question was not the great John but a local builder and property owner) and in the 1970s it was developed out of existence, being buried beneath the Barbicon complex. See also DRUDGE and HACK.

grunt. An infantryman. "There was always the grunt, the American infantryman, who actually had to fight those extra enemy soldiers, the ones that weren't supposed to exist" (former CIA analyst Samuel A. Adams, testimony, *Westmoreland v. CBS*, 1/10/85). Although the term had a prior military existence, referring in the Army Signal Corps to an assistant who did the heavy work, the modern meaning seems to have been established ca. 1960 by Marine Corps aviators, who did not intend it as a compliment for the men who fought on the ground. As one infantryman told Sergeant Major Dan Cragg: "They call us 'grunts' because that's what you do when you shit" ("A Brief Survey of Some Unofficial Prosigns Used by the United States Armed Forces," *Maledicta*, Winter 1980).

Of course, people in the different military services have hardly ever spoken well of one another; see *dogface* in DOG and *horse marines* in HORSE. Despite its origin—or, more likely, because of it—the term was adopted by Army and Marine infantrymen in Vietnam, who reveled in talking tough, and it subsequently became generic for a foot soldier in any man's army. Thus, a Western observer said of the Iraqi Army: "The senior commanders here must realize by now that the people who have to do the dirty work—the grunts—are not steadfast in action" (*New York Times*, 2/28/86).

In the seventeenth and eighteenth centuries, the sheer animality of the word caused cleaner-uppers of Shakespeare to change Hamlet's "grunt and sweat" (III, i, 77) to "groan and sweat." The trailblazer here was Sir William D'Avenant, who edited a number of Shakespeare's plays at the end of 1660 for presentation in the theaters, just being reopened by the restored Charles II, albeit with concessions to the sensitivities of the Puritans who had closed them by Act of Parliament on September 2, 1642. Other editors followed in D'Avenant's footsteps and, more than a hundred years later, in 1765, Dr. Samuel Johnson allowed *groan* to stand, though he knew it was wrong. "All the old copies have, to *grunt* and sweat," but the word "can scarcely be borne by modern ears," Johnson explained (from Noel Perrin, *Dr. Bowdler's Legacy*, 1969).

Grunt is onomatopoetic in origin, imitating the bodily sound. Its Indo-European root is *gru-*, which makes it a first cousin of *grouch* and *grudge*. The animalistic *grrr* also shows up in *growl* and possibly (the case is less clear) *grouse*, to complain, and *grunge*, filth, nastiness.

guinea. Originally (*OED*, 1748), a black person, presumably one who had been transported from the Guinea coast of West Africa, but later (from 1896), reflecting changes in the demographics of immigration to the United States, an Italian—or a Spaniard, or anyone else of swarthy complexion. "Senator Jeremiah Denton, Republican of Alabama, addressed a speech in Westchester County to his 'fellow Republicans and Democrats, Americans all, guineas, micks, and polacks' and he said today his audience 'thought it was great' " (UPI, 10/10/83). See also the *Guinnie boats* in PADDY.

Senator Denton, by the way, made a fine distinction between the "familiar terms," which he said he had used in jest, and the "bad terms," such as "wop—that would make somebody mad." See also GINZO and, of course, WOP.

gull. A simple fellow, so credulous that he is easily deceived. This sense of *gull* dates to at least the sixteenth century. The origin of the metaphor is not known. It may derive from one of the older senses of the avian gull, referring not to an adult of the species but to an immature bird, especially a gosling, who is young and therefore easily fooled. Another possibility, which appeals because it makes a neat parallel with CANARD, is that the credulous *gull* alludes to the alacrity with which these birds will swallow almost anything—hook, line, and sinker. Finally, there may have been some confusion in the past between the simple-minded *gull* and the equally foolish *cull*—the now obsolete *cullibility*, from 1728, predates the oldest recorded *gullibility* by sixty-five years. See also CONY, CULL(Y), DODO, DUPE, FOOL, GREENHORN, MUG, PATSY, PIGEON, and, for an example of a Shakespearean *gull*, refer to GEEK.

gunsel. A loathsome person; specifically, a catamite. The term is an Americanism, popularized by hoboes. It dates to at least the early twentieth century and derives from the German *gänslein*, gosling, little goose, via the Yiddish *genzel*. The word also has acquired a secondary, nonsexual meaning, apparently thanks to Dashiell Hammett, who enjoyed a private little joke on an editor, who had been watering down his language, by sneaking *gunsel* into *The Maltese Falcon* (1939) in a context that suggested a gunman was meant. " 'Another thing,' Spade repeated, glaring at the boy: 'Keep that gunsel away from me while you're making up your mind. I'll kill him.' " The word was retained in the film that was made from the book (1941), indicating that the people who administered the Motion Picture Production Code at the time didn't know the term's true meaning either. The relationship between Kasper Gutman (Sidney Greenstreet) and his young hit-man companion, Wilmer Cook (Elisha Cook, Jr.), is made fairly clear in the movie, but the overt mention of sexual perversion would have been deleted if the censors hadn't made the same mistaken assumption as Hammett's editor. See also GOOSE and PUNK.

gutless. Weak, irresolute, cowardly. "Now you see what a gutless poor worm I am" (L. A. G. Strong, *The Bay*, 1941). ". . . gutless and unprincipled" (a Chicago alderman's characterization of his city's mayor, "Nightline," WABC-TV, 5/9/83). "Paul Keating, Australia's Treasurer, has used harsh words in Parliament to describe the opposition: 'sleazebag,' 'harlot,' 'gutless spiv' [where *spiv* is British slang, from the racetrack, for a tout or swindler] and 'piece of criminal garbage' " (*New York Times*, 1/6/87).

As a collective plural for intestines, *guts* is Standard English of considerable venerability, dating to before 1000. The word was used by Shakespeare and other well-established writers on its own and in such figurative phrases as *greedy guts*, a voracious eater; *gut matter*, something pertaining to appetite or nourishment; and *rotgut*, bad beer or liquor (from 1597). Victorian reticence about mechanical aspects of the body affected the use of the term, however, with the *Oxford English Dictionary* noting that *guts* was "Formerly, but not now, in dignified use with reference to man" (Volume G, 1897–1900). Such delicacy also was prevalent in the United States, where the word was cited as coarse or obscene by 59 out of 361 students at Emory University in a study conducted by J. M. Steadman, Jr., in the late 1920s and 1930s. See BELCH for details.

As the standard intestinal sense of *guts* was being shunted aside, the modern slang sense of *guts* as courage, nerve, or intestinal fortitude began to evolve. The oldest examples of the latter come from *Slang and Its Analogues* (J. S. Farmer and W. E. Henley, 1893), e.g., "He (or it) has no guts—He (or it) is a common rotter [a good-for-nothing]." See also LILY-LIVERED.

guttersnipe. A purveyor of filth. In the words of President Harry S Truman: "I never met you, but if I do you'll need a new nose and plenty of beefsteak and perhaps a supporter below. Westbrook Pegler, a guttersnipe, is a gentleman compared to you" (letter, 12/6/50, to Paul Hume, music critic, on the morning after a severe appraisal by Mr. Hume of a concert by the president's daughter, Margaret, then essaying a career as a singer).

Guttersnipe dates to the mid-nineteenth century as a designation for the long-billed bird that usually resides in marshes rather than in gutters in cities. Aside from newspaper columnists of Pegler's ilk, the term also has been applied to (1) gatherers of rags and other refuse from gutters: (2) slum children and other URCHINS who spend most of their time in the streets; (3) disreputable people generally (Churchill characterized Hitler as a "bloodthirsty guttersnipe"); (4) the small printed handbills or posters (shortened to *snipe* today by politicians who pay to have them posted on lampposts and other places around town at election time); (5) cigar or cigarette butts (especially when collected by a hobo); and (6) securities dealers who operate on the curb because they are not members of the Stock Exchange: "He belongs to that class of beings in New York . . . known by the ornithological appelation of *guttersnipes:* (Q. K. Philander Doesticks [Mortimer Neal Thomson], *The History and Records of the Elephant Club,* 1856). See also BIRD.

gyp. To swindle or cheat; a swindle; a swindler. The last sense is the oldest, being an Americanism dated to the 1880s. The word probably is a shortening of *Gypsy,* which makes it an ethnic slur, and Gypsies, particularly, are sensitive about its uses. When William Safire referred to the "gypped generation" in one of his political columns, he received protests such as this, from Ms. Cara De Silva, an official of the Gypsy Lore Society: "Because the etymology of words such as *welshed* and *gypped* are not as obvious as that of a word such as *jewed,* many of your readers will not feel the full weight of your use of a defamatory term, but there are many who will" (*New York Times Magazine,* 12/5/84).

Gypsy itself comes from *Egyptian* as a result of a misapprehension by the English, who assumed that the dark-skinned Romany, who started showing up in their country in the sixteenth century, must have come from Egypt, though they actually are of Hindu origin. By the seventeenth century, *gypsy* was being used in a figurative sense to mean a "cunning rogue," whether or not a member of the Romany. The word also has been applied to women, both contemptuously and playfully, e.g., in the latter case, the famous stripper, or ecdysiast, Gypsy Rose Lee, *née* Rose Louise Hovick (1914–70).

H

hack. A writer for hire, usually a tired, worn-out one, whose prose reflects his condition, i.e., a journeyman or DRUDGE; formerly, also, a woman for hire, i.e., a prostitute, typically a tired, worn-out one. *Hack* in both senses is a shortening of *hackney*, originally meaning a saddle horse, as opposed to a war horse, hunting horse, work horse, and so on. From early times, hackney horses (perhaps from Hackney, the section of London where they were raised) were rented out and, like rented cars today, were not always in the best of condition. Thus *hackney* came to mean a poor steed, a JADE, and the *hack* who is a cab driver is a direct descendant of the *hack* who drove a *hackney*, or rented, carriage in the seventeenth century.

The opprobrious connotations survived the transition in denotation from rented horses (dating to the fourteenth century), to rented women (from the sixteenth century), to rented writers (*hackney pen* also comes from the sixteenth century). "Fielding has really a fund of true humour, and was to be pitied at his first entrance into the world, having no choice (as he said himself) but to be a hackney writer or a hackney coachman" (Lady Mary Wortley Montagu, letter, 7/23/1754, to her daughter, Lady Bute, commenting on the work of her cousin Henry, whom she greatly admired, and who admired her in return, having dedicated his first play to her).

Hack and *hackney* have since been extended to include tired and uninspired workers in other fields. Thus, the world has been graced with *hack* and *hackney attorneys, hack* and *hackney preachers,* and, in politics, *party hacks. Hack* writers naturally produced *hackneyed* writing, though prose of this sort was churned out long before this name for it was devised: ". . . if hackneyed expressions turn up in Old English writing, it's all right. They're called kennings then" (J. L. Dillard, *American Talk*, 1976). See also GRUBBY, HORSE, and TACKY.

hag. An ugly woman, usually an old one; a WITCH. Combining the senses: "Have done thy charm [here meaning "curse"], thou hateful, withered hag" (William Shakespeare, *Richard III*, 1592–93). A woman who is neither ugly nor old nor a witch may be a *fag hag*, i.e., one who associates with male homosexuals: ". . . Fag Hag, or Fruit Fly" (*Screw*, 10/18/69). See also FAG.

ham. A poor performer, often an actor, especially one who overacts or *hams it up*, but also applied to inept pugilists, ballplayers, and other amateurish types, particularly graceless, *ham-fisted* or *ham-handed* ones. "A squalid little ham actress" (Ngaio Marsh, *Final Curtain*, 1947). The theatrical sense dates to the late nineteenth century and is of obscure origin. It may come from *hamfatter*, "a term of contempt for an actor of low grade" (*The Century Dictionary*, 1889). *Hamfatter*, in turn, is said to come from a minstrel song, "The Ham-Fat Man." And it has been suggested that this phrase, in its turn, may derive from the practice of poor (and poorly paid) actors of using ham rind instead of a more expensive but less odiferous oil as a base for their makeup. Another, less plausible guess is that the word became incorporated in theatrical lingo as a result of Tony Pastor's giving away hams to attract patrons to his opera house in New York City about 1850. See also HOT DOG.

hard-off. A woman who arouses no sexual interest whatsoever. "As my buddy in the marines used to say, those women are hard-offs" (personal communication, 11/8/86).

harebrain(ed). Giddy; anything foolish, reckless, crazy, dumb, or LAMEBRAIN. "He could *think* the idea [of his wife's] was harebrained; thinking is not a sin. But contrary to popular notion, not all feelings should be expressed in marriage" (E. James Lieberman, M.D., *Washington Post*, 10/25/83).

The foolishness traditionally ascribed to the hare probably stems from the wild behavior of the male while rutting; hence, *mad as a march hare*. This expression has been around since at least the sixteenth century (though hares actually rut at intervals for up to ten months a year). When not in a state of sexual frenzy, the hare is a shy beast; for this reason, timorous people sometimes are said to be *hare-hearted*. Finally, to *make a hare [of someone]* is to make that person ridiculous, i.e., to show up the person as a fool. See also CONY and RABBIT.

harlot. Now essentially a euphemism for the harsher WHORE, *harlot* is a prime example of a word that began as a masculine term but underwent a sex change as its pejorative meanings became dominant. Dating from the early thirteenth century, *harlot* originally had the same meanings as the Old French word from which it derived—*herlot*, (*h*)*arlot*, a vagabond or beggar. During the next couple hundred years, its denotations were extended to include men who were rascals, loose livers, fornicators, itinerant jesters, buffoons, jugglers, servants, and—playfully—regular fellows or good guys. Female *harlots* begin appearing in the written record in the fifteenth century (*OED*, 1432), again with a range of meanings, referring to actresses, women jugglers, dancers, unchaste women, strumpets, and prostitutes. The modern female, whorish sense became dominant in the sixteenth century. This shift probably was aided by the adoption of *harlot* in translations of the Bible. Thus, the Geneva Bible of 1560 (the version used by Shakespeare) rendered *Isaiah*, 1:21 as "How is the faithful city become an harlot!," where the two Wyclif translations in the 1380s had used "strumpet" and "hoore." *Harlot* continues to have some attack value. As Prime Minister Stanley Baldwin said of the press barons Beaverbrook and Rothermere: "What the proprietorship of these newspapers is aiming at is power, and power without responsibility—the prerogative of the harlot through the ages" (speech, 3/18/31). For more about similar gender shifts, see GIRL.

harpy. A rapacious person, usually a woman; a SHREW. "Was it my mother-in-law, the grasping, odious, abandoned, brazen harpy?" (William Makepeace Thackeray, *The Virginians*, 1859). The Harpy of classical literature was a hideous creature, with the head and breasts of a woman and the wings and claws of a bird. It filled the air with stench and filth, contaminating all about, and was associated with storms and whirlwinds.

harridan. A vicious old woman, a scold; a corruption of the French *haridelle*, meaning a worn-out horse or mare, a JADE. *Harridan*'s modern meaning, as bad as it is, is better than it used to be. The word came into English around 1700, meaning a woman who is "half Whore, half Bawd" (B.E., *Dictionary of the Canting Crew*, ca. 1698–99) and this remained its primary meaning ("A decayed strumpet" in Johnson's *Dictionary* of 1755) for the next century or so, when the connotations of mere disagreeableness began to come to the fore. See also HACK and STRUMPET.

has-been. Over the hill, past one's peak, of no account anymore. "The only people here are has-beens" (Dorothy Guider, at a party attended by, among others, the author; New York City, 1972). "So he decided to get back verbally. 'McDonald, you're a been-has!' yelled Watson" (*New York Times Magazine*, 6/16/85). *Has-been* has been around for a while; the *Oxford English Dictionary* dates its first appearance in the form of *hes-beene* to 1606.

hash. A chopped up mixture of leftover foods, a mess. "This old, tired reheated hash, déjà vu Democratic demagogy" (Secretary of Education William J. Bennett on the Democratic response to President Ronald Reagan's State of the Union message, *New York Times*, 1/29/87). *Hash* in the sense of a mess or jumble, often in the phrase *to make a hash of*, dates to the first part of the eighteenth century, and *to settle [one's] hash*, to silence, subdue, or bring to account, goes back at least to the start of the nineteenth. A person who talked a lot of nonsense, i.e., who made a *hash* of his words, also used to be called *a hash*. As far back as 1655, according to the *OED*, a Henry Hedley was fined 3s. 4d. for calling William Johnson, a steward of the Company of Bricklayers and Plasterers, "a slavering hash." See also BALONEY.

hatchet man. One who specializes in cutting attacks upon others, such as the politician who leads the way in defaming the opposition or the functionary who assumes for superiors such unpleasant tasks as firing employees. "I think Senator [Bob] Dole has richly earned his reputation as a hatchet man tonight. Does he really think there was a partisan difference over our involvement in the fight against Nazi Germany?" (Senator Walter F. Mondale, vice-presidential candidates' debate, 10/15/76, responding to Dole's charge that 1.6 million Americans had been killed or wounded "in Democratic wars in this century"). This is a far cry from the original *hatchet man*, who in the time of the French and Indian war used his axe to cut a trail through the forest for an army. "I think it will be advisable to detain both mulattoes and negroes in your company, and employ them as Pioneers or Hatchetmen" (George Washington, *Writings*, 1755). The modern political sense may stem in part from the use of *hatchet man* in the nineteenth century to describe Chinese who were hired to commit murders in the U.S. "Some of them are called hatchet-men. They carry a hatchet with the handle cut off" (G.B. Densmore, *Chinese in California*, 1880). See also HENCHMAN.

hawk. One who believes that international differences are best settled through the display or use of military strength, as distinguished from a DOVE. The political sense is a shortening of *war hawk*, a metaphor that was introduced into American political speech by Thomas Jefferson, who did not intend it as a compliment when he noted in a letter in 1798: "At present, the war hawks talk of septembrizing, deportation, and the examples for quelling sedition set by the French executive." Subsequently, *war hawk* (also *war dog*; see DOG) was used to tar those who favored the War of 1812 with Britain and the dispute over the boundary between Canada and Oregon (settled in 1846 without going to war). "With the war-hawks, the catchword is honor, but the meaning is fight" (L. Baker, *Letter to John Quincy Adams on the Oregon Question* 7, 1846). See also BUZZARD.

haywire.. Crazy, mixed-up. "A married man . . . and absolutely haywire on the subject of another woman" (John O'Hara, *Appointment in Samarra*, 1934). The term is an Americanism, a product of New England logging camps. Prior to mechanization, the camps required large quantities of hay to feed the horses and oxen that hauled logs through the woods. They hay came in bales and it was discovered that the binding wire could be put to a great many other uses, from repairing a fence, to strengthening a cracked axe handle, to serving in lieu of a clothesline. By about the turn of this century, any logging camp that was short of good equipment—and so seemed to be held together by haywire—was known contemptuously as a *haywire outfit* or *rig*. Pretty soon, the word was being used to denote anything that was broken, substitute, confused, or out of order. And from this, it was but a step to apply the term to people, too. See also MAD.

heathen. An irreligious person, *or* one who believes in some god or gods other than the God of the Jews, Christians, and Mohammedans. *Heathen* comes from the Old English *hæthen*, a savage, one who lives on uncultivated land, i.e., a dweller on the heath. Thus, the term is basically an ethnic slur, its pejorative connotations reflecting the view of early, citified Christians toward unwashed, unconverted rustics. In sense as well as origin, *heathen* parallels PAGAN. See also HICK and HOYDEN.

Hebe (Heeb). A Jew. "*Variety*, which is owned and mainly staffed by Jews, reduces *Hebrew* to *Hebe*, obviously with jocose intent" (H. L. Mencken, *The American Language, Supplement I*, 1945). The writers at *Variety* could get away with it, but the word has a different ring when employed by others and is commonly regarded as derogatory, as in "He should've been a nigger or a hebe instead of Irish" (James T. Farrell, *Young Lonigan*, 1932). See also JEW (DOWN), TO; SHEENY and, for similar reductions, JAP.

heel. A low-down fellow; a petty thief; a BOUNDER, CAD, or DOUBLE-CROSSER (especially of women). "She had not only treated me foully but managed at the same time to put me in the wrong and make me feel a thorough heel" (Robert Graves, *Seven Days in New Crete*, 1949). The contemptible sense of *heel* surfaced in American criminal slang about the time of World War I. Its origin is obscure. It apparently is related to *shitheel*, as in "I'm not sophisticated, but I do know a real shitheel when I see one" (*Goodbye New York*, film, 1985). It may be that *shitheel* is simply an intensive version of *heel*, with the latter alluding to the use of the heel when kicking someone in a sneaky way. Or it may be that *heel* is a euphemistic shortening of the longer term. See also ROUND-HEELS.

heifer. Sometimes a young and pretty woman, but more likely a talkative one: "To call a hill woman a *heifer* is to call her a meddlesome gossip . . ." (Vance Randolph and George P. Wilson, *Down in the Holler*, 1953). See also COW.

Heinie. A German, especially a soldier; from *Heinrich* and with some additional derogatory value thanks to the *hiney* on which one sits. Dated to 1904 (*OED*), the term was used more often in World War I than World War II. See also GERMAN and PADDY.

hell. The place of torment where bad people are said to go after death, used as an expletive, *oh hell!,* as well as other parts of speech, e.g., as a negative adverb, *the hell you are;* a super-superlative, *hotter* (or *colder*) *than hell;* a general adverb, *run like hell;* an intensifier, *hell yes!;* a noun, *go to hell;* a synonym for turmoil or uproar, *to raise hell;* a verb, *to hell around;* and an adjective, *hell-bent.* The term also appears in such combinations as *hellcat* (a female scold or SHREW), *hell-dog* (a fiend), and *hellhound* (a wicked fellow), as well as in many phrases and proverbial expressions, such as *to be hell on wheels, to catch hell, to give [someone] hell, to hell and gone* (or *back*), *hell and high water, hell of a [something]* and *helluva, hell's bells and panther tracks, hell to pay, to hell with you, not a chance of a snowball in hell, to play hell with,* and *what the hell.*

The profusion of hellish expressions suggests a lack of serious belief in eternal punishment or, at the very least, substantial disrespect for the devil and his works. Even the religious use the word figuratively, as in "You're going to have a solid minority of bishops raising hell" (a forecast by the Reverend Richard P. McBrien, chairman of the theology department at the University of Notre Dame, *New York Times,* 10/28/86). On the other hand, when the videotape record showed that an eleven-year-old boy preacher, Duffey Strode, had used the term literally, telling the principal of the Eastfield Elementary School in Marion, North Carolina, to "go to hell," not, as his father asserted, "you'll go to hell," he was suspended for ten days (AP, 8/22/88).

The word's traditional shock value is evidenced by its employment in such contexts as the following, a song from the 1840 presidential race that was part of a smear campaign against Martin Van Buren, who lost:

> Who would his friends, his country sell,
> Do other deeds too base to tell,
> Deserves the lowest place in Hell—
> Van Buren!

Also indicative of the word's power in the Victorian era is the frequency with which our ancestors sidestepped it, employing such euphemisms as *blazes, Halifax, heck, Jesse, Sam Hill,* and *thunder.* (*Hell-dog,* meanwhile, was reduced to *fire-pup.*) As if this were not enough, nineteenth-century editors also made fine distinctions between the term's figurative and literal meanings. Thus, in *Mr. Midshipman Easy* (1836), by Captain Frederick Marryat, who had a distinguished naval career before he took up writing and who undoubtedly knew every "bad" word extant, readers were allowed to view the terrible term when used as an intensifier: "What the hell are you making such a howling about?" Some eighty pages later, however, the fires of hell are dampened with a dash when the word is employed as a noun in a more or less literal sense: "He then applied to Gasgoigne, who told him in a very surley tone to go to h-ll."

Before laughing too hard at such primness, it should be remembered that the same trait has been exhibited in the fast-stepping twentieth century. For example, *hell* was one of the words banned from film soundtracks by the Motion Picture Production Code of 1930 (see DAMN for details) and the card game, Oh Hell, introduced in New York City card clubs in the 1930s, was described in family-oriented publications as *Oh Pshaw* or *Blackout*. As late as 1954, in the Marlon Brando film, *The Wild Ones*, the Hell's Angels motorcycle gang was called *the Black Rebels* instead.

Even in the liberated 1980s, *hell* continued to be expurgated. This is one of the words that often is dropped from children's books when they are converted from hardcover to paperback for distribution by clubs to the unwashed masses in the nation's grammar schools. According to a 1983 report by the American Library Association's young-adult services division, the clubs "may remove four-letter words, including 'damn' and 'hell,' change 'Oh, God' to 'Oh, Lord,' remove mention of parts of the anatomy, such as 'thigh' or 'breast,' remove any connotation of anything sexual and sometimes remove violence as well." What's more surprising is that efforts still are made to shield adults as well as children from the terrible word, e.g. "It sometimes seems that Mike Tomczak [Chicago Bears quarterback] makes up his mind at the snap where he is going to throw the ball, and come you-know-what and high water he delivers" (WABC-TV, "Monday Night Football," 12/14/87). So the Victorian strain remains very much alive. See also DEVIL and GODDAMN.

hen. A woman—alone and in many combinations, e.g., *hen college* (a women's college); *hen coop, henhouse, hen pen, hen ranch*, and *hennery* (all residences for women and all verging on obsolescence, now that living arrangements on college campuses, in the military, and in real life are becoming coed); *hen-hearted* (cowardly); *hen party* (a get-together of them); *old hen* (one that is older than you are); and *wet hen* (an angry one, usually in the phrase, *as mad as a wet hen*). The basic *hen* analogy is venerable (dated to ca. 1626 in the *OED* and probably much older), and so are some of the combinations. Back in the eighteenth and nineteenth centuries, a *moon-eyed hen* was a woman with a squint, and a *hen frigate* was one on which the captain's wife was aboard, the implication being that she bossed him around or otherwise interfered with standard operating procedure. Such a man might be said to be *henpecked*, a term that has been dated to the late seventeenth century but never used more elegantly than by George Gordon Lord Byron in *Don Juan* (1819–24):

> But—oh! ye lords of ladies intellectual,
> Inform us truly, have they not hen-peck'd you all?

See also CHICKEN.

henchman. A trusted underling; specifically, in politics, one who does dirty work for his leader. "A mercenary adherent; a venal follower; one who holds himself at the bidding of another" (*Century Dictionary*, 1889). "The word [*henchman*] is only used pejoratively; nobody ever claims to be anybody else's henchman" (William Safire, *Safire's Political Dictionary*, 1978). *Henchman*, apparently meaning a groom, squire, or page (there were also *henchboys*), is a fourteenth-century word that had been out of circulation for more than two hundred years when it was rediscovered and popularized by Sir Walter Scott, who used it in the sense of the principal attendant or right-hand man of a Scottish highland chief in *The Lady of the Lake* (1810) and *Waverly* (1814).

The *hench* root is much more ancient, deriving from the Old English *hengest*, a male horse, usually a gelding. This also was the name of one of the two brothers,

Hengest and Horsa, who led the first Saxon band to England, ca. 449. Horsa was killed in battle against the Britons and Hengest became king of Kent, beginning the Anglo-Saxon monarchy. See also HATCHET MAN and LACKEY.

Hessian. A hireling; from the employment by the British of Hessian troops during the American Revolution. The term was much favored in the South during the Civil War for describing Northern citizens and soldiers, but its use need not be confined to actual zones of war. "The extent to which the placing of state politics upon a Hessian basis has gone deserves to be exposed" (*Springfield*, [Massachusetts], *Weekly Republican*, 10/13/1905). In an extended sense, a *Hessian* is anyone who is rough, boorish, and of low moral character. In the Ozarks, the term usually is "applied to a vicious or meddlesome old woman" (Vance Randolph and George P. Wilson, *Down in the Holler*, 1953). See also KRAUT and LACKEY.

hick. A country dweller, especially one easily taken advantage of. "Baileyville [Maine] people, one woman said, were being 'made to look like hicks' " (*New Yorker*, 1/16/84). A pet form of *Richard*, analagous to *Bob* for *Robert*, *hick* is another example of the pejorative use of nicknames; see PADDY for details. This one has been dated to 1565. The insulting connotations were firmly in place by the end of the seventeenth century when *hick* was defined in the *Dictionary of the Canting Crew* as "any Person of whom any Prey can be made . . . ; also a silly Country Fellow" (B.E., ca. 1698–99). *Hick* also serves as a building block in such combinations as *hick college*, *hick town*, and the generic *hicksville*. "A hick town is one where there is no place to go where you shouldn't be" (Robert Quillen, *ed.*, Fountain Inn [South Carolina, population 1,500] *Tribune*, in Alexander Woollcott, "The Sage of Fountain Inn," *Cosmopolitan*, 9/33). "We aren't just a little hick town and I didn't come in off a turnip truck" (C. Scott Parker, mayor of Liberty, Texas, population 10,000, *New York Times*, 11/24/87).

Hick is merely one of a great many opprobrious terms for people who reside in rural areas. Many of these are of considerable venerability and some have acquired wider but nonetheless disparaging meanings: The overlap with synonyms for stupidity is large. As a group, these terms provide a remarkable demonstration of the animosity (or lack of understanding, to put the best face on it) that seems always to have existed between town and country. Because the literary record is largely the creation of "cultured" city dwellers, their biases are better preserved for posterity than those of their country cousins. The disdain is mutual, however, and rural opinions of city slickers occasionally show through; see the presumed etymology of *cockney* in COCK, for instance. Most of the disparagements of rural residents follow standard insult techniques. Herewith, a sampling of them, grouped according to their method of formation:

Personal names. Unless among friends, calling an adult by his first name is almost always to be interpreted as an insult. See PADDY and UNCLE TOM for background on this topic. As for country dwellers, in addition to *hick*, names and nicknames that have been used disparagingly as generics include: *Bill Shears*, *bob* (a pet form of *Rob*, itself an abbreviation of either *Robert* or *Robin*), *Hiram*, *hodge* (from *Roger*), *jake* (from *Jacob*), *jasper* (an old name, also rendered as *Caspar* and *Gaspar*, traditionally that of one of the Three Wise Men in the Bible), *Jeff Davis* (a Southern *hick*), *John Farmer* (or *John Family*, *John Hoosier*, or simply *John*—or, for that matter, simply *farmer*, which can be turned into an insult with the proper intonation), *Oscar, Ralph, Reuben* (see RUBE), *Sam,* and *Silas.*

Intelligence, lack thereof. No one likes to be called a BLOCKHEAD or DUMMY. Stupidity is implied in *hick's* secondary sense of being easily deceived, of course. Unintelligent synonyms for *hick* include: *booby* (see BOOB), CLOWN, JAY, LOON, LOUT, SWEDE, and YOKEL.

Agricultural products. Just as different nationalities can be insulted in terms of their favorite foods (see KRAUT, for instance), so those who live close to the land can be demeaned in terms of what they grow upon it. For example: *apple-knocker* (see APPLE, BAD), *buckwheat, chawbacon, (Ameri)corn-fed* (see CORNY), *cotton-picker* (a term of reproach as a noun as well as in its adjectival form, see COTTON-PICKING), GOOBER-GRABBER (a Georgian, specifically), *grass comber, hayseed, hay shaker, pea-picker, pumpkin* (see *pumpkinhead* in BLOCKHEAD), *sorghum lapper, squash,* and *turnip sucker.*

Topography. Paralleling the product slurs, these include: *acrefoot, Boetian* (for details, see PEORIA), *brush hog* (see also HOG), *brush yankee* (see also YANKEE), *bush-whacker* (an illegitimate child, a *bush baby,* as well as a backwoodsman), *country-clod* (or *-egg, -hick,* or *-jake), desert rat,* DIRT-EATER, HILLBILLY, *jake-from-the-sticks* (as in the famous *Variety* headline, "Sticks Nix Hick Pix," 7/17/35), *river rat, shitkicker, sodbuster, swamp angel, timber rat,* WOODCHUCK, and *wood-hick* (or *-tick*). See also BOONDOCKS and PODUNK.

Back-country words. City folk have always looked down upon the *provinces;* hence, the pejorative connotations of *provincial,* i.e., "Not of the mother country; rude; unpolished" (Samuel Johnson, *Dictionary of the English Language,* 1755). Other geographically related slurs include: BOOR, BUMPKIN, *churl* (originally, any man, especially a married one, then a freeman, then a tenant or serf, then a countryman or rustic, and so on down the social scale, finally denoting a rude, low-bred fellow, especially a hard, stingy one), CLODHOPPER, CRACKER, HEATHEN (literally, a dweller on the heath), HOYDEN (originally, a rude fellow or rustic), PAGAN (from the Latin *pagus,* a district, the country), PEASANT (ultimately from the same Latin root as *pagan*), PECKERWOOD, RUSTIC (stemming from the Latin *rus,* country), and VILLAIN (originally a serf, from the Latin *villa,* meaning the manor to which he was attached).

See also POOR WHITE TRASH and REDNECK.

hillbilly. Technically, a resident of the mountainous portions of the southeastern United States, but with so many connotations of backwardness, coarseness, and ignorance that one should be careful about employing it except when referring to a particular brand of country music. ". . . many hillfolk regard it as a fightin' word. John O'Neill shot and killed Elmo McCullers, of St. Louis, in 1934, because the latter called him a *hillbilly"* (Vance Randolph and George P. Wilson, *Down in the Holler,* 1953). And the hillfolk still feel much the same way. "In our part of the country, we call each other hicks and hillbillies and that's O.K. But if somebody from California moves in and they refer to us as hillbillies, we get angry" (Lois Bostic, of Gould, Arkansas, AP, 10/16/88).

Hillbilly is of comparatively recent vintage. The oldest printed citation comes from the turn of this century, when the derogatory meaning was not yet established: "In short, a Hill-Billie is a free and untrammelled white citizen of Alabama, who lives in the hills, has no means to speak of, dresses as he can, talks as he pleases, drinks whiskey when he gets it, and fires off his revolver as the fancy takes him" (*New York Journal*, 4/23/1900). Popularized in its present range of meanings in the 1930s, *hillbilly* is only the most common of a large subset of synonyms to describe the folk who live in the uplands. These terms are derogatory most of the time. Among those cited by Randolph and Wilson: *acorn-cracker, briar-hopper, bush-buster, brush-ape, flint-buster, fruit jar sucker, haw-eater, hog-ranger, puddle-jumper, rabbit-twister* (how one gets food when one is too poor to buy bullets), *ridge-runner, sprout-straddler, squirrel-runner, 'tater-grabber,* and *weed-bender.* See also HICK and OKIE.

hireling. An employee; a mercenary or LACKEY. A neutral word on the face of it, *hireling* almost always is used disparagingly, sometimes in conflicting senses. On the one hand, the *hireling* may be lacking in zeal, as in Christ's parable: "I am the good shepherd: the good shepherd giveth his life for the sheep. But he that is an hireling, and not the shepherd, whose own the sheep are not, seeth the wolf coming, and leaveth the sheep, and fleeth. . . . The hireling fleeth, because he is an hireling" (*St. John*, 10:12–13). On the other hand, *hireling* may refer to someone ready to do almost anything for money, as exemplified by the attack of Senator Charles Sumner (Free Soil, Massachusetts) on supporters of slavery as "hirelings picked from the drunken spew and vomit of an uneasy civilization" (speech, U.S. Senate, 5/19/1856).

In particular, Sumner flayed Senator Andrew P. Butler (Democrat, South Carolina) as a Don Quixote whose Dulcinea was "the harlot slavery," and Senator Stephen A. Douglas (Democrat, Illinois) as Sancho Panza, "the squire of slavery, ready to do it humiliating offices." Sumner paid dearly for these remarks three days later when Representative Preston S. "Bully" Brooks (Democrat, South Carolina), a remote cousin of Butler's, avenged Southern honor by catching the Massachusetts congressman unawares at his Senate desk, and beating him senseless with a stout cane. This put Sumner out of action for most of the next three years, though Massachusetts reelected him in the interim, on the theory that his empty seat was the most eloquent reproach to slavery. Meanwhile, Southern admirers presented Representative Brooks with a large collection of suitably inscribed cudgels. For more about Sumner and this speech, see SKUNK.

hockey (hocky). Variously: semen, excrement, nonsense, e.g., "Great big blooping hunks of dog hocky" (William Styron, *Set This House on Fire*, 1960). The origin of the term is not known; it may come from HOKUM. If its meaning of nonsense really is the original one, then *hockey* is an exception among words of this sort, which ordinarily evolve in the opposite direction. See also BULLSHIT, CRAP, and SHIT.

Hockey seems fairly euphemistic; nevertheless, it has been tabooed in some square circles, especially in the Southern United States. "A casual mention of hockey will paralyze any Ozark audience, for the word hockey means nothing but dung in the hill country. There is a game that they play on ice in the North, which we who were brought up in the South almost instinctively blush at the mention of,' writes Burton Rascoe [of Oklahoma]" (Vance Randolph and George P. Wilson, *Down in the Holler*, 1953). See also BUNK.

hog. A greedy person or, as a verb, to take more than one's share, with a strong suggestion of uncleanly messiness, hogs not being particular about where and how they wallow. The type specimen of the human *hog* is the much-maligned King

Richard III—called an "abortive rooting hog" toward the start of Shakespeare's play about him (1592–93). This was a derogation of Richard's badge, a blue boar, and Shakespeare was not the first to make the demeaning connection. In 1484, the king and his chief henchmen (or "ministers"), Sir William Catesby, Sir Richard Ratcliff, and Francis, Viscount Lovell, were jointly attacked by William Colyngburne in a couplet, copies of which were posted on the door of St. Paul's and other prominent places in London:

> The catte, the ratte and Lovell our dogge
> Rulyth all England under a hogge.

For this offense, Colyngburne suffered grievously: He was apprehended and taken to Tower Hill where, according to the *Great Chronicle of London*, he was "at first hanged and straight cut down and ripped, and his bowels cast into the fire."

Nowadays, the greediness of the *hog* is most evident on the highways, where the motorist who takes up more than one lane, or his half of the road, from the middle, is known as a *road hog*, e.g., "That man is worse than a murderer—he is a road hog" (W. C. Fields speaking, *If I Had a Million*, film, 1932). Similar off-the-road combinations include *bed hog*, *beer hog*, and *chow hog*. A person showing such piggy tendencies may possibly be shamed into better behavior if bluntly told: "You're a hog—all but the bristles and they're sprouting!" See also PIG.

hogwash. Nonsense; anything weak, inferior, worthless, and, by extension, false or insincere. "[Alfred A. Knopf] impressed John Hersey in 1965 as 'the sworn enemy of hogwash, bunk, gas and rubbish, and a scourge of hypocrites and shoddyites' " (*New York Times*, 8/12/84). *Hogwash*, appearances to the contrary, has nothing to do with cleaning hogs. Rather, it is the swill, or garbage, that is fed to them. The term has been applied contemptuously to inferior liquor and other worthless things since ca. 1700. See also BUNK.

ho-hum. Dull, boring, tedious, humdrum; an exclamation, dated only to 1924 (*OED*). "So the Composers' Guild of Great Britain wants the Arts Council to twist the arms of orchestral managements to make them perform more works by British composers. Ho-hum" (*Jewish Chronicle*, 1/19/73). See also UGH.

hoity-toity. Pretentious, arrogant, quick to take offense; children's talk for cutting a pompous person down to size. "The show-off or conceited person is also known as . . . a 'porky prig', a 'snobby', a 'stuck-up peacock', Miss Prim and Proper, Miss Hoity-toity . . ." (Iona and Peter Opie, *The Lore and Language of Schoolchildren*, 1959). Dated to 1668, the phrase apparently derives from the obsolete *hoit*, to romp, with the sense being influenced both by HOYDEN and by *high* (a variant is *highty-tighty*). The feminine associations have always been strong. For instance, Captain Francis Grose defined the term this way: "A hoity-toity wench; a giddy, thoughtless, romping girl" (*A Classical Dictionary of the Vulgar Tongue*, 1796). See also SNOOTY.

hokum. Nonsense, especially when it is laid on thickly and insincerely. "It is all pure hokum to suggest that all authors are always interesting" (*Publishers' Weekly*, 6/16/28).

Probably a blend of *hocus-pocus* and *bunkum, hokum* seems to have originated within this century in American theatrical circles, referring at first to material that was hackneyed but guaranteed to appeal to an audience's sentimentalities. The underlying *hocus-pocus* is pseudo-Latin, long used by conjurers to refer to their tricks and themselves. Clerical opponents of magic have asserted that the phrase parodies the words spoken at the most solemn moment of the mass, *hoc est Corpus,* but considering the punishments that the Church meted out to those who practiced the black arts, it seems likely that any parallel was unintentional. The phrase apparently was popularized by a real magician who took Hocus Pocus as his stage name in the time of James, King of Scotland (1567–1625) and of Great Britain (1603–25). The first illustrated book on magic in English is entitled *Hocus Pocus Junior, The Anatomy of Legerdemain* (1634). As for *bunkum,* the other presumed progenitor of *hokum,* see BUNK.

homo. Homosexual and, like the short forms of many other words (see JAP and PADDY, for instance), an abbreviation that lends itself easily to assaults. "The teen-agers at first taunted the two young men, shouting 'Homos!' and 'Fags!' she said" (*New York Times,* 8/24/88). In this case the verbal assault was the prelude to a physical one, with the two young men being beaten and stabbed.

Homo has been dated to 1929 and *homosexual* to 1892. The latter is an irregular word, appropriately enough, part Greek (*homo,* same) and part Latin (from *sexualis*). From the beginning, it disturbed some people: " 'Homosexual' is a barbarously hybrid word and I claim no responsibility for it" (H. Havelock Ellis, *Studies in Psychology,* Volume 1, 1897). The word originally was a neutral one, compared to other choices available at the time, such as *invert, pervert,* and *Miss Nancy,* but it has since been superseded, of course, by GAY. See also QUEER.

honky (honkey). A white person. The term was popularized by militant blacks during the 1960s and quickly adopted by other minority groups, as in a song of the American Indian movement about the B.I.A., or Bureau of Indian Affairs:

> B.I.A., I'm not your Indian any more.
> You belong to white man now,
> So farewell, good-bye to you, honky.
> (Alice Marriott and Carol K. Rachlin,
> *Plains Indian Mythology,* 1975)

The word and, more importantly, the way it was spoken, produced a visceral reaction for the typical white person, who wasn't used to being labeled in this way. "The first time I heard *honky,* I knew just what it meant. It was a successor to *ofay* but meaner and more hate-filled. 'Rap' Brown said it on a TV newscast. No one had to wonder what a honky was, and no one doubted for a moment that it was an expression of loathing. I think every white American who watched that newscast was jolted in one way or another by that word *honky,* spoken with such vituperation. . . . If we'd first heard *honky* spoken by, say, Walter Cronkite—' "Rap" Brown today revealed a word he uses for white Americans; he calls them *honkies*'—we'd have known it to be a racist slur. But the power to jolt is in the context, not the word" (Thomas H. Middleton, *Saturday Review/World,* 1/25/75).

Honky, dating from the immediate post–World War II period, is of uncertain origin. Many scholars think it is a variant of *hunky* (see HUNK). Black people themselves tend to derive the term from the honk of a car horn, the idea being that whites, especially liberals, "honk their horns a lot, i.e., make noise, but don't actually do much about what they profess to believe. In short, a *honky* is a hypocrite. . . . The 'horn-honking' explanation may well be wrong, but I got it from various black militants I used to know" (Merritt Clifton, *Maledicta*, 1978). See also OFAY and WHITEY.

hoodlum (hood). A young rowdy, a tough guy, a gangster. The term seems to have originated in or around San Francisco about 1871. In its first known appearance in print in the local *Daily Union* of April 27 of that year, the word is capitalized and enclosed within quotation marks, indicating its newness: "Kelly and Dunn, San Francisco 'Hoodlums,' who were arrested at the Sarsfield guard picnic excursion on Sunday last, are doing duty in the chain gang on the streets of that city; which, together with the fact that a third 'Hoodlum' got his throat cut by an Indian at the same place, gives great satisfaction to our citizens."

Many theories of *hoodlum's* origin have been offered. For instance, it has been proposed that *hood* is not a contraction of *hoodlum* but the base word, deriving either from a Hood who led a San Francisco gang or the hood-like caps of the city's militia. The most popular explanation for many years was that *hoodlum* came from the family name Muldoon. According to John Russell Bartlett's *Dictionary of Americanisms*, (fourth edition, 1877): "A newspaper man in San Francisco, in attempting to coin a word to designate a gang of young street Arabs under the beck of one named Muldoon, hit upon the idea of dubbing them *noodlums*—that is, simply reversing the leader's name. In writing the word, the strokes of the *n* did not correspond in height and the compositor, taking the *n* for an *h*, printed it *hoodlum*." This story makes such a pretty parallel with HOOLIGAN, also said to come from a family name, that one wants very much to believe it. On balance, however, this theory seems less probable than the suggestion that the word derives from the Bavarian dialect term *hudelum*, disorderly. Aside from the linguistic parallel, this explanation has the virtue of fitting with the ethnic data, since Germans seem to have constituted the largest group of non-English speakers in San Francisco around 1870.

See also CROOK, GANG, GOON, GORILLA, KNUCKLE-DRAGGER, PLUG-UGLY, RACKETEER, and THUG.

hooey. Nonsense; from the 1920s and common since then, often in the phrases, a *bunch* (or *load*) of *hooey*. Of unknown origin, the term has suspicious resonances with the sideshow barker's exaggerated *ballyhoo*, the derisive *fooey*, and the baby-talk *pooey*. The last seems especially likely, considering that *hooey* frequently appears as a euphemistic substitute for *(horse)shit*: "My prof's full of hooey. He doesn't know a C theme from an A one" (Percy Marks, *The Plastic Age*, 1924). See also BUNK.

hooligan. A juvenile delinquent, a young ruffian, a street tough. The term probably is employed more often today in Russia than the West, especially in its extended form, *hooliganism*, a catchall characterization for antisocial or dissident behavior, not necessarily by a juvenile. "He was also charged with hooliganism, as the Soviet judicial system calls disorderly conduct" (*New York Times*, 1/14/77). The principal difference between Russian *hooliganism* and disorderly conduct in the United States is that the Soviet penalties are stiffer, corresponding to those for a felony, with the result that conviction for *hooliganism* can land you in a prison camp. One of the charges against Mathias Rust, the West German who flew a small plane over the Russian border in 1987 without permission, circled Red Square, and landed near the Kremlin wall, was *malicious hooliganism.* He was sentenced to labor camp for four years.

Hooligan has been dated to the summer of 1898, presumably a long, hot one, when it surfaced as London police slang for a young tough or member of a street gang. "The constable said the prisoner belonged to a gang of young roughs, calling themselves 'Hooligans' " (London *Daily News,* 8/8/1898). The word's exact origin is not known. It may derive from *Hooley,* as in *Hooley's gang,* or from the surnames *Hoolihan* or *Houlihan,* which are sometimes spelled *Houlighan.* Previously, the name was a laughing matter, not a criminal one. A music-hall song of the period featured a rowdy family named *Hooligan* and Mark Twain used the surname satirically when he introduced it into *The Gilded Age* (with Charles Dudley Warner, 1873) in a scene in which a bookstore clerk tried to make a sale: "Have you ever read this, ma'am? I am sure you will like it. It's by the author of 'The Hooligans of Hackensack.' [See also PEORIA.] It is full of love troubles and mysteries and all sorts of such things. The heroine strangles her own mother." See HOODLUM and MALARKEY.

hoper. An Irishman who wishes he wasn't one. "We are not 'hopers,' Irish who go to bed hoping that when they wake up they will be Yankees" (Alice Hennessy, vice president of the West Roxbury, Massachusetts, Historical Society, *New York Times,* 7/22/86). See also IRISH.

hornswoggle. To cheat, to deceive, to con. "One practical working theory in advertising circles is that the ad's chief function is to hornswoggle the consumer" (*Boston Herald,* 6/27/04). "In my judgment, Mr. [Robert] Wallach hornswoggled him" (former Deputy Attorney General Arthur I. Burns, on the relationship between Mr. Wallach and Attorney General Edwin Meese III, testimony, Senate Judiciary Committee, 7/26/88).

Hornswoggle is an Americanism, from the early nineteenth century, and of mysterious origin (as are the synonymous BAMBOOZLE and HUMBUG). One suspects that a penile horn is at the root of the matter, however, in view of *hornswoggle's* secondary meaning, to seduce. See HORNY in this connection. *Hornswoggle* also bears more than a passing resemblance to *honeyfuggle,* another Americanism of the same period, which means to copulate, especially with a young girl, as well as to deceive, especially through flattery or the use of honeyed words. The latter may be an alteration of the English dialectical *connyfugle,* a word that also has strong associations with sex as well as duplicity. See CONY.

horny. To be sexually excited, lecherous, randy; HOT. "Horny Koch (misprint) must walk with his hands behind his back or else take Hecker's Self-raising Buckwheat" (broadside, ca. 1893, issued by the Yale Class of '96, referring to a member of the Class of '95). "Cagey, *pruney, rollicky,* and *horny* are the conventional words for sensual, and are not used in polite conversation. . . . The Devil is often called Old Horny, but not in polite conversation between men and women" (Vance

Randolph and George P. Wilson, *Down in the Holler*, 1953). Women as well as men may be described as being *horny* though, technically, the term should be reserved for men, since the noun on which the adjective is based refers to the penis, especially when erect. Thus, Captain Francis Grose defined *horn colic* as "A temporary priapism" in *A Classical Dictionary of the Vulgar Tongue* (1785).

Horns are an ancient symbol of fertility and power, often identified with the crescent moon, the sexually potent bull, the rutting stag, the lickerish goat, and various gods and demons. For example: Shiva may appear either as a bull or a lingam, the devil wears horns, powdered horn is considered in some cultures to be an aphrodisiac, a cornucopia (Latin for *cornu* = horn) is a horn of plenty, and the Hebrew *geren* translates either as "horns" or "beams of power"—a confusion that resulted in Michelangelo and other artists protraying Moses as having horns after descending from Mount Sinai with the tablets bearing the Ten Commandments.

To be horned, hornified, or *made to wear horns* is to be cuckolded. This kind of *horn,* dating to the first part of the fifteenth century in English, and common in other European languages, too, may derive from the medieval practice of engrafting the spurs of a castrated cock onto the root of its excised comb, with the result that they will grow into horns several inches long (the German word for cuckold, *hahnrei,* originally meant "capon"). Or the allusion could be to the male deer in heat: In Greek mythology, Actaeon, the hunter who spied upon Artemis bathing, and who was then changed into a stag and torn apart by his own hounds, was also, as a stag, the emblem of men with unfaithful wives. See also BULL, CUCKOO, and DEVIL.

horse. A big, strong but somewhat stupid fellow, especially a plain or ugly one, a *horseface.* "I tell thee what, Hal, if I tell thee a lie, spit in my face, call me 'horse'" (William Shakespeare, *Henry IV, Part I,* 1596). "With a Horse-face, a great ugly head" (Thomas Otway, *The Soudlier's Fortune: A Comedy,* 1681). Or in modern parlance, honoring Roy Rogers' best friend:

> Hubba hubba, ding ding,
> Catherine's [insert name of choice]
>   got everything.
> What a face,
> What a figure,
> Two more legs,
> Look like Trigger.

Horse and the colloquial variant *Hoss* occasionally make personal nicknames (e.g., Hall of Fame baseball pitcher Charlie "Hoss" Radbourne and the Hoss character on the "Bonanza" television series). People also have been known to brag of being "half horse, half alligator." Frontiersmen, especially river boatmen, were using this one in the early nineteenth century, and it seems to be etched indelibly in the American psyche. As Ernest Borgnine tells Spencer Tracy in the 1954 film *Bad Day at Black Rock,* "I'm half horse, half alligator. You mess with me, I'll kick a lung out of you."

For sheer verbal exuberance, however, it is hard to match Colonel Davy Crockett (1786–1836), who served three terms in the House of Representatives, distinguishing himself in Washington with addresses such as this:

Mr. Speaker.

Who—Who—Whoop—Bow—Wow—Wow—Yough. I say, Mr. Speaker; I've had speech in soak this six months, and it has swelled me like a drowned horse; if I don't deliver it I shall burst and smash the windows. . . . I'm a screamer, and have got the roughest racking horse, the prettiest sister, the surest rifle and the ugliest dog in the district. I'm a leetle the savagest crittur you ever *did see*. My father can whip any man in Kentucky, and I can lick my father. I can outspeak any man on this floor, and give him two hours start. I can run faster, dive deeper, stay longer under, and come out dryer, than any *chap* this side the big *Swamp*. I can outlook a panther and outstare a flash of lightning, tote a steamboat on my back and play at rough and tumble with a lion, and an occasional kick from a *zebra*. To sum up all in one word *I'm a horse*. Goliath was a pretty hard colt but I could choke him. . . . I can walk like an ox, run like a fox, swim like an eel, yell like an Indian, fight like a devil, spout like an earthquake, make love like a mad bull, and swallow a nigger whole without choking if you butter his head and pin his ears back.

For better or for worse, they do not make congressmen—or anyone else—like this anymore.

Galloping through the pages of linguistic history are a herd of other *horses*, as is only befitting, considering the traditional importance of this animal to human kind. For example:

Caligula's horse. The Roman emperor Gaius Caesar Germanicus (A.D. 12–41), nicknamed "Caligula" (Little Boots), is said to have intended to appoint his horse, Incitatus, to the office of Consul. Whether true or not, the rumor, mentioned by Suetonius, established a memorable image. Thus, acid-tongued John Randolph of Roanoke said of the appointment of Richard Rush as Secretary of the Treasury (1825): "Never were abilities so much below mediocrity so well rewarded; no, not when Caligula's horse was made Consul" (from Edward Boykin, *ed.*, *The Wit and Wisdom of Congress*, 1961). See also SCOUNDREL.

gift horse. One that should never be looked at in the mouth; specifically, a present that should not be examined too critically, from the practice of determining a horse's age by inspecting its teeth. "No man ought to look a geuen [given] horse in the mouth" (*OED*, 1546).

high horse, on one's. To put on airs, to act superior; also, *to ride* (or *mount*) *the high horse.* The phrase has been dated to the eighteenth century but may well go back to the time when arrogant knights bestrode great horses.

horse, to. An old term for copulation, *to horse* a woman being to mount her. "An I could get me but a wife in the stews, I were manned, horsed, and wived" (William Shakespeare, *Henry IV, Part II*, 1596–97). This sense remains current, e.g., " 'This is a respectable band,' he said, 'and there ain't goin' to be any immoral horsin' goin' on. Whoever you start sleepin' with this trip, that's how you end the tour!' " (Stephen Longstreet, *The Real Jazz Old and New*, 1956). *Horse* also has sexual overtones in *to horse around* and *horseplay* when the frisking takes place between males and females. Of course, sex isn't everything and context determines precise meaning, e.g., "The President is very frustrated. He felt very strongly about the way Congress is horsing around on Nicaragua" (Senator Bob Dole [Republican, Kansas], *New York Times*, 5/22/85).

horse and buggy. Countrified, old-fashioned, of little account. In baseball, the minor leagues are *horse-and-buggy leagues.*

horse collar. Nothing, a zero, a goose egg. A baseball player who goes hitless is said *to wear the horse collar.*

horse feathers. Horses do not have them, therefore: nonsense, rubbish; a euphemism for *horseshit* (see below). "Mr. William DeBeck, the comic-strip comedian . . . assumes credit for the first actual use of the word horsefeathers" (*American Speech,* IV, 1928).

horse marines. An imaginary military corps, composed of men who are out of their natural element, i.e., seagoing soldiers (marines) aboard horses; hence, in the singular, an awkward, bumbling fellow, as is a soldier aboard a ship. The expression dates at least to the War of 1812, when the British brought coastal shipping to a standstill, so that goods had to be sent from city to city by wagon train instead. In place of shipping schedules, newspapers began listing the arrival and departure times of the wagon trains, terming them *Horse Marines* or *Horse and Ox Marines* (George Earlie Shankle, *American Nicknames,* 1955). Today, the *horse marines* are remembered when singing "I'm Capt. Jinks of the Horse Marines, / I feed my horse on corn and beans" (*Broadside Ballad,* ca. 1870). In the nineteenth century, though, the *horse marines* and even the regular *marines* symbolized gullibility in a common phrase for expressing disbelief: "Tell that to the marines [or horse marines], the sailors won't believe it." Byron used a variant of this in *The Island* (1823)—" 'Right.' quoth Ben, 'that will do for the marines' "—and explained in a footnote that this "old saying" was "one of the few fragments of former jealousies which still survive (in jest only) between these gallant services." For other examples of inter-service rivalries, see FLATFOOT, GALOOT, GRUNT, and *dogface* in DOG.

horse opera. A Western film.

horse's ass. An idiot, dumbhead, or ignoramus; especially one whose coarse behavior embarrasses others if not himself; often, a person who is not as shrewd as he thinks he is and who does stupid things as a result. "A prominent New York accountant said privately yesterday that he thought the offenses for which Nixon now faces removal from office were relatively trivial. 'He should be impeached, instead, for being a horse's ass' " (William F. Buckley, *New York Post,* 8/8/74). "The world is full of horse's asses; in fact there are more *horse's asses* than there are horses" (personal communication, David F. Costello, 1983). See also ASS.

horseshit. Nonsense; comparable to BULLSHIT; often softened into *hooey, horse,* or *horse feathers;* and frequently used as an exclamation of disbelief. *Horseshit* is more or less opposite to *horse sense,* i.e., plain, common, good sense. See also BALONEY.

one-horse town. A small and unimportant town, a wide place in the road. See ONE-HORSE.

stalking horse. In the beginning, back in the sixteenth century, a stalking horse was a steed trained to provide concealment for a hunter stalking wild fowl. Within a hundred years, however, the term was widened to include people who were acting as decoys, concealing the nefarious schemes of others, e.g., "You . . . were made his engine and his stauking horse, To undo my sister" (John Webster, *The White Divel,* 1612).

Trojan horse. A deception, from the wooden horse containing Greek soldiers that the Trojans foolishly hauled into their city—a *gift horse* that should have been looked at much more closely.

war-horse. A battle-scarred politician; a musical or dramatic production that has been mounted so many times as to become *hackneyed; see* HACK.

wheel horse. In politics, a party regular—dependable but uninspired—virtually synonymous with the political *war horse* above. Originally, a wheel horse was the stronger in a team; harnessed nearest to the front wheels, it followed the leader and pulled more of the load.

See also HACK, HARRIDAN, JADE, MULE, MUSTANG, NAG, ONE-HORSE, SCALA-WAG, and TACKY.

hot. Sexually excited, lustful, HORNY, RANDY. That passion elevates the temperature has long been known: "So hote he lovede that by nyghtertale [nighttime] / He slepte namoore than dooth a nyghtyngale" (Geoffrey Chaucer, *The Canterbury Tales,* General Prologue, 1387–1400). Some of our ancestors have preferred not to recognize this fact, however. Thus, when Henrietta Maria Bowdler produced the first edition of *The Family Shakespeare* (1807), she excised the nasty *hot* from Prince Hal's line about "the blessed sun himself a fair hot wench in flame-colored taffeta" (*Henry IV, Part I,* 1596). But times change and today the term crops up commonly in such expressions as *hot and bothered, hot pants* (not only an article of clothing, also called *short shorts,* but a state of sexual arousal, as in *to have hot pants for [someone]*), *hot tamale* (see TAMALE), *hotter than a little red wagon* (wagons, like other vehicles, usually are considered to be feminine), and *hot to trot.* In the present liberated age, even women may admit openly *to having the hots for [someone].* Thus, Helen Gurley Brown has advised her *mouseburger* readers to get the attention of males by giving them presents bearing the initials *I. H. T. H. F. Y.,* meaning—to those who know the code—"I Have The Hots For You" (*Having It All,* 1982). Henrietta Maria Bowdler, no doubt, is spinning in her grave. See also COLD.

P.S. *Mouseburgers* are women who, in Ms. Brown's words, are "not prepossess-ing, not pretty, don't have a particularly high I.Q., a decent education, good family background or other noticeable assets." A *mouseburger,* then, is very similar to a DOG or MUTT.

hot dog. A show-off or, as a verb, to show off; specifically, in sports, an athlete who manages to turn routine plays into dazzling exhibitions of physical prowess; formerly called a *grandstand player* or *showboat.* "Crybabies and 'hot dogs,' or show-offs, always earned Larry's contempt, and . . . he was capable of a venemous dislike of a ball player who prolonged a protest or laid on the histrionics to show up the umpire before the fans" (Red Smith, on umpire Larry Goetz, *New York Herald Tribune,* 11/3/62). "A leading *hot dog* is Reggie Jackson, and going back a few years there was nothing like Vic Power, a fancy-dan first baseman who had the habit of catching every ball with one hand" (Zander Hollander, *ed., The Encyclopedia of Sports Talk,* 1976).

Hot dog, hot dogger, and *hot dogging* were popularized initially by the stunts of skiers and surfers, starting about 1960. The basic expression may derive from the exclamatory "Hot dog!", uttered in approval of some remarkable feat. In the general sense of proficiency, *hot dog* goes back to the turn of this century, and is very nearly as old as the name of the sausage that inspired it. The sausage name, from ca. 1890, was popularized by the cartoonist T. A. Dorgan, who punned visually on *barker,* slang for "sausage," with a drawing of an elongated dachshund on a bun. Other factors may also have been at work: "*Hot dog* arose in conjunction

202

with the widespread belief (not without justification) in the 19th century that sausages were often composed of dog meat" (Gerald L. Cohen, *Newsletter of the American Dialect Society*, 9/87). See also DOG, HAM, and SHOW-OFF.

Hottentot. A person of inferior intellect and/or rude, uncivilized ways; a savage. "He disputes with heat, and indiscriminately; mindless of the rank, character and situation of the several gradations of familiarity or respect . . . Is it possible to love such a man? No. The utmost I can do for him is to consider him a respectable Hottentot" (fourth Earl of Chesterfield, *Letters to His Son*, 2/28/1751). According to the 1976 supplement to the *OED*, "This derogatory sense, which was based on a failure to understand an alien culture, appears now to be very rare." See also ZULU and, for another notable *Hottentot*, WENCH.

hoyden. A bold girl, a saucy one, a HUSSY; another example of the conversion of a masculine word with a bad meaning into a feminine term (see also HARLOT and GIRL in this connection). The earliest examples of *hoyden* in writing come from the sixteenth century. The word referred then to a rude or ignorant fellow, a boor or bumpkin, e.g., "I'le make every hoydon bestowe a faringe on his dore, his wall, his windowe" (*OED*, 1597). Before the end of the next century, the word was being applied to rude, ill-bred, and noisy girls and women. It probably comes from the Dutch *heiden*, heathen, originally heath-dweller rather than a nonbeliever. This theory squares with the word's early application to rustics. The term might also be connected, however, with *hoit*, an old word meaning "to romp inelegantly" (*OED*), as bold and saucy girls are wont to do. "HOYDON. A romping girl" (Captain Francis Grose, *A Classical Dictionary of the Vulgar Tongue*, 1796). See also HEATHEN and HOITY-TOITY.

humbug. A hoax or deception; a person who practices to deceive; the act of deceiving; in a general sense—nonsense. Thus, following the death of a woman who was said to be 161 years old, the New York *Sun* editorialized: "DISSECTION OF JOICE HETH.—PRECIOUS HUMBUG EXPOSED.—The anatomical examination of the body of Joice Heth yesterday, resulted in the exposure of one of the most precious humbugs that ever was imposed upon a credulous community" (2/25/1836). In truth, the examining surgeon believed the woman, who had been advertised as having been George Washington's nurse, probably was not over eighty. The person who imposed this *humbug*, the first in a long and fruitful career, was Mr. P. T. Barnum.

Humbug dates to about 1750, when it suddenly appeared out of nowhere. "There is a word very much in vogue with the people of taste and fashion, which though it has not even the 'penumbra' of a meaning, yet makes up the sum total of the wit, sense, and judgement of the aforesaid people of taste and fashion! . . . I will venture to affirm that this Humbug is neither an English word, nor a derivative from any other language. It is indeed a blackguard sound . . . a fine make-weight in conversation . . ." (*Student II*, 1/1751). Etymologists still don't know the word's origin. See also BAH, BAMBOOZLE, BUNK, and HORNSWOGGLE.

hump. An innocent enough term in such phrases as *to hump it* or *to get a hump on*, meaning to move quickly or to exert oneself, but in other contexts, whether as a verb, *to hump*, or a noun, *a hump*, the functional equivalent of another four-letter word, FUCK. "I miss the circus. I miss watching the elephant's trunk and the camel's hump" (Joe E. Lewis, Copacabana Club routine, 1956). "You win one more game, and you're going to be humping your fist for a long time" (*The Color of Money*, film, 1986).

Hump, referring to a deformity of a person's back, dates to the early eighteenth century and is apparently a clipping of the older *humpback(ed)*, in turn a derivative of *crump-back.* The term's sexual sense is at least a couple of hundred years old. As far back as 1785, for example, Captain Francis Grose described this as a "once fashionable word for copulation" (*A Classical Dictionary of the Vulgar Tongue*). Sexually, it always seems to have a feminine object, i.e., "he humped her," never "she humped him," which perhaps reflects a cultural bias for the missionary position. Whatever, the thought is basically the same as in Iago's breathless report to Brabantio that "your daughter and the Moor are now making the beast with two backs" (William Shakespeare, *Othello*, 1604). In our own time, the word was repopularized, if not made altogether "fashionable," by Edward Albee in *Who's Afraid of Virginia Woolf* (1962) when, toward the middle of Act Two, George suggests that a good party game for the evening would be "Hump the Hostess," i.e., Martha, his wife.

Hun. A brutal, barbaric person; specifically, a German (especially during and soon after World War I, with a modest revival in World War II).

Hun was used pejoratively prior to 1900, but then the allusion was to the Huns who overran much of Europe in the fifth century or to the Hungarians of recent times. The Germans managed to pin the *Hun* label on themselves, thanks to a speech by Wilhelm II to German troops who were about to embark for China on July 27, 1900, to help quell the Boxer Rebellion. The German minister to Pekin had been murdered and the Kaiser was anxious to teach the Chinese a lesson. He exhorted his soldiers in this manner: "No quarter will be given, no prisoners will be taken. Let all who fall into your hands be at your mercy. Just as the Huns a thousand years ago under the leadership of [Attila] gained a reputation in which they still live in historical tradition, so may the name of Germany become known in China so that no Chinaman will ever again even dare look askance at a German" (London *Times*, 7/30/1900).

The proper adjective is *Hunnish* and the Germans themselves were said as a result to come from *Hunland.* See also GERMAN.

hunk (or **hunkey, hunkie, hunky**). Originally, from the 1890s, an immigrant from east-central Europe, but today, usually a descendant of these immigrants; a BO-HUNK. "The average Pennsylvanian contemptuously refers to these immigrants as 'Hikes' and 'Hunks.' The 'Hikes' are Italians and Sicilians. 'Hunks' is a corruption for Huns, but under this title the Pennsylvanian includes Hungarians, Lithuanians, Slavs, Poles, Magyars and Tyroleans" (*New York Herald*, (1/13/1896). As we approach the end of the twentieth century, the *hunks* have been in place long enough that the term can be used tongue in cheek, at least among each other, e.g., an alternative publication in Pittsburgh, *The Mill Hunk Herald.* Non-*hunks*, however, tend to worry about using the label, and sometimes they overdo it. For example, the Human Rights Commission in Victoria, British Columbia, caught some flak for spending "many months and tens of thousands of dollars in an action against a Hungarian restaurant for calling itself 'Hunky Bill's' " (*New York Times*, 8/30/83). See also HONKY.

hussy. A variant of "housewife"; originally the mistress of a household, a thrifty woman, but since the seventeenth century, a rude way of addressing a woman—"You are mistaken Hussy" (*OED*, 1650)—or a woman herself, meaning that she is a lower-class, ill-behaved, altogether impudent female, a HOYDEN—or worse—a JADE, MINX, or STRUMPET. "It is common to use *housewife* in a good, and *huswife* or *hussy* in a bad sense" (Dr. Samuel Johnson, *Dictionary of the English Language*, 1755). Just to be sure that everyone understands the pejorative meaning of the once-positive word, it is often qualified: *bold hussy, brazen hussy,* or *shameless hussy.* Of course, with the raising of feminine consciousnesses, *housewife* also has become an insult in liberated circles; the safer term to use today is *homemaker.* For more about the tendency of feminine words to acquire negative meanings, see GIRL.

hyena. A despicable person. John Milton used the term in this sense in the seventeenth century (*Samson Agonistes*, 1671) and it remains current in the twentieth. "Colonel, I congratulate you on your decorum in the face of those ill-bred hyenas putting you through hell" (letter to Lieutenant Colonel Oliver L. North, on his performance before the Senate-House Iran-Contra committees, in *The New York Times*, 7/11/87). See also JACKAL.

Hymie. A Jew; also in the compound, *Hymietown,* i.e., New York City. "The Rev. Jesse Jackson acknowledged tonight that he had used the words 'Hymie' and 'Hymietown' in private conversations to refer to Jews" (*New York Times*, 2/27/84). *Hymie* is a pet form of *Hyman,* a common Jewish name. It means "life" in Hebrew and is the masculine counterpart of *Eve.* The Reverend Jackson's use of the terms clouded his campaigns for the Democratic presidential nomination in 1984 and 1988. Most people interpreted the references as a slur, and he apologized for his choice of words. At the same time, he insisted that their true meaning was not bad—that he had merely been using "noninsulting colloquial language" (*Newsweek*, 4/1/84). He told *Newsweek* that he had first heard *Hymie* twenty years earlier in Chicago. "If you can't buy any suits downtown, you go to Jewtown on Maxwell Street, and you start negotiating with Hyman and Sons," he said. "Understand? 'Jewtown is where Hymie gets you if you can't negotiate them suits down,' you understand? That's not meant as anti-Semitic." It would have been different, the reverend conceded, "If one had used something as derogatory as 'kike,' that's mean-spirited." See also JEW (DOWN), TO; KIKE; and, for more about the abuse of first names, PADDY.

hype. A swindle or deception, especially through inflated words in high-pressure advertising or promotion campaigns. Thus, President Ronald Reagan criticized the "so-called peace movement," saying that "peace is a beautiful word," but those who abuse it are engaged in a campaign of "modern hype and theatrics" (Seattle, Washington, 8/23/83, addressing a convention of the American Legion).

Hype dates to the 1920s and was popularized during the '60s and '70s by purveyors of records and books with reference to the use of high-pressure sales tactics and exaggerated claims to turn their products into best-sellers. The word probably comes from the underworld use of *hype* to refer to a technique for short-changing people or from carnival lots where it meant to overcharge for merchandise. And where these senses of *hype* came from, no one knows. It has been suggested that *hype* is related to *hustle,* which is used in much the same way; that it comes from the North English *hipe*, to find fault with, to slander; that it is a condensation of *high-pressure*; and that it is a clipping of *hyperactive* (which *hype artists* often are). The resemblance to *hoke* (*hoke up*, to cheat = *hype up*) also is suspicious; see HOKUM. Finally, in modern parlance, it seems likely that the association of *hype* with overblown language is influenced subliminally by *hyperbole*—and perhaps even HYPOCRITE. The word's origin, in other words, is obscure. See also BUNK.

hypocrite. One who does not believe what he or she professes, ordinarily a bad person who pretends to goodness; a dissembler; from the Greek *hypokritēs*, an actor. This is an especially good attack word because the charge is so difficult to refute. "As to you, sir, treacherous to private friendship (for so you have been to me, and that in the day of danger) and a hypocrite in public life, the world will be puzzled to decide whether you are an apostate or an imposter, whether you have abandoned good principles or whether you ever had any" (Thomas Paine, letter to George Washington, 7/30/1796). See also PHARISEE.

I

icky. Sickly sweet. "So many things seem wrong and boring and silly and sad about the Miss America Pageant . . . It is dull and pretentious and racist and exploitive and icky and sad" (Shana Alexander, *Life* Magazine, 9/20/68). The term's origin is uncertain. It has been dated to the 1930s and it may simply be a nauseating combination of *sick, sickly,* and *sticky.* The intensive is *icky-poo.*

idiot. Technically, a person with the lowest measurable intelligence and, broadly, any stupid person, often in the phrases *blithering idiot, congenital idiot,* and *mongolian idiot.* "Reader, suppose you were an idiot. And suppose you were a member of Congress. But I repeat myself" (Mark Twain, ms. note, ca. 1882). And in an extended sense: "The law is a ass, a idiot" (Charles Dickens, *Oliver Twist,* Mr. Bumble speaking, 1838). The term derives from the Greek *idiōtēs,* a private person, plebian, or lay person, (i.e., one without professional knowledge and, hence, ignorant). See also MONGOLISM and MORON.

ignoramus. One who does not know very much about anything at all, and particularly not about the topic under discussion, whatever it is; a dummy. In Latin, *ignoramus* means "we do not know." The term came into English as a legalism, *ignoramus* being the expression used by a grand jury when refusing to approve a bill of indictment because it felt the prosecutor lacked sufficient evidence for going to trial. The word began acquiring a new dimension as a personal insult after 1615, thanks to a play entitled *Ignoramus* by George Ruggle (1575–1622). The lead character in this drama, which satirizes the arrogance and ignorance of the legal profession of that time, so very long ago, is a lawyer named Ignoramus. Several generations later, following the refusal in 1681 of a grand jury to indict the Earl of Shaftesbury for treason, the phrase *ignoramus jury* became common. Today, grand juries that decline to indict carefully sidestep the issue of ignorance and report "not a true bill," "not found," or "no bill," instead of the now-damning *ignoramus.*

imbecile. A mentally deficient person. ". . . I say here, in my place in the Senate of the United States, that I never did see or converse with so weak and imbecile a man as Abraham Lincoln, President of the United States" (Senator Willard Saulsbury [Democrat, Maryland], speech, 1/29/1863). In the kind of speech that isn't often heard nowadays, the gentleman from Maryland continued: ". . . if I wanted to paint a tyrant; if I wanted to paint a despot, a man perfectly regardless of every constitutional right of the people, whose sworn servant, not ruler, he is, I would paint the hideous form of Abraham Lincoln." Of course, Lincoln also was known to his detractors as a BABOON and a GORILLA.

Back to *imbecile:* Traditionally, an *imbecile,* with a mental age of roughly six to nine years, ranked ahead of an IDIOT and below a MORON. In a famous ruling,

Oliver Wendell Holmes pronounced, "Three generations of imbeciles are enough" (*Buck v. Bell*, 1927), thus upholding a Virginia law requiring the compulsory sterilization of the feeble-minded. Scholars later discovered, however, that neither the woman in question, Carrie Buck (who lived until 1983), nor her daughter Vivian (who died young, but whose school report cards showed her to be an average student) were *imbeciles* in any sense of the word (see Stephen Jay Gould, *Natural History*, 7/84).

imperialist. One who advocates extending a nation's power beyond its borders; a supporter of one of the Western governments, i.e., a capitalist, in the Communist lexicon, or, turning the term back upon its users, a supporter of the Soviet *de facto* empire.

The first *imperialists*, dating to the early seventeenth century, were adherents of an emperor, usually the German one. Later, the term was applied to supporters of the Bonapartes in France, the Manchus in China, and to those who thought it proper that England should rule a large part of the world, e.g., "The Imperialist feels a profound pride in the magnificent heritage of empire won by the courage and energies of his ancestry, and bequeathed to him subject to the burden of many sacred trusts" (*Contemporary Review*, 3/1899). In time, the opinion of some Englishmen changed, of course. "Kipling *is* a jingo imperialist, he *is* morally insensitive and aesthetically disgusting" (George Orwell, in a basically friendly essay, "Rudyard Kipling," 1942). Today, the term is encountered most frequently in such contexts as: "The article [by the Soviet Defense Minister] was also noteworthy for the harshness of its references to the United States, which the marshal equated with Nazi Germany as an aggressive 'imperialist' country" (*New York Times*, 5/10/83). Or, cutting in the other direction: "The Soviet Union stood revealed for what it now is—an imperialist power" (London *Times*, 8/12/69). See also SATELLITE.

Indian giver. One who gives a present, then takes it back. In Colonial times, an *Indian giver* was one who expected a present in return. Thus, from Thomas Hutchinson's *History of the Colony of Massachusets Bay* (1764): "An Indian gift is a proverbial expression, signifying a present for which an equivalent return is expected." Within a hundred years, *Indian giver* was being used in its modern sense by children in the New York area, according to John R. Bartlett's *Dictionary of Americanisms* (1848).

Indian is unusual among ethnic terms for not having much pejorative value until comparatively recently. In the early 1970s, however, activist Indians began calling themselves *Native Americans* (from the peyote-using Native American Church, incorporated in 1918 in Oklahoma and subsequently in other states). The newer term, aside from disassociating its users from the reservation life of the past, was a form of one-upsmanship, since it reminded whites just who was on the premises first. Naturally, sympathetic whites began to shun the old word, too, most notably at Dartmouth College, where the school's traditional symbol, the Dartmouth Indian, was banned as being insulting to the indigenous people for whose education the institution had been founded in 1769.

The negative senses of *Indian* may also have been enhanced at about this time by the revival of *Indian Country* (from 1715, *Dictionary of American English*) by the military in Vietnam to refer to unsecured—i.e., enemy dominated—territory. "In Vietnam American officers liked to call the area outside [the Saigon government's] control 'Indian country.' It was a joke, of course, no more than a figure of speech, but it put the Vietnam War into a definite historical and mythological perspective; the Americans were once again embarked upon a heroic (and for themselves) almost painless conquest of an inferior race" (Frances FitzGerald, *Fire in the Lake*, 1972). Of course, the same metaphor also is utilized by domestic armed forces, as exemplified by the police station in the badlands of New York City, known far and wide as *Fort Apache, The Bronx* (film title, 1981). See also DUTCH and INJUN.

infamy. Evil fame, from the fifteenth century, but most famously in our own time, when Franklin D. Roosevelt substituted *infamy* for "world history" in a draft of his speech asking Congress to declare war against Japan after its attack on Pearl Harbor: "Yesterday, December 7, 1941—a date which will live in infamy—the United States of America was suddenly and deliberately attacked by naval and air forces of the Empire of Japan." No one, however, not even Voltaire, who rejected all superstition with *Éscrasez l'infâme!*, Down with the infamy! (letter to Jean le Rond d'Alembert, 1/27/1762), ever used the term with so much feeling as Hiram Johnson, the Progressive candidate for governor of California in 1910. He was goaded by *Los Angeles Times* publisher Harrison Gray Otis into producing the following diatribe—one of the great passages of "bad" talk in American history— which appeared on page one of the rival *Los Angeles Express*:

> In the city of San Francisco we have drunk to the very dregs of infamy; we have had vile officials; we have had rotten newspapers. But we have nothing so vile, nothing so low, nothing so debased, nothing so infa-mous in San Francisco as Harrison Gray Otis. He sits there in senile dementia, with gangrened heart and rotting brain, grimacing at every reform, chattering impotently at all things that are decent; frothing, fuming, violently gibbering, going down to his grave in snarling infamy.

Otis was not one to be left at a loss for words, and the *Times* responded with a story with the kind of headline that you don't see anymore: "JOHNSON IS VITUPERATIVE, Qualified as a Circus Clown and Rioter" (from Marshall Berges, *The Life and* Times *of Los Angeles*, 1984). Nevertheless, "Holy Hiram," as the *Times* constantly called him, won the election.

informer. A spy, stool pigeon, or, putting the nicest face on it, from Ray Brad-bury's *Fahrenheit 451* (film, 1967):

> "But he's an informer."
> "No—he's an informant."

An *informer* originally (from the fourteenth century) was an instructor or teacher, i.e., one who informs. Subsequently, the meaning was widened to include communicators of information or intelligence generally. The specific sense of informing the authorities about the actions of another person has been dated to the early sixteenth century. This is a necessary business—police work would collapse without it—but not a pretty one, and the word has been badly tarred as a result. See also PIGEON, SNITCH, and SQUEAL.

Injun. A colloquial form of Indian, often in the phrases *Injun giver, to play Injun,* and *honest Injun,* the last usually said with a crooked smile as *Injuns* are not considered especially trustworthy. "No more attention was paid to the shooting of an 'Injun' than if he were a coyote" (Kirk Munroe, *The Golden Days of '49,* 1889). To address a Native American as an *Injun* today would be asking for trouble, of course, since the term is considered to be on a par with such other nonstandard forms as NIGGER and POLACK. See also INDIAN GIVER.

insect. An insignificant, repulsive person, especially an enemy who is about to be stepped on. *Insects* frequently come out of the woodwork during times of political unrest, e.g., "The little, meagre, shrivelled hopping, though loud and troublesome *insects* of the hour" (Edmund Burke, *Reflections on the Revolution in France,* 1790). Similarly, V. I. Lenin proclaimed in a 1918 essay, "How to Organize the Competition," that the common purpose should be to purge "the Russian land of all kinds of harmful insects"—meaning not only class enemies, but "workers malingering at their work." See also FLY, LOUSE, MIDGET, NIT, PEST, ROACH, SPIDER, TERMITE, TICK, and VERMIN.

intellectual. A serious insult in a macho society. " 'I am not an intellectual!' Benjamin said. . . . 'If you want to stand there and insult me I'd appreciate it if you stopped short of that' " (Charles Webb, *The Graduate,* 1963). See also EGGHEAD, ELITIST, EUNUCH, LONGHAIR, and SNOB.

Irish. A derogatory prefix in many phrases, dating from at least the seventeenth century, first in England and then in the United States, reflecting the universal opinion that indwellers have of immigrants and demonstrating the same brand of good-natured humor that is evident to everyone (except Poles) in the Polish jokes of today. Exemplifying the traditional American opinion of Irish newcomers is a folk rhyme of ca. 1875:

> The dirty, dirty Dutch [here meaning *Deutsch,* Germans]
> They don't amount to much,
> But they're a damned sight better than the Irish.

Herewith a sampling of some of the more common *Irish* expressions that have flourished in English, especially in the nineteenth and early twentieth centuries:

Irish, get up one's. To become angry. "She'd got up her Irish now and din't keer a scratch for bars and nothin else" (Mark Twain, *The Adventures of Thomas Jefferson Snodgrass,* 1856). Or, as another American original put it: "Her Irish was up too high to do anything with her" (Colonel Davy Crockett, *A Narrative of the Life of David Crockett,* 1834).

Irish apricot. An Irish potato. Captain Francis Grose noted this one in the first edition of *A Classical Dictionary of the Vulgar Tongue* (1785). Synonyms include *Irish apple, Irish grape,* and *Irish lemon.* For reasons that should not seem terribly obscure, the Irish potato also have been known as a *bog orange, Donovan,* MICK, or *murphy.* The last of these probably is the most common and the oldest, too, having been dated to 1811 (Anon., "A member of the Whip Club," *Lexicon Balatronicum*).

Irish arms. Legs, especially thick ones. According to Captain Grose: "It is said of Irish women that they have a special dispensation from the Pope to wear the thick end of their leg downwards."

Irish as Paddy's pig, as. Very Irish. The importance of the pig in Irish culture has long been recognized. Thus, from a song that was sung by children before the First World War in the Pittsburgh, Pennsylvania, area (and Lord knows where else):

> Oh, they kept the pig in the parlor,
> They kept the pig in the parlor,
> They kept the pig in the parlor,
> And the pig was Irish, too.
> (personal communication, Catherine A. Rawson, 1985.)

Irish banjo. A shovel, from the Civilian Conservation Corps of the 1930s; also called, in the military, an *Army banjo.*

Irish battleship or *man-of-war.* A barge.

Irish beauty. "A woman with two black eyes" (Grose, *op. cit.,* 1796).

Irish blunder. ". . . to take the noise of brass for thunder" (Jonathan Swift, *Wood the Ironmonger,* 1725).

Irish buggy (or *baby buggy* or *chariot*). A wheelbarrow, said to be the world's greatest invention because the Irish learned from using it how to walk on their hind legs.

Irish bull. A contradictory statement. "How could we make any entirely new improvement by means of tonnage duties? . . . The idea that we could, involves the same absurdity as the irish bull about the new boots. 'I shall never git em on' says Patrick 'till I wear em a day or two, and stretch em a little' " (Representative Abraham Lincoln [Whig, Illinois], speech in the House, 6/20/1848). See also BULLSHIT.

Irish cherry. A carrot; twentieth-century soda jerk slang.

Irish clubhouse. A police station.

Irish compliment. A backhanded one.

Irish coat of arms. A black eye.

Irish confetti. Bricks.

Irish daisy. A dandelion.

Irish diamond. Rock crystal (*OED,* 1796). Also called *Welsh diamond.*

Irish dinner. Nothing to eat, in nineteenth-century usage, but now that the Irish have money to spend on food, we have it on the high authority of the Wizard of Id that the "famous seven-course Irish dinner" equals "a boiled potato and a 6-pack" (comic strip, 7/75).

Irish dividend. An assessment on stock.

Irish draperies. Cobwebs.

Irish evidence. Perjury; "False witness" (Grose, *op. cit.,* 1785).

Irish fan. A shovel.

Irish(man's) fart. "If he mentions his family, they're like an Irishman's fart: always making a lot of noise and raising stink, and never want to go back where they came from" (Gershon Legman, "A Word for It!", *Maledicta,* Summer 1977).

Irish(man's) fire. A fire that burns only on top.

Irish fortune. A woman's genitals and a pair of clogs; "A cunt and pattens" (J. S. Farmer and W. E. Henley, *Slang and Its Analogues,* 1896). Farmer and Henley characterized the expression as "old" at the time.

Irish harp. A long-handled shovel.

Irish hint. A broad one.

Irish hoist. A kick in the pants.

Irish horse. Corned beef, on the tough side. "Our provisions consisted of putrid salt beef to which the sailors gave the name Irish horse" (Tobias Smollett, *The Adventures of Roderick Random*, 1748).

Irish hurricane. A dead calm with a drizzle of rain.

Irish kiss. A slap in the face.

Irish local. A wheelbarrow (because it makes so many stops).

Irish marathon. A relay race.

Irish mahogany. The common alder.

Irish musket. A club; ca. American Revolution.

Irish mutton. Syphilis.

Irish nightingale. A bullfrog, from ca. 1850–52 and the American tour of Jenny Lind, "The Swedish Nightingale."

Irish pennant. A loose end of rope, flapping in the wind.

Irish promotion (or *raise*). A demotion or pay cut.

Irish root. The penis.

Irish shave. A defecation.

Irish sidewalk. The street.

Irish spoon. Irish laborers used many different kinds of shovels.

Irish theater. A military guardroom.

Irish toothache. Depending on context: (1) A persistent erection; (2) Pregnancy. The first sense has been dated to the late nineteenth century and the second, which seems to depend upon it, to the early twentieth. For delicacy's sake, the latter may be abbreviated *I.T.A.*

Irish toyle. A rogue who pretends to be a beggar and one of the oldest of the Hibernian breed: "An Irish toyle . . . useth to show no wares until he have his alms; and if the goodman and wife be not in the way, he procureth of the children or servants a fleece of wool, or the worth of twelve pence of some other thing, for a pennyworth of his wares" (?John Awdeley, *The Fraternity of Vagabonds*, 1661).

Irish triplets. "Irish triplets, she explained, is having three children in three years" (*New York Times*, 11/27/84).

Irish turkey. Corned beef and cabbage (tramp talk); hash (Army talk).

Irish way, the. Anal intercourse between man and woman (a form of birth control).

Irish wedding. Emptying a cesspool.

Irish wedding, to have danced at. To have two black eyes (after having danced with an *Irish beauty?*).

Irish whist. Copulation; a card-playing metaphor from the nineteenth century for a "trick" in which the *jack* (a *John Thomas* or penis) takes the *ace* (or *ace of spades*, the female pudendum). Conversely, a woman of this period might say she had *played her ace to take his jack.*

All this may seem a bit rough on the Irish, but they are not alone; see DUTCH, SCOTCH, and WELSH for starters. And for more about the Irish, continue with FLANNEL-MOUTH, HOPER, MICK, NARROWBACK, PADDY, and TURK; also note the *potato eater* and *spud* in KRAUT and the *Bridget* in MOLL.

it. A person reduced to the status of a thing. Thus, Berowne says as the French courtier Boyet appears on the scene: "See where it comes!" (William Shakespeare, *Love's Labor's Lost*, 1588–94). The epithet probably is applied most often to stupid people, mean or contemptible ones, and infants. A variation, for a snooty person who is not as smart as she thinks she is: "Gloria thinks she's Madame Ittsky." See also THOU.

Italian. As a rule, the Italians, like the Germans, are disparaged more often in terms of their nicknames (e.g., DAGO, GUINEA, WOP) than their national name. But every rule has its exceptions, and here are some:

Italian fashion (or *manner*). Sodomy; specifically, anal copulation. The expression may have arisen among the French. An early example, at any rate, comes from Benvenuto Cellini's stay in France, when his model (and mistress) Catarina and her mother made this charge against him, thinking he would pay them off to drop it. "They made up their minds to have the law of me, and consulted a Norman advocate, who advised them to declare that I had used the girl after the Italian fashion; what this meant I need hardly explain" (*The Autobiography*, 1558–71, *tr.* John Addington Symonds, 1927). Cellini vociferously denied the accusation, telling the judge that "so far from being the Italian fashion, it must be the French habit, seeing she knew all about it, while I was ignorant," and he managed to get off the hook. See also GREEK.

Italian football. A hand bomb, also called a *guinea football*.

Italian hurricane (or *storm*). Spaghetti with garlic.

Italian perfume. Garlic.

Italian quarrel. "Death, poison, treachery, remorselessness" (J. Redding Ware, *Passing English*, 1909) but, we are assured by Eric Partridge, now virtually obsolete (*A Dictionary of Slang and Unconventional English*, 1970). Whew!

See also EYETALIAN, GREASEBALL, MACARONI, and MEATBALL.

J

Jack. A familiar form of address to any man whose name is not known, as in *I'm All Right, Jack* (film, 1960), a title that was discreetly condensed from the much older catchphrase (ca. 1880, according to Eric Partridge), *Fuck you, I'm all right, Jack.* The name has a long history of contemptuous use and, as a pet form of the most common name, *John*, is especially suitable for addressing representatives of the common classes. " 'Go fro the window, Jakke fool,' she said" (Geoffrey Chaucer, *Canterbury Tales*, 1387–1400). See also *tomfool* in TOM-.

Jack is a male determinative in the case of animals, e.g., JACKASS and *jack hare* (the *jackrabbit*, of either sex, gets its name from its long, jackass-like ears), as well as in various occupations, e.g., *lumberjack* and *steeple jack*, the generalized *jack-of-all-trades*, the redundant *man jack*, the child's *jack-in-the-box*, the playing card also known as the KNAVE, and the broken-crowned *Jack* in "Jack and Jill" (see MOLL for more about *Jill*).

Jack's house and *Jack's place*, meanwhile, are old terms for a privy. *Jack* in this sense probably comes from the still older *jacques* or *jakes*, also for a privy and, before that, a chamberpot, and this kind of *Jack* apparently is the ancestor of the modern *john* that flushes.

Because of its essential maleness, *Jack* also has acquired various sexual meanings (in addition to such nonsexual meanings as *jack* for money). In the nineteenth century, for instance, *jack* was British slang for the penis (more formally referred to as *John Thomas*), while as a verb the word meant to copulate. The sexual senses are preserved in the current, masturbatory *jack off* (it also means to goof off). "As kids [about the time of World War I], we used to tell each other we went to the railroad station to see my uncle Jack off on the train" (David F. Costello, letter, 2/22/83). See also JERK, JOCK, and PADDY.

jackal. A skulking henchman; one who does another's dirty work, from the old belief that jackals went before lions, stirring up prey for them; in extended use, any detestable person, comparable to HYENA. "The British press was outraged and called Serov [then head of the KGB] 'a thug' and 'a jackal' as he conferred with Scotland Yard on security for the forthcoming Bulganin-Khrushchev visit to England" (*Life*, 4/2/56). See also LACKEY.

jackanapes. An impertinent or mischievous person. The word surfaces first in written records in connection with William de la Pole, Duke of Suffolk (b. 1396; beheaded at sea, 1450). Powerful but unpopular, in part because of prejudice against *nouveau riche* upstarts, his family being one of the first to rise from the merchant class to nobility, de la Pole was widely known as "Jack Napes." This apparently was a nickname for any captive monkey and it alluded in de la Pole's case to his badge, which featured a ball and chain of the sort used to restrain such a pet. Why captive apes were called "Jack Napes," however, is not known. It may be that the common name "Jack" often was applied to tame monkeys or that the phrase comes from "Jack of Naples," referring to an early importation into England of one or more apes from Italy. See also APE, JACK, and MONKEY.

jackass. A stupid person, a fool. ". . . if, as an increasing number are predicting, the economy may be turning down next summer and autumn, the Democrats could nominate a jackass and probably win" (Richard M. Nixon, confidential memo to friends that somehow made it into *The London Sunday Times*, 10/18/87).

The *jackass* is a well-known political figure, of course. When Thomas Nast first drew the cartoon symbol of the Democratic Party, the caption identified the animal as a "Jackass," not as the more refined "Donkey" preferred by Democrats today (*Harper's Weekly*, 1/15/1870). *Jackass* also was the operative term in a famous riposte by John Randolph of Roanoke in the House of Representatives in the 1820s. Though not included in official records, the exchange between him and Tristam Burges of Rhode Island is mentioned in many other sources. It began with Burges referring to Randolph's alleged sexual impotence:

> MR. BURGES: Sir, Divine Providence takes care of his own universe. Moral monsters cannot propagate. Impotent of everything but malevolence of purpose, they can no otherwise multiply miseries than by blaspheming all that is pure and prosperous and happy. Could demon propagate demon, the universe might become pandemonium; but I rejoice that the Father of Lies can never become the Father of Liars. One adversary of God and man is enough for one universe.
>
> MR. RANDOLPH: You pride yourself upon an animal faculty, in respect to which the slave is your equal and the jackass infinitely your superior.

See also ASS, DONKEY, and JACK.

jackdaw. A person who talks too much, a prattler; from the seventeenth century. The loquaciousness of the jackdaw (originally "jack the daw") was attributed to its having a split tongue. A *jackdaw* might also be an ordinary fellow pretending to be someone special, from an old fable, *a jackdaw in peacock's feathers*. Hence W. S. Gilbert's lyric in *H.M.S. Pinafore* (1878):

> Things are seldom what they seem,
> Skim milk masquerades as cream.
> High-lows pose as patent leathers,
> Jackdaws strut in peacocks' feathers.

See also JACK and PEACOCK.

jade. A loose woman; originally, from the fourteenth century, a contemptuous term for a horse, and by the sixteenth century, applied contemptuously to women in the same way as HACK, HARRIDAN, and NAG. Human *jades* often are tired, worn-out specimens—in a word, *jaded*. But not always. For instance, here is a quick peek at one of history's more attractive *jades*, Nell Gwyn, on the evening of November 6, 1668, when she was a mere eighteen and already a notable figure, though not yet official mistress to Charles II: ". . . to the King's playhouse, and there saw 'The Island Princess,' . . . We sat in an upper box, and the jade Nell come and sat in the next box; a bold merry slut, who lay laughing there upon people . . . Thence home and to the office to do some business . . ." (Henry B. Wheatley, *ed.*, *The Diary of Samuel Pepys*, 1896). See also HUSSY, SLUT, and WHORE.

jake it. To loaf or goof off. "The [New York Yankee] players think that they are playing with Steinbrenner on their backs. They think he overstated the charge that Piniella said Henderson was 'jaking it' " (*New York Times*, 8/13/87). Unrecorded in either the *New Dictionary of American Slang* (1986) or the pertinent supplement to the *Oxford English Dictionary* (1976), this bears little resemblance to the use of *jake* since about World War I to mean satisfactory, okay, or even excellent, as in "Everything's jake." Probably, it is a variant of *jack off*; see JACK.

Janus. A two-faced person, from the Roman deity of this name. Janus was the god of beginnings (hence, January, the first month of the year) and of doors and gates, and he was commonly depicted with two faces that faced—as doors do—in opposite directions.

Jap. Japanese. "What's the matter with the fat Jap" (Spiro Agnew, pondering the sleeping form of Baltimore *Sun* reporter Gene Oishi, on a campaign plane, en route from Las Vegas to Los Angeles, 9/20/68). Short forms of ethnic, national, or regional names almost always have derogatory overtones. For example, consider the vibes that emanate from *Argie* (see WOG), *Arkie, Belgie, gee* (Portuguese), HEBE, *Jug* (Yugoslavian), *Lit* (Lithuanian), NIP, OKIE, *Ruskie,* and WHITEY. (The same rule applies to personal names and labels; see PADDY and FAG.)

Dated to ca. 1880, *Jap* was used commonly, almost unthinkingly, for many years, e.g., "Ladies' short silk waists, made of plain colored Habutai Jap silk" (*Montgomery Ward Catalog*, 1895), and, nearly forty years later, "Doctor down the hall treated a man for yellow jaundice for eleven years—then found he was a Jap" (W. C. Fields, in *The Dentist*, film, 1932).

The term's latent derogatory meaning came quickly to the fore with the approach of World War II, which began, as far as the United States was concerned, with the Japanese air raid on Pearl Harbor; hence, *to pull a Jap* or *to Jap [someone]* became synonymous with a sneak attack of any kind. Earl Thompson's novel, *Tattoo* (1974), conveys the spirit of the time: "For from the moment of December 7 to the present moment, to *Slap a Jap* and *Stun a Hun* had been his most abiding and hopeful ambition." Contributing to the wartime popularity of the three-letter word was the ease with which it fit into headlines, such as "I Saw Jap Torture" (*Photo Story*, 3/43) and "Jap Rats Stop at Nothing—See This. It Will Make You Fighting Mad" (World War II ad by Joseph E. Levine for the film *Ravaged Earth*). Almost every good American, from the president on down, casually used the epithet, e.g., "This country is ready to pull the trigger if the Japs do anything" (Franklin D. Roosevelt, Oval Office tape recording, 10/8/40).

The Japanese had protested the short form before the war, but it was not until after they lost it that they began to have much success with their linguistic campaign. They were helped, of course, by the generally increased public concern for the sensitivities of others, inspired by civil rights movement of the 1960s. Thus, Mr. Agnew's use of the word created enough furor that he found he had to apologize publicly for it, saying no offense had been intended. (His apology included his reference to Polish-Americans as POLACKs: "I confess ignorance because my Polish friends have never apprised me of the fact that when they call each other by that appelation it is not in the friendliest context," *New York Times*, 9/24/68). Also indicative of the new concern for the feelings of our former enemies was a "sense of Congress" resolution introduced in 1986 by Representative Mike Lowry (Democrat, Washington) that the standard abbreviation for *Japanese* be changed to *Jpn.* from you-know-what. See also SKIBBY.

JAP (Jap). An acronym for Jewish-American Princess (or Prince), as in *The Official J.A.P. Handbook* (Anna Sequoia, 1982). The acronym, dating to the 1970s, trades somewhat on the negative associations of the preceding entry. Always portrayed as rich, spoiled, and straitlaced, the non-Oriental *JAP* is a figure of much fun, especially the female model, e.g., "The big news is The Return of the Jewish Woman, or Jewish-American Princess, as it were. Many have been to Tibet. Others have faithfully attended Masturbation Class. A lot of them kiss back" (Bruce Jay Friedman, *The Lonely Guy's Book of Life*, 1978). In time, however, the humor began to wear thin, and *JAP* jokes were the subject of a 1987 Conference on Current Stereotypes of Jewish Women, sponsored by the American Jewish Committee. Speakers asserted that the jokes were rooted in anti-Semitism as well as sexism. "What had started as humor has escalated into attacks," said Ms. Susan Weidman Schneider. "Imagine for a moment that you are an 18-year-old female Jewish student at a college football game. And when you get up to get a soda you hear someone yell 'JAP! JAP! JAP!' Then the cry is picked up by everybody sitting in the stadium" (*New York Times*, 9/7/87). See also JEW (DOWN), TO and WASP.

jay. A chatterbox; a DOLT, especially one who can be easily duped; frequently a rustic or HICK. The well-known thievery of jays may also have contributed to *jayhawk*—a bird that does not exist in real life. This term first appeared as *jayhawker*, referring to the guerrillas who fought over slavery in Kansas and other border states before and during the Civil War; later applied to any marauder or robber, it remains current as a nickname for Kansas, the Jayhawker State. Meanwhile, the basic doltishness of the bird remains dominant in *to jaywalk*, which is not considered a smart thing to do when autos are whizzing by. See also BIRD.

jazz. Not a bad word now, but almost certainly of extremely low origin, referring to copulation before it was applied to music, dancing, and nonsense (i.e., *all that jazz*). "If the truth were known about the origin of 'Jazz' it would never be mentioned in polite society . . . The vulgar word 'Jazz' was in general currency in those dance halls thirty years ago or more" (Clay Smith, *Etude*, 9/24). "According to Raven I. McDavid, Sr., of Greenville, S.C., the announcement, in 1919, of the first *jazz band* to play in Columbia, where he was then serving in the state legislature, inspired feelings of terror among the local Baptists such as what might have been aroused by a personal appearance of Yahweh. Until that time *jazz* had never been heard in the Palmetto State except as a verb meaning to copulate" (H. L. Mencken, *The American Language*, Raven I. McDavid, Jr., ed., 1963). " 'She never stepped out of line once in all the years we been teamed up. I can't sell her on jazzing the chump now' " (William Lindsay Gresham, *Nightmare Alley*, 1946).

Jazz arose during the late nineteenth century in the better brothels of New Orleans, which provided music and dancing as well as sex. The original jazz band, according to Herbert Asbury's *The Latin Quarter* (1938), was the Spasm (sic) Band, made up of seven boys, aged twelve to fifteen, who first appeared in New Orleans about 1895. They advertised themselves as the "Razzy Dazzy Spasm Band." When, about 1900, another band adopted the same billing for an appearance at the Haymarket dance hall, the Spasms loaded their pockets with rocks and dropped by to protest the infringement. This prompted the owner to the hall to repaint his advertising placards to read: "Razzy Dazzy Jazzy Band!" If the memories of Asbury's sources were correct—and he talked to two surviving members of the Spasms— this represents the word's earliest-known appearance in print.

Jazz probably comes from a Creole or perhaps African word, but exact connections have not been proven. Whatever, the presumed sexual origin is quite in accord with the development of many other related words, most notably:

boogie-woogie. Used in the nineteenth century by blacks in the American South to refer to secondary syphilis.

gig. The musician's engagement probably derives immediately from the *gig* that is a dance or party, but *gig* and *gigi* (or *giggy*) also are old slang terms for the vulva; the first has been dated to the seventeenth century. See also JIG.

jelly roll. Black slang from the nineteenth century for the vulva, with various related meanings, i.e. sexual intercourse, a loving woman, a man obsessed with finding same. " 'What yo' want?' she asked softly. 'Jelly roll?' " (Thomas Wolfe, *Look Homeward Angel*, 1929). The term probably derives from *jelly*, meaning semen: "Give her cold jelly to take up her belly, And once a day swinge her again" (John Fletcher, *The Beggar's Bush*, 1622). Related expressions include *jelly bag*, referring both to the scrotum and the female genitals; *jerk [one's] jelly*, to masturbate; and *jelly*, a good-looking woman. *Jelly roll* appears in many blues songs, such as "I Ain't Gonna Give Nobody None o' this Jelly Roll," "Nobody in Town Can Bake a Jelly Roll Like Mine," and "Jelly Roll Blues," the last by Ferdinand Joseph LaMenthe "Jelly Roll" Morton (1885–1941). And for more about food and sex, see EAT.

juke. The modern *jukebox* was preceded by *juke house*, which was a brothel to Southern blacks, the basic term coming from a Gullah word meaning disorderly or wicked.

swing. A partial exception to the rule, referring to music (from 1899, *OED*) some decades before it was applied in its modern sense to wife-swapping and related activities involving one or more partners of either sex (from 1964, or earlier, depending on the interpretation one gives to Frank Sinatra's 1956 record album *Songs for Swinging Lovers*). The related, now archaic *swinge*, however, was used for many years as a synonym for copulation ("= swive," according to the *OED*'s discreet definition). Note the quote from 1622 in *jelly roll* above. Or as John Dryden put it: "And that baggage, Beatrix, how I would swinge her if I could" (*Enemy's Love*, 1668). The oldest meanings of both *swinge* and *swing* deal with beating, striking, and whipping (i.e., the swing of a weapon predates the back and forth swaying of a swing or the rhythmic swing of music). For reasons that are not hard to guess, the conjunction of violent and sexual senses within the same word is very common, as noted in the entry on the great *F-word*.

See also FUNKY and KAZOO.

jellybean. A stupid person, a fool; from ca. World War I. "The jellybeans I went to school with" (Richard Bissell, *A Stretch on the River*, 1950). The gelatinous candy metaphor works because a person's head also is a *bean*.

jelly-belly. A fat person. "He was . . . an Outrageous Stinker, a Jelly-bellied Flag-flapper . . ." (Rudyard Kipling, *Stalky & Co.*, 1899). See also FAT.

jerk. A fool or dummy; a person of absolutely no importance. "In an age of jerkism, which we're in, the jerks are winning" (Mike Royko, *New York Times*, 1/15/84). And as evidence of the way world history is preserved by oral tradition among children, here is a jingle that was at least forty years old when collected at a Boy Scout installation, Camp Mattatuck, in Plymouth, Connecticut, in August 1986:

> Whistle while you work,
> Hitler is a jerk.
> Mussolini
> Cut off his weenie,
> And now it won't even work.

In another version, sung by young Pennsylvanians in the 1950s, the refrain goes: "Mussolini / Bit his weenie / Now it doesn't squirt" (personal communication, Mark Hurst, 2/23/89).

A superlative fool is a *jerkola, royal jerkola,* or, more contemptuously, a *jerk-off*. The person who lazes about or goofs off, i.e., acts the fool, is said to *jerk around* or *jerk off,* while to *jerk [someone] around* or *off* is to abuse, victimize, or make a fool of that someone, e.g., "I just want you to bear in mind that while we're sitting here and smiling at each other and you're jerking me around and I'm feeling like a real asshole that I know precisely what you're up to and that I can only take so much of it" (Ernest Thompson, *On Golden Pond*, 1979). See also FOOL.

The various *jerks* all derive from the *jerk-off*, who is a masturbator. The sense development is from *jerk* meaning a sudden, sharp movement (sixteenth century), to the self-indulgent *jerk off* (eighteenth century), to the dumb *jerk* (twentieth century). The underlying idea, of course, is that the dumb *jerk* has gotten that way from masturbating too much, as people used to believe would happen. This popular myth also shows up in *puddinghead* (see BLOCKHEAD), *lost some marbles* (see SCREW LOOSE, A), and WACKO. See also DODO, DOPE, FOOL, MORON, NINCOMPOOP, OAF, SCHNOOK, STUPID, and YO-YO.

jerry. A German, especially a soldier, from World War I and revived for World War II; see HEINIE. The term may derive from the shape of the German helmets, which looked to English eyes like chamber pots, *jerry* being nineteenth-century slang for *jeroboam,* a chamber pot or jordan, as well as the name of a large wine bottle. If so, then *jerry* comes ultimately from *Jeroboam,* a King of Israel, who provided the bottle's name because he was "a mighty man of valor" but nevertheless "did sin, and made Israel to sin" (*I Kings,* 11:28, 14:16). This usage, then, would parallel that of *jordan* (from the River Jordan?), which also is a time-honored (from the fourteenth century) term of abuse for a person, especially a FOOL, as well as yet another name for that much-maligned utensil, the chamber pot. Or the modern *jerry* could simply be an alteration of GERMAN. See also PADDY.

Jesus. The most heavily tabooed of Christianity's sacred names, as indicated by the avoidance of its use as a personal name (except among Hispanics); by its comparative power as an oath (*By Jesus!* carries greater weight than *By God!*, partly because it is heard less often); and by the variety of euphemisms that have been devised in place of it (including, among others, *gee, gee whillikers, jeepers creepers, Jeez, Jiminy Christmas, Jiminy Cricket,* and *jingo*). ". . . Latin immigrants to the United States have had relatively little difficulty in retaining their often beautiful given-names, though occasionally a Mexican named *Jesus* is constrained to change to *Jose* or *Joe* in order to allay the horror and check the ribaldry of 100% Americans . . ." (H. L. Mencken, *The American Language, Supplement II,* 1967). See also GODDAMN.

Jew (down), to. To bargain (down). "Just as some Gentiles use 'Jew' as a contemptuous synonym for too-shrewd, sly bargaining ('He tried to Jew the price down,' is about as unappetizing an idiom as I know), so some Jews use *goy* in a pejorative sense" (Leo Rosten, *The Joys of Yiddish,* 1968). See also GOY.

Jew has been used in an opprobrious sense for several hundred years at the very least. As a synonym for a usurer or driver of hard bargains, *Jew* has been dated to 1606 (*OED*), and it and the adjective *Jewish* have appeared over the years in a great many more or less disparaging phrases, e.g., *Jew boy* (or *girl* or *man*); *Jew(ish) flag,* a dollar bill; *Jewtown* (see HYMIE); and *Jew York,* the city across the Hudson from *Jew Nersey.*

The conversion of *Jew* into a verb seems to have been accomplished first by Americans in the early nineteenth century, with Jews as well as non-Jews using the word this way. The *Dictionary of Americanisms* dates *to Jew* to 1824 and *to jew down* to 1870. An early student of Americanisms, the Reverend R. Manning Chipman, of New Lisbon, Connecticut, observed that *Jew* is used as a verb "all over the U.S. In New England Jews themselves use it in the same way" (undated note, from 1859–77, in *American Speech,* 5/50). And consider how *The American Israelite* pridefully reported on the career of Joseph Choynski, a Jewish boxer from California (10/13/1892): "Our Jew-boys are fast gaining upon the Betzemer [an Irisher to a German Jew] bruisers, and before long the descendants of the Maccabees will be able to give the Sullivan slugging set two points in the game and beat them at their own castor" (*American Speech,* 12/63).

A curious effect of the long and largely successful campaign of Jews in the first half of this century to eliminate the use of *Jew* as a verb was that many people, including numerous Jews, started to avoid employing the word in any sense at all. Thus, *Hebrew* gained acceptance as a euphemism in such expressions as *Hebrew holidays* and *Hebrew comedian,* and the instrument known since the late sixteenth century as the *Jew's harp* metamorphosed into the *juice harp* or *jaw harp.* Today, the word is no longer shunned to the same degree, but even so, careful speakers are more likely to say "He is Jewish" than "He is a Jew." As noted by Lenny Bruce: "Now I'll say 'a Jew' and just the word *Jew* sounds like a dirty word and people don't know whether to laugh or not. . . . So there's just a silence until they know I'm kidding, and then they'll break through" (*How to Talk Dirty and Influence People,* 1972).

Not everyone is kidding, of course. Consider, as an example of low-key anti-Semitism, the following lines from T. S. Eliot's "Gerontion" (*Collected Poems 1909–1935,* 1936):

My house is a decayed house,
And the jew squats on the window sill, the owner,
Spawned in some estaminet [small cafe] in Antwerp

Then there is the more vociferous poem by Leslie Campbell, a black schoolteacher in New York City, dedicated to his union president, Albert Shanker, and read by the poet over a local radio station during the 1968 school strike:

Hey there, Jew boy, with that yarmulke on your head,
Hey there, Jew boy, I wish you were dead

See also HEBE; HYMIE; JAP; KIKE; MOCKY; *children of Satan* in SATAN; SHEENY; and YID.

Jezebel. A shrew, a whore. " 'Mr. Slope,' said Mrs. Proudie, catching the delinquent at the door, 'I am surprised that you should leave my company to attend on such a painted Jezebel as that' " (Anthony Trollope, *Barchester Towers*, 1857). The reference is to the Biblical Jezebel, wife of Ahab, a king of Israel. Their relationship was similar to that of Lord and Lady Macbeth: "But there was none like unto Ahab, which did sell himself to work wickedness in the sight of the Lord, whom Jezebel his wife stirred up" (*I Kings*, 21:25). See also MOLL and WHORE.

jig (jigaboo). A black person. "Mr. [Mark] Lane contended racist tendencies could be discerned in such articles [in *National Review*] as one . . . headlined, 'The Jig Is Up for Adam Clayton Powell Jr.' Mr. [William F.] Buckley testified that he had no idea back then, in 1958, that the word 'jig' could be used as a racial slur" (*New York Times*, 10/26/85).

Jigaboo has been dated to 1909 and *jig* to 1924. The term's origin is uncertain. It may derive from the *jig*, which is a dance, perhaps via the all-black *jig band* that played in a *jig show* during the era of minstrel shows and vaudeville. As with other terms, such as JAZZ, which are associated with music and with blacks, there is a strong suggestion of sexuality here, *jig-jig* and *jig-a-jig* standing for copulation since at least the nineteenth century. The sexual sense derives from the lively, up-and-down movement of the dance (as does the refrain of the nursery rhyme, "To market, to market, to buy a fat pig, / Home again, home again, jiggety-jig"). See also GIGOLO, NEGRO, and ZIG-ZIG.

jinx. A person or thing believed to bring bad luck; as a verb, to change fate for the worse. The word is an Americanism and surprisingly new, dated so far only to 1911. It apparently is a misspelling of *jynx*, which is the name of an Old World bird, also called the wryneck (from the way it writhes its head and neck when disturbed). A member of the woodpecker family, the jynx was thought to have magical powers. Witches used its feathers in making love philters and other potions, with the result that by the sixteenth century the bird's name was synonymous with "charm" or "spell." Thus, it seems, the jynx became a *jinx*. See also VOODOO.

jock. An athlete or an athletic supporter; the former is usually but not always an object of admiration, the latter never. "Ivy Leaguers learn that 'jock' can be a pejorative. 'At some universities, athletes are treated like kings: snap your fingers and it's yours,' says [Dallas Cowboy Jeff] Rohrer. 'Try snapping your fingers for a glass of water at Yale and you could die of thirst' " (William Safire, *New York Times,* 12/7/86).

The term derives via *jockstrap* from *jockum* (also *jockam*), which was slang for the penis from the mid-sixteenth century through the early nineteenth. As a verb, during much of this period, *jock* or *jockum-cloy* meant to copulate, while a *jockum-gagger* was a man who lived off his wife's earnings from prostitution. (Curiously, during the eighteenth and nineteenth centuries, *jock* also denoted the private parts of a woman.) The modern *jocker,* originally a homosexual hobo who lived off the earnings of his boy companion, is an aggressive male homosexual or WOLF. And, going back to the beginning, *jockum* probably came from the personal name, *Jock,* which is a form of *John,* comparable to JACK. As a personal name, *Jock* also may be employed as a casual form of address to any Scotsman whose real name is not known. See also PADDY.

joker. Any man or guy; usually derogatory, the implication being that the fellow is a CLOWN or, worse, a trickster or WISEACRE, and that he is likely to misbehave in an unpredictable way, i.e., that he is a *joker in the deck.* "The Bishop of Durham is a dangerous joker who by some error has been allowed to creep into the Congregation of Bishops" (Nicholas Winterton, M.P., "Poles Apart," BBC, 10/28/84).

The term may be applied to things as well as people, again usually in a pejorative sense—especially when the topic is hidden clauses in contracts or legislation, e.g. "They are all nervous over the possibility that there may be a hitherto unperceived joker in the present bill" (*New York Evening Post,* 5/11/04). In theory, *joker,* in the sense of "he who jokes," derives from the Latin *jocus,* joke, but the slang use of the word to refer to any man appears to be older than the jesting sense (Pepys mentioned having "a very good dinner among the old jokers" in 1665), which suggests an overlap here from an early date with the male meanings of JOCK. See also FOOL.

Jonah. One who brings bad luck to others. "Does it mean that Billy was a Jonah?" (New Orleans *Lantern,* 9/22/1886). "The men consider you a Jonah" (Richard McKenna, *The Sand Pebbles,* 1962). The allusion is to the Hebrew prophet, of course, who sought to escape the Lord by boarding a ship for Tarshish, whereupon the Lord created a great storm to stop him. This frightened the crew. "And they said every one to his fellow, Come, and let us cast lots, that we may know for whose cause this evil *is* upon us. So they cast lots, and the lot fell upon Jonah" (*Jonah,* 1:7). See also ALBATROSS.

Judas. A traitor of the very worst sort; from Judas Iscariot, the Disciple who betrayed Jesus Christ for thirty pieces of silver (*Matthew,* 26:14–15). "Every great man nowadays has his disciples, and it is always Judas who writes the biography" (Oscar Wilde, *The Critic as Artist,* 1891). "Louis Farrakhan, who heads the Chicago-based Nation of Islam, publicly called Milton Coleman . . . a 'traitor' and a 'Judas' and used language that some, including Coleman, interpreted as a death threat to the reporter" (*Columbia Journalism Review,* 7-8/84).

The traitorous meaning also is evident in *Judas hole,* a peephole, especially in the door of a prison cell; *Judas kiss,* one of betrayal; *Judas money,* payment for betrayal; and *Judas trick*, a very sneaky one. Then there is the *Judas goat*, originally an animal used to lead others into the slaughterhouse, and later a human decoy or DOUBLE-CROSSER, e.g., "But Mikoyan had been with Khrushchev at Sochi . . . when the leadership crisis developed. I thought he was there as a Judas goat, to keep down Khrushchev's suspicions about the plot to remove him" (Harrison E. Salisbury, *A Journey for Our Times*, 1983).

See also BENEDICT ARNOLD and TRAITOR.

junk. Rubbish; anything that is inferior, shoddy, or fit to be discarded, as in *junk bond, junk jewelry, junk mail, junk man, junk pitch* (a slow but tricky baseball pitch, such as a knuckleball), *junk shop, junkyard*, etc. "It's irresponsible for 60 *Minutes* to try to push such junk on the American people" (*Columbia Journalism Review*, 9-10/83). And from the works of that prolific poet, Anonymous:

> There's a wonderful family called Stein,
> There's Gert and there's Epp and there's Ein;
> Gert's poems are punk,
> Epp's statues are junk
> And no one can understand Ein.

The *junk* that is fit for discarding is a relatively new term, a nineteenth-century spin-off from *junk* as used by sailors to refer to worn-out cables, ropes, and other marine equipment. The nautical *junk* probably derives from the Latin *juncus*, rush, reed, also the ancestor of the prettier *jonquil*; of *junket*, a custard originally served on rushes or prepared in a rush mat; of the *junket* that is a picnic or expedition; and of the *junketeer* who goes on one (unless he is a congressman, in which case the *junket* is called "a fact-finding trip").

Of course, *junk* also is slang for drugs, especially heroin, a usage that has been dated only to the 1920s but probably goes back at least to the turn of the century. In its turn, this *junk* has produced such terms for confirmed users of narcotics as *junk freak, junk hog, junker*, and *junkie*, the last of which has been extended to include other less dangerous addictions, e.g. *newspaper junkie* and *publicity junkie*. "For all I know, people may exist who like to see their names in print. John Lennon and Yoko Ono were said to be print junkies" (Germaine Greer, *Listener*, 11/15/73). See also GROUPIE.

In the case of *junk*, the senses of worthlessness and addiction are combined most notably in the form of *junk food*.

See also BUNK, PUNK, and the *pothead* in BLOCKHEAD.

K

kaffir. A black person, especially in South Africa. "When we . . . were young people the word 'kaffir' meant nothing more than to indicate a Black man. . . . It has deteriorated to such an extent that it offends people with dark coloured skin and . . . we try to avoid it" (debate, Senate, South Africa, 5/17/73). "Sorghum beer [in South Africa] was known as 'kaffir beer' until *kaffir* became acknowledged as a pejorative, and was then known as 'bantu beer' until *bantu* took on the connotations of *kaffir*" (David E. Koskoff, *The Diamond World*, ms., 1980). See also COOLIE and ZULU.

Kaffir comes from the Arabic *kafir*, infidel, and was used disparagingly by Muslims of non-Muslims before being adopted by Christians. There are *white kaffirs*, too, meaning whites who associate too closely with blacks; for an American parallel, see UNCLE TOM.

kangaroo (court). A sham court, often one in which prisoners "try" fellow inmates, or a real court that dispenses sham justice; in either case, the implication is that verdicts are decided in advance of testimony. Curiously, *kangaroo court* is an Americanism, not an Australianism, with the *OED*'s earliest example coming from Texas in 1853. The connection between the kangaroo and frontier justice is not clear. Perhaps the original reference was to claim "jumpers." Whatever, the image has become firmly embedded in the American language and has inspired other phrases, such as *kangaroo convention*, an irregular or rump convention, and *kangaroo justice*, as provided by a *kangaroo court*.

kazoo. The anus or vagina. "He made this big blow-up of her private parts . . . everybody looking up her old kazoo" (Bruce Jay Friedman, *Steambath*, 1972). The term has a number of variants. Thus, when Senator Alan Simpson (Republican, Wyoming) told reporters just before a press conference by President Reagan on March 19, 1987, that "You're asking him things because you know he's off-balance and you'd like to stick it in his kazoo," the word was rendered by *The Wall Street Journal* as *gazoo* and by *The Litchfield County* (Connecticut) *Times* as *bazoo* (the latter also happens to be an old slang term for the mouth).

Kazoo usually is associated with the instrument of that name, whose sounds are appreciated mainly by kazoo players. "The New Deal is now playing hearts and flowers thru a kazoo instead of a Stradivarius" (*Chicago Tribune*, 11/1/47). The instrument itself was invented in the United States, perhaps as early as the 1840s, and most likely by a black musician, as it is similar to merlitons used by Africans to make buzzing sounds. No one is sure where the kazoo's name comes from. It may imitate the instrument's sound. Given the strong associations in this period between sex and the earthy music of American blacks, however, one can't help wondering if *kazoo* isn't related to the nineteenth-century British *kaze* or *caze*, meaning the female pudendum, or to the modern *cooz* (also rendered *coosie, coozie, cuzzy,* etc.), referring both to the female genitals and, by extension, to a female in her entirety. See also BAZOO and JAZZ.

kibitz. To offer unwanted advice; to stick one's nose, or beak, into another person's business (*beak* because the word stems from the German name for a bold bird, *kiebitz,* the lapwing); specifically, to look over other people's shoulders while they are playing cards, chess, or another game. The intruder who does all these nasty things is, naturally, a *kibitzer,* i.e., a BUTTINSKI or *meddlesome matty* (see MOLL). *Kibitz* is a Yiddish modification of the German original (in German, *kiebitzen* means to look over a card player's shoulder). The word was popularized in the United States in the 1920s, especially by a hit comedy of 1929, *The Kibitzer,* which helped make a star of the actor who coauthored it, Emmanuel Goldenberg (Edward G. Robinson).

Getting back to the lapwing: This member of the plover family, also called the pewit (from its cry), has long been a symbol of forwardness. This is because the young lapwing is active so soon after hatching that people like to think it runs around with its head still in its shell. Thus, Hamlet's friend Horatio characterized the elegant, effeminate courtier Osric: "This lapwing runs away with the shell on his head" (William Shakespeare, *Hamlet,* 1601–02). See also PEEWEE.

kibosh. A mysterious something that quashes, spoils, ruins, or terminates, most often in the phrase *to put the kibosh on [someone* or *something].* The word and the phrase have been dated to the 1830s. "Put the kye-bosk on her" appears in "Seven Dials," one of Dickens' *Sketches by Boz* (1833–35). The term's origin has been much debated. It sounds as though it might be Yiddish, but an appropriate ancestor has not been discovered. Another possibility, suggested by Padraic Colum, the Irish poet, is that it derives from the Gaelic *cie bais* (pronounced "bawsh"), meaning "cap of death," apparently referring to the black cap put on by a judge before pronouncing a sentence of death. *Kibosh* also has been used since the nineteenth century to mean nonsense (along with the more elaborate *kiboshery*), leading some to suspect a connection with the *bosh* (ex Turkish *boş*) that is BUNK.

kike. A Jew. "Sit down and I'll tell you everything, you little kike" (Dore Schary, *Heydey,* 1980, recalling a *tête-à-tête* with movie mogul L. B. Mayer).

Kike is an Americanism of uncertain etymology, dating to the late nineteenth century, and, like HEBE, perhaps not pejorative when first used, though it quickly became so. It has been suggested that *kike* derives from (1) the German *kieken,* to peep, as a spy would in the clothing business; (2) the common *-ski* or *-sky* ending of Slavic-Jewish surnames (which would make *kike* a relative of BUTTINSKI); and (3) the Yiddish word for "circle," *kikel.* The last of these, put forth by Leo Rosten in *The Joys of Yiddish* (1968), seems to be the most plausible. According to Rosten, the word developed on Ellis Island in New York when Jewish immigrants, who did not know Roman-English letters, signed their entry forms with circles (as opposed to the usual X, which was abhorrent to them, being also the symbol of the Christian cross). As a result, immigration inspectors began referring to anyone who signed with a circle as a *kikel,* which was eventually shortened to *kike.* Rosten's authority for this is Philip Cowen, cited as "the dean of immigration inspectors," who also founded and served as first editor of *The American Hebrew.*

Whatever its genesis, *kike* seems to have been popularized in society at large principally by assimilated German Jews who looked down upon newcomers from Eastern Europe. "A 'kike' . . . was any Eastern Jew, especially the noisy ones. 'Stop acting like a kike' was a frequent admonition to noisy, badly behaved children—or adults as well—who offended the middle-class mores of the German Jews" (Paul Jacobs, *Is Curly Jewish?*, 1965). The epithet has long since become internationalized, e.g., "Mr. [Kirill] Upensky recalled that shortly before he left Leningrad for the United States, three men on the street started shouting that he was a 'kike' (Mr. Upensky is not Jewish) and a 'stinking anti-Soviet' " (*New York Times*, 11/16/82). See also HYMIE and JEW (DOWN), TO.

kinky. Full of kinks, bent, twisted, weird, perverted, especially in sexual matters. "But much of the large format paperback is an unremarkable series of Voguish fashion shots and kinky cheesecake for bondage and discipline fans—a Frederick's of Hollywood catalogue for muscle freaks" (Los Angeles *Reader*, 4/1/83). Sexual *kinks* are a relatively new phenomena, by that name at least, dating only to ca. 1960, but mental *kinks*, meaning odd, fantastic, or mad notions, are a couple hundred years old, or more. "Should the judges take a kink in their heads" (Thomas Jefferson, letter, 11/24/1783). See also PERVERT, SADIST, and TWISTED.

kiss off. A rude dismissal or the act thereof. "Sorry, Fella, but if you don't have a high school diploma, *kiss off!*" (*National Lampoon*, 10/71). For regional variations, see *California* in PEORIA.

kite, go fly a (your). Go away, mind your own business, get off my back. ". . . if the offended party appears inclined to make the matter one for blows, he may be challenged with 'Fly your kite!' " ("Folk 'Sayings' from Indiana," *American Speech*, 12/39).
   Children have been flying paper kites since at least 1664 (*OED*). Another kind of paper that can be *kited*, without benefit of string, is a bad check. *To fly a kite* in the financial sense has been dated to the eighteenth century. The idea is that the check, like the child's toy, is supported by nothing but air. Both forms of paper *kite* come from the hawklike bird of the same name, noted for its soaring abilities. Probably once the most common bird of prey in Great Britain, kites scavenged the streets of London and other large cities several centuries ago. As a predator, its name became an epithet for the human who preys upon his fellows, a sharper, as well as for the simple fellow who becomes his victim (a common confluence of opposite meanings, see ROOK). More generally, as a consumer of garbage, the bird became a symbol for any loathsome individual. Which is what King Lear had in mind when he addressed his daughter Goneril: "Detested kite! Thou liest" (William Shakespeare, *King Lear*, 1605–06.) See also BIRD.

klutz. A clumsy person, a bungler, a fool. A *klutz* is the functional equivalent of a BLOCKHEAD or CHUMP, the word deriving from the Yiddish *kluhts*, a log, in turn from the German *klotz*, a block (of wood). "Think for a moment about the stereotypical absentminded professor found on every campus, who has a disheveled appearance, or who always drops papers, books, or pens. A male professor fitting this description would usually be labeled 'eccentric,' while a female professor would be called 'a slob' or 'klutz' " (Janice Hanson, assistant professor of communications, Rutgers University, *Psychology Today*, 2/83). See also CLOD.

knave. A rogue; a crafty fellow, lacking in principles. Originally, going back to about the year 1000, a *knave* was simply a boy child, from the Old English *cnafa*, boy, lad. Paralleling GIRL, also originally a neutral term (once applied to young males as well as young females), *knave* began acquiring pejorative connotations through its frequent application to serving boys and others from the lower classes. From this, it was but a step to regard the KNAVE in the modern sense as a ROGUE. Illustrating the way the two meanings—servant and SCOUNDREL—naturally gravitated together is the Duke of Kent's tirade in *King Lear* (1605–06), when Goneril's servingman, Oswald, is so foolish as to ask "What dost thou know me for?" And Kent replies:

> A knave, a rascal, an eater of broken meats; a base, proud, shallow, beggarly, three-suited, three-hundred pound, filthy, worsted-stocking knave; a lily-livered, action-taking knave; a whoreson, glass-gazing, superserviceable, finical rogue; one trunk-inheriting slave; one that wouldst be a bawd in the way of good service, and art nothing but the composition of a knave, beggar, coward, pandar, and the son and heir of a mongrel bitch—one whom I will beat into clamorous whining if thou deniest the least syllable of thy addition.

See also CAITIFF, MINION, RASCAL, and VARLET.

knock up. To impregnate, from 1813 in the United States, but not in Britain. "Fielding's guidebook considerately explains that a male host may quite casually tell a female American house guest that he will 'knock you up at 7:30 tomorrow morning.' The term, of course, conveys nothing more than a rapping at the door until one is awakened" (*National Observer*, 2/3/73).

Knock up also has enjoyed other meanings in British English, e.g., to accomplish or to achieve; to put something together hastily, as by nailing; and to tire or to exhaust, which presumably is what Jane Austen has in mind when she wrote, "If Fanny could be more regular in her exercise, she would not be knocked up so soon" (*Mansfield Park*, 1814).

The pregnant sense, however, is in keeping with the earlier use of *knock* to mean copulation and *knocker* to mean the penis, with such derivative expressions as *knocking-house*, a brothel, and *knocking-jacket*, a nightgown. The copulative *knock* may derive from the *knock* that is a rap or blow or from the *nock* that is a *notch* in an arrow or in a person's anatomy. Both possibilities have much to recommend them, since (1) images of sex and violence often are united in the same term (see FUCK, for example), and (2) physical descriptions of the *notch* sort are a prime source of sexual slang (see NOOKIE).

Knock has been used to refer to coition since at least the sixteenth century: J. S. Farmer and W. E. Henley included an illustration from *Nice Wanton*, a play of 1560: "Goldlocks She must have knocks, Or else I do her wrong" (*Slang and Its Analogues*, 1896). The expression probably is much older, however; see NAMBY-PAMBY for a *knock-knock* joke of ca. 1470.

know-nothing. Specifically and historically, in the 1850s, a member of one of the secret orders of white native-born Americans, who were opposed to immigrants in general and Roman Catholics in particular, and who came to be called Know-

Nothings because, when questioned, they professed to know nothing of their underground societies. In extended use, both before and after this episode, an ignorant person. "The fellow is a know-nothing" (James Fenimore Cooper, *Red Rover*, 1823). ". . . the white-jacketed priests of the Security Cult, the Know-Nothings, the Yahoos, the Galloots are never far distant" (Harrison E. Salisbury, lecture, "The Book Enchained," Library of Congress, 9/28/83).

knuckle-dragger. A thug. ". . . I immediately wrote a radio script which featured no less than five stabbings (realistically consummated by a sound effects man stabbing a watermelon close to the microphone), two brutal fist fights, and a sleazy bedroom scene between a has-been actress and a young knuckle-dragger" (George Lefferts, *Litchfield County* (Connecticut) *Times*, 7/6/84). See also GORILLA.

kook. An odd or outright crazy person, especially one with far-out political views, whether of the left or right. " 'She was deeply religious, but she was not an extremist or a kook' " (Newton, Connecticut, *Weekly Star*, 4/21/86). The adjective is *kooky*.

The term dates to the 1950s and probably arose in the entertainment business on the West Coast. It was sighted in the form of *cuk* in San Francisco at the end of 1957 and it is almost certainly a modern, with-it clipping of the old and equally pejorative CUCKOO (Peter Tamony, *Maledicta*, Winter 1977). In the political arena, the term was popularized as a label for the right-wing extremists who followed Senator Barry Goldwater's banner in the 1964 presidential primaries. When their chief antagonist, Governor Nelson A. Rockefeller, appeared at that year's Republican National Convention, they furiously tried to shut him down: "This was the man who called them kooks, and now, like kooks, they responded to prove his point" (Theodore H. White, *The Making of the President, 1964*, 1965). See also EXTREMIST.

kraut. A German, especially but not necessarily a soldier. Thus, Reinhold Aman, founder and editor of *Maledicta*, explained how to improve one's verbal-abuse techniques: "Look for a distinguishing characteristic. Each of us is deviant in some way. For instance, I wear glasses, I'm five-foot-seven, 20 pounds overweight, have short hair and a Kissinger accent. So you could start off calling me a fat, four-eyed, runty, reactionary, sewer-mouth Kraut" (*Time*, 1/9/78).

Kraut, short for *sauerkraut*, was popularized during World Wars I and II, but is substantially older, having been dated to 1841 (*American Speech*, Spring–Summer 1972). Early variations include *kraut eater* and *kraut-head*, as in Ty Cobb's announcement to Pirate shortstop Honus Wagner just before their first encounter at second base: "Hey, Kraut-head, I'm coming down on the next pitch" (Jack Sher, "The Flying Dutchman," *Sport*, 6/49). Cobb got the base plus three stitches, where Wagner tagged him in the mouth with the ball. See also BOCHE and the *cabbagehead* in BLOCKHEAD.

Kraut is one of the leading examples of the culinary insult. (You are—to your enemies, especially—what you eat.) Among the more common ones: *bean, bean eater, beaner,* and *beano,* all for a Latin American, usually a CHICANO, except for *bean eater,* which also is a resident of Boston, a.k.a. *Beantown; butter box,* a Dutchman; *cabbage eater,* a Russian; *cabbagehead,* a Dutchman or German; *chili* or *chili eater,* a Mexican (members of the Border Patrol are sometimes known as *chili chasers*); *chow* or *chow mein*, a Chinese; *fish eater*, a Roman Catholic (see FISH); FROG and *frog eater*, a Frenchman; *frijole eater*, a Mexican; *herring choker* or *-snapper*, a Scandinavian; *Hans Wurst*, a German; *lemon eater* or *-sucker*, an Englishman; *lime juicer* or LIMEY, an Englishman; MACARONI, an Italian; MEATBALL, an Italian; *pea soup*, a Frenchman; *pepperbelly*, a Mexican; *pork eater* and *porker*, a Jew (see PIG): *potato eater*, an Irishman; *sausage*, a German; *spaghetti* and *spaghetti-bender* or *-eater*, an Italian; *spud*, an Irishman; *taco eater*, a Latin American, usually a Chicano (if female and attractive, then a *taco belle*); TAMALE, a desirable Mexican (female); and *Tio Taco* (a Mexican UNCLE TOM).

For more about foods, see BALONEY, EAT, OREO , TWINK, and the agricultural terms in HICK; for more about *krauts*, see GERMAN.

kvetch. A constant complainer or whiner; as a verb, to complain. "She's got a disgusting father and a *kvetsch* of a mother" (Saul Bellow, *Herzog*, 1964). The term comes from the Yiddish *kvetsh*, in turn from the German *quetsch*, squeezer, crusher. No one likes a *kvetch*; hence, the epithet has acquired the extended meanings of SAD SACK or WET BLANKET. "Don't invite them to the party; he's a *kvetch*" (Leo Rosten, *The Joys of Yiddish*, 1968).

L

lace-curtain. Middle-class, or lower-class with pretensions toward respectability. The epithet usually is associated with Irish-Americans, who put up lace curtains as they rose from the serving class. Herewith, a definition of "Lace Curtain Irish," offered by one of Ann Landers' correspondents: "People of Irish descent who have fruit in the house when nobody is sick" (Danbury, Connecticut, *News-Times*, 3/4/88). The term can be applied to other ethnic groups, however, e.g., "Mrs. Ruskay's folks were lace-curtain Jews; they had a piano and a Polish maid" (*Saturday Review of Literature*, 6/25/49). See also BOURGEOIS and SHANTY IRISH.

lackey. A servant, especially a footman; hence, one who follows in another's footsteps, or dances in attendance upon someone else; a gofer; a toady or SYCO-PHANT. Like other words for people in menial positions (see BOY, GIRL, and KNAVE, for example), this one acquired pejorative meanings a long time ago. Consider *lackey*'s company in the following: "A sort of vagabonds, rascals, and runaways, A scum of Bretons, and base lackey peasants" (William Shakespeare, *Richard III*, 1592–93). In this century, the term was popularized as a political epithet by Marxist writers, as in "American bankers . . . have already stepped into the role of lackeys of British imperialism" (*American Mercury*, 4/41). See also FELLOW TRAVELER, FLUNKY, HENCHMAN, HESSIAN, HIRELING, MINION, PAWN, PUPPET, STOOGE, and TOOL.

la-de-dah. A *veddy* refined man, and as an adjective, one who is too affected for words, and thus can be described only in terms of otherwise meaningless syllables. "Some lah de dah with a cane" (Ben Hecht and Charles MacArthur, *The Front Page*, 1928). Eric Partridge dates the expression to ca. 1860 and attributes its popularity to a line in a music-hall song of 1880: "He wears a penny flower in his coat, La-di-da!" (*A Dictionary of Slang and Unconventional English*, 1970). See also SISSY.

lamebrain. A stupid person, i.e., a mental cripple, one who is BRAIN-DAMAGED. " 'Well, Miss "Lame Brain," ' he retorted sardonically, 'maybe you had better stop galvanizing around at nights and pay attention!' " (S. J. Perelman, *Crazy Like a Fox*, 1945). *Lamebrain* has been dated only to 1929, but *lame* has been used in the same way for many years: "Being not deficient, blind, or lame of sense" (William Shakespeare, *Othello*, 1604).

Casting aspersions at people's brains is traditional operating procedure in the insult business: "Thou hast no more brains than I have in mine elbows, an assinego [a little ass] may tutor thee" (William Shakespeare, *Troilus and Cressida*, 1601–02). Or again, from the same play: "Here's Agamemnon, an honest fellow enough and one that loves quails [see QUAIL], but he has not so much brain as earwax."

In modern times, complicated variations on this theme have been devised, such as "Your brain is so small that if you shoved it up an ant's ass it would rattle around like a jelly bean in a boxcar" and, conveying the same thought in slightly more refined terms, "Your brain is so small that you could suck it up through a straw and it wouldn't touch the side" and "You were at the end of the line when brains were passed out" (all personal communications, all supposedly in jest).

As a suffix, -brain is synonymous with -head. For instance, addlebrain, featherbrain, fiddlebrain, giddybrain, and peabrain all have their -head counterparts; for details, see BLOCKHEAD. Other notable -brains include:

amoebabrain. A single-celled brain, in other words.

beetlebrain. "Bettle-braines cannot conceive things right" (OED, pre-1604). The reference here may not be to the insect, but to a heavy implement, also called a beetle, used in various pounding, ramming, and stamping operations. This kind of beetle usually is made of wood (see BLOCKHEAD). The phrase as dumb as a beetle dates to the sixteenth century. The modern comic-strip character Beetle Bailey isn't very bright either.

birdbrain. "Bird brain. Nobody knows more about chickens than Frank Perdue" (ad, New York Times, 8/3/83). Birdbrain dates to the 1940s. It was preceded substantially by bird-witted (1605). The names of many particular species of birds are synonymous with stupidity: see DODO for details.

chickenbrain. See CHICKEN.

crackbrain. From the sixteenth century, with connotations of craziness as much as foolishness or stupidity. See also CRACKPOT.

fatbrain. A predecessor of fathead; see FAT.

fleabrain. Primarily an allusion to size, with the added implication of a mind that jumps quickly and randomly from one topic to another; see also FLEA.

harebrain. As with crackbrain, the overtones of craziness are strong; see HAREBRAIN.

lackbrain (or -wit). "What a lackbrain is this!" (William Shakespeare, Henry IV, Part I, 1596). See also NITWIT.

nutbrain. "He may walk in and call me 'nut brain' and ask what I'm doing here" (Cleavon Little, New York Times, 6/15/86). See also NUT.

pea-brained. ". . . about as much as I miss being partners with that pea-brained husband of yours" (WCBS-TV, 3/11/87).

peanut-brained. "Come on, you dog-gone, bullnecked, beetlebrowed, hogjowled, peanutbrained, weaseleyed fourflushers, false alarms and excess baggage!" (James Joyce, Ulysses, 1922). See also PEANUT.

scatterbrain. One whose thoughts are disconnected, from the eighteenth century. "Though I have seen you but once . . . I have found out that you are a scatter-brain" (William Cowper, letter, 7/31/1790).

scramble-brained. Disordered.

shallow-brained (or -minded, or -pated or -witted). Or simply shallow, as in the Shakespearian character Justice Shallow—"deep Master Shallow," as Falstaff calls him (Henry IV, Part II, 1596–97). Irving Stone elaborated the metaphor nicely, characterizing William Jennings Bryan thusly: "His mind was like a soup dish, wide and shallow; it could hold a small amount of nearly everything, but the slightest jarring spilt the soup into somebody's lap" (They Also Ran, 1968).

soft-brained. ". . . a soft brained boy; one who is lacking in intellect" (Benjamin H. Hall, A Collection of College Words and Customs, 1856).

stinkbrain. See DUMB/DUMMY for the epithet in use, as well as STINK.

lard. Fat, in various combinations, e.g., *lard ass, lardball, lard bucket,* and *tub of lard,* all referring to a grossly overweight person, and *lardhead,* to a dumb one. See also FAT.

laughingstock. An object of mirth, usually referring to a person rather than a thing; from 1533 and still much in evidence: "But [George] Steinbrenner mistakes the interest of people . . . on the street for adulation and affirmation of his works. He is an object of curiosity, sometimes even a laughing-stock" (Ira Berkow, *New York Times,* 8/16/87).

lawyer. A professional practitioner of the law—a term that has acquired so many pejorative connotations that most lawyers now prefer to be called *attorney* or *counsel.* ". . . in Columbus, Ohio, the quintessential American city, the place where Proctor & Gamble of Cincinnati sends new products to be test-marketed, the Yellow Pages listing for 'Lawyer' is followed with a terse 'See Attorneys, Patent Attorneys,' and 'Lawyers' Reference Service' with 'See Attorney Referral Service' " (*New York Times,* 6/21/76).

It is not hard to see why *lawyers* want to shuck this term, considering how it has been used in the past, e.g., "Lawyers are accounted knaves over all the country" (Anonymous, *The Countryman's Care,* 1641); "A good lawyer, an evil neighbor" (John Ray, *English Proverbs,* 1670); "God works wonders now and then; Behold! a lawyer, an honest man" (Benjamin Franklin, *Poor Richard's Almanac,* 1733). And, of course, there is Shakespeare's advice: "The first thing we do, let's kill all the lawyers" (*Henry VI, Part II,* 1590–91).

It is possible, too, that learned counsel have become sensitive to some of the secondary meanings of *lawyer.* These include, in Britain, a long bramble, and in the United States, a bird, the black-necked stilt, which, as the OED notes "is sometimes called the *lawyer* on account of its long bill." The pejorative connotations show up particularly when the word is used as a suffix, as in *armchair lawyer, barracks lawyer, jailhouse lawyer,* and *sea lawyer,* indicating long-winded, opinionated talk by someone who doesn't know too much about what he is saying. The distinguished members of the bar, it seems, have a great deal to live down. "I assume you already know the one about the shark's not eating the lawyer—'professional courtesy'—and that the difference between a rooster and a lawyer is that a rooster gets up every morning and clucks defiance" (Andrew Tobias, *Playboy,* 3/82). See also APOLOGIST, LIP, MOUTHPIECE, PETTIFOGGER, SHYSTER, and TRIMMER.

lay. To copulate and, as a noun, a woman—or, lately, thanks to women's liberation, also a man—considered solely as an object of sexual gratification. This is a comparatively mild term, known to most uneducated speakers of English, and to those who are uneducated as well, but some people still profess to be shocked by it. Thus, in A.D. 1987, the word was banned by the advertising acceptability department of *The New York Times,* which caused the title of a new film, *Sammy and Rosie Get Laid,* to be abbreviated to *Sammy and Rosie* in the paper's ad pages. (As the newspaper of record, the *Times* felt compelled to print the full title in its review on October 30, while an ad on the same day began "While London burns . . . *Sammy and Rosie,*" without explanation of what happened during the fire.)

Lay is considered an Americanism and of surprisingly recent vintage, according to established sources. It is dated only to 1932 in the OED (1976 supplement) and to 1930 in the *Dictionary of American Slang* (1960). The oldest *DAS* example is from a short story by James T. Farrell: "Both agreed that the two girls looked like swell lays . . ." Like most slang words, however, this one undoubtedly was used freely in speaking, if not in writing, long before its first certified, recorded appearance in type. Thus, *to lay the log* was reported in the sense of "to hold intercourse" in an article on "Prostitutes and Criminal Argots" by David W. Maurer (*American Journal of Sociology*, 1/39). The word also was bandied about in the past tense from an early date, e.g., "And there was that wholesale libel on a Yale prom. If all the girls attending it were laid end to end, Mrs. [Dorothy] Parker said, she wouldn't be at all surprised" (Alexander Woollcott, *While Rome Burns*, 1934). Our colonial ancestors also knew the term in this form. Thus, in America's first comic opera, *The Disappointment*, apparently written by a Philadelphia merchant, Andrew Barton, and initially performed in that city in 1767, a prostitute named Moll Placket (a *placket* is a slit in a petticoat and an old slang term for the vagina) boasts that she has "rais'd and laid 500 in my time" (from Kenneth Silverman, *A Cultural History of the American Revolution*, 1976).

Most likely, *lay*'s sexual sense arose from the word's use as the past tense of *lie*. Since at least the twelfth century, *lie with* and *lie by* have referred to sexual intercourse as well as to being in bed for the purpose of sleeping. The construction appears frequently in the King James Bible (1611), e.g., "Come [said Lot's eldest daughter], let us make our father drink wine, and we will lie with him, that we may preserve the seed of our father. . . . and the first-born went in and lay with her father" (*Genesis*, 19:32–33).

Shakespeare also seems to have been using *lay down* with more than pure recumbancy in mind when a character in *Henry VIII* declares that "The sly whoresons have got a speedy trick to lay down ladies" (*Henry VIII*, 1613). And two hundred years later—and more than a century prior to the earliest American example of the sexual *lay* in the present tense—Dr. Thomas Bowdler also demonstrated his appreciation of the word's double meaning. Thus, in *The Family Shakespeare* (1818), he toned down a reference to Anne Boleyn in *Henry VIII*—"Believe me, sir, she is the goodliest woman that ever lay by man"—changing *lay by* to *sits by*. (Curiously, Bowdler allowed Shakespeare his use of *lie with* in sexual contexts; perhaps, as Noel Perrin suggests in *Dr. Bowdler's Legacy*, he was extra-fastidious in Boleyn's case out of deference to Royalty.)

Today, overly careful speakers still pay tribute to the power of the sexual *lay* by avoiding it in any sense whatsoever. This results in such sentences as "He has lain the newspaper down" or, evading the issue entirely, "He has put the newspaper down," in lieu of the perfectly correct, non-salacious "He has laid the newspaper down." Nor would many writers nowadays venture Macaulay's line: "The coarse jollity of the afternoon was often prolonged till the revelers were laid under the table," by which he meant only that the revelers were prone (*History of England*, 1849). Macaulay, it seems, lacked the exquisite sensitivity to language possessed by Dr. Bowdler—and ourselves.

leech. A person who clings to other people, frequently with intent to borrow money that will not be repaid; a SPONGE. Doctors used to be called *leeches*, from ca. A.D. 900, probably from the common use of these worms to suck blood from their patients. See also BLOODSUCKER, PARASITE, and VAMPIRE.

left. Politically radical, as opposed to reactionary, with strong overtones of craziness, awkwardness, and inferiority; often used as an attack term by conservative politicians, who profess not to see—or who cannot see—any difference between *left*, *leftist*, and *left-winger* on the one hand and LIBERAL on the other. "A second-place [Doublespeak] award was voted to Vice President George Bush, who in a speech said that the Sandinistas 'are Marxists-Leninists. They are not liberals as Mr. Mondale says they are.' Later, Mr. Bush admitted that Mr. Mondale had never called the Sandinistas liberals. 'He's called them leftists. Maybe I used the wrong word.' But he then said he saw no difference between the two terms" (*Quarterly Review of Doublespeak*, 1/85). "President Reagan ridiculed the 'new realism' of Walter F. Mondale today, saying the leaders of the Democratic Party have gone 'so far left, they've left America' " (*New York Times*, 7/26/84).

The prejudice against *left* is ancient and by no means limited to politics where it reinforces the traditional seating arrangement of Continental legislatures, with the radicals on the left, facing the speaker, and the conservatives on the right. Thus, the Latin word for *left* is *sinister* and the French one is *gauche* (as opposed to *dexter* and *droit*, Latin and French for *right*, which produce such "good" words as *dexterous* and *adroit*). As for the English *left*, it comes from the Old English *lyft*, weak, useless, as in *lyftadl*, paralysis or "left-disease." At one time, *a left* was a mean, worthless person, as in "His wyf, that cursyd lyfte, Brewed the childys deth that nyght" (*OED*, ca. 1425). The bias against lefties also shows up in such phrases as:

left-handed. Clumsy, maladroit, inferior, insincere, as in *left-handed compliment*, not a real compliment; *left-handed flattery*, which is not to be believed; *left-handed security*, poor security; and *left-handed wife*, a concubine, alluding to the ancient custom of giving an inferior woman one's left hand when wedding her in what is called, naturally, a *left-handed marriage* (in French, *mariage de la main gauche*).

left-legged. Clumsy, inept, inefficient; somewhat archaic, along with *to see with the left eye*, *to work with the left hand*, and *left-witted*, all implying poor performance. Today the clumsy one is said *to have two left feet*, but John Dryden preferred *left-legged*, which he used in "Faction Displayed" (1705), when characterizing Jacob Tonson, his publisher, in such terms as almost to make one feel sorry for publishers:

> With leering look, bull-faced and freckled fair,
> With frowzy pores poisoning the ambient air,
> With two left leggs and Judas coloured hair.

out in left field. Crazy, erratic, weird, wrong; unexpected, as in a question (or anything else) that *comes out of left field*. In old-time, pre-AstroTurf ballparks, left field usually was larger than right field, with the result that some fielders seemed lost in the larger space, but the metaphor probably has as much to do with the assumed craziness of lefties—or *southpaws* if they are baseball pitchers.

over the left (or *left shoulder*). A phrase signifying that one doesn't mean whatever has just been said. This often was shortened to *over the left* and accompanied by a hand gesture, as explained by Charles Dickens: "Each gentleman pointed with his right thumb over his left-shoulder. This action imperfectly described in words by the very feeble term of over the left . . . is one of light and playful sarcasm" (*Pickwick Papers*, 1836–37). Earlier generations took the "light and playful sarcasm" rather more seriously, however, e.g., "The said Waters, as he departed from the table said, 'God bless you over the left shoulder.' The court ordered a record to be made thereof forthwith. A true copie" (*Record, Hartford* [Connecticut] *County Court*, 9/4/1705).

The semantic bias against *left* may reflect reality as observed casually, collectively, and almost unconsciously ever since people began to use words. Only in recent years have scientific studies begun to suggest that left-handers do suffer proportionately more from allergies, migraine headaches, learning disorders such as dyslexia, and autoimmune disorders such as rheumatoid arthritis. More profoundly, and most ironically, however, it also is beginning to appear that the universe has a left-handed bias, evidenced on many levels, from the rotation of the spiral galaxies to the structure of amino acids in living tissue. The latter observations raise very large questions indeed: "Was it purely a matter of chance that left-handedness became the preferred direction of our universe, or is there some reason behind it? Did the sinister bent of existence that scientists have observed stem from a roll of the dice, or is God a semiambidextrous southpaw? Stay tuned" (Malcolm W. Brown, *New York Times*, 4/25/86). See also COMMIE, FRINGE, LIBERAL, and RIGHT-WINGER.

lemon. Something bad, especially a poorly made product, such as a car; an unlikable person. "Mr. White says his success in wheedling a new car out of General Motors Corp. shows the effectiveness of Connecticut's nine-month-old lemon law, the first such law in the country. General Motors disagrees. . . . GM says lemon laws are unnecessary, encourage litigation and 'mislead customers into thinking some new right is being bestowed on them' " (*Wall Street Journal*, 7/12/83). "If she is unpopular, she is *a pill, a pickle, a lemon*" (Eric Partridge, *Slang Today & Yesterday*, 1950). *To hand [someone] a lemon* is to cheat that person by giving him or her a substandard or flawed item instead of good one. *Lemon* dates to the early twentieth century as a symbol for inferior things and to the mid-twentieth in its application to people. In both cases, the metaphor is based on the tartness of the fruit, which leaves a bad taste in the mouth. See also LIMEY and PRUNE.

leper. An outcast, an untouchable, one who is anathema. "The battle heated up quickly, with Mayor Koch publicly proclaiming the [subway fare] cheaters 'lepers' and 'pariahs' " (*New York Times*, 11/7/85).

Leper has acquired so many fearful associations through the years that its use in medical contexts has been banned by the World Health Organization and the International Leprosy Association. Leprosy itself is known officially today as *Hansen's disease* (or, if one is being finicky, *Hansen disease*, since Hansen did not have it), after Armauer Hansen (1841–1912), the Norwegian physician who in 1871 discovered the bacillus that causes leprosy. It is of passing interest that *leper* spelled backwards is *repel*. See also PARIAH.

lewd. Lascivious, lustful. Originally, going back to the ninth century, a *lewd* person was a *lay* person, meaning one who had not taken holy orders. In medieval times, *lewd* people were considered less refined than clerics, with the result that the term came to mean illiterate, ill-bred, ill-mannered, vile, wicked, and, by the fourteenth century—the surviving sense—licentious and unchaste. A *lewdie* in the vernacular of modern singles' bars is a "Married woman looking for a one-night stand" (Thomas E. Murray, *American Speech*, Spring 1985). It has been suggested that this is an acronym—compression would be more like it— of "let out for the evening wife," but it seems likely that *lewd's* association with rampant sex provides sufficient explanation for *lewdie's* origin. The connection certainly was clear enough in Noah Webster's mind. Substitutions in his bowdlerized edition of the Bible of 1833 included *lewd* and *lewd woman* for *whore*, while *to play the whore* became *to be guilty of lewdness. Lewd* also is the starting and ending point for a famous palindrome: "Lewd I did live ere evil did I dwel." See also WHORE.

liar. One who does not tell the truth; for emphasis, a *baldfaced liar, barefaced liar, boldfaced liar, brazen liar, congenital liar, liar and a cheat*, and so on, e.g., "[Drew] Pearson is an infamous liar, a revolting lair, a pusillanimous liar, a lying ass, a natural born liar, a liar by profession, a liar of living, a liar in the daytime, a liar in the nighttime, a dishonest, ignorant, corrupt and groveling crook" (Senator Kenneth McKellar [Democrat, Tennessee], in Donald Hook and Lothar Kahn, *The Book of Insults and Irreverent Quotations*, 1980). A syndicated newspaper columnist, Pearson (1897–1969) made many enemies among the people he wrote about; for another senator's opinion of him, see SON OF A BITCH.

From ancient times, *liar* has been one of the strongest of all terms of personal reproach: "I hate a liar" (Plautus, *Mostellaria*, ca. 200 B.C.). The word is heard fairly often on grammar school playgrounds ("Liar, liar, your pants are on fire"), but adults tend to avoid it for fear of being caught up in libel suits. A notable exception in American history came during the presidential campaign of 1884, when Democrats tarred the Republican candidate with

> Blaine! Blaine! James G. Blaine,
> The Continental liar from the State of Maine!

(The Republicans got their licks in when it was revealed that the opposing candidate, Grover Cleveland, had fathered a child out of wedlock, leading them to chant "Ma! Ma! Where's my pa?" but the Democrats had the last laugh when Cleveland won, enabling them to complete the couplet, "Gone to the White House, Ha! Ha! Ha!") Another exception, a highlight—or lowlight?—of recent sports history was New York Yankee manager Billy Martin's assessment of outfielder Reggie Jackson and team owner George M. Steinbrenner III: "The two of them deserve each other. One's a born liar, the other's convicted" (*New York Times*, 7/25/78, with Mr. Steinbrenner's distinctions including his admission of guilt to charges of making illegal political campaign contributions in a Watergate-related case four years earlier.) This remark concluded the first of Mr. Martin's many tours as manager of this team, as he was required to resign his job within hours of making it. See also ANANIAS and LIE.

liberal. One who favors political, economic, and social changes, especially those that aid the less fortunate members of society. Today, the term almost always is used in a derogatory way: "I never use the words Republicans and Democrats. It's liberals and Americans" (James Watt, Republican Secretary of the Interior, *Philadelphia Inquirer*, 1/30/82). "In announcing the cancellation [of his radio talk show] Tuesday, the [white] separatist, Dwight McCarthy, blamed what he called the 'liberal-Marxist-homosexual-Zionist coalition' for the show's demise" (AP, 12/16/87). See also UN-AMERICAN.

Liberal's political meaning thus has come almost full circle. The word was introduced into British politics toward the beginning of the nineteenth century by opponents of the progressive section of the Whig party. It was not meant as a compliment, the term having been used earlier to describe Jacobins and other revolutionaries on the Continent; the idea was to tar the domestic *liberals* with the foreign, radical association. (This was in the grand British tradition of political name-calling: a *whig* originally was a yokel or country bumpkin and a *tory* was a wild Irish outlaw.)

Isaac D'Israeli noted the change in *liberal*'s meaning in his "History of New Words": "It is curious to observe that as an adjective it had formerly a very opposite meaning to its recent one. It was synonymous with 'libertine or licentious'; we have 'a *liberal* villain' and 'a most profane and *liberal* counsellor'; we have one declaring 'I have spoken *too liberally.*' This is unlucky for the *liberals* . . ." (*Curiosities of Literature*, 1791–1823). D'Israeli guessed wrong about the term's political fortunes, however, at least for the near future. Since it also had various "good" meanings—bountiful, ample, generous, open-minded—the political *liberals* proved glad enough to adopt it. Others soon followed, as noted by Isaac's son: "I consider it a great homage to public opinion to find every scoundrel nowadays professing himself a liberal" (Benjamin Disraeli, *The Infernal Marriage*, 1834).

Today, though, all has changed. In the United Kingdom, the once mighty Liberal Party hardly exists, while in the United States, *liberal* politicians have been describing themselves as *moderates* since at least the 1960s. When *liberal* is used, it usually is as an attack term by conservatives. For emphasis, it often is embellished, as in *closet liberal, flaming liberal, knee-jerk liberal, lakefront liberal* (in Chicago), *limousine liberal, rancid liberal, reactionary liberal* (see REACTIONARY), and *ultraliberal*. Still another contemputous variant is *gliberal*.

Testifying, too, to the strength of the epithet is its frequent abbreviation, e.g., "In the last few years the word liberal has been so taboo that it is referred to jokingly as 'the L word' " (*New York Times*, 4/23/87). Of course, not everyone is joking: "You'll never hear that 'L' word—liberal—from [the Democrats]. They've put on political trench coats and dark glasses and slipped their platform into a plain brown wrapper" (President Ronald Reagan, radio address, 7/23/88). This line of attack seemed so effective that it became one of the main Republican themes in the 1988 presidential campaign, with Mr. Reagan sounding the first note at the GOP National Convention (8/14): "The masquerade is over. It's time to talk issues; to use the dreaded L-word; to say that the policies of our opposition and the Congressional leadership of his party are liberal, liberal, liberal." See also BLEEDING HEART ELITIST, INTELLECTUAL, and LEFT.

lickspittle. A parasite or sycophant of the most abject sort. The word's etymology is apparent from its parts. "Gib, Lick her spittle / From the ground. This disguiz'd humilitie / Is both the swift and safest way to pride" (Sir William Davenant, "Albovine," 1629). Ambrose Bierce assigned this term to a particularly obnoxious form of newsman, defining *lickspittle* as "A useful functionary, not infrequently found editing a newspaper. In his character of editor, he is closely allied to the blackmailer by the tie of occasional identity" (*The Devil's Dictionary*, 1911). Obsolete variants, available for use by those with a taste for reviving the past, include *lick-pan, lick-plate,* and *lick-spigot.* See also TOAD.

lie. A prevarication, a fabrication; the presentation of such a deception. The shorter, blunter word is considered so strong that it is not often used, and when it is, the user should be prepared to defend it in court. The *OED*'s note on *lie* (Volume L, 1901–03) still holds true: "In mod. use the word is normally a violent expression of moral reprobation, which in polite conversation tends to be avoided, the synonyms *falsehood* and *untruth* being often substituted as relatively euphemistic." *Lie* can hardly be used in public, even in telling a joke. Thus, when Chicago White Sox president Jerry Reinsdorf said of the New York Yankees owner, "Do you know when George Steinbrenner is lying? When you see his lips move," the commissioner of baseball hit Mr. Reinsdorf with a $5,000 fine (*New York Times* 11/9/83). Then there was the case of Mary McCarthy, who was asked by Dick Cavett, during the course of a discussion of the work of Lillian Hellman, "What is dishonest about her?" To which Ms. McCarthy bravely replied: "Everything. But I once said in some interview that every word she writes is a lie, including 'and' and 'the' " ("Dick Cavett Show," taped October 1979 and aired the following January). This prompted Ms. Hellman to initiate a $2.5-million libel suit that was terminated only by her death in 1984. In fact, she won a preliminary round in court before she died, when a New York State Supreme Court judge refused to dismiss the suit, declaring that Ms. McCarthy's statements seem "to fall on the actionable side of the line— outside what has come to be known as the 'marketplace of ideas' " (*Publishers Weekly*, 5/25/84). See also LIAR.

lightweight. Anyone or anything that need not be taken seriously because he, she, or it lacks solidity, profundity, or intelligence. "May we not see in them the handwriting on the wall . . . the end of the government of light-weight princes" (*OED*, 1809). The original reference probably was to boxing (lightweight boxers range from 126 to 135 pounds), perhaps with some reinforcement from *lightweight* as applied to coins of less than true weight. See also FEATHERWEIGHT.

lily-livered. Cowardly. "You come down here, you lily-livered, yellow-bellied, egg-sucking dog, bed-wetter, pinko Commie" (Washington, D.C., disc jockey Gary D. Gilbert, quoted by Walter Goodman, *New York Times*, 5/20/84). "Well, what you have around here are a bunch of lily-livered, weak-kneed people, particularly in the newspaper industry" (James A. Hail, editor and publisher of *North Idaho Press*, Wallace, Idaho, in *Columbia Journalism Review*, 1-2/85). The epithet, dating at least to Elizabethan times, reflects the folk belief that the liver is the seat of violent passions in general (and love, in particular). A coward's liver, presumably, is a sickly thing, with no blood in it. "For Andrew, if he were opened and you find so much blood in his liver as will clog the foot of a flea, I'll eat the rest of his anatomy" (William Shakespeare, *Twelfth Night*, 1600–02). *White-livered* formerly was used in the same way, as was the noun, *white-liver*, a coward. Naturally, the *lily-livered* person's face also grows pale, as blood rushes from it. "Go prick thy face and overred [make red] thy fear, Thou lily-livered boy" (Shakespeare, *Macbeth*, 1606). See also COWARD.

limey. A Britisher. "General Joseph W. Stillwell . . . was a rabid hater of the British and became angry with the way they deliberately diminished the importance of the Chinese effort. 'It was wonderful the way we slapped the limeys down' he said afterward," (Leonard Mosley, *Marshall: Hero for Our Times*, 1982).

Limey is short for the older *lime juicer*, both generally considered to be of American coinage, though *lime juicer's* first appearance in print came in Australia in 1859 (*OED*) as a slang term for a person who had just got off the boat from England. The epithet almost certainly was applied first to British sailors, who were issued lime juice (it replaced lemon juice adulterated with seawater) as protection against SCURVY, from 1795 in the Navy. Naturally, *limeys* are said to come from *limey land*. If in doubt about the essentially pejorative nature of the term, consider the following example, wherein guilt is demonstrated through association: "Then out with you, go back where you came from, you dago, you hunky, you scoovy [Swede], you heinie, you mick, you sheenie, you limey!" (Theodore Irwin, *Strange Passage*, 1935). See also ENGLISH and LEMON.

lint-head. A worker in a cotton mill, especially in South Carolina; often a HILLBILLY who has moved to town. " 'You damn lint-head,' Buck said contemptuously" (Erskine Caldwell, *God's Little Acre*, 1933).

lip. Abusive, impudent talk—usually on the loud side. " 'Don't you give me none o' your lip,' says he" (Mark Twain, *Huckleberry Finn*, 1884). *Button your lip* is another way of telling an insolent person to shut up. A *lip* also is an attorney specializing in criminal cases. See also LAWYER and LOUDMOUTH.

loafer. An idler. "The men appeared to be the laziest people upon the face of the earth; and indeed . . . there are no people to whom the newly invented Yankee word of 'loafer' is more applicable than to the Spanish Americans" (Richard Henry Dana, Jr., *Two Years Before the Mast*, 1840). *Loafer* apparently derives from the German *landläufer*, vagabond. It has been dated to 1830, which means that it appeared in American English at just about the same time as the similar BUM; another import from Germany. See also DEADBEAT, FEATHERWEIGHT, GOLDBRICK, NO-GOOD, SHIRKER, SLACKER, and TRAMP.

loco. Crazy; also a verb, e.g., "You're locoed man, plum locoed" (Glenn Balch, *Tiger Roan*, 1938). Coming from the Spanish *loco*, insane, the word appeared in the American southwest in the 1830s, usually in connection with horses or cattle that acted crazy after eating any of several varieties of plants known generally as *locoweed* (marijuana also is known in some circles as *locoweed*).

Although the *Locofocos* who composed the radical or Equal Rights wing of the Democratic Party in the 1830s also were considered to be on the crazy side by the bankers and businessmen who opposed them, it was not because of anything they ate. Rather, they got their name because the conservatives who controlled Tammany Hall tried to end a meeting at which they were outnumbered on October 29, 1835, by turning off the gas lights, whereupon the insurgents lit candles, using newly invented Loco-foco friction matches, and continued the session. Newspapers quickly dubbed the Equal Righters *Locofocos* and the Whigs (there were no Republicans yet) subsequently applied the term derisively to all Democrats, whether radicals or not. Just why the matches were called Loco-focos is not known; it may have been a play on *locus-focus*. See also MAD.

longhair. A brainy person, especially an aesthete (from the early 1900s); a performer or devotee of classical or *longhaired* music (from the 1920s); a counter-cultural hippie or beatnik (from the 1960s). The expression is more or less pejorative, depending on how real men are wearing their hair at the time. Thus, in the 1950s, when crew cuts were still in fashion: "Every campus gets what it deserves and deserves what it gets / So what do you want on yours—a lot of pinko longhairs, or red-blooded athaletes and drum majorettes" (Ogden Nash, *You can't get there from Here*, 1957). See also EGGHEAD, FUZZY-WUZZY, and INTELLECTUAL.

loon. A demented person, whether the mental disarray is strictly psychological (*as crazy as a loon*) or attributable to alcohol (*as drunk as a loon*); also, a stupid person (and, formerly, a LOUT, lad, or STRUMPET as well). The demented *loon* and the stupid *loon* have converged from separate sources. The former derives from the awkward bird with the loud cry, perhaps with some reinforcement from LOONY. The stupid *loon*, meanwhile, comes from a fifteenth-century word, variously spelled *loon, loun,* or *lown*, meaning a scoundrel, rascal, idler, BUMPKIN, or other worthless person. This is the kind of *loon* that Macbeth had in mind when he yelled at his servant: "The Devil damn thee black, thou cream-faced loon!" (William Shakespeare, *Macbeth*, 1606). See also BIRD.

loony. Crazy or, in attenuated form, simply silly. "You're that looney sort of chap that lives over younder, ain't ye?" (Bret Harte, "The Heiress of Red Dog," 1872). *Loony* derives from LUNATIC, rather than from the equally demented LOON. It has engendered such compounds as *loony doctor*, who is not a crazy doctor but one who treats the mentally afflicted; *loony bin*, an insane asylum; and *Looney Tunes*, crazy, demented, from the Warner Brothers animated cartoon series, devised by Hugh Harman and Rudolf Ising (Harman-Ising) to compete with Walt Disney's Silly Symphonies. ". . . we are especially not going to tolerate these attacks from outlaw states run by the strangest collection of misfits, Looney Tunes, and squalid criminals since the advent of the Third Reich" (President Ronald Reagan, speech to the American Bar Association, July 1985). See also MICKEY MOUSE.

loser. An incompetent person, a failure; for emphasis, *a born loser*. "I don't think the American people want a President who is a whiny loser" (Pat Robertson, referring to Vice President George Bush, *New York Times* 10/19/87). One who fails and then gets mad about it is, of course, a *sore loser*. See also DUD.

loudmouth. A person who habitually talks at the top of his or her voice, often boastfully or indiscreetly. "He was a loudmouth and a good one-punch fighter" (John O'Hara, *Appointment in Samarra*, 1934).

Loudmouth seems to be a twentieth-century American creation, though *loudmouthed* and the simple *mouth* are much older, the latter being used in British slang for a silly person or a dupe as well as a noisy fellow—what we call today a *big mouth* and what Shakespeare termed a *large mouth*, e.g., "Here's a large mouth indeed, That spits forth death and mountains, rocks and seas . . . Zounds! I was never so bethumped with words Since I first called my brother's father dad" (*King John*, 1594–97?).

The *loudmouth* typically is said *to run off at the mouth* or *to shoot off his* [or *her*] *mouth*, as in "A Dutch married woman . . . was taxed $17.80 for 'shooting off her mouth' against the virtue and morality of a neighboring maiden" (Denver, Colorado, *Rocky Mountain News*, 8/3/1864). The Dutch married woman fell, in effect, to the common challenge: "Put your money where your mouth is." A variant, used for putting down a person who expresses poor judgment: "Your taste is all in your mouth." See also LIP, MOTORMOUTH, and MOUTHPIECE.

240

louse. An insignificant or contemptible person; a mean or bad one. *Louse* has been a favorite among derogatory terms since at least the seventeenth century. Thus, Alfred Lord Tennyson's memorable putdown (ca. August 1888) of critic John Churton Collins as "a louse upon the locks of literature" almost certainly reflected the poet's reading of *Humphry Clinker*: "He damns all other writers of the age. . . . One is a blunderbuss . . . another a half-starved louse of literature . . ." (Tobias Smollett, 1771). Much more malevolently, *louse* can be used in the same way as INSECT and TERMITE to help justify the extermination of unwanted people. The Nazis, for example, repeatedly compared Jews to vermin. In the words of the chicken farmer who ran the S.S., Heinrich Himmler: "Anti-Semitism is exactly the same as delousing. Getting rid of lice is not a question of ideology; it is a matter of cleanliness. In just the same way, anti-Semitism for us has not been a question of ideology but a matter of cleanliness" (Nora Levin, *The Holocaust*, 1968).

Louse also has appeared in various combinations over the years, among them:

lobby lice. Men who hang around hotel lobbies.

louse land. Scotland (so defined by Captain Francis Grose in *A Classical Dictionary of the Vulgar Tongue*, 1796), and one of a number of similar national epithets; thus, Prussians call lice *Franzosen* (Frenchmen) and the French pass it on, calling the same critters *espagnols* (Spaniards).

louse trap. A small-toothed comb (Grose); also a hat or cap (recorded in Indiana in 1938, *American Speech*, 2/41).

prick louse. A tailor, from the phrase, "to prick a louse," and from the sixteenth century.

The pejorative connotations of *louse* carry over to the verb, *to louse up,* to botch up, and the adjective, *lousy,* a catch-all for anything that is poor, worthless, inferior, or generally unpleasant. As Dorothy Parker said, in a *New Yorker* review of a new work (1931) by Channing Pollock, "*The House Beautiful* is the play lousy." *Lousy* also may mean "prolific" or "teeming," as lice commonly are, e.g., "I'm not kidding, the hotel was lousy with perverts" (J. D. Salinger, *The Catcher in the Rye*, 1951).

Lousy seems to be even older than *louse* in an abusive sense, dating to the fourteenth century (Chaucer used *lousy* this way), but it was in nineteenth-century America that the term took root and flourished. Thus, Andy Gordon, who had gone to California in search of gold, noted in his diary on July 12, 1849: "I wish I could never hear the word *lousy* again. I am willing to bet that Tommy Plunkett uses it fifty times a day, but he is no worse than the others. It is 'lousy' this and 'lousy' that. The rain is lousy, the trail is lousy, the bacon is lousy, and Gus Thorpe, losing in the card game, has just said that he has had a lousy deal" (in W. E. Woodward, *The Way our People Lived*, 1944).

High-minded censors have attempted to eradicate both words from the language (*lousy* was banned from the Keith vaudeville circuit in 1929 and the Hays office suggested *stinkbug* as a substitute for *louse* in a 1942 Hollywood production), but without notable success. Robert Graves, for one, complained that the American *lousy* had infiltrated Great Britain via the movies and "taken all the bite out of 'louse' " (*The Future of Swearing and Improper Language*, 1936). Then there was the old lady who reproved her granddaughter: "My dear, you really must do something to improve your vocabulary. There are two words you use over and over again. One is 'swell' and the other is 'lousy.' "

"Yes, ma'am," replied the granddaughter. "And what are the two words?"

See also CRUMB and NIT.

lout. A clumsy oaf or stupid fellow; originally a rustic, BUMPKIN or GALOOT. "James Spader, who plays Joey, is all-American ingenuous. He may have grease under his fingernails, but clearly he's no lout" (*New York Times*, 1/31/85). The term has never been a compliment, as evidenced by the earliest citation (pre-1548) in the *OED*: "Callying them cowardes, dastardes, and loutes." Before it appeared as a noun, the word was used as a verb, meaning to bend low, to bow, which is what rural *louts* did when nobility rode by. It derives from the Indo-European root, *leud-*, and its cognates include *little* and—something else *louts* often do—*loiter*. See also HICK.

lowlife. A coarse, vile person; one who will stoop to anything; in effect, a SNAKE. Thus, following a meeting of Republican leaders on Staten Island, New York, at which the discussion grew so heated that the cops had to be called, "Mr. [George M.] Hart said Mr. [Guy V.] Molinari 'created a riot.' Mr. Molinari said Mr. Hart was 'a lowlife and disgrace' " (*New York Times*, 10/1/87).

lug. A fellow or guy, especially a big, clumsy, stupid one. The term seems to be an Americanism, with the earliest example in the *OED* coming from *Broadway Brevities* (10/19/31): "Is his only sin the fact that he was born a lug?" Its origin is uncertain. In a general sense, it probably derives from *lug*, meaning something heavy and clumsy, which is hard to *lug*, or drag, in turn from the Middle English *lugge*, flap or ear, which is what one grabs on to when *lugging* something around. (It is no coincidence that people also *lug* their *luggage*.) In a particular sense, however, the modern *lug* also echoes the very old, now obsolete *lug-loaf*, glossed by Farmer and Henley as BLOCKHEAD in "She had little reason to take a cullion lug-loaf, milksop slave, when she may have a lawyer, a gentleman" (*Wiley Beguiled*, a play of 1606, in *Slang and Its Analogues*, 1896). See also LUMMOX.

lummox. A big, clumsy person; often a stupid one as well. "Those great lummoxes would chew a little thing like you to the bone" (John Steinbeck, *East of Eden*, 1952). The term has been dated to the early nineteenth century and is of uncertain origin. It fits naturally with both the dialectical *lummock*, to move heavily or clumsily, and with the common perception of the big, stupid person as a *dumb ox*. See also GALOOT.

lump. A stupid fellow, especially a large, awkward one; a person without feeling or soul. The human kind of *lump* started out (pre-1400) as a *lump of clay*. This phrase also served as the point of departure for stronger expressions, such as Lady Anne's imprecation to the Duke of Gloucester (who had killed her husband and her father-in-law and whose wife she was about to become): "Blush, blush, thou lump of foul deformity" (William Shakespeare, *Richard III*, 1592–93).

The etymology of *lump* is uncertain, but it probably is related to to the Low German *lumpen*, a rag, and *lump*, a ragamuffin, and so to LUMPENPROLETARIAT.

lumpenproletariat. The ragged poor; Karl Marx's term, from 1850, for the poorest and most degraded members of the working class. "The financial aristocracy, in its methods of acquisition as well as in its enjoyments, is nothing but the reborn *Lumpenproletariat*, the rabble on the heights of bourgeois society" (*Marx's Class Struggles in France*, H. Kuhn, tr., 1924). The term combines the German *lump*, ragamuffin, and *proletariat*, the class of wage-earners. (*Proletariat* derives from the

Latin *proles*, offspring. In ancient Rome, the *proletarius* constituted the poorest class of people. The *proles* owned so little that they were exempted from taxation and military service, with the result that their only contribution to the state was the children that they begot; hence, their name.) *Lumpenproletariat*, also translated as "social scum," has taken on secondary connotations of boorishness and stupidity, as has *lumpen* itself, which now can be used conveniently as a prefix, signifying "unenlightened," for almost any other word, e.g., *lumpen-aesthetics, lumpen-avant-garde, lumpen-linguist, lumpen-sexist,* and so on. See also BOURGEOIS and LUMP.

lunatic. A crazy person. As German Chancellor Helmut Schmidt remarked during the course of a running feud with Israeli Prime Minister Menachem Begin, it had taken the Jews two thousand years to found a state, but "then 30 years later, along comes a lunatic like Begin and puts everything at risk" (*Time,* 5/18/81). People have been described as *lunatic* since the thirteenth century, when astrology was even more popular than now, and it was thought that those poor souls with recurring bouts of insanity were affected by the cycles of the moon, i.e., that they were *moonstruck* or MAD. Today *lunatic* shows up most often in politics in the phrase *lunatic fringe.* See also FRINGE and LOONY.

lunk. A stupid person. ". . . you thick-headed lunk" (*Harper's Weekly,* 5/25/1867). An Americanism, *lunk* apparently is shorthand for *lunkhead.* See BLOCKHEAD.

M

macaroni. An Italian; a fop. Both senses originated in Britain. The oldest example of the first in the *OED* comes from a letter of December 15, 1845, by the celebrated actress Fanny Kemble, in which she refers to her travels "among frogs or maccaronis." The second sense dates to 1760–75, and commemorates a group of London dandies with foreign tastes in food as well as fashion who banded together in the Maccaroni Club. It is the foppish sense of *macaroni* that is preserved in the "Yankee Doodle" song. See also ITALIAN, KRAUT, and YANKEE.

Machiavellian. Cunning, deceitful, unscrupulous. "Is it pestilent Machiavelian policie that thous hast studied?" (Robert Greene, *A Groatsworth of Wit Bought with a Million of Repentence*, 1592). The name of Niccolò Machiavelli (1469–1527), who might best be described as a clear-eyed secular humanist, became a byword for evil doings a couple of generations before *The Discourses* and *The Prince* were translated into English (1636 and 1640, respectively). This is largely because the political techniques that he described were being used to consolidate the nation-states of Europe, thereby reducing the secular power of the Church, with the result that his works were placed on the Index in 1577. In England, before many people had had a chance to read Machiavelli firsthand, the popular conception of him was influenced greatly by a French book that attacked him, Innocent Gentillet's *Contre-Machiavel* (1576, tr. 1602). The figure of Machiavelli looms large in Elizabethan drama, providing the intellectual basis for such characters as Iago and Richard III. In the words of the latter: "I can add colors to the chameleon . . . And set the murderous Machiavel to school" (*Henry VI, Part III*, 1590–92). See also *Florentine* in PEORIA.

machine. An organized group of people, especially in politics; an attack term, usually applied to those in power by those (the GOO-GOOs) who want to kick the ins out. An Americanism, the term has been dated to 1858, as *Masheen*. Associated most closely historically with New York, Boston, and other of the nation's older, larger cities along the Eastern seaboard, *machine* was adopted widely to describe political operations during the Gilded Age. Thus, as early as June 22, 1880, the San Diego, California, *Daily Union* had occasion to refer to "the manipulation of machine politics" in the state. See also BOSS.

mackerel. A pimp, a bawd or madam; from ca. 1400 and still current. "As some get their livings by their tounges, as interpreters, lawyers, oratours, and flatterers; some by tayles [see TAIL], as maquerellaes, concubines, curtezanes, or in plaine English, whores" (John Taylor, *The Great Eater of Kent*, 1630). This sense of the word is preserved in underworld slang, where a *mac* or *mack* is a PIMP (from the nineteenth century). The exact connection with the fish is not clear. The bawdy word may be a translation of the French *maquereau*, a mackerel, as well as a pimp or brothelkeeper; it may allude directly to the characteristics of the fish itself, which is abundant, elegantly shaped, carnivorous, and spotted; or it may be a corruption of the *mackle*, Standard English for a blur or spot (printers speak of *mackled*, or doubled, impressions). The fish itself definitely was meant, however, when one of America's masters of invective, John Randolph, of Roanoke, Virginia (1773–1833), said of a fellow member of the House of Representatives (and future Secretary of State), Edward Livingston: "He is a man of splendid abilities, but utterly corrupt. Like rotten mackerel by moonlight, he shines and stinks." If this seems too harsh on Livingston, it should be remembered that his distinctions included acting as a mob lawyer, hiring out his "splendid abilities" to the notorious pirate Jean Lafitte. The fish also is meant in *mackerel snapper*, a Roman Catholic. See also BAWD, MADAM, PIMP, and, for more on Randolph, SCOUNDREL.

mad. In order of increasing innocuousness: Crazy, insane, mentally deranged, mental. Of these, *mad* is the oldest, dating to before 1000, and the worst. As noted in the *Oxford English Dictionary*: "The word has always had some tinge of contempt or disgust, and would now be quite inappropriate in medical use, or in referring sympathetically to an insane person as the subject of an affliction" (Volume M, 1904–08). "Sometimes I get worried. The President is like a madman" (Secretary of State Henry A. Kissinger, on the subject of Richard M. Nixon, 10/73, in Bob Woodward and Carl Bernstein, *The Final Days*, 1976). Not that madness is an altogether negative quality. What red-blooded male would not wish to have for an epitaph Lady Caroline Lamb's assessment of Byron: "Mad, bad, and dangerous to know" (*Journal*, March 1812)? See also BONKERS, CRAZY, HAYWIRE, LOCO, LUNATIC, OFF THE WALL, SICKO, WACKO, and WEIRDO.

madam. The mistress of a brothel. Originally, and still within proper circles, a term of respect, from the Old French *ma dame*, my lady, and ultimately from the Latin *domina*, the wife of the *dominus*, or lord, but used derisively since the sixteenth century for an affected female, a bold woman or HUSSY, a kept mistress, a prostitute, and a keeperess of prostitutes. The *OED* suggests that the opprobrious meanings of *madam* may reflect British prejudices against foreign women and dates the managerial sense to the early twentieth century, though it may well be appreciably older. Thus, from Thomas Heywood's *The Captives*, of 1624: "Naye, make his honest and chast wyfe no better / Then a madam makarell," i.e., a BAWD. See MACKEREL and MISTRESS.

maggot. One who feeds off others. ". . . Sgt. James Erne, second vice president of the local [Cleveland, Ohio] chapter of the Fraternal Order of Police, called the killing, 'justifiable extermination of another of society's maggots' " (UPI, 9/10/82). "Mr. [Neil] Kinnock is making a considerable effort to purge the [Labor] party of what he denounces as 'maggot' extremists . . ." (*New York Times*, 8/27/86).

Maggot has overtones of corruption, stemming from the old belief that the legless larva of the housefly and other insects generated spontaneously in decaying matter. Thus colonists in old New York complained to Queen Anne that Edward Hyde, Lord Cornbury, their governor from 1702 until his removal in 1708, was a "peculiar detestable maggot." Cornbury's corruptions included embezzling £1,500 from the monies appropriated to defend New York harbor as well as a predilection for dressing up in women's clothes (to honor his cousin the queen, so he said). See also PARASITE.

malarkey. Nonsense, exaggerated talk. "Naw—malarkey—not a word of truth in it" (*Made for Each Other*, film, 1939). Dated to the 1920s, the word's origin is unknown. See also BUNK.

martinet. A strict disciplinarian, one who demands strict obedience to petty rules; from Jean Martinet, a lieutenant colonel who introduced a system of drill and training that helped make the army of Louis XIV into one of the first modern ones. The troops seem to have disliked the colonel's methods so much that his name was used disparagingly within his own lifetime. As early as 1676, the term had jumped the channel, appearing in a negative context in William Wycherly's *The Plaine Dealer*: "you martinet rogue . . . d'ye find fault with martinet? Let me tell you, sir, 'tis the best exercise in the world . . ." The English reference came just four years after Colonel Martinet was killed at the seige of Duisburg (1672) by what today is termed "friendly fire"—a French artillery round in his case. Killed at the same time was a Captain Soury, leading to the witticism that Duisburg had cost the king only a martin and a mouse (*souris*).

maverick. An independently minded person, a nonconformist, a lone ranger; from unbranded *maverick* calves that roam free, in turn from Samuel A. Maverick (1803–70), who neglected to brand many of the calves on his Texas ranch. By the 1880s, the term was being applied especially to politicians who felt no compulsion to abide by party discipline, and it has since been broadened to include anyone who is so unorthodox as to march to the tune of his very own drummer, e.g., "The suit further contended that he had failed to disclose . . . that he had had conversations with Ted Turner, the maverick Atlanta broadcaster . . ." (*New York Times*, 4/11/84). See also COW, MUGWUMP, and, for more about the Maverick family, GOBBLEDYGOOK.

mealymouthed. Unable to speak plainly; from the sixteenth century. "Carry your point, whatever it costs. Be not mealy-mouthed" (John Wesley, *Works*, 1788). See also MUSH.

meatball. A stupid person, an oaf, especially an obnoxious, distasteful one. " 'You tell our meatball President I'll be there in a few minutes,' he once snapped to a secretary who had summoned him to a meeting with Nixon" (Dr. Henry A. Kissinger, in Bob Woodward and Carl Bernstein, *The Final Days*, 1976).

Meatball is more or less synonymous with *meathead*. Thus the film *Call Me Meathead* (1981) was rereleased as *Meatballs, Part II* (1984). See also Archie Bunker's *meathead* in BLOCKHEAD.

mediocrity. A person of average abilities; almost always used disparagingly. Herewith, from the Nothing-New-Under-the-Sun Department: "He [the American President] is now always an unknown mediocrity, or a man whose reputation has been acquired in some other field than that of politics" (John Stuart Mill, *Dissertations and Discussions*, 1840). The adjective, *mediocre*, from the Latin *mediocris*, halfway up the mountain (*medius*, middle + *ocris*, peak), generally has the same negative vibrations. Thus, Senator Roman L. Hruska (Republican, Nebraska) did as much as anyone to kill President Nixon's nomination of G. Harrold Carswell to the United States Supreme Court in 1970 when he tried to defend Carswell with the inept argument that "Even if he is mediocre, there are a lot of mediocre judges and people and lawyers. They are entitled to a little representation, too, aren't they?" Note also the *mediocrity* of *Caligula's horse* in HORSE.

meow. An example of how even the most apparently innocent of words can be turned into an attack term, given the proper circumstances. Thus, when a police sergeant, accompanied by a German shepherd, ordered a group of youths in York, England, to move along, one of them, Lawrence O'Dowd, turned to the dog and said, "Meow." Result: O'Dowd was fined the equivalent of $126 for using threatening and abusive words and behavior (Reuters, 11/17/84).

Meow, by the way, has been dated only to 1632 (in the form of *meaw*), though it seems likely that cats were not entirely inarticulate before that.

Mexican. Inferior, in many combinations, some inspired by the Mexican War (1846–48), but today essentially a southwestern counterpart of the older, northeastern DUTCH.

Mexican athlete. One who fails to make the team.

Mexican breakfast. A glass of water and a cigarette.

Mexican chrome. Silver paint (hot-rod talk).

Mexican hairless. A well-used tennis ball.

Mexican iron. Rawhide (cowboy talk).

Mexican money. Foreign currency, originally and especially that of the Philippines (armed forces talk, from the Spanish-American War).

Mexican overdrive. Disengaging the clutch and coasting down a hill, also called *Jewish overdrive* (trucker talk).

Mexican promotion. The promotion ordinarily given to reserve officers on active duty as they are demobilized; if they have the bad luck to be called back to active service, the promotion will be taken away.

Mexican rank. In the Army in the post–Civil War period, a brevet rank, an honor that carried no increase in pay or authority. George Armstrong Custer, for instance, was brevetted a major general in the regular Army during the war but was assigned to the 7th Cavalry with the rank of lieutenant colonel after it.

Mexican seabag. A paper bag in which a sailor who cannot afford a more durable container carries his belongings.

Mexican standoff. A battle that no one wins, a stalemate; also, a cold-blooded killing, as in "The men were the victims of the St. Valentine's Day massacre in Chicago, when seven men were given the Mexican stand-off against the inside wall of a gang garage" (John O'Hara, *Appointment in Samarra*, 1935).

Mexican strawberries. Beans, usually reddish.

See also CHICANO, GREASER, SPANISH, WETBACK, and the food terms in KRAUT.

Mick. An Irish man; a Roman Catholic, not necessarily of Irish extraction. The term is an Americanism, first appearing not long after the great potato famine brought huge numbers of Irish to these shores. The earliest example in print comes from Mark Twain, then writing for the *Butte Record* in Oroville, California: "One of the 'bucks' jerked something from his belt, that glistened in the moonlight, and looked very much like an 'Arkansas toothpick'; and made for a Mick, when there was such a gettin', in less than no time, not an 'inemy' was to be seen" (9/20/1856).

Mick is short for Michael, and it is reinforced by the Mc of many Irish surnames. In England and Ireland, the diminutive of the personal name, mickey or micky, also is one of the many male names used to refer to the penis (for others, see DICK). As Molly Bloom puts it in her peroration that provides the climax of James Joyce's Ulysses (1922): "Ill put on my best shift and drawers let him have a good eyeful out of that to make his micky stand for him . . ." See also IRISH and PADDY.

Mickey Mouse. Stupid, inane, mindless; inferior, lousy, worthless; simple, unnecessary, insignificant; a white person (to a black one, or, alternatively, a black person who acts like he has a white face).

This unsavory complex of meanings seems to have evolved from the expression's original use in the military during World War II, when training films, especially those designed to scare the troops from doing anything that would give them V.D., were called Mickey Mouse films, an ironic tribute to the immortal mouse (b. 5/15/28, Plane Crazy, though this film was not released until after Steamboat Willie, 11/18/28).

The expression appears both as noun and adjective, e.g., "There's a lot of Mickey Mouse to this job—to every job" (Senator Paul E. Tongas, Democrat, Massachusetts, characterizing his own job, New York Times, 2/8/84). "I think the inference that Yale has a 'Mickey Mouse' operation is pertinent!" (Yale Alumni Magazine, 12/84). And as President Reagan said of the Russians: "If they want to keep their Mickey Mouse system, that's O.K." (as quoted by a "senior White House official," New York Times, 6/13/84). An old Hollywood actor, the President often seemed to think in cartoon terms; see the Looney Tunes in LOONY.

P.S. The organist at the Omaha (Nebraska) Royals' baseball stadium was ejected by an umpire on May 26, 1988, simply for playing the theme song of the "Mickey Mouse Club" TV show while the club manager and other officials were discussing a call at home plate (AP, 5/28/88). And the behavior of American athletes at opening ceremonies of the 1988 Olympics was termed "scandalous" in an official letter from the president of the International Olympic Committee to the U.S. team's chief of mission because, among other offenses, some of the Olympians donned Mickey Mouse ears for the occasion.

midget. A tiny person. "Have you heard about the voiceless midget who receives unemployment compensation? Just one more example of THE MUTE TINY ON THE BOUNTY" (Louis Phillips, The Phillips Book of Atrocious Puns, ms., 1984). A midge is a gnatlike fly and midget is its diminutive, which helps explain why small people don't like the term. They prefer to be known as pituitary dwarves, short-statured people, or, as in the name of their national organization, Little People of America. In extended use, the term can be used to characterize anything that is small, e.g., "One letter-writer called her [Rose Elizabeth Bird, former Chief Justice of the California Supreme Court] a 'ding-a-ling' while another . . . called her a 'mental midget' " (New York Times, 2/13/88). See also FLY, MUNCHKIN, PEEWEE, PIPSQUEAK, PYGMY, RUNT, SHORT, SMALL, WHIPPER-SNAPPER, and Lilliputian in PEORIA.

militant. Activist; an attack word, similar to AGITATOR. Thus, describing the editorial stance of the St. Louis Globe Democrat: "Civil rights activists, until quite recently, were routinely referred to as 'militants' in a way leaving little doubt as to the meaning of the epithet" ([MORE], 5/74). The first *militants* weren't actually military. The oldest example of the term in the *OED* comes from 1413 and the reference is to the "chirche militant." See also PAGAN.

Activists are a much newer breed: The first ones were not politically minded but adherents of the philosophical theory of activism (from 1907). See also RADICAL.

milksop. A weak, effeminate boy or man; from the thirteenth century. "And who doth lead them but a paltry fellow . . . A milksop, one that never in his life Felt so much cold as over shoes in snow?" (William Shakespeare, *Richard III*, 1592–93). A *milksop* originally was a piece of bread soaked with milk or, the underlying image that makes the word an insult, an infant, specifically, one still in the suckling stage. See also COWARD and MOLLYCODDLE.

milquetoast (milktoast). A timid, ineffectual person. "Upborn by the pulpit fervor that seems to infect so many writers for the Sunday [New York] *Times*, the usually mild and milquetoasty [Bosley] Crother had written: 'The critic must speak out boldly and let his anxieties fall where they may' " (Albert Goldman, from the journalism of Lawrence Schiller, *Ladies and Gentlemen, Lenny Bruce!!*, 1974). The epithet honors Caspar Milquetoast, a character created by New York *Herald Tribune* cartoonist H. T. Webster in 1924 and syndicated nationally. Caspar was the eternal scaredy-cat, afraid of his own shadow, doing whatever he was told, and with no more spine than the dish for which he was named. See also WIMP.

minion. A subordinate or follower, usually contemptuous, as in the cliché "Here come the minions of the law." The word has enjoyed much better meanings in the past. It comes from the French *mignon*, dainty, which is also responsible for the *filet mignon* steak. A *minion* originally—going back to the early sixteenth century— was a beloved object, as a lady-love or darling. In time, the term was transferred to paramours, mistresses, obsequious attendants and dependents at court, then to hussies, jades, and other servile creatures—with the result that the original estimable sense has been almost entirely lost. See also LACKEY.

minx. A saucy, flirtatious girl or woman. "Damn her, lewd minx! O, damn her!" (William Shakespeare, *Othello*, 1604). The word has been dated to the mid-sixteenth century and seems to have been used for pet dogs a couple generations before it was applied to women, especially forward or outright wanton ones, including prostitutes. It comes from the Low German *minsk*, hussy, in turn from the Indo-European *man-* or *mon-*, which happens also to be the root of the masculine *man*. See also HUSSY.

mistress. A woman who has a long-term sexual relationship with a man to whom she is not married; especially one who earns her keep this way. "Those women, whom the Kings were to take for their Wives, and not for Mistresses, which is but a later name for Concubines" (John Donne, *Sermon*, lxiv, pre-1631). *Mistress* also was the crusher in one of the most famous comebacks of all time, administered ca. 1763 by John Wilkes (whose radicalism is commemorated in the name of Wilkes-Barre, Pennsylvania) to John Montagu, fourth Earl of Sandwich (for whom the sandwich and the Sandwich, or Hawaiian, Islands were named). As recorded by Sir Charles Petrie in *The Four Georges* (1935):

THE EARL: 'Pon my honor, Wilkes, I don't know whether you'll die on the gallows or of the pox.

WILKES: That must depend, my Lord, on whether I first embrace your Lordship's principles, or your Lordship's mistresses.

Mistress comes from the French *maistre*, master, and its primary meanings revolve around the sense of a woman who has command over servants, children, a household, a territory, a state, or—getting to the issue at hand—a man's heart. The negative meaning, in place since the fifteenth century, has gradually overcome the positive ones. MADAM, denoting the mistress of a brothel, has traveled a parallel path. See also DAME.

mob. A criminal network or GANG. "Mr. [Barry I.] Slotnick built his reputation by representing some of New York's more infamous organized crime figures but he bristles at being called a 'mob lawyer.' 'That's a pejorative term,' he said in an interview. 'I represent people who are accused of crimes, many of them unjustifiably' " (*New York Times*, 5/16/87).

The organized, criminal sense of *mob* seems to be an American contribution to language, dating from the 1920s. The word itself is a seventeenth-century clipping of the Latin *mobile*, in turn shortened from *mobile vulgus*, meaning a movable, excitable crowd of common people, i.e., the rabble or (the Greek equivalent, also often used contemptuously) *the hoi polloi*. See also UNWASHED.

mocky (mockey, mockie). A Jew. "Love thy neighbor if he's not a seventh-day adventist or a nigger or a greaser or a ginzo or a hunkie or a bohunk or a frog or a spik or a limey or a heinie or a mick or a chink or a jap or a dutchman or a squarehead or a mockie or a slicked-up grease-ball from the Argentine" (Ira Wolfert, *Tucker's People*, 1943). The term has been dated to 1931 and is of uncertain origin, perhaps deriving from the Yiddish *makeh*, a boil or sore. See also JEW (DOWN), TO.

moll. Any woman, especially a prostitute or gangster's companion; a *gun moll*, though her *gun* comes from the Yiddish *gonif*, a thief, and she is, professionally speaking, a pickpocket rather than a bearer of small artillery. The generic *moll* is a diminutive of the proper name, *Mary* (as is *Molly*, which has been used since the eighteenth century to designate an effeminate man, or MOLLYCODDLE). By the early 1600s, if not before, it was being used disparagingly. The notoriety of a London thief, Moll Cut-Purse, may have helped fix the bad meaning. She flourished in the first half of the seventeenth century. Later, Daniel Defoe gave the name to the heroine of his novel *Moll Flanders* (1722); the choice of name was almost inevitable, considering that her career included, according to Defoe's subtitle, "Twelve Year a Whore, Five time a Wife (whereof once to her own Brother), Twelve Year a Thief, Eight Year Transported Felon," etc. See also WHORE. The attaching of negative meanings to female names is standard operating procedure. The usual connotations when this happens are of childishness, coarseness, looseness, and familiarity, especially in the case of nicknames. Herewith, a sampling:

Aspasia, a literary euphemism for a whore, from the name of the MISTRESS of Pericles in the Golden Age of Athens (fifth century B.C.). Other famous consorts whose names have attained general currency in the same way include *Dulcinea*, the lady-love of the hero of *Don Quixote de la Mancha* (1605, 1615); the Biblical Ahab's wife, JEZEBEL; Robin Hood's great and good friend *Maid Marian;* and *Thais,* the Athenian courtesan who is said to have inspired Alexander the Great to set fire to Persepolis (330 B.C.).

Biddy, a variant of *Bridget,* generic from the eighteenth to the early twentieth century for an Irish serving girl; gradually extended to include maids of any ethnic extraction and then to women of any occupation, usually as *old biddies,* elderly gossips or fussbudgets. (The *biddy* that is a young person, male or female, derives from the *biddy* in the sense of a hen or newly hatched chick; see CHICKEN.)

Cassandra, the legendary prophetess of doom, whose name has since been applied to men, too. Thus, speaking of an American secretary of state: "Mr. [George P.] Shultz, whose mission ended today as he left Cairo for a North Atlantic Treaty meeting in Madrid, sounds like a Cassandra" (*New York Times,* 6/8/88).

Delilah, a treacherous temptress, from she who deprived Samson of his strength by shearing his hair and then betrayed him to the PHILISTINES.

Doll and *Dollie,* pet forms of *Dorothy* that cast the woman in the role of plaything; see DOLL.

Jane, as in *plain Jane, Calamity Jane* (generic for a pessimistic woman, from Martha Jane Burke, 1852?–1903, made famous as the heroine of a dime novel by Edward L. Wheeler, *Deadwood Dick on Deck, or Calamity Jane the Heroine of Whoop Up*), and the anonymous *Jane,* wife to *John Doe* or *Richard Roe.* (The *Roe* in *Roe v. Wade,* the 1973 Supreme Court decision legalizing abortion, was a *Jane Roe,* who later revealed herself as Norma McCorvey.) A *jane* also is a toilet for women, i.e., a female *john.*

Jenny, from *Janet,* used to describe female animals (analogous to JACK for males), such as the *jenny ass;* also an epithet for an effeminate man, similar to *Nancy* below, and a euphemism for a whore, *a jaded jenny.*

Jill, as in that famous couple, *Jack and Jill,* where JACK is any man and *Jill* is any woman, but especially a wench or wanton girl, the name deriving from *Gill,* in turn a diminutive of *Gillian,* the old English form of *Juliana.* The proper name also is the probable ancestress of *jilt,* described as a "new cant word" in 1674. It originally had a stronger meaning than today, implying conscious deception at the outset of a relationship, both as a noun and a verb, e.g., "JILT. A tricking woman, who encourages the addresses of a man whom she means to deceive and abandon" (Captain Francis Grose, *A Classical Dictionary of the Vulgar Tongue,* 1796).

Judy, often denoting a foolish, stupid, or ridiculous woman, thanks to the leading female role in Punch and Judy shows, and occasionally extended to males who act that way. "They [a group of men] was up and a stirrin' I tell you; they called a meetin', and they made a chairmin and seketarie, and passed resolutions, and made perticklar Judies of themselves ginerally" (Philip Paxton [Samuel A. Hammett], *Piney Woods Tavern; or Sam Slick in Texas,* 1858).

Juggins, a simpleton, a dupe, probably from *Jug,* a pet form of *Joan* and *Judith,* whence also *jughead* see (BLOCKHEAD). *Jug* dates to the sixteenth century as a disparaging term for a woman, especially a serving woman, a homely woman, a mistress, and—with better vibrations—a sweetheart. *Juggins,* for a fool of either sex, dates to the nineteenth century. The contemptuous connotations carry over into the word's use as a verb: "He's making it a point to screw all the good-lookin' bitches in the neighborhood. There were few women around the neighborhood that Johnny wanted to jugg and didn't jugg, even if they were married" (Claude

Brown, *Manchild in the Promised Land,* 1965). In the plural, *jugs* are breasts, and it is possible, though not proven, that this is the connection by which the feminine name came to be applied in the sixteenth century to the hollow vessel for holding milk and other liquids.

Kate, a wanton woman; a prostitute, especially an attractive one. The usage is old and perhaps puns on the sexual senses of CAT.

Kitty, a pet form of *Catherine* and also a pet.

Lizzie, an effeminate man; sometimes, for emphasis, *lizzie boy.* "A swell bunch of Lizzie boys and lemon suckers and pie-faces" (Sinclair Lewis, *Babbitt,* 1922). A *lizzie* may also be a female homosexual, but then the term probably comes from *lesbian* rather than *Elizabeth.*

Lulu, the pet form of *Louise,* for something remarkable, and often used ironically rather than with unalloyed admiration. "[The CIA] has been a bit like the late Mayor La Guardia in that its mistakes tended to be 'lulus' " (Charles Mohr, *New York Times,* 6/13/85).

Magdalen, a former prostitute or a reformatory for prostitutes, from "Mary called Magdalene," who washed Christ's feet with her tears. Her name also is the source of *maudlin,* thanks to the effusiveness of her repentance.

Mary, a male homosexual, especially one who assumes the female role, *or* a female homosexual; dating to the 1890s, and perhaps obsolete, are *Mary-Ann* and *Charlotte-Ann* for effeminate gentleman and/or practicing sodomites.

Matty, a diminutive of *Martha* or *Mathilda,* as in *meddlesome matty,* one who interferes in other people's business; from the title of a poem in *Original Poems,* A. and J. Taylor (1814). "Good gracious child, what a meddlesome matty you are" (D. Holman-Hunt, *My Grandmother & I,* 1960).

Meg, from *Margaret,* traditionally a virago, after a real one, Long Meg, also called Meg of Westminster, whose exploits in the time of Henry VIII were remembered well enough some two generations later to form the basis of a comedy (1582).

Messalina, a voracious, avaricious woman, after Valeria Messalina, third wife of the Roman emperor Claudius, who might have lived longer despite her licentiousness if only she had not lusted also for power. As it was, she was executed by order of her husband in A.D. 48, aged twenty-six. " 'Unfaithful bitch!' he cried. 'Messalina! Medusa! Gorgon!' " ("J. Lymington," *Spider in Bath,* 1975).

Nancy, a rhyme on *fancy,* and usually reserved for effeminate men or outright catamites, as in *Miss Nancy* or *nancy-boy,* both popular since 1800 but probably older. (The abbreviated *nan-boy,* for an effeminate man, has been dated to 1691, while *nanny* and *nanny-house,* for WHORE and whorehouse, respectively, are from the same period, and *Nan,* as generic term for a serving girl, dates to at least the sixteenth century.) The effeminate sense may have been popularized in part by the actress Anne Oldfield, nicknamed *Miss Nancy,* who first trod the boards in Drury Lane in 1692, aged nine. See also NANNY GOAT.

Nelly, a sissy, weakling, or silly person; a homosexual or lesbian. Also conforming to the feminine stereotype, a *nervous Nelly* is a person who is easily upset or scared; a *nice Nelly* is a prude.

Poll, an alteration of *moll,* and the name usually awarded to parrots and to people who act like them. Thus, David Garrick produced a mock epitaph for Oliver Goldsmith, whose conversation verged, by all accounts, on the incoherent:

Here lies Nolly Goldsmith, for shortness called Noll.
Who wrote like an angel, but talked like poor Poll.

Polly, which is to *Poll* as *Molly* is to *Moll,* also has acquired some pejorative connotations, e.g., "When a teacher told a hillman that his son was fighting the other pupils, the man said, 'Well, I don't aim to have Bill a-settin' round *like Polly in the primer,'* meaning that he didn't want the boy to be a sissy" (Vance Randolph and George P. Wilson, *Down in the Holler,* 1953). See also NED IN THE FIRST READER and PARROT.

Pollyanna, a foolish optimist, from Pollyanna Whittier, child heroine of *Pollyanna* (1913), by Eleanor M. Porter. The Pollyanna of the novel was noted for her skill at "the glad game," which consisted of always managing to find a silver lining no matter how dark the cloud of disaster surrounding her. The name quickly became attached to those who exhibited this trait in real life: "I should not like to hold stock in a company with Pollyanna as president" (*Collier's,* 6/11/21).

Sadie Thompson, a prostitute, from the heroine of *Miss Thompson* (1921), a short story by W. Somerset Maugham, better known as dramatized under the title *Rain.* Meanwhile, *sadie-masie* is shorthand for *S and M.*

sapphism, female homosexuality, from the name of the poetess Sappho. She was born toward the start of the seventh century B.C. (612?), but use of her name to characterize sexual relations between women is not recorded before 1890. See also *lesbian* in PEORIA.

Sheila, a girl or a woman in Australia and New Zealand, from 1828 (*OED*). "They made the usual jokes about the local Sheilas" (D. Seaman, *Committee 63,* 1977). *Sheila* is the natural counterpart of PADDY.

Susie, a prostitute, especially as *sidewalk susie.*

Tabby, a name traditionally (from the mid-eighteenth century) reserved for old maids, either from *Tabitha* (gazelle, in Aramaic) or from the association between elderly spinsters and *tabby* cats (from striped tabby cloth, in turn from the Arabic *'attābī,* after the quarter of Baghdad, Al-'attābīya, named after Prince Attab, where the cloth originally was manufactured).

See also ANN, JEZEBEL, TAWDRY, and XANTHIPPE.

mollycoddle. A pampered, overprotected weakling; an effeminate man or boy; a MILKSOP or SISSY. "You have been bred up as a mollycoddle, Pen, and spoilt by the women" (William Makepeace Thackeray, *Pendennis,* 1849). The term, which also can be used as a verb, to pamper, derives from the personal name, *Molly* (or, in full, *Miss Molly,* + *coddle*), where the *Molly* is a an effeminate fellow, often a practicing SODOMITE. The word has enjoyed some use in politics, notably by Theodore Roosevelt, who characterized opponents of his Big Stick policies as "the large mollycoddle vote, people who are soft physically and morally" (*Theodore Roosevelt, An Autobiography,* 1913, in *Safire's Political Dictionary,* 1978). See also MOLL.

mongolism. Down syndrome; a type of congenital retardation. Children born with this condition (the result of an extra twenty-first chromosome) tend to have broad, flat faces, narrow eyes, and other characteristics associated (by non-Mongols) with the Mongolian race. Curiously, the Japanese think that children born with this condition look like occidentals.

Mongolism was coined in 1866 by Dr. J. Langdon Down, medical superintendent of Earlswood Asylum for Idiots in Surrey, England. In common use for about a century, the racial term is gradually being expunged from polite vocabularies. "When lexicographers understand that the use of *mongoloid* for 'person with Down syndrome' is now perceived by people involved with mental retardation as tantamount to the use of *nigger* as a synonym for *black*, they will realize that commercial dictionaries have a way to go in handling these terms" (*Newsletter of the American Dialect Society*, 5/87). See also IDIOT.

mongrel. Someone or something (a *mongrel* religion, say, or a *mongrel* language) of mixed or dubious ancestry. In human terms, the word has been used to denote specifically the offspring of different races or nationalities, almost always in a contemptuous manner. As a generalized epithet, the term is the functional equivalent of BASTARD. Thus, heaping well-deserved abuse on Goneril's steward, Oswald, the Duke of Kent calls him, among other things, "a knave, beggar, coward, pander, and the son and heir of a mongrel bitch" (William Shakespeare, *King Lear*, 1605–06). See also DOG.

monkey. A person who is not quite a person. "I simply will not have these monkeys [in the United States Congress] telling us what we can and cannot do" (President Dwight David Eisenhower, in Emmet John Hughes, *The Ordeal of Power*, 1963).

In its broadest sense, *monkey* (possibly from the Middle Low German, *Moneke*, the name of the son of Martin the Ape in a 1498 version of *Reynard the Fox*), stands simply for "man," often appearing as a suffix in such occupational terms as *grease monkey* and *powder monkey*.

Monkey also can be used playfully, even affectionately, as Jonathan Swift did when writing to Stella: "Well little monkeys mine, I must go write; and so good-night" (11/2/1710). Howard Cosell also tried to use *monkey* this way when commenting on a football player who had just caught a pass: "That little monkey gets loose, doesn't he? (WABC-TV, 9/5/83). Trouble is, the word has acquired so many bad associations that it is almost impossible to get away with it in an affectionate sense anymore especially when, as in Cosell's case, the person referred to is black. (The player himself said he was not offended, but other people were.)

The popular perception of *monkey* is conveyed more accurately by the *bon mots* attributed to Thomas Carlyle: "How long will John Bull allow this absurd monkey [Benjamin Disraeli] to dance on his chest?" and Aneurin Bevan: "Why should I question the monkey [Foreign Secretary Anthony Eden] when I can question the organ grinder [Prime Minister Winston Churchill]?"

Many of *monkey*'s pejorative senses reflect the inquisitive, meddling, uninhibited nature of the beast, e.g., *to monkey around* or *monkey with* (to fool around or interfere with as in the nineteenth-century cowboy yell: "I'm a two-gun man and a very bad man and won't do to monkey with"); *monkey business* (foolish or shady business); *monkey face* (a funny, monkey-like face, from the sixteenth century); *monkey jacket* and *monkey suit* (a fancy jacket, tux, or uniform, from the getup worn by organ grinders' monkeys); *monkeyshines* (capers, pranks, and an Americanism, dated to 1847); and *to make a monkey of* (to deceive someone, whence, perhaps, the surprised exclamation, "I'll be a *monkey's uncle*").

The uninhibited sex life of the monkey also has inspired such phrases as *lecherous as a monkey* (William Shakespeare, *Hamlet*, 1601–02) and *hot as monkeys* (William Shakespeare, *Othello*, 1604), not to mention the mating dance, *the monkey*, performed in discothèques from the 1960s. *The monkey* also is a nineteenth century Americanism for the vulva; hence, *to spank the monkey*, to masturbate. Because of the anatomical meaning, polite people in the Ozarks steer clear of using the phrase *monkeyin' around* in mixed company. Those who congregate in singles bars tend to be more outspoken, and Thomas E. Murray, who spent nearly five hundred hours recording language usage in such establishments in and around St. Louis, Missouri, in 1982, reported both "I'm a monkey tamer" (used only by males to females) and the feminine counterpart "My monkey's wild" (*American Speech*, Spring 1985). Each of these conversational icebreakers was used seven times during Murray's study, putting them substantially ahead of "My dong is two feet long" (male to female, one time only); about on a par with "I love lollipops" (female to male only, 8 times); and somewhat behind "I love cherries" (male to female only, twenty-two times). The most popular opening line, however, remained the prosaic "My name is . . ." (110 times).

Two other commonly encountered *monkeys* are the *monkey on [one's] back*, which is a drug habit, and the *monkey wrench*, which is so often thrown or hurled into the works. The druggy *monkey* may actually be a variant of the older *turkey on [one's] back* (note that to be suddenly deprived of drugs is *to go cold turkey*), perhaps influenced by the British *take the monkey off [one's] back*, to cool off, to calm down. It is also possible that the *monkey wrench*, despite its name, has a non-simian ancestry. The earliest known example of the *monkey wrench* appears in an 1858 British dictionary of trade terms, but it seems unlikely that the word is of British origin since the British call this tool a "spanner" or, in full, an "adjustable spanner wrench." Different theories of the word's origin have been bruited about, e.g., that the profile of the wrench, with its adjustable jaw, is reminiscent of that of a monkey, or that it was invented by a London blacksmith, Charles Moncke. A better guess is based on an undated (ca. 1932–33) clipping from the *Boston Transcript*, which reports that such a wrench was invented about 1856 by a Yankee named Monk, while in the employ of Bemis & Call, of Springfield, Massachusetts. This tool, according to the newspaper account, soon came to be called *Monk's wrench* and then *monkey's wrench*. As one of this country's leading lexicographers, Mitford M. Mathews, pointed out: "This explanation is suspiciously easy and 'pat,' but it is somewhat odd that the date given, 1856, tallies pretty well with that of the first occurrence in the *OED*" (*American Speech*, 2/53). Whatever, the monkey wrench remains with us, actually and figuratively, e.g., "The panel was established in June because of widespread discontent over . . . 'monkey-wrench politics'—the willingness of members [of the U.S. Senate] to throw a monkey wrench into things to achieve their own goals, no matter what the larger cost" (*New York Times*, 11/25/84).

Remember what Ike said at the head of this article?

See also APE, BABOON, CHIMPANZEE, GORILLA, and JACKANAPES.

monster. A person who is markedly cruel, depraved, hideous, and/or wicked, from the Old French *monstre*, originally a divine warning and hence, something marvelous, extraordinary, or unnatural. Human *monsters* with various supposedly inhuman and monstrous traits have been among us since at least the 1500s. Toward the end of that century, for instance, Robert Greene described "our English courtezans—to be plain, our English whores" as a "multitude of monsters" (*A Disputation*, 1592). And nearly four hundred years later, during a crackdown on BOURGEOIS tendencies in the People's Republic of China, members of the militia entered a hotel in Shanghai and "caught 'monsters' . . . mingling with the guests" (*New York Times*, 7/26/76). And so it goes.

One of the nicer *monsters* ever sighted comes from a putdown that Cotton Mather genially reported on himself: A Quaker who apparently had a difficult time getting a word in edgewise when Mather was talking, remarked, *"Thou are a Monster, all Mouth and no Ears"* (*Decennium Luctuosom*, 1699, from Kenneth Silverman, *The Life and Times of Cotton Mather*, 1984). See also ANIMAL.

moocher. A beggar, a borrower, especially one who borrows with no intention of returning; a petty thief, a dawdler, a lurker about. Part of hobo lingo since at least the mid-nineteenth century, the term got a big boost from Cab Calloway's song about "Minnie the Moocher," a "low-down hootchie-cootcher" (1931), and the Nat Fleischer film cartoon that was based on the song character (1932). The modern sense is in keeping, however, with the *OED's* oldest example of *mooch*, from the fifteenth century, apparently meaning "to act the miser" or "pretend poverty," as well as with the similar, thirteenth-century *miche*, to pilfer, in turn from the Old French *muchier*, to hide, to skulk. See also BEGGAR, CADGER, CHISELER, FREELOADER, PANHANDLER, and PARASITE.

moonshine. Foolishness, nonsense; from the fifteenth century. The idea is that *moonshine* has about as much substance as moonlight. Captain Frederick Marryat made the comparison explicitly in *Mr. Midshipman Easy* (1836):

"Is she as handsome as Agnes, Ned?"
"Twice as handsome by moonlight."
"That's all moonshine, and so will be your courting."

The ultimate in *moonshine* is Carlyle's "transcendental moonshine, cast by some morbidly radiating Coleridge" (*Life of John Sterling*, 1851). (The *moonshine* that comes in bottles, by the way, predates Prohibition by many years. The term was used in England in the eighteenth century for smuggled liquor, brought into the country at night, and also known as *moonlight*. Subsequently, Americans began applying the term to illicitly manufactured liquor, especially whiskey.) See also BUNK.

moose. A prostitute, MISTRESS, or girlfriend; military use since the occupation of Japan following World War II. The term comes from the Japanese *mus*, short for *musume*, a young girl or inamorata. A PX catalog is known also as a *moose maintenance manual*. See also WHORE.

mope. A fool, a stupid person. " 'Hell, they're all mopes,' Studs said" (James T. Farrell, *Young Lonigan*, 1932). The foolish *mope* dates to the sixteenth century, as does the gloomy, listless, apathetic verb, *to mope*. Both may come from the Middle Dutch *mopen*, to be dazed or dreamy. See also FOOL.

moron. A stupid person, a DUMMY. "I can't stand illiterates. I am not going to stand here and talk to a moron like John Lewis" (Ed Tyll, talk-show host, WGST-AM,

Atlanta, Georgia, AP, 7/14/87). For making this remark, Mr. Tyll was suspended for a week without pay.

The *moron* is a figure of near-mythic proportions in American lore, the subject of many jokes, not all of them so funny, e.g., Q. Why did the moron cut off his arms? A. He wanted to wear a sleeveless sweater. *Moron* also enjoyed a vogue in newspapers for several decades, starting in the 1920s, as a synonym for "degenerate" or "sex pervert," e.g., headlines such as "Whole Family Wiped Out by Moron" and "Moron Attacks Child" (*American Speech*, 12/25). This moronic extension of the word's meaning was especially notable in the Chicago area, where it persisted until comparatively recent times: "Removing shrubbery and lagoons will not improve the morals of a moron" (*Chicago Daily News*, 3/25/49).

Moron, based on the Greek *moros* (stupid, foolish), was coined by Dr. Henry H. Goddard, director of research at New Jersey's Vineland Institute for Feeble-minded Girls and Boys, and adopted in 1910 by the American Association for the Feeble-minded as the official designation for mentally defective people with the least amount of impairment, i.e., adults with mental ages in the eight-to-twelve-year range. See also CRETIN, IDIOT, IGNORAMUS, IMBECILE, NITWIT, and SIMPLETON.

mossback. An extreme conservative or, as an adjective, one who acts that way. "He's mossbacked and close to a fascist, but he's perfectly sincere" (George V. Higgins, *A City on a Hill*, 1975).

The epithet appeared first as *mossyback* during the Civil War when it was applied to Southerners who fled into the woods or swamps in order to escape conscription into the Confederate Army. Some of them seem to have remained hidden so long that moss grew on their backs. There may also be an allusion here to a large old fish, such as a bass, called a *mossback* by anglers on account of the marine growth on its back. In the 1880s, the term surfaced again, this time in politics, when it was applied to Western farmers in general and to a conservative faction of the Ohio Democratic Party in particular. "Everyone rejoices over the passage of the bill . . . except a few intense mossbacks, who were known during the war as copperheads" (*Boston Journal*, 3/5/1885). See also COPPERHEAD and FOGY.

motherfucker. A generalized expletive; as a participle, *motherfucking*, an intensifier of all work; as a noun, a despicable person, hardly ever to be taken literally, except as the counterpoint to the pun in the grafitti, "Oedipus was a motherfucker."

The expression seems to have originated among American blacks and it had a considerable amount of shock power for some years, especially for whites not previously familiar with it. Thus, Robert E. Rothenberg, M.D., clearly remembered the time he first heard the term, around 1930, when a black woman in a New York City hospital emergency room shouted, "You motherfucking cop, leave me alone." Her ear was being sewn on, after having been almost bitten off by another woman, at whose gentlemen friend she had made a pass (*Recall: Life as a Surgeon*, ms., 1987).

Integration of the Army at the end of the 1940s, followed by the swelling of military ranks during the Korean conflict, spread the word to society at large—the male portion of it, at least. The oldest example of the expression in the *OED* comes from a post-Korea article on "Army Speech and American English": "The linguistic vacuum [created by the overuse, and resulting enfeeblement, of *fuck*] is being filled by a new obscenity symbol, *motherfucker*, which goes beyond the simple obscenity symbol itself by outraging the most ingrained of human sensibilities" (*American*

Speech, 5/56). The degree of outrage was evidenced by the number of euphemisms that were devised for the expression, e.g., *granny-jazzer, mammy-jammer, mommy-bopper, mother-grabber, mother-jumper,* and *mother-lover,* among others, along with such variations on the unstated theme as *M. F., Marshall Field,* and *Mister Franklin;* the slurred *mo'-fo'* and *muh-fuh;* the rococo *triple-clutcher,* popularized by black truck drivers in army construction battalions; and the clipped *momma, mother,* and *muther.*

As late as 1960, the word was still printed as *motherf****** in a piece by James Baldwin in the spring issue of *Partisan Review.* And Lenny Bruce's use of the word—"Where is that dwarf motherfucker?"—when complaining about the handling of the lights during his act at the Troubadour nightclub in Los Angeles on October 24, 1967, helped lead to his arrest for violating Penal Code Section 311.6, i.e., uttering obscene words in a public place.

By this time, however, the word had come into general circulation. When students confronted members of the Ohio National Guard at Kent State University on May 4, 1970, this was one of the most frequently hurled epithets. "Girls were particularly abusive, using the foulest language and taunting the Guardsmen with being 'shit-heels, motherfuckers and half-ass pigs.' Others called them less explosive but equally hurtful names: 'toy soldiers, weekend warriors, fascists.' . . . Scores of Guardsmen went through this experience; within half an hour they would be facing these same girls with loaded rifles" (James A. Michener, *Kent State: What Happened and Why,* 1971). And when the guardsmen replied to this torrent of verbal abuse—with fifty-five M1 rounds, five pistol shots, and a shotgun blast—four students were killed and nine wounded.

So often and so widely was the word used during this period that the taboo against it began breaking down, as Christopher Lasch explains: "In the late sixties, white radicals enthusiastically adopted the slogan 'Up against the Wall, Motherfucker!' But the term has since lost its revolutionary associations, like other black idioms first popularized among whites by political radicals and spokesmen for the counterculture, and in slightly expurgated form has become so acceptable that the term 'mother' has everywhere become, even among teeny-boppers, a term of easygoing familiarity or contempt" (*The Culture of Narcissism,* 1978). See also UP AGAINST THE WALL.

Indeed, by the mid 1970s, the abbreviated form was being heard regularly on TV, which usually bleeps anything that is at all exceptionable, e.g., "You know, if I don't defrost this momma [a refrigerator] pretty soon, I can rent it to Peggy Fleming to rehearse in" ("Cher," CBS-TV, 6/1/75). Newspapers all over America also were printing the short form by this time, as in Erma Bombeck's observation about recalictrant supermarket shopping carts: "No state requires a license to drive these little mothers" (syndicated column, *Honolulu Star-Bulletin,* 1/7/75). Then there was the picket sign carried by a striking telephone company worker: "Ma Bell Is A Cheap Mother" (New York City, 8/15/83).

While public proprieties are preserved with the use of only the single word, the second part of the combo almost inevitably comes to mind. It is a bit like hearing someone drop a shoe and waiting for the second to follow. The net result is that people have grown so accustomed to thinking the thought that most of the emotional power has been drained out of it, and the phrase, whether in full or abbreviated form, now has about as much punch to it as BASTARD or BITCH. The difference is that the effective lives of the latter words were measured in centuries, while *motherfucker* was a force to be reckoned with for only a few decades. As many observers have noted, the pace of modern life is swift.

motormouth. An excessively talkative person. Back in the 1890s, before motor cars had begun to clog the roads, the term was *automatic mouth*, as in the poetic retort by Representative Marriott Brosius (Republican, Pennsylvania) to another congressman, who had been interrupting him (from Edward Boykin, *ed.*, *The Wit and Wisdom of Congress*, 1961):

> You love your automatic mouth;
>> You love its giddy whirl;
> You love its fluent flow;
>> You love to wind your mouth up;
> You love to hear it go!

Or as Thomas B. Reed (Republican, Maine), Speaker of the House in this period, is said to have said, loudly, when annoyed by the chattering of two other members: "They never open their mouths without detracting from the sum of human knowledge."

Closely related to the *motormouth* are the *bigmouth*, BLABBERMOUTH, and LOUD-MOUTH; the obsolete British *all mouth* and *all jaw* (*like a sheep's head*); and the modern *flap*, as in the British *flap* [*one's*] *mouth* and the more vivid American *flapjaw*. See also BLATHERSKITE, CHATTERBOX, and WINDBAG.

mouthpiece. A lawyer. When *Barron's National Business and Financial Weekly* ran a letter from Frank Sinatra's lawyer, Milton A. "Mickey" Rudin, on January 11, 1979, under the headline "Sinatra's Mouthpiece," Mr. Rudin sued for libel, with *his* attorney (or counsel or lawyer or whatever) contending that *mouthpiece* conjured up the image of a "fast-talking guy with a derby who . . . has got a bail bondsman in his pocket, a couple of judges in his other pocket" (*Columbia Journalism Review*, 5-6/83). *Mouthpiece* has been used as a general term since 1805 for one who speaks on behalf of another and since 1857 in the modern legal sense. Whether or not *mouthpiece* is libelous *per se*, most attorneys don't like it. Of course, they also are rather down on LAWYER.

muckmouth. A dirty talker. "Look, muckmouth . . . you cut that out!" (Edward Albee, *Who's Afraid of Virginia Woolf?*, 1962). A *muckmouth*, taken literally, is someone who talks a lot of SHIT, the oldest sense of *muck* (ca. 1250) being the dung of cattle as used for manure. This meaning survives, e.g., "The mucky end of the stick" (headline, *Bookseller*, 12/11/82). In addition to *muckmouth*, the basic term has other extensions, including *mucker*, a rude, coarse, vulgar, and boorish person; *muckerdom*, the world of *muckers*; *muckerism*, their distinguishing traits; *muckrake*, the instrument for spreading it; *muckraker*, a journalist who specializes in exposing corruption *or* a pornographer; and *muckheap*, a pile of it, as in the opening sentence of the *Scots Observer's* review (7/5/1890) of Oscar Wilde's *The Picture of Dorian Gray*, "Why go grubbing in muck heaps?" None of these *mucks* should be confused with the euphemistic *muck, muckabout, muckup*, and *mucking*, where the *m* is merely a substitute for an *f*, or with the *high muck-a-muck*, a self-important person, from Chinook jargon, *hiu*, plenty + *muckamuck*, food (from 1856). See also MUDSLINGER.

mudslinger. A dealer in abuse but, depending on one's perspective, not necessarily untruth. "Before that she [Kitty Kelley, biographer of Frank Sinatra, among other celebrities] had been 'hiding out' in New York, in a subleased apartment, during which time 'modern mudslinging's miniscule mistress of malice' (according to Sinatra's alliterative PR minions) kept a lunch date with an old friend" (*Publishers Weekly*, 11/25/83).

Mudslinger has been dated to 1896. Before that, there were *flingers* and *throwers* of *mud*, e.g., "These people fling mud at that elegant Englishman . . . and make fun of him" (Mark Twain, *A Tramp Abroad*, 1880). And before that, going back to the seventeenth century, scurrilous sorts were said to *cast*, *fling*, or *throw dirt*. Meanwhile, the basic *mud*, as a stupid person, has been dated to the early eighteenth century, and as the lowest part of anything, to the sixteenth century, e.g., the characterization of Talleyrand, attributed to Napoleon: "A silk stocking filled with mud." See also MUCKMOUTH and SLUR.

mug. A sucker. " 'Get out, mugg. While you can still walk' " (Raymond Chandler, *The High Window*, 1942). The *mug* that is a person probably comes from *mug* meaning a person's face, this in turn deriving from the eighteenth-century custom of decorating drinking mugs with grotesque human features. Hence, too, the photograph that is a *mug shot* and the verb, *to mug*, to make a funny face.

The *mug* that is a dolt or inexperienced person, not in the know, has been dated to the mid-nineteenth century: " 'We sometimes have a greenhorn wants to go out pitching with us—a mug, we calls them' " (Henry Mayhew, *London's Labour and London's Poor*, 1851–61). This form of *mug* seems to have given rise to *to mug*, meaning to attack someone, especially by applying a strangle hold; a *mug*, meaning a tough guy, especially a rough, ugly one, and often a criminal; and, finally—an American breakthrough of the last century—the *mugger* who specializes in *muggings*. The latter senses probably resulted from the predilection of criminals for picking out *mugs* as their victims, as evidenced by the earliest citation for *mugger* in the *OED*: "The Muggers, like most bullies and ruffians, manifested a fine discrimination, respecting the party they attacked, selecting those they thought they could rob with little resistance and entire impunity" (J. H. Brown, *Four Years in Succesia*, 1865). See also GULL.

mugwump. A political independent, especially a Republican who has decided not to support his party's candidate, or, worse, actually crossed over and voted for the Democrats. "So attractive was [Grover Cleveland's] record that liberal Republicans called Mugwumps defected to his camp after [James G.] Blaine had been nominated" (*Wall Street Journal*, 4/3/84).

Mugwump is Algonquin for "chief" and was used by the Reverend John Eliot in place of "duke" when translating the Old Testament for the benefit of Native Americans (1663). By the 1830s, the term was being applied more or less derisively to men who were important, or merely self-important (see SWELLHEAD). It became affixed to maverick Republicans as a result of the presidential race between Cleveland and Blaine in 1884: "We have yet to see a Blaine organ which speaks of the Independent Republicans otherwise than as Pharisees, hypocrites, dudes, mugwumps, transcendentalists, or something of that sort" (*New York Evening Post*, 6/20/1884). The classic definition of a *mugwump* is "a man with his mug on one side of the fence and his wump on the other" (*attr.* to Harold Willis Dodds, president of Princeton University, 1933–37, in Alfred H. Holt, *Phrase and Word Origins*, 1961). See also MAVERICK, NABOB, and POOH-BAH.

mule. A stubborn, stupid person, from ca. 1470—"Though he were an asse herd or a dulle mule" (George Ashby, *Active Policy of a Prince*)—and still very much with us, though sometimes as a euphemism: "Bill Hickok, you ornery son of a mule" (Jean Arthur to Gary Cooper in *The Plainsman*, film, 1936). People also can be said to be *mulish* or *mule-headed*. Then there is Major Houlihan: "She looks like an Army mule with bosoms" ("M*A*S*H," Channel 5, New York City, 9/30/80). See also HORSE.

mumbo jumbo. Obscure talk or writing, nonsense, gibberish. "Chesterton is like a vile scum on a pond . . . All his slop—it is really modern catholicism to a great extent, the *never* taking a hedge straight, the mumbojumbo of superstition dodging behind clumsy fun and paradox" (Ezra Pound, 1885–1972, on G. K. Chesterton, 1874–1936, in Donald Hook and Lothar Kahn, *Book of Insults and Irreverent Quotations*, 1980).

Mumbo jumbo is an import from Africa, coming from the name of a guardian of villages in the Sudan, symbolized by a masked priest who not only scared away evil spirits but kept tribal women in their places. "A dreadful Bugbear to the Women, call'd Mumbo-Jumbo . . . which is among the Mundingoes a kind of cunning Mystery . . . This is a Thing invented by the Men to keep their Wives in awe" (Francis Moore, *Travels into the Inland Parts of Africa*, 1738). The sense development was from a grotesque object of worship, to an object of unintelligent veneration (see POPINJAY for an example), to meaningless incantation, to—by the end of the nineteenth century—sheer nonsense. See also BUNK.

munchkin. A small person, often figuratively, i.e., a person of small importance. "Tom DeCair, a Justice Department spokesman, characterized Miss [Barbara] Honegger [whose resignation from the Department was accompanied by a blast at the Reagan Administration's record on women's rights] as a 'low-level munchkin,' whose salary was $37,000 a year" (*New York Times*, 8/25/83). The original *munchkins* were dwarfish inhabitants of the land ruled by *The Wonderful Wizard of* Oz (L. Frank Baum, 1900). See also MIDGET.

mush. Meaningless talk, especially of a sickly sentimental sort; nonsense. "Franklin is two-thirds mush and one-third Eleanor" (*attr.*, Alice Roosevelt Longworth, 1884–1980, speaking of her cousins). In a broader sense, *mush* is anything that is soft, pulpy, and yielding. "Mondale is mush. He's weak, and his managers know it, and they're scared" (Senator Gary Hart, Democrat, Colorado) on former Vice President Walter F. Mondale, *New York Times*, 1/6/84).

Variants include *mushmouth*, for someone who talks as though as his mouth were filled with it (which is a redundancy, since *mush* by itself also is slang for the mouth) and *mush-head*, for someone who is none too bright. And we have it on the authority of Senator Gordon J. Humphrey (Republican, New Hampshire) that the U.S. State Department is "full of weaklings and sissies and people with mush for brains" (*New York Times*, 8/19/82).

The original *mush* that is porridge dates to the seventeenth century and apparently arose as an alteration of *mash*. The figurative senses began to appear in the nineteenth century, e.g., "I hate, where I looked for . . . a manly resistance, to find a mush of concession: (Ralph Waldo Emerson, "Friendship," 1841). See also BALONEY, MEALYMOUTHED, PAP, SAP, and the *mush* in WIMP.

mustang. A wild or half-wild person, as well as a wild or half-wild horse, especially in the military, where a *mustang* officer is one who has been promoted from the enlisted ranks or who has jumped directly from civilian life to officer rank. Both meanings date to before the Civil War, but the first is more common today. See also HORSE.

mustard, can't cut the. Unable to perform satisfactorily; not able to hack it, so to speak. The expression has been dated to the early twentieth century, appearing first in positive form: "I looked around and found a proposition that exactly cut the mustard" (O. Henry, *Heart of the West*, 1907). The precise origin of the metaphor is unclear. It has been suggested that the phrase is an alteration of *can't pass muster;* that it alludes to the difficulty of cutting mustard plants, which may grow twelve feet tall but have to be brought down gently in order to avoid scattering seed; and, most likely, that it derives from the earlier slang use of *mustard* in the phrases *the proper mustard* and *all the mustard,* meaning that which was the genuine article, the best thing, in turn from the hotness and sharpness of really good mustard. Note that it does not follow that life is over just because one *can't cut the mustard,* anymore. As a not-so-sweet young thing tells a gracefully aging Paul Newman in *The Color of Money* (film, 1986): "If you're too old to cut the mustard, you can still lick the jar." See also CANDLE TO, CAN'T HOLD A.

mutt. A woman, especially a homely one; a DOG. "The consultant, testifying for the defense in Miss [Christine] Craft's $1.2-million sex-discrimination trial, was heard on tapes played for the jury to say: 'Is she a mutt?' " (AP, 8/3/83). A variation on the theme: "You should have seen my high school picture. What a bow-wow!" (Joan Rivers, TV ad for MCI, Channel 8, Hartford, Connecticut, 4/29/85).

Current connotations to the contrary, the homely *mutt* actually is a sheep, not a mongrel dog. An Americanism from around the turn of this century, *mutt* is an abbreviation of *muttonhead,* meaning a stupid, bumbling BLOCKHEAD (remember the *Mutt and Jeff* comic strip?). With the acquisition of a feminine sense, the term has come practically full circle: *mutton* being an old epithet (from the sixteenth century) for a loose woman, often in the phrases *laced mutton* or *piece of mutton.* The term also referred to sexual intercourse (a man might be said *to be fond of his mutton* or, if a frequenter of brothels, *to be a mutton-monger*) as well as to a woman's private parts (prostitutes were said *to hawk their mutton*). A common Cockney expression from the nineteenth century for an old woman attired as a young one was *mutton dressed up to look like lamb.* This seems to have derived from *old ewe, drest lamb fashion,* recorded by Captain Francis Grose in *A Classical Dictionary of the Vulgar Tongue* (1796). Eric Partridge has suggested that the shift in the metaphor from the animal to the animal's flesh may have corresponded with the disappearance of sheep from metropolitan London. See also SHEEP.

N

nabob. An important or—more to the point—a self-important person, most famously in an alliterative phrase devised by William Safire, while serving as a speechwriter for Vice President Spiro Agnew: "In the United States today, we have more than our share of nattering nabobs of negativism" (address, San Diego, California, 9/11/70).

A *nabob* or *nawab* originally was a viceroy or deputy governor in the Mogul Empire. The term was extended by the British rulers of India in the eighteenth century to anyone of high rank or great wealth, particularly an Englishman who returned home with a large fortune. In the United States, the word was associated especially with Southern plantation owners, usually in a disrespectful context, e.g. "The nabobs of highborn Virginia would run before an old woman" (Anne Royall, *Mrs. Royall's Southern Tour*, 1830). For similar honorifics, see MUGWUMP and POOH-BAH.

nag. To scold; a scold, or a horse. "A Woman with Horse Sense Never Becomes a Nag" (sign, Satsuma Gardens restaurant, Crescent City, Florida, noted by Calvin Trillin, *Third Helpings*, 1983). See also SHREW.

The scold, almost invariably female, and the horse, usually a worn-out one, actually represent two different words. The sense of constant complaining or tormenting comes from the Old Norse *gnaga*, to bite, while the *nag* that is a horse derives from the Middle Dutch *negghe*, in turn most likely from a German root that imitates the sound that a horse makes, i.e., *neigh*. The convergence of the two meanings, as exemplified by the Crescent City sign, probably has been aided by the secondary use of *nag*, horse, to refer to any woman, especially an oft-ridden one, i.e., a whore. For example, in Shakespeare's play, when Cleopatra deserts Antony at the battle of Actium, one of the Roman commander's friends terms her a "ribaudred nag," which translates as "foul mare" (Antony and Cleopatra, 1606–07). Of course, lewd women frequently are characterized as horses; see also HACK, HARRIDAN, and JADE.

namby-pamby. Weakly sentimental, insipid, ineffective, WISHY-WASHY. "I do not want you to think this conservative approach, this safe approach, which I think is the proper thing to do, is going to be a namby-pamby shuttle program" (Admiral Richard H. Truly, director of NASA's space shuttle program, *New York Times*, 3/26/86).

Namby-pamby is a living relic of a famous literary feud: It is a rhyme on *Amby*, a diminutive of *Ambrose*, the reference originally being to Ambrose Phillips (1675?–1749), who had the curious misfortune of having his pastoral poems praised too highly. The misfortunate part was that this praise aroused the jealousy of another author of pastorals by the name of Alexander Pope. He proceeded to assault Phillips and, though he really didn't need help in battles of this sort (see WASP), his friends rushed to his aid. Among them was the poet Henry Carey, who in 1726 parodied some verses Phillips had written for children. In the process, Carey coined *namby-pamby*:

> Namby Pamby's doubly mild,
> Once a man, and twice a child . . .
> Now he pumps his little wits
> All by little tiny bits.

Pope approved highly and incorporated the insult into one of the preliminary versions (1733) of *The Dunciad*: "Beneath his reign shall . . . Namby Pamby be prefer'd for Wit."

Poor Phillips! He seems to have been unjustly maligned, considering that he also edited *A Collection of Old Ballads . . . With Introductions Historical and Critical*, which contained such golden oldies as:

> And Joan of Arc play'd in the dark with the Knights
> of Languedock,
> But Jane Shore met King Edward, and gave him Knock
> for Knock.

The pun in this gem of country wit is on *nock*, which means "notch," as in the nock in the butt of an arrow, or the notch that is found in a person's butt—or elsewhere. The exact date of its composition is unclear, but Jane Shore attracted the notice of Edward IV around 1470 and became his mistress shortly thereafter, making this an early example of the use of *knock* in a sexual sense, prefiguring the modern KNOCK UP. It also suggests that Ambrose Phillips was not so namby-pamby after all.

nanny goat. A female goat (*nanny* is a diminutive of *Nancy*), as distinguished from a billy goat, and a generalized insult from the eighteenth century to the present. "Telling me that my father was a beggar man and my mother a nanny-goat" (Thomas Day, *History of Little Jack*, 1788). "Egypt has become a hostage to Israel and the Americans. It has been transformed into a nanny goat feeding their children while Egypt's people starve" (Colonel Muammar el-Qaddafi, Libyan head of state, *New York Times*, 8/20/84).

Nanny goat also appears prominently in a rhyme that children often recite when a police officer is in sight, though not close enough to hear:

> Brass buttons,
> Blue coat,
> Go chase
> A nanny goat.

This rhyme was popular in the suburbs of New York City in the 1940s. Undoubtedly, it is much older. Just how much older is impossible to say. It seems significant that *blue* and *blew coate* for "policeman" go back to Elizabethan times. See also COP, GOAT, PIG, and *Nancy* in MOLL.

narrowback. An American of Irish extraction, who either cannot or will not perform honest labor. "Irish informants use . . . *narrowback* for a second generation

Irishman who has neither the need, the desire nor the physical equipment to do the work his father had to do" (American Dialect Society, *Publications*, 1964, XLII). See also IRISH.

narrow-minded. Small-minded, bigoted; from 1625 (*OED*). Ernest Hemingway (1899–1961) did not endear himself to the citizens of Oak Park, Illinois, when it was reported that he had characterized his birthplace as a town of "broad lawns and narrow minds."

nasty. Disgusting, filthy, offensive, indecent. The noxious meanings of *nasty* loomed so large in the minds of Americans in the nineteenth century that they expunged the word itself from their vocabularies. As noted in the *OED* (Volume N, 1906–07), "*nasty* is not commonly used by polite speakers" in the United States. Thus, *nasty* was one of the words expurgated by American publishers of *Tom Brown's School Days* (1857). As late as 1935, *nasty* was cited as a "coarse" or "obscene" word by eighteen of J. M. Steadman's students at Emory University in Atlanta, Georgia, tying it for sixteenth place (with *slobber*) on his list of taboo terms; see BELCH for the grim details. *Nasty* is of additional interest for having a surprisingly obscure etymology. One guess is that it comes from the Old French *nastre*, bad, strange; another is that it is related to the Dutch *nestig*, from *nest*, as in bird's nest—specifically, in the case of the *nasty nestig*, a foul and filthy one.

nebbish. A pitiful, ineffectual, helpless, hapless, luckless excuse for a person; a nobody; a LOSER. "You want me to be a nebbish and do nothing—not prosecute—when we get tough cases which could go either way?" (Bronx, New York, District Attorney Mario Merola, *New York Times*, 5/28/87).

Nebbish is Yiddish, a softened pronunciation of *nebekh* (rendered variously as *nebech, nebbech, nebbich,* and so on). It may also be used as an interjection to express dismay or commiseration. The oldest example of the word in the *OED* is from Israel Zangwill's *Children of the Ghetto* (1892). *Nebbish* jokes are legion, e.g., "A nebech is sometimes defined as the kind of person who always picks up—what a *shlemiel* knocks over" and the wisecrack "When a *nebech* leaves the room, you feel as if someone came in" (Leo Rosten, *The Joys of Yiddish*, 1968). See also SCHLEMIEL.

Ned in the first (or **third**) **reader.** Not so bright, inept, naïve. The expression was a favorite of Casey Stengel's: "Naïveté was 'Ned in the Third Reader,' often used in reverse: 'He ain't no Ned in the Third Reader, you know'" (Robert W. Creamer, *Stengel: His Life and Times*, 1984). Casey was from K.C. (Kansas City), and the expression is an old one in that part of the country. For example, President Harry S Truman was castigated on the editorial page of the *Stone County News-Oracle* in Galena, Missouri, for "ineptness that makes him look like Ned in the first reader" (3/5/48, in Vance Randolph and George P. Wilson, *Down in the Holler*, 1953). See also MOLL for *Polly in the primer* and RIBBON CLERK.

Negro. Black. "And while the lawyers [Alton H. Maddox, Jr., and C. Vernon Mason] speak of building coalitions among blacks, they have alienated black elected officials and civic leaders by calling them 'Uncle Tom' or—their ultimate insult—'Negro'" (*New York Times*, 6/9/88).

Negro has been riding a linguistic roller coaster for the past several hundred years, regarded as a "good" word in the eighteenth century, as a "bad" one for much of the nineteenth century, then as a "good" one, and now as a "bad" one again. It means simply *black*, deriving from either the Spanish or Portuguese word for that color, *negro*, and ultimately from the Latin word for black, *niger*, which also is the ancestor of NIGGER. It has been employed in English to refer to black people from Africa since at least 1555 (*OED*).

Originally a neutral term, *Negro* was used in the eighteenth century as a euphemism for SLAVE. For example, *Negro quarter*, first recorded in 1734, is considerably older than *slave quarter*, from 1837. It was because of the association of the word with slavery, however, that after the Civil War onetime slaves preferred to be called *freedmen, freedwomen, colored people*, or *Afro-Americans*.

The return of *Negro* to public favor can be dated to 1890, when the Census Bureau adopted this term on the advice of Booker T. Washington; previously, the bureau had tried to classify dark people by the shade of their skins, from *black* through *mulatto* and *quadroon* to the almost white *octoroon*. Still, it was the National Association for the Advancement of *Colored* People that was founded in 1909, and *colored gentleman* and *colored lady* were considered more refined than their *Negro* equivalents by many people for many years thereafter.

During most of this period, it also was considered poor form to use the English word for *negro*, i.e., *black*, as this word was freighted with many negative associations, all opposed to the "goodness" and "purity" of *white*. Thus, the great cabaret singer Bricktop (short for Ada Beatrice Queen Victoria Louise Virginia Smith) recalled how she started her career in Chicago about 1910: "I was in the chorus of a Negro theater at 15—don't say 'black,' I hate 'black,' I'm 100 percent American Negro with a trigger Irish temper" (*New York Times*, 1/1/84).

The avoidance of *black* created a linguistic vacuum that was filled over the years by a host of other color-related terms. Among them: *blue* (a very dark black), *chocolate drop*, CROW, *darky* (from 1775, most famously in "The Darktown Strutters Ball" of 1915, and a word whose inclusion in Stephen Foster's songs has contributed to the decline in their popularity), DINGE, *dusky, ebony* (a nineteenth-century term that continues to enjoy some use, as in *Ebony* magazine, founded in 1945, and the Ebony Horsewomen, a riding club organized in Bloomfield, Connecticut, in 1984), EIGHTBALL, *ink* (remember the singing group the Ink Spots?), *moke* (from mocha), *pink-toes* or *pinky* (a light-complexioned black woman), SCHVARTZE (Yiddish for *black*), *shade, shine* ("A 'shine' is always a negro, so called, possibly, from the highlights on his countenance," Jack London, *The Road*, 1907), *smoke*, SPADE, and YELLOW (or *yaller* or *high-yaller*, often applied to a very light-skinned woman). Of course, black people also use color terms for Caucasians; see WHITEY.

Black began to become beautiful in the 1960s, less than a decade after the major TV networks banned (1957) Stephen Foster's "Old Black Joe" because of the then-noxious word. *Black's* ascendancy was due partly to pride at seeing Africans take charge of their own countries (Ghana became independent on March 6, 1957) and partly to the domestic influence of the Black Muslims (founded in 1931), especially Malcolm X (assassinated in 1965). Claude Brown, writing before the Black Panthers had been formed (the Student Nonviolent Coordinating Committee adopted the black panther as a political emblem in 1965) and before *black power* had become a rallying cry (1966), noted the phenomenon: "He started raising his voice and screaming this stuff about the white devils and the great black man. This was funny, because Alley was a very light-skinned guy, and he'd always been aware of it. It seemed as though, under this new Muslim movement, everybody was becoming real black and becoming proud of it" (*Manchild in the Promised Land*, 1965). The panther image, by the way, almost certainly came from M. S. Handler's introduction to Malcolm X's *Autobiography*, published the year before he was killed; in it, Handler noted that his own wife, after meeting Malcolm for the first time, remarked, "You know, it was like having tea with a black panther."

It followed inevitably that as *black* was adopted proudly by young activists, *Negro*, now associated with an older, seemingly more subservient generation, once more became a pejorative, as exemplified in the verbal attacks mounted by Messrs. Maddox and Mason, noted at the beginning of this entry, or, from the preceding decade: "Upon spotting the Afro-American, the Ghanians shouted out, 'Hey, Negro!' The other . . . retorted angrily, 'I'm a Black Man, not a Negro. Don't call me Negro' " (*Black World*, 5/73).

And the pendulum continues to swing, most recently with the promotion of *African-American* as a replacement for *black*. "To be called African-Americans has cultural integrity. It puts us in our proper historical context. Every ethnic group in this country has a reference to some land base, some historical cultural base. African-Americans have hit that level of cultural maturity" (Reverend Jesse Jackson, AP, 12/21/88). Substitution of *African-American* for *black* would leave the Bureau of the Census with a puzzling contradiction in terms, however. What about the Chinese, Indians, Arabs, and others who have come to this country from Africa? Some of them may have to be counted in Bureau records as *white African-Americans*.

See also ANN, BOOGIE, BOY, COON, JIG, KAFFIR, OREO, PICKANINNY, SAMBO, SPOOK, UNCLE TOM, and ZULU.

nerd (nurd). A stupid person, especially one who is socially unacceptable. "If you've seen one nerd—a four-eyed, egg-headed individual with a plastic pencil holder in his breast pocket and a song in his heart—have you seen them all?" (*New York Times*, 7/11/87, review of the film *Revenge of the Nerds II: Nerds in Paradise*).

Nerds come in both sexes, e.g., "I was a nerd. I was skinny, flat-chested and miserable. I spent a lot of Saturday nights dancing with the doorknobs in my room" (Anne Beatts, *Wall Street Journal*, 10/4/82). The word has even been converted into feminine form, as in "One day he met a girl that was just his type, if you know what I mean. She was a nerdess, a girl nerd" (Michael McGrath, Booth Free School, Roxbury, Connecticut, *Printing Press*, 4/85).

Nerd seems to have arisen among students in the 1960s. The 1975 supplement to the *Dictionary of American Slang* gives an example of the word's use from 1965, but it was recorded earlier as *nard* by Lawrence Postman III in the May 1964 issue of *American Speech*. The term might have originated as an alteration of *nert* (itself from NUT), but the *urd* spelling makes a rhyme with TURD equally probable. It has been established that use of the word among adults is almost, but not quite, libelous: "The town councilman wouldn't allow wet t-shirt contests in a local pub. So a local D.J. called him a nerd. The councilman sued for libel. But the D.J. won. And ERC paid the contest fees" (ad for Employers Reinsurance Corp., *Columbia Journalism Review*, 3-4/83). See also DORK, DWEEB, FOOL, GEEK, JERK, and SQUARE.

nester. A farmer or other homesteader in cattle-grazing region, according to the cattle raisers; also called a *landsucker*. Preserved in Western books and movies, the term had a real bite to it at the outset: "[A sheep man is] a tramp, an ingrate, a 'Nester,' and a liar" (Fort Griffin [Texas] *Echo*, 1/3/1880). See also HICK.

nigger. A black person, unless otherwise qualified, as in "Arabs were called 'sand niggers' in discussions about State Department issues in the Middle East" (Terrel H. Bell, recalling discussions in the Reagan Administration, during his tenure as Secretary of Education, 1981–84, *New York Times*, 10/21/87). And in the primary sense: "Today Borrego Springs [California] residents have forgotten—or have never known—that once this place was known as Nigger Springs. It was called that in the 1870s after a black man named Jim Green who lived and explored in the valley" (*Borrego Sun*, 3/2/89). (*Nigger* was once a fairly common place name. It has been replaced in most instances by *Negro*, as in Negro Mountain, Maryland, and Negrohead Mountain, California. Meanwhile, the newer, nicer name of the desert town of Borrego is Spanish for "lamb"; the term was used generally in the American Southwest when referring to sheep and appears in other place names, e.g., Borrego Arroyo, New Mexico.)

Nigger itself is a prime example of how a word's meaning depends on context. Among most educated white people today, this is a hateful term, rarely employed, yet among blacks, it continues to be used casually, often approvingly. Thus, discussing the word's nuances for blacks: "In the singular, the word was always applied to a man who had distinguished himself in some situation that brought [my family's] approval for his strength, intelligence or drive. 'Did Johnny *really* do that?' 'I'm telling you that nigger pulled in $6,000 of overtime last year. Said he got enough for a down payment on a house.' When used with a possessive adjective by a woman—'my nigger'—it became a term of endearment for husband or boy-friend. . . . In the plural, it became a description of some group within the community that had overstepped the bounds of decency as my family defined it: Parents who neglected their children, a drunken couple who fought in public, people who simply refused to look for work, those with excessively dirty mouths or unkempt households were all 'trifling niggers' " (Gloria Naylor, *New York Times*, 2/19/86).

It is a major mistake, of course, for a black person to use the word in front of a white one: "Before I realized what I was doing, I said 'Minetti . . . tell that nigger not to do it no more 'cause you ain't playin' with him. That's all you gotta do.' Tucker looked at me and said, 'Brown, damn, man, you shouldn't have done that.' It was real wrong to call somebody a nigger in front of a paddy boy" (Claude Brown, *Manchild in the Promised Land*, 1965). And it is even wronger, naturally, for a white to use the word in front of a black: "He started to call me a dirty yellow-bellied nigger . . . So I was glad when he was shot" (*Home of the Brave*, film, 1949).

With their talent for latching on to words that hurt, children used to use this one a lot. Recalling her youth in New Orleans, Alice Moser Claudel reported in *American Speech* (Spring–Summer 1975) that white children sometimes teased black ones with:

> Nigger, nigger, never die,
> Black face and shiney eye!

The standard reply to this for a black child, if a girl, was to flick up the back of her skirts and yell, "Your maw!" Or the white child's taunt might be topped with:

I don't eat cabbage
And I don't eat hash.
I'd rather be a nigger
Than poor white trash.

See also POOR WHITE TRASH.

Nigger stems from the Latin, *niger*, black, as does *Negro*, but whereas the latter came directly from the Spanish or Portuguese word for black, *negro*, the former was adapted from the French *nègre*, with the same meaning. The first appearance of *nigger* in its modern spelling is in a poem of 1786 by Robert Burns, but this was preceded by such variants as *negar*, *neeger*, *neger*, *niger*, and *niggor*, reflecting the different dialects of people from northern England and Ireland. Thus, John Rolfe, husband to Pocahontas, recorded in his journal the first shipment of blacks to Virginia: "there came in a Dutch man-of-warre that sold us 20 negars" (8/20/1619). And in the North, the inventory of an estate in the town of Gravesend, now part of Brooklyn, New York, included "One niggor boy" (12/12/1689). Over a period of years, the same person might use different spellings. For instance, Judge Samuel Sewall (best remembered for presiding over the Salem witchcraft trial, then publicly repenting his role), noted in his diary for July 1, 1676, that "Jethro, his Niger, was then taken" by the Indians. (Five days later, Jethro was glad to be "re-taken.") But forty years afterward, Sewall used the modern, preferred form of the word, reporting that "I essay'd . . . to prevent Indians and Negros being Rated [i.e., assessed for taxation] with Horses and Hogs; but could not prevail" (6/22/1716). Typifying the confusion was Noah Webster, America's premier lexicographer, who used *neger* all his life (1758–1843), and who also rendered *zebra* as *zeber* until his revision of 1828.

Amazingly, by today's standards, *nigger* was being used openly, and sometimes without contempt, well into the twentieth century, e.g., Edward Sheldon's play, *The Nigger* (1909) and Carl Van Vechten's novel, *Nigger Heaven* (1926). The first of these is, in effect, a plea for racial tolerance (the governor of a Southern state is told he is part Negro, he is threatened with exposure of this secret, his fiancée rejects him, and then accepts him), while the second, whose title comes from the slang term (from 1875) for the upper balcony of a (usually segregated) theater, is a deeply sympathetic portrait of life in Harlem. The Tulsa, Oklahoma, *Tribune* expressed rather different sentiments, however, when it blamed that city's ghetto uprising in 1921 on "the bad niggers . . . the lowest thing that walks on two feet" (6/1/1921). Or as one of the masters of racist rhetoric, Governor Eugene Talmadge of Georgia, put it in his own inimitable way: "No niggah's 's good as a white man because the niggah's only a few shawt year-ahs from cannibalism" (William Bradford Huie, *American Mercury*, 2/42).

Resistance against use of *nigger* increased during the 1930s, as black newspapers campaigned forcefully against the nonstandard term, often while managing to avoid printing it in full; n----r and N----- were typical evasions. Soon, children were being taught that in "eeny, meeny, miny, mo," it was a "rabbit" or "tiger" that was caught by its toe. By the 1940s, sensitivities were sufficiently aroused for Joseph Conrad's *The Nigger of the Narcissus* (1897) to be removed from open shelves in school libraries; for Marjorie Kinnan Rawlings's *The Yearling* (1938) to be released in a "school edition" (1940) that omitted two passages containing the word; and for Agatha Christie's play *Ten Little Niggers* (1939) to be retitled for American consumption as *Ten Little Indians* and then, even more innocuously, as *And Then There Were None*. Mark Twain still suffers from this backlash, with *Huckleberry Finn* (1885) continually being threatened by school censors because it features a noble character called "Nigger Jim." Most notably, *Huckleberry Finn* was banned for a short time in 1982 at—of all places—the Mark Twain Intermediate School in Fairfax, Virginia.

The taboo has grown so strong that such phrases as *to work like a nigger* (*OED*, from 1836), *nigger in the woodpile* (1852), and *nigger-lover* (1909, but most likely hurled at abolitionists many years before) have gone by the boards. No one of any refinement eats *nigger toes* (Brazil nuts) or *nigger heels* (hazel nuts) any more. Nor is it recommended that any white person today tell any black person that he or she is acting *niggardly*, even though this word, probably from the Middle English *nig*, miser, has nothing in common with the other but its sound.

Not even as a joke can a member of the outgroup (i.e., a white) now use the word safely—as Lenny Bruce found to his cost on December 12, 1964, when he appeared before the New York State Court of Appeals, whose members included Thurgood Marshall, later to become the first black member of the Supreme Court of the United States. Acting as his own lawyer, Bruce, who had been convicted for giving an "indecent, immoral, impure" performance at the Café Au Go Go in Manhattan, went into his nightclub routine in an effort to demonstrate to the judges that it was not obscene. As New York lawyer Martin Garbus remembers the event:

> The judges listened with interest. Lenny first talked about America's misuse of Christ symbols. He then went into a sketch commenting on the kinds of justice white men can expect from black juries, pointing out that black men would treat whites as badly as they themselves had been treated. He concluded with his imitation of the outraged liberal saying, "They gave me twenty years for raising my voice—those niggers!" Marshall's head jerked up and he nearly dropped a pen from his hand. Bruce saw Marshall's face, stumbled, tried bravely to explain the joke, but could not. Then he knew he had lost his case and sat down (in Albert Goldman, from the journalism of Lawrence Schiller, *Ladies and Gentlemen, Lenny Bruce!!*, 1974).

It was just about the time of Bruce's misstep that *black*, for many years also a pejorative term, was becoming beautiful. For more on this topic, see NEGRO.

nincompoop. A fool, a BLOCKHEAD. "We are fools, dolts, and nincompoops" ("To Serve Them All Our Days," WNET-TV, New York City 10/17/82). "NINKUMPOOP, or NINCUMPOOP. A foolish fellow; also one who never saw his wife's ****" (Captain Francis Grose, *A Classical Dictionary of the Vulgar Tongue*, 1796, asterisks in original).

Samuel Johnson suggested in his dictionary (1775) that *nincompoop* derived from the Latin *non compos* [*mentis*], of unsound mind, but etymology was not his strong point, and early forms of the word suggest some other origin. It may come from a personal name, Nicholas or Nicodemus (in French, *nicodème* is a fool), plus the obsolete *poop*, to deceive or to befool. There's a web of similar meanings here and they tend to reinforce one another. *Nicodème* also is the source of *noddy*, an old English word for a fool, while *poop* in the sense of "to cheat" comes from the Dutch *poep*, a fool. In addition, the two English terms have been combined into *poop-noddy*, another obsolete word for a fool or SIMPLETON but one that certainly seems colorful enough to warrant revival. See also FOOL, NINNY, and POOP.

ninny. A fool, a SIMPLETON; from the sixteenth century, and probably from *Ninny* as the nickname for *Innocent* (a parallel to *Ned* for *Edward*), with some reinforcement from the combining of "*an innocent.*" John Byrom wedged the word nicely into an epigram (1725) on the rivalry between George Frederic Handel and his former associate, Giovanni Battista Bononcini:

> Some say that Signor Bononcini,
> Compared to Handel's a mere ninny;
> Others aver, to him, that Handel
> Is scarcely fit to hold a candle.
> Strange that such high dispute should be
> Twixt Tweedle-dum and Tweedle-dee.

See also BLOCKHEAD; CANDLE TO, CAN'T HOLD A; and FOOL.

Nip. A Japanese, as in *Bugs Bunny Nips the Nips*, a Warner Brothers cartoon short, released 4/22/44. The derogative clipping of *Nipponese* was coined as part of the American war effort within a month or two of the Japanese attack on Pearl Harbor on December 7, 1941. The term is patterned on the older JAP.

nit. An insignificant or stupid person. The insignificant sense is the older, dating to at least the sixteenth century: "Thou flea, thou nit, thou winter cricket thou!" (William Shakespeare, *The Taming of the Shrew*, 1593). The stupid *nit*, meanwhile, seems to be a twentieth century innovation, perhaps inspired by the longer NITWIT. A *nit* is very small, of course, being either the egg or young of a LOUSE; hence a person who niggles or *nitpicks* over trifling details is a *nitpicker*.

Nit also has been used to dehumanize people one intends to exterminate. Thus, Colonel John M. Chivington, the "Fighting Parson," instructed the Third Colorado Volunteers as they approached a Cheyenne camp on Sand Creek early on the morning of November 29, 1864: "Kill and scalp all, big and little; nits make lice" (Alvin M. Josephy, ed., *The American Heritage Book of Indians*, 1961). His soldiers followed orders with a vengeance, killing some 200 to 450 Cheyenne, most of them women and children. The operative phrase was not original to Chivington, by the way: *Nits will become lice* has been dated to the early eighteenth century in the sense of "small matters that become important."

Finally, coming to the heart of the matter, there is the *nitty-gritty*. "Get down to the nitty-gritty" was popularized by black civil rights workers in the early 1960s. The phrase is of obscure origin. For sixty years or so, and probably for long before that, many Southern blacks have understood *nitty-gritty* to mean the anus, specifically the area where you hit something, presumably when picking out the nits that used to infest all parts of the bodies of all races in the Southern United States.

Whatever anatomical association the term once had, however, this has been forgotten so completely that even the most fastidious speakers and writers no longer hesitate to use it, e.g., "Soft Soap and Nitty-Gritty" (headline, *New York Times*, 3/31/85).

nitwit. A person with a very small brain—nit-sized, apparently (see NIT), though it also has been suggested that the term derives from the Dutch *niet wit*, "I don't know." *Nitwit* appeared on the scene in the 1920s and has been used more or less continuously ever since. "To be sure, the great Mr. Dickens . . . flagrantly employed his mother as his model for the nit-wit Mrs. Nickleby" (Alexander Woollcott, column from 2/33 in *Long, Long Ago*, 1943). " 'Nitwits,' the new publisher says conversationally, referring to her editorial description of the eight major candidates for the Democratic Presidential nomination . . ." (Nackey Scripps Loeb, of the Manchester, New Hampshire, *Union Leader*, in *New York Times*, 2/23/84).

Similar constructions include *dimwit, fat-witted* (see FAT), *half-wit, short-witted, woolly-witted* (see *wooly-headed* in BLOCKHEAD), and, of course, *witless*. Shakespeare was very good at this sort of thing, long before *nitwit* was ever thought of. For example: "Thou hast pared thy wit o' both sides and left nothing i' the middle" (*King Lear*, 1605–06) and "Look, he's winding up the watch of his wit. By and by it will strike" (*The Tempest*, 1611). See also LAMEBRAIN and MORON.

no-good. A worthless person or thing; the modern form (*OED*, 1908) of *good-for-nothing* and *ne'er-do-well*, both dated to the early eighteenth century; sometimes elaborated as *no-gooder* or *no-goodnik*, as in "A parasite, a leech, a bloodsucker—altogether a five-star nogoodnik" (S. J. Perelman, *Crazy Like a Fox*, 1944). See also LOAFER and, for more about the *-nik* family, NUDNIK.

nookie. Sexual intercourse or a woman considered as a sexual partner. "Lenny . . . could never get enough of nookey" (Albert Goldman, from the journalism of Lawrence Schiller, *Ladies and Gentlemen, Lenny Bruce!!*, 1974). It has been reported that military personnel stationed in Hawaii during World War II suffered grievously from *lackanookie*, also called *lackanookemia* or "that old Hawaiian disease" (*American Speech*, 12/47).

Nookie has been dated to 1928; it is used in *The Front Page*, by Ben Hecht and Charles MacArthur, which opened that year. The word's origin is uncertain. One possibility is that it derives from *nook*, in the sense of a small corner or recess, which would be in keeping with the traditional slang use of *cleft, crack, crevice*, SLIT, and similar terms for the female pudendum. Another is that *nookie* is a variant of *nug*, used from the seventeenth through the nineteenth centuries to refer both to coition and to a woman, sometimes fondly, as in "She's my nug." If the latter theory is correct, then the sexual *nookie* is a relative of the playful *nudge*. See also PUSSY.

Nosey Parker. One who snoops or pries into other people's business. It has been suggested that the phrase honors Matthew Parker, Archbishop of Canterbury (1559–75), who kept close watch on what other people were doing. The earliest written example of the phrase comes only from 1907, however. This appears to favor the alternate explanation that *Nosey Parker* originally referred to a loiterer in London's Hyde Park who tried to sneak looks at couples making love. *Parker*, then, may not be an eponym, but simply a person who frequents a park (park keepers used to be known as *parkers*). The inquisitive *nosey*, meanwhile, also seems to be of fairly modern vintage, having been dated just to 1882, though *to nose*, meaning to detect or discover, is underworld slang from the eighteenth century, as is *a nose*, meaning an informer. By the early 1800s, *nose* referred specifically to a paid spy for the police. (A *nose*, thus, was the same as a *nark*, a current term for such a person, which also dates to the nineteenth century and which derives from *nak*, a Romany word meaning—no surprise here—*nose.*) See also BUTTINSKI, PEEPING TOM, SNITCH, and SNOOP.

notorious. Infamous, as in *notorious criminal, notorious gambler, The Notorious Landlady* (film, 1962), and so on. *Notorious* started out in the sixteenth century as a neutral term for characterizing that which was well-known, a matter of common knowledge, but the label was used so often to point out conspicuously bad people or things that its meaning was affected for the worse. As late as 1866, in the Brampton Lectures that established him as the greatest Anglican preacher of his time, the Reverend Henry P. Liddon could churn out such a sentence as "The worship of Christ by the early Christians was a living and notorious practice." But *notorious* has become too *notorious* to use this way today.

nudnik. An obnoxious pest, an irritating bore. "The writer who writes about himself all the time must become a bore, just like the man who talks all the time about himself. When the writer becomes the center of his attention, he becomes a *nudnik.* And a *nudnik* who believes he is profound is even worse than a plain *nudnik*" (Issac B. Singer and Richard Burgin, *Conversations with Issac Bashevis Singer*, 1985).

Nudnik is a classic Yiddish word, based on the Russian *núdnyĭ*, tedious, boring, plus -*nik*, one who. The -*nik* suffix has enjoyed considerable use in English since World War II—especially since the orbiting of the first *Sputnik* on October 4, 1957. The ending often has a derogatory connotation, as in *nudnik*, and is particularly useful for stigmatizing those who are going against society's mainstream, e.g., *beatnik* (coined by *San Francisco Chronicle* columnist Herb Caen, 4/2/58), *draftnik*, *no-goodnik, peacenik, refusenik* (a Russian term for Soviet citizens, usually Jews, who have been refused permission to emigrate), *sicknik*, and *Vietnik*. The suffix also may be employed humorously, however, as in the *Daily Worker* headline, following the launching of *Sputnik* 2, with the dog, Laika, aboard: "Every Dognik Has Its Daynik" (5/15/58). See also SCHMUCK.

numskull. A stupid person, a BLOCKHEAD, from the eighteenth century, and from *numb*, in the sense of unfeeling, incapacitating paralysis, plus *skull*. "I remember not to have known a great numbskull than thou art" (Jonathan Swift, letter, pre-1724). See also DUMMY.

nut. A crazy, stupid, silly, or eccentric person. The meaning of *nut* has tended to soften in time as polite people have come to realize that crazy people have feelings, too. "On the N.B.C. network, it is forbidden to call any character a nut; you have to call him a screwball" (*New Yorker*, 12/23/50).

In its heyday, from roughly 1900 through 1950, *nut* demonstrated its power by spawning a remarkable number of expressions, all deriving from the earlier use of *nut* as slang for the head. Thus, the crazy one might be said to be a *nutbrain* or *nuthead*; to be *nuts, nutsy*, or even *as nutty as a fruitcake*; to belong in a *nut college* or *nuthouse*; to be in need of a treatment by a *nut doctor* or *nutpick*; or *to be off his* (or *her*) *nut*. " 'Kill you?' said Scully again to the Swede. 'Kill you? Man, you're off your nut' " (Stephen Crane, "The Blue Hotel," 1898). See also SQUIRREL.

Context is everything, of course, as *nuts* also are testicles. Captain Francis Grose recorded *nutmegs* in the testicular sense in *A Classical Dictionary of the Vulgar*

Tongue (1796). Because of this ulterior meaning, the rude dismissal *Nuts!*, or, in full, *Nuts to you!*, is the functional equivalent of *Balls!* or *All balls!* See also BALONEY.

The anatomical connection, no doubt, was responsible for the flowering of the euphemism *nerts* (from ca. 1925) as well as for the banning of *nuts* from Hollywood soundtracks under the Motion Picture Production Code. "Please eliminate the expression 'nuts to you' from Egbert's speech" (request from the Hays Office regarding the script of *The Bank Dick*, 1940). It also leads to such puns as, from Ray Allen Billington's *Limericks Historical and Hysterical* (1981):

> A woman's leader named Stutz
> Is known to have plenty of guts.
>   When asked what she'd need
>   To be totally freed,
> She snarled at her questioner, "Nuts."

O

oaf. A stupid, clumsy fellow. "You great ill-fashioned oaf, with scarce sense enough to keep your mouth shut" (Oliver Goldsmith, *She Stoops to Conquer*, 1773). *Oaf*, from the early seventeenth century, is a variant of *auf*, from the Old English *aelf*, i.e., elf. Originally, then, an *oaf* was an elf's child, a changeling, deformed in mind or body, who had been substituted for a normal human child by the little people, as in "Though he be an aufe, a ninny, a monster, a goos-cap" (Robert Burton, *Anatomy of Melancholy*, 1621). See also JERK.

obtuse. Dull, dumb, i.e., not acute, whether in intellect, sensitivity, or both, and sometimes by design, as in "Stop being so obtuse, dear—you know very well that tomorrow is my mother's birthday." People as well as objects have been described since the sixteenth century as *obtuse*, from the past participle of the Latin *obtundere*, to blunt. See also DUMB.

O.D. An intensifier, usually in the phrase "That's pure O.D. nonsense." This is a common Southern expression, which probably does not stand for *Olive Drab*, though it was often heard in the Army in the mid-1950s, before the uniform was switched to bus-driver green. Various guesses have been made at what the initials stand for: *Ox Dung* (an analogy with *B.S.*); *Old Devil*; a reversal of *Darn Old*; and *Old Damn* (perhaps through elision of *Old* to *Ol'* to *O*). Whatever, it seems the initials serve a euphemistic function, toning down an even more intense thought.

oddball. A queer or crazy person, an eccentric, sometimes a BORE or DRIP; popular since World War II. "Lenny and Mr. Bamford are part of a four-man comedy act called the Oddballs, whose specialty is a striptease dance done with balloons" (*Wall Street Journal*, 11/4/85). See also DORK and FOUL BALL.

ofay (or **fay**). A white person, to a black one—or to a white one pretending to be a black one, as in Jonathan Winters' impersonation of a Harlem disc jockey's pitch for hair straightener: "You cats want to score for those fine ofay broads, don'tcha? Well, man, you gotta get *straight*" (bootleg record of an impromptu recording session, ca. 1955).

Ofay, dated in writing only to 1925, is of uncertain origin. Explanations that have been offered include—in order of increasing probability—that it comes from the French *au lait* (milk); that it is Pig Latin for *foe*; and that it derives from the Yoruba *ófé*, to disappear, as from a powerful enemy, the theory here being that slaves transferred the word that was said for self-protection to the source of the threat itself. See also WHITEY.

off the wall. Eccentric, bizarre, CRAZY. "This is totally off the wall" (Chicago Bears quarterback Jim McMahon, denying a report that he had called the women of New

Orleans "sluts," *New York Times*, 1/24/86). "During my tenure as Secretary [of Education], however, proponents of the doctrines of the far right advanced many far-reaching and, in my view, radical and off-the-wall ideas" (T. H. Bell, *Phi Delta Kappan*, 3/86).

Off the wall, from the 1960s, fills a void that was created as *off [one's] trolley*, from ca. 1900, was rendered obsolete by changing modes of public transport. The precise origin of the modern metaphor is not known; it may stem from the erratic bounces that sometimes occur in squash, handball, etc. Walls, however, have loomed large in allusions to craziness, probably ever since people were confined behind them, e.g., such phrases as *to go up the wall, to climb the wall(s)*, and, for emphasis, *to drive [someone] up one wall and down the other*. See also MAD; SCREW LOOSE, A; and UP AGAINST THE WALL.

Okie. A migrant worker, originally an Oklahoman refugee from the Dust Bowl of the 1930s, but quickly extended to include to any person of rural origin and manners. "Okie use' ta mean you was from Oklahoma. Now it means you're a dirty son-of-a-bitch" (John Steinbeck, *The Grapes of Wrath*, 1939). See also HILLBILLY, PIKER, and, for other examples of insulting condensations of generic names, JAP.

old maid. An elderly spinster, or a timid, fussy person who acts like one. A tombstone epitaph, recorded in *American Speech* (4/26):

> Here lies Ann Mann; she lived an
> Old maid and died an old Mann

Old maid, from 1530, almost always appears in a negative context, e.g., from *The Ladies Calling* (1673) "By the author of The Whole duty of man:" "An old Maid is now . . . look'd on as the most calamitous Creature in nature." (The card game, by the way, has been dated to 1831.)

The *old* modifier is not always used in a disparaging way. It can connote expertise, as in *old hand* or *old pro*; authority, as in *the old man*, who is the captain of a vessel; or even camaraderie, as in the *old boy network*, whose members help each other out, or those type specimens of white, Southern masculinity, the *good old boys*. In most instances, however, *old* functions as a perjorative intensifier. A sampling:

old bat. An old woman, especially a gossip.

old cocker (or *gaffer* or *fart*). An old man, especially a silly or senile one; often as *alter kocker*, a Yiddish-German expression for the same type of person. This last, frequently abbreviated to *A. K.*, translates as "old shitter," from *alter*, old + *kock*, excrement. Middle-aged men may attain *A.K.* status by acting older than their years.

old fogy. An old person, especially one with outmoded ideas and attitudes; see FOGY.

old goat. An old man, especially with reference to sexual desires if not performance. After Alfred Kinsey's first report, *Sexual Behavior in the Human Male*, was published in 1948, *Time* quoted a little old lady as saying, in effect, "Why bother to do such a study? Everybody knows men are old goats." See GOAT.

old hat. Old-fashioned, outmoded, trite; from 1911 (*OED*), but used previously, in the eighteenth century, with an entirely different meaning: "Old hat; a woman's privities: because frequently felt" (Captain Francis Grose, *A Classical Dictionary of the Vulgar Tongue*, 1796).

old lady. A wife, or woman who serves in that capacity (a girlfriend or mistress) as in *my old lady*; a mother; a man with womanish qualities. "Henry James is one of the nicest old ladies I ever met" (*attr*. William Faulkner, 1896–1962).

old man. A husband, or man who serves in that capacity (a boyfriend, lover, pimp); a father, as in the not-so-witty retort, "So's your old man," or, another piece of Americana (ca. 1900):

> Everybody works but father,
> He sits around all day
> Warming himself by the fire,
> Smoking his pipe of clay.
> Mother takes in washing,
> So does sister Ann.
> Everybody works at our house,
> But my old man.

Old Nick. One of many old nicknames for the devil, e.g., *the Old Gentleman, Old Harry, Old Roger*, and *Old Scratch*.

old woman. A wife, mother, or timid, old-womanish FUSSBUDGET, in disparaging use from the fourteenth century unto our own time. "But surely the worst of your old-women are the male ones" (Ezra Pound, *Pavannes & Divisions*, 1918).

one-horse. Small, unimportant—especially as applied to towns; from the nineteenth century. "This poor little one-horse town" (Mark Twain, *The Undertaker's Chat*, 1875). See also PODUNK.

The epithet also has been applied over the years to many other items besides towns, e.g., *one-horse politician, one-horse college, one-horse grocery, one-horse lumber camp*, and, as Oliver Wendell Holmes put it, "I have seen a country-clergyman with a one-story intellect and a one-horse vocabulary" (*The Autocrat of the Breakfast Table*, 1858). See also HORSE.

opportunist. A pragmatist; an attack term in politics, the implication being that the *opportunist* has sacrificed principle on the altar of expediency. Rival politicians also may be said to engage in *opportunist politics*, or act *opportunistically*, and to practice *opportunism*. "The word grew popular in the political lexicon in the fifties, although Arthur Krock accused Senator Robert Taft of playing 'obvious or even opportunistic politics' in 1946" (William Safire, *Safire's Political Dictionary*, 1978). The term had earlier political incarnations, however, being a part of the Socialist-Communist lexicon since ca. 1900, e.g., "Axelrod and Martov . . . have dropped into the opportunist wing of our Party. . . . They have to repeat opportunist phrases . . . to seek . . . some kind of justification for their position" (J. Fineberg, *tr., Selections from Lenin*, 1929). And before that, going back into the nineteenth century, the term was used in French politics, especially with reference to supporters of Léon Gambetta (1838–82), and at the Vatican Council of 1870, where an *opportunist* was one who believed that the time was ripe for promulgating the doctrine of Papal Infallibility. See also TRIMMER.

Oreo. A black person who acts like a white one, according to another black. The term comes from the trade name of the layered cookie, which is black on the outside and white inside. It has been dated to 1968 (*OED*). In extended use: "The Oreo bandit teams were popular for a while. If they hit in a white neighborhood, the white bandit would be the wheel man and his black partner would ride on the floor. Vice versa in a black neighborhood" (Joseph Wambaugh, *The Glitter Dome*, 1981). For another example, see UNCLE TOM; for more about food insults, see KRAUT.

ostrich. A stupid person; specifically, one who ignores reality, from the belief that an ostrich will try to escape a pursuer by burying its head in the sand, thinking it cannot be seen if it itself cannot see. The oldest example in the *OED* of an "Austridge" hiding its head comes from 1623, and the metaphor remains current: "Mrs. [Prime Minister Margaret] Thatcher has described other European leaders as 'ostriches' for not realizing the need for changes in the agricultural structure [of the Common Market]" (*New York Times*, 3/20/84). Ostriches actually do put their heads into the sand, but according to ostrich farmers, it is because they are hungry and searching for something to eat. For more about supposedly stupid birds, see DODO.

out to lunch. Stupid, unaware, not all there, socially unacceptable; sometimes abbreviated *O.T.L.* by teenagers, as in "Who would want to date Henry? He is O.T.L." And if Henry is truly beyond the pale, the phrase might be amplified: "Henry is out to lunch—and closed for the season."

With a few exceptions, such as *out of sight*, which has been "to be excellent" since at least 1896 (*OED*), it is not good to be *out*, e.g., *out in left field; out of [one's] depth, out of [one's] head (gourd or skull); out of it, out of [one's] league; out of line; out of the loop* (or chain of command); *out of the woodwork* (where creepy, crawly things come from, usually political conservatives); *out on a limb; out on [one's] ass*, to be fired, as from a job; and *out to pasture*, to be retired.

ox. A big, strong, awkward person, especially a slow-witted one, typically in such phrases as *clumsy as an ox* and *dumb ox* (see also DUMB). Because he sat in class without saying very much, schoolmates of Thomas Aquinas (ca. 1227–1274) are said to have called him *the dumb ox*, but his teacher Albertus Magnus knew they were wrong, predicting that "The dumb ox will one day fill the world with his lowing" (*Brewer's Dictionary of Phrase and Fable*, rev., Ivor H. Evans, 1970). For more about bovines, see COW.

oyster. A close-mouthed, uncommunicative person. "I never knew anybody so close, you old oyster you!" (J. B. Priestley, *Angel Pavement*, 1930). Then there was William Travers, "the stammering wit of Wall St." (d. 1887), who, after having had to sit through a long monologue on the natural history of oysters, was asked by the speaker if he thought the bivalves had brains. "Well, y-yes," said Travers. "Just enough to keep their mouths shut" (Richard O'Connor, *Courtroom Warrior: The Combative Career of William Travers Jerome*, 1963). Travers, for whom the Travers Stakes, the oldest race for thoroughbreds in the United States, is named, also is credited with a line that later became a fixture in vaudeville acts. Hearing him creep into their bedroom in the wee hours of the morning, his wife awoke and asked, "Is that you, Bill?" His immortal reply: "Y-yes. Wh-who did you expect?" See also CLAM.

P

Paddy. An Irish person, since at least the eighteenth century, or, in the twentieth-century lingo of blacks and other minorities, any white person. Captain Francis Grose knew the Irish sense and explained its origin correctly: "PADDY. The general name of an Irishman: being the abbreviation of Patrick, the name of the tutelar saint of that island" (*A Classical Dictionary of the Vulgar Tongue*, 1796).

The Irish *Paddy* has been elaborated in various ways, e.g., *Paddyland*, the place where the *Paddies* come from; *paddy wagon*, a police car or van, from the period when the Irish dominated American police forces; *paddywhack*, a stout Irishman, a rage or passion, and a thrashing or firm blow—the kind of smack or whack an angry *Paddy* might give you; and *Paddy boat*, a fishing cutter: "First built in the late [eighteen] fifties by Irish immigrants, the 'Paddy boats' were themselves really immigrants, being modeled after the Galway 'hookers' native to the west coast of Ireland. . . . Toward the end of the century, the Paddy boats faced strong competition from a large fleet of 'Guinnie boats,' manned by rugged Italian immigrants who commonly rowed fifteen or twenty miles in a day" (W. H. Bunting, *Portrait of a Port: Boston 1852–1914*, 1971). See also IRISH.

The extension of *Paddy* to include any white person began among blacks around the time of World War II; see Claude Brown's reference to a *paddy boy* in NIGGER. Or in the words of Piri Thomas, a Puerto Rican who grew up in Harlem: "I dug her paddy-fair face. . . . But I didn't know her name, and I couldn't just start yellin', 'Here I am, paddy girl' " (*Down These Mean Streets*, 1967). See also IRISH and WHITEY.

Personal names frequently are used as generic characterizations and means of addressing individuals whose real names are unknown, with the pejorative connotations coming through most clearly when the names are shortened into their familiar forms. (Everyone knows what familiarity breeds.) Besides *Paddy*, other generics include: *Abe* and *Abie*, a Jew and Jewess; ANN, a white woman; *Biddy*, an Irish maid (from *Bridget*); *Billy*, as in HILLBILLY; *Boris*, a Russian, or Russia itself, as in "Complex geopolitical issues invariably are reduced to a tug-of-wars between the free world and the lackeys of 'Ivan' or 'Boris' " (*Columbia Journalism Review*, 11-12/83); *bud* or *buddy* (thought to have originated as a childish pronunciation of *brother*, and sometimes used as a personal name as well as a nickname, e.g., Lou Costello's partner, Bud Abbott, whose real first name was Winston); CHARLIE, any male, especially a white one; *Chico*, (see CHICANO); *Cuffy*, a black man; DAGO, an Italian, Spaniard, or Portuguese (from *Diego*, James); *Fritz*, a German; *Hans Wurst*, also a German (see KRAUT); HEINIE, another German (from *Heinrich*); HICK (from *Richard*); *hob* (from *Rob*) and *hodge* (from *Roger*) for rural residents; HYMIE, a Jew (from *Hyman*); *Ike* or *Ikey*, also a Jew (from *Isaac*, and note ALIBI IKE's complaint in YID); *Izzy*, yet another personification for any male Jew (from *Isadore*); JACK, any man; *Jack Canuck*, a Canadian (see CANUCK); *jake*, a rude country fellow (from *Jacob* and perhaps related to YOKEL; *Jean* or *Johnny Crapaud*, a Frenchman (see FROG); JERRY, a German; *Jock*, a Scotchman (see JOCK); *Joe*, an average guy, as in *Joe Blow, Joe Schmo, Joe Six-pack*, and *G.I. Joe*; *John*, any man, generally less opprobrious than the less formal JACK or JOCK, whether alone, as in the prostitute's faceless *john*, or in such combinations as *John Bull* (an Englishman), *John Chinaman* (see CHINAMAN), *John Doe, John Farmer, John Lack-Latin*, and *John Thomas*; *Liza*, a black woman; *Mack*, any man, but especially a Scotchman; *Mandy*, a black woman; MICK and *Mike*, both Irishmen; *Nicholas Frog*, a Dutchman (see FROG); *Olaf* and *Ole*, both Swedes; *Pat*, another Irishman; PATSY, a dupe or fall guy; (*Chief*) *Rain-in-the-Face*, an American Indian; *Rastus*, a black man; RUBE (from *Reuben*); SAMBO, brother to *Rastus*; *Sawney*, a Scotsman and also a fool (from *Sandy*); *Sitting Bull*, an American Indian; *Taffy*, a Welshman (from *Davy*, short for *David*, patron saint of Wales) and most famously, in a rhyme that already was old in the seventeenth century, "Taffy was a Welshman, Taffy was a thief"; *Teague*, a predecessor of *Paddy*, current from the late sixteenth century to ca. 1900 (from the Irish name *Tadhg*), and used in the name of the hulking, stupid antihero of Frank Norris's *McTeague* (1899); *Tom*, any male, often a stupid one, a *tomfool* (see TOM-); *Tony*, an Italian; UNCLE TOM, a black man who kowtows to whites; and YANKEE, a person from the United States, especially a New Englander (probably from the Dutch *Janke*, Little John).

For similar use of short forms of national ethnic, regional, and other names and labels, see FAG, HICK, and JAP. For the pejorative use of female names, see MOLL.

pagan. One who is neither Christian, Moslem, nor Jew—or who has no religion at all. *Pagan*, from the Latin *paganus*, peasant, and *pagus*, a district, the country, parallels HEATHEN (ultimately: a dweller on the heath) both in sense and origin. *Pagan* traveled a more circuitous route, however. First *paganus* became an epithet among Roman soldiers for *civilian*. Then, the contemptuous usage was adopted by early Christians, who saw themselves as soldiers, *milites*, of Christ, and who naturally extended *paganus* to anyone who wasn't converted. See also HICK, PEASANT, and RENEGADE.

palooka. An inept or inferior person, often a big, dumb one; especially, a prizefighter who is no prize. "I don't want commissioners to ever be able to say to me, 'I could not perform because you decided to give me palookas' " (New York City Mayor Edward I. Koch, *New York Times*, 3/16/86).

Palooka was introduced in 1925 by *Variety* staffer Jack Conway, according to H. L. Mencken (*The American Language*, Raven I. McDavid, Jr., ed., 1963). No one knows whether Conway made the word up out of thin air or modeled it on some other term, such as POLACK or, perhaps, *palouser*. (An old slang word with essentially the same meaning as *palooka*, *palouser* may come from the Palouse Indians of the northwestern United States; whence also the *Appaloosa* horse.) In boxing, a *palooka* usually turns out to be a slap-happy, slug-nutty, punch-drunk, stumble-bum—not at all like Ham Fisher's bluff, tough comic strip character, Joe Palooka, who hung up his gloves in 1984, after a fifty-four-year career of battling bad people in the ring and without. He retired to Wilkes-Barre, Pennsylvania, and is believed to be living comfortably nearby on the lower reaches of Joe Palooka Mountain. See also DUMB/DUMMY.

pander. A caterer to the base desires or weaknesses of others; as a verb, the act of so doing. "To go out yesterday and say 'I'm going to reach out to the Catholic vote by saying I'm against abortion'—I mean that was the most outrageous kind of pandering" (New York Governor Mario Cuomo, attacking the campaign tactics of President Ronald Reagan, AP, 7/27/84).

The word comes from the personal name of the Trojan prince, Pandarus, who acted as go-between for his niece, Cressida, and one of King Priam's sons, Troilus. The characters are Homeric, but the story is medieval, with Pandarus first appearing as a *pander* in Boccaccio's *Il Filostrato* (1344). Boccaccio's tale provided the basis for Chaucer's *Troilus and Cressida* (ca. 1385) and Shakespeare's play of the same name (1601–02). The pejorative meaning of the name was well-established by Shakespeare's time, as indicated by Pandarus's remark in act three to the lovers: "If ever you prove false to one another, since I have taken such pains to bring you together, let all pitiful goers-between be called to the world's end after my name—call them Pandars . . ."

See also JUDAS and PIMP.

panhandler. A seeker of alms; one who *panhandles*. The term is an Americanism from the 1890s, and it may have nothing to do with the metal pan that alms-seekers might possibly hold. Earlier in the nineteenth century, *pan* alone was used to mean bread or money, from the Spanish *pan*, bread, and the Latin *panis*. Herewith, an early example of people looking for *pan*: "Since the first outbreak of the late excitement, the Indians in the vicinity have kept themselves aloof from the city; but lately they begin to show themselves in search of *pan* and whiskey" (San Diego, California, *Herald*, 2/21/1852). See also BEGGAR.

pansy. A homosexual who plays the female role; broadly, any effeminate man. "In one issue of 'The Duck Book,' [Robert White, the publisher] said his aim was to 'put the fear of God into each of the pacifist, pansy "patriots" who gave away our canal, killed the B-1 and have virtually disarmed us for their mad, insane socialist welfare programs' " (*New York Times*, 6/2/86).

The homosexual sense of *pansy* dates at least to the nineteenth century, and is probably much older. Originally, among homosexuals, *pansy* was not derogatory. For example, it was the pseudonym-of-choice of one of the homosexuals that the equally pseudonymous "Earl Lind" encountered about 1895 in New York City's Paresis Hall, a gathering place for gentlemen of the opposite persuasion. In Lind's words: "In a few minutes, three short, smooth-faced young men approached and introduced themselves as Roland Reeves, Manon Lescaut, and Prince Pansy— aliases, because few refined androgynes would be so rash as to betray their legal name in the Underworld" (*Autobiography of an Androgyn*, 1918). The scornful connotations of *pansy* came to the fore soon after the term entered general circulation in the 1920s (a common progression; see FAIRY, for instance). Thus, Robert Graves, writing in 1936, told of a madam who mourned the passing of the good old days "when men were men and pansy was still the name of a flower" (*The Future of Swearing and Other Improper Language*).

The modern round-faced pansy—meaning the flower—is an artificial production, perhaps no more than a couple of centuries old, but the name was first applied to its wild ancestor about 1500. The English *pansy* comes from the French *pensée*, thought, the contemplative name by which this flower still is known across the Channel. A century after the anglicized form appeared, William Shakespeare knew the term's meaning: "And there is pansies, that's for thoughts" (*Hamlet*,

1601–02). Aside from its intellectual associations, the pansy also was much admired by the Church, since it is the only flower showing three colors, thus relating to the Trinity. In addition, the flower always had strong sexual associations since it was believed to be the key ingredient in preparing a powerful love potion. Some of the common names of its wild ancestor reflect this belief: *heartsease, kiss-me-at-the-garden-gate, tickle-my-fancy,* and *love-in-idleness* (where *idle* means *fruitless,* not *lazy,* the full name translating as *love-in-vain*). Shakespeare, well-versed in all this lore, too, called the pansy "Cupid's flower," and this is the flower that Oberon tells Puck to pick in *A Midsummer Night's Dream* (1600):

> Fetch me that flower, the herb I showed thee once.
> The juice of it on sleeping eyes laid
> Will make man or woman madly dote
> Upon the next live creature that it sees.

The pansy potion is for Queen Titania, of course, and when she awakens, the first creature she sees—and falls in love with—is a man with an ass's head. Strong stuff indeed!

See also QUEER.

Pantaloon. A silly, doddering old man, from a stock character in Italian comedy. "He became a withered and shrivelled pantaloon" (Thomas A. Trollope, *Marietta,* 1862). The name comes from *Pantaleone* ("all lion"), a popular saint in Venice and the patron saint of physicians. Because a lot of Venetians were named after the saint, and because Venetians started wearing trousers before most other Europeans, the comic character was attired this way, giving rise in due course to the names of various garments that replaced knee breeches and related clothing, including *pantaloons, pantalettes, pants, panties,* and *scanties,* not to speak of *panty raids, panty hose,* and *hot pants.* Of course, *pants* and *trousers,* too, were regarded as taboo words in the nineteenth and early twentieth centuries; hence, the many euphemisms that were devised to avoid mentioning them, such as *inexpressibles, unmentionables, unutterables, nether garments, sit-down-upons,* and so on. What the English thought of *pants* at the start of this century is evident from the *OED's* definition of the term: "A vulgar abbreviation of *Pantaloons* (chiefly U.S.)" (Volume P, 1904–09). And in the United States, *panties* still did not appear in *Webster's Second* until 1939, though most normal people, even advertisers, were using the word by then. See also PANTYWAIST.

pantywaist. A sissy or coward; a weak, effeminate male; from the 1930s. The term may also be hurled as an adjective: "Some goddam British poet with one of those pantiwaist names, like Vere de Vere" (Anthony Burgess, *MF,* 1971). See also PANTALOON and SISSY.

pap. Nonsense, especially statements that have all the solidity of baby food; from the sixteenth century and still current: "But members of the Fed's board of governors deny that Volcker is trying to pressure Congress. 'The notion is nonsense, absolute pap,' asserts a board member" (*Wall Street Journal,* 3/9/84). See also BALONEY and MUSH.

Papist. A Roman Catholic. *Papist* usually is employed in, as the *OED* puts it, a "hostile or opprobrious" manner, e.g., the title of a tract from 1534, *A Litel Treatise* *ageynst the Mutterynge of some Papists in Corners.* The implication is that the *Papist* believes more in the Pope than in God. *Popery* and *Romanism* (as in the charge, first made in the 1884 presidential campaign, that the Democrats are the party of Rum, Romanism, and Rebellion) have the same attack value. On an even less elevated level, so do *crossback* and *statue-worshipper.* See also *fish eater* in FISH.

parasite. One who lives off another; a BLIGHTER, BLOODSUCKER, LEECH, MAGGOT, MOOCHER, SPONGE, SUCKER, or VAMPIRE. Deriving from the Greek *parasitos,* fellow guest, in turn from *para,* (eating) besides + *sitos,* food, *parasite* was applied to humans long before biologists began making use of the term in the eighteenth century. In ancient Greece, the word referred to professional diners-out, who paid for their meals by flattering their hosts. The sense of *parasite* as a sycophant and hanger-on, now a secondary meaning, remained strong through the nineteenth century. To-day, when human *parasites* are encountered, it usually is in a Marxist nation; for an example, see SHIRKER.

pariah. A social outcast; from a proper noun, the name of the very large, very low caste of agricultural and domestic workers in southern India. "Qaddafi deserves to be treated as a pariah in the world community" (President Ronald Reagan, press conference, 1/7/86).

The Pariahs are Tamils, originally hereditary drummers, and the name comes from *parai,* the Tamil word for drum. The extension of the meaning was begun by upper-caste Hindus, who regarded the Pariahs as unclean and therefore shunned them as if they were outcasts. Europeans adopted the term in the eighteenth century, applying it first to any low-caste Indian and then to other Europeans, regarded as degraded, despicable outcasts. See also LEPER.

parrot. A person who repeats (or *parrots*) words mechanically, having memorized but not understood them; typically, a student. People have been dismissed con-temptuously as *parrots* since at least the sixteenth century. See also DODO, *poll* in MOLL, and POPINJAY.

patsy. A dupe; one who is easily victimized; the butt of a joke or, if it is not a laughing matter, a fall guy. "I do not pretend I am some kind of patsy . . ." (John O'Hara, *Pal Joey,* 1939). "[Frank] Carlucci is tough. He's not a patsy" ("a senior Administration official," *New York Times,* 11/4/87).

Patsy is an Americanism, dated to the early 1900s, and of unknown origin. It has been suggested that *patsy* comes from the diminutive of *Patrick;* from the Italian *pazzo,* fool; and from the use of *Patsy* among Italo-Americans as the English equivalent of *Pasqualino,* the diminutive of *Pasquale.* Expanding on the latter theory: "*Pasqualino* is used to designate a vulnerable, weak, and small boy or man, and is probably based in this sense at least partly on the relation between *Pasqua* 'Easter,' the derivative names *Pasquale* and *Pasqualino,* and the notion of the Pascal sacrifice or Pascal lamb as an innocent victim" (Robert L. Chapman, *ed., New Dictionary of American Slang,* 1986). See also GULL.

pawn. A person who is at another's beck and call; in political discourse, frequently a *capitalist pawn,* the functional equivalent of a LACKEY or TOOL. The pejorative personal *pawn* comes from the chess piece, the least valuable in the game, in turn from the Old French *pebon, pedon,* a foot soldier or walker, and ultimately from the Latin *pes,* foot (all of which makes a *pawn* a relative of a *peon*). People have been disparaged as *pawns* since at least 1589 (*OED*).

peacock. A vain person; one who ostentatiously struts his or her stuff; a dandy or fop. "Proud as a peacock" appears in Chaucer (ca. 1374). Solid citizens have never approved of *peacocks.* "Play not the Peacock, looking everywhere about you, to see if you be well deck't" (George Washington, *Rules of Civility,* 1745). See also BIRD.

peanut. Something small, insignificant, or worthless, such as a person, whether a child, as in the featured players in Charles Schulz's comic strip *Peanuts* (from 1950), or an adult, as in "They were your pea-nut fellows, I suppose" (William Dunlap, *The Memoirs of a Water Drinker,* 1837). The term often appears as a derogatory modifier, e.g., *peanut-brained, peanut-headed, peanut gallery* (the cheapest seats, in the upper balcony), and *peanut politician* (not necessarily a Southern politician, but a spin-off from the nineteenth-century *peanut politics,* as practiced originally—judging by the earliest known examples of the phrase—by petty politicians in the North).

Political *peanuts* arose in Columbus, Ohio, according to Al G. Field's autobiography, *Watch Yourself Go By,* which includes this reminiscence of city council hearings in 1880: "All ate peanuts. Special appropriations were requested by John Ward, city hall janitor, to remove the peanut hulls after each talk fest. And thus it was that peanut politics and peanut politicians came to be known in Columbus. Peanut politics like all infections spread until the whole political system became affected." Field's autobiography was not published until 1912, however, a quarter of a century after the oldest-known example of *peanut politics* in print: "If the Governor would consent not to play pea-nut politics" (*New York Mail & Express,* 5/27/1887). This makes David B. Hill, governor of New York, 1885–92, the first certifiable *peanut politician.* See also GOOBER-GRABBER and POL.

peasant. An uncouth, simpleminded rustic of the lowest social and economic class; from the Latin *pagus,* a district, the country, and thus a first cousin of PAGAN. The word entered English in the fourteenth century and, like BOOR, was reserved at first for small farmers and agricultural laborers in foreign lands. By the sixteenth century, it had become a term of abuse, e.g., "Base beardgroom, coward, peasant, worse than a threshing slaue" (*Troublesome Raigne of John King of England,* 1591). The lower-class connotations remain very strong. Thus, discussing race relations in New Zealand, Internal Affairs Minister Peter Tapsell explained, "New Zealand Europeans, and I am not saying this in a bitter way, are peasants. That is how it is. What we have here is aristocratic Maoris and peasant Europeans. Really, that's the problem" (*New York Times,* 10/29/85). The non-bitter Mr. Tapsell, it needs to be noted, happens to be a Maori. See also HICK, PLEBEIAN, RIFFRAFF, and WRETCH.

peckerwood. A white person, originally and especially a poor, white, Southern farmer; black use, also rendered as *peck, pecker,* and *peckawood.* "When I tried to get into the black caucus, they said 'No peckerwoods allowed in here, Sonny,' " (*New York Times,* 9/7/67).

Peckerwood is a straight reversal of *woodpecker,* often used in the South for the bird as well as a person. "Peckerwood means woodpecker, but it also means the sort of farmer who 'collars' [girdles] trees in the backwoods, instead of clearing land for his cornpatch" (Vance Randolph and George P. Wilson, *Down in the Holler*, 1953). The disparaging sense also seems to trade, however, on *pecker* as slang for the penis. Because of this association, refined hillfolk in the South have been known to refer to the *sapsucker* or *woodchuck*, rather than sully their lips with *peckerwood* or *woodpecker*. See also BIRD and POOR WHITE TRASH.

peddler. A traveling salesman; originally, from the fourteenth century, a neutral term, but now used only in a negative way, e.g., *dope peddler, drug peddler, influence peddler*. Though employed earlier in England in a contemptuous sense, referring to one who dealt in trifles or worked in an ineffective way, the modern meaning of the term derives from nineteenth-century American underworld use of *peddler* to mean a seller of stolen or illicit goods. The transition in *peddler's* connotations is typical of words that denote people who sell things to others, e.g., CADGER, *hawker, huckster, monger* (see WHOREMONGER), and TOUT. This seems to be the customers' revenge.

Peeping Tom. A voyeur, from the story of Lady Godiva, who rode through Coventry (ca. 1040) without benefit of clothes, thus redeeming a promise by her husband, Earl Leofric of Mercia, who had said, too casually, that he would relieve the inhabitants of certain taxes only if she were to do this. The grateful townspeople stayed indoors and hid their eyes except for Tom, a tailor, who snuck a look, and for this he was struck blind, or so the story goes. The original Tom, by the way, probably engaged in *peeking*, not *peeping*, as the *peep* form didn't appear until the late fifteenth century. The two words still travel in parallel, however. Thus, one may take a *peek* in a *peep* show, or play *peekaboo* with *Little Bo Peep*. In each case, a quick or furtive glance is involved. In China, such a voyeur is a Beijing Tom (formerly: Peking Tom or Peiping Tom). See also NOSEY PARKER.

peewee. Small, insignificant; especially a short person or a child. Thus, speaking of hypopituitary dwarfs, who are tiny people, but normally proportioned: "Peewee, shrimp, shortstop, snuffbox—there's a fair amount of invective leveled at these kids" (Professor Brian Stabler, University of North Carolina, *Wall Street Journal*, 6/24/83). An exception here is baseball Hall of Famer, Harold "Peewee" Reese, who gained his nickname not because he was short of stature but because a *peewee* also is a small marble, and he was a marble champion before he became shortstop for the Brooklyn Dodgers.

Peewee, dated to the mid-nineteenth century, is basically a rhyme compounded upon *wee*, but the application to children may be influenced by the *peewee* that is a bird, the lapwing. (The bird's name comes from its cry, rendered variously as *peewee* and *pewit*, another name for the fowl.) It is the newly hatched lapwing, by the way, that is traditionally pictured as running around with its head still in its shell. See also KIBITZ and MIDGET.

pelican. An old car or jalopy, a big eater or glutton, a tough woman or prostitute. The last sense is the least common and may have been limited to New Orleans, largest city in the Pelican State. Herewith, a sighting of this *rara avis* in her natural habitat: "Tillie Thurman . . . who keeps a joint on Basin street . . . is certainly a Pelican of the first water. Boys, if you are looking for a good time and wish to save a doctor's bill we severely advise you to give the above establishment all the room possible. When it comes to the real thing in low-down tarts, then this is the house you are looking for" (New Orleans *Sunday Sun*, 1/31/1904).

In bygone times, the pelican also has served as a symbol of Jesus Christ, of devoted parenthood, and of ungrateful children. All these images tied into the medieval belief that pelicans fed their young with their own blood, and that the children nevertheless turned upon their parents when they grew strong enough to do so. Supposedly, this provoked the parents then to kill their children. After three days, however, the mother returned to the nest and pierced her own breast so that her blood would restore the young birds to life. And it was unkind children that King Lear had in mind, of course, when he exclaimed: " 'Twas this flesh begot those pelican daughters" (William Shakespeare, *King Lear*, 1605–06). See also BIRD.

penny-ante. Insignificant, contemptible; CHEAP. "They're fed up with this penny-ante, picky business . . ." (Senator Gary Hart [Democrat, Colorado], *New York Times*, 4/2/84). The term comes from the form of poker with the lowest possible ante. The extended sense dates to at least the Civil War period. e.g., "Look at those fellows now! . . . ain't they a 'penny ante' lookin' lot?" (*The Nation*, Volume I, 1865).

Penny-ante is one of a large number of poker terms that have entered general circulation, most of them in a pejorative sense and many of them, peculiarly enough, associated with the practice of politics. Among them: *ace in the hole; ace up [one's] sleeve; bargaining chip*, a weapons system that is developed only in order to gain a concession when negotiating an arms limitation treaty; *big deal* (frequently ironic) and *no big deal; blue chip* (as a stock); *bluff, to bluff* and *to call a bluff; the China card*, played by the United States in 1978 when closer ties with China were viewed as a means of putting pressure on the U.S.S.R.; *to deal from the bottom of the deck; to deal [one] in* or *out; to double-deal.* and DOUBLE-DEALER; *to perform a fast shuffle* or simply *to shuffle [something*—a president's cabinet, for instance]; *to feed the kitty*, meaning a fund of any sort; *to have whatever it takes for openers; to find a joker in the deck; to play it close to [one's] vest* or *chest; to pack [something*—as a political convention]; *to pass*, especially in the publishing and movie businesses where *pass* is the standard euphemism for *reject* when turning down a book or film project; *to pass the buck* and *the buck stops here* (the latter saying was on a sign that President Harry S Truman kept on his desk); *to have a poker face; to give [someone] a raw deal* (as opposed to Truman's *Fair Deal*, Franklin D. Roosevelt's *New Deal*, and Teddy Roosevelt's *Square Deal*); *to be lost in the shuffle; to stand pat; to sweeten the pot;* and *wheeler dealer.* The parallels between card playing and politics have been noted by, among others, Colonel Davy Crockett, who put it this way: "Statesmen are gamesters, and the people are the cards they play with. And it is curious to see how good the comparison holds as to all the games, the shuffling and the tricks performed. . . . From 'three up' to 'whist;' from a 'constable' to a 'president,' the hands are always dealing out; and in both cases, the way they cut and shuffle is a surprise to all young beginners." (*Life of Martin Van Buren*, 1835). See also FOUR-FLUSHER, PIKER, SNOOKER, and TWO-BIT.

Peoria. A medium-size town in Illinois (1980 population 124,160), whose name comes from an Indian word meaning "place of fat beasts," and which often is regarded as the intellectual and cultural center of the United States, typically in the phrase *It'll play in Peoria*. In the Nixon White House (1969–74), this was the standard test for the acceptability of any plan, program, plot, or scenario. The phrase was popularized by presidential aide John D. Ehrlichman, who told William Safire that he first used the expression at a school for political workers that he had conducted in New York City in 1968. Explained Ehrlichman: "Onomatopoeia was the only reason for Peoria, I suppose. And it personified—exemplified—a place, remote from the media centers on the coasts, where the national verdict is cast, according to the Nixon doctrine" (*Safire's Political Dictionary*, 1978). Vaudevillians probably used the phrase pre-Ehrlichman, however, and baseball players also made a lot of jokes about Peoria, which was part of the St. Louis Cardinals' farm system. During the Branch Rickey era in St. Louis (1917–42), so many players passed through Peoria that a song was dedicated to the city at the annual show of the New York Baseball Writers. Written and sung by Arthur Mann, its refrain was:

> Rickey said . . . "I wish we had more o' ya."
> Yet I wind up that fall in Peoria.

It also is clear that *Peoria*'s use as a cultural symbol dates at least to the early years of this century. Thus, Ambrose Bierce, who composed his *Devil's Dictionary* at intervals from 1881 to 1906, noted in his entry on *dullard* that "the New England dullard is the most shockingly moral" but "the intellectual centre of the race is somewhere about Peoria, Illinois."

Poor Peoria. It also used to be known as *Whiskey Town* on account of its prominence in the distillery business. It is, however, only one of a large number of place names that have acquired negative meanings. As a class, these names exemplify the common attitude of people toward strangers, and they parallel the terms that have been devised for those who speak strange tongues (see BARBARIAN), who come from different countries (see DUTCH), from different cultures (see GOOK), and who live off the land (see HICK) or in small towns (see PODUNK) in the hinterlands (see BOONDOCKS). Place names with derogatory meanings include:

Afghanistanism, in the news business, the overemphasis on happenings in faraway places, while neglecting to report important stories on one's own doorstep. "Dart: to the *St. Louis Post-Dispatch*, for a minor epidemic of Afghanistanism, domestic-type. . . . the paper gave ample coverage to Gay Pride demonstrations in New York, Chicago, Los Angeles, San Francisco, Houston, and Columbus, but ignored the marching contingent in St. Louis itself; similarly, the *P-D* ran a piece examining the skyrocketing rents in twenty-six U.S. cities that did not include its own hometown" (*Columbia Journalism Review*, 11-12/83).

Albany, the capital of New York State, as in the old joke: *Joe*. Now, you take Albany, New York. *Moe*. No, *you* take Albany, New York.

Bedlam, as in a madhouse, from *Bedlem*, which is Middle English for *Bethlem*, short for *Bethlehem*. The association with madhouses and, by extension, any scene of tumult and uproar, comes from the priory of St. Mary of Bethlehem, or Bedlam, established in London in 1247, but mentioned as "a hospital" as early as 1330 and as a lunatic asylum in 1402. "To Bedlam with him! Is the man grown mad?" (William Shakespeare, *Henry VI, Part II*, 1590–91).

Billingsgate, as in foul, abusive talk, from the seventeenth century and the London fish market of this name. "We disapprove the constant billingsgate poured on them officially" (Thomas Jefferson, *Writings*, 1799). The vituperative sense of the word has outlasted the market itself, which was moved down the Thames on

January 12, 1982, to a new building, also called Billingsgate, but considerably less redolent with history, fish, and language. See also *fishwife* in FISH.

Boetian, meaning a stupid, boorish person, from the ancient reputation of Boetia, the central agricultural district of Greece, whose inhabitants were said by their neighbors to be as dull as their air. See also ZANY.

Bohemian, referring to an unconventional person, especially an artist or writer. The French applied *bohémien* to gypsies from the fifteenth century, thinking they came from Bohemia, and later extended the term, to include vagabonds, adventurers, and others with free-floating life-styles. Thackeray introduced the word into English in *Vanity Fair* (1848) and straitlaced types soon recognized its pejorative value, e.g., "In persons open to the suspicion of irregular and immoral living—in Bohemians" (Ralph Waldo Emerson, *Letters and Social Aims*, 1875). See also GYP.

Bridgeport, a thriving town in Connecticut, once the home of P. T. Barnum, but at some remove from the center of Western civilization: "Once you're out of New York, it's all Bridgeport, isn't it?" (Russell Baker, *New York Times*, 9/5/87). Or in the words that adorned a pewter ashtray on the desk of Paul Volcker, chairman of the Federal Reserve Board, 1979–87: "When you've left New York, you ain't going nowhere." South of the Rio Grande, the saying is, "Outside Mexico City every place is Cuauhtitlán."

Bronx, as in *Bronx cheer*, which is not a cheer but a jeer; see BIRD and RASPBERRY.

Brooklyn, in bowling, a hit into the wrong pocket, opposite the bowler's delivering hand—the 1–3 pocket if the player is right-handed and the 1–2 if the player is left-handed; also called a *Jersey* or *crossover*. The idea that Brooklyn is so far off the beaten track as to be totally out of it was epitomized by New York Giants manager Bill Terry's rhetorical question in 1934: "Is Brooklyn still in the league?" (But on the last day of the season, the Dodgers beat the Giants, enabling the St. Louis Cardinals to win the pennant.)

Buncombe County, North Carolina, as in BUNK.

Burbank, as in the ironic *beautiful, downtown Burbank*, popularized on TV by Johnny Carson on "The Tonight Show" (1962 ff) and by "Rowan and Martin's Laugh-In" (1968–73). "Send a masochist to Burbank for the summer" ("Laugh-In," encore presentation, 5/28/84, WOR-TV, New York City).

byzantine, as in devious and full of intrigue; see BYZANTINE.

Calcutta, an international symbol of teeming masses in abject poverty, as in "The ragged man shuffling through the bus terminal . . . the wild-eyed woman bundled in sweaters and coats on a 90-degree afternoon: Such are the symbols of a failed mental health policy. This summer, the number of them roaming the streets in fear and fantasy seems, Calcutta-like, to have increased sharply" (editorial, *New York Times*, 9/2/87, describing conditions in New York City).

California, as in *California kiss-off*, a very rude dismissal or brush-off, also called a *New York kiss-off*. "California is a great place to live in—if you happen to be an orange" (attr. Fred Allen, 1894–1956). And as it happens, *a California breakfast* consists of a cigarette and an orange. California also is known as *the land of fruits and nuts*. The verb is *Californicate*.

Canada, our much-maligned neighbor to the North, as in the remark attributed to Al Capone (1899–1947): "Canada? I don't even know what street Canada is on." From the very beginning, however, Canada has gotten a bad press. Thus, from one of the first white men to view it: "I am rather inclined to believe that this is the land that God gave to Cain" (Jacques Cartier, *La Premier Relation*, 1545).

Cape Cod turkey, a tongue-in-cheek euphemism for dried salt codfish, and one of a large subset of place names that have been used to flavor different foods, e.g., *Alaska strawberries*, dried beans; *Albany beef*, sturgeon (going back to the eighteenth century when the Hudson was rather cleaner than today); *Arkansas chicken*, salt pork; *Chicago* or *Cincinnati olive*, pork; *Chicago* or *Cincinnati oysters*, pig testicles; *Coney Island head*, as in a glass of beer lacking a head; *Montana gin*, Lysol—to a Crow Indian; *Pennsylvania salve*, apple butter; and *Rocky Mountain oysters*, lamb testicles. See also KRAUT.

Chicago, the eternal *second city*, though it actually has ranked third in population among the nation's cities (after New York and Los Angeles) since 1984. Natives of Chicago are called *Chicogorillas*. Sometimes they play *Chicago pianos*, which are submachine guns (also called *Chicago coffee grinders, Chicago mowing machines, Chicago sewing machines*, etc.).

Coventry, in the phrase, *to send [someone] to Coventry*, that is, to ostracize a person by agreeing not to speak to him or her, frequently for a specified period of time. The phrase has been common since the eighteenth century. Various explanations of its origin have been offered. It might come from the English Civil War, when Royalist prisoners were sent to Coventry, then a Parliamentary stronghold. It is also said that the women of Coventry would not speak to soldiers (for fear of being tattooed by fellow citizens), so that soldiers stationed in the town were cut off from social (and other) intercourse. Of course, this is not Coventry's only claim to fame; see PEEPING TOM.

Cretan, a liar, from the remark attributed to Epimenides (sixth century B.C.), "All Cretans are liars," which is actually a paradox since Epimedides himself was a Cretan. "He was perfectly truthful toward men, but to women he lied like a Cretan" (Thomas Hardy, *Far from the Madding Crowd*, 1874).

Cucamonga, in the derisive phrase *that's strictly from Cucamonga*, popularized on the Jack Benny radio show (1932–55). The effect of the phrase depends largely on the convergence with CUCKOO. In real life, Rancho Cucamonga in Southern California has a population of 55,250 souls (1980).

Dubuque, as in Harold Ross's announcement of his intentions upon founding *The New Yorker* (1925): "*The New Yorker* will not be edited for the old lady from Dubuque."

Florentine, usually a complimentary term, the exception coming in the phrase *Florentine politics*, as originally enunciated by Niccolò Machiavelli (1469–1527) and now practiced worldwide. See also MACHIAVELLIAN.

Foggy Bottom, a disparaging nickname for the U.S. State Department, popularized in 1947 by James Reston of *The New York Times*, but earlier used, according to him, by Edward Folliard of *The Washington Post. Foggy Bottom* is the old name of the marshy area near the Potomac River where the department is located, but the nickname stuck because of the fogginess of official documents. "In addition to the usual defects of Foggy Bottom prose, the paper was filled with bad spelling and grammar" (Arthur Schlesinger, Jr., *A Thousand Days*, 1965).

gasconade, vainglorious boasting or the act thereof, from the province of Gascony in southwestern France, whose inhabitants were very poor but notoriously proud. ". . . vulgar people of all countries are full of gasconade" (Sydney Smith, *Works*, 1818). See also GASCON.

Gehenna, a place of suffering, a hell, a prison; from the Valley of Hinnom (Hebrew *Ge-Hinnom*), near Jerusalem, where children were sacrificed to Baal and Moloch.

Georgia, as in a *Georgia credit card*, which is a short hose for siphoning gasoline out of someone else's tank.

Gotham, now usually applied in a complimentary way to New York City and other metropolitan centers (the comic-book characters Batman and Robin live in Gotham), the original reference was to a village in Nottinghamshire, home of the so-called *wise men of Gotham*, who actually were simpletons. Many stories were told about them, such as the one about the twelve Gothamites on a fishing expedition who feared that a member of their party had been drowned because each man forgot to count himself. It is also said, however, that when King John proposed to establish a hunting lodge nearby, the townsmen, fearing the expense of supporting royalty, engaged in all sorts of idiotic tasks, such as trying to drown an eel in a pond and to trap a bird by building a hedge around it. Convinced that the Gothamites were quite mad, the king decided to locate elsewhere, whereupon the townsmen congratulated themselves, saying "We ween there are more fools that pass through Gotham than remain in it." The sense of *gothamite*, then, has gradually improved, from "fool" to "wise fool" to—as first applied to New York by Washington Irving in *Salmagundi* (1807)—"wiseacre" or "know-it-all," and, finally, in today's parlance, to "sophisticate." *Gotham*, as a home of fools, has analogues in other cultures. Continental Europeans tell similar tales about the inhabitants of the imaginary villages of Chelm and Kocourkov, as well as of Mistelbach, a real town near Vienna. The story about the twelve fishermen, meanwhile, has been recorded in Iceland, India, and other countries in between.

guinea, usually an Italian or other dark-complected person; originally, a black person from the Guinea coast of Africa. See GUINEA.

Hackney, a borough of London and the likely source of tired horses, women, and writers; see HACK.

Hoboken, which is just across the Hudson River from New York City and is therefore considered to be in the hinterlands, i.e., nowhere, literally and metaphorically. "Everything outside the A.F.L.-C.I.O. is Hoboken" (Lane Kirkland, AFL-CIO president, *New York Times*, 7/11/82). Admittedly, Oscar Wilde hedged a bit when asked about the aesthetic value of the view across the river: "Might beauty then be in both the lily and Hoboken?" (reporter's question, upon Wilde's landing in New York, 1/3/1882). Oscar's reply: "Something of the kind." Modern comics, however, have found that mere mention of *Hoboken* almost always gets a laugh. The same is true of other New Jersey towns with odd-sounding Indian names, such as *Hackensack, Ho-ho-kus,* and *Parsippany,* not to mention *Piscataway*. New Jersey's state gem is concrete; the state flower is dead; its best-known river is the Piss-on-Me. Note Mark Twain's use of *Hackensack* in HOOLIGAN.

Hollywood, an epithet for anyone or anything that is flashy, affected, synthetic, or fake, thus representing the less appetizing aspects of the film business. "As an adjective, the very word 'Hollywood' has long been pejorative and suggestive of something referred to as 'the System.' . . . The System not only strangles talent but poisons the soul, a fact supported by rich webs of lore" (Joan Didion, "I Can't Get That Monster Out of My Mind," 1964, in *Slouching Towards Bethlehem,* 1968). See also TINSELTOWN.

lapland, meaning the female pudendum or female society in general; an example of a euphemism extended into a geographical pun.

lesbian, from the Greek island of Lesbos, home of the poetess Sappho, who was accused by later generations (not her own, apparently) of this "vice." The earliest example of *Lesbian love* in the *OED* comes from a medical dictionary that was published as recently as 1890. Thus, *lesbian* predates slightly the hybrid *homosexual* (*OED*, 1892), which is part Greek, from *homos*, same, and part Latin, from *sexus*, sex. See also GREEK, HOMO, *Sapphism* in MOLL, and *Sodom* below.

Lilliputian. Anything or anyone that is small, of little account, petty; especially, a dwarf or a person of limited intelligence; a MIDGET. Public imagination was so captured by Jonathan Swift's description of Lilliput, whose inhabitants were only six inches tall, that the adjective was being used in an extended sense within two years of the publication of *Gulliver's Travels* (1726).

Liverpool, as in *Liverpool kiss,* sailor-talk for a kick in the chin, and *Liverpool weather,* which is dirty weather.

Los Angeles, widely regarded as a state of mind and the butt of many jokes, even by its residents. "Q. What's the difference between Los Angeles and yoghurt? A. Yoghurt has an active culture" (Los Angeles *Reader,* 4/1/83). "Seventy-two suburbs in search of a city" (*attr.* to Dorothy Parker, Alexander Woollcott, and others).

Missouri, as a symbol of somewhat obtuse skepticism in the phrase *you've got to show me, I'm from Missouri,* which has long since become generic, e.g., "In the words of the current slang phrase, every Wisconsin legislator 'comes from Missouri' and you have to 'show him' " (C. McCarthy, *Wisconsin Idea,* 1912).

Neanderthal, a crude, rude, stupid, old-fashioned, ultraconservative person, having a Stone Age mentality; from the name of a valley near Düsseldorf, West Germany, and the hominid remains found there in 1856. The term has been applied disparagingly to modern hominids since at least the 1920s. William Safire has traced its conservative political associations to a reference to "the Neanderthal men of the Republican party" in an unsigned memo (probably by Judge Samuel Rosenman) to President Harry S. Truman on June 29, 1948 (*Safire's Political Dictionary,* 1978). See also TROGLODYTE.

Neapolitan, as in the *Neapolitan disease,* or syphilis, sixteenth–eighteenth centuries, a.k.a., depending on which nationality one wanted to blame, *English disease, French disease, Italian disease, Spanish disease,* etc. See also FRENCH and, for a Shakespearian allusion to the *Neapolitan* variety, TAIL.

netherlands, an old term for the private, or nether, parts of a man or woman; a geographical pun on the order of *lapland* above.

New York, as in *New York minute,* which is a very quick one, especially to Southerners. "I could close this place in a New York minute" (*The Best Little Whorehouse in Texas,* film, 1982).

Niagara, usually a reference to something large, especially a torrent of some sort, but also the subject of an unforgettable putdown by Oscar Wilde: "When I first saw the falls I was disappointed in the outline. Every American bride is taken there, and the sight must be one of the earliest, if not keenest, disappointments in American married life" (press interview, New York, 1892).

North Dakota, as in the many jokes told about that state, especially by residents of neighboring Montana, e.g., Do you know what the official tree of North Dakota is? . . . No? It's a telephone pole. "Fact is, we've become sort of a national synonym for Nowheresville, a place so remote that it's comic. . . . it is difficult to take seriously a state where towns are named Hoople, Gackle and Zap" (University of North Dakota professor Wynona H. Wilkins, *New York Times,* 10/27/81).

Norwegian, as in *Norwegian steam,* which is a maritime expression for "brute manpower, doing it the hard way. From the tradition of the fine sailing ships where there was no use of the principles of mechanics except for the block and tackle" (*American Speech*, 4/44).

Oakland, which is San Francisco's *Hoboken*-across-the-Bay. It can never recover from Gertrude Stein's lapidary "When you get there, there is no there there."

ozark, as a verb, to cheat, to defraud, as in "I've been ozarked out of my property," quoting a woman who felt she had been cheated by a realtor (in Vance Randolph and George P. Wilson, *Down in the Holler*, 1953). *To arkansaw* means the same. See also the origin of CHARLATAN.

Philadelphia, a *Hoboken*-in-spades, being even further from New York; most memorably gored by W. C. Fields: "I went to Philadelphia one Sunday. The place was closed" and, in his proposed epitaph, "On the whole, I'd rather be in Philadelphia." Then there is the classic contest award: "First prize: one week in Philadelphia. Second prize: two weeks in Philadelphia." Traditional underworld nicknames for Philadelphia include *Sleepy Town* and *The Morgue*.

Pocatello, as in *you can't go back to Pocatello*, referring to politicians who have become so accustomed to life in Washington, D.C., that they remain in the capital even after they've left office rather than return to Pocatello, Idaho, or other outposts of civilization in the nation's interior. The phrase was coined in 1943 or 1944 by Richard L. Neuberger, later a senator from Oregon, and Jonathan Daniels, then an aide to FDR, and popularized by the latter's 1946 memoir, *Frontier on the Potomac* (from Safire, *op. cit.*).

Redfern, as in *getting off at Redfern*, an Australian expression that is too good to pass up: it refers to coitus interruptus, the point being that Redfern is the last station before Sydney Central.

Salt River, in the phrase *to row [someone] up Salt River*, to give [someone] a sound beating, physically or, in an extended sense, politically. The expression may come from the name of a river in Kentucky or from *Salt River roarer*, a nineteenth-century American frontier braggart: "A 'Salt River Roarer.' One of these two fisted back-woodsmen, 'half horse, half alligator, and a little touched with the snapping turtle' " (Hamilton, Ohio, *Western Intelligencer*, 12/26/1826).

Scotland, the subject of much humor due to the alleged penuriousness of its inhabitants. Q. Why does the landscape in Scotland always look so white when you fly over it? A. Because the people have hung out their toilet paper to dry. See also SCOTCH.

Shanghai, a traditional sink of iniquity, as evidenced by the verb, *to shanghai*, to kidnap, originally referring to sailors who were drugged or otherwise rendered unconscious, then brought aboard ships that needed more crewmen.

Siberia, any remote and inhospitable place, especially one of banishment or imprisonment: "Guillam departed for the siberias of Brixton" (John Le Carré, *Tinker, Tailor, Soldier, Spy*, 1974). Faraway places everywhere also have been characterized as *Dakota* and *Outer Mongolia*. In chess, a *siberian move* is a blunder—alluding to the probable destination of Russian chess players who make too many mistakes.

sleazy, as in squalid, sordid; if not from Silesia, then strongly associated with it. See SLEAZE.

Sodom, one of the two (with Gomorrah) cities of the plain, destroyed by he Lord on account of the unspeakable vices of their citizenry (*Genesis*, 19:24). "You media stars from Sodom and elsewhere will never get your calls returned. Mother taught us never to associate with prostitutes" (message to outside reporters on the telephone answering machine of Charles McCluskey, editor of *The Hudson Valley Hornet*, Wappingers Falls, New York, *New York Times*, 2/26/88). See also SODOMITE.

Tasmania, which is Australia's *Hoboken*, and thus the object of many jokes by the "mainlanders," e.g., Q. How many Tasmanians does it take to screw in a light bulb? A. Only one—if a ship is coming in this month with a supply of bulbs and it has a crew that is able to row to Australia with an extension cord. Of course, Australia itself seems like *Hoboken* to some people. As Ava Gardner is said to have said after filming *On the Beach* (1959) on location Down Under: "I couldn't imagine a better place for making a film on the end of the world."

Thames, as in—usually in the negative—*[someone* or *something] won't set the Thames on fire*, i.e., will not work any wonders or otherwise excel. The phrase has been dated to 1778. Other rivers may be substituted. Thus, from George Palmer Putnam's "Advice to a young publisher": ". . . learn to resist the seductions of plausible and excellent authors, who are so very certain that their works are going to set the North [Hudson] River on fire, and that the world stands on tiptoe to receive the earliest copy" (*Publisher's Circular and Literary Gazette*, 8/15/1863).

Tijuana, as in *Tijuana Bible*, a pornographic book, from the easy availability of esoteric literature in this Mexican border town. According to the *Dictionary of American Slang* (1975), the expression is used mainly by teenagers in Southern California, which suggests where the principal demand for *Tijuana Bibles* comes from.

Timbuktu, a place so far away it might as well be nowhere, often in the phrase *go to Timbuktu*, which is the same as saying "Go to hell" or "Go hang yourself." Variants are *go to Halifax*, *go to Jericho*, and *go to Putney*.

Vermont, a symbol of cheapness, as in *Vermont charity*, which is what hobos call sympathy when it is accompanied by nothing else, and *Vermont kindling*, which are rolled-up newspapers used in place of wood.

Washington, not yet a fully developed metaphor, but on its way to becoming one, as politicians who want to go there spend increasing amounts of time campaigning against everything it represents. "Washington is a city of Southern efficiency and Northern charm" (John F. Kennedy, in William Manchester, *Portrait of a President*, 1962).

pervert. A gay. Originally, from the fourteenth century, *pervert* was a verb, meaning to turn upside down or to upset. The homosexual noun didn't arise until the nineteenth century, with the earliest example in the *OED* coming from Havelock Ellis's *Studies on the Psychology of Sex* (1897): "A pervert whom I can trust told me that he had made advances to upwards of one hundred men." *Pervert* always had a judgmental air to it, however, and it has not been used much since the 1960s when gays began coming out of the closet—except when making attacks on them, e.g., "We have got to call a spade a spade and a perverted human being a perverted human being" (Senator Jesse Helms [Republican, North Carolina], when introducing an amendment to bar Federal Centers for Disease Control from funding AIDS programs that "promote, encourage, or condone homosexual activities," (*New York Times*, 11/7/87). It is still possible, but just barely, to make jokes on the subject: Q. What is small and white and crawls up your leg? A. Uncle Ben's perverted rice. See also KINKY and QUEER.

P.S. Senator Helms's amendment was approved, overwhelmingly.

pest. A person who is a decided nuisance. Originally, going back to the sixteenth century, *pest* was a general term for any deadly epidemic, such as the bubonic plague or other pestilence. The term soon was extended to include unwanted people, however. Thus, from a speech in 1609 by James I: "They that persuade them to the contrary are vipers and pests, both against them and the Commonwealth."

Pétain. A dictator. "On a recent trip to London, I found that calumny is in fine form among the leaders of the Labor Party. Dennis Healey was using alliteration to calumniate Prime Minister Margaret Thatcher: 'not just a female Franco but a Pétain in petticoats'" (William Safire, *New York Times*, 4/24/83). Marshal Henri Phillipe Pétain, who rallied the French against the Germans at Verdun (1916), collaborated with them as head of the Vichy government (1940–42), an episode that most French preferred to forget after World War II was over. In Paris, *Avenue du Maréchal Pétain* was renamed *Avenue de la Division Leclerc*, after the Free French unit that led Allied forces into Paris in 1944. See also QUISLING.

peter. The penis; a euphemism that has failed in some parts of the world because its underlying meaning is in the forefront of practically everyone's mind. "The proper name *Peter* . . . is so universally used by children and facetious adults as a name for the penis that it never quite loses this significance. Very few natives of the Ozarks will consider naming a boy *Peter*" (Vance Randolph, *Dialect Notes*, VI, 1928).

The anatomical use of *peter* probably is reinforced by the assonance of the first syllable with *pee* and with the beginning of *penis*. It also has been suggested that there is an association here with *petard*, a sixteenth-century device for blowing holes in fortress walls and gates (in turn from the French *peter*, to fart). This last theory is in accord with the common analogy of the penis to a weapon (see PRICK). Whatever, the name also is appropriate in its own right, *peter* deriving from the Greek, *petros*, stone, rock, and thus connoting strength and solidity. (This is how the Apostle Simon became Saint Peter: in the words of Jesus, "thou art Peter, and upon this rock I will build my church," *Matthew*, 16:18.) Of course, *peter* also is just one of many proper names given to this particular piece of anatomical equipment; see DICK.

pettifogger. A quibbling lawyer, especially an unscrupulous one. Talking about the lawyers who gathered at the old New York City prison, the Tombs: "Ignorant blackguards, illiterate blockheads, besotted drunkards, drivelling simpletons, *ci devant* mountebanks, vagabonds, swindlers and thieves make up, with but few exceptions, the disgraceful gang of pettifoggers who swarm about its halls" (New York City *Subterranean*, 7/22/1843).

Pettifogger has been dated to the sixteenth century and it has always had a pejorative meaning. Captain Francis Grose defined the term this way in his *Classical Dictionary of the Vulgar Tongue* (1796): "A little dirty attorney, ready to undertake any litigious or bad cause." He thought the word came from the French *petit*, small + *vogue*, credit, reputation, but latter-day etymologists are not so sure about the *fogger* part. Other possibilities are that it derives from the Middle Dutch *voeger*, an arranger of things; the obsolete English *fogger*, a deceiver for gain; or even from *Fugger*, the merchant-banking family of Augsburg in the fifteenth and sixteenth centuries. The theoretical chain in the last instance is from *Fugger* to the Dutch *focker*, monopolist and, ironically, a peddler or huckster (in Flemish slang, *focken* = to cheat), and finally to the *fogger* of *pettifogger*. The origin of the epithet is, in a word, foggy. See also LAWYER.

Pharisee. A hypocrite, especially one who observes formalities sanctimoniously and self-righteously. The term comes from the ancient Jewish sect the Pharisees, who observed the Torah so strictly and in some cases so ostentatiously that other people, including Jesus, doubted that they could be as pure on the inside as they seemed to be on the outside: "Woe unto you, scribes and Pharisees, hypocrites! for ye are like unto whited sepulchres, which indeed appear beautiful outward, but are within full of dead *men's* bones, and of all uncleanness" (*Matthew*, 23:27). The influence of the Bible is so strong that the term continues to be employed, even by citizens of officially atheistic nations. Thus, the chief of the Soviet Foreign Ministry's press department, Vladimir B. Lomeiko, said of Western human rights advocates: "They travel to debauch young girls of developing countries, and after that put on their fancy suits and make speeches and try to teach other countries to live by their standards. That is Phariseeism, hypocrisy and unparalleled demagoguery" (*New York Times*, 7/26/85). See also HYPOCRITE.

Philistine. An uncultured, middle-class materialist; a BABBITT. "The Philistines in their vilest forms have seized upon you" (Oscar Wilde, letter to W. E. Henley, July 1889). It is not clear just what the inhabitants of ancient Philistia did to acquire such a bad reputation, though as competitors with the Hebrews, they naturally did not receive a very good press in the Old Testament. (Goliath was a Philistine.) The modern meaning was popularized by Carlyle and Arnold. They appear to have picked the word up from the slang of University students in Germany, who contemptuously referred to townspeople as *die Philister*. The expression seems to have started out in the seventeenth century at Jena, where *Philister*, originally a colloquialism for a tall man (an allusion to Goliath?), was applied first to members of the town guard (with whom the students had frequent altercations), and later to townies in general. Tradition has it that the wider meaning was fixed in 1689 when, following a brawl in which a student was killed by townsmen, the Rector of Jena took as his text for the funeral sermon a phrase from *Judges*, 16:9, "The Philistine be upon thee, Samson"—the same line, as it happens, that Oscar Wilde also had in mind. See also BOURGEOIS and SNOB.

phony. Fake, counterfeit, as in a *phony diamond, phony war*, or the person who is a *phony*. "I think he's a phony, period, as far as representing the black people of South Africa" (Reverend Jerry Falwell, referring to Bishop Desmond Tutu, *New York Times*, 8/24/85).

Phony has been dated only to 1900, but most likely is the living relic of a very old confidence game, described in detail as early as 1561 (?John Awdeley, *The Fraternity of Vagabonds*). The supposition is that *phony* comes from *fawney*, a finger ring (in turn from the Irish *fainne*, a ring). The connection is via a con game called the *fawney rig*. As originally played in the sixteenth century, the swindler, or *ring-faller*, would surreptitiously drop (let fall well, if you will) a copper or brass ring that had been gilded to make it appear very valuable. When another person spotted the ring, the con man would pretend that he also had just seen it and cry out "Half part!" This would lead to a negotiation, with the con man eventually agreeing, as a favor, to sell his share of the ring for much less than its supposed value to the victim, who had been led to think that he was cheating the cheater. The same game has been played over the years with meerschaum pipes, pocketbooks, and other items.

P.S. Reverend Falwell did feel constrained to offer a qualified apology for his "unfortunate choice of words," saying, "The word 'phony' I should not have used. I should have used the word that he was incorrect or wrong."

See also PSEUDO.

phooey (fooey, fooy, pfui). A generalized exclamation of disgust, contempt, or disbelief (comparable in the last case to BALONEY or BUNK). "The governor's advisers, spoilsports, have said 'Phooey' to the technicalities" (*Boston Globe*, 3/30/67). *Phooey* was popularized ca. 1930 by the newspaper columnist Walter Winchell, who probably picked it up from the Yiddish *fooy* or the German *pfui*, both meaning *phooey*, but the exclamation also has English antecedents in *phoo* ("Phoo! Phoo! Do not be so shamefaced," Jane Austen, *Mansfield Park*, 1814), which, in turn, derives from the elemental, physiological *phew*. See also UGH.

picayune. Petty, trifling, paltry, insignificant, and sometimes as a noun: "The very fathers of our country were a pack of jealous picayunes, who bickered while the army starved" (*Scribner's Magazine*, 4/03). *Picayune*, from the French *picaillon*, small copper coin, appeared in American English about the time of the Louisiana Purchase (1803). Used in New Orleans and other areas previously controlled by Spain, the *picayune* was equivalent to half a Spanish real, or about six American cents. Its purchasing power seems to have varied rather widely. On the one hand: "One can't buy anything [at New Orleans] for less than a six cent piece, called a *picayune*" (J. F. Watson, *Journal*, 11/4/1804). And on the other, speaking of the recreations of the men who brought flatboats to New Orleans in the 1820s: ". . . for a picayune (six cents) a boatman could get a drink, a woman, and a bed for the night—and the practical certainty of being robbed and perhaps murdered as soon as he fell asleep" (Herbert Asbury, *The French Quarter*, 1938). See also TWO-BIT.

pickaninny. A black child. Thus, from a book that was being sold in 1987 in order to raise money for the state of California's observance of the bicentennial of the United States Constitution: "If the pickaninnies ran naked it was generally from choice, and when the white boys had to put on shoes and go away to school they were likely to envy the freedom of their colored playmates" (Fred Albert Shannon, essay on slavery, 1934, in *The Making of America*, W. Cleon Skousen, ed., 1985).

Pickaninny arose among slaves in the West Indies, where it was recorded as early as 1653. The original users based the term either on the Portuguese *pequenino*, little child, or its Spanish equivalent. They employed the term affectionately, of course, and, on the evidence of Captain Frederick Marryat, who was a sensitive recorder of language, applied it to small children generally, regardless of color, e.g. "And den, Massa Easy, you marry wife—hab pickaninny—lib like gentleman" (*Mr. Midshipman Easy*, 1836). But no white person can get away with this today. The essential informality of the word makes it seem too condescending, too offensive, to most modern sensibilities. The California Bicentennial Commission, in fact, halted the sale of *The Making of America*, and issued a formal apology for having authorized it in the first place, after this use of *pickaninny* was called to their attention (along with other matters, the text also concluding that "slave owners were the worst victims of the system [of slavery])." See also NEGRO.

piece. A woman as sexual partner or the act of sex itself. "When a hillman says he got him a piece, he means that he has had sexual intercourse" (Vance Randolph and George P. Wilson, *Down in the Holler*, 1953). The term also appears commonly in such constructions as "She is quite a piece" or "I would like to have [or tear off] a piece." The human *piece*, dating to the thirteenth century, is older than, but synonymous in all respects with, *piece of ass* (or *tail*); see also ASS and TAIL. The short form has not always had a negative meaning, however. It was formerly applied to men in such positive contexts as, "King James . . . selected him as his choicest piece, to vindicate his regality" (*OED*, 1651). Nor did Shakespeare intend an insult when referring to the infant who was to become Queen Elizabeth as a "mighty piece" (*Henry VIII*, 1613). Demeaning connotations tended to come to the fore, however, in such combinations as *piece of calico* (i.e., a *skirt*), *piece of goods* (or *drygoods*), *piece of muslin*, *piece of mutton* (a sexually loaded term, see MUTT), *piece of stuff*, *piece of trade* (the *trade* in this instance being the world's oldest profession), and *piece of work* (often used sarcastically of men as well as women). In the eighteenth century, Captain Francis Grose understood *piece* in essentially the modern sense: "PIECE. A wench. A damned good or bad piece; a girl who is more or less active in the amorous congress" (*A Classical Dictionary of the Vulgar Tongue*, 1796). Cambridge wits of the period also punned on the term when delivering the toast, "May we never have a *piece* (peace) that will injure the constitution" (Anonymous, "A Member of the Whip Club," *Lexicon Balatronicum*, 1811). Unrecorded is the logical rejoinder: "And may it be a peace (*piece*) with honor." See also POONTANG and the *patch* in CROSSPATCH.

piffle. Nonsense, foolish talk. "Though free to challenge conclusions on a touchy subject, the reviewer should . . . avoid his own tendentious piffle" (letter, *Yale Alumni Magazine*, 3/88). The term is of mysterious origin; it might be onomatopoeic, similar to *puff*, with a diminutive ending. It arose in the mid-nineteenth century and also can be used as a verb, *to piffle*. The adjective, *pifflicated*, means "to be drunk." See also BUNK and UGH.

pig. (1) A woman, (2) a police officer, (3) a contemptible person, not necessarily a fat, greedy, or slovenly one, (4) broadly speaking, any man, especially a male chauvinist.

(1) The association between pigs and women dates to classical times. "Of course, if your taste is for pig-meat, he begs us to pity his daughter" (Aristophanes, *The Wasps*, 422 B.C., Douglass Parker, tr., 1962). The connection here is based on a favorite pun of the old Greeks—*choiros*, meaning both "pig" and "female genitalia." In modern times, *pig* often is used on women who are ugly or who are reputed to have loose morals (*pace* Miss Piggy). If the women are in college, they may live in a *pig house* (sorority house).

(2) Pigs and police officers also have been associated for a good many years—longer, probably, than most of the antiwar protestors of the 1960s and '70s realized when they shouted *off the pigs*. Police *pigs* date to about 1800. This sense of the word does not appear in Captain Francis Grose's *A Classical Dictionary of the*

Vulgar Tongue (1796), but is one of the additions made to that work by the anonymous "Member of the Whip Club," who reissued it as the *Lexicon Balatronicum* (1811). The gentleman from the Whip Club put it this way: "Pig. A police officer. A China-street pig; a Bow-street officer." He gave as an example of the term's use "Floor the pig and bolt," which translated in the slang of the day as "knock down the officer and run away." The *pig* of this period, also called a *grunter*, was a plainclothesman or detective. The term fell into disuse, but either was not quite forgotten or else independently reinvented. Thus, in Richmond, Virginia, prior to what Virginians call the War Between the States, local police were known as *blind pigs*. Here, too, lurks a pun. A *blind pig* (also *blind tiger*) is a place where liquor is sold illegally; at the same time, members of the Richmond Public Guard had the initials P. G. on their hats, which led some unknown local wit to point out that P. G. without an *i* is *pig* without an *eye*, that is, a *blind pig* (*American Speech*, Spring 1980). Not surprisingly, police have become sensitive about the word. In 1977, for example, the Illinois Police Association denounced William Steig's *Sylvester and the Magic Pebble* (1969) because its animal characters included pigs in cops' uniforms, even though the "officers" were sympathetically portrayed. In the underworld, meanwhile, *pig* had a second meaning—that of "informer," i.e., one who squeals.

(3) The contemptible *pig* also is of some venerability. For instance, Martin Luther (1483–1546) started with this term when heaping abuse on Henry VIII, whom he called "a pig, an ass, a dunghill, the spawn of an adder, a basilisk, a lying buffoon, a mad fool with a frothy mouth . . ." Nowadays, it is harder to get away with this kind of talk. For example, after the wife of the mayor of Pine Hill, New York, called a reporter a "fat pig," she was convicted of "verbal assault" and fined $250 (*New York Times*, 11/20/84). The fatness of pigs also has produced the verbs, *to pig [it]* and the newer *pig out*. A slovenly *pig*, meanwhile, may be said *to live like a pig* or to reside in quarters that resemble a *pigpen* or *pig sty*. When the phrase, "Clean up this camp. You live like a pig," was included in a bilingual primer, *Spanish for the California Farmer*, some Mexican-Americans objected (AP, 3/24/83). A person who is obstinate as well as stupid is *pig-headed*.

(4) The *male chauvinist pig*, also known as an *oink-oink* or M.C.P., is a product of the rise in feminine consciousness during the 1960s. "Hello, you male chauvinist racist pig" (*New Yorker*, 9/5/70). Gloria Steinem explained the theory behind the epithet this way: "Another symbolic confusion was the invention of *male chauvinist pig*, a hybrid produced by trying to combine feminism with leftist rhetoric, which was often anti-feminist in itself: in this case, a willingness to reduce adversaries to something less than human as a first step toward justifying violence against them" (*Outrageous Acts and Everyday Rebellions*, 1983). See also CHAUVINIST and SEXIST.

A variant on the *pig* theme is *porker*, a derogatory term for a Jew. This usage is relatively old. The word is included in this sense in Grose's dictionary of 1796 and it is not entirely obsolete. As recently as 1985, *pork eaters* was one of the epithets shouted during a tumultuous debate in, of all places, the Israeli Parliament (*New York Times*, 1/17/85). The power of the insult derives, of course, from Jewish dietary prohibitions against eating pork. Rabbi Avraham Shapira, leader of an Orthodox party with a long history of seeking to ban the sale of pork in Israel, subsequently explained to the *Times*: "Pork is a symbol. When someone does something you don't like, you say that what he has done is 'pork,' that it is 'schweinnarai' " (7/20/85).

See also HOG, SHOAT, and SWINE.

pigeon. A woman, especially a young one (also sometimes called a *squab*); a mark or gambler's victim (usually male, but inexperienced and easily outwitted); in the underworld, an informer.

Deriving from the Latin *pipire*, to cheep, *pigeon* originally denoted a young bird. It was extended in the sixteenth century to include women in much the same way as CHICKEN, QUAIL, and BIRD itself. Centuries ago, *pigeon* was used affectionately, but today it would ruffle the feathers of most right-thinking adult females. Take, for example, Germaine Greer: "The basic imagery behind terms like . . . *pigeon* is the imagery of food" (*The Female Eunuch*, 1970).

Of course, it doesn't help that since the sixteenth century, *pigeon* also has signified SIMPLETON, meaning one who is easily fooled, both as a noun (often in the phrase *to pluck a pigeon*) and as a verb (*to pigeon [someone]* or *to be pigeoned*). In this sense, *pigeon* parallels the dumb DODO and the gullible GULL. Good gamblers continue to live off inexperienced *pigeons*. Thus, speaking of a poker game during the filming of *Under the Volcano*: "It is the pigeons who lose the most . . . Perhaps the pigeons are not bad players either, but simply not acclimated to John Huston's presence" (*New York Times*, 8/23/83). Somewhat confusingly, in betting circles, a *pigeon* also is a professional gambler, often a sharper. This usage apparently dates to one of the standard swindles of the eighteenth century (described by Grose, 1796), in which the winning numbers of a lottery were sent by mounted messenger (a *carrier pigeon*, in other words) to an office where bets still could be placed.

As an informer, *pigeon* is comparable to CANARY, but where the latter alludes to "singing," the former is shorthand for *stool pigeon*. Originally, a *stool pigeon* was a decoy pigeon tied to a stool or other perch in order to attract birds of the species. In the opening decades of the nineteenth century, professional gamblers adopted *stool pigeon* to refer to the human decoy who lured potential victims, or *pigeons*, into their clutches. At about the same time, police started using the term for thieves who informed on other thieves: "He appealed in turn to the police representations then in attendance, to a committee of 'shysters' from the tombs, and to a deputation of stool-pigeons . . ." (New York City *Subterranean*, 9/9/1843). Subsequently, *stool pigeon* in this sense was clipped front and back to the modern *pigeon* and its alternate, *stoolie*.

In the past, *pigeon* also meant COWARD, frequently in the phrases *pigeon-hearted* or *pigeon-livered* (the latter occurs in *Hamlet*, 1601–02), but it seems to have been superseded in this sense by CHICKEN, which is used in the same combinations. *Pigeon-eyed*, i.e., drunk, also has gone by the boards, or slid under the table, but politicians and other deferrers of action still *pigeonhole* proposals, a turn of phrase that has outlasted the compartmentalized writing desks that inspired it. See also DOVE and ROOK.

piker. A worthless person; a timid plodder, who takes no risks; a tightwad; especially in gambling, one who makes only small bets. "The thing that distinguishes our American commonwealth from the pikers and tin-horns . . . is our Punch" (Sinclair Lewis, *Main Street*, 1920). The word's origin is obscure. It could come from the British *piker*, meaning a tramp or vagrant, i.e., one who traveled along a turnpike. Or it might have evolved from *Piker*, meaning a poor white from Pike County, Missouri. From Gold Rush times, both *Pike* and *Piker* were used contemptuously on the West Coast to refer to former Missourians in much the same way that later migrants to the promised land were tarred as OKIES. "There are about 350 inhabitants, miners, gamblers, sharpers, Jews, Pikes, Yankees, loafers &

hoc genus omne" (C. W. Wilson, *Mapping the Frontier*, 1860). See also PENNY-ANTE, TIGHTWAD, and, for an even worse way to abuse a Missourian, PUKE.

pill. An objectionable person; someone who is hard to endure or something that is hard to swallow. As applied to things, the figurative sense has been dated to 1548 (*OED*), some sixty years after the original medicinal *pill* appeared in the language. Human *pills* came still later. They seem to have been an American innovation: "In the patois of her locality, she was called a 'pill'; a girl whom Harvard men carefully avoid until it is rumoured that her family shortly intends to 'give something' in the paternal pill-box" (Charles M. Flandrau, *Harvard Episodes*, 1897). Pills, real and figurative, often are described as being bitter, as in *a bitter pill to swallow*, meaning something difficult to accept. For a similar taste sensation, see LEMON.

pimp. One who supplies the services of a prostitute; as a verb, to act as a procurer. "A pimp is a . . . McGimp, fish and shrimp, lover, Latin lover and many others" (H. L. Mencken, *The American Language*, Raven I. McDavid, Jr., ed., 1963). For many years, the word was considered so strong that American newspapers wouldn't print it. Thus, *The New York Times* reported in the early 1960s that blacks in South Africa called informers *impimpsi*, a term that the newspaper explained only by saying it was a common English word with a Swahili prefix and suffix. (*Pimp* also is used to mean informer or stool pigeon in Australia and New Zealand.)

Pimp has been dated to the early seventeenth century and is of obscure origin. Ernest Weekley suggested in his *Etymological Dictionary of the English Language* (1921) that it might derive from the Old French *pimpreneau*, a word that was defined in Cotgrave's French-English dictionary of 1611 as meaning "a knave, rascall, varlet, scoundrell." See also BAWD and PANDER.

pinko. Radical, left-leaning, LIBERAL. "Some call the [*National Geographic*] magazine's editors 'un-American,' 'traitors' and 'pinko Communists' for using the metric system" (*Wall Street Journal*, 7/2/87).

Pinko has a more aggressive sound to it than *pink* or its effete elaboration, *parlor pink*. In whatever form, the implication is that the *pink* person is almost RED, that is, a COMMIE, and perhaps a sissy as well. (Pink, of course, is the traditional color for girl babies, as opposed to blue for boys, leading to such childhood taunts as "Pink, pink, your panties stink." It may also be significant that the Nazis made homosexuals in concentration camps wear pink triangles.) The association of the color with radicalism, however, predates not only the rise of Bolshevism but even the publication of *The Communist Manifesto* (1848), e.g., "Amusing it is to look back upon any political work of Mr. Shepherd's . . . and to know that the pale pink of his Radicalism was then accounted deep, deep scarlet" (Thomas De Quincey, *Tait's Magazine*, 2/7/1837). See also SCARLET LADY.

pipsqueak. An insignificant person, usually but not necessarily a short one, too. "He [Admiral Ernest King] had never liked Roosevelt and refused to look sad at his death; he thought Truman was nothing more than 'a pipsqueak haberdasher'" (Leonard Moseley, *Marshall*, 1982). The expression has been dated to 1910. It may be applied to things as well as people, e.g., referring to a monotonous book, "Mighty blasts on the tooter herald the arrival of just another pip-squeak" (Marshall McLuhan, *The Mechanical Bride*, 1967). See also MIDGET.

pisher. An insignificant person or thing; literally, a bed wetter, from the Yiddish *pisher*, in turn from the German *pissen*. "He bought this pisher grocery in a dead neighborhood where he didn't have a chance" (Bernard Malamud, *The Magic Barrel*, 1958).

piss. Urine or to urinate, nowhere more elegantly employed than by Byron in an epitaph for the British statesman, Robert Stewart, second Marquess of Londonderry (1769–1822), better known as Lord Castlereagh:

> Posterity will ne'er survey
> A nobler grave than this;
> Here lie the bones of Castlereagh.
> Stop, traveller . . . [sic]

That Byron did not actually have to write the word in order to call it to the reader's mind merely demonstrates how well acquainted most people are with the vulgarity. (And for more about Byron on Castlereagh, see EUNUCH.)

This word was not always regarded as a "bad" one. It was used fairly commonly for some five hundred years, starting from the thirteenth century. The verb seems to have arisen before the noun. It derives from the Middle English *pissen*, the Old French *pissier*, and appears ultimately to be of onomatopoetic origin. (The French word also was adopted in German, Swedish, and other Teutonic languages, originally as a euphemism.) The term adorns the works of Chaucer, More, Shakespeare, Dryden, Sterne, and Swift, among others. It was the word of choice in the Wyclif translation of the Bible (completed 1388) as well as the King James, or Authorized Version, of 1611, e.g., 2 *Kings*, 18:27: "the men which sit on the wall . . . may eat their own dung, and drink their own piss." (The *Revised Standard Version*, of 1952, uses "urine" in this passage.) *Piss* also became part of many other common words and phrases. Among them:

pissabed. A name for the dandelion and also a term of abuse, as in the old nursery rhyme (from *Tommy Thumb's Pretty Song Book*, 1744, but not included in modern Mother Goose collections):

> Piss a Bed,
> Piss a Bed,
> Barley Butt,
> Your Bum is so heavy
> You can't get up.

Or as Byron put it in a brief critique of the work of a fellow poet: "Here are Jonny Keats' piss-a-bed poetry . . . No more Keats, I entreat . . . there is no bearing the drivelling idiotism of the Mankin." (Byron also referred to Keats as "that dirty little blackguard.") The name became associated with the dandelion on account of the plant's diuretic action, a quality also recognized by its French name, *pissenlit*, where *lit* = bed. (*Manger les pissenlits par la racine*, to eat dandelions by the root, however, is to be dead, comparable to pushing up daisies.)

pissant. An ant, so called because of the smell of the formic acid that it secretes; also known as the *pissmire* and, a nineteenth-century euphemism, the *antmire*.

pissing evil. An old name for diabetes.

pissing pins and needles. To have gonorrhea.

pissing post. An early form of public urinal.

piss pot. An unrefined chamber pot. (*To piss by the pot* was a colloquialism for committing adultery.)

piss prophet. A physician who diagnosed diseases by conducting what is now known as a *urinalysis.* (A standard test was to taste it; sweetness indicated the *pissing evil.*)

piss proud. A priapism, esp. upon awakening. As defined by Captain Francis Grose: "Having a false erection. That old fellow thought he had an erection, but his ---- was only piss-proud; said of any old fellow who marries a young wife" (*A Classical Dictionary of the Vulgar Tongue,* 1796).

In the first part of the eighteenth century, even so intellectual and refined a person as Lady Mary Wortley Montagu could still use the term casually. Thus, reporting on the visits of English high society to the wife of a French ambassador, who had given birth to a son shortly before, Lady Mary wrote to her sister, Lady Mar (December 1724): "Madam de Broglie makes a great noise, but 'tis only from the frequency and quantity of her pissing, which she does not fail to do at least ten times a day amongst a cloud of witnesses." The scene was sufficiently rococo to English sensibilities, however, to inspire Lady Mary to produce the following verse:

> One would think her daughter of a river,
>   As I heard Mr. Miremont tell,
> And the best commendation that he could give her
>   Was that she made water excellent well,
>   With a fa la la, etc.

Even as late as the middle of the eighteenth century, polite people could use the term in polite contexts, e.g., from the *Philosophical Transactions of the Royal Society* of 1743: "They hold a Piss-pot over the Womens Heads whilst in Labour, thinking it to promote hasty Delivery." (Which it might well have—anything to get rid of that pot!)

By this time, though, some sensitive souls were beginning to shy away from the elemental term. Thus, a Harvard College regulation of 1735 stated that "No freshman shall mingo against the college wall or go into the fellows' cuzjohn." (Here, *mingo* is a Latin evasion for you-know-what—the verb in Latin is *mingere*—and the *cuzjohn,* or *cousin john,* just happens to be the oldest example in the OED of a *john* that is an outhouse.) Prejudice against *piss* increased as the Victorian Age approached, and in 1833, four years before Herself ascended the throne, Noah Webster censored this word (along with BREAST, STINK, WHORE, and other rousers) when editing a new edition of the Bible. His aim, as he explained in a letter of 1836, was to remove words and phrases that "cannot be uttered in families without disturbing devotion." To this end, the men on the wall in Webster's version of 2 *Kings* wound up eating "their vilest excretions."

Today, the word is still debarred from most formal writings, though it is heard often enough, usually in figurative senses, e.g., *horse piss* and *panther piss,* referring most often to raw whiskey and cheap wine, respectively; *piss and vinegar,* which is what an energetic man may be said to be full of; *pisscutter,* a term of admiration for someone or something of excellence; *pisser,* an extraordinary person or thing, not

302

always in a disagreeable sense; *pisshead*, a despicable person; *piss off*, an exhortation to someone to depart the scene; and *piss poor* which is very poor. The most common form, however, probably is the reflexive *pissed off*, to be angry, once euphemized as *peed off* or *P.O.'d* but now used bluntly by women (in New York City, at least), as well as by men. This expression is dated in the *OED* to 1946, but it goes back at least to the preceding war years. Thus, after Felix, a Scottie dog belonging to General Dwight D. Eisenhower and his driver, Lieutenant Kay Summersby, urinated on a campaign map at Allied headquarters during the Battle of the Bulge (1944), thus eliminating, so to speak, all trace of the enemy attack, staff officers joked that the perfect reply to the question "Where's the enemy?" was "Pissed off" (Leonard Moseley, *Marshall*, 1982).

The term also appears in various folk expressions, such as *go piss up a rope*, go away, get lost, go chase yourself; *piss away*, to squander (*piss money against the wall*, with the same meaning, dates at least to the fifteenth century); and *piss through the same quill*, referring to two people who are so intimate as to have no secrets from each other. Even the high and the mighty relish such expressions. For example, Senator William E. Jenner (Republican, Indiana) described New York Governor W. Averell Harriman this way: "He's *thin*, boys. He's thin as piss on a hot rock" (President Richard M. Nixon, tape, recalling Harriman's announcement that he would run for the presidency in 1956, CBS-TV broadcast, 4/84). And one of Nixon's predecessors, Lyndon B. Johnson, explained his retention of J. Edgar Hoover as director of the FBI by saying, "I'd much rather have that fellow inside my tent pissing out than outside my tent pissing in" (John Kenneth Galbraith, *Guardian Weekly*, 12/18/71). Still, there are limits, even in the White House. Thus, President Jimmy Carter's staffers retracted a 1977 change in the nomenclature of presidential orders, from National Security Study Memorandums to Presidential Study Memorandums, as soon as it was realized that the relevant acronym, would shift from NSSM (Nissim) to the unpronounceable PSSM.

In fact, the taboo against *piss* remains strong enough to have affected some of the euphemisms that have been devised for it, making them also available as attack terms. Thus, a traditional insult among schoolboys is for one to say of another, "He pees sitting down" (i.e., he is a girl). Variations on the same theme include the translation of the initials of the Chicago, Rock Island & Pacific Railroad (CRI&P) as "Come Right In & Pee," and the question posed by a first-grader at Packer Collegiate Institute, Brooklyn, New York, "Ask me if I can spell 'iccup,'" to which, if one is foolish enough to say "How?", the reply is "I.C.U.P." (David Costello, then working as a gandy dancer, heard the first one some fifty years ago, and I bit on the second, 9/18/83). Much more elegantly, Ben Bradlee, executive editor of *The Washington Post*, told a critic, Reed Irvine, chairman of Accuracy in Media, that "You have revealed yourself as a miserable, carping, retromingent vigilante" (*Columbia Journalism Review*, 9-10/81). *Retromingent*, from *retro*, backward + the past participle of that Latin *mingere*, is antique (*OED*, from 1646), but well worth reviving. Of course, it usually is applied to animals (the lion and the elephant are *retromingent*, for example) . . . which makes its insult value for humans all the greater.

pits, the. The lowest, the worst. "TV SUPERMOM, JUNE LOCKHART: MOTHERHOOD'S REALLY THE PITS" (headline, *New York Post*, 5/9/83).

Pit usually is taken as an abbreviation of *armpit*, and in this context it carries the connotation of a bad body odor. Whatever is *the pits*, then, really stinks. Sometimes

303

the term appears in full. Thus, quoting Tiger pitcher Milt Wilcox: "I get tired of people talking about Detroit as the armpit of the world" (*New York Times*, 10/12/84).

In former times, from the thirteenth century, if not before, *the pit of hell* or *the bottomless pit* was a place to be avoided by all true Christians. It has always been permissible, however, to consign thine enemies to these deeps, e.g., "I hope I never see ye again, till I see ye a-burnin' in the middle pits of hell!" (Springfield, Missouri, *News & Leader*, 3/18/34). Many people also continue to agree with Dr. John Arbuthnot, who drew on this image in his famous (it fixed the present image of "John Bull") story of a legal suit, entitled *Law is a Bottomless Pit* (1712).

plebeian. Common, crude, low, vulgar; from the Latin *plebeius*, belonging to the common people, or *plebs*. The depreciatory applications, dated to the seventeenth century, were popularized at the time of the French Revolution. As epithets go, this is the social equivalent of the rural BOOR or PEASANT. See also BOURGEOIS, SANS-CULOTTE, and VULGAR.

plow (plough). To copulate. "Royal wench! She made great Caesar lay his sword to bed. He plowed her, and she cropped [became pregant and gave birth]" (William Shakespeare, *Antony and Cleopatra*, 1606–07). The metaphor probably has been around since shortly after the plow was invented. Lucretius (98?–55 B.C.) used the phrase "to plow [*arare*] the fields of women." A wonderful variation, probably referring to the varying length of rows in irregular clearings, is the Ozarkian *short rows*, meaning the last moments before orgasm, e.g., the report by a frustrated backwoods philanderer: 'We was just *gettin' into the short rows* when I heerd the front gate slam!" (Vance Randolph and George P. Wilson, *Down in the Holler*, 1953).

plug-ugly. A ruffian. Dating from the 1850s, the term is associated particularly with the fair city of Baltimore. "In Baltimore there is but little direct slave interest. Indeed, the number of slaves there held can scarcely be regarded as involving so much wealth as the piratic slave-trade, in which Plug-Uglymore is known to bear her part most gallantly" (New York *Tribune*, 1/15/1861). John Russell Bartlett reported in his *Dictionary of Americanisms* (1860) that *plug-ugly* was bestowed originally on certain of Baltimore's fire companies. The *plug* part probably does not refer to fireplugs, however, but to stovepipe hats, also called *plugs*, which were popular in this era. See also HOODLUM and UGLY.

podunk. The quintessential small town; an insignificant place, inhabited by presumably insignificant people. "In opposition to the repeated commands and entreaties of her parents, she ran away with the needy but handsome P., who was once the terror of the staid mothers and frigid maids in the town of Podunk, but who is now the dignified and steady double-chinned aristocrat of the 'change . . . in the city of New York" (*New Mirror*, 12/2/1843).

Podunk—along with its variants, *Squedunk* and *Podock* (a portmanteau with BOONDOCK)—usually is taken as a fictive town, though the term crops up in place names in Connecticut, Massachusetts, and New York, e.g., Podunk Brook, which empties into the Connecticut River near Hartford. The distribution is natural, since the word is Algonquian, from *pot-*, to sink, plus *-unk*, a locative, the expression thus translating as "a boggy place" (W. W. Tooker, *The Indian Place-Names on Long Island and Islands Adjacent*, 1911). Allen Walker Read, the man who nailed *podunk* down linguistically (*American Speech*, 4/39), showed how the word gained notoriety as a joke name during the 1840s when Americans indulged themselves in a tremendous amount of wordplay. (*O.K.*, from *orl korrect*, a jocular alteration of *all correct*—and perhaps Walker's greatest discovery—also dates from this period, with the earliest example yet found coming from 1839). Other imaginary towns of the era included *Bottomless Bogs, Buzzardsborough, Catsville, Coonsborough, Crow Corners, Dogtown, East Punkinton, Ganderfield, Skunk's Misery, Squashborough, Turkeytown, Upper Bugbury*, and *Weazletown*. The level of wit in this period also may be gauged by such gems of repartee as these, collected by Read from New York City newspapers of 1839 (*American Speech*, 2/63):

> What town in the south would be a capital place for a dentist? *Tusk-ah!-looser*. (Tuscaloosa, commonly spelled.)
> What is the best city for laundresses to reside in? *Washing*-ton.

As for *podunk*, though earlier used in a fictive sense, its popularity apparently stems from a series of anonymous "Letters from Podunk," which appeared in the Buffalo, New York, *Daily National Pilot* in 1846. The initial letter, dated January 5, begins:

> MESSRS. EDITORS: I hear you ask, "Where in the world is Podunk?" It is in the world, sir; and more than that, is a little world of itself. It stands "high up the big Pigeon," a bright and shining light amid the surrounding darkness.

And the last letter in the series (3/6/1846) informs us:

> Podunk is a huge town, not distinguished exactly as the geographies have it, for its "fertile soil, salubrious and healthy climate," but for some of its characters that do here congregate.

Podunk has retained its vigor into our own time and has been joined by a host of other derogatory terms for small and unremarkable places. A few of these are the names of actual towns or other locales that have attained generic status, representing places of the same sort everywhere; see PEORIA for details. Others are essentially imaginary, though it sometimes happens that an actual place with the same name exists. For example, President Reagan was mildly embarrassed in 1982 when he challenged reporters for calling it news when "some fellow in South Succotash someplace" lost his job, whereupon the press retaliated by locating a real Succotash in Rhode Island and proceeded to file stories on unemployment there. And there really is a thriving town of *Hicksville* on Long Island. Many of the imaginary places appear in various forms, e.g., *Rube Center, Rube Junction, Rube Town*, and *Rubeville*, and many are based on words that have considerable pejorative value in their own right, e.g., BOOB, CHUMP, CLOD, and so on, through to YAHOO, YAP, and YOKEL. Herewith a sampling of these geographic derogations:

Apple-knocker town; Boobopolis; Bugville; burg (as in the old New England joke, wherein the city slicker stops at a general store and asks, "Where is X-burg?" To which the reply is, "Don't you move a goddamned inch!"); *Chump Junction; Clodville; Clunksville; cow town* (going against the grain, Fort Worth, Texas, calls itself "Cowtown, U.S.A." in opposition to the big-city pretensions of neighboring Dallas); *cross roads; Dog Patch* (cartoonist Al Capp's updating of *dog town*); *dump; East Jesus; four corners; ghost town; God-forsaken place; Gopherville; Goose Hill; grease spot in the road; Hard-scrabble; hayseed town; hell's half acre; hick town* (or *-ville*); *Hodgeville, Hoosierville; Jackass Gulch* (thus, on a proposal in 1870 to remove the nation's capital to California: "Jackass Gulch can hardly meet with opposition. Jack is a jolly fellow. Ass is the superlative stentorian verbose orator. Gulch means a nice shady place with rippling waters, where gold may be found. Who could wish for more—jolly fellows, long thundering speeches, plenty of money, and lying in the shade?" [Representative James A. Johnson, Democrat, California]); *Jakeville; Jayville; jerkwater town* (from nineteenth-century railroading, when crews of locomotives with small boilers used buckets to jerk water from pans that were set between the tracks at towns that were so small they weren't worth stopping at); *Junkville; Mudville* ("There is no joy in Mudville—mighty Casey has struck out," Ernest Lawrence Thayer, "Casey at the Bat," 1888); *Noplaceville; one-eyed* ("A little one-eyed, blinking sort of place," Thomas Hardy, *Tess of the D'Urbervilles*, 1891); *one-horse town; one-lung town; Palooka Center; Pumpkin Center; prairie dog town; Rubeville* (and *Rube Center*, etc.); *shirt-tail bend; shitburg; shit-poke town* (the shitpoke also is the small green heron, so-called on account of its tendency to evacuate its bowel when taking to wing: as a place name, slightly euphemized, quoting a boy on his visit to Neosho, Missouri, "I hate these little shike-poke towns," Vance Randolph and George P. Wilson, *Down in the Holler*, 1953); *Squash Corner; Stickville; tanktown* (slightly larger, theoretically, than a *jerkwater town*, since trains actually stopped to take on water at *tanktowns*); *Thistle Stop; tinhorn village; Toonerville* (the famed Toonerville Trolley in Fontaine Fox's comic strip, *Toonerville Folks*, which ran for forty years, starting in 1915, was inspired in part by the notoriously unreliable Brook Street line in Louisville, Kentucky); *whistle-stop* (a town where trains did not stop except upon whistle signals, usually called a *flag station* or *flag stop* by railroaders, but incorporated into the vocabulary of politics as *whistle-stop* to describe the brief halt of a campaign train for a speech at a small town, as a result of President Harry S Truman's national train tour in 1948); *wide place* (or *-spot) in the road* ("Fountain Inn [South Carolina] is just a desolate wide place in the road," Alexander Woollcott, *Cosmopolitan*, 9/33); *yahoo town* (New York City is *Yahooville-on-the-Hudson*, according to Sinclair Lewis, *Main Street*, 1920); *yap town* (an underworld nickname for Cleveland, in particular); *Yokelville;* and *Yokelania*. See also BOONDOCKS, HICK, ONE-HORSE, and PEORIA.

pogey bait. Candy, sweets; specifically, a treat that is used to lure a young male—the *pogue*—into a homosexual encounter. Popularized in the U.S. Navy and Marines, the expression dates to at least World War I. Both *pogey bait* and *pogue* have been generalized considerably. The first may be used in completely nonsexual situations, e.g., talking about loading transports while it rained in Wellington, New Zealand, prior to the invasion of Guadalcanal in 1942: "Marine workers in drenched dungarees groaned to see cartons of cigarettes and candy, or 'pogey bait,' turn soggy" (Richard Wheeler, *A Special Valor*, 1983). *Pogue*, meanwhile, has been extended in the Marines to denote one who serves behind the lines in a combat zone or who is more or less incompetent. "In the strictest sense, the word refers to pederasty . . . [but it] can be either a deadly insult or a term of amiable affection, depending entirely on who uses the word, the tone of voice and to whom it is being applied . . ." (Jeremiah O'Leary, letter to William Safire, *New York Times*, 1/1/84).

Pogue's origin is unknown. Among the guesses: that it comes from the Gaelic *pogue*, a kiss, or, an alternative of a rather different sort, from *pogy*, as used for various fish, including the porgy and the menhaden; that *pogey bait*, for catching fish, was extended to sweets for catching young males, through association with the young (below the legal age of consent) women who are known as *jailbait*; and that the term has a Chinese root, remembering that Marines served in China from the time of the Boxer Rebellion (it may be significant that *pogee* is modern Korean slang for the female genitals). Finally, and perhaps most likely, *pogue* also is a variant of *poke*, which has long been fraught with sexual meanings. *To poke* is to thrust or jab and, hence, also to copulate. At the same time, a woman is a *poke* (usually *a good poke* or *a bad poke*), not only because of the action but also because a *poke* is a pocket, sack, pouch, or, the modern feminine equivalent, a BAG.

pol. Politician. The short form reeks of smoke-filled rooms and is almost always used pejoratively. "'Pol' is to politician what 'cop' is to policeman" (Fletcher Knebel, 1964, in [William] *Safire's Political Dictionary*, 1978). See also PEANUT, THROTTLEBOTTOM, and TINHORN.

Polack/Polock. A Pole or a person of Polish descent. Archie Bunker (1971–83) loved this one, often referring to his son-in-law, Mike Stivic, on the TV show "All in the Family," as that "Polack pinko meathead" (Stivic being mildly liberal politically). The show's huge success helped popularize the term, especially in the form of Polish jokes, such as *Mad* magazine's 1973 parody of Johnny Carson's "Amazing Carnak" mentalist routine:

CARNAK: The answer is "Dope Ring"!
ANNOUNCER: And what is the question?
CARNAK: Describe six Polacks sitting in a circle.

The epithet was by no means original either to Archie Bunker or his chief creator, Norman Lear. Americans have been using the word, usually insultingly, since the end of the nineteenth century—and they were just picking up on well-established European usage. For example, that great liberal Karl Marx once threatened to sue a London newspaper, *The Daily Telegraph*, which he described as being owned by "polack Jews" (letter to Freidrich Engels, 2/9/1860, in Saul Padover, *Karl Marx, An Intimate Biography*, 1980). Nor was Marx the first in the field: "You from the Polack wars, and you from England, Are here arrived" (William Shakespeare, *Hamlet*, 1601–02). And so it goes, back into the mists of time. The *OED's* earliest example of the word (as *Polakes*) comes from a letter by Sir Philip Sidney, indited November 27, 1574. And there isn't any reason to think that Sidney invented the word. Of course, neither he nor Shakespeare had the same choices that we do today, the modern polite form, *Pole*, apparently not arising until the mid-seventeenth century (*OED*, 1656). The retention of the archaic form for purposes of insult is paralleled by the use of the old but nonstandard INJUN for *Indian* and NIGGER for *Negro*. See also PALOOKA and note Spiro Agnew's apology for *Polack* in JAP.

polecat. Not rally a cat at all, but a weasel-like animal (in Europe) or a skunk (in the United States). Both Old and New World animals are noted for their ability to emit a powerful STINK. Hence, they serve equally well as epithets for noxious individuals, especially in the past, whores and courtesans, e.g., "Out of my door, you witch, you rag, you baggage, you polecat, you ronyon!" (William Shakespeare, *The Merry Wives of Windsor*, 1597).

The *pole* in *polecat* probably comes from the Old French *pole* (*poule*), a chicken, reflecting the animal's preference when raiding the barnyard for food. A domesticated variety of the *polecat* is the ferret (from Latin *fur*, thief), which can be trained to hunt rabbits and rodents. This animal's ability to root out hidden things is preserved in the verb, *to ferret* or *ferret out*. See also RUNNION, SKUNK, and WEASEL.

pooh-bah. A pompous person. The epithet converts an important person into a self-important one. It comes from Pooh-Bah, a character in *The Mikado* (W. S. Gilbert, 1885). The English began using the term generically within a few years of the comic opera's opening and Americans soon picked it up, too. See also BAH.

pooh-pooh. An exclamation of contempt, denial, or impatience, a reduplication of the elemental human *pooh*, caused by rapidly expelling air from the lungs. The *pooh* part appears in writing first as *puh*, e.g., "Affection, puh! You speake like a greene girle" (William Shakespeare, *Hamlet*, 1601–02). *Pooh-pooh* has been dated to 1679 (as *pough-pough*), and it continues to see service. "The securities industry . . . doesn't want to know what's happening or pooh-poohs the extent of cocaine abuse—at least publicly" (*Wall Street Journal*, 9/12/83). See also PHOOEY.

poontang. Sexual intercourse or a woman regarded as a sex object; *poon* in short. "What's the matter with having a little poontang? Ain't nothing dirty about it unless you feels dirty in your mind" (William Lindsay Gresham, *Nightmare Alley*, 1946). The word probably is a Creole pronunciation of the French *putain*, whore, though Chinese and West African sources also have been suggested. See also PIECE.

poop. A bore; an ineffectual person. "You pedantic boring old poop" (*The Wrong Box*, film, 1966). On rare occasions, the term is used affectionately, e.g., "You poop. I love you" (Ernest Thompson, *On Golden Pond*, 1979). More often, though, the *poop* who *poops out* is derided as a *party poop(er)*. The boring *poop* has been dated only to 1915 (*OED*). The term may be a shortening of the older NINCOMPOOP, or the obsolete *poop-noddy*, a fool, but it is likely that the modern meaning has been reinforced by onomatopoetic potty talk, which also is of some antiquity. For example, *poop* in the sense of "to break Wind backwards softly" appears in Nathan Bailey's *English Dictionary* of 1721. As applied to a person, then, an *old poop* is similar etymologically to an *old fart*. See also BORE, CLINCHPOOP, and WET BLANKET.

poor white trash. The lowest of the low; the earliest examples of the phrase suggest that it originated among black slaves as a disparagement for Southern whites at the very bottom of the region's socioeconomic ladder. "The slaves themselves entertain the very highest contempt for white servants, whom they designate as 'poor white trash' " (Fanny Kemble, *Journal*, 1/6/1833). Certainly, blacks continued to use the phrase, and variations of it, for many years. Thus, from an 1899 novel by a black author: ". . . but dis yer Ole Nick wa'n't nuffin but a po' buckrah, en all de niggers 'spised 'im ez much ez dey hated 'im, fer he did n' own nobody, en wa'n't no bettah 'n a nigger, for in dem days any 'spectable pusson would ruther be a nigger dan a po' w'te man" (Charles W. Chesnutt, *The Conjure Woman*). See also BUCKRA, PECKERWOOD, REDNECK, TACKY, TRASH, WHITEY, and the black child's ditty in NIGGER.

popinjay. A fop, a stuck-up person, one who is conceited without having anything to be conceited about. "Whoso belongs only to his own age, and reverences only its gilt Popinjays or soot-smeared Mumbojumbos, must needs die with it" (Thomas Carlyle, *On Boswell's Life of Johnson*, 1832).

What we call PARROTs today originally were *popinjays*, the latter word entering the English language around 1300, a couple hundred years before the other. The contemptuous senses of *popinjay*, dating to the early sixteenth century, derive from the bird's gaudy plumage and its ability to repeat words without understanding them. Now that *parrot* has taken over as the label for the bird, *popinjay* is left with its contemptuous senses only.

poppycock. Nonsense. "You won't be able to find another pack of poppycock gabblers as the present Congress of the United States" (Charles Farrar Browne, *Artemus Ward: His Travels*, 1865). "Executive poppycock" (Senator Sam J. Ervin, Jr. [Democrat, North Carolina], 4/2/73, on the Nixon Administration's offer to have its high-ranking members testify before the Senate Watergate committee, but only in nonpublic sessions).

Poppycock is a Dutch contribution to English. It derives from *pappekak*, soft dung, and ultimately, on the *kak* side, from the Latin *cacare*, to defecate, whence also the childish *ca-ca*. See also BUNK and CRAP.

pregnant. Carrying a developing fetus in the uterus; gestating; breeding. Now considered an innocuous word, *pregnant* was a taboo term until after World War II, when the troops returned home and the baby boom began, with so many women becoming pregnant at once that both the condition and the word for it became socially acceptable. Previously, mothers-to-be generally were described on formal occasions as *anticipating* (a *blessed event*), *enceinte*, *expectant* or *expecting*, *in a family way*, *in a delicate* (or *interesting*) *condition*, *preggers* (or *preg*, *preggo*, and *preggy*, if British, though *preggers* sometimes is used in the United States by Americans with transatlantic pretensions), and the simple but essentially euphemistic *with child* (as far as the phrase goes, the child might as well be on a leash as on an umbilical cord).

Many quaint country expressions for pregnancy have been recorded. In the Ozarks, for instance, a man might say (provided no women are around to hear him) that "his wife is *ketched*, or *pizened*, or *springin'*, or *sprung*, or *too big for her clothes*, or *knocked up*, or *comin' fresh*, or *lookin' piggy*, or *otherwise*, or *teemin'*, or *with squirrel*, or *fallin' apart*, or *fallin' to pieces*, or . . . *that she has swallered a watermelon seed*" (Vance Randolph and George P. Wilson, *Down in the Holler*, 1953). If an unmarried woman has the misfortune to get pregnant, she might be said *to stump her toe*. Variations on this theme, all casting the event in terms of an accident, include *sprain* (or *break*) *an ankle*, *break a leg*, and *break a leg above the knee*. But such verbal roundabouts have not been confined to the hills of Missouri, Arkansas, and Oklahoma. In England, for example, Captain Francis Grose recorded *sprain an ankle* in the pregnant sense in *A Classical Dictionary of the Vulgar Tongue* (1796). And in the northeastern United States in the 1930s, to the question, "How do you say, 'She is pregnant?' " interviewers for the *Linguistic Atlas of New England* (Hans Kurath, *ed.*, 1939–43) elicited such answers as *she's getting out of shape, she's wearing her apron strings high, she's coming in soon,* and *she's been knocked higher than a kite.* This was provided the New Englanders didn't clam up entirely when questioning turned to this particular topic. As noted by Falk Johnson (*American Mercury*, 11/50), "Some of the people hesitated slightly before replying. Some replied in whispers though no one was in the room except the interviewer and the person being interviewed. And some refused to discuss the matter at all, even in whispers. So strong was the resistance to this question, say the editors of the *Atlas,* that 'In some cases the field-workers thought it advisable to refrain from asking for these words.' One investigator dropped the question entirely."

The gradual easing of the taboo on the term is indicated by the progressive changes in the title of one of the classic books on childbirth: *Pregnancy, Birth and Family Planning* (Alan F. Guttmacher and Irwin H. Kaiser, revised edition, 1986). It was initially published in 1937 as *Into This Universe,* then revised and republished in 1947 with the title, *Having a Baby.* Not until the 1950s did *pregnancy* make it into the title (*Pregnancy and Birth,* 1956), with the almost-as-controversial *Family Planning* being added in 1973. (In 1961, seven thousand copies of another work coauthored by Dr. Guttmacher, *The Complete Book of Birth Control,* were returned to the printer by the Chicago Post Office, and it took some months before authorities in Washington conceded that an error had been made and allowed the copies to resume their passage through the mails.)

We have come, as the saying goes, a long way, baby.

prick. An obnoxious fellow; the penis. "I did not write S.O.B. on the Rostow document . . . I didn't think [Canadian Prime Minister John] Diefenbaker was a son of a bitch. I thought he was a prick" (President John F. Kennedy, in Donald Hook and Lothar Kahn, *Book of Insults and and Irreverent Quotations,* 1980). The term may be elaborated in many ways, e.g., *silly prick, stupid prick, prick face,* and *prick tease(r).*

As a personal epithet, the word has been dated only to 1929 (*OED*), but this usage is certainly much older, considering the antiquity of the penile sense (from the sixteenth century in writing and no doubt much earlier in speech) and the well-established tradition of referring to people in terms of their intimate anatomy (see COCK, PUTZ, and SCHMUCK, as well as, on the distaff side, PUSSY and TAIL). The word's penile meaning follows logically from the primary sense of a prick being produced by something sharp and piercing, and it fits with other metaphors for the penis as a weapon (e.g., *gun, pistol, short arm,* or *truncheon*—take your pick) for use in what is sometimes referred to as "amorous combat." The Romans thought of this *affair, apparatus, business, gadget, instrument, member, organ,* or *thing* (again, take your pick) as a *gladius,* or sword, for placement in a *vagina,* or sheath. See also DICK, DORK, SCHLONG, SCHMUCK, SHAFT, SNAKE, and TOOL.

Shakespeare, Jonson, Heywood, Beaumont, Fletcher, and Dekker, among others, used *prick* with anatomical intent in works that were performed before live audiences in the sixteenth and seventeenth centuries. It was even used during this period as a term of endearment. Not until the latter part of the seventeenth century does it appear that much of a taboo became attached to the term. Thus, discussing the word's use as an endearment, the translator ("H.M., gent.") of *The Colloquies or Familiar Discourses of D. Erasmus* noted in 1671: "One word alone hath troubled some, because the immodest maid soothing the young man, calls him her Prick. . . . He who cannot away with [i.e., stand for] this, instead of 'my Prick,' let him write 'my

Sweetheart.' " The onset of this taboo closely coincides, not so coincidentally, with the first appearance in the written record of the Latin *penis* (literally, tail). The oldest example of this term in the *OED* comes from a medical text that was translated in 1684 and published in 1693.

By the eighteenth century, people were resorting to asterisks and dashes to blot out the now-offensive word. Even Captain Francis Grose waffled a bit on this one, including an entry on "GOBBLE P---K," defined as "A rampant, lustful woman" in his *Classical Dictionary of the Vulgar Tongue* (1796), though he later dispensed with the dashes in his entry on "PRICK" itself. And just fifteen years later, when Grose's work was revised by "A member of the Whip Club" and republished as the *Lexicon Balatronicum*, the "gobble" entry was deleted, while the main entry was softened to "P---K." Thus, Victorianism flowered before the queen ascended to the throne (1837).

Naturally, the new niceness created something of a quandary for the Bowdlers and their ilk, when faced with such speeches as that by Touchstone in *As You Like It* (1599–1600):

> He that sweetest rose will find
> Must find love's prick and Rosalinde.

As Noel Perrin reports in *Dr. Bowdler's Legacy* (1969), Henrietta Maria Bowdler slashed away, cutting ten lines here when preparing the first edition of *The Family Shakespeare* (1807). Her brother Thomas, with greater restraint, cut only two lines in the second edition (1818). Epes Sargent, another editor, or bowdlerizer, omitted four lines at this point. The objection was pinpointed, however, by William Chambers and Robert Carruthers in *The Household Edition of the Dramatic Works of William Shakespeare* (1861). They changed but a single word, making the passage read:

> He that sweetest rose will find
> Must find love's "thorn" and Rosalinde.

Ah, well—proprieties are still preserved. In the case of JFK's remark about Mr. Diefenbaker, for example, official historians have left accounts of varying degrees of vagueness. Arthur Schlesinger, Jr., summed up the incident this way: "Kennedy thought the Canadian insincere and did not like or trust him. The round of talks in Ottawa [May, 1961] was civil enough, though a confidential memorandum from Walt Rostow to the President setting forth our objectives at the meeting somehow fell into Canadian hands and caused trouble later" (*A Thousand Days*, 1965). Theodore C. Sorenson included a few more details: "Kennedy had inadvertently left behind one of the staff papers he had been using. Diefenbaker not only expropriated the paper but threatened to expose it publicly, claiming that it referred to him as an s.o.b. (Apparently this was a typically illegible reference to the OAS, which the President was urging Canada to join. 'I couldn't have called him an s.o.b.,' commented Kennedy later. 'I didn't know he was one—at the time')" (*Kennedy*, 1965).

End of official story.

prima donna. A spoiled, conceited, temperamental person; from the Italian for "first lady," as of an opera company, but by no means limited to women in its extended sense. ". . . he [General George C. Marshall] kept reminding Eisenhower that all generals were apt to be 'a bunch of prima donnas' and never to forget that 'Montgomery is about the only hero the British have' " (Leonard Mosley, *Marshall*, 1982). The transfer of the term from music to other fields took place during the first part of the nineteenth century. The word also may be used as a verb: "Stop prima-donnaing and accept the fact" (Ernest Hemingway, *For Whom the Bell Tolls*, 1940). The adjective is *prima donnaish* and the preferred form of address, for anyone who dares use it, is *Your Prima-donnaship*.

prune. A disliked person, especially a prude; a fool or simpleton. The expression seems to have arisen in the United States prior to 1900. It is still current: "I think she's a bit of a prune" (Judith Krantz, *Scruples*, 1978). See also LEMON.

prushun. A boy who travels with a hobo, begs for him, and, usually, is his catamite. "I once knew a kid, or prushun, who averaged in Denver nearly three dollars a day" (*Century Magazine*, 11/1893). The term probably comes from *Prussian*, either as an aspersion on the manliness of German soldiery, or from (*my*) *prooshan blue*, a nineteenth-century term of endearment reflecting the temporary popularity of Prussians in England, owing to their help in defeating Napoleon at Waterloo (1815). See also GERMAN and PUNK.

pseudo. An insincere person, a fake. "The undiscriminating, arty chat of a campus pseudo" (*Observer*, 5/28/67). In the case of a really smooth *pseudo*, the word may be pronounced *suedo*. The term has been around for a while, e.g., "How men shal knowe siche pseudos" (John Wyclif, *English Works*, ca. 1380). *Pseudo* also is an excellent prefix for denigrating that which the user of the word considers to be inauthentic, false, or fraudulent, as in *pseudoartist, pseudoevent, pseudofact, pseudofolk* (*music*), *pseudohippy, pseudointellectual, pseudophilosopher, pseudorebel, pseudoscientist*, etc. See also PHONY, SO-CALLED, and ULTRA-.

puke. To vomit, or the matter ejected; also an old name for a Missourian. " 'That's tough, Joan, because I don't like you. You make me puke, if you want to know' " (Sylvia Plath, *The Bell Jar*, 1961).

Puke is labeled "coarse" in the 1982 supplement to the *Oxford English Dictionary*, but people were not always so queasy about using the term. For example, Sir James Murray did not bother to append a usage note to *puke* when he prepared Volume P of the original edition of the *OED* in 1904–09—and he was usually quite sensitive in matters of this sort.

The term's origin is not known, but it may well be onamatopoetic, so to speak. The derivative, *pukishness*, has been dated to 1581, but the word as we now know it appears first in Shakespeare's "All the world's a stage" speech: "At first the infant, Mewling and puking in his nurse's arms" (*As You Like It*, 1599–1600).

The extended, Missourian sense has been dated to 1835: "The inhabitants . . . of Michigan are called *wolverines* . . . of Missouri, *pukes*" (A. A. Parker, *A Trip to the West and Texas*). Many explanations have been offered for this locution, e.g., that it is a corruption of *Pike*, as in Pike County, Missouri (see PIKER); that the first settlers of St. Louis suffered an epidemic of nausea after eating wild greens; that the residents of that city used to dose themselves with *puke-root* as a remedy for fever and ague; and that so many Missourians had left home that it seemed as though the state had vomited them up. "Whatever the origin of the name, there are men in

Arkansas and Oklahoma today who always refer to Missouri as the *Puke Territory* or the *Puke Nation*" (Vance Randolph and George P. Wilson, *Down in the Holler*, 1953). See also BARF, BELCH, and, for the people who live across the river from the *pukes*, SUCKER.

punk. An inexperienced person, a nobody, someone or something of little account or inferior value; a young ruffian or HOODLUM; earlier, a catamite; and still earlier, a prostitute.

The origin of *punk* is not known. The sense progression, from harlot to homosexual, parallels that of GAY. *Punk's* whorish meaning, which has been dated to the early sixteenth century, remained dominant through the nineteenth. The word was used in this sense by Jonson, Shakespeare, Dekker, and other writers, e.g., from a broadside ballad of 1620–55: "A woman that will be drunk, / Will eas'ly play the punck." At the end of the eighteenth century, Captain Francis Grose defined *punk* as "A whore; also a soldier's trull," and at the end of the nineteenth century, the anonymous author of *My Secret Life* also knew the term in this sense: "At London I at first took fancy again for women in the suburbs, punks who would let me have them for half a crown . . ." The latest example of *punk* as prostitute in the *OED* comes from Aldous Huxley's *Point Counter Point* (1928).

The conversion of the word from feminine to masculine denotation, and from heterosexual to a homosexual orientation, seems have begun around the turn of this century among hoboes, sailors, and prison inmates—in isolated all-male societies, in other words. The *punk* then was the boy or young man who played the passive, female part (the tramp's traveling companion, for example), usually with the implication that the *punk* had been coopted into the role. This usage remains current; e.g., from a glossary of slang compiled at Washington State Prison in Walla Walla: "PUNK IN A BUNK. An expression commonly used referring to prison sex relationships. 'Got to have a punk in the bunk to take care of the house' " (Inez Cardozo-Freeman, with Eugene P. Delorme, *The Joint*, 1984). See also PRUSHUN and QUEER.

The *punk* as criminal has been dated to 1917: "By failing to get up . . . I escaped departing with the bums mutts and jeffs (not to say ginks, slobs, and punks) who came over with us" (e.e. cummings, letter, 6/4/17). This sense of the word seems to have been popularized by detective story writers of the 1930s, though it is likely that Dashiell Hammett had the homosexual meaning in mind, too, when writing such lines as (Sam Spade to Kaspar Gutman): "I told that punk of yours that you'd have to talk to me before you got through" (*The Maltese Falcon*, 1930). For more on Gutman's relationship with his *punk* and, not so coincidentally, another word that originally denoted a catamite, see GUNSEL. The criminal sense probably is responsible for the aggressive *punker* or *punk rocker* (whose mate is the *punkette*), as well as for the verb, *punk out*, which is to adopt the style of a *punker* or, an earlier meaning, to quit, especially on account of fear, e.g., "Well; the boy had said, wavering, he had promised B . . . that he would go through with the hold-up. He didn't want to 'punk out' " (*New York Times Magazine*, 3/21/54).

Then there is the worthless *punk*, whose meaning may depend in part on an entirely different kind of *punk*, referring to the spongy, rotten wood or fungus used because it is slow burning to light fireworks and other explosives. (The smoldering *punk* makes an intriguing musical covergence with the malodorous *funk*, as in *funky jazz*; see FUNKY.) The connection with the *punk* that burns has been credited to

Thomas Carlyle (1795–1881), who characterized nonsensical or foolish writing as "phosphorescent punk and nothingness." (He seemed to like glowing metaphors; see MOONSHINE.) It is not unlikely, however, that the sense of inferiority was reinforced by the *punk* you could get for half a crown in the same way that CHIPPIE has been extended to include anything that is small and amateurish, as a *chippie habit.* Whatever, we now have *punk ideas, punk poetry* (see JUNK for an example), *punk athletes,* and so on, together with the generalized *punk,* as in the following example, with which these notes must end as it is impossible to top (or, some would say, sink lower than): "A man had two daughters, Lizzie and Tillie, and Lizzie is all right but you have no idea how punctilious" (attributed to George S. Kaufman, F.P.A., New York *Evening Mail,* 6/3/23).

puppet. An individual or nation controlled by another. The metaphor has been dated to 1550 (the reference being to "kynges" who are "poppetes") and it remains popular, with Communist speakers often using it to disparage their non-Communist opponents and vice versa. Thus, from the account by General Van Tien Dung, North Vietnam's Chief of Staff, of the final offensive in 1975 that led to the conquest of South Vietnam: "The morale and combat strength of the puppet troops were clearly declining" (*New York Times,* 4/26/76). On the other hand, there is the memo written in August 1944 by George F. Kennan, then minister-counselor at the American embassy in Moscow, criticizing rules proposed by the United States for the United Nations: "We ignore completely the time-honored conception of the puppet state which underlies all political thought in Asia and Russia, and occasionally appears in Eastern and Central Europe as well. . . . Try asking the head of the Outer Mongolian Republic whether Mongolia has any grievances against Russia. He will pale at the thought" (*New Yorker,* 2/20/84). See also LACKEY, PUPPY, ROBOT, and SATELLITE.

puppy. A young man, especially an inexperienced or conceited one; often an *impudent, insolent,* or *silly puppy.* Such a youth may also be *puppy-headed* (stupid), have *puppy fat* (baby fat), and be afflicted with pangs of *puppy love.* Or pulling out all stops: "Shane Lautenslager . . . says the [National Survival Game] offers a release from the confines of corporate behavior. 'Out there,' he says, 'I can yell, scream, call people slime puppies, chicken molesters, whatever' " (*Wall Street Journal,* 5/22/84).

It used to be that women also could be classed as *puppies.* ". . . I carelessly led forth my youth, and wantonly spent the flower of my years, holding such maidens as were modest, fools, and such as were not wilfully wanton as myself, puppies, ill brought up and without manners" (Robert Greene, *A Disputation, Between a Hee Conny-catcher, and a Shee Conny-catcher, whether a Theefe or a Whoore, is most hurtful in Cousonage, to the Common-wealth,* 1592). The word's feminine sense flowed from *puppy's* earliest (late fifteenth century) meaning as a lady's dog, or lap dog, with this in turn deriving from the French *poupée,* a doll or a woman likened to a doll, a plaything. (From *poupée* also comes PUPPET, with which *puppy* originally was interchangeable.) See also DOG, WHELP, and Dr. Johnson's use of *puppy's mother* in BITCH.

pussy. A woman as well as the most common of the current euphemisms for the ancient, Standard English, but heavily tabooed "cunt"; also, a man regarded disparagingly as a woman.

Both feminine senses (along with the synonymous *puss* and *pussycat*) appear to derive from CAT, which has been used for some centuries to denote either a whole woman or this particular part of her. The use of the same word for both is common. Others with this double meaning include BEAVER, *bit, bunny,* CONY, *cookie, cooz,* CUNT, FISH, MONKEY, *mouse, mutton* (see MUTT), PIECE, QUIM, SNATCH, SQUIRREL, TAIL, and TWAT. The conjoining of the two meanings in these words obviously says much about the attitudes toward women in the sectors of society where they are used most frequently. But it should be remembered that men also are treated this way; see COCK and PRICK.

In the sense of "adult human female," *pussy* is at least four hundred years old, e.g., "The word pussie is now used of a woman" (Philip Stubbes, *The Anatomie of Abuses,* 1583). The anatomical sense probably is equally old, though it is hard to say for sure since precise meaning often depends upon context and the documentary evidence prior to the nineteenth century is not always as clear as one might wish. Thus, in their monumental *Slang and Its Analogues* (1902), J. S. Farmer and W. E. Henley illustrated the anatomical sense with a toast from 1664: "Aeneas, here's a Health to thee, / To Pusse and to good company." The editors of the 1982 supplement to the *Oxford English Dictionary* questioned the citation, however, noting that it "may not exemplify this meaning, claimed for it by Farmer and Henley."

Over such nuances, great lexicographers do battle. Arguing in favor of the *OED*'s interpretation is the fact that *puss* and *pussy* were used endearingly of women through much of the nineteenth century, and it seems unlikely that the words would have gained wide currency in this form if the other meaning were well-known. Not many Americans today would address a young woman in this manner: " 'What do you think, pussy?' said her father to Eva" (Harriet Beecher Stowe, *Uncle Tom's Cabin,* 1852). On the other hand, it also is possible that the editors of the *OED* have a bit of a blind spot here, since they give for the phrase, "to eat pussy," the rather opaque definition, "of a man, to engage in sexual intercourse."

Related phrases include *pussy posse* (police talk for the vice squad); *pussy power* (defined by Germaine Greer in *The Female Eunuch,* 1970, as the manipulation of men by "wheedling and caressing, instead of challenging"); •*pussy talk* (gossip among women); *pussy-whipped* (of a man, to be bossed around by a woman or simply henpecked); *pus-pus* (an example of reduplicative Pidgin English from Melanesia, meaning "[to have] sexual intercourse"); and *PCOD* (a military abbreviation for "pussy cut-off date," meaning the last day on which a serviceman can have sexual intercourse and still be treated for venereal disease, should the need arise, before embarking on a long and otherwise possibly painful voyage).

As a quintessentially feminine word, *pussy* ordinarily is a great insult when applied to a man. *Puss* and *gentlemen puss,* along with *pussy,* imply that the male is effeminate, old-maidish, and perhaps overtly homosexual—or, putting the best possible construction on it, merely a timid weakling, e.g., talking about a male hockey team, "They came here to scout the toughest team in the Federal League—not this bunch of pussies" (*Slap Shot,* film, 1977). The masculine application of *pussy* is in line with a common linguistic transformation, one that mirrors society's pecking order: while "male" words with "bad" meanings become attached to women (see HARLOT, for example), "female" words with "bad" meanings tend to be foisted off on homosexuals (see SISSY).

putz. An obnoxious fellow, a fool; the penis. " 'You,' she said, enunciating clearly, 'are a putz, a schmekel, a schmuck, a schlong, and a shvantz. And a WASP putz at that" (Judith Krantz, *Scruples,* 1978). As should be obvious from this example, the term is Yiddish. It derives from the German *putz*, decorations, ornaments, and has been dated to 1934 in the anatomical sense and to 1964 in the extended, personal sense. It was one of the words that got Lenny Bruce in trouble in Los Angeles in 1962 (see EAT). "*Putz* is not to be used lightly, or when women or children are around. It is more offensive than *shmuck;* the latter may be used in a teasing and affectionate way, vulgar though it is, but *putz* has a pejorative ambience" (Leo Rosten, *The Joys of Yiddish*, 1968). See also PRICK, SCHLONG, and SCHMUCK.

pygmy. An insignificant person; anyone or anything as small figuratively as a real pygmy is physically. "I was sore at pygmies trying a great man like Oppenheimer" (I. I. Rabi, explaining his support of J. Robert Oppenheimer, who was declared a security risk in 1953, *New York Times*, 1/12/88).

The existence of pygmies has been known since ancient times (they are mentioned by Homer and Herodotus, and depicted in Egyptian tombs), but the name of this people does not seem to have been used disparagingly in English until the sixteenth century, e.g., "The King doth smile at, and is well prepared / To whip this dwarfish war, this pigmy arms, From out the circle of his territories" (William Shakespeare, *King John*, 1594–97?). See also MIDGET.

quack. One who does not know what he is talking about; especially, a pretender to medical knowledge. "America's first great quack was Dr. Elisha Perkins (1740–1799)" (Martin Gardner, *Fads and Fallacies in the Names of Science*, 1957). The term is an old one, dating to the seventeenth century, and is sometimes elaborated, depending upon need, into such forms as *psychoquack, quackery, quackster,* and *quackupuncture.* It comes from the older, sixteenth-century *quacksalver* (where the *salver* is salve or ointment and the *quack* probably refers to the way itinerant medicine men sold the stuff, i.e., *to quack*). Whether or not they actually made duck-like noises, the reputation of *quacksalvers* was no better than that of modern *quacks,* e.g., from *The Virgin Martyr* (1622) by Philip Massinger and Thomas Dekker:

> Out, you imposters!
> Quack salving, cheating mountebanks! your skill
> Is to make sound men sick, and sick men well.

Dr. Perkins, by the way, believed that diseases could be drawn out of the body by passing one of his patented (1796) Metallic Tractors downward over the ailing part of the body. He sold his tractors for five guineas each. Customers included George Washington, whose entire family used the device. See also CHARLATAN, DUCK, and, for a look at how *quacks* used to work, consult *toad-eater* in TOAD.

quail. Once upon a time (Chaucer's time), a timid person, but in our time, usually a woman, often a young and attractive one (see *chick* in CHICKEN) and sometimes a prostitute or WHORE. A subspecies is the *San Quentin quail,* a young woman who inspires lustful thoughts that are better repressed since she is below the legal age of consent—*jailbait,* in other words.

Quail is the leading example of the use of the names of game birds to refer to prostitutes. Others include *bird, bird of the game, game hen, game pullet, lone dove, lone duck, partridge, pheasant,* and *plover.* At one time, to go searching for such women was *to go grousing.* In the case of *quail,* the allusion to hunting may be reinforced by what the OED refers to as "the supposed amorous disposition of the bird." True or not, the idea has been around for some centuries, e.g., "Here will be Zekiel Edgworth, and three or four gallants with him at night, and I have neither plover nor quail for them; persuade this . . . to become a bird of the game" (Ben Jonson, *Bartholomew Fair,* 1614). See also BAT and the *Winchester geese* in GOOSE.

queen. A male homosexual, especially one who plays the female part. ". . . *queen* can be used defiantly but is essentially derogatory . . . the word implies both effeminacy and elegance, though *butch queens* would not appreciate being described as 'elegant' (or maybe as *queens*) and *disco queen* is more neutral, descriptive" (Leonard R. N. Ashley, *Maledicta*, Winter 1980).

The homosexual sense derives from the longstanding British use of *quean* (cognate to the royal *queen*) as a term of disparagement. This word has been used since before the year 1000 to designate a bold or ill-behaved woman, a HUSSY or JADE, and especially (in the sixteenth and seventeenth centuries) a WHORE. The oldest example in the *OED* of a homosexual *queen* is from 1924, but this meaning of the word goes back at least to the 1880s. Thus, when John Saul, a male prostitute involved in the Cleveland Street scandal of 1889, was asked in court the following year if he lived with "a woman known as Queen Anne in Church Street, Soho," the reply was "No, it is a man. Perhaps you will see him later on" (in H. Montgomery Hyde, *The Cleveland Street Scandal*, 1976). See also QUEER.

queer. Homosexual. "*Queer, fairy, faggot,* and *swish* were familiar to all ten of the heterosexual informants, and they agreed that these words have unpleasant connotations. Homosexuals indicated that they knew the words, but felt that they were more properly to be regarded as heterosexual slang. Several of the homosexuals pointed out that their use of one of these hetero terms is always understood as an insult and has no nonpejorative meaning" (Julia P. Stanley, *American Speech*, Spring–Summer 1970). Note that *queer*, though originally applied to men, has become bisexual, e.g., "Some girls said that I was queer and that she shouldn't be friendly with me" (letter to Dr. Franzblau, syndicated newspaper column, 5/21/56).

Queer is a relatively new word, dated only to 1508 (*OED*), and of uncertain origin. It perhaps derives from the German *quer*, across, adverse, perverse, though the earliest examples of its use suggest that it might also be of Scottish origin. *Queer* became something of a vogue word in the eighteenth century, appearing in many slangy phrases such as *queer as Dick's hatband* (out of order), *queer birds* (rogues released from prison), and *queer bit-makers* (counterfeiters)—which are just three of the twenty-three *queer* entries in Captain Francis Grose's *Classical Dictionary of the Vulgar Tongue* (1796).

The homosexual sense, apparently an Americanism, has been dated only to 1922, with the earliest example in the *OED* coming from a publication of the Children's Bureau of the U.S. Department of Labor. Here, the use of quotation marks around the word suggests that it was not widely known at the time: "A young man, easily ascertainable to be unusually fine in other characteristics, is probably 'queer' in sex tendency" (*The Practical Value of Scientific Study of Juvenile Delinquency*). Homosexuality seems to be implicit, however, in the advertisement that was placed by Diana and Norma, of 213-215 North Basin St., New Orleans, in the *Blue Book*, a directory of Storyville, the city's red-light district, which was published annually for several years, from ca. 1902: "Their names have become known on both continents, because everything goes as it will, and those that cannot be satisfied there must surely be of a queer nature." It seems, too, that the denizens of Storyville knew the word in an off-beat heterosexual sense since the preface to the *Blue Book* uses the terms "Sporting District" and "Queer Zone" interchangeably. If so, this would not be unusual; another word that managed to encompass both heterosexual and homosexual meanings at about the same time was GAY.

The homosexual sense has nearly submerged the rest of the word's meanings. Thus, for fear of misunderstanding, it is hardly ever said nowadays that Sam, say, is *queer on* Janet, meaning that he is in love with her, or that he is *on Queer Street*, meaning that he is bankrupt, or almost so. The tendency of other meanings to atrophy once a word becomes associated with homosexuals is common, of course. See also DYKE, FAG, FAIRY, FLIT, FREAK, FRUIT, GUNSEL, HOMO, MOLLYCODDLE, PANSY, PERVERT, POGEY BAIT, PRUSHUN, PUNK, QUEEN, SISSY, SODOMITE, SWISH, and the various female given names, such as *Lizzie* and *Nancy*, in MOLL.

quim. The female pudendum, the vulva. "Were you brushing the cobwebs off a few quims?" (James Joyce, *Ulysses*, 1922). "Please note that Scene #131 gives you an excellent shot at the fantastic winner-quim of our beautiful young girl star" (letter, Terry Southern to Lenny Bruce, 7/31/64, Albert Goldman, from the journalism of Lawrence Schiller, *Ladies and Gentlemen, Lenny Bruce!!*, 1974). As with so many of its synonyms (see PUSSY), this word also is used to refer to women collectively, as in "The key to success in this contest is a flashy car; and if the car is both expensive and impressive, 'you have to beat the quim off with a hockey stick' " (*Saturday Night*, Toronto, 1/74).

Quim was one of the four-letter words discreetly omitted from the first edition of the *Oxford English Dictionary* (Volume Q, 1902), but included in its supplement (1982). The term has been dated to the first part of the eighteenth century and may well be older. Captain Francis Grose speculated that it came from the Spanish *quemar*, to burn (*A Classical Dictionary of the Vulgar Tongue*, 1796). Other, probably better possibilities, suggested in the *OED*, are that it is related to *quaint* (in the sense of a woman's "priuities," according to the great dictionary's exceedingly reticent 1902 entry on that term) or to the obsolete *queme*, with such provocative meanings as "to act so as to please (one)"; "to be suitable or fitting for"; "to join or fit closely"; and "to slip in."

quisling. A traitor. "Mr. Karaeen found his dialogue with the Israelis dwindling away. Palestinians were either dealt with as quislings who cooperated with the occupation or they were banished to the margins, he said" (*New York Times*, 12/28/87).

Thus, we remember the role of Major Vidkun Quisling, Norwegian Nazi leader, who helped the Germans prepare to conquer his country in World War II, then served as premier during their occupation of it. (*b.* 1887, *d.* by firing squad, 1945). Usually it takes some time for an individual's name to become a generic term, but in Quisling's case this feat was accomplished practically overnight—a measure of his dastardy. The Germans invaded Norway on April 9, 1940. Ten days later, Edward R. Murrow said in a CBS broadcast from London: "I don't think there were many Quislings in the Norwegian Army or Navy." The new meaning of the name was ratified by the highest authority: "A vile race of quislings—to use the new word which will carry the scorn of mankind down the centuries" (Winston Churchill, speech, 6/12/41). See also BENEDICT ARNOLD, FIFTH COLUMNIST, JUDAS, PÉTAIN, RENEGADE, TOKYO ROSE, and TRAITOR.

quitter. One who gives up without a fight; an Americanism from the late nineteenth century (*OED*, 1881). "A man may shirk and be a 'quitter,' as they call him, in the class room, if he pleases, but he cannot be a 'quitter' on the football field and retain his position on the team" (*Churchman*, 9/22/06). "I have never been a quitter. To leave office before my term is completed is abhorrent to every instinct in my body" (Richard M. Nixon, address to the nation, 8/8/74, announcing his resignation of the presidency as a result of what he called "the Watergate matter").

R

rabbit. A person of no account, especially a timid one, a novice (in schools, freshmen are *rabbits*), or a poor and easily victimized gameplayer (a CONY). As a general expression of contempt: "Away, you whoreson upright rabbit, away!" (William Shakespeare, *Henry IV, Part II*, 1596–97).

racist. One who emphasizes the differences between races, almost invariably to the benefit of his own; a bigot. "I recently heard a man denounced as a racist for having observed that the rate of illegitimacy in New York is 14 times as high among the Negro population as among the white" (*San Francisco Examiner*, 4/14/65). Currently one of the strongest of all political attack terms, *racist*, strangely, is much newer than the phenomenon. Dated only to 1932 in the OED, it is a condensation of the older *racialist* (from 1917). The latter—the more common of the two in Britain—occasionally is encountered in the United States, as in Herman Badillo's characterization of New York City Mayor Edward I. Koch as "a petty racialist who fans the flames of racism" (*New York Times*, 12/12/85). See also SEXIST.

racketeer. Originally a gangster and, by extension, anyone in business, politics, or another endeavor who makes use of supposedly illegal, often strong-arm tactics. The oldest examples of *racketeer* as well as the basic *racket*, referring to organized criminal activities, come from Chicago of the 1920s (though *racket* as slang for a dodge, scheme, or line of business goes back to the early nineteenth century).

"What is the NRA? The National Racketeers Arrangement . . . Nuts Running America . . . Never Roosevelt Again" (Senator Huey P. Long [Democrat, Louisiana], filibuster, 7/35, against extension of the National Recovery Act). "I spent thirty-three years and four months in active service as a member of our country's most agile military service—the Marine Corps [in Nicaragua, Mexico, Haiti, Honduras, Cuba, the Dominican Republic, and China]. . . . And during that period I spent most of my time being a high-class muscle man for Big Business, for Wall Street, and for the bankers. In short, I was a racketeer for capitalism" (Major General Smedley Butler, USMC, Retired, *Common Sense*, 11/35).

The term continues in more or less extended use: "[The Nicaraguan Contras are] a small ragtag army of racketeers, bandits, and murderers" (Thomas P. [Tip] O'Neill, with William Novak, *Man of the House*, 1987). See also THUG.

radical. Extreme, far out; a political attack term, both on its own and in such combinations as *radical chic, radical conservative, radical liberal* (condensed by Vice President Spiro Agnew, in 1970, to *radic-lib*), and *radical right*. "A radical is a man with both feet firmly planted—in the air" (President Franklin D. Roosevelt, radio speech, 10/26/39).

Deriving from the Latin *radix*, root, the term entered politics with the Radical Reform movement in the late eighteenth century, when the more advanced members of the Whig Party began pressing for thorough, or radical, changes to democratize the British constitution and society in general. Naturally, their enemies often applied the term reproachfully to them, e.g., "Radical is a word in very bad odour here, being used to denote a set of blackguards" (Sir Walter Scott, letter, 10/16/1819). The word's connotations improved following passage of the Reform Bill of 1832, but the Radicals never managed to form a parliamentary party, becoming extreme Liberals instead. In the United States, the term was associated first with socialists and others of the LEFT, many of them of European origin. Thus, to most Americans, *radicals* always seemed to have a tinge of un-Americanism. "There is a foreign atmosphere about him, the stamp of an alien radical, a strong resemblance to the type Anarchist as portrayed, bomb in hand, in newspaper cartoons" (Eugene O'Neill, *The Iceman Cometh*, 1946). See also EXTREMIST, LIBERAL, MILITANT, and UN-AMERICAN.

raghead. An Arab, a Hindu; any Asian who wears a turban or other cloth headgear. "Seventy-five percent of Americans surveyed could not locate the Persian Gulf on a map (like we're supposed to care where these ragheads swim)" (Bill Duryea, *New Milford* [Connecticut] *Times*, 8/4/88). The term has been dated to 1921. It may have originated at the University of California, where foreign students with turbans were a common campus sight. See also ASIATIC and GOOK.

randy. Wanton, lecherous, sexually aroused. "She'll be randy directly her belly is filled" (Anonymous, *My Secret Life*, 1890). The sexual sense, dated only to 1847, flows naturally from the word's older meanings, i.e., to be rude, coarse-spoken, obstreperous, dissipated, unruly. *Randy* seems to be a seventeenth-century offshoot of the Scottish *rand*, itself a variant of *rant*, which for many years had much the same set of meanings as *randy*. Thus, from *Slang and Its Analogues*: "RANTING, *adj.* = (1) in high spirits; and (2) amorous" (J. S. Farmer and W. E. Henley, 1902). See also HOT.

rape. Forced sexual intercourse. *Rape* was long banned from print and polite discourse. Instead, when the crime was reported, such euphemisms were used as *assault, attack, interference* (primarily British), and *molestation*. Books also were censored. Thus, speaking of the period between the wars: ". . . publishers, aware of the market among women readers, who liked sexual content but objected to taboo vocabulary, diligently pasteurized all manuscripts. For example, in Faulkner's *Sanctuary* [1931], the term *rape*, taboo even in newspapers, was sacrificed" (David W. Maurer, *American Speech*, Spring–Summer 1976). A notable exception, which may have helped people get used to seeing the term in print, was the not-so-metaphoric "rape of Nanking" (12/13/37), when "Japanese troops wantonly slaughtered some 40,000 civilians and ravaged [sic] thousands of women" (David Eggenberger, *A Dictionary of Battles*, 1967).

The taboo on *rape* pretty much went by the boards during the postwar years, when other four-letter words, of far greater power, began to see the light of day (in books, if not newspapers). Still, in the late—presumably liberated—1970s, Canadian processors of rapeseed felt they had to change the name of their product to *canola* in order to gain greater market acceptance.

rascal. A dishonest person, a ROGUE. "What will be their policy aside from 'Get the rascals out,' a good slogan but not a policy" (Nathan Glazer, *New York Times*, 11/12/87).

Dating to the fourteenth century, *rascal* is of obscure origin. It may derive from the Old French *rasque*, mud, filth. The term was first applied to people of the lowest class—the rabble of an army, camp followers, or common soldiers. The word's political associations have been strong for many years, however. Thus, the slogan "Turn the rascals out" seems to have been popularized by Charles A. Dana, when attacking the Tweed ring in the New York *Sun* (ca. 1871). But a century earlier, Dr. Samuel Johnson, who commonly referred to Whigs as *rascals*, expressed essentially the same thought, telling Boswell what he would do if he had a lot of money: "If I were a man of great estate, I would drive all the rascals whom I did not like out of the country at an election" (3/31/1772, Boswell's *Life of Johnson*, 1791). Then there is the fine distinction attributed to John P. Hale, of New Hampshire, a former Democrat who represented his state as an Antislavery senator (1847–53, 1855–65): "I did not say that all Democrats were rascals; only that all rascals were Democrats." (Horace Greeley later converted this one into: "I never said all Democrats were saloonkeepers. What I said was that all saloonkeepers are Democrats.") The term also may be used as a verb, e.g., "But being rascalled out of my election, I am taken all aback" (*Colonel [Davy] Crockett's Exploits and Adventures, Written by Himself*, 1837). See also KNAVE and SCALAWAG.

raspberry (razzberry). A derisive sound made by putting the tongue between the lips and blowing out; a Bronx cheer. " 'Razzberry' is on the Association's list of unacceptable words and expressions and could not be approved" (advice from the Motion Picture Association of America's Johnston Office—Eric Johnston having succeeded the better-known Will Hays in 1945—to the producers of *Bedtime for Bonzo*, 1951, starring Ronald Reagan and a chimpanzee).

The sound of a *raspberry*, properly made, is indicated by the term's etymology (of which the motion picture censors evidently were aware), i.e., *raspberry* is short for *raspberry tart*, with the *tart* part being Cockney rhyming slang for the noise that is made when a person vents, or breaks, what is politely called "wind." The medium, then, truly is the message.

Raspberry tart has been dated to the late nineteenth century. The clipped form, *raspberry*, was popularized in theatrical circles around 1900, often in the phrase *to give [someone] the berry* and, apparently an American innovation of the post-World War I period, *to razz [someone]*. Besides denoting the particular sound, the various terms have been extended to include general disapproval, dismissal, heckling, and teasing, e.g., "The Red Swede got the grand razz handed to him" (Sinclair Lewis, *Main Street*, 1920). See also BERK, BIRD, and Prince Hamlet's contemptuous "Buzz, buzz" in ASS.

rat. A despicable person; a sneaky, dishonest one; especially a police informer, i.e., one who *rats* or SQUEALs on his pals, also called—among other bestial terms—a CANARY, *long-tailed rat* (a rat of the very worst sort), *mouse, nightingale*, PIGEON, *ring tail* (or, in full, *ring-tailed skunk*; see SKUNK), and WEASEL. In the general, despicable sense: Secretary of the Interior Harold L. Ickes, a CURMUDGEON of the first water, described Governor Eugene Talmadge of Georgia as looking "more like a rat than any other human being I know . . . [with] all the mean, poisonous, and treacherous characteristics of that rodent" (Arthur M. Schlesinger, Jr., *The Politics of Upheaval*, 1960).

Rat has been used in a disparaging way at least since the reign of Richard III (1483–87), when one of the king's men, Sir Richard Ratcliff, was known, not so fondly, as *the ratte* (for details, see HOG). In the sixteenth through the nineteenth centuries, the epithet was applied to lowlife of various sorts, including DRUNKs; pirates; politicians who deserted their parties (reflecting the belief that rats, sensing danger, will leave a house that is about to fall or a ship that is destined to sink); workmen, especially printers, who either refused to join a strike or agreed to do their jobs for less than union wages (see SCAB); and to college students or cadets, usually freshmen or other newly admitted pupils.

The meaning of *informer* is a comparatively recent one. This sense is included in *Slang and Its Analogues* (J. S. Farmer and W. E. Henley, 1902), but without their usual illustrative examples, which suggests the usage then was too new to have been committed frequently to paper. The term's continuing strength was underlined by a 1984 decision of the Connecticut State Supreme Court: "A man convicted of killing three guards during an April 1979 robbery of a Purolator armored-car depot in Waterbury has won a new trial because a prosecutor called him a 'rat,' a 'merciless killer' and other names" (AP, 10/6/84).

The pejorative meanings of *rat* carry over to other forms of the word. Thus, *rats!* is an expression of annoyance or disgust (probably, however, from *rot*, which is used the same way, rather than from the animal); *to give [someone] rats* is to rebuke that someone or to make trouble for the other person; and anything that is disreputable, mean, or shabby may be said to be *ratty*. Other commonly encountered kinds of *rat* include:

boonierat. One who lives in the outback, especially an infantryman, from the amount of time these soldiers spend in the BOONDOCKS; also *field rat.*

rat fink. An extremely odious person; see FINK.

ratfuck. Antisocial behavior, ranging from practical joking to unsavory and/or downright illegal political activities, such as bugging offices, planting spies, forging letters, stealing documents, and disrupting opposition rallies. This expression was popularized in the late 1950s at Stanford and other centers of higher education on the west coast. In 1963, the initials "R. F." were burned into the grass of the Stanford football field prior to the game with the University of California. Ten years later the expression was burned into the American consciousness when it was revealed during the course of the Watergate scandal that some employees of the White House had engaged in *ratfucking* on a national scale during the 1972 presidential election. The point man in these activities, Donald H. Segretti (in Italian, his name means "secrets"), and a number of his associates had learned their lessons at the University of Southern California. "All belonged to a campus political party called Trojans for Representative Government. The Trojans called their brand of electioneering 'ratfucking.' Ballot boxes were stuffed, spies were planted in the opposition camp, and bogus campaign literature abounded" (Carl Bernstein and Bob Woodward, *All The President's Men*, 1974). For an example of *ratfucking* as practiced in national politics, see CANUCK.

rat line. A route used by a *rat*. ". . . Army intelligence officers told their civilian counterparts falsely that they had lost contact with Mr. [Klaus] Barbie, and smuggled him out of Europe in early 1951 through an underground railroad for Soviet bloc defectors and informants dubbed 'the rat line' " (*New York Times*, 8/2/83).

rat pack. A gang, originally teenage use, from ca. 1950; glamorized in the early 1960s by the Hollywood *rat pack*, led by Frank Sinatra.

rat race. Life; mindless striving for short-term rewards. The phrase has been dated only to the 1930s. It seems to have started out as an allusion to a mad scramble or whirl. "A cadet's first flight comes in 'rat race' (great swarm of planes at Corry Field") (*Life,* 8/26/40).

rats in the attic (or *garret, loft, upper story*). To be eccentric, weird, or just plain crazy; from the nineteenth century, if not earlier. See also SCREW LOOSE, A.

rug rat. A Jew, to an anti-Semite. "The Alberta [Canada] Teachers Association has been criticized for strongly defending Mr. [James] Keegstra's unfettered right of free speech, which student notes indicate included references to Jews as 'rug rats' " (*New York Times,* 5/26/83).

smell a rat, to. The phrase dates to the sixteenth century and remains useful. For instance, one of the pieces of evidence that CBS introduced in its defense against a libel suit brought by General William C. Westmoreland was a 1968 letter from an intelligence analyst in Vietnam, who told his wife that investigators from the Defense Intelligence Agency were examining American estimates of enemy strength because they had "smelled a rat . . . They know we've been falsifying the figures, but can't figure out which ones and how" (*New York Times,* 1/14/85).

Finally, in the canyons of Wall Street, home of the bull and the bear, there also lurks a *rat* of acronymic proportions: "But it's too late; as he barks out the command, 'the Rat' has already entered the market, snapping up $40 million of the issue from a Becker salesman. The Rat, as traders call Merrill Lynch's Ready Assets Trust, is the biggest of the money funds" (*Wall Street Journal,* 7/20/83).

rattlesnake. A dangerous person; frequently a cunning one as well. Thus the Reverend Cotton Mather, in one of his less ecumenical moods, described the Anglican ministers that dared invade his Congregational turf as ". . . Ignorant wretches, and such debauched and finished villains, that, like the rattlesnakes in our country, they carry with them what warns and arms our people against being poisoned with them" (Kenneth Silverman, *The Life and Times of Cotton Mather,* 1984).

The image has easily withstood the test of time. For example, when Representative Wright Patman (Democrat, Texas) began showing his age (eighty-one), Representative Richard Bolling (Democrat, Missouri) allowed as how "The old man has always been a rattlesnake and now he is senile" ([MORE] magazine, 4/75). Using the term as a verb, General William C. Westmoreland complained after an interview with CBS's Mike Wallace, "I have been rattlesnaked" (*New York Times,* 11/20/84). The general was not the first to use the word this way, however. "We must cut this, and not be rattlesnaked into any more of the like" (John Keats, letter, 2/3/1818). See also SNAKE.

raunchy. Indecent, smutty, filthy. "Mr. [Rupert] Murdoch's raunchier British newspapers, the News of the World and the Sun, continue to bring in millions. Their formulas emphasize crimes, sex and sob stories" (*Wall Street Journal,* 12/9/83).

Raunchy seems to be comparatively new, but is of unknown origin. It surfaced first in the late 1930s as Army Air Corps slang, meaning inept, awkward, or sloppy, and was soon broadened (by 1941 or before) into a general term for anything in bad shape or dirty. After the war, the word was popularized by college students (many of whom had been in the armed forces) and its meaning was extended from simple dirtiness to sexual earthiness. The back-formation, *raunch,* dates from the 1960s. It has the same range of grubby, vulgar meanings, but is more versatile, since it also can be employed as a verb, one that reduces the act of sexual intercourse to its shabbiest, crudest level, e.g., ". . . she's raunched a few law students" (*National Lampoon*, undated, in Robert L. Chapman, *ed.*, *New Dictionary of American Slang*, 1986). See also CRUD.

reactionary. One who responds to action by moving in the opposite direction; in a political sense (from the mid-nineteenth century), an opponent of revolution, progressivism, or liberalism. The inherent sense of backwardness in *reactionary* makes it a fine attack term, whether one is lashing out to the right or the left, e.g., "I can find you hundreds of the most sordid rascals, or the most densely stupid reactionaries, with all these qualifications" (George Bernard Shaw, *Back to Methuselah*, 1921). Or, flailing away in the other direction, there was the tirade by Patrick J. Buchanan, White House director of communications, against Mario Cuomo, governor of New York, in which Mr. B. called Gov. C. a "glib, fast-talking lobbyist for a reactionary liberalism that would kill tax reform in its crib" (*New York Times*, 6/16/85). Technically, "reactionary liberalism" is an oxymoron, or contradiction in terms, meaning nothing. See also EXTREMIST.

Red. Communist or seemingly Communist. Thus, referring to veterans of the Abraham Lincoln Brigade, which fought on the Republican side in the Spanish Civil War: "They were labeled 'Reds' or even 'premature antifascist' " (*New York Times*, 12/28/86). The color makes a convenient target for attacks, especially in such combinations as *red baiter* and *red hunter*. Headline writers also find the short word to be a useful one, as in "Red newspaper won't be read in town library" (Waterbury, Connecticut, *Republican*, 1/21/88, reporting a decision by the library in neighboring Southbury to stop accepting free copies of the weekend edition of *The People's Daily World*).

Long a symbol of violence, as the color of blood and fire, *red* has been the particular color of Communism since the revolutions of 1848. "The 'Red Republicans' have justified their name. They have filled the streets of Paris with blood. . . . The working classes, or 'Red Republicans,' were imbued with the doctrines of Communism" (*Illustrated London News*, 7/1/1848). A century later, during the Cold War years, the associations of *red* in the United States were so pejorative that some people strove to avoid it even in nonpolitical contexts. For instance, the Cincinnati Reds began calling themselves the *Redlegs*. The team, the first to play baseball on a professional basis, had begun life in 1869 as the Red Stockings, but *stockings* was no longer acceptable in a sporting context; hence the substitution of *legs*. (For another, very fine distinction of this sort, see DEVIL.) Of course, this also was a period when *Better Dead Than Red* (Stanley Reynolds, 1964) was considered a serious reply to the disarmament slogan "Better Red Than Dead." See also PINKO and SCARLETT LADY.

red dog. (1) In nineteenth-century America, a bill or note of a private bank; such notes, of shifting and often little value, also were called WILDCAT money, and they were issued by *red dog* or *wildcat* banks. (2) A low grade of flour, better suited for feeding animals than humans. (3) Either of two poker games, most commonly a five-card game, also called high-card pool, a favorite "for social groups who want a betting game in which the action is fast and the demands on brainwork not too great" (Albert H. Morehead and Geoffrey Mott-Smith, *Hoyle's Rules of Games*, 1983).

The canine in each of the foregoing instances is a symbol of inferiority, as is usually the case; see DOG. In football, a *red dog* is an aggressive defensive maneuver in which a linebacker charges the quarterback. But this exception to the rule is apparent, not real. In football, the *dog* derives from *to bulldog*, which is what cowboys do when they seize a calf (like a bulldog) and wrestle it to the ground, while the *red* comes from Don "Red" Ettinger, of the New York Giants, who said after executing such a play in 1949 that he had been "just doggin' the quarterback a little" (Tim Considine, *The Language of Sport*, 1982).

red herring. A diversion, distraction, or misdirection that draws attention from the main subject at hand. "And [the House Un-American Activities Committee hearings] are simply a 'red herring' to keep from doing what they ought to do" (President Harry S Truman, press conference, 8/5/48).

Herring, which turn red when smoked, originally were used to teach dogs how to follow a scent. "The trailing or dragging of a dead Cat, or Fox, (and in case of necessity a Red-Herring) three or four miles . . . and then laying the Dogs on the scent" (Nicholas Cox, *The Gentleman's Recreation*, 1686). It probably wasn't too long after this that some smart felon figured out that dogs could be distracted by drawing a red herring across his trail. By the late nineteenth century, the term was being used in the present, figurative sense: "The talk of revolutionary dangers is a mere red herring" (*Liverpool Daily Post*, 7/11/1884). See also FISH.

redneck. A poor, white, rural Southerner, especially a racist, but often used loosely as an attack term. "I'll bust that little redneck in the mouth" (New York Mets right-fielder Darryl Strawberry, upon learning that second baseman Wally Backman had questioned his desire to play; *New York Times*, 7/5/87).

Redneck is usually but not always derogatory, the principal exception to the rule coming when politicians seek to gain votes by identifying themselves with *redneck* values. Thus, from a recapitulation of the prepresidential career of Jimmy Carter: "He had appealed to the supporters of Gov. George C. Wallace of Alabama in his successful campaign [for governorship of Georgia] in 1970, and he frequently described himself as a 'redneck,' a synonym for the traditional racial attitudes of the Deep South" (*New York Times*, 7/15/76).

Redneck has been dated to 1830. Initially applied to Presbyterians in Fayette-ville, North Carolina, it probably alludes to the sunburned neck of the typical field-worker. The image may have been reinforced by the effects of pellagra, formerly endemic in the South. The lesions produced by this disease, the result of dietary deficiency, are aggravated by sunlight and, in chronic cases, may form a ring that follows the line of the victim's shirt collar. " . . . 'redneck' is the only opprobrious epithet for an ethnic minority still permitted in polite company. . . . Within living memory [it] was not a pejorative but the opposite, a populist honorific for an honest son of toil" (C. Vann Woodward, *New York Times Book Review*, 2/5/89). See also DIRT-EATER, HICK, and POOR WHITE TRASH.

regime. A government that is opposed by the user of the term. "[Russia] seemed to me one vast prison in which the jailors were cruel bigots. When I found my friends applauding these men as liberators and regarding the regime they were creating as a paradise, I wondered in a bewildered manner whether it was my friends or I that was mad" (Bertrand Russell, *The Theory and Practise of Bolshevism*, 1920). "But if *Time* [magazine] makes a regressive contribution to literary language, it nonetheless does so with enormous care. Socialists not only plan, they 'concoct'; they rarely have governments, they have 'regimes'; Marx's laws of history were not scientific, they were 'scientific' " ([MORE] magazine, 5/78).

The chief people in a *regime* frequently are said to be *bosses*, e.g., Communist party *bosses*, not *leaders*, or to constitute a *clique*, as opposed to the ruling *circle* of a friendly nation. (Note that the United States itself is blessed with an intelligence *community*, and, some say, a military-industrial *complex*, not an intelligence or military-industrial *clique*.)

The negative connotations of *regime* probably are the result of the word's association with pre-Revolutionary France, i.e., the autocratic *ancient* (*l'ancien*) or *old regime*. They are also in keeping, however, with the *regime*'s etymology, from the Latin *regere*, to rule, which makes it basically a more authoritarian word than *government*, from the Latin *gubernāre*, to direct or steer (as a ship). See also BOSS and TERRORIST.

renegade. A traitor. This was originally a term of religious abuse, from the Medieval Latin *renegatus*, one who has denied the faith; specifically, by converting from Christian to Mohammedan. It came into English in several forms, including *renegate* and *renegado*, as in "He was a Renegado, which is one that first was a Christian, and afterwards becommeth a Turke" (Richard Hakluyt, *The Principall Navigations, Voiages and Discoueries of the English Nation*, 1599). The same Latin word gave rise to *renege*, which is what people are said to do when they fail to keep their commitments, whether in real life or, in particular, at cards, e.g., "Reneging or renouncing, that is, not following suit when you have it in your hand, is very foul play" (Charles Cotton, *The Complete Gamester*, 1680). See also PAGAN and QUISLING.

reptile. A loathsome person, especially a groveling, sneaky one, since the seventeenth century; from the Latin *reptilis*, crawling. "This work, may, indeed, be considered as a great creation of our own, and for a little reptile of a critic to presume to find faults with any of its parts without knowing the manner in which the whole is connected . . . is a most presumptuous absurdity" (Henry Fielding, *Tom Jones*, 1749). And the term remains in service. Witness the sign posted in the lobby of an apartment house in Brooklyn, New York, to greet the landlord, who had accumulated so many violations that he was sentenced to live for a time in his own building: "Welcome you reptile. Bad m'gmt plus poor services equals unhappy tenants" (*New York Times*, 2/13/88). See also CROCODILE and SNAKE.

rhubarb. (1) A noisy argument or brawl, especially on a baseball diamond; (2) nonsense or any other worthless thing; (3) in the military, a low-level mission in search of targets to strafe or bomb; (4) in the plural, a metapor for rusticity in the phrase *out in the rhubarbs*; and, (5) a symbol for the genitals, usually male.

The first two senses may derive from the theatrical practice of having actors simulate crowd noise by mumbling, "Rhubarb-rhubarb." (The similar sounding "hubba-hubba" also is used, but note that foods often serve as metaphors for nonsense; see BALONEY. It may also be significant, considering that both these senses involve worthless confusion, that rhubarb is a mild emetic.) The third, military meaning may refer either to the close-up view pilots have of gardens when they are on strafing missions or to the resemblance of bullet spatters to luxuriant rhubarb plants; one guess seems to be as good as another. The fourth, rustic sense appears to be a play on *suburbs* with a dash of RUBE thrown in.

When it comes to the final, sexual meaning, one is reduced to considering the length of rhubarb stems and to tracing the faintest of etymological trails. The *rhu*-part of *rhubarb* apparently comes from *Rha*, a former name of the Volga River (on whose banks rhubarb grew), deriving in turn from the Indo-European root, *ers*, to be wet, which also has given us, among other words, the modern *arse*, or ASS (as well as the Old Persian *arshan-*, man, which, in its turn, produced the second syllable of *Xerxes*, meaning "ruling over men"). The *-barb* part of *rhubarb*, meanwhile, represents the stem of the Latin *barbarus*, with the name of the plant translating as "foreign rhubarb" (see also BARBARIAN).

Whatever the force of the underlying linguistic associations, there seems to be no doubt about *rhubarb*'s sexual significance in both Great Britain and the United States. Under this heading, Eric Partridge included the definition, "Genitals, male or, occ., female: low: late C. 19–20. E.g. 'How's your rhubarb, missis?' or 'How's your rhubarb coming up, Bill?'" (*A Dictionary of Slang and Unconventional English*, 1970). And on the American side of the Atlantic, in *Down in the Holler* (1953), Vance Randolph and George P. Wilson cited as an example of *rhubarb*'s "off-color" meaning, the following fragment of a folk song, collected in Sulphur Springs, Arkansas:

> The cat couldn't kitten an' the slut couldn't pup,
> An' the old man couldn't git his rhubarb up.

ribbon clerk. An amateur; an ineffectual person. "In poker . . . a player with a good hand may say as he raises the pot, 'Let's keep the ribbon clerks out!' This is pure gamesmanship, employed to needle other players into meeting the raise lest they be thought too timid" (Albert Z. Carr, *Business As a Game*, 1968). See also NED IN THE FIRST READER.

riffraff. Worthless, disreputable people or trashy things. Thus, referring to the white inhabitants of New Zealand: "The pakeha are riffraff, the flotsam and jetsam of British culture" (Atareta Poananga, *New York Times*, 10/29/87). *Riffraff* dates to the fifteenth century in the sense of the scum of society and to the fourteenth century as *rif and raf*, meaning one and all, every single bit. It derives from an Old French phrase that translates roughly as "spoiled sweepings." Probably, its alliterative nature has helped it to survive. See also FLIMFLAM and PEASANT.

right-winger. A conservative in politics. "Don't call us right-wingers—that's a slander" (Richard V. Allen, former national security adviser to President Reagan, as quoted by William Safire, *New York Times Magazine*, 8/18/85). *Right-winger* is an exception—and a comparatively recent one at that—to the rule that the connotations of *right* are all right, while those of LEFT are bad. Mr. Safire explains: "A generation ago, people on the political right did not mind being called *right-wingers. . . . right wing* had a sassy connotation—even the 'moderate' among us counted ourselves as a hardy band of conservatives, murmuring 'I'd rather be right' as we consigned ourselves, legs bowed but heads unbowed, to the clubbiness of permanent minority status. . . . [but] it became the term used by those on the left to attack us, and instead of reveling in that attention, we took umbrage" (*op. cit.*). See also EXTREMIST.

rip off. To steal or the act of stealing (a *rip-off*). The term did not have such bad connotations when it was popularized in the counterculture of the 1960s. "In defying the law, young people claim not only a special innocence of wrong-doing but a special kind of moral superiority. 'Ripping off the Establishment,' they insist, is a political act" (Dr. Joyce Brothers, *Good Housekeeping*, 2/66). "The implication is that the telephone company, the rich or corrupt are being taught a gentle lesson when the coins, the TV set or some merchandise on display are 'ripped off,' like a superfluous appendix" (Grace Hechinger, *Wall Street Journal*, 10/27/71). The term's euphemistic veneer wore through fairly quickly, however, as it was applied to thefts of all sorts, including those perpetrated by the Establishment, e.g., "Spiro [Agnew] got caught ripping off tax money" (*Black Panther*, 3/16/74).

Rip-off may have arisen from underworld slang; *rip-and-tear mobs* are among the lower, less artistic orders of pickpockets (as the name implies, they tear pockets instead of picking them). Or *rip off* may simply be a variant of *tear off*, with which it shares a number of meanings. For example, *rip off some sleep* and *tear off some sleep* are synonymous for "to take a nap." Both phrases also refer to having sexual intercourse, as in "Let's rip one [or someone, always a "her"] off," or, "Look, you come down and tear off a piece anytime. And the wine—*Asti Spumante*—she is on me. I stand the wine. The girls, that is up to you" (Stephen Longstreet, *The Pedlocks*, 1951).

See also TRASH.

roach. A contemptible person. The term can be used in the same way as INSECT to blot out the humanity of one's opponents, e.g., "Its [the Tehiya party's] stellar figure is former chief of staff Rafael Eytan, who said while in office that he would treat the Arabs in occupied territories so firmly that they would be like 'drugged roaches in a bottle' " (*New York Times*, 7/30/84).

Over the years, *roach* also has carried such specific meanings as (1) a police officer, (2) an ugly or unpopular coed, and (3) a local reporter who boards a presidential candidate's airplane for only one leg of a campaign flight (the top national correspondents who stay for longer stretches are known, ominously, as *big feet*).

Roach is a nineteenth-century euphemism for *cockroach*, which is not a compliment either: " ' . . . you hain't got the invention of a cockroach' " (Robert Louis Stevenson, *Treasure Island*, 1883). The euphemization of *cockroach* (*rooster roach* also has been reported) actually is quite unjust, since the word has nothing to do with that foul fowl, the *cock* (see COCK). The bug's name comes from *cacarootch*, which is how Captain John Smith (of Pocahontas fame) rendered the Spanish *cucaracha* in his *Generall Historie of Virginia, New England and the Summer Isles* (1624).

robot. A mindless person; one who acts mechanically; an automaton. "Mr. G. Bernard Shaw defined Robots as persons all of whose activities were imposed upon them" (*Westminster Gazette*, 6/22/23). The term was popularized by Karel Čapek's play *R.U.R.*, featuring Rossum's Universal Robots, but was coined by his brother Josef (the two often collaborated), who used it initially in a short story. The word began to be used widely in 1923, immediately after the play (1920) was first produced in English. It comes from the Czeck *robata*, work hard labor, servitude. The *Rossum* also is significant: It alludes to the Czeck *rozum*, intelligence, reason. See also FRANKENSTEIN, PUPPET, and ZOMBIE.

rogue. A scoundrel; an unprincipled or undisciplined animal or person, especially one with a savage, destructive disposition, as a *rogue elephant* or, in the intelligence business, a *rogue agent.* "Opinions on whether Colonel [Oliver L.] North and Admiral [John M.] Poindexter were heroes or rogues vary, but the [naval] officers who were questioned were universally astonished and puzzled over the events in which they played a role" (*New York Times*, 3/10/87). See also ELEPHANT.

A *rogue* originally (from the sixteenth century) was an idle BEGGAR or vagabond and, as such, a common term of abuse. Thus, from Robert Greene's *The Second Part of Cony-Catching* (1592): "At last the elder called the younger rogue. 'Rogue, thou swain,' quoth he, dost thou or darest thou dishonour me with such a base title?' " Shakespeare also employed the epithet with some feeling, as in this conversation from *Timon of Athens* (1606–07?):

> TIMON: Away thou tedious rogue! I am sorry I
>   shall lose
>   A stone by thee. (*He throws a stone.*)
> APEMANTUS: Beast!
> TIMON: Slave!
> APEMANTUS: Toad!
> TIMON: Rogue, rogue rogue!

The origin of *rogue* is not entirely clear. It might derive from *roger*, an obsolete word for *beggar*, in turn from the Latin *rogare*, to ask, to plead (whence also the church's Rogation Days of special prayer). On the other hand . . . *roger*, from the personal name, also is an old slang term for the penis (recorded from 1653 but no doubt much older), as well as for the act of copulation. In this case, the *roger-rogue* might well be construed in the more familiar sense of DICK or PRICK.

The copulative *roger*, by the way, was once considered quite a strong term, so much so that some of its letters often were replaced by dashes even when it was written in a private diary. Thus, James Boswell recounted an adventure on the evening of June 4, 1763, which began when "a little profligate wretch" decided to raise her fee in mid-stride, so to speak, having "allowed me entrance. But . . . refused me performance." This caused Boswell to push the "miscreant" up against the wall. She screamed, a parcel of whores and soldiers came to her rescue, and Boswell started talking fast: " 'Brother soldiers,' said I, 'should not a half-pay officer r-g-r for sixpence? And here she has used me so and so.' I got them on my side . . . and then left them. At Whitehall I picked up another girl . . ." (*Boswell's London Journal, 1762–1763*, Frederick A. Pottle, ed., 1950).

See also KNAVE, RASCAL, SCOUNDREL, and VILLAIN.

rook. To cheat or swindle, from the same word as a noun, a cheater or SWINDLER, both forms dating to the sixteenth century and deriving from the name of the Old World bird, the rook, a member of the crow family adept at stealing seed from farmers' fields. Rooks also are gregarious, nesting in huge numbers in rookeries; by extension, a *rookery* is any place crowded with characters of low repute, e.g., a slum tenement, a military barracks, or a brothel.

Rook parallels KITE and PIGEON in that it can refer either to the predatory sharper or to the novice or simpleton who is preyed upon—who is, as the metaphor goes, *rooked.* The sense of *rook* as simpleton also dates to the sixteenth century: "Hang him, rook he! why, he has no more judgement than a malt-horse" (Ben Jonson, *Every Man in His Humor*, 1598).

In modern usage, the novice *rook* probably is influenced by *rookie*, an inexperienced person, who is prone to making lots of errors, whether as a baseball player, police officer, or soldier. But *rookie* itself is of uncertain origin. Possibly a corruption of *recruit*, it may also be—closing the circle—partly influenced by the basic *rook* that is a bird-swindler-simpleton. See also DODO and SIMPLETON.

root. The penis. "The noun root designates the male organ and must be used cautiously in decorous conversation" (Vance Randolph and George P. Wilson, *Down in the Holler*, 1953). As an example of its indecorous use, the authors cite a ditty formerly sung by vulgar boys in Stone County, Missouri:

> The gals up Rainy Creek they are full grown,
> They'll jump on a root like a dog on a bone.

The term was common in the nineteenth century. Walt Whitman used *manroot*, while Frank Harris preferred the short form, as in "I got into bed on her and slipped my root into her" (*My Life and Loves*, 1925). It dates at least to the sixteenth century and probably is substantially older. Shakespeare went to some lengths to work it into a series of sexual allusions, beginning with an *F-word*, in *The Merry Wives of Windsor* (1597):

SIR HUGH EVANS: What is the *focative* case, William?
WILLIAM PAGE: Oh, *vocativo*, O.
EVANS: Remember, William. Focative is *caret* [missing].
MISTRESS QUICKLY: And that's a good root [also "carrot"].
EVANS: 'Oman, forbear.

And so on, the conversation continuing with a question about the "genitive case," which turns out to be *horum, harum, horum*.

In Australia, *root* refers either to copulation or to the woman involved, as in "Johnny Bickel . . . thought she'd be an easy root and began to take notice of her" (D. Ireland, *The Glass Canoe*, 1976). See also PRICK.

rot. Nonsense, rubbish. Both *rot* and the extended *tommyrot* have been dated only to the nineteenth century, as in the critique of a "Sonnet by M. F. Tupper" as "A monstrous pile of quintessential rot" (H. C. Pennell, *Puck on Pegasus*, 1861). See also BUNK and TOM-.

rotter. An objectionable person; especially one who is soft and *rotten* inside, lacking moral fiber; a good-for-nothing. "A regular rotter; that man is about as bad as they make 'em" (George Moore, *Esther Waters*, 1894). Or, referring to a 1922 attempt to climb Mount Everest: "The majority opinion at the time was that oxygen would be used only by 'rotters' " (*New Yorker*, 6/7/82).

round-heels. One who is easily pushed over, as an incompetent pugilist or, the more usual context, a compliant woman. "But little round heels over there . . . she's a blonde" (Raymond Chandler, *The Lady in the Lake*, 1943).

Round heels has been dated to 1926 in the sexual sense; *round-heeler* and *round-heeled* also have been sighted. The image is basically the same as the older *light-heeled* (from at least the sixteenth century), *loose-heeled*, and *short-heeled*. For example, in *A Classical Dictionary of the Vulgar Tongue* (1796), Captain Francis Grose defined a *light-heeled wench* as "one who is apt, by the flying up of her heels, to fall flat on her back, a willing wench." (Even better, according to Grose, was the *thorough good-natured wench*, i.e., "One who being asked to sit down, will lie down.") See also WENCH.

rubbish. Nonsense; anyone or anything that is worthless; GARBAGE, TRASH. "Rubbish! Abolute rot! Is there no end to human foolery?" (A. L. Rowse, commenting on new theories as to the identity of "Mr. W. H.," dedicatee of Shakespeare's sonnets, *New York Times*, 3/3/87). Or, as children say when a disliked person departs the scene, "Good riddance to bad rubbish."

Rubbish has been dated to the fourteenth century; it is of obscure origin but may be related to *rubble*. Although seemingly a fairly innocuous term, its use can, under the right circumstances, lead to a lawsuit. Thus, the eminent critic John Ruskin described a painting by James Abbott McNeill Whistler: "It was a daub professing to be a 'harmony in pink and white' (or some such nonsense); absolute rubbish, and which had taken about a quarter of an hour to scrawl or daub—it had no pretence to be called painting" (*Fors Clavigera*, 1877). Whistler sued for libel, in part (the language aside) because the market value of paintings was influenced, then even more than now, by the length of time required to paint them, as evidenced by their finish and intricacy. (Asked in court how long it had taken him to execute a certain "impression," Whistler replied, "All my life.") See also BUNK and, for the outcome of this suit, COXCOMB.

rube. A resident of a rural area, a rustic, especially a dim-witted one; from the personal name *Reuben*. The expression is an Americanism, dating to the last century. "If I had time I'd go over to that church and make a lot of them Reubs look like thirty-cent pieces" (George Ade, *Artie*, 1896). The term was popularized by traveling circus and carnival workers, who extended it to include townspeople as well as farmers, typically in the cry *Hey, Rube!*, a call for help when one or more *rubes*, realizing that they had been cheated, threatened to get even with their fists. See also HICK.

runnion (ronion, ronyon). An old insult for a woman that warrants revival if only because no one is sure exactly what it means. Shakespeare used it in *The Merry Wives of Windsor* (see POLECAT for the unseemly context) and in *Macbeth* (1606), where one of the witches described a sailor's wife as a "rump-fed ronyon." Lexicographers have more or less thrown up their hands at this. The *Oxford English Dictionary* simply calls it "An abusive term applied to a woman." Samuel Johnson treated the different spellings as different words, defining *ronion* as "A fat bulky woman" and *runnion* as "A paltry scurvy wretch." In the first of these entries, however, he offered the disclaimer: "I know not the etymology, nor certainly the meaning of this word" (*A Dictionary of the English Language*, 1755). For that matter, Shakespearean editors are not even agreed on the meaning of "rump-fed" in the example from *Macbeth*. They have offered such diverse explanations as "fed on the best rumpsteak," "fed on scraps," and "large-bottomed" (*Shakespeare, The Complete Works*, G. B. Harrison, *ed.*, 1952). So next time you get angry at a woman, try "rump-fed runnion!" It may leave her speechless . . . for a moment or two.

runt. A small person; one of little account. A *runt* is a small animal, of course, especially, in the phrase *the runt of the litter.* The term may derive from the Dutch *rund*, small ox. It was once used in a more general sense as an epithet for anyone, regardless of size, who was considered ignorant or uncouth, e.g. "Sir, you are a welsh Cuckold, and a prating Runt, and no Constable" (Ben Jonson, *Bartholomew Fair,* 1614). The sense of smallness was in place by 1700 and at that end of that century, Captain Francis Grose defined *runt* as "A short squat man or woman; from the small cattle called Welsh runts" (*A Classical Dictionary of the Vulgar Tongue*, 1796). See also MIDGET.

Russian. Fierce, brutal, difficult, as in:
Russian boots. Leg chains.
Russian law. "A 100 blowes on his bare shins," from 1641, in Eric Partridge, *A Dictionary of Slang and Unconventional English*, 1970.
Russian love. Sadomasochism, possibly a nonce term. Thus, describing the tumultuous nine-month marriage of the American dancer Isadora Duncan and the Russian poet Sergei Esenin: ". . . their romance began when the drunken Esenin slugged Duncan at a party after one of her Moscow recitals, awakening an unsuspected masochistic streak in her and arousing her appetite for what she called 'Russian love,' all too often expressed in black eyes . . ." (*New York Times Book Review*, 5/9/76).
Russian roulette. A game played by loading one chamber of a revolver, spinning the cylinder, holding the barrel to one's head, and pulling the trigger. Those who really hate life can easily change the odds: " 'Did you ever hear of Russian Roulette?' . . . With the Russian army in Rumania, around 1917, . . . some officer would suddenly pull out his revolver, . . . remove a cartridge from the cylinder, spin the cylinder, snap it back in place, put it to his head and pull the trigger" (*Collier's*, 1/30/37).
Russian socks. Rags bound about the feet of soldiers on a march
See also DUTCH.

rustic. A simple-minded, oafish country-dweller; a BOOR or PEASANT. Stemming from the Latin *rusticus*, from *rus*, country, the term has been applied pejoratively to residents of rural areas since at least the sixteenth century. "A Rustick Fellow, one without City or School breeding, without cleanliness, and of a slovenly Speech" (Randle Holme, *The Academy of Armory*, 1688). See also HICK.

S

sadist. One who derives pleasure from another's pain; after Count (though commonly called "Marquis") Donatien Alphonse François de Sade (1740–1814), author of *Justine* (1791) and other works exemplifying this form of behavior. De Sade's name is so firmly attached to the trait that it comes as a mild surprise to find that *sadist* and *sadism* have been dated in print only to 1897 and 1888, respectively. By contrast, *sadism's* natural (or "unnatural," if you prefer) complement, *masochism*, made it into print in 1892, within the lifetime of its namesake, Leopold von Sacher-Masoch (1836–95), another author whose works revealed his private pleasures. The two terms often are coupled and abbreviated *S.M., S/M, S&M,* and so on, especially in advertisements of a personal nature. Even in innocent contexts, the terms may prove disturbing to right-thinking, straight-thinking people. Thus, a United States Army memorandum, issued in August 1985, on behalf of Chief of Staff John A. Wickham, Jr., explained that the Pentagon disliked the use of "S.M." as an abbreviation for "service member" because " 'S.M.' is a vapid construct which evokes sensings of computer-jargon cipher" (AP, 8/28/85).

Different strokes for different folks, as the saying goes. See also KINKY.

sad sack. An ineffectual, unlucky, not very bright person; if feminine, a *sadie sack.* The expression was popularized by Sergeant George Baker's cartoon character, Sad Sack, who first appeared in 1942 in the Armed Forces newspaper *Yank.* Baker did not actually invent the name of his forlorn private. Rather, he obtained it by abbreviating a common military expression of the era, *sad sack of shit (American Speech,* 12/46). Much earlier, in the eighteenth century, a *shit sack* was "A dastardly fellow; also a non-conformist" (Captain Francis Grose, *A Classical Dictionary of the Vulgar Tongue,* 1788). See also DOPE.

Sambo. A black person, especially a male. ". . . Sambo has been put up as your idol of worship, and while you keep him as your god you will fail" (Senator William Saulsbury [Democrat, Delaware], speech, 1/29/1863).

A popular personal name among blacks during slave times, *Sambo* was used generically from at least the early eighteenth century—and not always in a contemptuous manner, e.g., "As for Sambo, whose wrongs moved the abolitionists to tears, there is some reason to believe that he suffered less than any other class in the South from its peculiar institution" (Samuel Eliot Morison and Henry Steele Commager, *Growth of the American Republic,* 1930).

Obviously part and parcel of traditional racial stereotypes, however, the term began to grate as sensitivities were raised among both blacks and whites after World War II. A notable casualty of this period was the much-loved folk tale *The Story of Little Black Sambo* (Helen Bannerman, 1923; about an East Indian child, actually), which is now difficult to find on library shelves. Soon, the word came to be regarded as an attack term, e.g., ". . . you serpents of pestilence you / samboes you green witches gnawing the heads of infants" (Welton Smith, "The Nigga Section," Dudley Randall, *ed.*, *The Black Poets*, 1971).

Sambo's generic use among whites may have been influenced by the American Spanish *zambo*, a black person, a mulatto, and also a kind of yellow monkey, in turn from the Spanish *zambo*, bandy-legged. The word's widespread use as a personal name, however, suggests that it is basically African in origin, probably stemming from a Hausa word meaning "second son" or "name of the spirit." It is only one of many popular given names of the slave era that fell by the wayside, once slavery was abolished, because of their servile associations. Others include *Cuffy*, from an African word for a weekday, Friday, and given so often to boy children that it, too, became generic for any black male; *Cudjo*, from an African word for "Monday"; *Liza*, short for *Eliza* (a lead character in *Uncle Tom's Cabin*, 1852); *Mandy*, traditionally from *Amanda*, but perhaps reinforced by the tribal name *Mandingo*, little mother; *Mungo*, popularized by the slave character in an English farce, *The Padlock* (1769); and *Rastus*, as in *Rastus in Zululand* and *How Rastus Got His Turkey*, film shorts in a series that Sigmund Lubin began producing in 1909 (he also did a *Sambo* series). *Rastus*, like *Sambo*, continues to have insult value, e.g., "You're out of your league, Rastus" ("Miami Vice," WNBC-TV, New York City, 9/16/84). See also PADDY and UNCLE TOM.

sans-culotte. A radical or revolutionary from the time of the French Revolution; originally derisive, applied by the upper classes to those beneath them. "The term plebs is convenient for the *sans-culottes* and similar movements made up mainly of small shopkeepers, artisans, journeymen; proletariat for factory workers" (*New York Review of Books*, 1/30/69). *Sans-culotte* translates as "without breeches." The usual explanation for the phrase's origin is that workers and other poor people were distinguished by their trousers (*pantaloons*, as they were called then) as opposed to the knee breeches worn by the upper classes. The "without breeches" may have had a more literal meaning, however, considering that "in caricatures of the time the 'nether garments' [of the revolutionaries] are conspicuous by their absence" (Ernest Weekley, *An Etymological Dictionary of Modern English*, 1921). See also PLEBEIAN.

sap. A fool. As Alice Roosevelt Longworth said of cousin Franklin D., he is "one-third sap and two-thirds Eleanor" (*New York Times*, 2/21/80). This was such a good line that she seems to have repeated it in different forms; see also MUSH. *Sap* is a nineteenth-century clipping of the older *saphead*, *sappate*, or *sapskull*. In each instance, the reference is to the fluid found in trees, meaning that the human *sap* is, in effect, a somewhat watery BLOCKHEAD. See also DRIP and FOOL.

Note: *Pa's a sap* is a palindrome.

Satan. An enemy, as in *The Great Satan*, i.e., the United States, in the lingo of Ayatollah Ruhollah Khomeini, of Iran, from 1979 to 1989. And domestically: "The 'enemies' about whom the [Dodge City, Kansas, FM radio] station has sounded the alarm . . . are legion: blacks, Roman Catholics, Asians, public officials, the courts, the Internal Revenue Service and, particularly, Jews, which KTTL broadcasts have described as 'the children of Satan' " (*New York Times*, 5/18/83). *Satan* has been applied to people as a term of abhorrence for some centuries, e.g., Prince Hal speaking: "That villainous abominable misleader of youth, Falstaff, that old white-bearded Satan" (*Henry IV, Part I*, 1596). The *OED* considered such use of *Satan* to be "Now *rare*," but that was back when the original S–Sh sections were being prepared (1908–14), well before KTTL went on the air. See also DEVIL.

satellite. A person or, more recently, a nation in thrall to another person or nation. "Cuba is not a satellite of the USSR in the same sense that other Latin American states are satellites of the USA" (M. B. Brown, *The Economics of Imperialism*, 1974).

The term is essentially demeaning, implying that the *satellite* has no will of his, her, or its own. The connotation nowadays is that of a *satellite* kept in its orbit by the gravitational force of a larger astronomical body. The personal sense of the word is the older, however. It derives from the Latin *satelles*, an attendant or bodyguard, which may in turn have come from the Etruscan *satnal*. It appears first in English in the sixteenth century referring to a yeoman of the guard. The astronomical sense has been dated to the seventeenth century and the political sense to the eighteenth. The transition seems to have been made by Thomas Paine in *Common Sense*: "In no instance hath nature made the satellite larger than its primary planet; and as England and America . . . reverse the common order of nature, it is evident that they belong to different systems: England to Europe, America to itself" (2/14/1776). See also IMPERIALIST, LACKEY, and PUPPET.

scab. A laborer who refuses to join a union; especially, one who works while others are on strike. Thus, a sidelight to the professional football players' strike in 1987: "In the hotel lobby, he hailed another training-camp Giant, Rob Dirico from Kutztown State. 'Hey, scab,' [quarterback Jim] Crocicchia called out. 'I mean replacement' " (*New York Times*, 9/25/87).

Scab—the allusion may be ultimately to syphilitic scabs—has been a term of serious reproach since at least the sixteenth century, as in "What's the matter, you dissentious rogues, That, rubbing the poor itch of your opinion, Make yourselves scabs?" (William Shakespeare, *Coriolanus*, 1608). See also SCURVY. The use of the word to characterize strikebreakers, in particular, seems to have arisen in the late eighteenth century. The earliest example of the word in this sense in the *OED* comes from a report on a strike of shoemakers in Bristol, England: "The Conflict would not been [sic] so sharp had not there been so many dirty Scabs; no Doubt but timely Notice will be taken of them" (*Bonner & Middleton's Bristol Journal*, 7/5/1777). This sense of the word was prefigured almost a century earlier, however, by the Reverend Cotton Mather: ". . . that man is a *Wen* [an excresence, a cyst] or a *Scab* rather than a member of this *Body Politic*, who shall decline the Service of his Countrey" (election sermon, 1690, *American Speech*, 2/50). Then there is the old proverb, included in John Ray's *A Collection of English Proverbs* (1678): "He that is a blab [a tattletale] is a scab."

See also DUNG, FINK, GOON, and RAT.

scalawag. A reprobate, a RASCAL; historically, a white Republican in the South who supported the congressional plan of reconstruction after the Civil War. The *scalawag* was the Southern counterpart of the northern COPPERHEAD (a Democrat in Union territory during the war). "Those who were born in the South and remained faithful to the Government, or have since joined the Republican party, are stigmatized as the 'scalawags,' or low persons of the baser sort" (*Congressional Globe*, 4/4/1871). The origin of the term is unknown. It first appears in western New York in the sense of "a mean fellow, a scape-grace" (John R. Bartlett, *Dictionary of Americanisms*, 1848). It also was used prior to the Civil War to denote a poor or worthless animal. This raises the possibility that the term may derive from *Scalloway*, the ancient capital of Mainland, the largest of the Shetland Isles, which are famous for their diminutive ponies and cattle. See also CARPETBAGGER and POL.

scarlet lady (whore or **woman).** A flagrantly venal person, especially, in bygone, pre-ecumenical times, a Protestant epithet for the Roman Catholic Church: "I will not dispute with you whether the Pope be or be not the Scarlet Lady of Babylon" (Sydney Smith, *Letters on the Subject of the Catholics, by Peter Plymley*, 1807). The reference is to "the great whore that sitteth upon many waters" in *Revelations*, 17:1–6: "I saw a woman sit upon a scarlet coloured beast, full of names of blasphemy, having seven heads and ten horns. And the woman was arrayed in purple and scarlet colour, and decked with gold and precious stones and pearls, having a golden cup in her hand full of abominations and filthiness of her fornication." See also WHORE.

This vivid biblical image seems to have tinged *scarlet* forever with sinful associations, e.g., Nathaniel Hawthorne's *The Scarlet Letter*, of 1850 (the letter in question being *A* for "Adultery") and the *scarlet women* of ordinary brothels. Thus, the *Sunday Sun*, a weekly that reported on doings in New Orleans' *red-light* district (from 1888), included a regular "society" column called "Scarlet World." The subheads for this column in the issue of January 31, 1904, went like this:

GAY GIRLS' ACTIONS
Guilded Vice in Silk and Calico.
Interesting Items About the
Every-Day Life of Women
of Crimson Circles.

See also RED.

schlemiel (shlemiel, schlemiehl, shlemihl). A fool, especially a clumsy person or one with consistently bad luck, a JERK. "Confronted by the evidence, the already tarnished hero at last confessed that he had killed not only the poor schlemiel in the morgue but Mrs. Wanderer as well" (Alexander Woollcott, *Long, Long Ago*, 1943). The word is Yiddish, of course, first surfacing in English in the 1890s. Israel Zangwill used it in *Children of the Ghetto* (1892). It probably comes from *Shelumiel*, a leader of the tribe of Simeon (*Numbers*, 1:6), who had bad luck on the battlefield. The truly unlucky person, however, is not the *schlemiel* but the *schlimazel* (among other spellings). As Representative Stephen J. Solarz (Democrat, New York) told Secretary of State George Shultz: "A shlemiel is the fellow who climbs to the top of a ladder with a bucket of paint and then drops it. A shlimazl is the fellow on whose head the bucket falls. I fear that you will become the shlimazl of American diplomacy because it's on your head that the bucket will fall" (*New York Times*, 2/6/86). See also NEBBISH, SCHMUCK, and SCHNOOK.

schlock. Defective, inferior, shoddy, trashy, originally applied to merchandise (*OED*, from 1915), as sold in a *schlock house, joint*, or *shop*, perhaps by a *schlockmeister*, but since extended to individuals and other entities. Thus, speaking of the accounting firm Arthur Young & Company: "They don't take clients that other companies would; they just don't take schlock clients" (Philip L. Defliese, former chairman of a rival firm, Coopers & Lybrand, *New York Times*, 8/23/84). The etymology of the term is not clear, but it most likely derives from the German *schlag*, a blow, perhaps via the Yiddish *shlak*, an apopleptic stroke, an evil.

schlong. The penis. " 'Why do you call it a *schlong?'* 'Sometimes we call it a peter,' I whispered. 'In parts of the upper south they call it a dong or a tool. Or a peter.' 'I've heard Nathan call it his dork. Also his *putz*' " (William Styron, *Sophie's Choice*, 1979). *Schlong* comes from the Yiddish *shlang*, snake, a common metaphor. See also DICK, DORK, PRICK, and PUTZ, as well as SNAKE.

schmuck (shmuck). A person who is not only stupid but obnoxious. "I had already been arrested on the West Coast for saying *schmuck*—by a Yiddish undercover agent who had been placed in the club several nights running to determine if my use of Yiddish terms was a cover for profanity" (Lenny Bruce, *How to Talk Dirty and Influence People*, 1972). "I never heard my elders, certainly not my father or mother, use *shmuck*, which was regarded as so vulgar as to be taboo" (Leo Rosten, *The Joys of Yiddish*, 1968).

The oldest example of *schmuck* in the OED is from Israel Zangwill's *Children of the Ghetto* (1892), also the source of the oldest SCHLEMIEL. The Yiddish word comes from the German *schmuck*, an ornament, but it translates as "penis" or, more precisely in the case of an obnoxious person, PRICK. Because of its vulgar meaning, *schmuck* was euphemized as *schmo(e)*. This was transmuted in turn by cartoonist Al Capp into the *shmoo*, an adorable little critter that was both prolific and bounteous (it gave milk, laid eggs, and tasted like chicken), and which became a great national fad in the late 1940s (shmoo dolls, shmoo pillows, shmoo ashtrays, and so on), without many people realizing just what the joke was all about. See also NUDNIK, PUTZ, and SCHNOOK.

schnook (shnook). A dope or sucker, especially a timid person, easily cheated, unable to stand up for himself, and more to be pitied than despised; a FOOL. ". . . off in the wings, like in a Greek tragedy, stands a schnook with a dilemma. What's a schnook? Well, it's a Yiddish word which loosely translates to mean somebody not real gifted in the smarts department, not reeking with couth and culture, and, for football, not really equipped. To watch, yes, to play, no" (Samuel Susser, *The Truth About Selling*, 1975).

Schnook probably derives from the German *schnucke*, a little sheep, but the expression almost certainly originated on this side of the Atlantic. It seems to have appeared first in the diminutive form, *schnukel* or *schnookel*, and H. L. Mencken recorded it as *schnuck*, "A customer easily persuaded, a sucker" (*The American Language*, Supplement II, 1948). By 1949, Jack Benny was using it in a more general sense on the radio: "Don't be such an apologetic schnook" (Harold Wentworth and Stuart Berg Flexner, *Dictionary of American Slang*, 1975). See also CHAMER, SCHLEMIEL, and SCHMUCK.

schvartze (schvartzeh, schwartze, shvartze, shvartzer, etc.). A black person. "She [the writer's mother] sews, she knits, she darns—she irons better than the *shvartze*" (Philip Roth, *Esquire*, 4/67). *Schvartze*, from the Yiddish *shvartz*, black, and the German *schwarz*, meaning the same, seems to have been popularized as a code term of sorts, used to refer to black servants when they were within earshot. Later, through the 1960s—and beyond, among the older generation—it was employed indiscriminately, and usually disparagingly, whether or not blacks were on the premises.

Jews were by no means the first to use this construction. As H. L. Mencken reported: "In Baltimore, in the 80s of the last century, the German-speaking householders, when they had occasion to speak of Negro servants in their presence, called them *die Blaue* (blues). In the 70s *die Schwarze* (blacks) had been used, but it was believed that the Negroes had fathomed it" (*The American Language: Supplement I*, 1945). Nor is the tendency to lapse into one's own tongue in this context limited to German and Yiddish speakers, e.g., "When I was growing up the Italian word melanzana had two meanings. One was its literal translation, which is eggplant. The other was what a dictionary might call a pejorative slang expression and was a reference to the dark skin of the vegetable. The older men in my grandparents' neighborhood used to mutter the word when a black man came walking by" (Anna Quindlen, *New York Times*, 12/30/87). See also NEGRO.

schweinhund. Bastard, dirty dog; literally "pig dog." "Finally, he swung around to face Hans and spat out the word *'Schweinhund!'* Though normally calm and easygoing, Hans turned red with fury and would have struck the cabby if Joan had not intervened. . . . At a loss to explain his reaction, Hans shrugged and said, 'Well, it loses something in the translation' " (Donna Woolfolk Cross, *Word Abuse*, 1979). See also PIG and DOG.

scofflaw. One who habitually ignores the law; now usually applied to minor offenses, such as the refusal to answer a summons for a parking violation. The word was coined in response to a contest announced in 1923 by Delcevare King, of Quincy, Massachusetts, who offered a prize of $200 for the best word to characterize the person who flouted the Eighteenth Amendment (Prohibition) by drinking liquor that was illegally made or obtained. Mr. King received more than twenty-five thousand entries. Two people—Henry Irving Dale and Kate L. Butler—submitted *scofflaw*, and they shared the prize. Mr. King announced the winning word on January 15, 1924, and it caught on immediately.

Scotch. A contraction of *Scottish*, and an accepted ethnic designation for a couple hundred years, starting ca. 1650, but used as a pejorative prefix in many phrases, especially among the English, whose traditional opinion of their northern neighbors is typified by Dr. Samuel Johnson's proclamation: "Norway, too, has noble wild prospects; and Lapland is remarkable for prodigious noble wild prospects. But, Sir, let me tell you, the noblest prospect which a Scotchman ever sees, is the high road that leads him to England!" (7/6/1763, in Boswell's *Life of Johnson*, 1791). Of course, Scotland in this period also was known to the *Sassenach* (not usually a compliment) as *Louseland*, *Itchland*, and *Scratchland*, and this was the same Johnson who remarked on another occasion that "Much may be made of a Scotsman if he be caught young" (Spring 1772). It says a great deal for Boswell's personal charm that he was able to overcome the doctor's prejudice against his race. But as Johnson noted: "I will do you, Boswell, the justice to say, that you are the most *unscottified* of your countrymen" (5/1/1773). Herewith a sampling of *Scotch* phrases, comparable to those depending upon IRISH and WELSH. As a group, they define the stereotypical English view of Scotland as a poor and backward nation of penurious people:

Scotch attorney. A name popularized in Jamaica (*OED*, 1864) for various vines of the *Clusia* species that entwine themselves so tightly around the trunks of trees as to kill them; also referred to as *a Scotchman hugging a Creole*.

Scotch blessing. "A vehement scolding" (Abraham Roback, *A Dictionary of International Slurs*, 1944).

Scotch boot. An iron boot used in late medieval Scotland when interrogating prisoners; a wedge would be driven into the boot until the suspect either confessed or had his (or her) leg bone shattered.

Scotch casement. The pillory; from the late eighteenth to the mid-nineteenth century (Eric Partridge, *A Dictionary of Slang and Unconventional English*, 1970).

Scotch chocolate. "Brimstone and milk" (Captain Francis Grose, *A Classical Dictionary of the Vulgar Tongue*, 1785).

Scotch coffee. Hot water flavored with burnt biscuit; obsolete. Partridge suggests that it was inspired by *Scotch chocolate* above.

Scotch douche. "A strong spray of warm water which was played at the naked patient as he stood shackled against a wall" (Robert E. Rothenberg, M.D., describing treatment of manic patients, ca. 1930, *Recall: Life As a Surgeon*, ms., 1987).

Scotch fiddle. Scabies, the itch caused by mites (Grose, *op. cit.*); also called the *Welsh fiddle*. As noted, another name for Scotland in this period was *Scratchland*.

Scotch Greys. Lice; nineteenth and twentieth centuries. *The headquarters of the Scotch Greys* was, naturally, the head.

Scotch hobby. ". . . a little sorry, scrubbed, low Horse of that country" (B.E., *Dictionary of the Canting Crew*, ca. 1690).

Scotch marriage. A common-law marriage, i.e., no marriage at all (Roback, *op. cit.*).

Scotch mist. "A sober soaking rain: a Scotch mist will wet an Englishman to the skin" (Grose, *op. cit.*). *Scotch mist* also is a sarcastic British catch phrase, dating to the 1920s, that implies someone is either not seeing things or failing to understand what is seen. " 'Are yer married?' " 'Course she is. What do yer think that is? Scotch mist?' Rube points to my wedding ring" (*New Statesman*, 5/18/62).

Scotch ordinary. An outhouse; seventeenth and eighteenth centuries.

Scotch organ, to play the. "To put money in the cash register" (Roback, *op. cit.*).

Scotch pint. "A bottle containing two quarts" (*Lexicon Balatronicum*, 1811).

Scotch prize. Nautical: A capture made by mistake; specifically, one that is worse than no prize at all, since it may hamper the captors or lead to heavy legal expenses (*OED*, from 1818).

Scotch rabbit. From 1747; the same meatless recipe as *Welsh rabbit*, a.k.a. *rarebit*. See also WELSH.

Scotch seamanship. Seamanship characterized by stupidity and strength only; from 1900.

Scotch Tape. A trade name, from 1945, though Minnesota Mining and Manufacturing Co. claimed use of *Scotch* since 1928 in its patent application. It seems the product was used initially by automobile manufacturers as masking tape when painting two-tone cars. To make it easier to remove the tape, at first only the edges had adhesive. The auto workers suspected, however, that the supplier was scrimping on adhesive in order to save money. So they started calling the product *Scotch tape*.

Scotch verdict. Anything inconclusive; technically, a verdict of "not proven," which in Scots law is the functional equivalent of "not guilty," except that the defendant is left saddled with the burden of moral guilt.

Scotch warming pan. "A wench; also a fart" (Grose, *op. cit.*). More specifically, the first kind of *Scotch warming pan* was a female bedfellow, apparently from the friendly custom in chilly Scotland of having a chambermaid climb into bed to warm it for the proper occupant—and sometimes staying to warm him, too. The *Scotch warming pan* dates to the seventeenth century, but seems now to be obsolete, alas.

Scotch woodcock. Another meatless dish: eggs on toast with anchovies or anchovy paste, from the second half of the nineteenth century and still current.

By the middle of the nineteenth century, *Scotch* had acquired so many negative associations that the natives of Scotland began to shy away from it. Today, they prefer to be called *Scots* or *Scottish*, and it is possible to get a rise out of them by applying the other term, e.g., "Professor Trevor Roper . . . tries to irritate and provoke by using the word 'Scotch' knowing well that many decent Scots . . . have come to regard this as a demeaning adjective" (London *Times*, 5/11/76). It remains permissible, of course, to drink *Scotch* whisky, to play *hopscotch* and *to scotch* (something)—a plan, for instance. The latter two are not ethnic terms, however, deriving from different words: *scotch*, meaning an incision or line on the ground (children have been playing *scotch-hoppers* since the seventeenth century), and *scotch*, meaning a wedge or block, used to keep a wheel from turning, or any other action from proceeding. On the whole, the Scots seem to have had much better luck in escaping their adjective than the Netherlanders; see DUTCH.

scoundrel. A thoroughly unprincipled person; a KNAVE, ROGUE, or VILLAIN. "Patriotism is the last refuge of a scoundrel" (Dr. Johnson, 4/7/1775, in James Boswell's *The Life of Samuel Johnson, LL.D.*, 1791).

Scoundrel popped into English in the late sixteenth century, apparently out of thin air. The word's etymology, at any rate, is not known. It makes a fine epithet, however. Thus, Abraham Lincoln, according to his secretary, John Hay, described John C. Frémont as being "the damndest scoundrel that ever lived, but in the infinite mercy of Providence . . . also the damndest fool." Then there is the famous comeback attributed to Henry Clay, of Kentucky, upon meeting John Randolph, of Roanoke (Virginia), on a narrow walkway in Washington. It was clear that one or the other would have to step aside into the mud to let the other pass, which led to the following exchange:

RANDOLPH: Sir, I never give way for a scoundrel.
CLAY (*gallantly stepping aside*): I *always* do.

This bon mot also has been credited to the Earl of Chesterfield and, reversing the above roles, to Randolph—a real possibility, considering the Virginian's reputation as a master of the art of insult; see also *Caligula's horse* in HORSE and MACKEREL.

screw. To engage in sexual intercourse or a person considered as a sexual object. This is essentially a euphemism, dating from the eighteenth century, for the older, more powerful four-letter *F-word*, which see. Still, some people profess to be shocked by *screw* in its sexually active sense, and there was much wagging of tongues after Jimmy Carter, then running for President, used it in the course of an interview with *Playboy*: "Christ says, Don't consider yourself better than someone else because one guy screws a whole bunch of women while the other guy is loyal to his wife" (11/76). Some newspapers could not bring themselves to reprint the remark. For example, *The New York Times* merely informed readers that "Mr. Carter used a vulgarism for sexual relations" (9/21/76). All this came as a surprise to the man who had conducted the interview (and probably to Carter, too): "When I finished interviewing Jimmy Carter for *Playboy*, I had no premonition that the words 'screw' and 'shack up' which he uttered would cause a furor. I just didn't know that they were still dirty words" (Robert Scheer, *New Times*, 10/15/76).

Whether "dirty" or not, it is true that the sexual meaning of *screw* has become strong enough that no writer today would commit to paper Jane Austen's observation about the head of an honest, old-fashioned boarding school: "Miss Goddard was the mistress of a school—not of a seminary or an establishment or anything which professed, in long sentences of refined nonsense, to combine liberal acquirements with elegant morality upon new principles and new systems, and where young ladies for enormous pay might be screwed out of health and into vanity . . ." (*Emma*, 1816). Ms. Austen, it seems, was not entirely familiar with the slang of her own time, as the copulative meaning is the first one given for *to screw* in both Captain Francis Grose's *A Classical Dictionary of the Vulgar Tongue*, 1796, and the updating of it that was done by "A Member of the Whip Club" and published as the *Lexicon Balatronicum* (1811).

screw loose, a. Crazy, dumb. "[William Blake] was quite mad, but of a madness that was really the elements of great genius ill-sorted: in fact, a genius *with a screw loose*, as we used to say" (Edward FitzGerald, letter to William Bodham Donne, 1833, in Robert Bernard Martin, *With Friends Possessed*, 1985).

A *screw loose* is one of many folk metaphors for describing a person who is not mentally or emotionally normal. Though some of these expressions are used mainly to denote madness and others stupidity, there is a large overlap here and many, such as *a screw loose*, can be used with either meaning in mind. As a group, these metaphors have an antique, countrified ring, but numerous older ones remain current while new expressions that draw upon the concerns of postindustrial society are in the process of creation, as demonstrated by the examples in the following list:

as bright as a bump on a log;

balmy in the crumpet; bats in the belfrey (see BAT); *both oars not in the water*, " 'I don't know about you, guy . . . Sometimes I'm not sure you have both oars in the water' " (Jim Shepard, *Flights*, 1983); *bread is not done*, usually reserved for the mentally deficient, and metaphorically comparable to *half-baked* below;

cannot see through a ladder; couldn't drive nails in a snowbank;

dead between the ears; doesn't have all [one's] buttons; doesn't have all [one's] cups in the closet, "Mrs. Rudolf Hess, who visits the prisoner [her husband, the erstwhile deputy Reichsführer] occasionally, says Dr. Thomas 'doesn't have all his cups in the closet' " (*New York Times*, 4/15/79); *doesn't have anything between [one's] ears but air* (see also *airhead* in BLOCKHEAD); *doesn't have enough sense to come in out of the rain; doesn't know a bee from a bull's foot; doesn't know [one's] ass from [one's] elbow* (see also ASS); *doesn't know beans; doesn't know dung from honey* (see also DUNG); *doesn't know which way is up; duller than a widder woman's ax* (see DULL);

[one's] elevator doesn't go all the way up, "Doesn't your elevator go to the top floor?" ("All My Children," WABC-TV, New York City, 3/22/82);

fifty cards in the deck;

half-baked, stupid, not well thought out or fully prepared, as in "Critics of feminist perspectives often charge a group of half-baked women is trying to subvert real science . . ." (Stephen Jay Gould, *New York Times Book Review,* 8/12/84); *half-boiled; half-brained; half-cracked; half-headed; half-wit(ted); head full of rocks;*

just fallen off the turnip truck, "Mr. Lewis spent 22 years in police precincts in Brooklyn and Manhattan. He had not, as they say, just fallen off the turnip truck" (*New York Times,* 4/5/84); *just not together;*

left [one's] dresser drawers open, "I think Col. Qaddafi must have left a few of his dresser drawers open" ("Best of Johnny Carson," himself, WNBC-TV, New York City, 4/11/84); *light upstairs; lost [one's] cookies* (comparable to *gone crackers* in CRACK-POT); *lost* (or *missing*) *some* (or *one's*) *marbles* (possibly from the old belief, also reflected in JERK, that masturbation causes idiocy, since *marbles* also are testicles and *to lose [one's] marbles* also means to experience orgasm);

narrow (or *small*) *bandwidth,* " 'Bandwidth' . . . is the amount of information in a conversation. It is derived from a technical term for the breadth of information in certain computer devices. You might want to end a conversation with someone whose bandwidth is small because he is probably not following very well" (*New York Times,* 2/19/84); *ninety-nine cents in the dollar; no bean in the pod; nobody home; no seeds in the pumpkin; not all there,* "He looked blank. He wasn't all there" (Police Officer Norman Phillips, describing a young man who had run amok and shot seven people, *New York Times,* 4/13/86); *not finished in the upper story; not furnished with brains; not playing with a full deck* (also an implication that someone is cheating); *not screwed on right,* "I mean, he just isn't well screwed on, is he?" (President Richard M. Nixon, discussing Watergate burglar G. Gordon Liddy, White House tape, 6/23/72, six days after the Watergate break-in); *not wrapped tight,* "Frances, she's not wrapped too tight, you know" (*Nutcracker,* WNBC-TV, New York City, 2/24/87);

officer material (an enlisted man who is short on brains); *off [one's] chump* (or *head* or *nut*); *off [one's] mental reservation; off [one's] rocker* (or *trolley*); OFF THE WALL; *one brick shy of a load,* ". . . there was something about the boy that bothered me, nothing I could put my finger on, but, as my boy says, kind of one brick shy of a load" (*New York Times,* 10/15/83, quoting a Texan's description of a teenager who helped his father kill two people); *one foot in the funny farm,* "T.J. enters a disastrous marriage with a woman who, as his uncle recalls, always had one foot in the funny farm" (*New York Times,* 2/10/84, review of TV miniseries based on Tommy Thompson's *Celebrity*); *out of [one's] gourd* (or *mind* or *skull*), "I knew he'd drive me out of my skull sooner or later" (*Archie's Double Digest,* 7/84); *out of it; out of [one's] tree* (see also APE); *out to lunch,* socially unacceptable as well as stupid (see OUT TO LUNCH);

playing with the squirrels (see also SQUIRREL);

rats in the attic (or *garret* or *loft* or *upper story;* see also RAT); *read-only memory,* " 'He's a read-only memory.' That's a rather nasty thing to say about someone. It means he never learns anything, keeps saying the same thing over and over again. It comes from ROM, or read-only memory, a computer part that cannot be altered by the user" (*New York Times,* 2/19/84); *room-temperature I.Q.,* "He had a room-temperature I.Q., which made him extremely obliging, hence an excellent artist's model and a pretty fair marine" (Joseph Wambaugh, *The Glitter Dome,* 1981);

scratching where it doesn't itch; soft in the upper works, "there was a fore-topman, of the name of Bill Harness, a good sort of chap enough, but rather soft in the upperworks," (Captain Frederick Marryat, *Jacob Faithful*, 1834); *standing behind the door* (or *at the end of the line*) *when brains were passed out*;

tile loose, a; touched (or *tetched*) *in the head; turned* (or *gone around*) *the bend,* ". . . I had put down the letter with the awful feeling that Svetlana [Alliluyeva, daughter of Stalin] . . . had turned the bend" (William F. Buckley, *Litchfield County* [Connecticut] *Times,* 11/16/84);

up the pole (and *halfway around the flag*);

weak (or *wrong*) *in the upper story; with a bee in* [one's] *bonnet* (also *bees in the brain* or *bees in the head*); *with a leak in the think tank; with an apartment to let; with an unfurnished attic* (or *garret*); *with a room for rent*. See also FOOL and MORON.

Scrooge. A miser, especially a mean one. "Many readers have written to object to the Government's playing Scrooge with the airlines' ticket giveaways for frequent fliers" (*New York Times,* 11/25/85). The original Scrooge was Ebenezer, antihero of Charles Dickens' *A Christmas Carol* (1843). Other literary figures whose names have become bywords for penuriousness include *Haragon*, the central character in Molière's comedy, *L'Avare* (*The Miser*), 1668, and *Silas Marner,* the gold-hoarding weaver in George Eliot's novel of the same name (1861). See also CHEAPSKATE and TIGHTWAD.

scum. The lowest of the low—paradoxically, since *scum* is that which rises to the top (from the Middle Dutch *schum*, foam). Vile people have been characterized as *scum* since at least the sixteenth century; see LACKEY for an example from Shakespeare. And the epithet remains in active service, e.g., "On rechecking his tapes, reporter David Sheff has found that he misquoted Dr. John J. Marshall. Dr. Marshall did not say that writer Cameron Stauth was 'a dirty rotten scum who got very greedy.' What he said was, 'He's an unscrupulous little [pause] gentleman' " (editorial correction, *People,* 7/5/82). The pejorative sense of *scum* in recent times probably has been increased by the slang use of the word to mean "semen," as in *scumbag* (a condom), *scumsucker* (a fellator), and *scumsucking* (anything disgusting or despicable), e.g., ". . . he considered them [the Mafia] scumbags" (unnamed FBI agent, UPI, 1/7/88). See also CONDOM, DIRTBAG, DOUCHE BAG, SLEAZE, and SLIME.

scurrilous. Vile, low, mean, abusive. Thus, President Ronald Reagan's first attorney general, William French Smith, hit the ceiling after it was reported that he had attended the birthday party of a man whose other friends happened to include mobsters. As reported in *The Washington Post*: "He labeled news reports questioning the propriety of his appearance at the party as 'nothing less than scurrilous,' repeating 'scurrilous' three times, until he finally added, 'Am I making myself clear?' " (William Safire, *What's the Good Word?,* 1982).

The word's meaning seems to be in the process of changing. It formerly referred to—and some dictionaries still give as its primary meaning—the use of coarse, indecent, foul-mouthed language, i.e., the sort of talk that only a professional fool or buffoon could get away with. This is reflected in its etymology. It comes from the Latin *scurrilis*, buffoonlike, *scurra*, buffoon, and possibly an older Etruscan term. See also FOOL.

scurvy. Vile, mean, contemptible; from the disease, whose symptoms include foul breath, bleeding gums, and livid spots on the skin. The word entered English in the early 1500s and was being applied in an extended sense before the century was out to people and things, "Get glass eyes [spectacles] And, like a scurvy politician, seem To see the things thou dost not" (William Shakespeare, *King Lear*, 1605–06). The disease itself is rarely seen, now that it is known to be caused by a deficiency of vitamin C, but the figurative use lingers on: "In the vast configuration of things, you're nothing but a scurvy spider" (*It's a Wonderful Life*, film, 1946). See also SCAB.

scut. A contemptible person or a menial, routine job—*scut work* or *scut* for short. The personal sense is the older, recorded first in Anthony Trollope's *Harry Heathcote* (1873): "I thought you was ringing trees for that young scut at Gangoil!" The *scut* that is work, meanwhile, has been dated only to 1960 (Harold Wentworth and Stuart Berg Flexner, *Dictionary of American Slang*). Possibly, *scut work* comes from the use of *scut* in hospital slang to mean a junior intern.

Scut's origin is not known. It might derive from *scout* in the sense of "spy" or of "servant." The latter would tie in with both modern meanings. The pejorative sense, however, could also stem from, or be reinforced by, the longstanding (sixteenth to twentieth centuries) slang use of *scut* to refer to the female pudendum (from the word's primary, aboveground meaning: the tail of a rabbit, hare, or deer). Shakespeare, among others, punned on the genital meaning, as in, from *The Merry Wives of Windsor* (1597):

MRS. FORD: Sir John! Are thou there, my deer? My male deer?
FALSTAFF: My doe with the black scut!

scuz(z). A filthy, nasty person or thing. "Didi pointed out the girls. 'I never can get over how you'll always see beautiful chicks with the most disgusting-looking guys, she said. . . . it was true. Talley saw gorgeous girls hanging on to what appeared to be sheer scuz" (Virginia Hamilton, *A White Romance*, 1987). The term has been dated to the 1960s and appears, on the face of it, to be an unappetizing blend of *scum* and *fuzz*. The proper adjective is *scuzzy* and the verb is *to scuzz (someone) out*. A truly despicable person may also be said to be *scuzzo*, a *scuzzbag* (the same as a *scumbag* or *sleazebag*), or a *scuzzball*. *Scuzz food* is junk food. See also GROSS OUT, JUNK, SCUM, and SLEAZE.

serpent. A deceitful, hateful, treacherous person, most famously in the comparison, "How sharper than a serpent's tooth it is To have a thankless child!" (William Shakespeare, *King Lear*, 1605–06). Serpents—human and other—evoke special horror because they also are believed to be highly intelligent: Thus, their hatefulness is all the worse for being the product of guile rather than dumb instinct. This image is ingrained deeply in Judeo-Christian culture, e.g., "Now the serpent was more subtile than any beast of the field which the Lord God had made" (*Genesis*, 3:1). See also DOVE and SNAKE.

sex. Gender; the genitals, both male and female; the act of sexual intercourse, as in the euphemistic phrase *to have sex*.

Sex, from the Latin *sexus*, in turn, probably, from *secare*, to divide (as into two sexes), was fairly heavily tabooed for the first half of the twentieth century. For example, in *The Male Animal* (Elliott Nugent and James Thurber), the word was never pronounced but always spelled out *S-E-X*. And this was on Broadway in 1940.

Of course, this also was the era when high-school girls took classes in *hygiene*, not *sex education*. (The boys took shop.)

As recently as 1987, it still was considered newsworthy when the Massachusetts State Board of Education amended guidelines for school health programs to mention "sex education" explicitly. As proposed by education department bureaucrats, the guidelines had waltzed around the subject, discussing programs "designed to develop critical thinking and individual responsibility . . . to encourage self-esteem, competence, and coping skills, decision-making and conflict resolution . . . [and focusing on] the dynamic relationship between physical, mental, emotional, and social well-being." The guidelines were amended after board member Mary C. Wright pointed out, "Sex education is what we are talking about, so why not just state it directly?" (AP, 5/29/87).

sexist. A sexual chauvinist.

The term seems to have been coined by Pauline M. Leet, Director of Special Programs at Franklin and Marshall College, Lancaster, Pennsylvania, in "Women and the Undergraduate," a talk that she gave at the Student-Faculty Forum on November 18, 1965. She said, in part: "When you argue . . . that since fewer women write good poetry this justifies their total exclusion [from English courses], you are taking a position analogous to that of the racist—I might call you in this case a 'sexist'—who says that since so few Negroes have held positions of importance relative to the majority race, their exclusion from history books is a matter of good judgement rather than discrimination." This speech was circulated in mimeograph form among feminists.

Sexist was popularized by Caroline Bird, who was the first to use it and the related *sexism* in print, according to Fred R. Shapiro, who traced the development of words associated with the women's movement in *American Speech* (Spring 1985). Ms. Bird used *sexist* (over the objections of a copy editor, who couldn't find the word in a dictionary) in the foreword to *Born Female* (with Sara Welles Briller, 1968) and she employed *sexism* in a speech, "On Being Born Female," published in *Vital Speeches of the Day* (1968).

Both words also seem to have been coined independently—and popularized, too—by Sheldon Vanauken, a professor at Lynchburg College, Lynchburg, Virginia, in a pamphlet, "Freedom for Movement Girls—Now" (1968). In a special note on words, Mr. Vanauken explained the attack value of *sexist*: "It's a better word than *male chauvinist* which is bulky, usually mispronounced, and imprecise in meaning. . . . *Sexist*, on the other hand, is short, precise, instantly understandable. It has a sharp, vicious sound; and it inherits the ugly overtones of *racist*. It is potentially a word of power." See also CHAUVINIST and RACIST.

shaft. To deceive, reject, or take cruel advantage of another person; as a noun, the instrument or act of such rejection. "[The media] have a right and a responsibility, if they're against a candidate—give him the shaft; but also recognize, if they give him the shaft, put one lonely reporter on the campaign who will report what the candidate says now and then" (Richard M. Nixon, press conference, 11/7/62, after losing the California gubernatorial election). "*Shaft* . . . was taboo as a verb until a generation ago, when Richard Nixon used it in his 'last press conference.' The odious term has become a synonym for *double-cross* or *harm* that is now printable in a family newspaper" (William Safire, *I Stand Corrected*, 1984).

The popularity of the film *Shaft* (1971) and its sequels may also have helped ease the taboo. Whatever, people do seem to have forgotten, or chosen to ignore, the word's strong associations with buggery, *shaft* being an old byword for the penis. *Shaft* appears to have started out as a euphemism of sorts, the earliest references to the penile sense in the OED being to the *shaft of Cupid* (1719) and the *shaft of delight* (1772). Hence, the original, low meaning of *to be shafted*. The phrase also has been embellished in various picturesque ways, e.g., *to get the purple shaft* (or *maroon harpoon*); *to get the shaft with barbs* (or *the order of the purple shaft with barbed-wire cluster*); and, allusively, *they screwed it in and broke it off*. See also STICK IT TO [SOMEONE].

shanty Irish. The poorest of the Irish in America. "I learned that there were even prejudices among the despised. The Neapolitans looked down on the Sicilians; the lace-curtain Irish thought themselves better than the shanty Irish" (Anna Quindlen, *New York Times*, 12/30/87).

Shanty is an Americanism (from 1820) of uncertain origin. Some etymologists, especially Hibernians, derive it from the Irish *sean tigh*, old house, while others trace it to the French Canadian *chantier*, log hut. The appearance of the term in Ohio in 1820, prior to the great potato famine and the accompanying exodus of the Irish from Ireland, argues in favor of the latter theory. *Shanty town*, where many Irish lived, has been dated to 1876, but the *shanty Irish* themselves don't enter in the written record for another half century, the earliest example in the OED being from Jim Tully's *Shanty Irish* (1928): "I'm just plain Shanty Irish an' I'll go to hell when I die." The phrase certainly was used widely before 1928, however—witness the baseball catcher, James Francis "Shanty" Hogan, who broke into the big leagues with the Boston Braves in 1925. See also IRISH and LACE-CURTAIN.

shark. A voracious, predatory person, a swindler—alone and in such combinations as *card shark, financial shark, land shark, loan shark,* and *pool shark.*

Among animal words, *shark* is atypical for apparently having referred to humankind before it became attached to the fish. The term was introduced into English by sailors in the sixteenth century. Thus, from a broadside of 1569, referring to a large specimen that Captain (later Sir John) Hawkins exhibited in London: "There is no proper name for it that I knowe, but that sertayne men of Captayne Haukinses doth call it a 'sharke.' " Where the sailors picked up the word is not known for sure, but it seems likely they got it from the German *schurke,* a rogue or rascal, especially a greedy parasite (and also the ancestor of *shirk* as in SHIRKER). Within thirty years of Captain Hawkins's display, the English were using *shark* on each other, both as a noun, to describe worthless, parasitical types, and as a verb for the act of sponging off, or preying upon, another person. These meanings are still current. See also CHEAT and FISH.

sheeny. A Jew. "Sheeny and Moses are . . . smoking their pipes before their lazy shutters in Seven Dials" (William Makepeace Thackeray, *The Book of Snobs,* 1847). The word is a slang term of uncertain origin. Ernest Weekley's guess that it comes from the German *schön,* beautiful, as pronounced by Yiddish-speaking peddlers and merchants when praising their own wares, is as good as any. *Sheeny* has been dated to 1816 (OED). It was used by Jews (jocosely) and by Gentiles up to the

1870s—without giving offense—according to Eric Partridge. Note the similar trajectory traveled by HEBE.

The opprobrious sense certainly has been dominant for at least a hundred years, however, and it has grown greater with time. For an example of casual anti-Semitism in the United States several generations ago, consider the following verses, from an Ohio State University songbook of ca. 1899:

> Oh my name is Solomon Levi
> And my store's on Beacon Street;
> That's where you buy the coats and vests,
> And everything else that's neat.
>
> Second-handed underpants
> And everything else so fine,
> And all the boys they trade with me
> At one hundred and forty-nine.
>
> *Chorus*
> Oh Solomon Levi
> Levi tra la la la,
> Poor sheeny Levi,
> Tra la la la la la la la la la la la.

See also JEW (DOWN), TO.

sheep. A mild-mannered, simpleminded, easily victimized person; one who is *sheep-headed* (dumb), *sheep-hearted* (cowardly), *sheepish* (bashful or embarrassed), or easily *fleeced* (cheated, robbed). These are only some of the undesirable qualities attributed to sheep and to people who act like them. Thus, *sheep* are said to follow each other blindly; they are easily led to the slaughter; they are prone to becoming lost; and some of them are ne'er-do-wells who disgrace their families (i.e., *black sheep*). See also CROCK, CRONE, and MUTT.

shiksa (shicksa, shiksah, shickseh). A female Gentile, especially a young one. Thus, from a tape that was made of Lenny Bruce's performance at the Gate of Horn in Chicago on December 6, 1962, one of the many occasions on which he was busted: "That is a *shiksa* [holding up a picture of a girl from a calendar], there's pink-nippled lady: that's one thing about the *goyim*, boy, they've got winner chicks. . . . [two people walk out] Before all of you escape, let me explain one thing to you. . . . It's God, your filthy Jesus Christ, made these tits, that's all." This idea was sufficiently disturbing to the arresting officers to be included in their official report: "Mr. Bruce held up a colored photograph showing the naked breast of a woman and said 'God, your Jesus Christ, made these tits' " (Bruce, *How to Talk Dirty and Influence People*, 1972). Of course, the fatal attractions of those winner chicks on the other side of the religious fence are well known: "His mother, a lady of the old school, had repeatedly and solemnly warned him that there is a yellow-haired, blue-eyed shiksa lying in wait for every good Jewish boy" (Judith Krantz, *Scruples*, 1978).

The Yiddish *shiksa* began appearing in English toward the end of the nineteenth century. It comes from the Hebrew *sheges*, a blemish, a detested thing (L. Bruce and Ia Krantz to the contrary). See also GOY.

shirker. One who evades work or other obligations. "The Polish Parliament passed a law today providing for forced labor, or even imprisonment, for 'shirkers' and 'social parasites,' who could not prove they had gainful employment" (*New York Times*, 10/27/82). As it happens, *shirker* derives from the obsolete (seventeenth-eighteenth centuries) *shirk*, a parasite, swindler, sharper—which makes the modern *shirker* kin to the predatory SHARK, also, among other things, a swindler. See also PARASITE and SLACKER.

shit. Excrement and the act of voiding it, but with a great many extended uses as an exclamation of surprise or disgust; as a personal insult; as a byword for trouble, worthlessness, nonsense, and lying; as a pejorative modifier and suffix; and so on, almost without end, not to mention its specialized use as a synonym for drugs, especially heroin.

The term is an extremely old one, dating to before A.D. 1000. It derives from the Middle English *shiten*, to void excrement; the Old English *scitan*, known from the compound *bescitan*, to befoul; and, ultimately, from the Indo-European root, *skei-*, to cut, to split. This makes the vulgar word a cousin of *science, conscience, schedule, shed* (in the sense of "to separate"), *sheath, shield, escutcheon*, and *squire*, among others. (The printable *excrement* has a similar, equally bland etymology, deriving from the Latin *ex*, out + *cernere*, to separate or to sift. So does TURD).

For many years, this classic four-letter word usually appeared in longer form as *schite* or *shite*. (The latter still crops up occasionally, but now as a euphemism, or as the name of a heron, the *shitepoke*, so-called on account of its tendency to defecate when taking to wing.) The past participle in olden times was *shitten*, as in "And shame it is, if a preest take keepe / A shitten shepherde and a clene sheep" (Geoffrey Chaucer, General Prologue, *The Canterbury Tales*, 1387–1400).

The modern spelling of the word dates to around the middle of the seventeenth century. Thus, Sir Thomas Urquhart used both forms when translating the opening book of Rabelais' *Gargantua* (1653), first telling how the hero's mother, Gargamelle, ate so much tripe that she swelled up "by the ingrediency of such shitten stuff," and then, describing her son's deportment, reporting that "He pissed in his shoes, shit in his shirt, and wiped his nose on his sleeve." The older spelling continued to be used for several generations, however, e.g., "I say, Sir, you're a meer shite-fire [a hot-tempered person, a bully]" (Edward Ward, *Helter Skelter*, 1704). As late as ca. 1731, the old form was still acknowledged—but now softened with dashes—as in "How the old Proverb lyes, that says sh——n luck's good" ("Windsor Medley," in J. S. Farmer and W. E. Henley, *Slang and Its Analogues*, 1903).

Though employed by Urquhart, Burton, Swift, and other literary lights, the term was one of the first of those dealing with bodily functions to come to be regarded as too vulgar for public discourse. For example, it does not appear in the works of Shakespeare (and he did use *piss* as in "I do smell all-horse piss; at which my nose is in great indignation," *The Tempest*, 1611). The divines who prepared the King James Bible (also of 1611) also went by Shakespeare's standard. Thus, the

S-word was avoided in 2 *Kings,* 18:27: "the men which sit on the wall . . . may eat their own dung, and drink their own piss."

In the next century, when the term was used, its offensiveness commonly was diluted with dashes, as in the 1731 rendition of the old proverb above, or in Captain Francis Grose's definitions of *sh-t sack* ("A dastardly fellow; also a non-conformist") and *sh-t-ng through teeth* ("Vomiting") in the 1788 edition of his *Classical Dictionary of the Vulgar Tongue.* And in the following, Victorian century, the word hardly ever appeared in print in any form at all. For the whole of the nineteenth century, the *OED* includes but a single citation of its use. This one example, however, does illustrate the different standards applied to written and spoken English. It is from a collection of words used by farmers in southwestern England: "*Shit,* a term of contempt. (Very com.) He's a regular shit. Applied to men only" (Frederick T. Elworthy, *The West Somerset Word-Book,* 1886).

Like other tabooed terms, this one was used with great frequency by soldiers in World Wars I and II, typically in such phrases as *chickenshit* (petty rules and regulations; see CHICKEN); *day the eagle shits* (payday); *shit in your mess kit, I hope to* (a promise of retaliation); *shit on a shingle* (creamed chipped beef on toast, often abbreviated *S.O.S.* and known in the Navy as *shit on a raft*); and *shit, shower, shave, and shine* (the way one gets ready for a day of duty or a night off-post).

The ban against the word in print continued until well into modern times, however. Thus, James Joyce used it in *Ulysses* (1922), and this was one reason, along with other "worse" words, that this book was not allowed into the United States until 1933. When e. e. cummings used the term in *The Enormous Room* (also 1922)—"My father is dead! Shit. Oh, well. The war is over."—the secretary of the New York Society for the Suppression of Vice, John Sumner, objected so violently that the publisher, Boni and Liveright, had the offending word inked out of all the copies of the first printing that remained in inventory. For the second printing, cummings translated the thought into French, which is how it appears—"*Mon père est mort! Merde!—Eh, b'en!*"—in the Modern Library edition. The translation satisfied Mr. Sumner, the euphemistic power of French being comparable to that of Latin.

Still later, when the *Atlantic Monthly* was putting together its centennial issue (11/57), Ernest Hemingway sent in a story that contained the *S-word* twice. As the magazine's editor, Edward Weeks, recalled in an interview with *Publishers Weekly* (2/19/82): "He did it deliberately to test us, and of course we printed it. But when you do that, you lose part of your subscription that goes for college reading courses—which for us meant a drop of 40,000 copies." Thus was decency preserved for young Americans in the Eisenhower years.

During the whole of this period, though heard commonly—and coming, since at least the end of World War II, from the lips of women as well as men—you could look for this word in some fairly good dictionaries, and not find it. The term is missing, for example, from the *Funk & Wagnalls Standard College Dictionary* (1963), *Webster's Seventh New Collegiate Dictionary* (1970), and *Webster's New World Dictionary* (1970). As society became more permissive, however, lexicographers could, too. Thus, the term was admitted to the *American Heritage Dictionary* (1969) and *Webster's New Collegiate Dictionary* (1973). The lacuna remains, however, like a ghostly hand from the past, in more recent editions of some older dictionaries that have been reissued with minor changes but not thoroughly revised and reset, e.g., *Webster's New Universal Unabridged Dictionary* (1983), which advertises 320,000 definitions, all of other words.

And there are, of course, publications that still refuse to print it. *The New York Times* is the most notable holdout; its classic evasion of the word came in a report on February 4, 1970, of the trial of the Chicago Eight, wherein readers were informed that one of the defendants, David Dellinger, had characterized a prosecution witness's testimony with a "barnyard epithet." ("Oh, bullshit!" is what he really said.) The *Times* also has sidestepped the issue on different occasions over the years with "barnyard vulgarity," "cow-pasture vulgarism," and "henhouse epithet."

By contrast, such other periodicals for general readers as *Reader's Digest* and *The New Yorker* have printed the word, as have some newspapers—though in at least one instance it seems to have been sneaked into print by an impish writer or printer, e.g., a caption in the Crystal Lake, Illinois, *Morning Herald*, accompanying a picture of a mother and son shoveling their sidewalk after a snowstorm in April 1984, which read: "Though a shitload of snow fell Saturday, snowplow crews had most major streets cleared by Sunday." (The "load" constituted almost seven inches of white stuff.)

Most children know the word, and they revel in jokes about it. Thus, if a youngster ever tells you that his brother has just been admitted to the Sam Houston Institute of Technology, *don't* say you've never heard of this seat of learning: "What! You've never heard of S.H.I.T.!" is the usual reply. (In the Army, officers who did not go to West Point have been known to disparage the military academy as the South Hudson Institute of Technology.) And if an angelic six-year-old asks, "Would you like to have some Sugar Honey Iced Tea?", the safest course is to pretend that you have suddenly gone stone deaf. Then there is the coded message that was being passed around among grade-schoolers at Brooklyn's Packer Collegiate Institute in 1984:

I got some money.	= $
I crossed a bridge.	= H
It started to rain.	= i
I put up an umbrella.	= T

In most cases, this word is used metaphorically rather than literally, a distinction that is typified by the story about the lady who stepped off the curb without looking and exclaimed, "Oh shit! I've just stepped in some dog doodoo." As evidence of the term's remarkable linguistic fecundity a sampling of the more picturesque of these expressions follows. If the list seems a bit much, it may help to remember that if trees could talk, their word for oxygen, which they excrete, probably would be a "bad" one, and that it would figure similarly in their rustling conversations. Herewith, the sampling:

act like [one's] shit doesn't stink, to. To act high and mighty; to presume to be superior to others; also *to think [one] is king shit.*

alter kocker. Yiddish-German for "old shitter," referring to a man. See *old cocker* in OLD MAID.

bad shit. Either very bad or, in black English, very good. "One dude said to another, noticing how he was dressed: 'You sho got on some bad shit,' which means he got on good shit, which means he's attractively dressed" (Geneva Smitherman, *Talkin and Testifyin*, 1977). See also BAD.

beat (or kick) the (living) shit out of (one), to. To trounce; to rout; to knock the living daylights out of [one].

built like a brick shithouse. Solidly constructed, not your usual wooden outhouse; often said admiringly of a well-built woman.

bullshit. Nonsense. See BULLSHIT.

crock of shit. Nonsense; often shortened to *crock*, the *crock* here being an earthen pot, i.e., a chamber pot. See also CROCK.

dipshit. A stupid person, a JERK; euphemized both as *dip* and *dipstick*; in Vietnam, during the American entanglement there, a native of that country. See also DIPPY.

diddly shit. A measure of insignificance, applied to anything of little or no value; a.k.a. *diddly poo, diddly squat*, or just plain *diddly*.

eat shit (and die), to. To be willing to accept or do anything. Explaining his use of *skite* in the *Arabian Nights* (1886), Richard Burton noted: "The allusion is to the vulgar saying 'Thou eatest skite!' (*i.e.*, thou talkest nonsense). Decent English writers modify this to 'Thou eatest dirt': and Lord Beaconsfield made it ridiculous by turning it into 'eating *sand*.' "

full of shit. Worthless, wrong, not to be believed; sometimes abbreviated *F.O.S.* "We are all beautiful (except white people, they are full of, and made of shit)" (Imamu Amiri Baraka [LeRoi Jones], *Black Magic*, 1969). Variants include *as full of shit as a Christmas goose* and *so full of shit his eyes were brown*. (If such a person has a bad attitude, an *ocularectomy* may be indicated. In this operation, the surgeon cuts the nerve that connects the anus with the eyeball, so the patient will no longer have such a *shitty* outlook on life.)

go shit in your hat (and pull it down over your ears), to. To go chase yourself, only more so; a most emphatic rejection, the implication being that the rejectee is so stupid as to follow the instruction. This also makes for a vivid image of self-mortification. As Edward Montagu, first Earl of Sandwich, told Samuel Pepys on October 7, 1660, it was an old saying of his father's that "he that do get a wench with child and marry her afterwards is as if a man should shit in his hat and then clap it on his head"—the topic of their conversation being the Duke of York, the future James II, who had impregnated the Lord Chancellor's daughter, Anne, and who was required by his brother the king to marry her—with hat in hand, presumably.

go through [someone or something] like shit through a tin horn, to. To accomplish something easily, completely, and rapidly.

holy shit. An unholy exclamation of surprise.

horseshit. Nonsense. See HORSE.

hot shit. Hot shot, hot stuff; often ironic, comparable to HOT DOG. Also an exclamation of amazement and appreciation.

in deep shit. In a lot of trouble. Or as Vice President George Bush delicately put it, when asked by *The Wall Street Journal* in February, 1986, what would have happened to a Chinese official in the 1970s who showed too much familiarity toward Americans: "He would have been in deep doodoo."

lower than dog shit. Of a person, very low indeed, but not *as low as whale shit*, than which nothing is lower.

not know shit (from Shinola), to. To not know anything. Shinola is a brand of shoe polish. The expression probably is military, dating to the period (pre-1956) when the shoes worn and polished were brown.

pile (or piece) of shit. Something worthless, inferior, or not to be believed. "Horse and Goose . . . raking up all the oldest gags in the world, saying 'How tall are you Pearson?' and he said '5'11",' and they said, 'We never seen a pile of shit so high before' " (Mark Harris, *Bang the Drum Slowly*, 1956).

Private Slipinshits. "The military equivalent of John Doe, but derogatory; used only of lower-ranking enlisted personnel" (John R. Elting, Dan Cragg, Ernest Deal, *A Dictionary of Soldier Talk*, 1984).

scare the shit out of [one], to. A reference to the tendency of terrified people to lose control of their evacuatory functions; *to shit in [one's] pants.* In the passive mode, *to be scared shitless.*

shit ass. A contemptible person; a twentieth-century updating of *shit-abed, shit-breeches,* and *shit-sticks,* all of which go back at least to the seventeenth century. See APE for an example of the first.

shit (or *shitty*) *end of the stick.* The worst end of any deal; bad treatment in general. The phrase often is prettied up as the *dirty* (or *short*) *end of the stick.*

shitburg. One of many epithets for small towns; see PODUNK.

shitface. Another contemptible person. Q. Why did the Lone Ranger shoot Tonto? A. He just found out that Kemo saby means *shitface* (teenage humor, ca. 1950). To be drunk is to be *shitfaced.*

shit fit, to have. To be very upset or angry. Variants: *to be as nervous as a cat shitting razor blades, to shit a brick* (or *bricks*), *to shit green.*

shit for the birds. Nonsense; see BIRD.

shithead. Still another contemptible person, sometimes oneself. "While he [Adolf Hitler] saw himself as a veritable Messiah of his people and spoke, often without knowing it, the very words of Jesus, he also referred to himself as a shithead (*Scheisskerl*)" (Walter G. Langer, *The Mind of Adolf Hitler*, 1972). More often, this epithet is applied to other people, of course, as in the graffito *Khomeini is a Shiite head* (ca. 1980).

shitheel. A despicable person; see HEEL.

shitkicker. A farmer or other resident of a rural area; see HICK for more on this topic.

shit list. A blacklist; a roster of enemies or other disliked people. A common WWII expression; the list itself usually is figurative, not actual.

shit on, to be. To be dumped on; to be jilted or flushed, as by one's date (also *to get the brown helmet*).

shit on wheels. Very remarkable; often ironic as applied to people who are not as good as they think they are.

shit or get off the pot. Make up your mind; go ahead or get out of [my] way; fish or cut bait. Usually expressed as a command, this may be euphemized, e.g., *pee or get off the pot, shoot or give up the gun.*

shit out of luck. Out of luck, really and truly; without a chance of success. The abbreviation, *S.O.L.,* was about as common in World War I as was *snafu* (Situation Normal, All Fucked Up) in World War II.

shit, piss, and corruption. An exclamation of shock, surprise, anger, etc.

shitwork. Menial, routine drudgery; scut work (see SCUT); particularly, in feminist writings, housework (*OED*, from 1968). In the military, a *shit detail.*

shoot the shit, to. To gossip; especially, to lie or to talk nonsense; also *to shoot the crap* (or *the bull*).

tough shit. Tough luck, always sarcastic; also *tough titty* and, in euphemized, abbreviated form, *T.S.,* as in *T.S. slip* (or *ticket*), a document which, when punched, entitles the bearer to sympathy but nothing else. (And sometimes not even that: "If you are looking for sympathy, you'll find it in the dictionary under 'S.' ") *T.S. slips* are usually imaginary forms, but some military chaplains have been known to print batches of them for distribution to complainers.

up shit creek (without a paddle). In serious trouble, lost, ruined; for emphasis, *up shit creek with a leaky paddle* (or *with leaky oars*). "Show me a veterinarian without any customers and I'll show you a doctor who is up Shit Creek without a poodle" (Los Angeles *Reader*, 4/1/83). The creek metaphor may be a twentieth-century updating of *to row [someone] up Salt River;* see *Salt River* in PEORIA.

when (or *then*) *the shit hits the fan.* When (or then) all hell breaks loose; a time of crisis or extreme tension. The expression is related to, and may well derive from, an old joke: A man in a crowded bar needed to defecate but couldn't find a bathroom, so he went upstairs and used a hole in the floor. Returning, he found everyone had gone except the bartender, who was cowering behind the bar. When the man asked what had happened, the bartender replied, "Where were you when the shit hit the fan?"

See also BLATHERSKITE, CRAP, DUNG, HOCKEY, HOOEY, POPPYCOCK, SAD SACK, SHYSTER, TRAYF, and TURD.

shoat (shote). An idler, a worthless person; an Americanism. The earliest example in the *OED* is from Parson Weems' hagiography of George Washington of 1800. The expression has been used within living memory in some-out-of-the-way places, e.g., " 'He's a pretty poor shoat' " (B. B. Ashcom, "The Language of the Bedford [Pennsylvania] Subarea," *American Speech*, 12/53). See also PIG.

short. Lacking in height, length, breadth, or quantity. "Society is obsessed with height, and our language reflects that obsession. We call impractical people *short*-sighted. Cheating at the cash register is described as *short*-changing the customer. In commodities trading, when we sell what we don't have, we sell *short*. When did a winner ever get the *short* end of the stick? Not enough food? Call it *short* rations. (But whoever heard of tall rations or long rations)" (John S. Gillis, *Too Tall Too Small*, 1982).

The classic exposition of the prejudice against shortness was the song "Short People" (1979), written and recorded by Randy Newman. Its lyrics asserted that "short people got no reason, got no reason to live." Among their other shortcomings, the song cited the small voices of undersized people and their beady little eyes. In addition, it noted the inconvenience of having to pick them up in order to say hello.

Short people all over the country rose up in high dudgeon and the record was even banned in Boston. Newman tried to defuse the protests by saying that he had intended the song as an ironic demonstration of the absurdity of all forms of prejudice, but this didn't satisfy his critics. Even those who took him at his word couldn't help but note what the road to hell is paved with.

Newman was far from the first to take pot shots at tiny targets, of course. In the words of Noel Coward (1899–1973): "He's a little man, that's his trouble. Never trust a man with short legs—brains too near their bottoms." Or as Thomas Hart Benton (1782–1851), who served first as senator and then as representative from Missouri, said of a fellow Democrat, Senator Stephen A. Douglas, "The Little Giant" of Illinois: "Douglas can never be president, Sir. No, Sir; Douglas can never be president, Sir. His legs are too short, Sir. His coat, like a cow's tail, hangs too near the ground, Sir." It also is reported on good authority that stunted arms are a liability: "For the theatre one needs long arms; it is better to have them too long than too short. An *artiste* with short arms can never, never make a grand gesture" (Sarah Bernhardt, *Memories of My Life*, 1907).

See also MIDGET and SMALL.

show-off. One who goes to unseemly lengths to impress others; also called a *show boat(er)* or *grandstander*. In the sense of a display or exposure of something, *show off* has been dated to the eighteenth century, but the present meaning is of recent vintage (*OED*, 1924). See also HOT DOG.

shrew. A scold; an evil-tempered, nagging woman, typified by Katharina, daughter to Baptista, a rich gentleman of Padua (Shakespeare, *The Taming of the Shrew*, ca. 1593). Now restricted to female applications, *shrew* started out as a masculine term, meaning a wicked or mischievous man—a rascal or villain. It also was an epithet for the devil. The malignant senses stem from folk beliefs that the tiny animal had magical powers. For example, it was thought a shrew could cause cattle to go lame by running over their backs. See also BITCH, CATAMOUNT, CROSSPATCH, HARPY, HARRIDAN, *hellcat* in HELL, NAG, TARTAR, TERMAGANT, VIRAGO, VIXEN, XANTHIPPE, and YENTA.

shrimp. A pint-sized person, especially a weak, puny one. The contemptuous sense of *shrimp* is so old that it may come directly from the word's Anglo-Saxon ancestor, akin to *scrimman*, to shrink, and meaning "a shrunken creature." Geoffrey Chaucer employed the term in the sense of "weakling" in *The Monk's Prologue* (1387–1400): "and we burel men [laymen] been shrimpes!" Etymology aside, when the insult is hurled, the crustacean usually is meant specifically. For example, when another U.S. representative told Alexander Hamilton Stephens of Georgia, who weighed in at less than one hundred pounds, "You little shrimp! Why I could swallow you whole," Stephens [whose long congressional career was interrupted by service as vice president of the Confederacy] replied: "If you did, you'd have more brains in your belly than you ever had in your head" (Edward Boykin, ed., *The Wit and Wisdom of Congress*, 1961). See also FISH.

shylock. An usurer, an extortioner; loosely, any lender of money or extender of credit; from Shakespeare's character in *The Merchant of Venice* (1596–98), who lends three thousand ducats without asking for any interest. Instead, Shylock sets a memorable condition: "If you repay me not on such a day . . . let the forfeit Be nominated for an equal [exact] pound Of your fair flesh, to be cut off and taken In what part of your body pleaseth me." The term may also be used as a verb. "Lieut. Remo Franceschini, the commander of the Queens District Attorney's detective squad, testified that reliable informants had told him that in the last year Mr. [John] Gotti had been involved in illegal activities, including gambling and shylocking" (*New York Times*, 4/30/86).

shyster. An unscrupulous lawyer (note that the definition presumes the existence of scrupulous ones); a PETTIFOGGER. ". . . I know an author who refers to his New York publisher as Slimy and Shyster . . ." (Richard Conniff, *New York Times Magazine*, 9/18/83).

Shyster was popularized in New York City in the 1840s by Mike Walsh, editor of what has to be termed an underground newspaper, *The Subterranean*. Initially, the reference was to incompetent lawyers, but Walsh almost immediately extended the meaning to characterize the unscrupulous, usually unlicensed lawyers who preyed upon the inmates of the city prison, the Tombs, extracting fees but rarely performing any services. Walsh picked up the word in a conversation with Cornelius Terhune, the most gifted of the *shysters* of the era, and first used it in print with a slightly different spelling on July 29, 1843: ". . . The Counsellor [Terhune] expressed the utmost surprise at our ignorance of the true meaning of that expressive appelation 'shiseter,' after which, by special request, he gave us a definition, which we would now give our readers, were it not that it would certainly subject us to a prosecution for libel and obscenity." The unearthing of this early quotation has enabled Gerald Leonard Cohen to pin down the much debated etymology of *shyster* ("Origin of the Term 'Shyster,' *Forum Anglicum*, 1982). The term does *not* come from—as suggested in various dictionaries—the surname Scheuster, supposedly a lawyer noted for shyster-like practices; from the name of the Shakespearean character, Shylock; from the Gaelic *siostair*, meaning one who commits barratry (originally the acquisition of church or state office by purchase and later, in a general legal sense, the incitement of quarrels or groundless lawsuits); or from any of the various meanings of *shy* (e.g., to be shy of money). Rather, as suggested by Walsh's fear of prosecution for "libel and obscenity," and as Cohen convincingly demonstrates, *shyster* evolved from the underworld use of *shiser*, a worthless fellow, which derived in turn from the German *scheisse*, excrement, via *scheisser*, an incompetent person (specifically, one who cannot control his bodily functions). See also LAWYER.

sicko. A severely disturbed person, a psychopath; also called a *sickie* or *sicky*. " 'I've never seen so many monsters in my life,' she said, referring to a group of photographers. 'You sickos' " (AP, 5/30/87). This was from a woman who had just been convicted of having killed her three-year-old adopted son through beatings and other forms of abuse. Apparently dating from the 1970s, *sicko* and *sickie* probably derive from the preceding fad for *sick jokes*, e.g., "The prototype of sick jokes is one that goes 'But apart from that, Mrs. Lincoln, how did you enjoy the play?' " (*Punch*, 9/2/59). See also MAD.

Simon Legree. A harsh taskmaster, a slave driver; loosely and sometimes jocularly, any foreman or boss; from the name of the cruel owner, a renegade Yankee, who whips Uncle Tom to death: "I don't keep none o' yer cussed overseers; I does my own overseeing; and I tell you things *is* seen to" (Harriet Beecher Stowe, *Uncle Tom's Cabin*, 1852). See also UNCLE TOM and YANKEE.

simpleton. "A silly mortal; a trifler; a foolish fellow. A low word" (Samuel Johnson, *Dictionary of the English Language*, 1755). *Simpleton* is a seventeenth century elaboration of *simple*, as in *simpleminded* or the famous *Simple Simon*, who "met a pieman, Going to the fair" (from 1764). The pejorative sense of the basic *simple* derives from the word's original meaning (from ca. 1220), i.e., to be free of duplicity, innocent and harmless, open, straightforward . . . which says a great deal about society's true estimate of these theoretically commendable qualities. See also FOOL and MORON.

sissy. A man or boy who acts like a girl; a weakling or coward; a male homosexual. "Most young boys who persistently act like girls grow up to be homosexuals or bisexuals, a 15-year study of 'sissy boys' has shown" (*New York Times*, 12/16/86). This particular study, done by Dr. Richard Green, was entitled *The 'Sissy Boy Syndrome' and the Development of Homosexuality* (1987). Sometimes elaborated as *sissy-britches* and *sissy-pants*, this classic denigration of women is a nineteenth-century Americanism. It derives from *sister*, of course, via the older, abbreviated *sis*. See also APRON STRINGS, TIED TO [SOMEONE'S]; COWARD, LA-DE-DAH; PUSSY; and WEAK SISTER.

skibby. A Japanese, especially on the U.S. West Coast. "The fact that the Japanese considered *skibby* particularly odious naturally increased the popularity of the word among the Jap-hating Californians" (Damon Runyon, New York *Mirror*, 2/11/42).

Skibby dates to the early twentieth century and seems to have referred originally to a prostitute or mistress, especially one involved with Occidentals. It probably comes from a Japanese term, but the precise origin has not been established. One possibility is *sukebei*, which translates as lechery, prurience, a bawdy person. See also JAP.

skinflint. A stingy person, a greedy one. "Next, it shows that not everyone is staring at television or reading the latest newspaper; somebody, somewhere—even as you read this—is reading an acid-stained climatology text or the letters of the author of 'Moby Dick' to his skinflint publisher" (William Safire, *New York Times Magazine*, 3/27/83). Dating from the late seventeenth century, *skinflint* apparently reflects the reputation that misers have of being willing to try to skin anything, even if it is as hard as a flint, in order to save money or gain something else. See also TIGHTWAD.

skunk. A contemptible person. Thus, New Hampshire newspaper publisher William Loeb, a recognized master of invective, termed presidential candidate Eugene McCarthy in 1968 "a skunk's skunk's skunk."

An Algonquian Indian word, variously transcribed as *scunk, squnck, squncke*, and so on, and roughly translating as "he who squirts," the term was picked up by English explorers as early as 1588. The contemptible human sense has been dated to 1840 as a noun. Soon afterward, the word also began appearing as a verb with various meanings, e.g., to thoroughly defeat another person (specifically, in games, not to allow a player to score a single point); to evade a debt; and to slink away from danger. In the nineteenth century, the term was considered such a powerful insult that in the most august circles it could only be alluded to— as in the colloquy between Senators Charles Sumner, of Massachusetts, and Stephen A. Douglas, of Illinois, that followed Sumner's HIRELING speech of May 19, 1856:

> MR. SUMNER: . . . no person with the upright form of a man can be allowed, without violation of all human decency, to switch out from his tongue the perpetual stench of offensive personality. . . . The noisome, squat, and nameless animal, to which I now refer, is not a proper model for an American Senator. Will the Senator from Illinois take notice?
> MR. DOUGLAS: I will; and therefore will not imitate you, sir . . .

MR. SUMNER: Mr. President, again the Senator has switched his tongue, and again he fills the Senate with its offensive odor.

MR. DOUGLAS: . . . I will only say that a man who has been branded by me in the Senate, and convicted by the Senate of falsehood, cannot use language requiring reply, and therefore I have nothing to say.

Today, the power of *skunk* as an epithet has degenerated somewhat, perhaps reflecting the increasing urbanization of American society. Hollywood has employed the term more or less as a euphemism ("You dirty skunk!" *Black Fury*, 1935) and its value as an insult seems to be appreciated most by preadolescents, typically in the quatrain:

> Roses are red,
> Violets are blue,
> A skunk smells bad,
> And so do you!

See also POLECAT and RAT.

slacker. One who shirks work or evades other obligations, especially during time of war. The term dates from the end of the last century and was popularized as an attack word during World War I by home-front warriors, who applied it to conscientious objectors, pacifists, and others who appeared reluctant to do their bit. See also LOAFER and SHIRKER.

slant. An Oriental, or any vaguely Oriental-looking person with slanted eyes. "To the G.I. the Vietnamese . . . is a 'gook,' 'dink,' 'slope,' or 'slant' " (*Time*, 12/5/69). *Slant*, dating from the start of World War II, is short for *slant-eye*. (The OED traces the adjective *slant-eyed* to 1865 in its Oriental sense.) *Slant-eye* is opposed, of course, to the Occidental *round-eye*. A variant of *slant-eyed* is *slitty-eyed*. During Queen Elizabeth II's visit to China in 1986—the first ever by a British monarch—Prince Philip remarked to a British student, who said he had been in China for six weeks, "If you stay over here much longer, you will go back with slitty eyes" (*New York Times*, 10/18/86). This wisecrack raised eyebrows of all sorts all around the world, resulting in such headlines back home as *The Sun*'s "Philip Gets It All Wong." See also GOOK.

slattern. An unkempt, slovenly woman; dating to the seventeenth century and apparently of basically onomatopoetic origin; stemming from the dialectical *slatter*, to spill, splash, slop, or splatter. See also SLUT.

slave. A submissive, servile, unmanly person, seemingly without free will, as a *slave of fashion*, a *slave of love*, or a *slavish imitator*. "Oh, what a rogue and peasant slave am I!" (William Shakespeare, *Hamlet*, 1601–02; the Prince speaking).

Slave is perhaps the oldest ethnic disparagement in English. It comes from *Slav*, so many of whom were enslaved that by the ninth century their racial name had been generalized to include any person who, through capture, purchase, or birth, had become another person's property. In the United States, even when slavery was legal, enough people sensed that there was something wrong about the custom that they avoided using the word *slave*. Thus, *servant* became a euphemism for *slave* in the eighteenth and nineteenth centuries (with the inevitable result that free white servants decided that they wanted to be called *the help* so as not to be lumped in semantically with unfree black *servants*). The full extent of *slave's* degradation, however, is measured by its fall from *slav*, which, in Slavic, means "glory." See also COOLIE, DRUDGE, and the origin of WELSH.

sleaze. Sordidness, squalor; (someone or something) that is disreputable, dirty, run-down, dilapidated, cheap, inferior, or immoral. "White House pollster Richard Wirthlin said Wednesday the resignation of Attorney General Edward Meese III doesn't erase 'the sleaze factor' for Vice President George Bush in the fall presidential campaign, but makes it easier for him to deal with it" (AP, 7/6/88).

Sleaze comes from *sleazy*, whose origin is obscure but which classes as a geographical derogation in view of its long association with the region of Silesia in Eastern Europe (once mainly in Germany but since the Potsdam Pact of 1945 mainly in Poland). The geographical connection dates to the seventeenth century when *sleasie, sleasy,* and *sleazy,* all recognized corruptions of *Silesia,* also were used to describe a kind of linen or cotton cloth that was flimsy, ill-made, and quick to wear out. The progression in textile nomenclature was from *Holland* cloth, a fine cloth first made, as the name implies, in The Netherlands (from the fifteenth century), to imitation *Sleasie Holland,* originally made in Germany, to the simple *sleazy.* See also CHINTZY.

In addition to the political *sleaze factor* (from 1984), other *sleazy* constructions include *sleazebag* (basically the same as a *scumbag* or *scuzzbag*), *sleazeball, sleaze merchant, sleazo,* and *sleazoid.* Of course, the basic *sleazy* also continues in service, as in, complaining about the bias of Northern newspapers against Southerners: "Suppose Hamilton Jordan and Bert Lance had been accused of using material stolen from the Ford White House to prepare Jimmy Carter for the 1976 debates. . . . Editorial demands for the White House to make a clean breast of it and jettison the sleazy Georgians . . . would have run throughout the land" (Jody Powell, *The Other Side of the Story,* 1984).

For more about geographical putdowns, see PEORIA.

slime. A thoroughly disgusting person or thing; for emphasis, *slimebag, slimeball, slimebucket.* " 'I think that they are just slime,' [Republican mayoral candidate Bernard] Epton said of Chicago's newspeople just after the polls closed on April 12" (*Columbia Journalism Review,* 7-8/83). *Slime* has been applied pejoratively to people since at least the fourteenth century. It is comparable as a epithet to SCUM—an equivalence that has been recognized for several centuries. Thus, from John Marston's *Antonio's Revenge* (1602):

ANTONIO: Scum of the mud of hell!
ALBERTO: Slime of all filth!

slit. The female pudendum. "The vagina . . . belittled by terms like . . . *slit*" (Germaine Greer, *The Female Eunuch,* 1970). The belittling term has been around for quite some time. From Robert Herrick's *Hesperides* (1648):

Scobble for Whoredome whips his wife; and cryes,
He'll slit her nose; but blubb'ring, she replyes,

Good Sir, make no more cuts i' th'outward skin,
One slit's enough to let Adultry in.

The underlying metaphor is common as well as old; see NOOKIE.

slob. An untidy, loutish, foolish fellow; often, one on the fat side as well. "[Warren G.] Harding was not a bad man. He was just a slob" (Alice Roosevelt Longworth, *Crowded Hours*, 1933). Deriving from the Irish *slab*, mud, the *slob* as person is a relatively new word, dated only to 1861 in the *OED*. It is distantly related to such other beauties as *slaver, slobber, slump,* and, most picturesquely, the unfortunately obsolete *slubberdegullion,* a slobbering, dirty, nasty fellow. People of Slavic extraction sometimes are said to be *Slobovians* (also *Slobbovians*), or to hail from *Lower Slobovia,* a region discovered and named by the cartoonist Al Capp (1909–79).

slope. An Oriental; specifically, during the war in Vietnam, a Vietnamese, but before that, usually a Chinese. "Why is there such good skiing in China? Because they have six billion slopes" (Merritt Clifton, "How to Hate Thy Neighbor: A Guide to Racist Maledicta," *Maledicta*, 1978).

The derogation—arguably the most offensive of those devised for Asians— seems to have been popularized by the military. It dates at least to the early 1940s and comes from the apparently older *slopehead* (1920s or before). Thus, from a novel about events in China in 1925: " 'They'll run,' Crosley said. 'Slopeheads always run' " (Richard McKenna, *The Sand Pebbles*, 1962). Another variant was used by the members of the American Volunteer Group (better known as the Flying Tigers), who went to China prior to American entry into World War II, and who referred to the Chinese on whose behalf they fought as *slopies, coosies, flange heads,* and *little brown brothers* (John Lancaster Riordan, "A.V.G. Lingo," *American Speech*, 2/48). Opinion is divided as to whether the original reference was to the slope (or SLANT) of Oriental eyes, or to the extreme roundness of some Oriental skulls. See also GOOK.

sloth. A lazy person, an idler, or laziness itself; from the Middle English *slowthe*, in turn from *slow*. The term denoted one of the Seven Deadly Sins long before Europeans encountered the arboreal animal, whose name in Portuguese, *preguica* (from the Latin *pegrita*, laziness), was translated in the early seventeenth century into the English *sloth*. See also SLUGGARD.

sluggard. An idler or lazy fellow; from the fourteenth century. The basic *slug* probably is of Scandinavian origin, akin to the Swedish *slogga*, to be slow, and the Norwegian *slugg*, a large heavy body. In English, *slug* parallels SLOTH in that it was applied to slow-moving, sluggish people (and also to vessels, vehicles, and animals of various sorts) for several centuries prior to its adoption (ca. 1700) as the name of the slimy land snail often found in gardens. The older, pre-snailish sense is preserved in *slug-a-bed*, defined by Captain Francis Grose as "A drone, one that cannot rise in the morning" (*A Classical Dictionary of the Vulgar Tongue*, 1796). People have been having trouble getting out of their beds since at least Elizabethan times: "Why Lady! Fie, you slugabed" (William Shakespeare, *Romeo and Juliet*, ca. 1595).

slur. A disparagement, a deliberate slight. The word itself is basically a slur on female-kind, apparently deriving from the middle Dutch *sloor*, sluttish woman, via the Middle English *sloor*, *slore*, mud. See also MUDSLINGER.

slut. A slovenly woman; one of loose morals; a prostitute, HUSSY, or JADE. "He got very drunk and brought back a sluttish girl to the house. He woke me later to tell me that he had just rogered her and her mama, too" (Evelyn Waugh, *Remote People* [in Kenya], 1931).

An old word, perhaps related to SLATTERN, *slut* was applied to women long before the nineteenth century, when it sank for a while to the animal level, becoming a euphemism for a she-dog, or BITCH. In very olden times, it was not restricted to women, e.g., "Why is thy lord so sluttish" (Geoffrey Chaucer, *The Canon's Yeoman's Tale*, 1387–1400). The feminine senses developed early, however, and they soon became dominant, which is usually what happens when "bad" words have both male and female meanings. Nowadays, only women are *sluts* or *sluttish*, the men having managed to get to escape the derogatory designation, just as they did with, for instance, GIRL, HARLOT, and SHREW. See also DOG.

small. Little; lacking in size, quantity, or importance, as contrasted with the "good" qualities that are deemed inherent in *big, broad, expansive, large*, etc. The prejudice against *small* has been alleviated lately, thanks in no small part to E. F. Schumacher's *Small Is Beautiful* (1973), but it remains evident in the continuing use of such phrases as *small beer, small change, small fry, small-minded, small potatoes, small talk,* and *small-time*. Of these, *small beer*, originally weak or inferior beer and, in extended use, anything trivial or inconsequential in nature, is one of the oldest, e.g., Shakespeare's line in *Othello* (1604): "To suckle fools and chronicle small beer." For sheer denigration, however, it is hard to improve upon the use of the word by Samuel Butler (1612–80) in his *Miscellaneous Thoughts*:

> The souls of women are so small,
> That some believe they've none at all.

See also SHORT.

smarmy. Smugly ingratiating, unctuous, oily. "Its official name is 'the Workshop,' and it is run by a rather smarmy doctor and highly officious nurse" (*Time*, 12/17/73). The term is of British origin, the adjective coming from the verb, *to smarm*, i.e., to flatter or toady (up to). *Smarm*, in turn, is the most usual modern form of the dialectical *smalm*, to smear, bedaub, first recorded in the nineteenth century.

snake. A treacherous person; the ultimate in LOWLIFE, as in the country saying "John is *as crooked as a barrel of snakes*," or as that most urbane British Prime Minister, Anthony Eden, said of an American Secretary of State, "[John Foster Dulles is] as tortuous as a wounded snake, with much less excuse" (Robert Rhodes James, *Anthony Eden*, 1987).

Snakes have been perceived as dangerous and deceitful since ancient times (see SERPENT). Aesop (ca. 620–560 B.C.) helped establish their character with his fable about a farmer who in the winter came upon a frozen snake. Feeling sorry for it, the farmer put the snake in his bosom, whereupon the critter, after thawing out, bit the farmer, killing him. Moral: The greatest benefit will not bind the ungrateful, or, as the farmer put it in his dying words, "I am rightly served for pitying a scoundrel." Two thousand years later, writers still drew upon Aesop's story as a symbol of treachery: "I fear me you warm the starved snake Who cherished in your breasts, will sting your hearts" (William Shakespeare, *Henry VI, Part II*, 1590–91). The proverbial *snake in the grass* is nearly as old, dating at least to Roman times— *Latet anguis in herba*, as Virgil put it in the third of his *Eclogues* (43–27 B.C.). Today, the *snake in the grass* probably appears most frequently in a spoonerism relished by adolescents:

Q. What is the difference between a snake and a goose?
A. One is an asp in the grass.

Snake has other uses as well. For example:

Snake is low slang for the penis, sometimes also referred to as a *one-eyed snake*. (See also SCHLONG.) A *snake* also may be a young girl or woman (perhaps an allusion to their treacherous nature). If the female person is a member of a campus sorority, she may be said to live in a *snake house* (not to be confused with a *snake ranch*, which is cheap bar, dive, or brothel). College campuses also are populated by male *snakes*, who are adept at deceiving women, and sometimes *snake away* with them at dances (by cutting in and not returning them to their proper partners). The male of the species also has been described as a *parlor snake*.

Snake juice, snake medicine, and *snake poison* are bywords for whiskey, often cheap rotgut, the terms perhaps deriving from *seeing snakes*, which is what happens to those who drink too much of it and suffer delirium tremens. *Snake pit,* an insane asylum, probably is based on the same delusion. *To snake* is to cheat, especially when gambling; *to be snakebit* or *struck* is to be slightly injured, sometimes with the implication that one is jinxed or accident prone, and to tell a *snake story* or *snake yarn* is to tell a long, convoluted, unbelievable one. *To wake snakes* is to get into trouble and to tell someone *to kill [their] own snakes* is to say that they should mind their own business. Finally, there is *snake oil,* once purveyed in bottles by traveling medicine show men, who thereby turned it into a symbol for any kind of misrepresentation, e.g., "The credibility of Mr. Richards . . . was assailed by Mr. Kaplan's lawyer [who] described Mr. Richards as a 'snake oil salesman' " (*New York Times,* 10/1/86). See also ADDER, DEAF AS AN; COPPERHEAD; RATTLESNAKE; and VIPER.

snatch. The female pudendum; sexual intercourse, quickly performed; a woman. "She . . . twisted away, fleeing far enough . . . for Yossarian to lunge forward and grab her by the snatch again" (Joseph Heller, *Catch-22,* 1961).

This slang term, like many of its synonyms, is of some antiquity, with the copulatory sense apparently being the oldest, e.g., "Why, then, it seems some certain snatch or so Would serve your turns" (William Shakespeare, *Titus Andronicus,* 1589–94). G. B. Harrison, the editor of a generally excellent text for college students, *Shakespeare: The Complete Works* (1952), glosses this example as "snack" or "taste," and it is true that *snatch* is also an old word for "hasty meal." The context suggests a pun, however, as it comes in the course of a discussion of the conquest of Lavinia ("She is a woman, therefore may be wooed; She is a woman, therefore may be won"). Robert Burton also used the term at an early date, and with clearer venereal intent: "I could not abide marriage, but as a rambler, I took a snatch when I could get it" (*The Anatomy of Melancholy*, 1621). See also PUSSY.

sneak. A cowardly, untrustworthy, despicable person. Of obscure origin, the word appeared at the end of the sixteenth century, when it was often treated as though it were a proper name, e.g., "Was she . . . wench to that Sneake-John?" (Ben Jonson, *Tale of a Tub*, 1633). *Sneak's* low meanings accord completely with the presumption that it is etymologically akin to the Old English *snican*, to creep, to crawl, just like its sound-alike the sneaky SNAKE.

Sneak also serves as an adjective and verb, of course. Thus, Americans generally refer to the Japanese air raid on Pearl Harbor on December, 7, 1941, as a *sneak attack*, though the makers of the Japanese film *The Tokyo Trial* (screened in New York in 1985) chose instead to term the event "a triumph of tactical surprise." See also SNOOKER.

snitch. An informer or to inform (on); also a thief or the act of stealing. A *snitch* is the lowest of the low (to the extent that there is honor among thieves), and the charge, accordingly, is an exceedingly strong one. "He employs that phenomenon of despicability . . . in Western parlance called a snitch . . . to work up the lawsuit" (*Atlantic Monthly*, 11/06). "Corporations, most of them anyway, are male-bonding fraternities, made up of team players. . . . The term 'whistle-blower' has no gender, but to snitch is not considered manly; 'one of the boys' is never a tattletale" (*New York Times Magazine*, 6/7/87).

Although popular in the American West, *snitch* was not original to it. The sense of "informer" was known to Byron, who used *snitch* in this way in a footnote to *Don Juan* (1800), as well as to Captain Francis Grose, who included the verb in the first edition of his *Classical Dictionary of the Vulgar Tongue* (1785). Probably, the informing sense comes from the earlier (seventeenth century) use of *snitch* to mean the proboscis, as *nose* also is an old cant term for an informer. See also INFORMER, NOSEY PARKER, PIGEON, SNOOP, and TATTLETALE.

sniveling. Weak, whining; applicable to things as well as people, e.g., "I have received a sniveling letter from Griffin, offering to make public submission and pay costs" (Tobias Smollet, *Humphry Clinker*, 1772). *Sniveling* gains its force from its original meaning, "running at the nose." Note, too, the number of derogative terms that begin with *sn*. The ess-en sound itself seems to be intrinsically negative. *Snack, snooze,* and *snuggle (up with)* are exceptions that prove the rule. See also SNOTTY.

snob. One who strives to associate with people of greater social, cultural, or intellectual attainments, and who looks down upon the rest of the world; an affected, effete person. "It is impossible, in our condition of society, not to be sometimes a snob" (William Makepeace Thackeray, *The Book of Snobs*, 1848). "A spirit of national masochism prevails, encouraged by an effete corps of impudent snobs who characterize themselves as intellectuals" (Vice President Spiro Agnew, speech, New Orleans, Louisiana, 10/19/69).

The principal present meaning of *snob* is due to Thackeray. A *snob* originally (from the late eighteenth century) was a shoemaker or shoemaker's apprentice. The term's origin is not known; it might be cognate to *snub*, i.e., to cut short, which is what shoemakers did to strips of leather before social *snobs* began *snubbing*, or cutting short, their presumed inferiors. The modern sense seems to have evolved over a period of about fifty years, proceeding from shoemaker, to townsman (in Cambridge slang, as opposed to a gownsman), to a person of the lower classes, to an uncultivated but ostentatious person, to the social *snob* delineated by Thackeray.

The earliest meaning is preserved in *the Snob's Horse*, the name of the figure of a horse that was cut by some cobbler's apprentices in 1845 in the chalky soil of the downs in Wiltshire, England. See also EUNUCH, INTELLECTUAL, and PHILISTINE.

snooker. To cheat; to deceive. "CBS feels it was 'snookered' by Ziff-Davis and their accountants Touche Ross, so much so that it filed suit against them with the SEC, charging a $3.9 million overstatement of earnings in the documents that CBS relied on when buying twelve Ziff-Davis consumer magazines" (*Authors Guild Bulletin*, Spring 1985). "Regan Testifies Reagan Felt Iran 'Snookered' Him" (headline, *New York Times*, 7/31/87).

Snooker, as a verb, usually employed in passive sense, and often in rueful manner, comes from the name of the game, invented in Jubbulpore, India, in 1875 by a British subaltern, Neville Chamberlain (later a colonel and knighted, but never a prime minister; the two men were unrelated). The game combines elements of pool and billiards, while providing more opportunities than either for defensive play, with the cue ball being left in a position so that one's opponent is unable to hit the ball at which he is supposed to be aiming. The opponent then is said to be *snookered*, or stymied. From such legitimate but crafty play, the sense of cheating developed.

The origin of the name of the game is uncertain. Chamberlain is said to have applied *snooker* first to a fellow officer, who played the game with a remarkable degree of ineptitude. The term may come from *snoke*, sneak, an old word (from the fourteenth century) that was used in the nineteenth century at the Royal Military Academy at Sandhurst to characterize first-year cadets—low fellows, apparently, who were always sneaking about.

See also CHEAT and FOUR-FLUSHER.

snoop. One who pokes his nose into other people's business, sometimes professionally, as a detective; the act of prying. A nineteenth-century Americanism, from the Dutch *snoepen*, to eat (dainties) on the sly, the term has been adopted by English speakers generally. Thus, when asked by an Israeli investigatory commission what he had done after learning about the massacre of Palestinian refugees at two camps in Beirut, Communications Minister Mordechai Zipori replied, "I reported that to the Foreign Minister. I usually trust him; and, besides, since perhaps I am considered a snoop, I stopped nosing around" (*New York Times*, 11/19/82). The word has been elaborated in various ways, e.g., *snooper, snoopy, snoopery*, and the military *snooperscope* that makes use of the infrared wavelengths to discern objects in the dark. See also NOSEY PARKER.

snooty. Supercilious, snobby, conceited; HOITY-TOITY. "I didn't like . . . the snooty way you talked" (Sinclair Lewis, *Babbitt*, 1922). The term seems to be an Americanism of the post–World War I period. It comes from the *snoot* that is a snout, or nose, which is what the *snooty* one has stuck up in the air, so to speak. See also SNOTTY.

snotty. Contemptible, nasty; stuck-up. "My old friend George [Bush] reacted through a press aide, by objecting to 'a number of inaccurate and, quite frankly, snotty criticisms of the Vice President' in this column" (William Safire, *New York Times*, 10/10/84).

The reference is to the mucus that descends from a runny nose, of course, *snot* being cognate to *snout*. From at least the early 1600s, *snotty, snotty nose*, and *snot* have served as epithets. Thus, Cambridge, Massachusetts, was dismissed as a "Snotty Town" by an Anglican minister, the Reverend Timothy Cutler, in a letter on April 2, 1725. (It may be significant that Cutler, an apostate from the Congregational ministry, also was a founder and former rector of Yale, upstart rival to a nameless Cambridge institution.) See also SNIVELING.

so-called. Dubious, spurious, illegitimate, fake. "Rose Macaulay [1881–1958] noticed a tendency to prefix 'so-called' to almost any adjective when it was used of those the speaker hated; the final absurdity being reached when people referred to the Germans as 'these so-called Germans' " (C. S. Lewis, *Studies in Words*, 1960). "During his latter years as F.B.I. Director, J. Edgar Hoover seemed to mistrust sociologists and called them 'so-called sociologists.' A listener once gibed that sociologists are so called because that's what they are, but for Mr. Hoover, the modifier made the term truly pejorative" (*New York Times*, 6/11/85).

Purported and *self-styled* can be used in much the same way as *so-called*. See also PSEUDO.

sodomite. (1) A homosexual, usually male (*sodomitess* is obsolete, on the high authority of the *OED*); (2) in a legal sense, often vaguely defined by statute, anyone, of whatever sexual orientation, who performs any "unnatural" act with man, woman, or beast (up until a couple hundred years ago, the poor beasts usually were punished with death for their part in such doings); (3) an inhabitant of the biblical city of Sodom (see PEORIA).

In the primary sense (and one of history's more famous accusations): "To Mr. Oscar Wilde, posing as a somdomist" (message on card, left at Wilde's London club, 4:30 P.M., 2/18/1895). The author of this billet-doux was the Marquis of Queensberry, father of Wilde's young friend Alfred, Lord Douglas, a.k.a. Bosie. Queensberry's penmanship left much to be desired, and the exact wording of the message has been questioned: "posing as" perhaps should have been read as "ponce and" (*ponce* meaning a man who is supported by a HARLOT). His Lordship does seem to have written *somdomist*, however, perhaps because he didn't know any better or perhaps because he was incoherent with rage. The message became famous because Wilde, against the advice of friends, sued for libel. He lost, then was tried and convicted of having violated a law, enacted just ten years previously, that made it a misdemeanor for any male to commit "in public or private . . . any act of gross indecency with another male person . . ." (Note that this Victorian statute did not contemplate the possibility of such gross misbehavior by females.) Sentenced to two years of hard labor at Reading Gaol, Wilde emerged a broken man. He died three years later, in Paris in 1900.

Sodomite has been dated to ca. 1380. The word originally referred to the act rather than the practitioner. It alludes, of course, to the ancient city of Sodom, which the Lord decided to destroy, along with its sister city, Gomorrah, on account of the sinfulness of their inhabitants. The nature of these sins is apparent from the story of Lot, a resident of Sodom. When two angels came to visit him overnight, all the men of the city surrounded his house: "And they called unto Lot, and said unto him, Where are the men which came in to thee this night? bring them out unto us, that we may know them" (*Genesis*, 19:5).

That the Sodomites here used *know* in its biblical sense of *carnal knowledge* is evident from Lot's offer, three verses later, to give his two virgin daughters to the men, if only they would leave his angelic guests alone—an offer the Sodomites declined. Instead, they tried to break down Lot's door. Protected by the angels, Lot and his family left town the next morning. After they had reached the safety of the small city of Zoar, the Lord rained brimstone and fire down upon Sodom and Gomorrah, and it was then that Lot's wife, looking back upon the destruction of her home, was turned into a pillar of salt.

See also QUEER.

soft. Weak, yielding; unmanly; foolish; excessively partial to—all in contrast to *hard*, which generally is perceived as a "good" quality. Thus, a *soft-brained* or *soft-headed* person is a FOOL or SIMPLETON (see also BLOCKHEAD), while a *hard-headed* person is a shrewd one; a *soft-boiled* fellow is easygoing, naïve, or impractical, in contrast to a tough, *hard-boiled* type (see EGGHEAD); *soft-core* pornography is a watered down version of the real *hard-core* thing; *soft currencies* are not as good as *hard cash*; and *soft drinks* don't have the kick of *hard alcohol*.

son of a bitch. A despicable person, usually a man but sometimes a woman; a nasty, troublesome, or difficult thing; and an epithet of all work, frequently used as an exclamation of surprise, an oath of disgust, an adjective (sometimes appreciatively), and even as a greeting among friends. In the classic negative sense: "I think we are going to fix that son-of-a-bitch. Believe me. We are going to. We've got to, because he's a bad man" (President Richard M. Nixon, White House tape 9/15/72, referring to Edward Bennett Williams, in his capacity as lawyer for the *Washington Post*).

Probably the most common American vulgarity from about the middle of the eighteenth century to the middle of the twentieth, *son of a bitch* has lost much of its shock power. Having superseded *son of a whore* and WHORESON, it has begun to be replaced in most of the uses enumerated above by the ruder, cruder MOTHERFUCKER. The onetime power and popularity of the term is demonstrated in a number of ways, including (1) the large number of euphemisms that were devised for it (such as S.O.B., from ca. 1850, *so-and-so, sonofa, son of a b., son of a sea cook, son of a gun,* and so on); (2) the refusal for many years of newspaper and book publishers to print it (even *son-of-a-* _____ caused an uproar when the New York *Daily News* used it in cartoon caption on October 4, 1939); (3) the inclusion of S.O.B. among the terms officially banned from Hollywood soundtracks in 1931 (*son-of-a* later was added to the list; see DAMN for other no-nos); and (4) substantial ancedotal evidence, e.g. Robert Graves' account of the Frenchman who commiserated with a Mrs. Beech upon her visit to Paris after World War I: "Ah, Mrs. Beech, Mrs. Beech, you are one of ze noble muzzers who gave so many sons to ze War" (*The Future of Swearing and Improper Language*, 1936). And, in fact, the French heard the Yanks in the AEF use the expression so often that they referred to the Americans as *les sommobiches*. (The fans of Sherlock Holmes, The Baker Street Irregulars, have included a group called "The Sons of the Copper Beeches.")

Though extremely popular in the United States, the expression was by no means a New World invention. The *OED* records it from 1688: "There stands Jack Ketch, that Son of a Bitch, that owes us all a grudge" (John Shirley, *The Triumph of Wit*, 1707). This, not so incidentally, is from the great dictionary's 1986 supplement, *son of a bitch* having been omitted from both the original Volume S (prepared 1910–15) and the first 1933 supplement. Prefiguring Shirley's example are such similar constructions as the "Biche-Sone" that appears in *Of Arthour & of Merlin* (anonymous, ca. 1330) and Shakespeare's "son and heir of a mongrel bitch" (*King Lear*, 1605–06; see KNAVE for the full quote). Indicating how standards change in regard to what is considered "bad," Henry Fielding employed his dash elsewhere when quoting a traveling salesman's instructions to a groom at an inn in Somersetshire: "D–mn your blood, you cock-ey'd son of a bitch, bring me my boots" (*Covent Garden Journal*, 4/25/1752).

The expression was particularly popular in the American West, as exemplified by the ditty that Charles E. Boles, better known as Black Bart, left in the Feather River Canyon at the scene of one of his many Wells Fargo stagecoach robberies in the 1870s and '80s (from Ralph Moody, *Stagecoach West*, 1967):

> I've labored long and hard for bread,
> For honor and for riches,
> But on my corns too long you've tred,
> You fine-haired sons of bitches.
>
> Let come what will, I'll try it on,
> My condition can't be worse;
> And if there's money in that box
> 'Tis money in my purse.
> —Black Bart, the PO8*

In the same period, the term (sometimes known as *the four-word epithet*) also served as the culmination of a famous sentence of death by Judge Isaac Charles Parker (1838–96), the "Hanging Judge" of Arkansas. (Similar pronouncements also have been attributed to Judges Kirby Benedict and Roy Bean; see CHINAMAN and GALOOT for more on the latter's brand of Western jurisprudence.) In Parker's case, a Mexican cook had killed a cowboy in a dispute over cards. Said the judge to the prisoner:

> I command the sheriff or some other officer or officers of this county to lead you out to some remote spot, swing you up by the neck to a nodding bough of some sturdy oak, and there let you hang until you are dead, dead, dead. And . . . further that such officer or officers retire quietly from your swinging, dangling corpse, that the vultures may descend upon your filthy body and pick the putrid flesh therefrom till nothing remains but the bare, bleached bones of a cold-blooded, copper-colored, bloodthirsty, chili-eating, guilty, sheep-herding, Mexican son-of-a-bitch (Ralph Emerson Twitchell, *Old Santa Fe*, 1925).

*Don't get "PO8"? Sound it out.

Echoes of this kind of Western "tall talk" are preserved in Senator William E. Jenner's (Republican, Indiana) appreciation of newspaper columnist Jack Anderson's mentor: "This Drew Pearson is a self-appointed, self-made, cross t'd, dotted i'd, double-documented, super-superlative, revolving s.o.b." (AP, 9/23/50).

The decline in the power of *son of a bitch* is illustrated by changing reactions to its use by public figures. For example, many people—especially Republicans—professed to be shocked by Harry S Truman's defense of his longtime friend and aide-de-camp, General Harry H. Vaughan, who had come under fire for accepting a medal from Argentina's fascist dictator Juan Perón. Said Truman at a meeting of the Reserve Officers Association in Arlington, Virginia (2/22/49): "I am just as fond of and just as loyal to my military aide as I am to the high brass, and I want you to distinctly understand that any SOB who thinks he can cause any of these people to be discharged by me by some smart-aleck statement over the air or in the paper, he has another think coming" (Bert Cochran, *Harry Truman and the Crisis Presidency*, 1973). Of course, Truman also expected the "high brass" to be loyal to him; thus, he couched his dismissal of General Douglas MacArthur in 1951 in these terms: "I fired him because he wouldn't respect the authority of the President. . . . I didn't fire him because he was a dumb son of a bitch, although he was, but that's not against the law for generals. If it was, half to three quarters of them would be in jail" (Merle Miller, *Plain Speaking: An Oral Biography of Harry S Truman*, 1984).

A small furor also followed the revelation, in April 1962, of John F. Kennedy's observation that "My father always told me that all businessmen were sons of bitches, but I never believed it till now" (Arthur M. Schlesinger, Jr., *A Thousand Days*, 1965). JFK was upset because he felt he had been double-crossed. He made the remark just after meeting (April 10) with Roger Blough, chairman of U.S. Steel, who announced a series of price increases—after having accepted Kennedy's help in persuading the steelworkers' union to agree to a noninflationary wage contract.

Kennedy softened his comment at a press conference, saying that actually his father had referred only to steel men: ". . . he was involved when he was a member of the Roosevelt administration in the 1937 strike. He formed an opinion, which he imparted to me. . . . I quoted what he said and indicated that he had not been, as he had not been on many other occasions, wholly wrong." Nevertheless, many businessmen never forgave the president for what he had said. Of course, Kennedy was quite angry. As he told Schlesinger and Adlai Stevenson a few days later: "They *are* a bunch of bastards—and I'm saying this on my own now, not just because my father told it to me."

Showing how times have changed, however, there was a noticeable lack of cluck-clucking in 1986 when Ronald Reagan casually referred to reporters as "sons of bitches," not realizing that the microphone in front of him was turned on. The remark was widely printed, the episode provoking nothing but mirth. (Of course, many people, including most of the president's most fervent supporters, agreed with his assessment.)

Nowadays, even an elderly woman of refinement can use the expression, and even family newspapers will report in full what is said. Thus, explaining why Supreme Court Justice Hugo L. Black was not bitter about being shunned by fellow Alabamans because of his liberal opinions, Virginia Durr, Black's eighty-two-year-old sister-in-law, said, "It's very difficult in the South to be self-righteous. We were all segregationists when we grew up. You can't say everybody else is a son of a bitch or wrong if you were exactly the same way yourself" (*New York Times*, 4/14/85).

As epitaph for the taboo that once was, here is a verse by Dorothy Parker, upon viewing a picture at San Simeon, palatial residence of newspaper publisher William Randolph Hearst and his actress-friend Marion Davies (in Joseph Alsop, *The Rare Art Traditions*, 1983):

> Upon my honor, I saw a Madonna
> Hanging within a niche
> Above the door
> Of the private whore
> Of the world's worst son of a bitch.

See also BASTARD and BITCH.

sophomoric. Immature, wet behind the ears. "I don't trust the *Columbia Journalism Review*. . . . I wrote them a letter a year or so ago, in fact, in which I described them as a playpen of sophomoric lefties" (*Washington Times* editor James R. Whelan, interview with *CJR*, 5-6/83). The word's use as a term of disparagement is in keeping with its descent from *sophism*, i.e., argument that is plausible and often ingenious but always fallacious and sometimes intentionally misleading.

sorehead. A constant (loud) complainer; a malcontent. "I was holding court with a lot of my customers, who were all telling me what a bunch of shit the whole business was, caused by a few soreheads" (Mario Puzo, *Fools Die*, 1978).

Sorehead seems to be a nineteenth-century Americanism, perhaps deriving from the expression "as mad as a bear with a sore head."

space cadet. An eccentric; one who seems disconnected from the real world, far out (in space). "Edward G. (Jerry) Brown Jr., the former Governor of California who has been alternately labeled a visionary and a 'space cadet,' was elected chairman of the state Democratic Party late Saturday" (*New York Times*, 2/13/89). Influenced by the use of *spaced* and *spacey* to describe people who are out of contact with reality because they are high on drugs, *space cadet* probably derives directly from a TV program, Tom Corbett, Space Cadet, widely watched by the kids of the 1950s who became the *spaced-out* generation of the 1960s.

spade. A black person. "The four Turlocks hated Negroes and never hesitated in voicing their disgust. 'Goddamned spades killed my cousin Captain Matt— one of them gets out of line with me, he's dead' " (James A. Michener, *Chesapeake*, 1978).

The allusion is to the card suit, and this kind of *spade* derives from the Italian *spada*, a broad sword, not the spade that is a shovel, though the two forms have the same Indo-European root, *sphe-*. See also NEGRO.

Spanish. A common ingredient in many phrases of a more or less derogatory nature, some of them dating to the sixteenth and seventeenth centuries when England was beginning to vie with Spain as a world power. Among them:

Spanish athlete. An expert at throwing the bull; modern. See BULLSHIT.

Spanish bath. A sponge bath, i.e., one that doesn't use much water; twentieth century.

Spanish castle (or *castle in Spain*). A daydream, a scheme that is unlikely to be realized, a castle-in-the-air; from before 1400. The French in the fourteenth century used *château en Espagne* interchangeably with *château en Asie* and *château en Albanie*, which suggests that the surviving Spanish phrase was rooted in the hopes of landless knights—younger sons probably—to establish themselves in other countries.

Spanish coin (or *money*). "Fair words, and compliments" (Captain Francis Grose, *A Classical Dictionary of the Vulgar Tongue*, 1785); from the exaggerated courtesy of Spaniards.

Spanish custom, an old. A jocular justification for an unauthorized or irregular practice of some years' standing (*OED*, 1932).

Spanish disease, gout, needle, or *pox.* Syphilis; the last seems to be the oldest, dating to the sixteenth century.

Spanish fly. A fabled aphrodisiac, Cantharides, made by crushing the cantharis blister fly or beetle; from ca. 1600 and still the subject of much curiosity, especially among teenagers, though they would seem to have the least need for it. Experimenters should keep doses very small, as the drug is highly toxic and 0.03 gram is enough to kill a person.

Spanish padlock. "A kind of girdle contrived by jealous husbands of the nation, to secure the chastity of their wives" (Grose, second edition, 1788).

Spanish pike. A tailor's needle; from the early sixteenth century.

Spanish trumpeter (also *King of Spain's trumpeter*). "An ass when braying" (Grose, 1785). In other words: Don Key.

Spanish walk (also *to walk [someone] Spanish*). A compulsory form of locomotion, accomplished on tiptoes, while being held by the back of one's collar and the seat of one's pants, and being propelled in the desired direction, typically toward an exit; from the early nineteenth century.

Spanish worm. "A nail: so called by carpenters when they meet with one in a board they are sawing" (Grose, 1785).

International rivalries frequently are preserved in phrases of this sort; for openers, see DUTCH, and FRENCH. And for more about the Spanish among us, continue with CHICANO, DAGO, GREASER, MEXICAN, SPIC(K), and WETBACK.

spic(k). A Spanish-American; or anyone of vaguely Spanish extraction, such as a Latin American, Mexican, Puerto Rican, or Filipino; or any foreigner at all; or anyone of apparently foreign ancestry. "The Mexican men they despise and call 'spicks' " (E. Peixotto, *Our Hispanic Southwest*, 1919).

Spic has been dated to ca. 1915 and its origin is uncertain. It may derive from *spig*, in turn from *spiggoty*. The oldest known *spiggoty* (*OED*, 1910) refers to Nicaraguans, but the word also was used for Italians at an early date, leading Stuart Berg Flexner to suggest that it may derive from *spaghetti* (*I Hear America Talking*, 1976). Another possibility is that it may come from *no spik Ingles*. Both theories are in line with standard naming practices, which include attacking people according to the foods they eat (see KRAUT) and for their failure to speak one's own language (see BARBARIAN). And see also SPANISH.

spider. An evil person; specifically, one who weaves intricate plans for snaring victims. Thus, speaking of Richard III: "Why strew'st thou sugar on that bottled spider Whose deadly web ensnareth thee about?" (William Shakespeare, *Richard III*, 1592–93). See also INSECT.

spineless. Weak, irresolute, lacking moral fiber; from 1885 (OED). "The 6-foot-5-inch, 275-pound [Los Angeles Raiders end Howie] Long called the 5-10, 170-pound [New England Patriots general manager Pat] Sullivan 'the jellyfish of Foxboro,' 'a wimp,' and 'spineless' " (AP, 1/5/86).

The idea that weak people lack spines has been developed over the years into a number of picturesque formulations. Thus, Ulysses S. Grant said of a later president, James A. Garfield, that "he is not possessed of the backbone of an angleworm," and Theodore Roosevelt, while assistant secretary of the Navy, said that President William McKinley had "no more backbone than a chocolate eclair" (a bon mot that may have been uttered first by Speaker of the House Thomas B. Reed). Subsequently, Winston S. Churchill characterized Ramsay MacDonald, a founder of the Labor Party and head of the first two Labor governments, as "The Boneless Wonder." The metaphor has even been updated to reflect advances in medical technology. Thus, Representative Pat Schroeder (Democrat, Colorado) admitted that "Spine transplants are what we really need to take [President Ronald] Reagan on" (*New York Times*, 1/14/85).

A *spineless* person is, technically speaking, an *invertebrate*, as in the screed by a disappointed author, D. H. Lawrence, upon the occasion of a publisher's rejection of *Sons and Lovers*: "Curse the blasted jelly-boned swines, the slimy, the belly-wriggling invertebrates, the miserable sodding rotters, the flaming sods, the sniveling, dribbling, dithering, palsied, pulseless lot that make up England today" (letter to Edward Garnett, 7/3/12).

See also CHAMELEON, COWARD, and EUNUCH.

sponge. (1) A drunkard; (2) a shameless borrower, a PARASITE. The absorbent capacity of the *sponge*, whether for alcohol, money, or other amenities, was well established by Elizabethan times. Shakespeare used the word in both senses: (1) "I will be anything, Nerissa, ere I will be married to a sponge" (*The Merchant of Venice*, 1596–98); (2) *Rosencrantz*: "Take you me for a sponge, my lord?" *Hamlet*: "Aye, sir, that soaks up the King's countenance, his rewards, his authorities" (*Hamlet*, 1601–02). See also DRUNK and MOOCHER.

spook. A black person. "I looked at Brew who was as black as God is supposed to be white. 'Man, Brew,' I said, 'you sure an ugly spook' " (Piri Thomas, *Down These Mean Streets*, 1967).

Spook, meaning a ghost or specter, comes directly from the Dutch *spook*, with the same meaning. As a ghost, the term has been dated to 1801 (*Dictionary of Americanisms*). The racial sense is much newer, not recorded until the 1940s. For example, black pilots in training at Tuskegee Institute during World War II called themselves the *Spookwaffe* (another example of how a racial slur can be used within the target group without giving offense; see also NIGGER in this respect).

The epithet may be based on the difficulty of seeing a black person at night. A *spook* may also be, among other derogatory meanings, a white person to a black one; an ugly girl or sometimes just a shy one; and an undercover agent or spy. See also BOOGIE.

square. Stodgy, old-fashioned, unsophisticated; someone or something with these qualities. The intensive forms are *cube* and *supercube*. "Canada is a country so square that even the female impersonators are women" (*Outrageous*, film, 1977).

Square was popularized in musical circles toward the end of World War II. "That G. L. [orchestra leader Guy Lombardo] . . . strictly a square" (Max Shulman, *Barefoot Boy with Cheek*, 1943). "*Square,* in musician's jargon, anyone who is not cognizant of the beauties of true jazz" (Baltimore *Sun*, 1/27/44). It quickly was adopted in other contexts, perhaps aided by association with the older *squarehead,* a stupid person (also a SWEDE or GERMAN); *square peg,* a misfit; and *square John,* an underworld term for a mark, especially a self-righteous person, on the square, who can be taken advantage of easily.

The modern usage also represents a revival to some extent of the word's senses, labeled "obsolete" in the *OED,* of "Precise, prim, solemn," as in "A serious, solemne, and supercilious face, full of formall and square gravitie" (Ben Jonson, *Cynthia's Revels,* 1599). See also BLOCKHEAD, CREEP, JERK, and NERD.

squeal. To inform upon or the act of so doing. "We have challenged [the Reagan Administration's] insistence on promulgating a rule requiring family planning clinics to squeal on teen-age patrons to their parents" (editorial, *New York Times,* 1/13/83). By labeling the requirement a *squeal rule,* opponents of the plan stacked the argument in their favor. See also ABORTION.

Squeal has been dated in the informing sense to 1865. It superseded *squeak,* used the same way for a couple hundred years previously. Both *squeak* and *squeal* fit with the image of an informer as a *mouse* or a RAT. See also INFORMER.

squirrel. A woman or her genitals; a parallel in both senses to BEAVER. Both meanings of *squirrel* were included in a glossary of "Razorback Slang," gleaned by Gary N. Underwood at the Fayetteville campus of the University of Arkansas (*American Speech,* Spring–Summer 1975), and they may have been fairly new when he encountered them. The word's feminine implications are of some antiquity, however. Captain Grose defined *squirrel* in *A Classical Dictionary of the Vulgar Tongue* (1796) as "A prostitute: because she, like that animal, covers her back with her tail." (If his definition seems confusing, consult TAIL.)

Squirrels—the furry animals—also hoard nuts, and this association has led to other meanings: a *squirrel* may be an odd person of either sex, and to say that someone is *food for the squirrels,* has *squirrels in the attic* (or *in the nut*), is *playing with the squirrels,* is *squirrelly,* or has *walnut storage disease* are just different ways of saying that other person is CRAZY, eccentric, or STUPID. See also NUT and SCREW LOOSE, A.

Stepin Fetchit. A gofer, an errand boy; specifically, a black male in a menial position. "Representative Henry B. Gonzalez called Samuel R. Pierce, Jr., the Secretary of Housing and Urban Development, a 'Stepin Fetchit,' and although Mr. Pierce termed that epithet 'vile, abusive and racist,' the Texas Democrat refused to apologize" (UPI, 9/22/82).

The expression was popularized by Lincoln Theodore Monroe Andrew Perry, who began appearing in movies as Stepin Fetchit in 1927 (*In Old Kentucky*). He became the first black actor in Hollywood to receive feature billing, but the comical roles he played were so racially stereotyped that his screen name (he took it from a racehorse on which he'd won some money) became an insult as times changed and jokes about lazy, shuffling blacks ceased to be funny. See also UNCLE TOM.

stick. A dull, awkward person; a stiff, wooden one; if particularly inept, a *poor stick* or *weak stick.* "He had had to hire white men to help him, but they were poor sticks and would be half the time drunk" (Frederick Law Olmstead, *A Journey in the Seaboard Slave States,* 1856). A different kind of *stick* is the conservative, unimaginative person who is a *stick in the mud* (from 1733). See also BLOCKHEAD and REACTIONARY.

stick it to [someone]. Put it to [someone], but with strong priapic reverberations. "I stick it to the audience and they love it" (Alan Berg, combative radio talk-show host, in an interview shortly before his assassination by neo-Nazis, *New York Times,* 6/20/84). The inherent sense of violent sex in *stick* is in accord with the oldest (pre-900) senses of the verb, i.e., to pierce, to thrust, as with a sword, knife, or spear. See also PRICK and SHAFT.

stiff. A person of little or no account, especially a dumb or disagreeable person, a *big stiff;* a hobo, a *bindle (bundle) stiff;* or an ordinary laboring fellow, a *working stiff.* "If a black man did buy a house, hey, we knocked on his door and said hello. And if he was a nice guy, great. If he was a stiff, well, I know lots of white stiffs, too" (*New York Times,* 1/8/75).

The disparaging use of *stiff* for a person of little worth, dating to the late nineteenth century, combines two older meanings: (1) a corpse, after rigor mortis has set in, and (2) to be dead drunk. The verb, *to stiff [someone],* that is, to cheat or otherwise take advantage of another person, follows naturally, since the victim, the *stiff* who has been *stiffed,* has been rendered, in effect, dead or senseless.

stink. (1) To smell, as in the reply to a not-so-innocent child's question: "If frozen water is iced water, what is frozen ink?" (Iona and Peter Opie, *The Lore and Language of Schoolchildren,* 1959); (2) to be disgusting, filthy, nasty, as in "We told the man we could . . . make such a scandal out of this, as should make his name stink from one end of London to the other" (Robert Louis Stevenson, *The Strange Case of Dr. Jekyll and Mr. Hyde,* 1886); (3) to bungle or perform poorly; for emphasis, *to stink on ice, to stink to high heaven,* as in "He sighed. 'I must be lousy,' he said. 'Boy, you stink,' I agreed" (Raymond Chandler, *The High Window,* 1942).

Back in the eighth century, when the word first appeared in English, *to stink* was to emit an odor of any kind, sweet as well as foul. (Its cognate, *stench,* also began with a neutral meaning.) Within a couple hundred years, however, the noxious senses began to take over the word, with *stink* being used for bad smells and *smell* for good or simply non-offensive stinks. Geoffrey Chaucer still qualified the word at the end of the fourteenth century, as in "Thy breath full sour stinketh" (*The Canterbury Tales,* ca. 1387–1400), but several generations later the *sour* was no longer required, e.g., "How his breth stynkyth" (J. Mirkus, *Mirk's Festial,* ca. 1450).

Eventually, *stink* became thoroughly contaminated. When Noah Webster bowdlerized the Bible in 1833, he knocked out every single *stink,* substituting such terms as *ill smell, ill savor,* and *odious scent,* with the result that ". . . the river shall stink" (*Exodus,* 7:18) became "shall be offensive in smell." And on the other side of the Atlantic, Leigh Hunt removed the "sour stinketh" from Chaucer, prettying up the aforementioned passage to read: "Thy breath resembleth not sweet marjoram" (Richard Horne, *ed., The Poems of Geoffrey Chaucer, modernized,* 1841). This delicacy continued well into the twentieth century, in some circles at least, with *stink* ranking second on the list of "coarse" and "obscene" words produced by J. M.

Steadman's students at Emory University in the late 1920s and early '30s (see BELCH for details).

Today, *smell* and *odor*, although technically neutral, also have been affected sufficiently by the underlying *stink*, so that, unless otherwise qualified, the usual assumption is that the vapor concerned does not please the nose. ("Good" vapors are called *aromas, fragrances,* or *scents.*) Thus, roses may be said "to smell good," but a deal that simply "smells" is bad, and so is the "odor" in the advertiser's B.O., or body odor (since the 1930s). This process has been going on for some time, e.g., "you are smelt above the moon" (William Shakespeare, *Coriolanus*, 1608).

Stink appears in many forms, most of them pejorative, e.g., *stinking* (especially *stinking drunk* or *stinking rich*); *stinky* (occasionally a more or less affectionate nickname); STINKER; and the intensive *stinkeroo, stinko,* and *stinkpot* (the last usually applying to people, not things). Note, however, that the meaning of *stink*, like that of BAD, can be reversed in certain situations. Thus, reporting on slang at the Children's Storefront School in Harlem: "If Kimathi tells Oneshia that she is wearing some 'mighty stink boots,' he means he loves the way they look. But if he turns to his brother and says 'you stink,' he means it is time for a bath" (*New York Times*, 2/2/89). It is even possible for *stink*, as bad as it usually is, to serve as a euphemism for something even worse; see SUCK.

stinker. A despicable person or thing, a failure; the modern form of *stinkard*, dating to the sixteenth century, as in "He asked with great emotion if I thought him a monster and a stinkard (Tobias Smollett, *Roderick Random*, 1748). "Perhaps it's time for [a rerelease of] 'Paris As It Sizzles.' I took Bill Holden, Audrey Hepburn. Marlene Dietrich, Noël Coward and the city of Paris and made an absolute stinker" (George Axelrod, *New York Times*, 2/24/88). See also STINK.

stooge. An underling; one who acts as foil or cat's-paw for another, doing what is asked, and without asking questions. "The happiest people in this country [over President Truman's dismissal of General Douglas MacArthur, 4/11/51] will be the Communists and their stoodges . . ." (Senator Richard M. Nixon [Republican, California], film clip in *MacArthur*, film, 1977).

Stooge is an Americanism of unknown origin. The earliest examples of its use (dating to pre-World War I) come from the theater, where a *stooge* was a stagehand or the assistant to a performer, especially the straight man who serves as the butt for the lead comedian's jokes. One suggestion is that the word is a corruption of *student*, since students often were employed as assistants in the theater. See also FELLOW TRAVELER and LACKEY.

strumpet. A prostitute. "France is a bawd to Fortune and King John, That strumpet Fortune, that usurping John" (William Shakespeare, *King John*, 1594–97?). "*Bosom* was uncompromisingly deleted every time it appeared even though on one occasion the bosom was that of an Egyptian mummy. So, of course, was the unthinkable, unspeakable *strumpet*" (Richard D. Altick, *The Scholar Adventurers*, 1988, on the posthumous editing of Nathaniel Hawthorne's diaries by his widow, Sophia).

Dating to the fourteenth century, *strumpet's* origin is unknown. Among the possibilities suggested are that it derives from the Late Latin *strumpum*, dishonor, violation, or from either of two Middle Dutch words, *strompe*, a stocking, or *strompen*, to stride, to stalk (a man, for instance). In the eighteenth and nineteenth centuries, *strumpet* often was abbreviated as *strum*. The short form is a good example of a word whose meanings differ widely according to context. As defined by Captain Francis Grose: "TO STRUM. To have carnal knowledge of a woman; also to play badly on the harpsichord or any other stringed instrument" (*A Classical Dictionary of the Vulgar Tongue*, 1796). See also HUSSY and WHORE.

stupid. Unintelligent. "Russell Reynaga . . . applied for a vanity license plate that read 'STUPID.' Mr. Reynaga, who had no problem getting the same plate in Texas and New York, was turned down by Connecticut [Department of Motor Vehicle] officials who said such a plate would be in poor taste and would reflect poorly on the state" (Newtown, Connecticut, *Weekly Star*, 2/1/88).

Stupid may be abbreviated to *stupe*, as in "Was there ever such a poor stupe!" (Isaac Bickerstaff, *Love in a Village*, 1762). The word also has a long form, *stoopnagel*, as in W. C. Fields' firm, Colonel Stoopnagel & Budd (*International House*, film, 1933).

The basic *stupid* comes from the Latin *stupere*, to be stunned, to have one's faculties benumbed, as from shock or grief (i.e., to be in a *stupor*). Slow-witted people have been disparaged as *stupydes* since at least 1541 (*OED*). This is a common evolutionary pattern. For example, *silly*, as in *silly-billy*, is an alteration of the older *seely*, to be happy or blessed, while *simple*, as in *simpleminded*, originally denoted innocence, openness, and absence of duplicity. See also *chowderhead* and *dunderhead* in BLOCKHEAD, as well as DAFFY, DUMB, FOOL, and SIMPLETON.

suck. To fellate; also, on occasion, to cunnilingue. Or as Allen Walker Read defined the term in *Lexical Evidence from Folk Epigraphy in Western North America* (1935): "To practise a certain form of sexual irregularity."

The opacity of Read's definition (in a book that was first printed privately in Paris in an edition of just seventy-five copies) demonstrates the onetime strength of the taboo on this word. And more than forty years later, the nation's newspaper of record would not print the term, although it was being widely used in public, by the newspaper's own account. Thus, in a column about the joys of being a Boston Red Sox fan at a ball game in New York's Yankee Stadium: "The enemy hordes chant in unison, 'The Red Sox stink!' ('Stink' is a word I've substituted for the one they actually use, which is forbidden in family newspapers)" (Sydney H. Schanberg, *New York Times*, 6/26/78). Nor can there be any doubt as to the true meaning of *stink* in this instance, since the behavior of Yankee fans also was noted at about the same time in a rival paper in these terms: "Or is George [Steinbrenner, principal owner of the Yankees] talking about those fans who loudly accuse the opposition of a sexual proclivity that their parents should have practiced, saving us their miserable conception" (Joe Flaherty, New York *Daily News*, 7/9/78).

The "irregularity" or "proclivity" is, no doubt, as old as humankind, but commonplace words for it (see also BLOW and EAT) were not put into writing until comparatively recently. The more acceptable Latinate *fellatio* and *cunnilingus* also are relatively new, having been dated only to 1897; the first derives from the past participle of *fellare*, to suck, in turn from *fe*, to suckle, while the second comes from *cunnus*, female pudendum, plus *lingus*, to lick. As for the sexual *suck*, it is dated only to 1928 in the *OED* (the citation being a graffito in Read's *Folk Epigraphy*), although it is not hard to find examples of the word's use—with feminine as well as masculine objects—in nineteenth-century literature, including the novel, *Flossie, a Venus of Sixteen* (Anonymous, undated); the autobiography, *My Secret Life* (Anonymous, ca. 1890), and *The Pearl, A Journal of Facetiae and Voluptuous Reading*, issued monthly in London from July 1879 to December 1880. No doubt, careful perusal of the special collections of major libraries would provide other pre-1928 citations.

Of the works just mentioned, *The Pearl* is of the greatest interest from a strictly literary standpoint, as it included sixty-five early examples of bawdy limericks, labeled "Nursery Rhymes" ("limerick" was not applied to light verse until the 1890s) in the seven issues over which they were distributed. The only older surviving collection of such verse, according to G. Legman's *The Limerick* (1969), is *Cythera's Hymnal, or Flakes from the Foreskin* (1870), which bears the sham imprint "Oxford: Printed at the University Press, for the Society of Promoting Useful Knowledge." The *Hymnal* was produced mainly by Captain Edward Sellon, author of erotic novels and a treatise on Hindu eroticism, and G. A. Sala, a well-known journalist and war correspondent of the time, with the help of several other Oxford men. Sala also is likely to have written the rhymes that appeared in *The Pearl*, including this, from the third issue (8/1879):

> There was a young man of Nantucket.
> Who went down a well in a bucket;
> The last words he spoke.
> Before the rope broke,
> Were, "Arsehole, you bugger, and suck it."

The taboo on *suck* apparently predates the blatantly sexual use. Thus, this was one of the words that Noah Webster removed from the Bible when he produced a watered-down text for family consumption in 1833 (see also STINK). In the Word According to Webster, *Matthew*, 24:19, ". . . woe unto them . . . that give suck in those days!" became " . . . that nurse infants in those days!" The point here, of course, is that a Latin-French word, immediately from *nourrice*, foster mother, was being substituted for a more vivid Anglo-Saxon term.

Refined people have been known to go to considerable lengths to avoid the plainer word. For example, Otto Jesperson cited the following newspaper item in *Growth and Structure of the English Language* (9th edition, 1938):

> The young lady home from school was explaining. "Take an egg," she said, "and make a perforation in the base and a corresponding one in the apex. Then apply the lips to the aperture, and by forcibly inhaling the breath the shell is entirely discharged of its contents." An old lady who was listening exclaimed: "It beats all how folks do things nowadays. When I was a gal they made a hole in each end and sucked."

The taboo may also have been reinforced by the pejorative uses of the word in such phrases as *suck around*, *suck ass*, and *suck up to* (to be a SYCOPHANT, or in British English, dating to at least the nineteenth century, a *bumsucker*); *suck-egg*, a contemptible person, in effect, a WEASEL, and also a young, inexperienced person; *suck the hind tit*, to get the worst of a situation; *suck in*, to cheat; and *sucker*, a sponger, an easy victim, and a euphemism for *cocksucker*, among other things (see SUCKER). Some of these are fairly antique. *Suck-egg*, for example, has been dated to 1609, and it remains in use. Thus, Senator Jesse Helms (Republican, North Carolina) "once invited a Raleigh newspaper reporter to a political gathering where he announced 'Your newspaper is a suck-egg mule' " (*Columbia Journalism Review*, 7-8/85).

The pejorative but traditionally printable meanings of *suck* seem to have fused with the sexual sense during the overheated 1960s to produce a figurative but powerful verb for expressing contempt or disgust, as in: "Polaroid sucks! For some time the Polaroid Corporation has been supplying the South African government with large photo systems . . . to use for photographing blacks for the pass books . . . every black must carry " (*It*, 6/2–16/70). This is an unusually versatile verb, suitable for use in almost any context, e.g., the graffito, "There is no gravity; the world sucks" (*Maledicta*, 1981), or, on a more personal level, "I suck at making beds" (complaint by an American nine-year-old, 7/19/84).

Finally, the widespread use of the word in nonsexual situations has helped diminish the taboo on its employment in public with the other, explicit meaning—in books, films, and other media, if not yet in family newspapers. Thus, Truman Capote encountered a young man at the Los Angeles International Airport in November 1970 who was outfitted with yellow jitterbug pants (ca. 1940), yellow wedgies, yellow cowboy hat, white leather windbreaker with an ermine lining, and a sweatshirt bearing the message SUCK DAMMIT, DON'T BLOW (*Music for Chameleons*, 1980). And a young woman in the 1979 film *The Electric Horseman* was characterized as "a girl who can suck the chrome off a trailer hitch." Combining sexual and nonsexual meanings, and thus closing the circle, was the poster for the 1987 film *Full Metal Jacket*, which was displayed prominently in public places: "In Vietnam the wind doesn't blow, it sucks."

sucker. Someone or something; a highly generalized but forceful characterization that trades on the term's sexual connotation, discussed in the preceding entry, as well as on its rhyme with *fucker*. "Get those suckers in the streets" ("Police Story," TV episode, 8/6/78). "Sign this sucker [a petition for the Equal Rights Amendment] or I'll ram the clipboard down your throat" (*B.C.*, comic strip, 10/28/84).

Sucker has enjoyed an inordinate number of other meanings over the years, among them: (1) one who lives off another, as the babe sucks nourishment from the mother; a PARASITE or SPONGE; (2) an easy victim or mark; earlier a FOOL or GREENHORN, i.e., one who has all the smarts of an unweaned animal; (3) the penis, as well as a euphemism for *cocksucker* (see COCK), whence also *suckster* and *suckstress*, the last two recorded by J. S. Farmer and W. E. Henley in *Slang and Its Analogues* (1904) but now apparently obsolete; (4) a lollipop or all-day sucker; and (5) a traditional nickname for an inhabitant of Illinois.

Of these, the first seems to be the oldest, having been traced in its broadest sense to 1500–20. The others have been dated to the nineteenth century, with the second probably being the most common today, if only because of the famous remarks attributed to P. T. Barnum. ("There's a sucker born every minute") and Edward F. Albee, of the Keith-Albee vaudeville circuit and grandfather, through adoption, of the playwright of the same name ("Never give a sucker an even break"). Or as they say on carnival lots: "A sucker's bankroll is like a dog's testicles—they're always out in plain sight" (*American Speech*, 5/53).

The *sucker* who hails from Illinois has been dated to the 1830s. This is one of many quaint nicknames applied to the citizens of the various states during the nineteenth century, some of which remain in use. Walt Whitman chronicled a number of them in an article on "Slang in America" in *North American Review*

(11/1885, and apparently cribbed to some extent on a clipping in his files from *Broadway Journal* magazine of 5/3/1845):

> Among the rank and file, [in] both armies [in the Civil War], it was very general to speak of the different States they came from by their slang names. Those from Maine were call'd Foxes; New Hampshire, Granite Boys; Massachusetts, Bay Staters . . . New York, Knickerbockers; New Jersey, Clam Catchers; Pennsylvania, Logher Heads . . . North Carolina, Tar Boilers; South Carolina, Weasels; Georgia, Buzzards . . . Illinois, Suckers; Missouri, Pukes; Mississippi, Tad Poles . . . Oregon, Hard Cases.

It was reported as early as 1833 that the nickname for Illinoisans came from the fish called suckers (*Catostomus commersoni*) whose migrations up and down rivers in the territory coincided with the seasonal comings and goings of itinerant laborers from southern Illinois who worked the lead mines in the north. Another story has it that crawfish left holes in the prairie where they descended to the fresh water beneath, and that early settlers in Illinois got their nickname through using long reeds to suck water out of these natural artesian wells. But it also could be that many settlers of Illinois were suckered into deals by land speculators. In any case, the nickname does not seem to be used much any more. Illinois calls itself "The Prairie State" nowadays, and it is not recommended that visitors to Chicago attempt to ingratiate themselves with the local denizens by addressing them as *suckers*. See also PUKE.

Swede. A blunderer, a DOPE; sometimes, for emphasis, a *big dumb Swede*. "What's dumber than a dumb Irishman? A smart Swede" (Notre Dame football coach Knute Rockne, *b.* in Norway, 1888, *d.* 1931, quoted by Raven I. McDavid, Jr., *American Speech*, 4/45). See also DUTCH.

swellhead. A vain person; one with delusions of grandeur. " 'Mugwump' . . . is synonymous with the New York term 'big bug,' or the Washington expression 'swellhead' " (*St. James Gazette*, 5/10/1884).

A *swellhead* (from 1845) is the same as a *big head*, of course, as in "Were I to use a western term, I would say they were troubled with a big head" (Brigham Young, *Journal of Discourses*, 1853). The condition also may be alluded to with such phrases as *your hat's too small for your head, your halo is on too tight*, and, an old folk saying, *[so-and-so] is all swelled up like a pizened pup.* See also MUGWUMP.

swindler. A cheat; a practitioner of fraud. " 'Do you mean to call me a swindler, sir,' replied Jack. 'Yes, sir, you——' " (Captain Frederick Marryat, *Mr. Midshipman Easy*, 1836).

The term, first recorded from 1774, is said to have been introduced to London by German Jews about 1762. It comes from *schwindler*, in turn from *schwindeln*, to totter, to be dizzy, to act in a giddy, irresponsible manner. Captain Francis Grose misspelled the German verb but the rest of his explanation is correct: "SWINDLER. One who obtains goods on credit by false pretences, and sells them for ready money at any price, in order to make up a purse. This name is derived from the German word *schwindlin*, to totter, to be ready to fall; these arts being generally practised by persons on the totter, or just ready to break.

The term *swindler* has since been used to signify cheats of every kind" (*A Classical Dictionary of the Vulgar Tongue*, 1796). See also CHARLATAN, CHEAT, and DOUBLE-DEALER.

swine. A low, coarse, greedy, or despicable person; from at least the fourteenth century, when the term also had lecherous connotations. Thus, in the modern contemptuous sense, one Alaskan politician referred to another: "Hammond may be a posie-sniffing swine but he hasn't given the state away to the oil companies" (*New York Times*, 10/13/82). Then there is the famous—one hopes not entirely apocryphal—occasion when Dorothy Parker and Clare Boothe Luce jockeyed for position in front of a revolving door. Miss Luce deferred, saying, "After you, my dear. Age before beauty, you know," to which Miss Parker replied as she charged ahead, "Yes—and pearls before swine."

Note: The biblical injunction about not casting "ye pearls before swine, lest they trample them under their feet, and turn again and rend you" (*Matthew*, 7:6) is a poetic mistranslation. Some medieval monk mixed up *margarite* (pearl) with *marguerite* (daisy). Saint Matthew probably was thinking about feeding flowers to pigs. See also PIG and SCHWEINHUND.

swish. An effeminate male, especially a homosexual; from the 1930s and probably from the swinging, swishy walk of a man with feminine traits. "The myth that all Frenchmen were slightly bisexual was widely believed, the *swish* of some deviants being confused with the affected mannerisms of the stereotyped French fop" (David W. Maurer, "Language and the Sex Revolution: World War I Through World War II," *American Speech*, Spring–Summer 1976). *Swish* is of onomatopoetic origin, the word for the movement coming from the sound, in this case, perhaps, that of a flowing dress. See also QUEER.

sycophant. A flatterer of the most loathsome sort, a toady; of interest here primarily because of its presumed etymology, from Greek *sukophantēs*, informer, in turn from *sukon*, fig + *phantēs*, shower, i.e., fig-shower. It was once argued that the term originally denoted a person who informed authorities about the unlawful exportation of figs. The consensus today, however, is that the word refers to a common obscene gesture, perhaps made by the ancient Greeks when denouncing criminals. See FIG, NOT TO GIVE and BOOT-LICKER.

T

tacky. In bad taste, inferior, shabby, CHEAP. "The presidential strategists . . . recognized dangers—the danger that the picture of President Nixon and his men that emerged would seem so tacky that it would further alienate the electorate . . ." (R. W. Apple, Jr., introduction, *The White House Transcripts,* 1974).

Tacky has been dated to 1800 as a term for a pony or a small scrawny horse of little value. During the nineteenth century, its meaning was extended to include people of the same ilk—poor Southern whites, specifically, e.g., "If Mr. Catlett will come to Georgia and go among the 'po' whites' and 'piney-wood tackeys'" (*Century Magazine,* 9/1888). The present, generalized usage also goes back more than a hundred years: "Two little cards (with his name printed on them in gilt. Tackey? Ugh.)" (Isabella Rittenhouse, *Maud,* 1883). The reduplicative *ticky-tacky* is a much more recent innovation, from the 1960s, apparently inspired by the flimsy construction of houses in many large suburban developments. See also HACK, POOR WHITE TRASH, and TAWDRY.

tail. A woman considered as a sex object, *a piece of tail;* the act of intercourse with the object, *to get some tail;* the human posterior; the human anterior, i.e., the pudendum, whether female or male. "Get me another drink. And then let's go and find a girl. You've got a piece of tail. I want a piece of tail, too" (Graham Greene, *The Quiet American,* 1955).

Women have been characterized as *tails* since at least the eighteenth century. At first, the term seems to have been reserved for prostitutes. Thus, the 1785 edition of Captain Francis Grose's *A Classical Dictionary of the Vulgar Tongue* included the question that a potential customer might ask of the madam of a bawdy house: "Mother, how many tails have you in your cab? How many girls have you in your nanny house?" See also WHORE. By the twentieth century, the term was extended to women in general. In the meantime, however, many picturesque phrases seem to have dropped by the wayside, among them: *tail feathers,* pubic hair; *tail fence,* the hymen; *tail fruit,* children; *tail wagging,* sexual intercourse; *warm in the tail,* wanton; and *hot-tailed,* infected with venereal disease.

The basic anatomical meanings of *tail,* masculine as well as feminine, are to be found in the works of Chaucer, Shakespeare, the Motteaux translation of Rabelais, and others. The idea that the penis is like a tail goes back at least to Roman times (*penis* in Latin means "tail"). For example, Shakespeare punned upon the penile sense of the word in *Othello* (1604):

> CLOWN: Why, masters, have your instruments been in Naples, that they speak i' the nose thus? [The allusion is to syphilis, the Neapolitan disease.]
> MUSICIAN: How, sir, how?

CLOWN: Are these, I pray you, wind instruments?
MUSICIAN: Aye, marry are they, sir.
CLOWN: Oh, thereby hangs a tale.
MUSICIAN: Whereby hangs a tale, sir?
CLOWN: Marry, sir, by many a wind instrument that I know.

And, going back into the mists of English literature, we have, from *Piers Plowman* (*attr.* William Langland, ca. 1362–87):

Heo is tikel of hire tayle . . .
As comuyn as a cart-wei to knaues and alle

(Where "heo" is the old form of "she"; "tikel" is pretty much what it means today—ticklish or excitable; and the "cartway" is a "common" or "public" one, and well-traveled.)

See also *piece of ass* in ASS and PIECE.

tamale. A Mexican woman; a CHICANO. "A judge who was quoted as calling Hispanic Americans 'cute little tamales and Taco Bells' . . . has been censured by the California Supreme Court" (AP, 5/22/82). If the person of Mexican extraction is especially sexy, then she is a *hot* (or *red-hot*) *tamale.* See also DAME and, for more about international cuisine, refer to KRAUT.

tart. A loose woman; a fast, forward one, sometimes a professional prostitute; also, in Britain, a young male friend of an older man, a catamite, sometimes a professional.

Tart (and *jam-tart*) began in the mid-nineteenth century as endearments, comparable to the modern *sweetie-pie.* "*Tart*, a term of approval applied by the London lower orders to a young woman for whom some affection is felt. The expression is not generally employed by the young men unless the female is in 'her best' " (J. C. Hotten, *The Slang Dictionary*, 1864). Within a few decades, however, the word began to acquire connotations of immorality (*OED*, from 1887). Somewhat unusually, the commendable or, at least, neutral meanings have continued to coexist with the negative ones in England, Australia, and New Zealand. In the United States, however, the sense of wanton women or WHORE has long been dominant; for example, see PELICAN for a "low-down tart" in New Orleans in 1904. Male *tarts,* meanwhile, have been dated to 1935, and they probably are responsible for the verbal phrase *to tart up,* i.e., to dress or decorate (someone or something) in a gaudy manner.

Thus, *tart* exhibits in varying degrees three common linguistic traits of feminine words: the casting of the woman as toothsome object (see EAT); the tendency of feminine terms to acquire pejorative meanings (see GIRL); and the use—and sometimes complete conversion—of feminine-heterosexual words into masculine-homosexual ones (see GAY).

tartar. A savage, especially one with a violent temper; frequently a woman, a SHREW. The epithet honors the fierceness of the Tartars who fought for Genghis Khan (1167?–1227), and who are now usually described by ethnologists as *Tatars,* partly for good etymological reasons and partly, no doubt, to avoid confusion with the transferred senses of *tartar*. The savage meaning dates to at least the seventeenth century: "I never knew your grandmother was a Scotchwoman: Is she not a Tartar too?" (John Dryden, *The Wild Gallant*, 1663). By the eighteenth century, the word had become truly generic as *tartar*, with a lowercase *t*.

To catch a tartar is to make the mistake of laying hands on someone who proves to be stronger than you. The expression seems to have arisen from an early Irish joke. As recounted by Captain Francis Grose: "This saying originated from a story of an Irish soldier in the Imperial service, who, in a battle against the Turks, called out to his comrade that he had caught a Tartar. 'Bring him along then,' said he. 'He won't come,' answered Paddy. 'Then come along yourself,' replied his comrade. 'Arrah,' cried he, 'but he won't let me'" (*A Classical Dictionary of the Vulgar Tongue*, 1796). See also BARBARIAN, PADDY, and TURK.

tattletale. A whistle-blower. "Mr. [Roger] Boisjoly's suit charges that, after the [1986 *Challenger* shuttle] accident, both NASA and Thiokol 'undertook a program to discredit' him and other engineers 'who had warned against the flight.' . . . It cited press interviews in which Thiokol spokesmen labeled Mr. Boisjoly a 'tattletale' . . ." (*New York Times*, 1/29/87).

Tattletale is a nineteenth-century American variation on the sixteenth-century British *tell-tale*. Both are heard more commonly in schoolyards than in press conferences, with the two forms even appearing in basically the same rhyme on both sides of the Atlantic. Thus, Iona and Peter Opie recorded in Britain (*The Lore and Language of Schoolchildren*, 1959):

> Tell tale tit,
> Your tongue shall be slit,
> And all the dogs in town
> Shall have a little bit.

And across the Atlantic, Horace Reynolds included the following version in an article on childhood language (*American Speech*, 2/56):

> Tattle tale tit,
> Tattle tale tit,
> Your tongue will be slit
> And every dog will get a bit.

It is apparent that this bit of wisdom has been handed down from one generation of children to another for a great many years. The ancestral rhyme is one of the thirty-eight in what generally is regarded as the first collection of nursery rhymes ever to be published, *Tommy Thumb's Pretty Song Book* (ca. 1744). As reprinted in *The Annotated Mother Goose* (William S. Baring-Gould and Ceil Baring-Gould, 1967):

> Spit Cat, Spit,
> Your tongue shall be slit
> And all the Dogs
> In our Town,
> Shall have a bit.

And there is no reason to think the rhyme was particularly new in 1744. See also SNITCH and, for other words related to *tattle*, TWADDLE.

tawdry. Showy and ostentatious, but cheap or without any real value at all; a corruption of the feminine name Audrey, via *tawdry lace*, originally St. Audrey's lace, worn about the neck as a tie or band, originally at fairs held on St. Audrey's Day, October 17, on the Isle of Ely (of which she was patron saint) and elsewhere. *Audrey*, in turn, is the English rendering of *Etheldreda*, which is the Latinized form of the Anglo-Saxon name *Æthelthryth*. The saint died of a throat tumor, which she apparently considered just retribution for the sin of having liked to wear necklaces when she was young. Since she was the daughter of a king of East Anglia, one assumes that her necklaces weren't as tawdry as those named after her. See also MOLL and TACKY.

tenderfoot. A raw, inexperienced, callow person; a newcomer. As *tenderfooted*, the term was applied to horses and other animals from the 1690s. Much later, it was transferred to new arrivals in the American West, e.g., the observation of a 49'er, Tommy Plunkett: "We saw a man in Sacramento when we were on our way here [San Francisco], who was a tenderfoot, or rawheel, or whatever you call'em, who struck a pocket of gold" (from the diary of Andy Gordon, in W. E. Woodward, *The Way Our People Lived*, 1944). The context usually was disparaging, as noted by General Custer's widow: "The frontiersman had then, as now, a great 'despise,' as they put it for the tenderfoot" (Elizabeth Custer, *Following the Guidon*, 1890). See also GREENHORN.

termagant. A quarrelsome woman, a scold—and yet another of the many negative words that have undergone gender shifts, from male to female (see HARLOT, for example). The Termagant originally was an imaginary Moslem deity that appeared in medieval mystery plays. Represented as a violent, turbulent figure, the Termagant was dressed Turkish fashion in long flowing robes, which led later generations to assume mistakenly that the character was a woman. The present meaning has been dated to 1659. See also SHREW.

termite. A person who bores from within, as an enemy guerrilla.

Termite was part of a complex insect metaphor used by Americans in Vietnam to dehumanize their opponents. Thus, General William C. Westmoreland explained why he could not use more than 525,000 American troops in early 1967: "If you crowd in too many termite killers, each using a screwdriver to kill the termites, you risk collapsing the floors or foundation. In this war we're using screwdrivers to kill termites because it's a guerrilla war and we cannot get bigger weapons. We have to get the right balance of termite killers to get rid of the termites without wrecking the house" (*Newsweek*, 3/27/67). Continuing this train of "thought," American advisers in Vietnam often spoke of *sanitizing* or *cleaning out* through *sweeping operations* the parts of the country that were *infested* by the *termites*. See also GOOK and INSECT.

terrorist. A guerrilla, commando, or freedom fighter. "The word 'terrorist' incenses Mr. [Menachem] Begin and he chided newsmen who asked about his experiences in the 1940s as commander of an underground band of Jews called the Irgun Zvai Leumi, Hebrew for the national military organization. 'Freedom fighter' is the correct description, he insisted" (*New York Times*, 5/22/77). Times change, of course, and so do points of view. Thus, Mr. Begin's "experiences" as a freedom fighter included the blowing up of British government offices in Jerusalem's King David Hotel (91 killed, 100+ wounded), and the British saw things differently at the time, with *The Annual Register for 1946* referring to this event as "The latest and worst of the outrages commited by the Jewish terrorists in Palestine . . ." See also BANDIT, PUPPET, and REGIME.

thou. The familiar, singular form of *you*, comparable to the French *tu*, and of considerable insult value before its virtual extinction from English. *To thou [someone]*, meaning to speak as though that someone was an inferior, has been dated to the fifteenth century. The pronoun also appeared frequently in the phrases *to thee and thou* or *to thou and thee*, i.e., to speak familiarly to somebody, not politely. (The French *tutoyer* means the same.) Shakespeare put it this way: "Taunt him. . . . If thou thouest him some thrice, it shall not be amiss" (Sir Toby Belch, goading Sir Andrew Aguecheek into fighting a duel, *Twelfth Night*, 1600–02). Or as Attorney General Sir Edward Coke said to Sir Walter Raleigh at the latter's trial in November, 1603: ". . . thou viper; for I thou thee, thou Traitor!" In the seventeenth century, non-Quakers were apt to take particular offense when addressed this way by plain-speaking Friends. According to William Penn, one nobleman took umbrage in these terms: "Thou me! Thou my dog! If thou thouest me, I'll thou thy teeth down thy throat" (introduction, *George Fox's Journal*, 1694 [1827]). See also IT and, for more about Raleigh's trial, VIPER.

Throttlebottom. A bumbling, incompetent politician. "David Lilienthal, chairman of the Tennessee Valley Authority, recorded in his journal that his response was one of 'consternation at the thought of that Throttlebottom, Truman [succeeding to the presidency, 4/12/45]. The country and the world doesn't deserve to be left this way, with Truman at the head of the country at such a time' " (Bert Cochran, *Truman and the Crisis Presidency*, 1973). "[Dan] Quayle, who often seems as lost as an actor missing half the pages of his script, struggled to overcome his own Throttlebottom image—and lost" (*Time*, 10/17/88).

The term comes from Vice President Alexander Throttlebottom, a character in the 1931 musical *Of Thee I Sing* (book by Morrie Ryskind and George S. Kaufman, music by George Gershwin, lyrics by his brother Ira, and starring, among others, George Murphy, a dance man who later became a Republican senator from California, helping to pave the way for another actor-politician). In the show, as is often the case in real life, the vice president was a nonentity. Poor Throttlebottom was even refused admission to the White House because guards didn't recognize him, with the result that he had to join a guided tour to get past the door. See also POL.

thug. A ruffian or tough; a HOODLUM. "But a raucous parliamentary debate on the subject [of burning bus shelters bearing posters of women in skimpy bathing suits] broke up in chaos, after a secular civil rights leader, Yossi Sarid, was removed from the hall for calling an Orthodox legislator who supports the bus-stop burners 'a thug' " (*New York Times*, 6/12/86).

Thug derives from the Hindi *thag* (thief, swindler) and was popularized by the Thugs of India—closely knit gangs with the trappings of a religious cult who made their living by killing and robbing travelers. Because they murdered people by strangling them, they also were known as *phansigars* (noose-operators). They flourished from at least the fourteenth century until the early 1830s, when the British conducted a vigorous campaign to eradicate them. It was at about this time that the word entered English in its modern sense, the earliest example in the OED being Thomas Carlyle's reference to "Glasgow Thugs" in his *Essay on Chartism* (1839). The first example in English of the similar *goonda* also comes from Glasgow; see GOON.

tick. An old term of contempt ("Yee nigling Ticks you," OED, 1613), but more commonly encountered today in such phrases as *tight as a tick* (very drunk), *lively as a tick in a tar-pot* (motionless), and *tick(ed) off* (angry). The last one does not come from the insect, however. It is a variant of *tee'd off*, in turn a euphemism for *pissed off*. See also INSECT and PISS.

tiger. A cruel or rapacious person. "There is no more mercy in him than there is milk in a male tiger" (William Shakespeare, *Coriolanus*, 1608). Of course, some outwardly fierce *tigers* are inwardly weak, e.g., "All reactionaries are paper tigers" (Mao Tse Tung to Anna Louise Strong, 8/1946, in *Peking Review*, 11/11/58). Credit for coining *paper tiger* is given to Chairman Mao in the 1982 supplement to the *Oxford English Dictionary*, but the phrase actually is much older. David Shulman provided three nineteenth-century examples of the expression in *American Speech* (Summer 1988), the earliest being "A blustering, harmless fellow they [Chinese] call a 'paper tiger' " (*Youth's Dayspring*, 3/1850).

tightass. A tense, inhibited person; a prig. " 'Jenny Cavilleri,' answered Ray. 'Wonky music type.' 'I know that one,' said another, 'a real tight-ass' " (Erich Segal, *Love Story*, 1970). The term derives from the older *tight-assed* or, in Britain, *tight-arsed*, the latter defined in *Slang and Its Analogues* (J.S. Farmer and W. E. Henley, 1904) as meaning "chaste; close-legged." Thus, the *ass* in *tightass* is basically an anatomical displacement, similar to that in *piece of ass*; see ASS.

tightwad. A stingy person, a miser. The term refers to the roll of bills, which the miserly person keeps in such a tight wad that he finds it impossible to extract one when the time comes to pay a check.

    Tightwad (from 1900) was preceded by the simple *tight* (1828) in the same sense. Although we still speak generally of *tight* money, the word may have been extended into *tightwad* as a personal characterization in order to avoid confusion with another sense of *tight*, i.e., tipsy or DRUNK, whick also dates from the first half of the nineteenth century.

    The stingy kind of *tight* has provided the basis for some picturesque characterizations of miserliness, e.g., *as tight as bark on a tree*, *as tight as the skin on his back*, and *so tight he squeaks when he walks*, as well as the simple *tight-fisted*. See also CHEAPSKATE, PIKER, SCROOGE, and SKINFLINT.

tinhorn. An inferior, contemptible person, especially a pretentious or flashy one; originally, in full, a *tinhorn gambler* but later extended to others with *tinhorn* characteristics, especially politicians, e.g., "Washington had not seen such a concentration of tinhorns for a quarter of a century. They were not only self-serving; they had the reflexes of backwoods Coolidges" (Bert Cochran, *Harry Truman and the Crisis Presidency*, 1973).

Tinhorn gambler has been dated to the late 1800s. "We have been greatly annoyed of late by a lot of tin horn gamblers and prostitutes" (*Weekly New Mexican Review*, 2/26/1885). These gamblers got their name from Chuck-a-Luck, according to George Willison's *Here They Struck Gold* (1931): "Chuck-a-luck operators shake their dice in a 'small churn-like affair of metal'—hence the expression 'tinhorn gambler,' for the game is rather looked down upon as one for mere 'chubbers' and chuck-a-luck gamblers are never admitted within the aristocratic circle of faro-dealers." (On modern carnival lots, the churn-like affair has been replaced by a spinning wire container, which looks like, and is called, a Bird Cage. The game is easily rigged, using metal-loaded dice and an electromagnet, and its operators still rank low in the gambling fraternity.)

Credit for coining *tinhorn politician*, meanwhile, is given by William Safire to William Allen White, who first used it in an editorial in the *Emporia* (Kansas) *Gazette* on October 25, 1901 (*Safire's Political Dictionary*, 1978). This improved upon the British use of *tin-pot politician* (from 1897) in the same sense. As a generic for that which is cheap, poor, shabby, worthless, and also, on occasion, pretentious, *tin-pot* has been dated to 1838. See also POL and the cheap but flashy *tin* in TINSELTOWN.

Tinseltown. Hollywood, in all its superficial splendor. "I confess: Growing up in Tinseltown, my childhood hobby was visiting cemeteries, seeking the resting places of my heroes" (Kenneth Anger, *Hollywood Babylon II*, 1984). The sobriquet has been dated to 1974 (*American Speech*, Winter 1985), but the basic idea is older, as evidenced by the acerbic remark attributed to Oscar Levant (1906–72): "Strip the phoney tinsel off Hollywood and you'll find the real tinsel underneath" (in Leslie Halliwell, *The Filmgoer's Book of Quotes*, 1973). See also PEORIA and TINHORN.

tit. A woman's breast.

Speaking of the publisher of the *Washington Post*: "Katie Graham's gonna get her tit caught in a big fat wringer if that's published" (John N. Mitchell, telephone conversation with *Post* reporter Carl Bernstein, 9/29/72, in Bernstein and Bob Woodward, *All the President's Men*, 1974). The comment by Mr. Mitchell, former Attorney General of the United States and the director of the campaign to reelect President Nixon in 1972, came in the course of a denial that he had controlled a special fund that financed the Watergate break-in and other Republican espionage operations against the Democrats. The *Post* printed the denial, except for "her tit," which was deleted on the instruction of Ben Bradlee, the editor. But a full account of the conversation was given to Mrs. Graham, who asked Mr. Bernstein the next morning if he had any more messages for her.

The vivid phraseology of the denial of Mr. Mitchell (who later did jail time for his part in Watergate) was not original to him. "Got his tit in a wringer," meaning "got himself in difficulty," was included in a list of common expressions collected about thirty years earlier in southern Indiana (*American Speech*, 2/44). Similar folk expressions include *cold as a witch's tit*, extremely cold; *live off the tit*, to live well, especially without working; *suck the hind tit*, to get the worst of something; and *useless as tits on a boar hog*, very useless. All of these, no doubt, are of considerable antiquity.

Tit is a good old Anglo-Saxon word (as *titt*), originally denoting the nipple only, but applied from an early date to the entire breast. (The word also has had a variety of other meanings, e.g., a small animal, often a horse, especially a filly; a young girl, especially a HUSSY; and a bird, such as a titlark or titmouse.) In its anatomical sense, however, the term was superseded by *teat* (from the French *tette*).

The adoption of *teat* is typical of what has happened to the stock of words involving sexually charged subjects, with Anglo-Saxon terms generally being eschewed in favor of those derived from other languages, especially French and Latin. The foreign words, it seems, have considerable insulation value. Thus, both *bust*, from the French *buste*, and *mammary gland*, based on the Latin *mamma*, are considered to be more polite than their Anglo-Saxon equivalent. In the case of *teat*, people further distanced themselves from the base term by reserving the word mainly for animals rather than women—"now usually [used] of quadrupeds," as the *OED* put it (Volume O, 1902–04). Another example of this distancing is Nahum Tate (1652–1715), poet laureate of England (from 1692) and dramatist, noted for rewriting Shakespeare's *King Lear* with a happy ending wherein Cordelia marries Edgar, but who also deserves to be remembered for changing his surname: Nahum's father's name was Faithful Teate.

The older Anglo-Saxon word did not die out, but went underground, surviving in dialect. As a provincial term, employed largely by unlettered people, it was not often reduced to writing, however. The first modern example in the *OED* of an anatomical *tit* is in the form of the diminutive *tetty*: "Es wont ha' my Tetties a grabbed zo" (*An Exmoor Courtship, Gentleman's Magazine*, 6/1746). Meanwhile, the modern plurals, *tits* and *titties*, were recorded first in a glossary of words collected in East Anglia prior to 1825.

In fact, the anatomical meaning of *tit* seems to have become dominant only within the last century or so. For example, neither *tit*, *tits*, nor *titties* are included in this sense in *A Classical Dictionary of the Vulgar Tongue* (Captain Francis Grose, 1796) and the anonymously produced updating of it, the *Lexicon Balatronicum* (1811). Both defined *tit* as "A horse; a pretty little tit; a smart little girl. A tit, or tid bit; a delicate morsel. Tommy tit; a smart lively little fellow." Moreover, the *Lexicon* used the word in its definition of *keep* in this way: "Mother, your tit won't keep; your daughter won't preserve her virginity." And approaching mid-century, a Lady Tavistock could let it be known that she thought the Queen Victoria "a resolute little tit," a term that she is unlikely to have used in this context had she been aware of the anatomical implication (*A Selection from the Correspondence and Diaries of the Late Thomas Creevey a 1838*, 1903).

The modern short forms also are missing from *Slang and Its Analogues*, by John S. Farmer and W. E. Henley, though this (also British) work does have *titties* in a list of synonyms for *dairy* (Volume II, 1891). Among the others in this collection: *bubbies, charlies, blubber, butter-boxes, berkeleys, diddies, globes, dugs,* and "*charms.*" (Quotation marks in original text.) Conspicuously absent from this listing are *boobs*, from the aforementioned *bubbies*, and *knockers*, perhaps inspired by the height and shape of old-fashioned door knockers or, another possibility, by their ball-like appearance, *knackers* and *knockers* also dating from the nineteenth century as slang for the testicles. See also BOOB.

As a standard, non-dialectical term, *tits* has been dated only to 1928, with the example coming not from a book or other publication, but a graffito recorded by Allen Walker Read on July 17 of that year in Fairhaven Park, Bellingham, Washington (*Lexical Evidence from Folk Epigraphy in Western North America*, 1935). This discovery, together with the omissions in the pioneering slang dictionaries, suggests that Americans should be credited with reviving the Anglo-Saxon *tit*, as well as its regular plural, during the opening decades of the present century. A notable contribution, indeed, and once since added to with such common phrases as *tit man*, a connoisseur of this portion of female anatomy; *tits and ass*, a display thereof, as in a magazine or show (British: *tits and bum*); *tits and zits*, having to do with the passion of teenagers; *tough titty*, hard luck; and *the tits*, excellent, the best, great!

Which is not to imply that the Anglo-Saxon term has yet come completely out of the linguistic closet. The *Washington Post*, as noted, deleted it from Mr. Mitchell's denial—not too surprising, considering that the owner herself was involved. And on a related matter, we have it on the authority of baseball commissioner A. Bartlett Giamatti that the top of the strike zone was defined in 1987 as being at the middle of the batter's chest because some baseball people feared the American public was not yet ready to hear TV announcers refer to "the nipple zone" (*New York Times Magazine*, 9/4/88).

Tits also contributed to one of Lenny Bruce's obscenity convictions. In a two-to-one court decision against him in New York City (11/4/64), the first of the "obscene references" cited in the majority opinion was "Eleanor Roosevelt and her display of 'tits.'" (In the routine in question, Mrs. Roosevelt was portrayed as sporting a lovely pair.) One of the most notable things about this opinion was the refusal of the newspaper of record in the field, the *New York Law Journal*, to print it. Even when pressed for more information by lawyers who were interested in obscenity cases, the editors of the *Law Journal* stuck to their guns, saying, "The majority opinion, of necessity, cited in detail the language used by Bruce in his night-club act, and also described gestures and routines which the majority found to be obscene and indecent. The *Law Journal* decided against publication, even edited, on the grounds that deletions would destroy the opinion, and without the deletions publication was impossible within *Law Journal* standard" (in Bruce, *How to Talk Dirty and Influence People*, 1972). Ironically, the *Law Journal* did print a cut-down version of the dissenting opinion in the case, since it omitted descriptions of the words and acts that the majority found to be criminal. For more on this case, see *haul ass* in ASS.

P.S. When John Mitchell died in 1988, *The New York Times* included the story of his advice to Katharine Graham in its obit but in the blandest of terms, reporting only that the former Attorney General had "warned that the publisher would be 'caught in a big fat wringer if that's published.'" (11/10/88). The publisher's sex was not even mentioned. See also BREAST.

toad. A low, loathsome individual; especially, among present-day teenagers, a parent, as in "My old toad won't let me have the car tonight." The ill repute of *toads* stems from the folk belief that they are poisonous. Thus, speaking of the Duke of Gloucester (and future king of England): "The time will come when thou shalt wish for me To help thee curse that poisonous hunchbacked toad" (William Shakespeare, *Richard III*, 1592–93).

The *toady*, who is a flatterer or PARASITE, comes from *toad-eater*, an eighteenth-century term for a SYCOPHANT—specifically, a poor relation or companion, usually a woman, who had to swallow all sorts of abuse as the price for being allowed to live with a great family. And this *toad-eater*, in turn, came from the *toad-eater* who assisted traveling medicine men in the seventeenth and eighteenth centuries. The assistant got this name because one of his less appetizing chores was to swallow (or, if sufficiently skilled at sleight of hand, pretend to swallow) a

388

supposedly poisonous toad in order that his master could proceed to demonstrate the curative powers of whatever nostrum he was peddling at the time. See also FROG and YES-MAN.

toilet. A can, commode, convenience, throne, stool, etc. "Without Hart in the equation, Simon will do well against Michael Dukakis in New Hampshire. With Hart in the race, Simon is in the toilet" (a political campaign manager's strategic insight, *New York Times*, 12/18/87).

The toilet as a symbol of dirtiness was analyzed most closely by that late professor of semantics, Lenny Bruce. (The word itself arose as a euphemism, *toilet room*, originally a dressing room, having evolved from the French *toilette*, a little cloth, or *toile*.) Here is the key portion of Bruce's analysis, taken from a performance at the Jazz Workshop in San Francisco on October 4, 1961 (for which he was arrested, with the result that a tape recording of his act was played in court on March 8, 1962):

> I want to help you if you have a dirty-word problem. There are *none*, and I'll spell it out logically to you.
> Here is a toilet. Specifically—that's all we're concerned with, specifics—if I can tell you a dirty-toilet joke, we must have a dirty toilet. That's what we're talking about, a toilet. If we take this toilet and boil it and it's clean, I can never tell you specifically a dirty-toilet joke about this toilet. I can tell you a dirty-toilet joke about the toilet in the Milner Hotel, or something like that, but *this toilet* is a clean toilet. Now obscenity is a human manifestation. This toilet has no central nervous system, no level of consciousness. It is not aware; it is a dumb toilet; it cannot be obscene; it's impossible. . . . Nobody can ever offend you by telling you a dirty-toilet story. . . .
> Now, all of us have had a bad early toilet training—that's why we are hung up with it. All of us at the same time got two zingers—one for the police department and one for the toilet. All right, he made a kahkah, call a policeman. All right, OK, all right. Are you going to do that anymore? OK, tell the policeman he doesn't have to come up now.

And then, making the next connection:

> Now, if the bedroom is dirty to you, then you are a true atheist. . . . if anyone in this audience believes that God made his body, and your body is dirty, the fault lies with the manufacturer. . . . He made it all; it's all clean or all dirty.

Bruce was acquitted this time, but he picked up a $100 fine for contempt of court in the process.

The toilet was a fixture in Bruce's nightclub act for many years; see also COMMIE.

Tokyo Rose. A traitor, especially one who makes treasonable broadcasts. "Mike Wallace has become today's Tokyo Rose" (letter to "60 Minutes," CBS-TV, 11/3/85). *Tokyo Rose* was the sobriquet of Mrs. Iva Ikuko Toguri D'Aquino, whose daily propaganda broadcasts included enough music and other entertainment to make them highly popular with U.S. troops in the Pacific Theater during World War II. Born in the United States, she was convicted of treason in 1949, sentenced to ten years in jail, and fined $10,000. See also QUISLING and TRAITOR.

Tom-. Any male, as in *Tom, Dick, and Harry*, from the eighteenth century, and earlier, as in Shakespeare's "Tom, Dicke, and Francis" (*Henry IV, Part I*, 1596). The generic *Tom* appears in many more or less disparaging phrases, among them:

blind Tom. A baseball umpire.

Tom and Jerry. Names that now conjure up images of a cartoon cat and mouse (starting with *Puss Gets the Boot*, 1940), but which were popularized as a duo by the lead characters in Pierce Egan's *Life in London* (1821), Corinthian Tom and Jerry Hawthorn, whose adventures were such that *Tom-and-Jerry shop* came to stand for a low pub and *Tom-and-Jerryism* for drunken, riotous behavior.

tomboy. Originally a boisterous boy, but from the sixteenth century and now, always, a boyish girl.

tomcat. A male who is on the make or, as a verb, to chase women, from the name of the hero of a bestseller of 1760 (see CAT).

tomfool. A half-wit, an idiot; formerly called a *Tom coney* or *Tom-noddy*, comparable to *jack fool* or, as Chaucer put it, *Jakke fool* (see JACK).

tommyrot. Nonsense, i.e., words uttered by a *tomfool*, though perhaps stemming from *tommy*, meaning the daily allowance of food, especially bread (from the eighteenth century), supplied to workmen, soldiers, and convicts (see ROT).

See also UNCLE TOM and, for more about first names, PADDY.

tool. A person used by another; in the Communist lexicon, *a capitalist tool*. The comparison of people to *tools* goes back at least to the mid-seventeenth century. Thus, from the *Dictionary of the Canting Crew* (B.E., ca. 1690): "Tool, an implement fit for any Turn, the Creature of any Cause or Faction; a meer Property, or Cat's Foot." See also *dog-bolt* in DOG and LACKEY.

Tool also has acquired a variety of other extended meanings, including what the *OED* (Volume T, 1909–15) terms "the male generative organ." This usage seems to be even older, dating to the mid-sixteenth century. It also remains current; see SCHLONG.

Ignorance of the anatomical meaning may result in peculiar sentences, e.g., from Henry James' first novel, *Roderick Random* (1876): " 'Oh, I can't explain!' cried Roderick impatiently, returning to his work. 'I've only one way of expressing my deepest feelings—it's this.' And he swung his tool."

Context is everything, of course, and it helps to know that the hero of James' novel is a sculptor. See also PRICK.

tout. An aggressive purveyor of frequently erroneous information, especially at a racetrack; as a verb, to solicit or to sell in a pushy way. The word is underworld slang from the eighteenth century (a *tout* originally was a lookout), and it has never escaped its seamy origins. Thus, a London producer, Ivan Caryll, is said to have given a new name to young actress, Hazel Tout (1890–1988), telling her, "You're just the one I want for my new play. But you must change your name. Tout is honest but impossible. You are so young, so fresh, so pink, you remind one of the dawn; you shall be Hazel Dawn" (*New York Times*, 8/31/88). See also PEDDLER.

traitor. A betrayer; specifically, one who commits treason against his country. "The same punishment that's due that no-good filthy traitor you'll get it yourself as his wife" (Black Muslim leader Louis Farrakhan to the spouse of the black newsman who reported the Reverend Jesse Jackson's use of HYMIE, *New York Times*, 4/9/84). *Traitor*, dating from the early thirteenth century, is one of the strongest charges that can be made against anyone. It stems from the Latin *trādere*, to hand over, to betray, and the Romans felt the same way about traitors that we do today, e.g., "Traitors are disliked even by those they favor" (Cornelius Tacitus, *History*, ca. 100). See also COPPERHEAD, DOUBLE-CROSSER, QUISLING, and TURNCOAT.

tramp. A promiscuous woman. " 'Hell, I won't pretend I've been the faithful little wife by the book. I was being humped by his best friend the night his squadron shipped out. I'm a tramp. He *liked* a tramp' " (Earl Thompson, *Tattoo*, 1974). The sense of sexual wandering is in keeping with other, older meanings of the word, e.g., the vagrant male tramp and the tramp vessel that does not have a regular route but roams from port to port. The term is an Americanism, dated so far only to 1922. See also BUM.

trash. A worthless someone or something; rubbish.

Herewith, some fatherly advice on the advantages of knowing a foreign language: "Our young countrymen have generally too little French, and too bad address, either to present themselves, or be well received in the best French companies; and, as proof of it, there is no one instance of an Englishman's having ever been suspected of a gallantry with a French woman of condition, though every French woman of condition is more than suspected of having a gallantry. But they take up with the disgraceful and dangerous commerce of prostitutes, actresses, dancing-women, and that sort of trash; though, if they had common address, better achievements would be extremely easy" (Lord Chesterfield, letter to his son, 6/5/1750).

Trash, of obscure origin, was used in the sixteenth century to refer to useless twigs or small branches that are lopped off a tree. It may derive from the Norwegian *trask*, rubbish, and be related to the Old English *trus*, brushwood. Whatever, the word's meaning quickly was extended: "Who steals my purse, steals trash" (William Shakespeare, *Othello*, 1604).

In particular, *trash* has enjoyed, almost from the beginning, a special application in the field of literary criticism, e.g., from a 1710 attack by a John Banister on the Reverend Cotton Mather:

> With undigested trash he throngs the Press;
> Thus striving to be greater, he's the less.

Although there was an element of truth here, Mather being a most prolific author, legal proceedings were instituted against Mr. Banister and his publisher, who were brought before Judge Samuel Sewall, and fined (from Kenneth Silverman, *The Life and Times of Cotton Mather*, 1984).

The term also is used as an adjective and verb. In the first case, it can mean "bad" or "poor" as well as "worthless," e.g. "Don't you put no trash mouth on me" (*The Great Santini*, film, 1979). Game animals that are taken inadvertently and then discarded also became *trash*, e.g. *trash ducks* (1940) and *trash fish* (1944).

The verb was popularized in the sense of "to destroy or vandalize" by rebellious young people during the 1960s: "The counter-culture is as deeply 'into' (to coin a phrase) the word pollution as the Establishment. . . . 'Trashing' was invented as a non-destructive cover for window-breaking and other mayhem, often at the cost of thousands of dollars" (Grace Hechinger, *Wall Street Journal,* 10/27/71). In an extended sense *to trash [someone* or *something]* is to destroy that person or thing figuratively through insult or other forms of deprecation.

See also POOR WHITE TRASH, RIP OFF, and RUBBISH.

trayf (tref). Nonkosher, unclean, extremely foul; from the Hebrew *teref,* torn to pieces, meaning an animal not killed in accordance with dietary laws. "Lopwitz's voice rose. 'Whaddaya mean they won't sell it to "trade"? . . . you tell 'em I got a word for them. *Trayf . . .* If I'm "trade," they're *trayf . . .* What's it mean? It means, like, "not kosher," only it's worse than that. In plain English I guess the word is *shit.* There's an old saying, "If you look close enough, everything is *trayf,*" and that goes for those moth-eaten aristocrats, too, Ronald' " (Tom Wolfe, *The Bonfire of the Vanities,* 1987). See also DRECK.

trimmer. A pragmatist, one who frequently changes sides, trimming his sails to suit the prevailing wind, especially in politics; also an unscrupulous lawyer. "He who wavers in seeking to do what is right gets stigmatized as a trimmer" (Washington Irving, *Knickerbocker's History of New York,* 1809). "There was an *esprit de corps* of reliability and honor in their practice; excluding such characters as are known as 'Shysters,' 'Tombs Lawyers,' 'Trimmers,' and lawyers guilty of 'sharp practice' " (S. M. Welch, *Home History. Recollections of Buffalo During the Decade from 1830 to 1840,* 1891). See also LAWYER. The principal, political sense dates to the 1680s, when George Saville, first Marquess of Halifax, who was neither Tory nor Whig, gained the sobriquet "Halifax the Trimmer," on account of his policy of compromise and willingness to change his positions to suit changed political circumstances. Halifax himself gladly accepted the label, contending in a pamphlet that "our climate is a Trimmer between that part of the world where men are roasted and the other where they are frozen; our Church is Trimmer between the frenzy of fanatic visions and the lethargic ignorance of Popish dreams; . . . true virtue hath ever been thought a Trimmer, and to have its dwelling in the middle of two extremes. . . . In such company, our Trimmer is not ashamed of his name" (*Character of a Trimmer,* 1682). See also OPPORTUNIST.

tripe. Intestines; when cooked, a dish that can be described as an acquired taste and, hence, pejoratively: (1) nonsense, and sometimes, for emphasis, *a bunch of tripe;* or (2) a contemptible person, and sometimes, for emphasis, *a bag of tripe.* "What th' hell do they have to give us that tripe for?" (Percy Marks, *The Plastic Age,* 1924). And conveying the flavor in a personal sense, from Ben Jonson's *Bartholomew Fair* (1614): "Alice: Thou Sow of Smithfield, thou. Ursula: Thou tripe of Turnebull." See also BALONEY and THOU.

troglodyte. An extreme conservative, a RIGHT-WINGER; a boorish, backward person. "I voted for Mario Cuomo for Governor of New York in 1982 because I liked what he was saying and because I thought his opponent, Lewis E. Lehrman, was a social Luddite and a moral troglodyte" (William Kennedy, *New York Times Book Review,*

5/13/84). ". . . . nose-picking, flatulence, scratching, slouching and mumbling had been brought pretty much under control by Dec. 3, 1947, when suddenly they all made a come-back. That was the night Marlon Brando threw a bloody package of raw meat at Kim Hunter in the New York opening of 'A Streetcar Named Desire.' The Age of the Intense Troglodyte had dawned" (Florence King, *Newsday*, New York edition, 9/22/87).

Troglodyte comes from the Greek *trōglodýtēs*, a cave dweller, one who creeps into (gnawed) holes, making it completely synonymous with *Neanderthal* (see PEORIA).

turd. A lump of excrement; a despicable person. ". . . SCUM will conduct Turd Sessions, at which every male present will give a speech beginning with the sentence: 'I am a turd, a lowly abject turd,' then proceed to list all the ways he is" (Valerie Solanas, *S.C.U.M. Manifesto*, 1968, where the acronym stands for Society for Cutting Up Men).

Turd is regarded as vulgar now, but this was not always the case. The word is extremely old, having been dated to ca. 1000 in its elemental sense, to pre-1250 as a symbol of worthlessness or vileness, and to ca. 1450 as a term of personal abuse. It comes from the Old English *tord*, and ultimately from the Indo-European root *der-*, to split, and, hence, that which is separated. (The etymology parallels that of SHIT.) The term was used in literature for some centuries in both excremental and extended senses. It appears in the Wyclif translation of the Bible (1388) and in the works of Shakespeare, Jonson, and other writers. The divines who produced the King James version of the Bible in 1611 did some sidestepping, however. Where Wyclif's translation reads, "Alle thingis . . . I deme as toordis, that I win Crist" (*Philippians*, 3:8), the King James has "I count all things but loss for the excellency of the knowledge of Christ."

Turd seems to have been one of the casualties of the rise of Puritanism in the seventeenth century. With the exception of *turd-bird*, as a provincial name for Richardson's skua (the scientific name of the thrush family, by the way, is *Turdidae*), the *Oxford English Dictionary* includes not a single example of the word, with all four letters spelled out, from 1651 to 1922. The term was used in the long interval, of course, but its power in print usually was neutralized with asterisks or dashes, as in "Out you nasty T--d colour'd dog" (Thomas Brown, *Walk Round London, Thames*, pre-1704). Even Captain Francis Grose, a specialist in coarse talk, did not print the word in full, e.g., "T--D. There were four t--ds to dinner; stir t--d, hold t--d, tread t--d, and must--d; to wit a hog's face, feet, and chitterlings, with mustard" (*A Classical Dictionary of the Vulgar Tongue*, 1796).

As with so many of our steamiest words, the reappearance of this one in twentieth-century literature is courtesy of James Joyce's *Ulysses*. Of course, that book was banned in the United States until 1933, and *turd* was not often seen in print until after World War II when legal and social restraints against the public use of taboo words were eased. Asked about his philosophy of life, President Harry S Truman, a farmboy at heart, replied: "Never kick a fresh turd on a hot day" (Richard Bolling, in Merle Miller, *Lyndon: An Oral Biography*, 1964). Nowadays, on a scale of three, *turd* rates as a two, falling midway between the innocuous *crap* and *dung* on the one hand and the stronger *S-word* on the other.

Turk. (1) A wild, fierce person; specifically, an Irishman, from the proverbial fierceness of Turks, perhaps reinforced by the Gaelic *torc*, a wild boar. (2) A pederast, from the reputed proclivity of Turks for this form of sexual activity. See also IRISH and GREEK.

The *Turk* as Irisher, dated to 1914, sometimes is confused with the well-known bird: "Terrible Turkey McGovern, ah, there was a sweet fighting harp for you, a real fighting turkey with dynamite in each mitt . . ." (James T. Farrell, *Young Lonigan*, 1932). Not, of course, the kind of thing to say of, let alone to, an Irishman today, in view of the pejorative meanings lately acquired by TURKEY. The second form of *Turk*, also from the early twentieth century, is encountered today most commonly in personal ads, where *Turkish culture* is a code phrase for anal intercourse.

Back in the sixteenth century, when the Turks were threatening to overrun parts of Europe, the term had other, stronger negative meanings. The *Oxford English Dictionary* lists such early transferred senses for *Turk* as "a cruel, rigorous, or tyrannical man; anyone behaving as a barbarian or savage; one who treats his wife hardly; a bad-tempered or unmanageable man." By the nineteenth century, however, *little turk* and *young turk* were being applied to mischievous children. (In politics, the *Young Turk* who breaks regular ranks may well be middle-aged, but the allusion here is to the Young Turks who overthrew the last Ottoman sultan, Muhammad VI, and established the Turkish republic in 1923.) See also DUTCH and the Turkic-speaking TARTAR.

turkey. An incompetent person, one who continually makes mistakes, a DUD; reported among students from before 1945 (*Dictionary of American Slang*) and now current at even the highest levels of society. For example, during the presidency of Jimmy Carter (1977–81), Republicans regaled one another by asking "Why does the president's staff always carry a frozen turkey aboard *Air Force One?*" Answer: "Spare parts."

This is only one of a number of pejorative meanings that have become attached to this bird, a native American despite its name (the result of sixteenth-century confusion with the Old World guinea-fowl, then also called the *turkey*). Thus, a *turkey* may be a coward; a failure, flop, or mistake (typically, a theatrical production that has been panned by the critics and required to close quickly); or a fake capsule of narcotics (one that contains sugar, chalk, some other white, noncontrolled substance, or nothing at all). *To have a turkey on one's back* is to be drunk, and *to go cold turkey* is to begin something without preparation, referring most commonly today to a period of withdrawal from drugs. In an extended sense, a *turkey* may be any unsuitable or worthless item, as in "The Shoreham [nuclear plant] is a $4 billion turkey" (*New York Times* editorial, 2/23/84).

Many of *turkey*'s meanings reflect the bird's traits, actual or imputed. For instance, *turkey* also can refer to an arrogant gait or walk, a strut; to grandiloquence or hot air, GOBBLEDYGOOK; to pretentious boasting (more gobbling); and to a suitcase or canvas bag (probably a tribute to the bird's size and shape).

John James Audubon described turkeys as "very wary and cunning" (*Birds of America*, 1831), but in the popular imagination they are, like most other birds (see DODO), considered to be stupid and easy to catch. Hence, a *turkey shoot* is a simple task or a helpless target, as in "The Marianas Turkey Shoot," of June 15, 1944, when the Japanese lost 330 planes to 30 for the Americans. And in a gloriously extended sense that *The New Yorker* found worthy of inclusion in its department of mixed metaphors, 6/3/85: "If somehow we lose control on the Senate floor and amendment after amendment after amendment is offered and a turkey shoot begins to unfold and the package begins to unwind, it will be well nigh impossible to pick Humpty Dumpty off the floor and reassemble the package" (budget director David Stockman in the Austin [Texas] American-Statesman).

Remarkably, considering all the word's negative meanings, to talk turkey is to speak simply and plainly, to get down to facts in a businesslike way. This expression seems to have evolved from the punch line of an old joke (ca. 1830) involving two hunters, one an Indian and the other a white man. When it came time to divvy up the game, consisting of turkeys and buzzards (or crows, in some versions), the white man allotted the birds, saying "I will take the turkey and you may take the buzzard," then "You may take the buzzard and I will take the turkey." And so on, until all were accounted for, leading the Indian to complain, "You never once said turkey to me." See also BIRD.

turncoat. A renegade; a person who switches parties or sides, especially one with reversible principles. Legend has it that the term comes from a Duke of Saxony who had a coat that was white (for France) on one side and blue (for Spain) on the other, and who changed colors depending on his policy of the moment. The word has been dated to 1557 in the sense of abandoning one party for another. The first turncoat that is a real coat, renovated by being turned inside out, doesn't appear in the record until 1726, although the practice of concealing wear and tear this way certainly is much older, e.g., "Petruchio is coming in a new hat and an old jerkin; a pair of breeches thrice turned" (William Shakespeare, The Taming of the Shrew, ca. 1593). See also CHAMELEON, RENEGADE, and TRAITOR.

twaddle. Empty talk, nonsense, rubbish. "Mr. Cheshire says the paper's current editor in chief, Arnaud de Borchgrave, pressed him to change an editorial that was critical of the South Korean government . . . 'That's twaddle,' Mr. de Borchgrave countered . . ." (New York Times, 4/17/87).

Twaddle is not heard as often nowadays as in the early 1780s when it was all the rage because fashionable people had a thing about it, as noted in a couplet in European Magazine (12/1785):

> The favorite phrases fall and are no more,
> The Rage, the Thing, the Twaddle, and the Bore.

Twaddle, from 1782, is a variant of the older twattle, from 1573, meaning idle talk or chatter. Twaddle, twattle, twittle-twattle, and tittle-tattle, all seem to be variants of tattle, as in TATTLETALE. See also BORE and BUNK.

twat. The female pudendum; a low, four-letter word for the still lower C-word. "According to one rather ornate theory, Joe Bob had for months been trying to sneak the word 'twat' past the two copy editors [at the Dallas, Texas, Times-Herald], and they were concentrating so hard on spotting it—examining each syllable in the name of any town that Joe Bob invented, searching any new organization for contraband acronyms—that they weren't paying enough attention to the content of the column" (Calvin Trillin, New Yorker, 12/22/86).

Like many synonyms for intimate female anatomy (and for comparable male anatomy, too, for that matter), this term frequently is used insultingly to refer to an entire person, usually a woman. Thus, one night on a stoop near Stanley's Bar, a joint on Manhattan's Lower East Side where blacks and whites mingled during the euphoria of the 1960s, a now well-known author, who will go nameless here because he later saw the light of feminism, delivered in a memorably loud voice the literary judgment: "Twat can't write!" (personal communication).

Twat is of obscure origin. Dated to 1650 in *Slang and Its Analogues* (J. S. Farmer and W. E. Henley, 1904), it may be related to the Old Norse *thveit*, cut, slit, forest clearing (*Random House Dictionary*, 1987). Sir James Murray, the great editor of the *Oxford English Dictionary*, admitted *twat* to Volume T, which he completed just before his death in 1915, though he had previously excluded *cunt* from Volume C (1888–93). He could not bring himself to define *twat* explicitly, however, merely referring the reader to a citation from Nathan Bailey's *Universal Etymological English Dictionary* of 1727. In a curious reversal, William Morris, editor of *The American Heritage Dictionary* (1969), the first general American dictionary to include *cunt* (and *fuck*), omitted the less highly charged *twat*.

The *T-word* occupies a special niche in literary history, however, thanks to a horrible mistake by Robert Browning, who included it in "Pippa Passes" (1841) without knowing its true meaning: "The owls and bats, / Cowls and twats, / Monks and nuns, / In a cloister's moods." Poor Robert! He had been misled into thinking the word meant "hat" by its appearance in "Vanity of Vanities," a poem of 1660, containing the treacherous lines: "They talk't of his having a Cardinalls Hat, / They'd send him as soon an Old Nuns Twat." (There is a lesson here about not using words unless one is very sure of their meaning.)

tweeb. A dilgent student. Thus, reporting on life at Yale: "Oh, yes, and the study 'grind' of yesteryear has been rechristened 'the tweeb' " (Julie V. Iovine, *Wall Street Journal*, 8/4/87). See also DWEEB and WEENIE.

twerp (twirp). An objectionable person, especially an insignificant one. "Those brainless twerps. People are killed and injured every day because of insults, but they refuse to study them because the subject is disreputable" (Reinhold Aman, founder of *Maledicta: The International Journal of Verbal Aggression*, commenting on the academics who denied him tenure at the University of Wisconsin–Milwaukee, *Time*, 1/9/78).

Various theories of the origin of *twerp* (from 1925) have been proposed—e.g., that it is related to the Danish *tver*, perverse, or that it is a variant of TWIT or maybe even TWAT—but the most appealing is that it is an eponym, after T. W. Earp, who matriculated at Exeter College, Oxford, in the fall of 1911. The 1986 supplement to the *Oxford English Dictionary* includes two citations that support this theory. The earliest is from a letter by the king of the Hobbits, J. R. R. Tolkien: "He lived in O[xford] at the time we lived in Pusey Street (rooming with Walton, the composer, and going about with T. W. Earp, the original twerp)" (10/6/44). The second reference suggests that T. W. Earp was considered a *twerp* because he kindled "Goering-like wrath" in "the hearts of the rugger-playing stalwarts at Oxford when he was president of the Union, by being the last, the most charming, and wittiest of the 'decadents' " (Roy Campbell, *Portugal*, 1957). See also JERK.

twigger. "It would be impermissible to print the proper—or, rather, improper—modern equivalent of this" (A. L. Rowse, *Christopher Marlowe*, 1964). Mr. Rowse's comment was made in the form of a footnote to *twigger* in the following fragment from Marlowe's *Dido, Queen of Carthage* (ca. 1593), wherein a bawdy old Nurse (who has much in common with Shakespeare's Nurse in *Romeo and Juliet*) addresses a young Cupid:

> That I might live to see this boy a man!
> How prettily he laughs! Go ye wag!
> You'll be a twigger when you come to age.

Etymology helps. *Twigger* apparently derives from *twig*, to do anything vigorously or strenuously, and is related to *twigle*, to copulate. A *twigger*, then, is an expert at sexual intercourse, a prostitute or wencher, a lascivious person; in the vernacular, a good fucker.

twink (twinkie, twinky). An attractive but soft-headed person, a *chicklet* (see CHICKEN); a homosexual; a weird person. "In spite of all the slapstick in her book, Linda Ellerbee is clearly serious about her journalism. She is contemptuous of the Twinkies—those perky, oleaginous, desperately amiable anchorpersons with their blow-dried brains who fill America's television screen" (*Columbia Journalism Review*, 7-8/86).

The term apparently derives from *Twinkies*, trade name of a soft-centered cupcake that is much loved by connoisseurs of junk food. Twinkies were introduced by the Chicago branch of Continental Baking Co. in 1930. Company legend has it that the name popped into the head of the creator of the confection, Jimmy Dewar, while traveling by bus to St. Louis, just as the vehicle passed a billboard with an ad for Twinkle Toes shoes.

See also KRAUT.

twisted. Perverted, from ca. 1900. "Snuff films . . . would have been made to be shown privately to wealthy individuals who got their pleasure in twisted, sadistic ways" (Sidney Sheldon, *Bloodline*, 1978).

Twisted also has other meanings, i.e., to be drunk, to be high on drugs other than alcohol, and, back in the eighteenth century, when hanging was in style, to be executed in this manner. The last sense was revived brilliantly by presidential adviser John D. Ehrlichman, and given new life as a metaphor for protracted agony: "Well, I think we ought to let him hang there. Let him twist slowly, slowly in the wind' (recorded phone conversation, with presidential counsel John W. Dean, III, 3/6/73). Mr. Ehrlichman was referring to L. Patrick Gray, III, then being asked questions to which he did not have good answers at Senate hearings on his nomination as director of the FBI. Mr. Gray was allowed to twist slowly in the wind until April 5, a month later, when the White House finally withdrew the nomination.

See also KINKY and WARPED.

twit. A stupid person, an insignificant one. "During his 15 years as commissioner of baseball, the fans often saw Bowie Kuhn as a supercilious twit and booed him vigorously at his public appearances" (*New York Times Book Review*, 3/8/87).

Dated to ca. 1925 by Eric Partridge (*A Dictionary of Slang and Unconventional English*, 1970), all the earliest examples of *twit* come from Britain. The word is of obscure origin. It might a euphemistic mispronunciation of TWAT, a blend of TWAT and TWERP (TWIRP), or NITWIT minus the first two letters. By whichever route, the intent clearly is derogatory. See also JERK and STUPID.

two-bit. Cheap, petty, vulgar, as in, with a pun on the original (1939) price of mass-market, softcover books, *Two-Bit Culture: The Paperbacking of America* (book title, Kenneth C. Davis, 1984). The adjectival *two-bit* dates from the early 1800s, when dollars and other coins sometimes were still being cut into parts, with eight bits (from the Spanish piece of eight, an old Spanish peso of eight reals) equaling a whole and *two bits* amounting to twenty-five cents. The modifier has become part of many fairly standard phrases over the years, such as *two-bit cigar, two-bit club, two-bit house,* and *two-bit saloon.* Or in Erskine Caldwell's words: "Tom said she used to be a two-bit slut" (*Tobacco Road,* 1932). See also CHEAP, PENNY-ANTE and PICAYUNE.

U

ugh. An exclamation of disgust, disapproval, horror, and the like. "It may have been a water-rat I speared, / But, ugh! it sounded like a baby's shriek" (Robert Browning, "Childe Roland," 1855).

The elemental *ugh* has been dated to 1765 as a represention of the sound of a person's cough and to 1837 as an exclamation expressing disgust. Most likely, it is older in life than in literature. See also BAH, BLAH, FEH, HO-HUM, PHOOEY, PIFFLE, POOH-POOH, and YUCK.

ugly. Unpleasant to the eye, repulsive, disagreeable. "Thus . . . a homely woman [is] 'ugly as sin,' 'ugly as a mud fence,' 'so ugly her face would stop a clock' " (Paul G. Brewster, "Folk 'Sayings' from Indiana," *American Speech*, 12/39). Similar expressions include the intensive *ugly as homemade sin; if I were as ugly as you, I'd sue my parents;* and from the wit and wisdom of Vice President George Bush, the figurative: "And I knew the minute I said 'card-carrying member of the A.C.L.U.,' a couple of your best columnists would jump all over me like ugly on an ape" (*New York Times*, 10/12/88).

Ugly once had a stronger meaning than it does today, referring originally (ca. 1250) not just to unsightliness but to an appearance that caused dread or horror in the beholder. It stems from the Old Norse *uggr*, fear. For artful spite, it is hard, as always, to improve upon George Gordon Lord Byron (letter to John Murray, his publisher, 7/12/1819):

> If for silver, or for gold.
> You could melt ten thousand pimples
> Into half a dozen dimples,
> Then your face we might behold,
> Looking, doubtless, much more smugly,
> Yet ev'n then 'twould be d----d ugly.

See also PLUG-UGLY.

ultra-. Extreme; going beyond acceptable limits, especially in such combinations as *ultra-left, ultra-liberal, ultra-nationalistic, ultra-patriot, ultra-right*, and so on. "The editorial [in official Chinese publications] said the four leftists whom it termed a 'gang of four,' had actually pursued 'an ultra-right line' " (*New York Times*, 10/26/76).

The prefix, dated to 1793 in the form of *ultra-revolutionary*, began to be applied widely from about 1830, with *ultra-Anglican, ultra-conservative, ultra-fashionable, ultra-refined, ultra-religious,* and *ultra-revolutionary* all coming from the nineteenth century. See also ARCH-, ARMCHAIR, CLOSET-, CRYPTO-, PSEUDO, and WEAK-.

un-American. American in name only; contrary to the values of the United States; traitorous. For example, Jefferson B. Sessions, III, U. S. attorney in Mobile, Alabama, testified at a Senate hearing on his nomination for a federal judgeship that he "once may have said something about the N.A.A.C.P. being un-American or Communist, but I meant no harm by it" (*New York Times*, 3/20/86).

Un-American arose soon after the United States became independent, being recorded first in a relatively innocuous context as an adjective for something not characteristic of the United States, e.g., "Ninety marble capitals have been imported at vast cost from Italy . . . and show how *un*-American is the whole plan" (Morris Birkbeck, *Notes on a Journey in America*, 1817). The term began to be bandied about in politics in the middle decades of the nineteenth century, becoming a deadly charge, especially during the lifetime (1938–75) of the House Committee to Investigate un-American Activities, when *un-American* Americans were cited for contempt, imprisoned, blacklisted, and generally villified. See also LIBERAL.

Note: The nomination of Mr. Sessions, who also said he thought Ku Klux Klan members "were OK until I found out they smoked pot," was rejected by the Senate Judiciary Committee.

Uncle Tom. A servile person; specifically, a black person who kowtows to white people or accepts their values. Thus, speaking of Brian Taylor, a basketball star at Princeton in the early 1970s: "Once, during warm-ups for a game at Memphis State, black players on the other team started riding him. They called him an Uncle Tom and an Oreo cookie" (Stan Adelson, assistant director of personnel at Princeton, *New York Times*, 5/4/83). The epithet has been generalized sufficiently for females also to qualify for it, though technically they should be referred to as *Aunt Thomasinas*. "An Akron woman won $32,000 in damages from a Cleveland newspaper because it called her an *Uncle Tom*" (Robert Hendrickson, *The Literary Life and Other Curiosities*, 1981).

Harriet Beecher Stowe depicted the hero of *Uncle Tom's Cabin* (1852) as a man of great innate nobility, whose spirit could not be broken, even by SIMON LEGREE. The original Uncle Tom died rather than reveal the hiding place of two escaped slaves, but he is remembered less for this than for his long-suffering humility and patience. In a perverse tribute to the novel's impact (three hundred thousand copies sold the first year), Tom's name was being used disparagingly within a year of its publication in such forms as *Uncle Tomitude, Uncle Tomitized,* and *Uncle Tomific*. The early epithets, however, were hurled by whites against whites; specifically, by those who supported slavery (a.k.a. the peculiar institution) against those with abolitionist views, e.g., "Our papers have coined a word—Uncle Tomitude—to sneer at the sympathy with the African" (1853, in Thomas S. Perry, *The Life and Letters of Francis Lieber*, 1882).

Among blacks, *Uncle Tom* and *Tom* have been used for many years, especially in Northern cities, to designate fellow blacks who have adopted a deferential, flattering posture toward whites. Gunnar Myrdal noted *Uncle Tom's* use in this sense in *An American Dilemma* (1944). Or, as Claude Brown put it, describing a job at Hamburger Heaven in New York City: "It was something terrible. It was on Madison Avenue, and you had to be a real Tom. . . . You had to smile at the white folks, hoping they'd throw a big tip on you" (*Manchild in the Promised Land*, 1965). The pejorative value of the characterization probably is increased by memories of the Southern custom, maintained well into the twentieth century, of addressing blacks as *Uncle* (or BOY or *Aunt* or *Auntie*).

Indicating the strength of the insult, other ethnic groups have adapted it for their own lexicons. Thus, an American Indian who cooperates unduly with the white establishment, or who fades into white society, may be dismissed as an *Uncle Tomahawk,* and a Mexican American who exhibits the same cultural failings may be labeled a *Tio Taco* (literally, Uncle Taco). See also COUSIN, NEGRO, and for more about the condescending use of first names, PADDY.

underwear. Clothing worn next to the skin and, hence, an unmentionable word for many years, especially in feminine contexts. Thus, speaking of linguistic and other changes following the First World War: "Short skirts, also a French importation, went with bobbed hair, which meant that the female leg was exposed to dazzling heights. . . . Obviously, there had to be some changes in the area of *underwear,* a word almost as taboo as *pregnant* or *menstruation*" (D. W. Maurer, *American Speech,* Spring–Summer 1976).

The delicacy of the whole subject also is shown by the way new sets of words for articles of intimate apparel continually evolve. As established terms become contaminated by their proximity to the naked body (and by the evil thoughts that they thus arouse), they are sloughed off and replaced by new ones. *Underwear* itself is relatively new, having been dated only to 1872 (though it is apparent from the *OED*'s earliest example—an ad for "Ladies' underwear" in the New Orleans *Picayune* of April 2—that the term must have been familiar by then to members of the general public). Before *underwear* appeared, people wore *inside clothes, small clothes, underclothing* and *undergarments.* In the same manner, in the mid-nineteenth century, *lingerie* replaced *linen,* and *chemise* replaced *shift,* which had earlier replaced *smock.* Meanwhile, *underpants* and *undershorts* are from the twentieth century, as are the euphemistic *panties, scanties, undies, briefs, brevities,* and *step-ins,* all in place of the older *drawers,* itself something of a euphemism, since that term describes the action of donning, or drawing on, the garment, not the unspeakable garment itself. Even in the present liberated age, mention of *underwear* continues to evoke unseemly thoughts, especially in small minds, as evidenced by such schoolyard rhymes (all gathered in the New York area) as:

> What's your name?
> Mary Jane.
> Where do you live?
> Down the drain.
> What do you eat?
> Pig's feet.
> What do you drink?
> A bottle of ink.
> What do you wear?
> Daddy's dirty underwear.

And:

> Hi-ho Silver
> Is on the air.
> Tonto lost his underwear.
> Tonto said, "Me no care.
> Lone Ranger buy me another pair."

Then there is the classic (dating at least to the early 1940s):

> I see London,
> I see France,
> I see [so-and-so's]
> Underpants.

Chanted properly, this taunt can reduce another child quickly to tears. And finally, an excellent way of bringing down to earth anyone who is acting high and mighty: "Aw—your underpants are on too tight."

unwashed. The common people, the masses, the working stiffs who get dirty on the job, often in the phrase *the great unwashed*. "Gentlemen, there can be little doubt that your ancestors were the Great Unwashed" (William Makepeace Thackeray, *Pendennis*, 1850). The epithet was applied originally (1830) to the English lower orders, but soon crossed the Atlantic, e.g. "A score of loafers from the 'unwashed democracy' had got together for the purpose of seeing a live President" (F. A. Durivage and G. P. Burnham, *Stray Subjects, Arrested and Bound Over*, 1848). See also MOB.

up against the wall. A command to assume a humiliating, defenseless posture, literally or figuratively, with the threat of violence if the order is not obeyed immediately and unquestioningly; for emphasis, *up against the wall, motherfucker*. "The door was open a crack when he heard, 'Up against the wall, mother-fuckers!' Jesus Christ, they *all* said that" (Joseph Wambaugh, *The Glitter Dome*, 1981).

In popular use since the 1960s, spreading from counterculture to culture, the phrase probably derives from the police officer's command to a person being arrested to lean forward against a wall, hands and feet outspread, so that the suspect can be controlled easily and frisked for weapons. (Robbers have been known to use the same technique and terminology on their victims.)

The basic image is quite old, however. *To go to the wall* dates to the sixteenth century in the sense of giving way or succumbing in a conflict and to the nineteenth century as a metaphor for bankruptcy or other difficulties (*to be up against it*). *To drive* (or *push*) *to the wall* also dates to the sixteenth century in the sense of driving (someone) to the last extremity (where one's *back is against the wall*), and *to set* (or *thrust* or *send*) *to the wall* is of equal antiquity in the sense of putting someone in a position of neglect. The last leads to Shakespeare's double entendre in the opening scene of *Romeo and Juliet* (ca. 1595):

> SAMPSON: I will take the wall [the place of honor] of any man or maid of Montague's.
> GREGORY: That shows thee a weak slave, for the weakest goes to the wall [another old saying, the wall here being a place of shelter].
> SAMPSON: Tis true, and therefore women, being the weaker vessels, are ever thrust to the wall. Therefore I will push Montague's men from the wall and thrust his maids to the wall.

Which is very close to the modern sense of *up against the wall*. See also OFF THE WALL.

up yours. An emphatic exclamation of contempt, rejection, or defiance. "Horse and Goose. . . raking up all the oldest gags in the world, saying . . . 'By the way, Bruce, what is your whole, complete name?' and he said, 'Bruce William Pearson, Jr.,' and they said 'Well, up yours, Bruce William Pearson, Jr.' "(Mark Harris, *Bang the Drum Slowly*, 1956). " *'Up yours*, sister! If you had as many stickin out of you as you've had stuck in you, you'd look like a goddamn porkypine' " (Earl Thompson, *Tattoo*, 1974).

The phrase, contrary to the implication of the second example above, is a condensation of *stick it up your ass*. Eric Partridge dated it to the late nineteenth century (*A Dictionary of Slang and Unconventional English*, 1970). Many variants have been recorded. Among them: *up your butt, up your gig, up your gigi* (or *giggy*), *up your pooperdoop*, and *up yours with a left-hand turn* or *a hard-wire brush*, or *a red-hot poker*, or whatever other implement comes readily to mind. All are comparable to *fuck you!*. See also *stick it* (or *stuff it*), *etc.* in ASS.

urchin. A scamp, waif, or street arab, usually dirty and raggedy as well as mischievous. "The tone of insolent superiority assumed by even the gutter urchins over their dusky companions" (Fanny Kemble, *Journal of a Residence on a Georgia Plantation in 1838–39*, 1863).

An *urchin* originally was a hedgehog. The word entered English in the fourteenth century, a translation of the Norman French *herichon*. As time went on, it was applied also to elves and goblins (from the belief that they could turn into hedgehogs), to sea urchins (once also called "sea hedgehogs" on account of their spines), and to prickly people of various sorts, including hunchbacks, roguish youngsters, ugly women, and bad-tempered girls.

V

vampire. A person who preys upon others; specifically, a woman who ruins men with her seductive wiles. "She was plainly a vampire, an evil woman, and he was her dupe" (Arnold Bennett, *Vanguard*, 1928).

Vampire is another exception to the rule that animal words become pejorative when applied to people. In this case, as with PARASITE and SHARK, the term initially referred to humans—or humanoids, to be precise. It was the vampire of folklore, a reanimated corpse that sustains itself by sucking blood from sleeping people, that inspired the name of the vampire bat. The word probably derives from the Turkish *uber*, witch, but comes immediately from Hungary, appearing first in English in the accounts of visitors to the Continent during the opening decades of the eighteenth century. The horrific idea was developed fictionally in the next century, beginning with Johann Ludwig Treck's "Wake Not the Dead" and culminating with Bram Stoker's *Dracula* (1897), the latter written around the real-life exploits of Prince Vlad Tepes, who was not actually a vampire but—just as bad—was known to citizens of Wallachia and Transylvania in the fifteenth century as "The Impaler."

In our own time, the word has been used in abbreviated form as both noun and verb, *a vamp* being an unscrupulous seductress and *to vamp* describing her manner of accomplishing her wicked ways. The type specimen of the *vamp* in the early twentieth century was Theda Bara (*née* Theodosia Goodman, 1890–1955), who achieved overnight notoriety in her first starring role, *A Fool There Was* (1915), a film based on Rudyard Kipling's poem "The Vampire." See also BLOODSUCKER and LEECH.

vandal. One who destroys or defaces another's property, from the name of the German tribe that invaded western Europe and northern Africa in the fourth and fifth centuries, plundering Rome in 455. The Vandals were a rough lot, no doubt, but the specific charge against them, implicit in our present use of their tribal name, may be false: "There does not seem to be in the story of the capture of Rome by the Vandals any justification for the charge of wilful and objectless destruction of public buildings which is implied in the word 'vandalism.' It is probable that this charge grew out of the fierce persecution which was carried on by [the Vandal king] Gaiseric and his son against the Catholic Christians, and which is the darkest stain on their characters" (*Encyclopaedia Britannica*, Thirteenth Edition, 1926). See also BARBARIAN.

varlet. Originally a page or groom, and a term of abusive address from the sixteenth to the nineteenth centuries, comparable to KNAVE and VILLAIN. The word is a variant of *valet* and comes from the Latin *vassus*, servant, which also produced *vassal*. For Shakespeare, the derogatory *varlet* also had a specialized meaning, as exemplified by the following exchange from *Troilus and Cressida* (1601–02):

THERSITES: Thou art thought to be Achilles' male varlet.
PATROCLUS: Male varlet, you rogue! What's that?
THERSITES: Why, his masculine whore.

vegetable. A dull or brain-damaged person; on college campuses, the epithet may be shortened to *veggie* (which also stands for vegetarian). In hospitals, a *vegetable* is a person unable to care for himself, or herself, usually because of a stroke.

Doctors and other providers of medical care isolate themselves from suffering by referring to incapacitated patients as *vegetables*—or *potatoes, carrots, cucumbers,* and so on. Collectively, such patients are said to constitute a *vegetable garden, rose garden, potato patch,* etc. The attendant who changes their intravenous feeding bottles is said to *water the garden* (C. J. Scheiner, "Common Patient-Directed Pejoratives Used by Medical Personnel," *Maledicta,* 1978).

The metaphor also applies outside hospital precincts. For example, Molly Ivins, columnist for the Dallas *Times-Herald,* has "a gift for the telling phrase, as in her line about the congressman who, if he were any dumber, would have to be watered twice a day" (*Columbia Journalism Review,* 11-12/83). The use of vegetable metaphors for apparent stupidity is in keeping with the negative values associated with many foods; see also BALONEY and the many food terms, such as *cabbagehead,* in BLOCKHEAD.

vermin. One or more noxious individuals; from at least the sixteenth century. "A coronation all unknown / To Europe's royal vermin" (Thomas Babington Macaulay, in George Trevelyan, *The Life and Letters of Lord Macaulay,* 1876).

In the United States, frontiersmen frequently used the variant *varmint,* especially when referring to Indians, who thereby were put in a class with pests to be exterminated, e.g., "We threw up a work of blocks, to keep the ravenous varmints from handling our scalps" (James Fenimore Cooper, *The Last of the Mohicans,* 1826). Human *varmints* have not yet been totally wiped out. Thus, quoting Mrs. Myrtle Clare, postmistress of Holcomb, Kansas: "All neighbors are rattlesnakes. Varmints looking for a chance to slam the door in your face" (Truman Capote, *In Cold Blood,* 1965). See also INSECT and RATTLESNAKE.

vice admiral of the narrow seas. A military rank rarely encountered in our own effete age, but worthy of preservation as a linguistic artifact of a less inhibited time; as explained by Captain Francis Grose, the *vice admiral, etc.* is "A drunken man that pisses under the table into his companions' shoes" (*A Classical Dictionary of the Vulgar Tongue,* 1796).

villain. A despicable person, a SCOUNDREL; the eternal antihero. (Boo! Hiss!) This is another rural word that has fallen on hard times. A *villain* or *veillein* originally was an agricultural worker, a serf, from the Latin *villa,* house, meaning the manor to which he was attached. The term has been used in a disparaging sense since at least the early fourteenth century and its flavor has not changed a great deal over the last several hundred years. For example, Randle Cotgrave became positively agitated when defining this epithet in his French-English dictionary of 1611: "*vilain:* a villaine, slave, bondman, servile tenant. Hence also, a churl, carle, boore, clown; and, a miser, micher, pinchpenny, pennyfather; and, a knave, rascall, varlet, filthie fellow; any base-humored, ill-born, and worse-bred hind, cullion, or clusterfist." For more about rural words, see HICK.

viper. A venomous, treacherous person, a villain. "I want words sufficient to express thy viperous Treasons. . . . There never lived a viler viper upon the face of the earth than thou" (Sir Edward Coke, as attorney general, prosecuting Sir Walter Raleigh, November 1603). This attack was so outrageous that it built up sympathy for Raleigh, whose sentence of death was deferred for another fifteen years. (Another memorable line of Coke's: "Thou hast an English face, but a Spanish heart.") See also THOU.

The *viper* metaphor was a popular one of the period, and it worked on two levels. Not only was the viper, or ADDER, a poisonous snake (the only one in Great Britain) but fable had it that vipers were born by eating their way out of their mother, killing her in the process. (*Viper* comes from the Latin *vivus*, living + *parere*, to bring forth.)

Viper also can be used in a generalized malignant sense: "But when he [John the Baptist] saw many of the Pharisees and Sad'-du-cees come to his baptism, he said unto them, O generation of vipers, who hath warned you to flee from the wrath to come?" (*Matthew*, 3:7).

Such *vipers* still exist, e.g., in a story filed from Peking: "A commentary in the [*People's Daily*] called for 'absolutely no leniency' prosecuting the human 'vipers and scorpions' who trafficked in women" (*New York Times*, 7/28/83). See also SNAKE.

virago. A bold, brassy, bad-tempered woman. *Virago* comes from the Latin *vir*, man, and was not originally a term of disparagement, but simply the female equivalent of *vir*. Thus, in the Wyclif translation of the Bible (1388), Adam says of Eve that she shall "be clepid virago, for she is takun of man" (*Genesis*, 2:23). In particular, a *virago* might be a strong, heroic woman—a female warrior or amazon. This sense was still extant in the early nineteenth century, e.g., "Did not the same virago boast that she had a Cavalry Regiment, whereof neither horse nor man could be injured" (Thomas Carlyle, *Sartor Resartus*, 1831). The word also has been used pejoratively since the fourteenth century to denote a loudmouthed female scold, however. And—as is usually the case, especially with feminine terms (e.g., GIRL, HARLOT, and HUSSY)—the bad meanings have displaced the good ones. See also SHREW.

virgin. A person who has not had sexual intercourse, especially a girl or woman, but not without other meanings, e.g., in the U.S. Army in World War II, a soldier who had not experienced the joys of V.D.

Although used commonly in churches, the term was taboo in secular contexts for a great many years. As H. L. Mencken reported: "Back in 1916 even *virgin* was a forbidden word, at least in Philadelphia. On February 26 of that year a one-act play of mine, 'The Artist,' was presented at the Little Theatre, and the same day the *Public Ledger* printed specimens of the dialogue. One of the characters was called 'A Virgin,' but the *Ledger* preferred 'A Young Girl'" (*The American Language*, 1937).

This taboo continued more or less intact, so to speak, until the 1950s, the big breakthrough coming in 1953 with the release of *The Moon Is Blue*, a film in which not only *virgin* but—horrors—*seduce* actually was mentioned out loud. Thanks to such shocking language, this otherwise tame little comedy was denied a seal of approval under the Motion Picture Production Code, was condemned by the Roman Catholic Legion of Decency, was banned in a number of cities, and became a box-office hit as moviegoers lined up to have their ears assaulted by the formerly forbidden words. The producer, Otto Preminger, sued several local censorship boards, and the U.S. Supreme Court eventually held that they could not prevent the film from being shown. This decision, together with an earlier one involving Roberto Rossellini's *L'Amore* (1948), in which the court held that a film could not be banned for "sacrilege," extended the protection of the First Amendment to the movies, thereby leading to the demolition of the nationwide film-censorship apparatus.

See also CHERRY.

vixen. A quarrelsome woman, a SHREW, perhaps from the fierceness of the she-fox with cubs. The term has been applied to female foxes (from the Anglo-Saxon *fyxe*, the feminine of "fox") since the fifteenth century and to female humans since the sixteenth. Thus, using an older spelling and heaping one term of abuse upon another: "She is a foole, a nasty queane, a slut, a fixen, a scolde" (Robert Burton, *The Anatomy of Melancholy*, 1621). See also FOX.

voodoo. Magical, with strong overtones of artful deception, as in George Bush's characterization (1980) of Ronald Reagan's announced intention to balance the national budget while cutting taxes as "voodoo economics"—a phrase that seems to have attained a permanent life of its own, e.g., speaking of salary negotiations with professional baseball players: "My outlook depends on how realistically they will assess our economic problems. If they continue to say it's voodoo economics, we have a real problem" (Lee MacPhail, spokesman for the major league baseball team owners, *New York Times*, 6/13/85).

Voodoo, the religion, also called *vodun*, is a West African word, probably from the Ewe *vodū*, demon. An American variant is *hoodoo*, with various meanings: to bring bad luck, bad luck itself, or the bearer of same. "The prospect of pleasing his party and at the same time escaping a hoodoo must be irresistibly attractive" (*New York Sun*, 3/20/1889). See also JINX and ZOMBIE.

vulgar. Boorish, offensive, smutty; from the Latin *vulgus*, the common people, and yet another class-conscious epithet; see also BOURGEOIS and PLEBEIAN.

Vulgar originally (from the fourteenth century) referred to that which was common or ordinary, as in *vulgar fractions*, meaning common ones as opposed to decimals; the *vulgar era*, meaning the Christian era; and *vulgar language*, meaning the language that everyone spoke, the vernacular. (Before anyone spoke English, the vernacular was Latin, as in the *Vulgate*, the version of the Bible—still the authorized version of the Roman Catholic Church—that Saint Jerome translated from Greek and Hebrew sources, starting A.D. 382.) In the sixteenth century, the word began to be applied in English to the lower classes, the *vulgar people*, and thanks to this association, within a hundred years the present senses of coarseness and offensiveness began to evolve.

Of course, vulgarity, like obscenity, is relative. Thus, Supreme Court Justice John Paul Stevens, Taking note of an earlier opinion in which it was pointed out that a "nuisance may be merely a right thing in a wrong place—like a pig in the parlor instead of the barnyard," concluded that "Vulgar language, like vulgar animals, may be acceptable in some contexts and intolerable in others" (dissent, *Bethel School District No. 403 v. Fraser*, 1986). See also FUCK for more on the Bethel-Fraser case.

vulture. A rapacious person; one who preys upon others. This sense of the word is dated to 1603 in the *OED* and it remains current: " 'Vultures' he [Bernhard Goetz] said, glaring at a group of reporters who had asked him if he wanted to say anything" (*New York Times*, 1/5/85). *Vulture* has enjoyed other specialized uses. In the jazz subculture of the 1940s, a *vulture* was a sexually aggressive woman, and those who flock to museums and concerts today are, of course, *culture vultures*. See also BUZZARD.

W

wacko (whacko). Crazy, weird, eccentric. "During his first term [1978–82] at City Hall, the Mayor [Edward I. Koch, of New York] so regularly denounced people he disapproved of as 'wackos'—sometimes spelled 'whackos'—that a reporter for the *News* asked some editors of dictionaries of American slang whether this apparent coinage of a new word might win Koch a footnote in their next editions" (*New Yorker*, 4/11/83).

The mayor himself recalled first using the word during the eleven-day transit strike of 1980, when encountering hecklers among the New Yorkers who were walking, jogging, and bicycling to work. "It was against this background of rugged self-confidence that I reintroduced 'wacko' into the Gotham lexicon . . . I have always loved hecklers and used them well. But when I discovered 'wacko,' I added a new dimension to my repertoire of antiheckler devices" (Koch, *Mayor: An Autobiography*, 1984). As Hizzoner acknowledged, the word was not coined by him. For example, speaking of professional basketball player Neal Walk: "[He] Went whacko a couple of years ago and hasn't been worth much as a ball player since" (Zander Hollander, *The Complete Book of Pro Basketball*, 1977).

Wacko and *wacky* come from *wacky* and *whacky*, or, in full, *wicky-wacky* and *whacky-brained*. The basic *whacky* is included in *Slang and its Analogues* (J. S. Farmer and W. E. Henley, 1904), but without citations. The sense of craziness probably derives from the way people's brains are scrambled when they are *whacked* too often on the head. (Note that *to be wacked out* is criminal slang for "to be killed.") The idea of craziness also may be reinforced by *out of whack*, meaning "out of order," which in turn derives from *whack*, meaning a share or portion of a larger amount (*to whack up* = to divide). At the same time, there is a subliminal sexual innuendo here, the *whack* that is a vigorous blow also having given rise to *whack it up*, British slang from ca. 1900 for copulation, and *whack off*, twentieth-century American slang for masturbation, an activity which, according to tradition, inevitably causes the self-abuser to go insane or, as they say, *whacky*. See also JERK and MAD.

wang (whang, whanger). The penis. "Q: Who had the first computers? A: Adam and Eve. She had an Apple and he had a Wang" (schoolyard humor, New York City, 1984). The penile *wang*, apparently a twentieth-century Americanism, probably derives from *whang*, a blow or whack, the semantic conjunction of sex, violence, and anatomy being quite common; see PRICK.

warped. Crazy, mentally twisted; perverted; distorted. "A good sort of man, though most ridiculously warped in his political principles" (Tobias Smollett, *Humphry Clinker*, 1771). The image comes from weaving, the *warp* of a fabric being the threads that run lengthwise in a loom, and which usually are twisted more tightly than the threads of the weft, or woof, at right angles to them. See also CRAZY and TWISTED.

wasp. An irascible person, who might—or might not—also be a WASP, i.e., a White Anglo-Saxon Protestant, or a White Southern Appalachian Protestant, or a member of the Women's Airforce Service Pilots (they ferried airplanes in World War II), or even one of the Wasp, a rock group, which denies that its name is an acronym for We Are Sexual Perverts.

Wasp and the adjective *waspish* usually are applied to those who have a talent for making stinging comments. Thus Alexander Pope was known to those he satirized as The Wicked Wasp of Twickenham, after the villa near London to which he moved in 1719. (See also NAMBY-PAMBY.)

As a general term of contempt, *wasp* is very old. For example, Aristophanes equipped with stings the doddering old men that comprise the chorus of *The Wasps* 422 B.C.). He might have used another metaphor if he had known that among flying wasps only the females have stings. Increasing knowledge of biology gradually led to semantic change, as evidenced by Captain Francis Grose's definition of *wasp*: "An infected prostitute, who like a wasp carries a sting in her tail" (*A Classical Dictionary of the Vulgar Tongue*, 1796).

The modern White Anglo-Saxon Protestant *WASP* also appears frequently in a derogatory sense, which is hardly surprising, considering that this once dominant group has been reduced to minority status, making its members fair game for ethnic slurs, along with everyone else. The term seems to have started off as a statistician's descriptive acronym (*OED*, 1962), but it soon became a buzz word among those who disliked what they perceived as the *WASP* (or *Wasp*) Establishment. For example, discussing Edward I. Koch's *Mayor: An Autobiography* (1984), Sydney H. Schanberg noted: "people are not identified by their character but as 'WASP' or 'Wall Street' or as 'high-toned Jews who look down on my Polish-Jewish antecedents.' (One man gets a multiple putdown as 'a Harvard-educated WASP turned Buddhist.')" (*New York Times*, 1/21/84). See also JAP, WHITEY, and YANKEE.

weak- (brained, headed, hearted, kneed, minded, willed, etc.). Different forms of stupidity and timidity, typically due to irresolution, tenderness of sensibilities, and faintness of nerve. *Weak-* has served as a disparaging prefix since at least the sixteenth century. "A weak-headed prince, who neither had a right to give his crown, nor a brain to know what he was doing" (Daniel Defoe, *The Consolidator*, 1705). "There is today a well-armed intellectual and political lobby that contends that Vietnam could have been won were it not for the weak-kneed media and their dovish handmaidens in Congress" (John R. MacArthur, *New York Times*, 2/24/85). See also BLOCKHEAD, FOOL, and ULTRA-.

weak sister. A weak person, especially a man who is timid, ineffectual, and unreliable as well as puny. "If the president of the college had asked me what I thought about Dewey McLean, I'd say he's a weak sister" (Dr. Luis W. Alvarez, critiquing a fellow academic, *New York Times*, 1/19/88). Like the foregoing WEAK-constructions, this expression has been around for a while, e.g., "G. W. Swerzy . . . is a 'weak sister' and a rather 'bad egg' " (*San Francisco Call*, 5/1/1857). The original context was religious, with *weak brother* (from 1525), *weak sister*, and *weak(er) brethren* having been used for many years to refer to believers whose faith was not solidly based. See also SISSY.

weasel. A sneaky fellow; one who *weasels out* of obligations; specifically, in prison parlance, an informer or RAT. "A lying weasel like you couldn't resist the chance" (Superman to Lex Luthor, *Superman II*, film, 1980).

The bad reputation of weasels stems from their ability to sneak into hen houses at night and suck eggs. Shakespeare referred to this in *Henry V* (1599): "For once the Eagle England being in prey, To her unguarded nest the weasel Scot Comes sneaking, and so sucks her princely eggs . . . "

Weasels, the world over, seem to be the same. Thus, just before President Ronald Reagan went to China in April, 1984, a clandestine Soviet radio station, broadcasting in Chinese, compared Reagan's visit to "the weasel going to pay his respects to the hen," this being a Chinese proverb for treachery (*New York Times*, 5/7/84).

The affection of weasels for hens' eggs also resulted in *weasel words*, which are bywords for ambiguous words, typically as uttered by politicians. The phrase's popularity dates to its use by Theodore Roosevelt in a 1916 speech attacking Woodrow Wilson's policies. TR put it this way: "You can have universal training or you can have voluntary training, but when you use the word *voluntary* to qualify the word *universal*, you are using a weasel word; it has sucked all the meaning out of *universal* The two words flatly contradict each other."

Finally, there is the weasel that goes pop in the nursery rhyme.

> All around the cobbler's bench
> The monkey chased the weasel.
> The monkey thought it was all in fun.
> Pop goes the weasel!

Various interpretations of this verse have been offered. One theory is that the *weasel* was an instrument used by cobblers (or tailors; authorities differ) that was regularly *popped*, or pawned, to pay for Friday night carousing. This explanation fits well with the nineteenth-century variant (attributed to W. R. Mandale in *The Oxford Dictionary of Quotations*):

> Up and down the City Road,
> In and out the Eagle.
> That's the way the money goes—
> Pop goes the weasel!

There is an erotic undercurrent here, however. Pop Goes the Weasel also is the name of a dance, which probably predates the song. In the dance, done as a square dance in the United States and a longways dance in England (Warwickshire), it is the woman who is "popped" under the raised arms of other dancers as she progresses from one couple to another until she rejoins her partner and they are "popped" together. In this context, the rhyme begins to look much less innocent, since *monkey* is symbolic of lechery in general and the vulva in particular. In this reading, then, the sneaky *weasel* that does the "popping" probably is not a tradesman's implement, though it might be described as a "tool." See also MONKEY.

weenie (weeney, weeny, weinie, wienie). A student who is despised for being diligent, as in the following exchange from the *Doonesbury* comic strip: "You're submitting your roommate as your psychology project?" "Yes, as an archetype weeny in the age of Reagan" (Gary Trudeau, *Litchfield County* [Connecticut] *Times*, 4/23/86).

Weenie, dating at least to the 1950s, probably derives from *weeny*, meaning a girl or girlish man (from 1929), in turn from *weeny*, meaning a child (from 1844), and ultimately from *weeny*, meaning something small (1790). There are other possibilities, however, including the *weenie* that is a small frankfurter (from *wiener-wurst*) and the *weenie* that is childspeak for the penis.

Weenie is only one of a number of similar terms for the industrious student (who, not so incidentally, makes lazier students look bad). The epithets vary over time and from one part of the country to another, e.g., "At San Diego State University, a flattering term for a hard student is a 'study bunny'; less so is 'squid' [a squirter of ink]. At the University of California at Santa Cruz, when 'nerds' travel in pairs they are referred to as 'Elroy and Melvin.' If they threw a party, the chances are it would be 'fully geeking.' In the East, at Yale, such characters are referred to as 'weenies,' and a carrel at the library is a 'weenie bin' " (*New York Times*, 4/12/87). Other synonyms include *pencil geek, grind, grub,* and *throat* (from "cutthroat," this being the kind of student who tears pages out of library books to prevent class-mates from reading them). See also TWEEB, WONK, and the *bookworm* in WORM.

weirdo (weirdie). A very odd fellow, often a crazy person or one with particularly perverse tastes. "Very interesting married young cpl in 30s seek attr couples versatile gals extra select males for discreet friendship and swinging fun. No fatties weirdos" (*Ace*, undated, ca., 1976).

Weird originally meant "destiny," and *the weird sisters* who appear in *Macbeth* (1606) once were the Fates, not witches. The word had practically dropped out of English when Shakespeare revived it, and its modern senses of the supernatural, and of fantastic, odd, or strange appearance or behavior, stem from his use of the term in this play. Shakespeare also is responsible for converting what had been a noun into an adjective. See also CREEP and MAD.

welsh. As a verb, to fail to fulfill an obligation; specifically, to decline to pay a bet that one has lost. As an adjective, a deprecatory modifier comparable to IRISH and SCOTCH.

The cheating sense arose in the mid-nineteenth century in sporting circles, particularly at racetracks, where bookmakers who took bets and then absconded were known as *welshers* or *welchers*. Presumably, some of them came from Wales, long regarded by the English as the home of thieves (see *Taffy* in PADDY). The term has been used to characterize the breaking of all sorts of promises since at least the 1930s, with the old *welch* spelling still being used occasionally, e.g., "When the brothers were captured on a bank raid, the British government welched on them, dropped them like a hot penny" (*Socialist Worker*, 11/2/74). Or, more simply and also more provocatively: "Raquel Welched" (graffito, in *American Speech*, Fall 1980). The adjectival form of *welsh* dates to the sixteenth century. Herewith, a selection of *welsh* phrases, a few of which remain current:

welsh ambassador. A cuckoo or an owl, two birds with loud, monotonous calls. "Thy Sound is like the cuckowe, the welch Embassador" (Thomas Middleton, *A Trick to Catch the Old-One*, 1607).

welsh comb. "The thumb and four fingers" (Captain Francis Grose, *A Classical Dictionary of the Vulgar Tongue,* 1796). "Dressed and welshcombed, I pocketed my luggage and went downstairs" (Anthony Burgess, *MF,* 1971).

welsh cricket. A louse, also a tailor, i.e., a *prick-louse;* see LOUSE.

welsh diamond. Rock crystal; the same as *Irish diamond.*

welsh ejectment. "To unroof the house, a method practised by landlords in Wales to eject a bad tenant" ("A Member of the Whip Club," *Lexicon Balatronicum,* 1811).

welsh fiddle. The itch caused by mites; also called the *Scotch fiddle.*

welsh mile. "Like a Welch mile, long and narrow. His story is like a Welch mile, long and tedious" (Grose, *op. cit.*).

welsh parsley. A hangman's noose. "This . . . Rascal deserves . . . To dance in Hemp . . . Lets choke him with Welch Parsley" (Thomas Randolph, *Hey for Honesty,* 1651).

welsh rabbit. Toasted bread and cheese; from the first quarter of the eighteenth century and from the reported fondness of the Welsh for cheese; sometimes euphemized on menus as *rarebit,* which is, technically, a non-word.

Welsh, by the way, is the name that the English hung on the inhabitants of Wales. It comes from the Anglo-Saxon *wealh,* (foreigner or SLAVE), a root that also helps form such words as *Cornwall, Wallace, Walloon, Walsh,* and *walnut.* The Welsh themselves prefer their ancient name, *Cymry* (compatriot). See also DUTCH.

wench. A young woman, but with many low associations. Thus, Algernon Charles Swinburne attacked Walt Whitman (whom he had earlier admired): "Mr. Whitman's Venus is a Hottentot wench under the influence of cantharides [Spanish fly] and adulterated rum" (*Whitmania: Studies in Prose and Poetry,* 1894). See also HOTTENTOT.

Wench, from the ninth-century *wenchel,* a child of either sex, was applied first to young girls, then to rustic ones, servants, and strumpets (a common complex of meanings; see GIRL). It also was the usual term for a black female slave (analogous to the male BUCK in America during the eighteenth and nineteenth centuries, e.g., "Richard Peronneau, a free Negro carpenter, gives this public notice . . . not to trust his wife, a free wench named Nancy, a mulatto, on his account . . . as she has eloped from him" (personal ad, *South Carolina Gazette,* 10/3/1771, in *American Speech,* 12/53).

Other *wenches* of the past include *the light-heeled wench,* "who is apt, by the flying up of her heels, to fall flat on her back," and *the Athanasian wench,* "a forward girl, ready to oblige every man that shall ask her" (Captain Francis Grose, *A Classical Dictionary of the Vulgar Tongue,* 1796). The second of these *wenches,* by the way, has a religious background, the reference being to the first words of the Athanasian creed, *quincunque vult* (whoever desires). See also ROUND-HEELS and WHORE.

wetback. An illegal immigrant from Mexico to the United States. "The use of *wet,* as in *wet cattle* and *wet stock,* to describe illegal or subrosa entry in the United States from Mexico dates from frontier times. The extension of *wet* to Mexican migrant labor began with head tax and visa requirements set up in 1924" (Atcheson L. Hench, *American Speech,* 2/61).

The allusion is to crossing the Rio Grande, of course. Those with enough money may avoid getting their backs wet, or anything else for that matter, by hiring someone to carry them across; see COYOTE.

The term has been used in extended senses. Thus, in a remark for which he later felt compelled to apologize, Senator Ernest F. Hollings (Democrat, South Carolina) asserted that he did poorly in a presidential preference poll of Iowa Democrats because "You had wetbacks from California that came in here for [California Senator Alan] Cranston" (AP, 10/12/83). See also MEXICAN.

wet blanket. Someone or something that spoils an occasion or ruins the fun for others; a person so gloomy that he depresses others; a *party pooper*, not necessarily limited to social gatherings, e.g., "Party leaders said the shake-up had thrown a 'wet blanket' on the momentum of the Mondale campaign" (*New York Times*, 7/16/84). The figurative use of the phrase has been dated to the eighteenth century, and otherwise festive gatherings have been dampened by *wet blankets* for well over a hundred years. See also BORE, DRIP, DROOP, DUD, KVETCH, and POOP.

whelp. A young person, especially an insolent one; from the fourteenth century. Thus, speaking of Thomas Chatterton, the young poet who had the nerve to pass off his work as that of a fifteenth-century monk: "This is the most extraordinary young man that has encountered my knowledge. It is wonderful how the whelp has written such things" (Samuel Johnson, 4/29/1776, in Boswell's *Life of Johnson*, 1791). See also CUB and PUPPY.

whipper-snapper. A small person, especially a saucy one; an insignificant fellow. "Silence, whipper-snapper! The beneficient Oz has every intention of granting your request" (*The Wizard of Oz*, film, 1939). An extension of *whip snapper*, the term has been dated to the seventeenth century. It was modeled on *snipper-snapper*, an insignificant but nevertheless conceited young man, from the fifteenth century. "Thou'rt a prick-eared foist . . . a knack, a snipper-snapper!" (John Ford, *The Fancies, Chast and Noble*, 1638). See also MIDGET.

white, to speak. To speak like a white man. "One of the most intolerant linguistic insults on record is the admonition 'Speak white!' occasionally used by Canadian English speakers to their French-speaking fellow nationals" (Mario Pei, *The Story of Language*, 1965).

white feather, to show the. To act in a cowardly manner. The expression dates at least to the eighteenth century. As explained by Captain Francis Grose: "He has a white feather; he is a coward: an allusion to a game cock, where having a white feather is a proof he is not of the true game breed" (*A Classical Dictionary of the Vulgar Tongue*, 1785). See also COWARD and FEATHERWEIGHT.

whitey (whitie, whity). A Caucasian; also a collective epithet. "But the term 'power structure' when translated down to the level of the street becomes the term 'whitey'—and 'whitey' in the Negro ghetto is as contemptuous as 'nigger' is in a Southern village" (Theodore H. White [sic], *The Making of the President 1964*, 1965).

In a white-dominated culture, *white* generally signifies that which is good, pure, innocent, honorable, and otherwise beyond reproach, as in "You've behaved to me like a white man from the start" (William Dean Howells, *A Woman's Reason*, 1883). The diminutive *whitey* converts the word into an attack term, however, with the earliest example in the racial sense in the *OED* coming from 1828 and, of all places, Australia: "The instant *blacky* perceives *whity* beating a retreat, he vociferates after him—'Go along, you dam rascal'" (Peter Cunningham, *Two Years in New South Wales*). In the United States, the usual form for many years (from the 1830s at least) was *white*, but in the explicitly disparaging phrases, *white trash* and POOR WHITE TRASH, both of which seem to have originated among Southern black slaves. Among American blacks, *whitey* and *white meat* also have had specialized meanings, designating Caucasian women, especially when considered as sexual objects. The *whitey* form was popularized during the civil strife of the 1960s, probably as a result of the preaching of the Black Muslims about *white devils*, but the term had merely been lying dormant, e.g., from the preceding decade: "A white-skinned girl . . . was called 'Whitey cockroach!'" (Samuel Selvon, *A Brighter Sun*, 1952).

Other colorful terms that blacks have used for whites include *bright skin, chalk, gray, milk, pale, paleface* (attributed to the American Indian but popularized by a non-Indian, James Fenimore Cooper, in *The Last of the Mohicans*, 1826, and now used mainly by black homosexuals to designate white homosexuals), and *pink* (as distinguished, sometimes barely, from *pink-toes*, a light-skinned black woman). For more on the complicated subject of skin coloring, see NEGRO, and for other characterizations of white people, continue with ANN, BUCKRA(H), CHARLIE, HONKY, OFAY, PADDY, PECKERWOOD, REDNECK, SPOOK (a word that goes both ways), TACKY, and WASP.

whore. A person who engages in promiscuous sexual intercourse, usually a woman and usually for hire; as a verb, to act this way; in an extended sense, one who sells his or her name or abilities to promote the causes of others. "My dear Sir, never accustom your mind to mingle virtue and vice. The woman's a whore, and there's an end on't" (Samuel Johnson, 5/7/1773, to James Boswell, who had had the temerity to defend the behavior of Lady Diana, eldest daughter of the Duke of Marlborough, who married Topham Beauclerk, a great grandson of Charles II and Nell Gwyn, two days after being divorced, by Act of Parliament, from Viscount Bolingbroke, in Boswell, *The Life of Samuel Johnson, LL.D.*, 1791). "And now that [Bill Cosby's] pitched for Pan Am, and most recently signed a major contract with Ford, he threatens to replace Arthur Godfrey as the 'whore' of endorsers" (*MORE*, 5/77).

Whore is one of the principal makers of society's sexual and linguistic hang-ups. Barred for many years from polite conversations and public print, the term's traditional shock value is indicated by the larger number of euphemistic substitutes that have been devised for it. Among them: *B-girl, call girl, courtesan, fallen woman, harlot, hooker, hoor* (an aural euphemism), *hustler, lady of the night, painted woman, prostitute, pure* (and *purest pure*), *sporting girl, streetwalker,* TRAMP, *woman of the town,* and *working woman,* among many, many others. But *whore* was not always considered such a terrible word. Dated to the eleventh century, it comes from the Anglo-Saxon (or Old English, as linguists prefer to call it) *hōre,* and is cognate to the Latin *carus,* dear. Possibly, it arose as a euphemism for some other term, so "bad" that it never entered humanity's literary record.

Until the end of the seventeenth century, *whore* was used commonly. Thus, when an unruly crowd surrounded her carriage in 1681, thinking it belonged to the king's Roman Catholic mistress, the Dutchess of Portsmouth, Topham Beauclerk's great-grandma calmed the citizens, saying "Pray, good people, be civil. I am the Protestant whore." The word also appears frequently in the works of Shakespeare and other writers of the period, as well as in the King James Version of the Bible (1611), e.g., "For a whore is a deep ditch; and a strange woman is a narrow pit"

(*Proverbs*, 23:27) and "the great whore that sitteth upon many waters" (*Revelations*, 17:1).

In the eighteenth century, however, this was one of the words (see also ASS) that people began to be nervous about using. As Alexander Pope put it: "I loathe a whore and startle at the name" (*January and May*, 1709). Later writers often were startled enough to dash out the term, as did Horace Walpole: "He would have piqued himself on calling the Pope the w---e of Babylon" (letter to Sir Horace Mann, 10/3/1743). Lord Chesterfield also made an extremely fine distinction at about this time, blanking out the term in literary-historical context, when referring to a quarrel between Achilles and Agamemnon "about a w---e," and then, in the very same letter, spelling the word in full in the religious context, explaining to his son that "The good Protestant conviction that the Pope is both Antichrist and the Whore of Babylon, is a more effectual preservative in this country against Popery than all the solid and unanswerable arguments of [William] Chillingworth" (2/7/1749). Dr. Johnson, on the other hand, pulled no punches when assessing the earl's letters to his son, observing that "they teach the morals of a whore, and the manners of a dancing master" (1754, in Boswell's *Life of Johnson*, 1791).

The taboo on *whore* grew stronger in the following century. Thus, Noah Webster dropped every *whore* out of the Bible when he produced a version for use by families in 1833, four years before Victoria ascended the throne. In Webster's text, the person that "sitteth upon the many waters" in *Revelations* became "the great harlot." In other cases, he substituted *lewd* and *lewd woman*, while changing *whoredom* to *carnal connection, idolatries, impurities, prostitution, lewd deeds*, and so on. See also LEWD.

The silence of the *Oxford English Dictionary* on the subject also is noteworthy: The relevant section (W–wo, 1922–27) includes not a single example of the word's use between 1818 and 1894. It was during this period, of course, that *abandoned woman, one of the frail sisterhood, unfortunate*, and similar Victoriana flowered. In one theatrical company of the time, it is reported that the confrontation between Othello and Desdemona in Act IV, Scene 2, was known as the "notta" because the line "What, not a whore?" was always broken off "before the last, unspeakable word" (Benedict Nightingale, *New York Times*, 1/29/84).

Concern about *whore* was so great that it extended to some of the word's softer synonyms. For example—a curious case of self-bowdlerization, noted by Noel Perrin in *Dr. Bowdler's Legacy* (1969)—Thomas De Quincy changed "prostitute" to "the outcasts and pariahs of our female population" when he produced a new edition in 1856 of *The Confessions of an English Opium-Eater* (1822). Then there was the anonymous editor of Alexander Pope's poems (Edinburgh, 1859), who watered down the opening verse of "A Farewell to London" (1715) from

> Dear, damn'd, distracting town, farewell!
> Thy fools no more I'll tease:
> This year in peace, ye Critics dwell,
> Ye Harlots, sleep at ease!

to

> Dear, droll [sic] distracting town, farewell!
> Thy fools no more I'll tease:
> This year in peace, ye Critics dwell.
> Ye Nobles sleep at ease!

Delicacy continued to be the rule until well into our own century. Thus, when John Ford's *'Tis Pity She's a Whore* (1633) was revived in New York City in 1930, *The New York Times* refused to print the title in full, reducing it to *'Tis Pity.* By contrast, the *Times* boldly printed (albeit in small type) the cast of characters of Sean O'Casey's *Within the Gates,* including the one called "The Young Whore," when the play opened in New York in 1934, and the *Herald-Tribune,* though omitting the cast, actually used the word in the third paragraph of its review. Not all of Sin City's newspapers displayed so much nerve, however. The *Sun* resorted to "The Young Prostitute," the *World-Telegram* to "The Young Harlot," and the *American* to "A Young Girl Who Has Gone Astray" (all originally noted by Robert Benchley, *New Yorker,* 11/3/34). It was at about this time, too, that *whore* finished with two more votes than BASTARD in a ranking of taboo words by students at Emory University; see BELCH for the grim details.

In informal situations, more leeway was allowed, even in the 1930s, e.g., the retort of a tugboat master on the Thames when a young gentleman on a pleasure outing complained that the tug had broken one of his oars: "Oh, I did, did I, Charley? And talking of oars, 'ow's your sister?" (Robert Graves, *The Future of Swearing and Improper Language,* 1936). This is the same vein that Dorothy Parker worked when she produced one of the more memorable Round Table luncheon lines in the '30s: "You can lead a horticulture, but you can't make her think." And a technical question from a slightly later period (the 1950s): "Do you know the difference between a vitamin and a hormone?" Answer: "You can make a vitamin." But note that even in these examples, the risque word on which the joke depends has not been spelled out in all its pristine glory. In the hinterlands, the word still caused difficulty in 1967, when the Performing Arts Company at Michigan State University was required to advertise John Ford's drama of 1633 as *'Tis Pity She's A ___.*

Most (but not all) of the vestiges of the taboo have since faded away. The *Revised Standard Version* of the Bible (1962) still uses "great harlot" in *Revelations,* 17:1, and the people in charge of ads on New York City buses declined to accept one for Carol Hall's musical, *The Best Little Whorehouse in Texas* (1977), which urged the public simply to "Come to the Whorehouse." The *Times,* however, which is always a bellwether when it comes to semantic sensitivity of this sort (see LAY for a recent example of how it blue-pencils ads) has printed the word in many reviews and news accounts. For example, and demonstrating the continuing strength of the term in other societies: " 'Charmouta!' one of the [Israeli] soldiers shouted in Arabic, using the word for 'whore' outside the Abu Shawish Insurance Agency. . . . 'Don't you call me charmouta,' bristled Samir Abu Shawish . . . The word is so insulting to an Arab's honor that he refused later to translate it literally for a foreigner" (1/28/88).

See also BAG, BAT, BAWD, BIMBO, BROAD, CHIPPIE, DOXY, FLOOZIE, GIRL, GROUPIE, HACK, HARLOT, HARRIDAN, HUSSY, JADE, JEZEBEL, LEWD, MADAM, MOLL, MOOSE, PIECE, PUNK, QUAIL, QUEEN, ROUND-HEELS, SCARLET LADY, SLATTERN, SLUR, STRUMPET, TAIL, TART, and WENCH.

whoremonger. Not, as commonly supposed, a pimp or procurer, but one who deals with whores in the sense of being a patron of prostitutes; a fornicator or lecher, e.g., "WHORE-MONGER. A man that keeps more than one mistress. A country gentleman, who kept a female friend, being reproved by the parson of the parish, and styled a whore-monger, asked the parson whether he had a cheese in his house; and being answered in the affirmative, 'Pray,' says he, 'does one cheese make you a cheese-monger?' " ("A Member of the Whip Club," *Lexicon Balatronicum,* 1811).

Although now archaic, if not entirely obsolete, *whoremonger* is of interest here as the leading historic example of the use of *-monger* as a pejorative suffix. Since the sixteenth century, it has signified not just a trader or dealer in a commodity, as *cheesemonger,* COSTERMONGER, *fishmonger,* and *ironmonger,* but a disreputable merchandiser, as in *muttonmonger* (see MUTT), *newsmonger* (Shakespeare has Prince Hal refer to "base newsmongers" in *Henry IV, Part I,* 1596), *rumormonger, scandalmonger, warmonger,* and *wordmonger* (not always contemptuous when applied to dictionary-makers and other harmless DRUDGEs). The negative associations of the suffix are in keeping with the word's origin. It comes from the Latin *mango,* whose standard translation as "salesman" hardly conveys the flavor of the term as it was understood in the sixteenth century. Thus, from the definition of *mango* in a Latin-French dictionary of 1573: "a baude that paynteth and pampereth up boyes, women or servauntes to make them seem the trimmer, thereby to sell them the deerer; an horse coarser [dealer] that pampreth and trimmeth his horses for the same purpose" (P. Cooper, *Thesaurus Linguae Romanae & Britiannica,* in Ernest Weekley, *Words Ancient and Modern,* 1946). See also PEDDLER.

whoreson. An execrable person or thing; literally, a son of a WHORE, i.e., a BASTARD or, the functional equivalent, a SON OF A BITCH. The term was much used from the fourteenth to the eighteenth centuries, frequently as an adjective. Thus, in good Elizabethan style, the Duke of Kent berates Goneril's steward, Oswald: "Thou whoreson zed! Thou unnecessary letter! My lord, if you will give me leave, I will tread this unbolted villain into mortar and daub the walls of a jakes with him" (William Shakespeare, *King Lear,* 1605–06). *Whoreson* is still seen occasionally in print, but only as a conscious archaism. Most of its power had drained away by the early nineteenth century, or else Sir Walter Scott, a greater collector of old words, would not have been able to use it in *Kenilworth* (1816): "Some of his whoreson poetry (I crave your Grace's pardon for such a phrase) has rung in mine ears."

wildcat. A savage, unruly, bad-tempered person, especially a woman, i.e., a spitfire or CATAMOUNT, from the sixteenth century. "But will you woo this wild cat?" (William Shakespeare, *Taming of the Shrew,* ca. 1593). A man may also brag of being a *wildcat* or related to one, as in the boast of the ferocious Mississippi keelboatmen: " 'Whoo-oop! I'm the bloodiest son of a wildcat that lives!' " (Mark Twain, *Life on the Mississippi,* 1883).

The unruliness of the wildcat is associated with illegality and rashness. For example, a *wildcat bank* in the nineteenth century, before passage of the National Banking Act of 1863–64, was a private bank that issued more notes—a.k.a. *wildcat* or *red-dog bills* (or *currency* or *money*)—than it could redeem; a *wildcat mine* is one of little or no value that serves as the bait in defrauding investors; a *wildcat oil well* is a successful but risky one, having been drilled by a *wildcatter* in a region not previously known to have oil; and a *wildcat strike* is an unauthorized walkout.

Summing up the dangers of dealing with a wildcat, albeit a real one, is the Ozark saying, used to characterize a difficult and hazardous enterprise: "It's just as easy as puttin' butter up a wildcat's ass with a hot awl" (from Vance Randolph and George P. Wilson, *Down in the Holler*, 1953). See also CARPETBAGGER, CAT, and RED DOG.

wimp. A weakling, a BORE or DRIP. "A wimp is a weak, ineffectual person, the 97-pound weakling on the beach. If you call someone a wimp, it implies that you, by contrast, are strong" (*New York Times*, 11/4/82).

Wimp probably comes from *whimper* rather than J. Wellington *Wimpy*, Popeye's hamburger-loving friend in the cartoon strip *Thimble Theater*. The term was popularized when an anonymous staffer on *The Boston Globe* changed the headline for an October 15, 1980, editorial about a speech by President Jimmy Carter on his anti-inflation program from "All Must Share the Burden" to "Mush from the Wimp." Previously, the word had circulated mainly among teenagers and college students, with its appearance having been noted in *American Speech* on campuses in California (ca. 1960), Nebraska (1964), and Arkansas (1970–72). One suspects a connection with *wimp*, meaning a young woman or girl, which was current among undergraduates at Cambridge in England as far back as 1909 (Eric Partridge, *A Dictionary of Slang and Unconventional English*, 1970). This would fit with the *whimper* theory of origin, since young women are thought by young men to do a lot of this. The sense of effeminacy also comes through a Sinclair Lewis's line about "Wimpish little men with spectacles" (*Arrowsmith*, 1925).

After the furor caused by the *Globe*'s use of the word in a headline, *wimp* quickly was applied to other politicians and elaborated in various ways. For example: "[New York Mayor Ed Koch's] pugnacious manner has often given the impression that he associates compromising with wimpishness" (*New Yorker*, 6/13/83); " 'I remember him as a kind of wimpy little guy,' Sergeant Lewis said" (*New York Times*, 7/3/84); " 'There's no question there's a wimp factor,' Rollins said [of Walter Mondale's presidential candidacy]" (*Portland Maine Sunday Telegram*, 7/22/84); and, finally, as a verb, " 'The publishers wimped out in terms of the pressure from the creationists and now the publishers are scared to death,' said Thomas A. Shannon, executive director of the National School Boards Association" (*New York Times*, 9/16/85). Clearly, the word is withstanding the test of time. "George Bush is a fake, a fool and a wimp" (Feiffer, New York *Village Voice*, 11/1/88). See also FOOL, MILQUETOAST, MUSH, SISSY, and WUSS.

windbag. A person who talks a lot, especially one who doesn't know what he is talking about. "I don't want people to think I am a windbag" (John F. Kennedy, explaining to Theodore C. Sorenson why he wanted his inaugural address in 1961 to be a short one, in Sorenson, *Kennedy*, 1965).

Wind has been applied to things that are empty or insubstantial, especially empty talk, since the thirteenth century, and *windbag*, meaning the bellows of an organ, has been dated to the fifteenth century. The *windbag* who is a person seems to be a nineteenth-century innovation (*OED*, 1827). The eipthet also figures in an elegant comeback, attributed both to the Reverend Sidney Smith (1771–1845), a well-known wit and sometime Canon of St. Paul's, and to President William Howard Taft (1857–1930). In the latter version, at a dinner before he became president, Taft was joshed about his girth by Chauncy Depew, an almost equally rotund lawyer.

DEPEW: I hope if it's a girl, Mr. Taft will name it for his charming wife.

TAFT: If it is a girl, I shall, of course, name it for my lovely wife. And if it is a boy, I shall claim the father's prerogative and call it Junior. But if it is, as I suspect, only a bag of wind, I shall name it Chauncy Depew.

Kennedy's speech, by the way, ran nineteen minutes, the shortest since Teddy Roosevelt's in 1905. See also *blowhard* in BLOW, BUFFOON, GAS, and MOTORMOUTH.

wiseacre. A fool, especially one who pretends to be wiser than everybody else. Thus, a specimen of nineteenth-century American wit: " 'May I ask, sir,' said Mr. Curran, 'how many acres make a *wise-acre?*' " (Boston *Courier*, 6/5/1838).

Wiseacre entered English in the late sixteenth century (*OED*, 1595), coming from the Middle Dutch, where it had a better meaning—*wijsseggher*, truth sayer, i.e., prophet or soothsayer, in turn from Old High German *wīzago*, prophet. In English, the word's meaning was bad right from the beginning, with Randle Cotgrave including "wisakers" as one of the equivalents for the French *fol*, fool, in his French-English dictionary of 1611. (Other equivalents in Cotgrave's list: asse, goose, calfe, coxcomb, ideot, naturall, ninnie, and noddie.)

In modern parlance, *wiseacre* often can be translated as *wise* (or *smart*) *ass* and *wise guy*, though it can be dangerous in some circles to make a mistake with the latter, since a *wise guy* also is a shrewd person (from 1896), and, in particular, a full-fledged member of the Mafia. "To become a made guy . . . is a satisfaction beyond measure. A made guy has protection and respect. You have to be Italian and be proposed for membership . . . and inducted in a secret ceremony. Then you are a made guy, 'straightened out,' a wise guy" (Joseph D. Pistone, *Donnie Brasco: My Undercover Life in the Mafia*, 1987).

See also FOOL, JOKER, and WISENHEIMER.

wisenheimer. One who pretends to know more than others; a WISEACRE. "We were nervous . . . at the statistics on child pedants and academic wisenheimers who grow up into faculty-recreation-room savants" (J. D. Salinger *Franny & Zooey*, 1957).

Wisenheimer has been dated to 1904. H. L. Mencken speculated in *The American Language* (Supplement I, 1945) that it was helped into American English by the influence of Yiddish, the suffixes of *-heimer* and *-ski*, as in BUTTINSKI, appearing at about the same time.

wishy-washy. Weak; watery; lacking in character, strength, or purpose. "He has no problems, wishy-washy, back and forth. He knows exactly what he wants to do and that's very important as a Chief Justice" (Thurgood Marshall, Associate Justice of the Supreme Court of the United States, assessing the qualifications of Chief Justice William H. Rehnquist, AP, 12/12/87).

Dating from the late seventeenth century, *wishy-washy* is one of many reduplications with negative meanings; see FLIMFLAM and NAMBY-PAMBY.

witch. One who practices, or is said to practice black magic; especially the female of the species, usually portrayed as an ugly, old hag. " 'He is a financial wizard' is praise without aspersion, but much more than financial acumen was implied when Hetty Green was called the Witch of Wall Street" (Casey Miller and Kate Swift, *Words and Women*, 1976).

Witch is quintessentially bad, deriving from the Anglo-Saxon *wicce*, witch, the feminine form of *wicca*, wizard (the latter also just happens to be the ancestor of *wicked*). Additionally, *witch* seems to be cognate to the Latin *victima*, victim, originally meaning a sacrificial animal, via the hypothetical root, *wiktima*. Noting this apparent relationship, Ernest Weekley suggested that *wicce* and *wicca* acquired their present meanings because "the priests of a suppressed religion naturally become magicians to its successors or opponents" (*An Etymological Dictionary of Modern English*, 1921).

wog. A foreigner, usually an Arab, Indian, or Oriental. ". . . the Falklanders have furiously opposed any link with Argentina. They call Argentines 'Argies'—a kind of local synonym for 'wog'—and dislike their language, politics, mores and even their food" (*New York Times*, 4/11/82).

Wog is comparatively new (*OED*, 1929) but of uncertain origin. Suggestions that it is an acronym for Westernized Oriental Gentleman, Wily Oriental Gentleman, or Worthy Oriental Gentleman, are not terribly convincing. More likely, it is a shortening of *golliwog*, a black-faced male doll with frizzy hair that became a popular toy in British nurseries following the publication of Bertha Upton's *The Adventures of Two Dutch Dolls—and a 'Golliwogg'* (1895).

An exception to *wog*'s derogatory meaning occurs in Australia and New Zealand, where it is perfectly acceptable to say that "Bertha is in bed with the wog," since *wog* here means a germ or illness, often the flu. See also FROG for another example of *wog*, GOOK for other kinds of *wogs*, and WOP for other spurious acronyms.

wolf. A rapacious person, one who devours others, especially a man who preys (sexually) upon women or younger men. The metaphor is composed in equal parts of the fierce disposition of the *wolf* and the defenselessness of its victims, known variously as *lambs* and CHICKENs.

Cruel and predatory people have been characterized as wolves for well over a thousand years, and the sexual connotations of the term have been apparent for most of that time. The wolf was a symbol of lust in the Elizabethan period and was used as such by Shakespeare; see GOAT. And referring to the denizens of Elizabeth's court, Sir William Knollys, ca. 1547–1632, wrote that "I will no way ffayle to deffend the innocent lamb [Mary Fitton] from the wolvyshe crueltye & fox-like subtletye of the tame bests of thys place" (from *American Speech*, 4/49).

The Reverend Cotton Mather meanwhile, used the term in its modern lecherous sense in 1721, describing an Anglican clergyman, James McSparran, as a "grievous wolf." The Reverend McSparran earned this epithet with an awkward attempt to seduce a young woman; she testified that "he put his Hand round my Waste, and shoved me along, and set me down on the Bed. . . . [and told me] that if I came to Naraganset I should not come home a Maid again" (from Kenneth Silverman, *The Life and Times of Cotton Mather*, 1984). From not-so-Puritanical *wolves* of this ilk we also have the verb *to wolf* (here meaning "to seduce" rather than "to gobble down food"); *wolf bait* (an especially attractive morsel of femininity); and *wolf whistle* (an appreciative whistle, used both as a noun and a verb), e.g., "The Governor of Mississippi today called for a complete investigation of the kidnap-killing of a Negro youth [Emmett Till] who allegedly wolf-whistled at a white woman" (AP, 9/2/55).

The *wolf* that preys upon men rather than women dates to at least World War I: "The sodomist, the degenerate, the homosexual 'wolf' . . ." (*New Republic*, 1/13/17). A generation later, Gershon Legman defined "wolf" as "A pedicator. The most common term at present" ("Language of Homosexuality," in George M. Henry, *Sex Variants*, 1941). This still seems to be the case, although the term may be broadening out to include overbearing behavior generally, especially in prisons, where *wolves* are endemic. For example, the glossary in *The Joint* (Inez Cardozo-Freeman, in collaboration with Eugene P. Delorme, 1984) gives "The aggressor in a homosexual situation" as the first meaning of *wolf* and "A prisoner who is physically aggressive; a troublemaker; a bully" as the second.

On occasion the sexually aggressive woman also has been labeled a *wolf, wolfess, wolfette,* or even *wolverine*. These *wolves* are seen most often on college campuses, in nightclubs, and in other dens of iniquity. They are, however, but pale imitations of "The She-Wolf of France," who was Isabella (1292–1358), wife of Edward II, of England. She gained her sobriquet by running away from her husband (whose interests, admittedly, did not run much to women), committing adultery with Roger Mortimer, and then leading the movement to overthrow, imprison, and murder (most cruelly, reportedly with a red-hot poker up his rectum) her husband, the anointed king. Isabella's wolfishness was in line with the medieval conception of this animal: "Wolves are known for their rapacity, and for this reason we call prostitutes wolves, because they devastate the possessions of their lovers" (*The Bestiary*, a twelfth-century ms., translated by T. H. White, 1954).

See also COYOTE, and DOG.

wonk. A notably industrious student or other hard worker. "Your basic wonk is a guy who studies all the time" (*To Race the Wind*, film, 1980). "Lawyers in the [Solicitor General's] office describe themselves as nerds, wonks, and idiot savants who wear dull gray suits and thick-soled wing-tips and sometimes relieve the intensity of analyzing cases with a quick game of darts" (*New Yorker*, 8/17/87).

Wonk has been dated to 1962 (*OED*). It is of uncertain ancestry, though the same term was used earlier by seafaring types to refer to a useless hand, naval cadet, or midshipman, and by Australians to refer to a white person (pejoratively) and, in particular, an effeminate or homosexual male. The word as used by American students may well be of some other, entirely different origin. Most likely, it is just a coincidence that *wonk* spelled backwards is *know*. See also WEENIE.

woodchuck. A rural dweller, especially a Northern REDNECK. "Vermont is full of woodchucks" (Frank Johnston, personal communication, 3/25/89). "But what could a 'greenhorn,' right from the land of woodchucks do?" (J. H. Ross, *What I Saw in New-York*, 1851). See also GREENHORN and HICK.

wop. An Italian or a person of Italian descent, alone and in such combinations as *wop house*, an Italian restaurant, *wop special*, a plate of spaghetti, and *wop stick*, 1940s jive talk for a clarinet.

Following the pattern of the older DAGO and GUINEA, *wop* has been extended on occasion to comprehend non-Italian peoples, usually but not always of southern

European origin, e.g., "The bosses had their own vernacular. . . . To some of these a Jew was a *sheeney*, the Pole a *wop*, and the Italian a *dago*" (Dale Chauncey Brewer, *The Conquest of New England by the Immigrant*, 1926). Though generally considered derogatory (the term was banned on the Keith vaudeville circuit as early as 1929), it still is encountered frequently in everyday blue-collar discourse. "The policeman's culture is that of the masculine workingman. It is of the docks, the barracks, the battlefield—Joe DiMaggio was a helluva good 'wop' center fielder, not an athlete of 'Italian extraction,' and similarly, the black man is a 'nigger,' not a member of an 'underprivileged minority' " (Jerome Skolnick, *Justice Without Trial*, 1966).

Wop frequently is said to be an acronym for WithOut Passport or WithOut Papers, which is how some immigrants arrived in the United States, or Working On Pavement, which is what many did afterward, but as etymologies go, these are in a class with those proposed for WOG and WOWSER. Almost certainly the term comes from the Neapolitan *guappo*, a tough guy, a showy ruffian, a fop. This word was used as a salutation by Sicilians in the United States during the late nine-teenth and early twentieth centuries. The oldest example of *wop* in writing comes from 1912 in *Courts and Criminals*, by Arthur Train, a former Manhattan assistant district attorney. The passage is worth quoting at some length, not only for its clear inclusion of the foppish sense of the Italian original but for its delineation of an immigrant lifestyle now associated with another minority:

> Curiously enough, there is a society of criminal young men in New York City who are almost the exact counterpart of the Apaches of Paris. They are known by the euphonious name of "Waps" or "Jacks." These are young Italian-Americans who allow themselves to be supported by one or two women, almost never of their own race. These pimps affect a peculiar cut of hair, and dress with half-turned-up velvet collar, not unlike the old-time Camorrist [the Camorra being the Neapolitan version of the Mafia], and have manners and customs of their own. They frequent the lowest order of dance-halls, and are easily known by their picturesque styles of dancing, of which the most popular is yclept the "Nigger." They form one variety of the many "gangs" that infest the city, are as quick to flash a knife as the Apaches, and, as a cult by themselves, form an interesting sociological study.

From this it is not hard to understand why *wop* developed disparaging connota-tions. The same thing seems to have happened in the Old Country, where *guappo* has been adopted in a derogatory sense to mean a Sicilian. See also ITALIAN.

worm. A lowly person. Thus, during a close vote in Israel's Parliament: "When Rabbi [Meir] Kahane's name was called out, another member . . . shouted in Hebrew, 'He's a worm!' " (*New York Times*, 1/17/85). The epithet is traditional: "But I am a worm, and no man; a reproach of men, and despised of the people" (*Psalms*, 22:6).

The word also has low connotations as a verb, *to worm out* meaning to renege or to crawl away, as from an obligation, or to extract information, as through persistent questioning. Equally insidious is the act of *worming [oneself] into [someone's] favor*. Then there is the *can of worms* that is a troublesome or complex matter, as in "Oh well, this is a can of worms as you know, a lot of this stuff went on" (President

Richard M. Nixon to John W. Dean III, discussing the initial Watergate indictments, 9/15/72, *The White House Transcripts*, 1974).

A detestable subspecies is the *bookworm*, or WEENIE, e.g., "Perverted and spoiled by a whoreson book-worm" (Ben Johnson, *Cynthia's Revels*, 1599).

Worms also have long signified death, from the belief that they nibble away on corpses, as in the grave pun: "He is gone to the diet of worms; he is dead and buried" (Captain Francis Grose, *A Classical Dictionary of the Vulgar Tongue*, 1796). See also SNAKE.

wowser. A puritanical person, a bluenose, a killjoy; hence, *wowserish* and *wowserism*, as in Canadian Prime Minister Pierre Trudeau's observation to Australians in 1970: "You have wowserism; we have Toronto" (*Wall Street Journal*, 6/27/83).

Wowser is an Australianism from the 1890s, originally—and still especially—referring to an ardent advocate of the prohibition of intoxicating beverages. The term's origin is not known. It has been suggested that *wowser* arose as an acronym for some reform organization's slogan: "We Only Want Social Evils Righted." Theories of this sort always should be taken with a grain of salt, however (see WOP). It does seem that John Norton, editor of *Truth*, popularized the word (the earliest *OED* citation is from this magazine), though he probably did not coin it, as he claimed: "I invented the word myself. I was the first man publicly to use the word. I first gave it public utterance in the City Council, when I applied it to Alderman Waterhouse, whom I referred to . . . as the white, woolly, weary, watery, word-wasting wowser from Waverly" (in Robert McCrum, William Cran, Robert MacNeil, *The Story of English*, 1986).

wretch. A miserable person; a low, mean, vile fellow. Thus, from a famous definition by a lexicographer with a grudge: "*patron*. One who countenances, supports or protects. Commonly a wretch who supports with insolence, and is paid with flattery" (Dr. Samuel Johnson, *A Dictionary of the English Language*, 1755). Johnson undoubtedly had Philip Dormer Stanhope, fourth Earl of Chesterfield, in mind. He had sought Chesterfield's patronage when he began his dictionary in 1748 and received the almost insulting gift of ten pounds cash. Chesterfield then managed to ignore Johnson for seven long years until, just as the dictionary was to be published, he sought to associate himself with the now much-heralded work by writing two essays commending it in a fashionable weekly, *The World*. Johnson replied with one of the great salvos in literary history. It reads in part:

> Is not a Patron, my Lord, one who looks with unconcern on a man struggling for life in the water, and when he has reached ground, encumbers him with help? The notice which you have pleased to take of my labours, had it been early, had been kind; but it has been delayed until I am indifferent, and cannot enjoy it; till I am solitary, and cannot impart it; till I am known, and do not want it. I hope it is no cynical asperity not to confess obligations where no benefit has been received, or to be unwilling that the Publick should consider me as owing that to a Patron, which Providence has enabled me to do for myself (letter to Chesterfield, 2/7/1755).

That wretch Chesterfield took all this in stride, leaving the letter out on a table for all to see. "This man has great powers," he told Johnson's publisher.

As for *wretch*, it is quite an old word, dated to before 1000. It derives from the Old English *wrecca*, an exile, one who is banished or driven away from his native land; hence, the senses of misfortune and affliction, as well as of vileness and reprehensibility, it commonly—and conveniently—being assumed that people in deep distress must be responsible for their own plight. Curiously, in German the word has taken an entirely different route, metamorphosing by way of *wreckeo*, exile, bandit, knight, into *recke*, warrior, hero. See also PEASANT.

wuss (wussy). A weakling, scaredy-cat, or CHICKEN; also a verb, as in, "Yeah, but wussing out is something I always remember," which was one of the replies by book critics to a survey question: "Is it ethical for a reviewer to decline to review a book he has already accepted to review, on the ground that he didn't like the book and doesn't want to say negative things in print?" (*National Book Critics Circle Journal*, 1/88).

Of apparently recent vintage, *wuss* is included in the *New Dictionary of American Slang* (1986) but not the preceding, 1960 edition of that work. The term might be a blend of *wimp* and *pussy*; a reduction of *pussy-wussy*; or a variant of the British rock-and-roller's *wuzzy*, girl, in turn from the French *oiseau*, bird (see BIRD). The last possibility is especially attractive considering the parallels between the use of *wuss* and *wimp* both as noun and verb, and the probable feminine antecedents of the latter; see WIMP.

X

Xanthippe. A bad-tempered woman, a scold, from the name of the wife of Socrates (470–399 B.C.), who got such a bad press from ancient writers that her name became generic for a SHREW. "An errant Vixen of a Wife . . . By this *Xantippe* he had two Sons" (Henry Fielding, *Tom Jones*, 1749). It has been suggested that (1) because of Xanthippe, Socrates didn't really mind having to take hemlock, and (2) the poor woman may have been driven around the bend by having a philosopher for a husband. See also MOLL.

Y

yahoo. An ignorant, vicious person. ". . . the white-jacketed priests of the Security Cult, the Know-Nothings, the Yahoos, the Galloots are never far distant" (Harrison E. Salisbury, "The Book Enchained," lecture, Library of Congress, 9/28/83). The original *yahoos* were the loathsome manlike critters encountered by Lemuel Gulliver in Houyhnhnmland: ". . . their Bodies were bare, so that I might see their skins, which were of a brown Buff Colour. . . . The Fore-feet of the *Yahoo* differed from my Hands in nothing else, but the length of the Nails, the Coarseness and Brownness of the Palms, and the Hairiness on the Backs. . . . they are cunning, malicious, treacherous, and revengeful. . . . but of a cowardly Spirit, and by Consequence insolent, abject, and cruel" (Jonathan Swift, *Gulliver's Travels*, 1726). By contrast, the best and wisest inhabitants of Houyhnhnmland were, of course, the horses. See also ANIMAL.

Yankee. Within the United States, a person from New England or (especially during the Civil War) any Northerner, but outside the country, any U.S. citizen, as in the common graffito, "Yankee go home" (from the 1950s), or, in Spanish-speaking lands, "Yanqui go home."

Yankee has a distinctly checkered history, though usually considered to be a "good" word today, at least within the northeastern states (with some exceptions, such as the disparaging use of *brush Yankee* and *swamp Yankee* for rural HICKs). But when the term surfaced in the eighteenth century, there was no doubt about its derogatory meaning, e.g., "It seems our hero being a New-Englander by birth, has a right to the epithet of Yankey; a name of derision, I have been informed, given by the Southern people on the Continent, to those of New England" ("a North Briton," note on "Oppression, a poem by an American," 1765). Or, as Captain Francis Grose defined the term: "YANKEY, or YANKEY DOODLE. A booby, or country lout: a name given to New England men in North America" (*A Classical Dictionary of the Vulgar Tongue*, 1796).

Yankee's origin remains uncertain though much discussed. As far back as 1789, a British officer who had served with Burgoyne during the Revolution derived the word from the Cherokee *eankke*, a slave or coward, which he said Virginians applied to New Englanders on account of their having failed to help the Southern colonists fight the Indians. Another guess, accepted for many years, was that *Yankee* came from *Yengees*, which was said to be the way North American Indians pronounced *English*. The consensus today, however, is that the word is Dutch, coming either from *Jan Kees*, i.e., John Cheese, a disparaging name for Hollanders, or, more likely, from *Janke*, Little John. Supporting the last theory is evidence of *Yankee's* use as a personal name or nickname from an early date, e.g., Yankey Duch, a pirate captain who operated in the 1630s, and a black slave named Yankee, listed in an estate inventory of 1725. Such a derivation also accords with the common use of diminutives of personal names to characterize entire national, ethnic, and racial groups; for other examples, see PADDY.

Yankee has opprobrious connotations of sharp practice and deceit (mirroring its positive sense of cleverness and ingenuity), which are apparent in such phrases as *Yankee trick* (from 1776) and *damn* (or *damned*) *Yankee*, a sentiment commonly attributed to Southerners, but which is recorded first (from 1798) as being expressed by Dutch inhabitants of New York in reference to *Connecticut Yankees* and other New Englanders with whom they traded. The word also has been used derogatorily as a verb, as in this comparison by John Russell Bartlett: "To *Jew* a person is considered, in Western parlance, a shade worse than to 'Yankee' him" (*Dictionary of Americanisms,* 1859).

The linguistic fortunes of *Yankee* are bound closely to its appearance in the "Yankee Doodle" song. The tune and the title are twenty years or so older than the words, at least as we now know them. Credit for the music, probably based on an old English country air, usually is given to Dr. Richard Schuckburgh, a British army surgeon. He is thought to have written the song about 1755, during the French and Indian War, while campaigning in northern New York State with Lord Jeffrey Amherst's mixed force of British regulars and Colonial troops.

The professional British soldiers looked down upon the rustic provincials, of course, and the *Yankee* part of the song's title certainly was not intended as a compliment. As for the *Doodle,* opinion is divided as to whether it referred to a *doodlesack,* a bagpipe; a *noodlehead* or simpleton (see BLOCKHEAD); or the penis (another meaning of *doodle,* already current in the eighteenth century, whence also *doodle-dasher,* a male masturbator, and, another kind of *doodlesack,* the vulva). Adding weight to the last theory is the appearance of an early version of "Yankee Doodle" in a brothel scene in America's first comic opera, *The Disappointment* (1767); see also LAY.

Whatever the precise meaning of the title, the sprightly air became a popular marching tune in the British Army—especially when Colonials were around to hear it. Thus, after British soldiers tarred and feathered a Boston man in March 1775, and stuck a sign on his back, proclaiming, "AMERICAN LIBERTY, OR A SPECIMEN OF DEMOCRACY," they added to the insult by having the fifes play "Yankee Doodle" as they paraded him around town. Then, on April 19, after a British expedition to seize rebel supplies at Concord met with unexpected resistance, the brigade that was sent out from Boston in relief played "Yankee Doodle" all the way.

This proved to be the turning point for *Yankee* as well as for American history generally. The British had a difficult trip back to Boston, as Minutemen from surrounding towns converged and subjected them to fire practically every step of the way. The rebels—the *Yankee Doodles*—had chased the Redcoats from the field, and they took the British song as their trophy. According to one newspaper account of the day's events, after the British got back to town, one officer "asked his brother officer how he liked the tune now? 'Damn them (returned he,) they made us dance until we were tired.' Since which Yankee Doodle sounds less sweet in their [British] ears" (in Kenneth Silverman, *A Cultural History of the American Revolution,* 1976). And later that summer, after the Battle of Bunker Hill, the *Pennsylvania Evening Post* reported (7/22/1775): "General Gage's troops are much dispirited . . . and . . . disposed to leave off dancing any more to the tune of Yankee Doodle."

The rebels, meanwhile, began playing the tune regularly themselves, and it wasn't long before they began thinking of it as an indigenous American air—and of

Yankee as a complimentary term. Various lyricists tried their hands at putting words to the music during this period. (For an example from the summer of '75, see FART). The version now sung, describing the visit of a father and son to General Washington's camp outside Boston, and concluding "Yankee Doodle went to town, / Riding on a Pony. / Stuck a feather in his cap, / And called it macaroni," probably was composed in early 1776 by Edward Bangs, then a Harvard sophomore as well as a Minuteman. See also MACARONI and, for more about *Yankees,* GRINGO and WASP.

yap. A dolt or other person easy to dupe; especially a country sucker, an inhabitant of *yap town,* a.k.a. *dog town* (see PODUNK). "Instead of his being the only 'yap,' as he calls it, in Congress, there were about two hundred other members" (C. H. Hoyt, *Texas Steer,* 1889). "Well, maybe I didn't con those yaps with that patriotic bluff" (George Ade, *The Sultan of Sulu,* 1903).

Yap has been dated to ca. 1894 in the doltish sense, predating slightly the *yap* that is a person's mouth, as in "Shut your big yap" (from 1900), and the *yap* that is idle chatter (from 1907). All are probably much older, however. The similar *yawp* or *yaup,* meaning to shout hoarsely or harshly, that is, to yelp like a dog, goes back to the fourteenth century.

Of course, the not-so-bright *yap* should not be confused with the *yap,* who is a Young Aspiring Professional (from 1984). Of course. See also YUPPIE.

yellow. Chiefly the color representing cowardice, but with many other noxious associations, e.g., diseases (*yellow jack,* a slang name for yellow fever as well as for the quarantine flag); treachery (in medieval paintings, Judas wears yellow); and heresy (those condemned by the Spanish Inquisition wore yellow as they were paraded to the stake). Yellow also was used to single out Jews, who were required to wear the *yellow badge* in some countries long before the Nazis devised the *yellow star.*

When referring to cowardice, the term frequently is embellished as *yellow belly* and *yellow streak,* as in ". . . you are an arrogant egomaniac with a large yellow streak running down your spine" (Ring Lardner, Jr., *The Ecstasy of Owen Muir,* 1954). The cowardly quality also may be alluded to in other ways, e.g., the sign on a Black Pearl taxicab: "We're not 'yellow.' We go anywhere" (Brooklyn, New York, 5/2/83), or the rhetorical question, popular during World War II: "What's the color of chicken?" Answer: "Yellow, yellow, yellow" (John R. Elting, et al., *A Dictionary of Soldier Talk,* 1984).

Yellow's association with cowards is of surprisingly recent vintage, dated only 1856: "We never thought your heart was yellow" (in P. T. Barnum, *Struggles and Triumphs,* 1869). Previously, going back to Elizabethan times, *yellow* was associated more with jealousy. At the end of the eighteenth century, Captain Francis Grose explained the color code this way: "YELLOW. To look yellow; to be jealous. I happened to call on Mr. Green, who was out: on coming home, and finding me with his wife, he began to look confounded blue and was, I thought, a little yellow" (*A Classical Dictionary of the Vulgar Tongue,* 1796). See also COWARD.

Other notable forms of this color include:

yellow. A Mongolian or, in the United States, a black (often as *yeller,* a light-skinned black, from 1834). The term's connotations in the racial context extend beyond the mere perception of color, however. Thus, reviewing Amiri Baraka's *The Autobiography of LeRoi Jones:* "By attending Howard University, he aspired to being 'yellow'—a Negro in the white man's system—and thereby turned his back on the true 'black' souls of his people" (*New York Times*, 1/23/84).

yellow-belly. Not only a coward but, at different times and in different places, a Mexican (from 1842, especially a soldier), an Oriental, a Eurasian, and, most curiously, a native of the Lincolnshire fenlands, "an allusion to the eels caught there" (Grose, *op. cit.*).

yellow-dog contract. A now-illegal agreement that keeps employees from joining a union; see DOG.

yellowfish. A Chinese who has entered the United States illegally; comparable to the WETBACK from Mexico.

yellow journalism. Sensational, unscrupulous journalism, as brought to new lows by William Randolph Hearst's *New York Journal*; from 1898. The *yellow* here comes immediately from Richard Outcault's comic strip, *Shantytown*, featuring "The Yellow Kid," whose costume was printed in yellow—the first use of color in a newspaper—but the metaphor fit naturally with, and was perhaps partially inspired by, the earlier use of *yellow back* and *yellow cover* to refer to cheap books and magazines of a sensational or trashy nature. The avant-garde London quarterly *The Yellow Book*, published 1894–97, also was on the sensational side, thanks especially to Aubrey Beardsley's decadent drawings.

yellow peril. Orientals, especially Chinese, as perceived by Europeans in fear of being overrun by the peoples of the East. The expression has been dated to 1900 in English, but was coined in the preceding decade in Germany (*die gelbe gefahr*).

To the Orientals, things look different, of course. Thus, in China, pornographic or decadent films, magazines, and other publications—materials that Westerners would describe as *blue*—are categorized as *huangse*, i.e., yellow.

yenta. A coarse woman, a gossip or busybody; a SHREW. The *OED*'s earliest example is from 1923: "The slattern *yentehs* lounging on these stoops . . . were transfigured" (A. Yezierska, *Salome of the Tenements*). Like many other words for women, this one has sunk a long way: It is American Yiddish, originally a female personal name, for *Yentl*, in turn from the Italian *gentile*, kind, gentle, and before that, noble, highborn. "*Yenta*, I am told was a perfectly acceptable name for a lady, derived from the Italian *gentile*—until some ungracious *yenta* gave it a bad name" (Leo Rosten, *The Joys of Yiddish*, 1968). See also DAME.

yes-man. One who never says no to a superior; an obsequious underling. Popularized through its application to assistant directors in the movie-making business in the early 1920s, credit for coining the term often is given to the cartoonist T. A. "Tad" Dorgan, who used it in a 1913 cartoon, showing several assistant editors of a newspaper, labeled "yes-men," bringing their critical facilities to bear as the editor-in-chief goes over the first edition to come off press. But Dorgan, a man of fertile imagination, who also introduced or helped popularize such landmarks of the language as *cat's pajamas*, *drugstore cowboy*, *skiddoo*, and HOT DOG, may be getting more than his due in this instance. The *OED*'s earliest example of the expression comes from the preceding year: "We're both yes-men, Edward. We've got to take orders now" (*Century Magazine*, 7/12).

The personality type predates the modern label for it, of course. In the eighteenth century, for example, such individuals were known as *amen* men, as in Captain Francis Grose's definition: "AMEN. He said Yes and Amen to every thing;

he agreed to every thing" (*A Classical Dictionary of the Vulgar Tongue*, 1796). And still earlier, the world was blessed with *yea-forsooth* types, who assented easily without really meaning it, as in Falstaff's complaint about "A rascally yea-forsooth knave" (*Henry IV, Part II*, 1596–97).

See also SYCOPHANT, the *toady* in TOAD, and ZANY (for another Elizabethan *yes-man*, the *please-man*).

Yid. A Jew. " 'What do you call me Ike for? I ain't no Yid' " (Ring W. Lardner, "Alibi Ike," *How to Write Short Stories*, 1924). " 'We aren't so concerned with keeping the Yids away—they generally stay clear of a place unless they know it's open—as with letting the white [sic] people know it's restricted' " (Ring Lardner, Jr., *The Ecstasy of Owen Muir*, 1954).

Yid is very much a Jewish creation, traditionally used by Jews themselves, as evidenced by the oldest example of the term in print: "*Yid*, or *Yit*, a Jew. *Yidden*, the Jewish people. The Jews use these terms very frequently" (J. C. Hotten, *The Slang Dictionary*, 1874). For example, Chaim Weizmann, the first president of Israel, ". . . would describe himself appealingly as just 'a Yid from Pinsk,' but he loathed Pinsk, as is shown . . . in the letters, when he lets his hair down in writing to Vera" (*New York Times Book Review*, 6/30/85).

The word comes from the German *Jude*, Jew, itself a shortened form of *Yehuda* (Judah, in English), the name of the Jewish Commonwealth in the period of the Second Temple (ca. 520–20 B.C.), and ultimately from another *Yehuda*, the name of one of Jacob's sons.

The term's insult value thus depends mainly on who employs it and how. The pronunciation also is important. "*Yid* [should be] pronounced YEED, to rhyme with 'deed.' (If you pronounce it YID, to rhyme with 'did,' you will be guilty of a *faux pas.* 'YID' is offensive—and the way anti-Semites pronounced it)" (Leo Rosten, *The Joys of Yiddish*, 1968).

See also JEW (DOWN), TO and note the *Ike* in PADDY.

yokel. A stupid country fellow, often in the phrase, *local yokel;* a HICK. "Thou art not altogether the clumsy yokel and the clod I took thee for" (R. D. Blackmore, *Lorna Doone*, 1869). "There is an influx of new people who have more money than the local yokels do" (Gail Leo, restaurant manager in Kent, Connecticut, *New York Times*, 6/9/88).

The term has been dated to the early nineteenth century. Opinion is divided as to its origin. It may come from the English dialectical *yokel*, a green woodpecker, or from the German personal name *Jokel*, Jacob. In either case, *yokel*'s derivation would follow tradition, since people often are disparaged by describing them as dumb birds as well as by addressing them familiarly with names that may not be their own; see DODO and PADDY.

yo-yo. A stupid person, since ca. 1950; before that, an indecisive person. Thus, Roy M. Cohn blasted a disciplinary committee of lawyers that recommended his disbarment as a "bunch of yo-yos" (*New York Times*, 11/26/85). Originally a trademark, the name of the spool that goes up and down on a string, the word comes from Tagalog, a language spoken in the Phillipines, where the toy was invented. See also JERK.

yuck (yeck). An exclamation of strong disgust or distaste, also rendered as *yuk, yecch, yech, yeck,* and even *eck*. The related adjectives for characterizing anything that is repulsive, gooey, messy, and sick-making are *yucky* and *yecky*. "In one seminar I attended, a personnel-placement specialist [asked] one young woman in the audience how she would react to the name of the Chase Manhattan Bank. 'You'd say it sounds awful, wouldn't you?' he said. 'Yuck! Who wants to work in a bank' " (Calvin Trillin, *New Yorker*, 3/7/77).

The basic terms have been dated to 1966 (*yuck*) and 1969 (*yeck*). They probably are of onomatopoetic origin, imitating the sound of retching. It seems significant that in the dialect of Newfoundlanders *yuck* is used as a verb meaning "to vomit." On the other hand, people have always despised fools, and *yuck* was recorded as a noun in this sense more than twenty years before the other meaning appeared: "*Yuck* is a word introduced into the language by Fred Allen. A yuck is a dope who makes a practice of going around appearing on quiz programs. That was its original definition; it now means a dope of any description" (H. Allen Smith, *Life in a Putty Knife Factory*, 1943). See also DOPE and UGH.

yuppie. Young Urban Professional. "There's something vaguely nauseating now about being a yuppie. No one wants to be called that anymore" (Gil Schwartz, thirty-four-year-old corporate PR executive and resident of Manhattan's Upper West Side, *New York Times*, 6/28/85). ". . . I'd like to address those of your readers who equate the word YUPPIE with dastardly people. I refer specifically to the reader who, on seeing your [glossy] new cover, said 'Oh no! They've gone YUPPIE! All is lost" (letter, *Old-House Journal*, 6/86).

Yuppie apparently broke into print for the first time in a syndicated column by Bob Greene about the "networking" parties run at a New York City disco by a onetime radical, Jerry Rubin, for rising young businesspeople: "While he and Abbie [Abbott] Hoffman once led the Yippies—the Youth International Party—one social commentator has ventured that Rubin is now attempting to become the leader of the Yuppies—Young Urban Professionals" (*Chicago Tribune*, 3/23/83). Greene did not coin the word, but overheard it in a bar. The "social commentator" was a fiction that he devised because he had no idea who had made up the term (*American Speech*, Summer 1986). Not wanting to go down in history as "The Father of the Yuppies," Greene has asked any earlier user of the word to get in touch with him, but at last report, was still waiting for someone else to step forward and relieve him of the honor.

Variations on the *yuppie* theme include *yap*, Young Aspiring Professional (see also YAP), and *yumpie*, Young Upwardly Mobile Professional. Both have been certified as legitimate words by the *Oxford English Dictionary* (1986 supplement). Nonce forms, yet to pass the test of time, are *guppie*, Grown-Up Urban Professional; *puppie*, Parent of Urban Professional; and *dink*, for yuppies who are living together and have Double Incomes, No Kids.

Z

zany. Comical, ridiculous; ultmately, by a circuitous route, a sixteenth-century aspersion on the mountain people of the province of Bergamo in Italy, who were regarded as simple, boorish fools by the ever-so-much-more sophisticated residents of cities on the coast. A *zany* originally was a buffoon; specifically, a clown's assistant, a jester's straight man, or a charlatan's attendant. The word comes from the Italian *zanni*, diminutive of *Giovanni*, John. The clownish sense was popularized in the *Commedia dell'arte* where the *zannis* were stock characters, usually lackeys or valets, presented as though they came from Bergamo, *zanni* having become generic for a servant from the inland uplands. (See PADDY for more on the disparaging uses of the diminutives of personal names.) Italian troupes featuring *zannis* played regularly in England from 1546, with the first known example of the word's use in English coming about forty years later: "Some carrytale, some pleaseman [a YES-MAN, in effect], some slight zany . . . That . . . knows the trick to make my lady laugh" (William Shakespeare, *Love's Labor's Lost*, 1588). See also CHARLATAN, FOOL, and *Boetian* in PEORIA.

zero. Someone or something that doesn't amount to anything; a nothing. The mathematical comparison is not new: "The other gentlemen are mere zeros" (Maria Edgeworth, *Patronage*, 1813). For emphasis, the truly worthless person may also be described as *a big zero*. See also ZIP.

zig-zig. To copulate and the act of so doing; a French expression, acquired by U.S. servicemen in World War I and reacquired in World War II. Thus, from the record of a court-martial in the European Theater (*American Speech*, 12/46):

> Q: Did you actually hear the accused talking French to this girl?
> A: Yes, sir.
> Q: Well, what did he say, if you know?
> A: He said, "No zig-zig ce soir, sweetheart."

Zig-zig is synonymous as noun and verb with *jig-a-jig*, dated to 1896 in English (J. S. Farmer and W. E. Henley, *Slang and Its Analogues*). The origins of these expressions are murky, but it seems likely the allusion in each case is to the lively dance, the *gigue*, jig. See also GIGOLO and JIG.

zip. A person of no account; specifically, an Oriental, to the American military in Vietnam, ca. 1961–73; see also GOOK. The term is said to be an acronym for Zero Intelligence Potential, but it also fits in with, and may derive from, the earlier use of *zip* meaning "nothing," which is what Vietnamese were thought to be worth. (The Z sound alone seems to imply nothingness, e.g., ZERO, *zilch*, and *zot*.)

Since the war in Vietnam, the epithet has been extended to other unimportant people, e.g., "One strength they [the Mafia] still possess is getting recruits from Italy. They are bringing over a lot of immigrants, so-called 'zips' to use at the lower levels" (Andrew J. Maloney, U.S. Attorney for the Eastern District of New York, *New York Times*, 3/8/87). These *zips* come from Sicily and the use of the epithet may be reinforced in this case by the fact that they speak in their native dialect so rapidly that it is difficult for other Mafia members to understand them.

The intensive form, for people who definitely aren't all there, is *zippo*, as in "Some people are real zippos" (Ed Boch, a water inspector in Old Westbury, New York, who has occasion to meet all types in his line of work, *New York Times*, 7/10/87).

zombie. A weird person, or one who is simply different; in particular, a dull, slow-witted (mentally dead) person. "Any performer [in the movie business] not a Caucasian is a *zombie*" (H. L. Mencken, *The American Language*, 1936). "*Zombie*. Soldier who falls in the next to lowest category in Army classification tests" ("Glossary of Army Slang," *American Speech*, 10/41). For the lowest category, see GOON.

Zombie is of West African origin, deriving from the Kongo *zumbi*, fetish, and referring originally to the snake god of voodoo cults. The *zombie* in the principal current sense of a reanimated corpse is not just the creation of B-movie-makers, by the way. It seems that Haitian sorcerers use a toxin, probably obtained from the puffer fish, to punish social offenders by paralyzing them so completely as to mimic death. ". . . the fear of a Haitian is not of being *attacked* by a zombie, but rather of being *turned into* one. Becoming a zombie is understood to involve having one's *ti bon ange*—roughly one's soul—stolen from one's body, and thus losing one's autonomy" (*New York Times Book Review*, 8/21/88, on Wade Davis, *Passage of Darkness: The Ethnobiology of the Haitian Zombie*). See also ROBOT and VOODOO.

zoo. A motley collection of people, specifically (1) a whorehouse containing women of various nationalities and races; (2) a prison; and (3) a sorority house (also called an *animal house, doghouse, pigpen,* and *snake house*).

In political campaigns, the *zoo plane* is the number two plane for the press; it contains the *animals*—the TV journalists and technicians, with their bulky equipment—as well as reporters from secondary print publications and others, sometimes as punishment for having incurred the candidate's wrath. But some prefer the second plane. "The kinkier members of the press tended to drift onto the Zoo Plane. The atmosphere was much more comfortable. There were tremendous amounts of cocaine, for instance" (Hunter S. Thompson, *Fear and Loathing: On the Campaign Trail '72*, 1973).

As an adjective, the term is synonymous with "wild," with overtones of sheer craziness. Thus, characterizing the second trial of Claus von Bülow: " 'It's been very zooy here,' said Alan Rosenberg, a reporter for the Boston Herald, who is writing a book about the trial, which offered a sultry mix of money, sex and society" (*New York Times*, 6/12/85).

Zulu. A black person; in the United States, usually deprecatory. ". . . witness the New York West Indian boy who was heard to call a Barbadian girl a 'bloody Zulu bastard' " (J. Brown, *Un-Melting Pot*, 1970). The derogatory connotations are strong enough that news also was made when New York City mayor Edward I. Koch, in his previous incarnation as a U.S. Representative, characterized a fellow House member, Ronald V. Dellums (Democrat, California) as a "Zulu warrior" and "Watusi prince" (*New York Times*, 12/5/85). The raising of eyebrows was only natural in view of the pejorative meanings that have become attached to the names of other African peoples, e.g., "Nigerian. Euphemism for *Nigger* . . . Not insulting when applied to a Nigerian national, but otherwise a fighting insult" (Merritt Clifton, *Maledicta*, 1978). And it has been years, of course, since anyone has told *Ethiopian jokes*, or gone to an *Ethiopian drama* or *opera*, all popular nineteenth-century entertainments. The great success of *Old Folks at Home* (1851) persuaded Stephen Foster that he should try to become "the best Ethiopian song writer," and it is partly because he did such a good job of incorporating the language of his day that some of his lyrics (e.g., "I hear the darkies calling") are not sung much any more. See also HOTTENTOT, KAFFIR, and NEGRO.